Tolley's Professional Partnership Handbook

Fourth Edition

by Smith & Williamson
Chartered Accountants

Tolley
LexisNexis™

Members of the LexisNexis Group worldwide

United Kingdom	LexisNexis Butterworths Tolley, a Division of Reed Elsevier (UK) Ltd, Halsbury House, 35 Chancery Lane, LONDON, WC2A 1EL, and 4 Hill Street, EDINBURGH EH2 3JZ
Argentina	LexisNexis Argentina, BUENOS AIRES
Australia	LexisNexis Butterworths, CHATSWOOD, New South Wales
Austria	LexisNexis Verlag ARD Orac GmbH & Co KG, VIENNA
Canada	LexisNexis Butterworths, MARKHAM, Ontario
Chile	LexisNexis Chile Ltda, SANTIAGO DE CHILE
Czech Republic	Nakladatelstv Orac sro, PRAGUE
France	Editions du Juris-Classeur SA, PARIS
Hong Kong	LexisNexis Butterworths, HONG KONG
Hungary	HVG-Orac, BUDAPEST
India	LexisNexis Butterworths, NEW DELHI
Ireland	Butterworths (Ireland) Ltd, DUBLIN
Italy	Giuffre Editore, MILAN
Malaysia	Malayan Law Journal Sdn Bhd, KUALA LUMPUR
New Zealand	LexisNexis Butterworths, WELLINGTON
Poland	Wydawnictwo Prawnicze LexisNexis, WARSAW
Singapore	LexisNexis Butterworths, SINGAPORE
South Africa	LexisNexis Butterworths, DURBAN
Switzerland	Stampfli Verlag AG, BERNE
USA	LexisNexis, DAYTON, Ohio

© Reed Elsevier (UK) Ltd 2002

A CIP Catalogue record for this book is available from the British Library.

ISBN 0 754 51200 2

Typeset by Tradespools, Frome, Somerset
Printed by Hobbs the Printers, Totton, Hampshire

Visit Butterworths LexisNexis *direct* at www.butterworths.com

Preface to the fourth edition

Updating the third edition of this book has brought into sharp focus how quickly the professional practices world is changing.

Partnership law itself is still under review by the Law Commission although likely changes have become clear and the legal framework for professional firms has moved on with fresh regulation, statute and case law.

Limited Liability Partnerships (LLPs') have become a reality with an increasing number of firms considering whether to convert to this structure. This edition not only brings up to date the chapters on LLPs and Taxation of LLPs, but also includes a new chapter on Accounting for LLPs.

Tax law continues to evolve. For example, the phasing out of retirement relief from capital gains tax is being counteracted by partners' potentially increased business asset taper relief.

This edition has been revised to take account of these and other changes in the overall environment.

Simon Mabey

Preface to the first edition

Partnership is a form of business organisation which has enabled a variety of professional practices to flourish. Professional partnerships may be large, medium-sized or small and exhibit many different styles of management. This perhaps explains why remarkably little literature is available on the practical aspects of running a professional partnership.

This handbook is designed to be of use to a broad range of individuals involved in the management of partnerships including senior and managing partners, finance partners and other partners as well as those considering partnership.

In the past, partners tended to consider themselves primarily as members of a profession, rather than as participants in businesses. In today's competitive environment, the reverse is more commonly true. Nevertheless whilst those responsible for the management of partnerships are generally highly expert in their own field, they have not always had the opportunity to acquire the range of skills needed to run a successful business.

While a handbook is no substitute for experience, this book is designed to provide information and advice on the wide range of issues that running a professional partnership involves. Between them, the contributors have many years' experience of advising professional partnerships as well as involvement in management in their own practices.

A professional partnership is a living entity that develops and succeeds through the skills and abilities of its people. This handbook is for all those who wish to ensure the success of their partnership.

Acknowledgements

Tolley's Professional Partnership Handbook has been written primarily by a team of experts at Smith & Williamson who advise professional practices. In addition I wish in particular to thank the other contributors.

Firstly, Richard Turnor and his team at international law firm Allen & Overy for their substantial contribution on the legal aspects, especially the first five chapters. I should also like to thank Richard Essex of The Hanover Park Group for his contribution to the Insurance Chapter, Bob Empson of White Maple Consulting for his contribution on Strategic Planning and Marketing, and John Robinson of Barclays Bank for his contribution to the Financial Management Chapter.

I also wish to thank my many colleagues at Smith & Williamson who contributed significantly in their professional areas of expertise. I particularly would like to mention audit specialists Jeremy Boadle, Yvonne Lang and Giles Murphy, information systems specialist Roland Brook, human resources director Jenny Chandler, pensions directors Mike Fosberry and Peter Maher, partnership tax specialist Colin Ives, corporate tax specialist John Newman and national tax director Francesca Lagerberg.

I am grateful to architects Sheppard Robson for the use of the image of the City Point building on the front cover.

Simon Mabey

Chairman, Professional Practices Group

Smith & Williamson

Disclaimer

Every effort has been taken to ensure the accuracy of the contents of this book. However, neither the authors nor the publishers can accept any responsibility for any loss occasioned to any person acting or refraining from action in reliance on any statement contained in the book.

Contents

Table of Statutes

References in the right-hand column are to Division and paragraph numbers.

Table of Statutory Instruments

References at the right-hand side of the column are to Division and paragraph numbers.

Table of Cases

Chapter 1

Introduction

Definition of partnership

1.1   In everyday speech, the word 'partnership' is used to describe almost any relationship involving collective activity by people of equal standing. As a matter of law, however, 'partnership' has a very particular meaning which is to be found in the *Partnership Act 1890* (see glossary).

Section 1(1) of the *Partnership Act 1890* defines partnership as 'the relation which subsists between persons carrying on a business in common with a view of profit'.

Section 4 of the *Partnership Act 1890* provides that persons who have entered into partnership with one another are collectively known as 'a firm'.

Two categories of partnership are now recognised under English law. The *Partnership Act 1890* defines the rights and obligations of partners in general partnerships and the *Limited Partnerships Act 1907* introduced the concept of limited partnerships. Limited partnerships are considered further in Chapter 3. The law of partnership is currently under review by the Law Commission. A consultative document ('Partnership Law', A Joint Consultation Paper, the Law Commission (Consultation Paper No 159) and the Scottish Law Commission (Discussion Paper No 111)) was published on 31 July 2000, and a further report with draft legislation is expected in early 2003. This edition describes the law as it currently stands.

Both forms of partnership consist of three essential elements.

There must be a business

1.2   *Section 45* of the *Partnership Act 1890* states that the expression 'business' includes every trade, occupation or profession. Almost every commercial activity, including a one-off commercial venture, can be a business for this purpose.

Section 2 of the *Partnership Act 1890* provides that co-ownership of property, and investing jointly in property, does not necessarily imply the existence of a partnership (see 1.7 below).

The business must be carried on by two or more persons in common

1.3   For a partnership to exist, two or more persons must carry on the business in common. [*s 1(1)*]. The term 'persons' includes corporations and unincorporated bodies (such as partnerships), as well as individuals.

The persons carrying on the business must act as principals and not as agents. If several persons carry on a business on behalf of a third party or parties, then a partnership will not exist. For example, two executors carrying on the business of a deceased sole trader are not strictly partners as they carry on the business on behalf of the deceased person's estate.

The words 'in common' dictate the necessity for a single business carried on jointly. A partnership does not exist where each 'partner' in fact carries on a different and distinct business. However, this is often a fine distinction to draw. For example, where several separate firms agree to co-operate over the referral of business, training and the maintenance of business standards but there is no further integration, a single partnership is unlikely to exist. However, where those firms also use the same name and share profits and losses, the separate firms may in fact be in the same position as branch offices of a single partnership. In such circumstances, the separate firms may be surprised to find themselves jointly liable for one another's debts.

The business must be carried on with a view of profit

1.4   In conducting a business in common, the partners must intend that the receipts of the business will exceed the expenses incurred in generating those receipts, leaving a profit. It is the profit motive of the partners which is essential, rather than the actual generation of profits. The making of a profit need not be the only motive. Even if the partners have an additional motive (e.g. administrative convenience or tax avoidance), the condition of conducting the business with a view of profit may be satisfied.

Prior to 1890, it was thought that, in order for a partnership to exist, the partners should not only intend to make a profit but should also intend to divide the profits between themselves. However, the *Partnership Act 1890* does not contain this requirement and it is now thought that a partnership may exist even where one or more of the partners are excluded from the profits, and perhaps also where the partners agree to pay the profits to a third party (provided that they are acting as principals). Even so, sharing the profits of a business is prima face evidence of partnership, although it will be a question of fact as to whether or not the recipients of those profits are all partners. *Section 2(3)* of the *Partnership Act 1890* describes specific circumstances where profit sharing will not create a partnership. For example the following do not in themselves make the recipient a partner:

(*a*)   repaying a debt or liquidated amount by instalments out of the profits of a business;

(*b*)   paying an employee or agent a share of the profits of the business under his or her contract for remuneration; and

(*c*)   paying the widow or children of a deceased partner an annuity from the profits of the partnership.

A partnership will only exist at a time when the business is 'carried on'. Therefore, even if the parties have entered into a partnership agreement, a partnership will not exist between them until such time as they begin to carry on a business together. This does not mean that trading must have commenced. In *Khan v Miah [2000] 1 WLR 2123*, which involved the establishment of a restaurant business, the House of Lords unanimously held, overturning the decision of the Court of Appeal, that preparatory activities including fitting out premises in view of carrying on a trading business, were indicative of the existence of a partnership relationship. It was not necessary for actual trading to have commenced. The Law Commission suggests that the partnership only needs to have as its objective the carrying on of a business, to make it clear that a partnership could exist prior to the commencement of a business. Query whether the House of Lords decision in *Khan v Miah* already achieves this.

What is not a partnership?

1.5   The definition of partnership in *section 1(1)* of the *Partnership Act 1890* is very wide, but the Act expressly limits its scope. The following situations do not give rise to a partnership.

A company

1.6   *Section 1(2)* of the *Partnership Act 1890* specifically provides that the relationship between the members of a company (whether registered under the *Companies Acts* or incorporated under Royal Charter) or between members of other special types of company is not a partnership. The fundamental difference between a company and a partnership is that a company is a separate entity capable of acquiring rights and incurring liabilities which are separate from those of its members. However, partners jointly own the assets of and rights relating to the partnership and are jointly liable for liabilities incurred by it.

Joint holding of property

1.7   *Section 2(1)* of the *Partnership Act 1890* provides that 'joint tenancy, tenancy in common, joint property, common property, or part ownership does not of itself create a partnership as to anything so held or owned, whether the tenants or owners do or do not share any profits made by the use thereof'. In order for a partnership to exist, the holders of the property must be carrying on a business (see 1.2 and 1.3 above).

The sharing of gross returns

1.8   The mere sharing of gross returns, as opposed to profits, does not give rise to a partnership.

Clubs and societies

1.9   Clubs and societies are not partnerships even if carrying on a business, provided that their objects do not include making profits.

Formalities of forming a partnership

1.10   A partnership exists when the three essential elements of a partnership are in existence, irrespective of whether or not the partners have entered into a formal written partnership agreement or deed. It is therefore quite possible for a person to incur liability as a partner unintentionally, without realising that the nature of his relationship with another person amounts to a partnership. Where there is a partnership but no express agreement, or the agreement is incomplete, the *Partnership Act 1890* will govern the relationship between the partners.

The case of *Joyce v Morrisey [1999] EMLR 233* concerned the pop group The Smiths. There was no formal agreement governing the relationship between the band members and therefore the relationship was governed by the *Partnership Act 1890*. *Section 24* states that there is a presumption of equality as to the distribution of profits between partners. The defendant argued that the profits should be shared unequally as a result of discussions between the band members. The judge held that the presumption in *section 24* could only be displaced if the plaintiff had actively accepted new terms of unequal profit sharing.

Where parties have entered into a partnership agreement but the three conditions are not satisfied, a partnership will not exist simply because the parties have said that it exists.

Restrictions on the number of partners

1.11   The current rule under *section 716* of the *Companies Act 1985* is that a partnership must be registered as a company if it consists of more than 20 partners. This restriction does not apply where the partnership in question is a professional partnership of solicitors, accountants (qualified as company auditors), stockbrokers, estate agents, chartered surveyors, engineers, architects, auctioneers, actuaries, authorised persons carrying on investment business, insolvency practitioners, general medical practitioners and limited partnerships which constitute collective investment schemes, all by virtue of a series of Partnership (Unrestricted Size) Regulations.

At the time of writing, a Draft Regulatory Order was before Parliament to abolish the restriction by repealing *sections 716* and *717* of the *Companies Act* and amending *section 4(2)* of the *Limited Partnerships Act 1907*. This follows the recommendation by the DTI that the limit should be removed, made in the light of responses to the consultation document on the issue, published in April 2001. The DTI consultation recognised that the restriction on the size of partnerships frequently poses practical problems. For example, it is important to note that, for this purpose, where one partnership is a partner in another, known as a sub-partnership, each partner in the first partnership is a separate partner in the sub-partnership. This follows from the fact that a partnership entity does not have legal personality separate from that of its partners.

One method of overcoming this problem is to create parallel partnerships carrying on separate businesses. This device is often used to allow non-members of a particular profession to enjoy partnership status in a form where this would not otherwise be allowed by law. For example, many firms of chartered accountants have established parallel firms of management consultants. A parallel partnership can be formed which provides for its partners to be remunerated and otherwise treated in exactly the same way as the partners of the original partnership. The two partnerships may provide services to each other and pay for those services in accordance with service and consultancy agreements between the two firms. These means of obviating the 20-partner limit will no longer be necessary once the limit is abolished.

Categories of partners

1.12   A partner is any individual or company that is a member of a partnership. In the context of a professional partnership, a person normally starts life as an employee. Having earned his spurs, he may then be invited to become a partner. Before becoming a full partner, otherwise known as an equity partner, he will often spend a number of years as a salaried partner so as to enhance his status but without having all the authority of a full partner. At the end of his career, he may simply retire, thus becoming a retired partner, or he may leave his capital in the firm and continue to share in the profits, becoming a sleeping or possibly a limited partner. The meaning of these terms is explained in the glossary.

Who may become a partner?

1.13   Anyone except an enemy alien can be a partner in a partnership. However, special rules apply in a number of situations and the key rules are set out below.

Companies

1.14   Both limited and unlimited companies are able to become partners. A partnership may consist of corporate bodies, individuals or a combination of corporate bodies and individuals. A company should be authorised to enter into a partnership by the objects clause in its memorandum of association. However, whether a corporate entity has a constitutional authority to join a partnership is less important than previously, following the amendment of the ultra vires rules. [See *section 35* of the *Companies Act 1985* as amended by the *Companies Act 1989*].

Limited Liability Partnerships

1.15   Limited Liability Partnerships formed under the *Limited Liability Partnerships Act 2000* have unlimited capacity. They are therefore able to become partners in much the same way as companies.

Persons of unsound mind

1.16   Where it is claimed by a partner that he was suffering from some form of mental disorder at the time he entered into the partnership agreement, he will continue to be bound by that partnership agreement unless he can show that his fellow contracting partners were aware of his disability at the time or that Court of Protection proceedings had been commenced before he entered into the agreement. Partnership agreements frequently provide for the automatic retirement of partners who are of unsound mind.

Bankrupts

1.17   Bankrupts can be partners, although a bankrupt is likely to be guilty of an offence under *section 360* of the *Insolvency Act 1986* if he obtains credit on behalf of the firm without disclosing his status. Most partnership agreements will provide for the automatic expulsion of bankrupts, and will usually override *section 33(1)* of the *Partnership Act 1890*, which provides for the automatic dissolution of the partnership upon the bankruptcy of any partner.

It is important to ensure that each partner in a professional partnership holds the required professional qualifications. At worst, the inclusion of an unqualified person could lead to an automatic dissolution of the firm as an illegal partnership.

Professional regulation and multi-disciplinary partnerships (MDPs)

1.18 Historically, the different professions have practised separately, so that partnerships have tended to include partners all of whom are members of the same profession. There have been some exceptions, for example, surveying firms have included partners who are qualified as chartered surveyors, land agents and auctioneers.

This separation of the professions has in some cases been a requirement of professional rules, for example, under Rule 7 (the fee-sharing provisions) of the Solicitors' Practice Rules 1990, solicitors are only permitted, subject to Law Society requirements, to enter into partnership with registered foreign lawyers and registered European lawyers. However, the accountancy profession has encouraged MDPs by reducing to 50% the required number of partners in a firm of chartered accountants that must be qualified as such.

The Law Society's MDP Working Party has been looking at interim measures which would allow non-solicitors to become partners in a solicitors' firm, such as the 'Legal Practice Plus' model, or to share fees with non-lawyers, such as the 'Linked Partnerships' model. These models are considered in the consultation document released by the Lord Chancellor's department on competition in the professions in July 2002, responding to a report of the same name from the Office of Fair Trading (OFT) in March 2001. The consultation document illustrates the impediments to permitting MDPs, listing necessary changes to the Law Society's rules and to legislation, but stipulates that the Government is keen to remove restrictive practices that are not in the public interest. Legal difficulties have so far prevented the introduction of even the interim measures.

The OFT issued a progress statement in April 2002 on competition in the professions. Of note are the repeal by the *Enterprise Act 2002* of the exclusion of designated professional rules from application of the provisions of the *Competition Act 1998* and the decision in *Wouters v Algemene Raad van de Nederlandse Orde van Advocaten [2002] All ER (EC) 193*. The competition provisions of the *Enterprise Act 2002* are expected to come into force in spring or summer 2003. *Wouters*, a decision of the Court of Justice of the European Communities, considered whether the Netherlands Bar rules preventing barristers from entering into partnership with accountants were incompatible with *Article 85* of the *EC Treaty* (which deals with competition issues). It was decided that the restrictions were necessary for the proper practice of the legal profession and therefore did not infringe *Article 85*. The current rate of change in the professions is not expected to slow in the near future.

The Canadian Bar Association, the Federation of Law Societies of Canada and the Law Council of Australia have also indicated that they favour the introduction of MDPs. The American Bar Association set up an MDP commission in August 1998. The work of the commission culminated in a vote taken by the ruling house of delegates against fee sharing with non-lawyers, the practice of law by non-lawyers and the sharing of control of law firms with non-lawyers. The view opposing MDPs is shared by the Law Society of Scotland.

Chapter 2

Issues Covered by a Standard Partnership Agreement

The importance of a written agreement

2.1   As noted in paragraph 1.10, it is not essential in law for a partnership to have a formal written partnership agreement. The rights and obligations of the partners may be agreed orally and may be inferred from a course of dealing. In the absence of agreement on specific issues, the *Partnership Act 1890* governs the rights and obligations of the partners.

A modern professional partnership should have a well-drafted written agreement. The following are some of the main benefits.

(*a*) *Certainty*. In the event of a dispute, a written partnership agreement is prima facie evidence of the terms upon which the partners have agreed to carry on business together though the terms of the partnership agreement may be determined and a written agreement overridden by a contrary course of dealing. [*Partnership Act 1890, s 19*]. In the absence of a written agreement, there is no convenient point from which to start ascertaining the partners' internal arrangements.

(*b*) *Concentrating the mind*. Discussing the terms of a draft partnership agreement and updating an existing agreement forces the partners to concentrate on the issues that concern them and to think through how the business will be run, and what their respective rights and obligations should be.

(*c*) *Overriding the Partnership Act*. There are many provisions in the *Partnership Act 1890* which will apply if not excluded by contrary agreement. Many of these provisions are wholly inappropriate for a modern professional partnership, and should be excluded by a carefully drafted written agreement.

For example, in the absence of contrary agreement:

(i) capital, profits and losses are to be shared or borne equally [*Partnership Act 1890, s 24(1)*];

(ii) a partner making an advance to the firm in excess of his agreed capital contribution is entitled to interest at 5% [*Partnership Act 1890, s 24(3)*];

    (iii) there is no other entitlement to interest on capital [*Partnership Act 1890, s 24(4)*];

    (iv) every partner can take part in management [*Partnership Act 1890, s 24(5)*];

    (v) no partner is entitled to any salary or fixed share of profits [*Partnership Act 1890, s 24(6)*];

    (vi) no new partner can be admitted without unanimous consent [*Partnership Act 1890, s 24(7)*];

    (vii) disagreements about ordinary matters relating to the business are decided by a simple majority but no change can be made to the nature of the business without unanimity [*Partnership Act 1890, s 24(8)*];

    (viii) no majority of partners can expel a partner [*Partnership Act 1890, s 25*];

    (ix) any partner can dissolve a partnership at will by giving oral or written notice (in the event that the partnership is constituted by deed) [*Partnership Act 1890, ss 26* and *32*];

    (x) the partnership will be dissolved automatically by the bankruptcy or death of a partner, and may be dissolved if a partner charges his share for his separate debts. [*Partnership Act 1890, s 33*].

(*d*)   *Evidence of the existence of the partnership.* Although not conclusive, a written partnership agreement is evidence of the existence of the partnership and its date of commencement.

(*e*)   *Avoiding disputes.* Few things can be more disruptive to a business than litigation between partners, and a clear agreement is the single most important way of avoiding this.

The form of a partnership agreement is often a deed, although this is not strictly necessary. If a deed is used, a debt owed under the partnership agreement will be a specialty debt and will become time barred after twelve years rather than the normal six-year limitation period. Otherwise, a written agreement is perfectly adequate.

It is common for supplemental agreements to be entered into, especially when a new partner joins the firm, or an existing partner retires from the firm, or the capital contributions or profit-sharing ratios of the partners are altered. The partnership agreement may be amended by a resolution of the partners (see paragraph 2.40). It is often helpful to produce regular consolidated versions of the partnership agreement as amended by supplemental agreements and resolutions. One partner may be made responsible for maintaining an up to date record of the agreement and its accompanying documents.

As explained above, a written partnership agreement can be varied with the consent of all the partners, and such consent inferred from a course of dealing, even if the formal amendment procedures established in the agreement have not been followed. It is therefore important to review the partnership agreement regularly to ensure that its terms reflect the firm's current practice. This is of particular significance when new partners are introduced to the firm, as they will be bound by the terms of the agreement as presented to them (usually the existing written agreement) until it is varied again with the agreement of all the partners (including the new partner), whether by way of resolution or by inference from conduct.

Typical clauses in a well-drafted partnership agreement

2.2 A model partnership agreement is set out in Appendix 4 and a checklist for preparation of partnership agreements is set out at 2.42 below. Every partnership is unique and will have its own individual requirements and the model agreement has been included for illustration purposes only. It is important that partners seek professional advice when preparing the agreement. Modern partnership agreements normally include clauses dealing with the matters described in the following paragraphs of this chapter.

The parties to the agreement

2.3 The parties will be those who are engaged jointly in the partnership business as principals, i.e. the equity partners including both sleeping and limited partners. Those who are not engaged in the business as principals, such as salaried partners, who are merely employees and not in receipt of any profit share although they are held out as if they were partners, will not normally be parties, although their rights and obligations should be fully set out in separate agreements.

The business to be carried on by the firm [clauses 1(1) and 2(1) of the model]

2.4 It is important to define the scope of the partnership business in the partnership agreement, and therefore the extent to which the partners authorise one another to bind the firm. However, some flexibility should be built in to accommodate future change.

Section 5 of the *Partnership Act 1890* provides that:

'Every partner is an agent of the firm and his other partners for the purpose of the business of the partnership; and the acts of every partner who does any act for carrying on in the usual way business of the kind carried on by the firm of which he is a member, bind the firm and his partners, unless the partner so acting has in fact no authority to act for the firm in the particular matter, and the person with whom he is dealing either knows that he has no authority, or does not know or believe him to be a partner.'

A partner will be bound by the acts of his fellow partners where those acts fall within the usual scope of the firm's business even if the acting partner is not actually authorised to carry out that particular act, unless the third party is aware of the acting partner's lack of authority.

Name of the firm [clauses 1(1) and 2(1) of the model]

2.5   The firm name should be stated in the partnership agreement, and the firm should ensure that it complies with

(a)   the provisions of the *Business Names Act 1985* where the name does not consist of the surnames of all the partners who are individuals and names of all the partners that are corporate entities; and

(b)   any professional regulations (for example, the Solicitors' Practice Rules 1990 Rule 11).

The *Business Names Act 1985* provides that the approval of the Secretary of State is required where certain words or expressions are used as or as part of a firm's business name. In addition, all business letters, written orders for goods or services, invoices and receipts and other similar documents issued in the course of business must state, in legible characters, the name of each partner and an address in Great Britain for the service of process. This last provision does not apply to a document issued by a partnership of more than 20 people which keeps at its principal place of business a list of the names of all the partners if:

(a)   none of the partners' names appear in the document except in the text or as a signatory; and

(b)   the document states the firm's principal place of business and says that a list of the partners can be inspected at that address.

The name may be a professional firm's most valuable asset. It is important to protect the name and any abbreviations or combinations of it by registration as a service mark, worldwide if appropriate. It is also important that the partnership agreement states that the name is a partnership asset and as such may only be assigned or licensed to third parties in agreed circumstances. The agreement should be drafted in such a way that the firm name cannot be used by a departing partner and provision should be made for devolution of the name on the retirement of a partner and on dissolution of the partnership. Where the partnership forms part of a national or international organisation which uses a common name, the agreement between member firms may dictate terms regulating and protecting the use of that name.

Duration of the partnership [clause 2(4) and 2(5) of the model]

2.6   This clause should state the date of commencement of the partnership (although this will not be conclusive proof of the actual date of commencement if it is not borne out by the facts (*Khan v Miah [1998] 1 WLR 477*)) and the circumstances in which the partnership will be dissolved.

If the duration of the partnership has not been agreed, the partnership will be a partnership at will and can be dissolved by any one partner giving notice to that effect. [*ss 26(1)* and *32(c) Partnership Act 1890*]. In the absence of an express provision to the contrary, the *Partnership Act 1890* also provides that a partnership will be dissolved by the death or bankruptcy of a partner. [*s 33*]. A partnership (whether of a fixed or certain duration) is also technically dissolved under general law whenever there is a change in the composition of the firm, for example, as a result of retirement, expulsion or the introduction of a new partner.

It is therefore important to override the position in law, as in most cases the partners will want the partnership business to continue when only some of their number leave. They will certainly want to avoid giving a single partner the ability to dissolve the firm unilaterally, thereby forcing the disposal of the firm's name and goodwill. This point should be addressed in the partnership agreement by providing either for a fixed duration of the partnership, or for a partnership for a certain term (often a term for the joint lives of any two of the partners). Either way, it should be specifically agreed that the partnership will not terminate when new partners join or existing partners leave the partnership, or where one partner serves notice of dissolution.

Place of business [clause 3 of the model]

2.7   It is usual to describe the place where the business is to be carried on, which is the place where the books must be kept, subject to contrary agreement.

Partnership property and goodwill [clause 4 of the model]

2.8   The partnership agreement should, wherever possible, make clear what is partnership property and what is property belonging to the individual partners, especially where some of the property used by the partnership is owned by individual partners. The agreement should also state whether the goodwill of the partnership belongs to one or more of the partners or is a firm asset, and whether or not an outgoing partner is entitled to a sum representing his share of the goodwill.

Legal title to land can be vested in a maximum of four individuals and it should be made clear in the title documentation, and possibly in the partnership agreement itself, that partnership land is held for the benefit of the partnership as a whole. It is often desirable for such property to be held in the name of a nominee company on trust for the partnership.

Partnership capital [clause 5 of the model]

2.9   A key decision for every partnership will be how to provide the firm's capital. The partners will have to decide whether to contribute equity or loan capital, and in what proportions. They should also agree the extent to which the capital is to be provided by loans from third parties, such as the firm's bank.

(*a*)   *Capital contributions*. The partnership agreement should specify how much capital is to be contributed, by whom, whether by way of equity or loan, whether in cash or in kind, how it should be owned and when contributions and withdrawals should be made. The agreement should also set out how the partners are to share paid-in capital, because if this is not dealt with, their entitlements will be treated as equal under *section 24* of the *Partnership Act 1890*. This is so even where partners have made unequal capital contributions (*Popat v Shonchhatra [1997] 3 All ER 800, CA*). The reasoning behind the statutory provision, that in the absence of express agreement to the contrary, equality should prevail between the partners, is the difficulty in evaluating a partner's contribution to the partnership in purely monetary terms.

(*b*)   *Interest on capital*. Sometimes firms agree to pay interest on the partners' capital contributions to the partnership, particularly if capital is contributed in proportions that are different from the proportions in which profits and losses are to be shared. If the agreement remains silent on this issue under the *Partnership Act 1890*, no interest will be payable [*s 20(4)*] unless the advance is greater than the partner's agreed capital contribution. [*s 24(3)* and *s 24(4) Partnership Act 1890*]. It may be appropriate for partners who make late capital contributions or early capital withdrawals to be charged interest.

(*c*)   *Outgoing partners*. The partnership agreement should provide for what happens to the capital contributed by an outgoing partner. This is usually dealt with in the outgoing partner provisions (see 2.27–2.33 below).

(*d*)   *Changes in capital*. The partnership agreement will usually provide for flexibility for the future by way of periodic revisions of the amount of capital needed (perhaps at the end of every accounting year). If no provision is made for additional capital contributions or withdrawals of capital, individual partners cannot be compelled to provide additional capital at a later date and no contributing partner is entitled to make a withdrawal. Agreements should normally specify what effect changes in the partners' profit sharing ratios have on the partners' capital contributions, and the time and manner in which additional capital is to be contributed or withdrawals made. In the model partnership agreement, each partner's capital contribution is linked to his profit share, so that if a partner's profit share decreases, he receives back a corresponding proportion of his capital contribution but the firm's capital base remains unchanged.

Sometimes agreements provide for periodic revaluations of the partnership property, with consequent debits and credits to the partners' capital accounts, but this is unusual because a revaluation can trigger a subsequent capital gains tax charge. Furthermore, such revaluations may cause confusion as, in the absence of express provision to the contrary, capital contributions cannot be withdrawn, unlike capital profits arising on revaluations.

Profits and losses [clause 6 of the model]

2.10   Under *section 24(1)* of the *Partnership Act 1890* profits are to be shared equally, but this is rarely what the parties intend. It is therefore important to agree how profits are to be shared. *Joyce v Morrissey [1999] EMLR 233* illustrates that where partners want to displace the presumption of equality, it has to be made absolutely clear to all the partners that profit sharing will be on an unequal basis. That cannot be achieved by simply circulating accounts to the partners showing an unequal distribution. The profits and losses of a firm are made up of those of a capital nature and those of a revenue nature. Capital profits or losses are those profits or losses arising on the realisation of capital assets (e.g. the sale of goodwill). Revenue profits or losses are those profits or losses arising from the firm's trading activities (e.g. professional fees and income on cash deposits).

The agreement should state clearly how both capital and revenue profits are to be shared and how capital and revenue losses are to be borne. Some agreements provide for partners to have a fixed profit share (akin to a salary), sharing any surplus profits in accordance with their agreed profit sharing ratios. If the profits fall short of the aggregate guaranteed profit shares, it is important to agree who will suffer the shortfall and in what shares. A court would normally conclude, in the absence of an express provision to the contrary, that losses should be borne by the partners in proportion to their profit shares. The partners may decide to share the profits and losses in different proportions. Chapter 6 discusses profit and loss sharing in more detail. The agreement must clarify how profits and losses are computed. As from the tax year 1999/2000, professional partnerships are subject to income tax on profits computed on an earnings basis and taxable profits (including work-in-progress) are computed for tax purposes on the basis of a true and fair view (see Chapter 18). Partners need to decide whether the accounts should be prepared on the same basis in order to determine the rights of the partners.

Problems may arise where a partner receives director's fees from a client company or holds shares in a company in connection with the partnership's business. The agreement should clarify whether the partner has a duty to account for such fees and any dividends or for any other income to the firm or whether he can treat them as his own.

Drawings [clause 7 of the model]

2.11 The profits of a partnership for a particular year of account may not be agreed for months after the year end, but the partners will need to draw money on account in their respective profit shares throughout the year. Even when profits have been agreed, it may be desirable for the firm to retain a proportion of each partner's profit entitlement, whether to meet working capital requirements or to provide for individual partners' tax liabilities.

Therefore, the partnership agreement should set out the partners' respective drawings entitlements very clearly, and deal with the consequences of over-drawings and under-drawings.

Books and accounts [clause 8 of the model]

2.12 The agreement will usually specify the firm's accounting date and state that annual accounts are to be prepared. There may be less provision for the accounts to be audited. The agreement should state whether the accounts are to take into account work-in-progress and goodwill. As from the tax year 1999/2000, partnerships have been required to take into account work-in-progress for income tax purposes. The firm's accountants are often named in the partnership agreement and most agreements specify where the books are kept. Each partner normally has a right to inspect and take copies of the partnership books. If particular partners' rights are to be restricted, this should be specified.

It is important that the partnership agreement reflects the firm's accounting practices and where it is intended that the accounts are produced on a different basis in specified circumstances, that this is set out clearly in the agreement. This was highlighted in *White v Minnis ([2000] 3 All ER 618, CA)*. In that case the agreement required that each year accounts were drawn up showing the capital at a 'just valuation'. Over the years, the firm's accounts had always been shown at historic cost. The personal representatives of a deceased partner argued that for the purposes of calculating the deceased partner's share in the capital of the partnership, the accounts should be shown at market value. The Court of Appeal held that as the partners had dealt with the property in the accounts on an historic basis for many years, that was a 'just valuation' within the meaning of the agreement.

Provision for tax liabilities [clause 9 of the model]

2.13 Under the old partnership taxation regime the income tax liability of a partnership was assessed on the partnership and apportioned between the partners. Under the self-assessment regime (which had its first full year in 1997/98) income tax is the responsibility of the individual partners. However, many professional partnerships continue to provide for tax retentions to be held by the firm until needed by the individual partner to meet his tax liability and many have chosen to continue the practice of the firm meeting the individual partners' tax liabilities direct. A typical tax retention clause will provide for the partnership to provide fully for all tax due and payable on all profits earned up to the end of each accounting period in that year's accounts. If the accounts date does not fall at the end of a tax year, consideration needs to be given to providing for a reserve for anticipated tax liabilities on the basis that a partner may retire in that accounting period. Thought needs to be given to the repayment of any excess retentions, interest payment and the appointment of a partner with responsibility for ensuring compliance with any statutory and Inland Revenue requirements. The partnership should provide the nominated partner with all necessary information and indemnify that partner in respect of liabilities incurred in the course of that role (other than those liabilities occasioned by his own wrongdoing).

Bank accounts [clause 10 of the model]

2.14   Partnership agreements normally name the firm's bankers and the partners who are to be authorised to sign cheques. Provision may be made for different levels of security, depending upon the value of the cheque.

Insurance [clause 11 of the model]

2.15   Most agreements contain provisions setting out the basic insurance cover to be maintained by the partnership, including employers' liability insurance, professional indemnity cover, third party liability insurance and cover for partnership assets.

Many partnerships provide for former partners to be given the protection of any insurance cover to the extent that they are liable for any partnership related claims.

Restrictions and duties [clause 12 of the model]

Duty of good faith

2.16   It is a fundamental principle that partners must act with the utmost good faith towards each other. The duty amounts to an obligation to be entirely honest, straightforward and open in all dealings between partners and to disclose all material facts. As part of this duty, partners are obliged by *section 28* of the *Partnership Act 1890* 'to render true accounts and full information of all things affecting the partnership to any partner or his legal representatives'. Although this is implied in any event, most agreements include an express provision to remind parties of this important duty.

The duty of good faith includes an obligation not to make private profits at the expense of the firm, and to share with the firm any private profits made in the course of the firm's business. [See *Partnership Act 1890, ss 29* and *30*]. A partner who uses information gained during the course of the partnership business to acquire a personal benefit will normally have to account for the profit that he makes. Similarly, a partner who obtains a directorship of a client company will generally be accountable for the fees that he earns. This duty to account may be overruled by contrary .agreement. The agreement should specify if a partner is to be allowed to keep any director's fees or other profits for his own benefit. It is important to have regard for any professional rules which may restrict the freedom of the firm or an individual partner in the firm to act for a client where a directorship or appointment is held with that client.

Full time and attention

2.17 It will normally be appropriate to specify in the partnership agreement that the partners' whole time and attention should be devoted to the partnership business. In the absence of such a provision, it may be impossible to show that a lack of commitment to the business amounts to a breach of duty.

The full time and attention clause will generally be coupled with an express prohibition against pursuing outside business interests, so that a partner who is in breach of this obligation can be forced to stop pursuing those interests by injunction, or be required to compensate the firm for loss.

In some cases, certain partners will want to have the freedom to pursue outside business interests and, if agreed, the partnership agreement should contain a mechanism to allow that partner to do so without being in breach of his general duty to spend his full time and attention on the partnership business.

To reduce the risk of a partner being unable to meet his share of any losses or liabilities, it is common to prohibit partners from joining any syndicate at Lloyd's, conducting any other business or holding any share in a company with unlimited liability.

To ensure that offices can be monitored, agreements often require partners to obtain the consent of the managing partner or a committee before accepting such a position and to specify whether the position is held for the account of the partnership or personally. If it is a partnership appointment it is normal for the partner to be fully indemnified by the firm in respect of all costs and liabilities incurred in that capacity. This consent requirement can help the firm avoid any partner putting himself in a position where his duties as a partner may conflict with those as a director or trustee.

Restrictions

2.18 *Section 5* of the *Partnership Act 1890* states that 'every partner is an agent of the firm and his other partners for the purpose of the business of the partnership'. A partnership agreement usually places specific restrictions on a partner's ability to bind the firm unless he obtains the partners' prior consent.

Such restrictions may include preventing a partner from compromising, compounding, releasing or discharging any debt, entering into any bond, bail, security or surety, lending any money or property of the partnership or giving credit or acting for or having any dealing with any person whom the partner has been requested not to deal with by the other partners.

Dealings with partnership interests

2.19   Partnership is essentially a personal relationship, and the *Partnership Act 1890* recognises this. *Section 31* provides that, subject to any contrary agreement, an assignee will have no right to participate in the management of the business, or even to inspect the books. He is simply entitled to his share of the partnership profits and, on dissolution, assets. In the context of a professional partnership, it is normally appropriate to go further and specify that partnership interests are non-assignable and that the partners may not charge their interests in the partnership. However, if the partnership is to be funded significantly by borrowings, the lender will often insist upon personal guarantees from the partners and perhaps a charge on all their personal assets, other than the partnership share itself. The partnership agreement should not prevent the partners from agreeing suitable terms with lenders.

Professional and regulatory rules

2.20   Professional partnership agreements usually provide that partners must comply with all regulatory and professional obligations. The inclusion of such a clause gives each partner a contractual duty to comply with these obligations, and in default other partners may be able to obtain damages from the defaulting partner or an order for specific performance.

Confidentiality

2.21   A partner, like anyone who occupies a fiduciary position implying trust and confidence, will be subject to a duty under general law not to disclose confidential partnership information, and this is often supplemented by express wording in the partnership agreement. This may make it easier for the firm to prevent a disaffected partner from disclosing confidential information to the trade press by injunction, or to obtain damages if the partner acts in breach of the restriction and the firm suffers loss.

Indemnity

2.22   It is common to include a clause whereby each of the partners agrees to indemnify the other partners if he breaches any of the obligations contained in the duties clause. This prevents the need for an action in damages against the defaulting partner and overcomes a technical difficulty, namely the uncertainty that exists as to whether co-partners can recover damages from a partner who is in breach of the partnership agreement.

Management and decision-making [clauses 14–16 of the model]

2.23   *Section 24(5)* of the *Partnership Act 1890* provides that every partner has a right to take part in the management of the business. *Section 24(8)* provides that differences between the partners in relation to ordinary matters connected with the partnership business may be resolved by majority decision, except that a change in the nature of the partnership business can only be resolved by unanimous decision. The basic position in the *Partnership Act 1890* is rarely sufficient for a modern firm and there is a trend among professional partnerships at present away from full partner involvement in the day-to-day decision-making process and towards a management team-led process: in an era of fast growing national and international practices it is increasingly difficult and ill-advised for all the partners of the firm to be actively involved in the management of its day-to-day affairs.

It is usual for agreements to specify that certain decisions will be taken by a senior or managing partner, or a committee, whilst other more important decisions require a specified majority vote of the partners. For example, routine decisions such as the purchase of stationery and the hiring and firing of secretarial staff are often delegated to a particular committee or officer. But major decisions, for example, dissolving the firm, admitting or expelling partners, appointing salaried partners, acquiring a company or business, merging with another firm, amending the terms of the agreement, acquiring or disposing of freehold or leasehold property, often require a specified majority decision. Partners should consider whether the requirement for unanimous decisions to be made in certain circumstances may allow a capricious or dissident partner to block decisions which are in the general interests of the firm.

Striking a balance

2.24   The partnership agreement must find a balance between:

(*a*)   enabling the firm to make fast and effective management decisions in an increasingly competitive market place;

(*b*)   enabling the firm to deal with sensitive issues, such as an under-performing partner, decisively but fairly; and

(*c*)   preserving the fragile atmosphere of co-operation and mutual benefit known as the 'spirit of partnership'.

The larger the firm, the harder it becomes to achieve the first two objectives without sacrificing the third. Those partnerships that choose to move towards a complex, corporate governance style of management must ensure that the management structure remains fully accountable and in touch with the partners. Some of the larger partnerships achieve this by establishing a policy board in addition to a management committee. The policy board represents the partnership as a whole, acting as a sounding board to the management committee and providing strategic direction to the partnership. Whatever governance procedures are chosen, it is important that they are described fully and clearly in the partnership agreement.

Deadlocks may arise where decisions have to be taken by majority decision. Ways round this difficulty are as follows:

(i)   not to have any specific provision in the partnership agreement dealing with deadlock but to try to resolve problems as they arise by negotiation (although if the negotiations fail, then dissolution of the partnership may be the only practical answer);

(ii)   providing a senior or managing partner with a casting vote in the event of a deadlock;

(iii)   giving partners differing numbers of votes depending on their capital contributions, seniority within the firm or some other factor; or

(iv)   giving one or more partners the right to veto certain decisions.

Under the self-assessment regime a partner is required to deal with the making of the partnership return and partnership statement and it is sensible to elect an individual to that position.

Partnership and committee meetings

2.25   The *Partnership Act 1890* says little about the conduct of partnership meetings, although the duty of good faith confers a right on every partner to have his point of view heard and discussed. Especially in the context of larger partnerships, it is desirable to agree some guidelines, and the partnership agreement can usefully set out a code governing the conduct of partners' meetings and committees. Such codes will deal with issues such as the notice required for meetings, quorum requirements and voting procedures including proxy voting and voting rights where a partner declares an interest in the question to be decided. Minutes of these meetings should be taken and circulated to the partners.

Incoming partners [clause 17 of the model]

2.26   The partnership agreement should make provision for the admission of new partners. Otherwise, a dissident partner may be able to block the appointment of a new partner who may be important to the future of the firm.

The partnership agreement should deal with the terms on which new partners will be admitted. A large majority in favour (such as 80% or 90%) is often required. In the absence of agreement, unanimity will be required.

A new partner does not become liable to the creditors of the firm for any debts and obligations incurred before he became a partner. [*Section 17(1) Partnership Act 1890*]. However, liabilities incurred before his appointment but first provided for in the profit and loss account after his appointment will have the effect of making him indirectly liable by decreasing the profits or increasing the losses of the firm for the relevant period.

The agreement should establish how much capital (if any) the new partner must contribute to the partnership and the new partners' profit and loss sharing ratios. In order to ensure that the new partner is bound by the terms of the existing partnership agreement, the existing partners may ask him to sign a supplemental deed confirming that the terms of the main partnership agreement apply to him and setting out any particular issues that relate solely to him.

It can sometimes be helpful to attach as a schedule to the partnership agreement a standard form of supplemental accession deed for use when new partners join the partnership.

The admission of salaried partners as employees is normally effected by a separate contract with the salaried partner concerned. The partnership agreement will often provide for a special majority decision of the partners to approve the appointment of a salaried partner.

Outgoing partners [clauses 19–22 of the model]

2.27   The agreement should specify the circumstances in which partners cease to be partners and the rights and obligations of outgoing partners. Under the general law, a partnership for an indefinite term is dissolved when a partner retires or dies, and it is important to provide in the agreement that, in these circumstances, the partnership continues between the remaining partners.

Expulsion and compulsory retirement

2.28   *Section 25* of the *Partnership Act 1890* provides that:

'No majority of the partners can expel any partner unless a power to do so has been conferred by express agreement between the partners.'

Therefore, unless the partnership agreement makes express provision for the expulsion of partners, the only way to expel a partner would be to dissolve the partnership. This would lead to the forced disposal of all the partnership assets, including its goodwill.

Most agreements include an expulsion provision providing that a partner may be expelled with immediate effect or on notice, where all or a substantial majority of the other partners agree. The agreement normally sets out a list of grounds for expulsion for cause, such as criminal activities and professional misconduct, infringement of the rules of any professional body regulating the firm, a serious or persistent breach of the agreement or insolvency and mental or physical incapacity preventing compliance with the terms of the partnership agreement. In the absence of such a clause, the mental incapacity of a partner can cause considerable inconvenience, making it necessary for the firm to deal with the relevant partner's attorney under an enduring power (where available), or with a Court of Protection Receiver.

One of the most difficult management issues is how to deal with underperforming partners who have not actually committed a breach of the agreement. Of course, prevention is better than cure, and a well-managed firm will monitor the performance of individual partners and give them the help and support they need to contribute everything that is expected of them. Unfortunately, however, it may be impossible for some partners to keep up, and it is important to ensure that the firm can avoid a situation in which underperformers hold the firm back to such an extent that the firm cannot satisfy the aspirations of its high-fliers. It is normally possible to resolve the situation by mutual agreement, but ultimately the firm must have the means to secure the compulsory retirement of a partner where it is impossible to reach agreement. This will generally require a substantial majority of votes.

Whether a partner is being expelled or compulsorily retired, this must of course be handled with the utmost good faith. It must be fully debated, and, in the case of an expulsion 'for cause', the outgoing partner must be given the opportunity to put forward his case.

With a view to protecting the interests of the firm, partners should consider incorporating gardening leave provisions in their agreement. This may provide that for the duration of any notice period, a partner who is subject to the notice may be denied access to the office, to clients and to staff, which helps isolate him. He could also be deprived of his right to participate in decision-making during this period. It may be unduly harsh to impose garden leave on an underperformer who is compulsorily retired.

Suspension

2.29   Some partnership agreements provide for the suspension of partners for a period of time (for example, where a criminal investigation is pending or continuing but where no findings have been published or convictions obtained). The *Partnership Act 1890* does not contemplate suspension, and suitable terms must be incorporated in the written agreement, where appropriate. The suspended partner may be excluded from the firm's offices, staff and clients during the period of suspension, may not be allowed to draw profits during the period of his suspension and may be deprived of his right to participate in all decision-making, depending on the agreement reached. However, because of the obvious scope for abuse of such a clause, considerable care has to be taken to ensure that the power is exercised in the utmost good faith.

Retirement

2.30   The *Partnership Act 1890* makes no provision for the retirement of partners and, in the absence of such a clause, the only means available to a partner who wishes to leave the firm is to dissolve the firm. The partnership agreement should therefore set out the circumstances in which partners may retire from the firm. Most partnership agreements provide that partners can give notice to retire, and for compulsory retirement at a specified age. Since partnership agreements generally provide for retiring partners to be able to withdraw their capital from the firm, and this can lead to serious cash flow problems, a limit is occasionally imposed on the number of partners who may retire in a particular year. However, the issue of restricting the number of partners that may retire at any one time is not straightforward, as the courts are generally reluctant to force partners to continue in partnership against their will. There is a danger that in a situation where a partner is prevented from retiring from a firm in this manner, he could apply to court to dissolve the partnership on the grounds that circumstances had arisen which made dissolution just and equitable. [*Section 35* of the *Partnership Act 1890*]. An alternative is to provide for the withdrawal of capital from the partnership in fixed instalments, thereby controlling the cash flow situation. Sometimes provision is made for retiring partners to have a continuing involvement with the firm, perhaps as consultants.

Death

2.31   The partnership agreement should state that the partnership will continue after the death of a partner. Otherwise, under *section 33(1)*, the partnership will automatically dissolve, unless the deceased partner was a limited partner. [*Limited Partnerships Act 1907, s 6(2)*]. Sometimes it is intended that the executors should continue in partnership until the expiry of a fixed term (although this would obviously be highly unusual in the context of a professional partnership), and this will have to be spelt out in the partnership agreement.

The agreement should also deal with how a deceased partner's share in the profits and capital of the partnership should be calculated and paid out to his personal representatives. It may also provide for any annuities that might become payable to the deceased partner's dependants, although annuity payments are becoming increasingly rare in the context of professional partnerships.

Bankruptcy

2.32   If it is intended that the partnership should continue following the bankruptcy of one of the partners, this must be clearly stated in the partnership agreement. Otherwise, *section 33(1)* of the *Partnership Act 1890* provides for the partnership to dissolve.

Entitlement of outgoing partners [clause 23 of the model]

2.33   The agreement should deal with the financial entitlements of outgoing partners and, where a partner has died, the entitlement of his personal representatives. Such entitlement will include a return of capital, the withdrawal of any further revenue or capital profits due and accrued interest on the partner's capital account (if any).

Often the partnership agreement will provide for the withdrawal of capital in instalments (with or without interest) to minimise cash flow problems when a partner leaves or even to discourage early leavers. The provision should deal with how any advances made to or overdrawings made by the outgoing partner should be repaid (normally by way of set-off against the outgoing partner's share). Some agreements include a retention provision to provide for unknown liabilities such as negligence claims incurred whilst the outgoing partner was still a partner. Sometimes these provisions only apply if the partner is retiring voluntarily to discourage partners from leaving the firm to join a competitor.

The partnership agreement may also seek to discourage outgoing partners from acting in breach of any restrictive covenants or in breach of the agreement in any other way by preventing a partner in breach from receiving some part of his expected financial entitlement on leaving the partnership. If such a provision is included, care should be taken to ensure the inclusion of a clause stating that the provisions of the agreement are independent of each other, so that if a court were to find the clause unenforceable the other provisions in the agreement would remain unaffected.

The partnership agreement should specify how the remaining partners are to acquire the outgoing partner's share. Partnership agreements generally provide either for the outgoing partner's share to accrue automatically to the other partners, or for the continuing partners to be able to elect to acquire that share. Whilst the latter approach provides for flexibility as it enables partners to assess the firm's financial viability before choosing to exercise the option, most professional partnerships favour the former approach. Despite the potential financial hardship to the continuing partners if the firm is struggling, an automatic accruer clause avoids the risk of a dissolution and stability and continuity are encouraged.

For the purposes of inheritance tax, it is important that the continuing partners should not be given a contractual right to purchase the outgoing partner's share because such a 'buy and sell' agreement would mean that the deceased partner's partnership interest would not be 'relevant business property' for inheritance tax purposes.

Care needs to be taken to ensure that, where the continuing partners can effectively buy out a bankrupt partner's share, the transaction is not vulnerable to attack by the trustee in bankruptcy as a 'transaction at an undervalue' for the purposes of the *Insolvency Act 1986*.

It is important that the partnership agreement clarifies whether an outgoing partner's rights are to be calculated by reference to the value of the partnership assets that appears in the firm's annual accounts or whether full market value is to be substituted. Sometimes it is intended that the partnership assets should be revalued on a partner ceasing to be a partner, so that any increase or decrease in value can be debited or credited to the outgoing partner's capital account on his departure. The capital gains tax consequences of such a provision are discussed in Chapter 19.

If retired partners and their dependants are to be entitled to an annuity from the firm, this should be spelt out in the partnership agreement, but this is increasingly rare and partners are normally encouraged to make their own provision for retirement.

Debt exposure

2.34   The exposure of an outgoing partner to debts of the firm is fully discussed in Chapter 3.

Outgoing partners' liabilities

2.35   An outgoing partner remains liable for the partnership debts and obligations, breaches of trust and contract, fraud (in the course of the partnership business) and negligence incurred while he was a partner, unless contrary agreement is reached with any creditors. [*Sections 9, 10* and *11 Partnership Act 1890*]. Thus, outgoing partners may remain liable for continuing obligations, for example, under the covenants of a firm's lease or under hire-purchase agreements. Similarly, where there is a claim for negligence after the partners who committed the wrong have left the firm, it is the partners who were partners at the time of the negligent action who are liable, not the partners in the firm at the time the cause of action accrues (although it is the partners at the time the cause of action arises who will be sued, they will be entitled to a right of contribution from the former partners).

Under *section 9* of the *Partnership Act 1890*, an outgoing partner ceases to be liable for any partnership debts or obligations incurred after he ceases to be a partner but he will continue to be exposed if he is held out as being a continuing partner or is an apparent partner, for example, if existing clients and contacts are not informed that he has left the firm. The holding-out doctrine and the agency principle of 'apparent' members do not apply to tortuous acts.

Given the above, most partnership agreements include an express indemnity for outgoing partners, although a right to indemnity from the continuing partners is generally implied in any event by the fact that the outgoing partner ceases to have a share in the firm's profits and losses.

Sometimes agreements provide for outgoing partners to remain liable for the consequences of professional negligence or breach of duty on the part of that partner alone. An account is drawn up as at the date he leaves the firm and provision is made for any known liabilities before he withdraws his capital from the firm and on occasions sums are retained to provide for unknown liabilities (see paragraph 2.33). The rationale for such an indemnity is that it achieves a clean break.

Restrictive covenants [clause 24 of the model]

2.36 In an age of increasing mobility of partners, it is desirable to protect the firm's goodwill, which depends on its partners and employees, from time to time. This protection is particularly important when a partner leaves to join a rival firm, and a clear set of restrictive covenants can help to avoid damage to the business of the partnership.

Restrictive covenants

2.37 Most major UK professional firms have restrictive covenants although, interestingly, most US law firms tend not to place restrictions on outgoing partners acting in competition with the firm.

Some argue that it is wrong as a matter of principle to interfere with a partner's right to work after his departure and a firm should not force a partner to stay but rather inspire partners to stay. On the other hand, partners are stakeholders in their firm and unless reasonable restrictive covenants are included in the partnership agreement the danger is that a firm facing a period of financial difficulty may become inherently unstable as partners seek to leave the partnership rather than help the firm work through its financial difficulties. Where outgoing partners have a complete indemnity, partner defections leave the remaining partners to meet the same overheads out of diminished turnover and a trickle of defections could turn into a flood. Generally in the UK it is thought perfectly legitimate for a firm to seek to protect its goodwill by discouraging defections and minimising the damage when they occur; especially as the courts have shown themselves willing to enforce reasonable restrictions and the trend in the market place is to include them.

The basic legal principle is that covenants are inherently anti-competitive, and they are therefore viewed as contrary to public policy and unenforceable if they go further than is strictly necessary to protect the legitimate interest of the ongoing business. In the context of partnership structures, restrictive covenants should be no more onerous than is reasonable to protect the goodwill of the partnership.

Three kinds of restrictive covenants are often used.

The model partnership agreement includes a traditional clause seeking to prevent an outgoing partner from practising at all in a specified area for a limited period. Such clauses must be very limited in terms of the geographical area and the period of application if they are to be reasonable. A more general non-compete clause, which simply prevents competition with the business for a specified period, is becoming increasingly popular given the relative ease with which those seeking to rely on them can argue that the effect of such restrictions is reasonable. Non-competition covenants prevent a partner from competing directly or indirectly with the firm for a fixed period of time after leaving the partnership. In a franchise case, *Kall-Kwik Printing (UK) Ltd v Rush [1996] FSR 114*, the courts interpreted competition to mean 'a business capable of competing with the [business] and not simply a business of the same type'. The courts view non-competition covenants as inherently self-limiting, and there is therefore no requirement for any geographical limitation on their operation.

Non-solicitation of and dealing with partnership client restrictions aim to prohibit a partner from soliciting clients or dealing with clients for a fixed period of time, irrespective of whether or not the partner initiated the approach. Careful consideration needs to be given to the definition of a partnership client in this context to ensure that the restriction is no wider than is reasonable, and it should be noted that if the services to be supplied by an outgoing partner to a partnership client are not the same as those that the partnership supplies, any attempt to rely on such a restriction would be likely to be deemed unreasonable.

Non-solicitation of staff covenants prevent a partner from 'poaching' staff by preventing an outgoing partner from encouraging a current employee to join him in a different business venture.

The term of such covenants has been a matter for debate in recent years. The current view is that, notwithstanding the five-year term upheld in the Privy Council decision in *Bridge v Deacon [1984] 2 All ER 19, PC*, partnerships should opt for a lower term and thereby increase the likelihood of being able to enforce the covenants. The principle borne out by subsequent cases is that such covenants will be enforceable only if they are reasonable, in the interests of the parties and the public and no wider than is required for the proper protection of the covenantee.

The *Competition Act 1998* came into force on 1 March 2000, and will affect partnership agreements containing non-compete clauses. Chapter I of that Act prohibits agreements which have as their object or effect the prevention, restriction or distortion of competition within the UK or a part of it. This is an as yet untried area of law. However, *section 60* of the *Competition Act 1998* provides that in applying the Act, a court must ensure that it is interpreted consistently with European law, the relevant provisions here being *Article 81(1)* (formerly *Article 85(1)*) of the *EC Treaty*, and the rules interpreting the EC Merger Regulation.

Article 81(1) prohibits agreements which have as their object or effect the prevention, restriction or distortion of competition within the EU or part of it. However, in the context of sale and purchase agreements, agreements containing restrictive covenants have been held to fall outside *Article 81(1)* of the *EC Treaty* where such clauses are reasonable in time and scope. This may shed some light on the provisions relating to the transfer of a partner's interest in the business to the other partners on his retirement. Under the EC Merger Regulation, specific provision is made in relation to non-compete clauses where they can be seen as ancillary restrictions. The legal rationale is that they guarantee the purchaser the full value of the asset acquired. To be enforceable, however, the restriction must be limited to a reasonable duration, geographic scope and subject matter. The current notice on Ancillary Restrictions states that a five-year period is appropriate for a non-compete covenant if the sale includes both goodwill and know-how, and a two-year period would be appropriate in cases where goodwill alone is included. However, proposals are currently before the Commission to amend these to a maximum of three and two years respectively.

Should these proposals be enacted they could have wider ramifications for the future consideration by the UK courts in interpreting Chapter I of the *Competition Act 1998*.

Even if reasonable restrictive covenants are included, in practice it can be very damaging to the partnership to insist that a particular client ceases to use the outgoing partner's services, and the partnership may feel that it cannot seek an injunction preventing this. In those circumstances, it may be necessary instead to claim damages for breach from the outgoing partner. Sometimes agreements specify how such damages are to be computed. The method of computation must be a genuine pre-estimate of the actual loss that the firm will suffer, as the court may otherwise strike it down as an unenforceable penalty, and exercise its own discretion to quantify the damage.

The individual restrictive covenants should be drafted as separate clauses, so that if the court thinks that any one of the covenants is unreasonable, then it can be struck out, leaving the remainder intact. A partnership agreement may encourage the partners to adhere to the restrictive covenants by way of financial incentives, for example, denying outgoing partners in breach of such restrictions some part of their financial package (see 2.33).

In practice, restrictive covenants are often not enforced but there is ample case law and market knowledge to rely upon them and such clauses maximise a firm's negotiating power if it faces a defecting partner situation.

Generally a well-drafted partnership agreement will also prohibit an outgoing partner from representing himself as a partner or using the partnership name in any way. An outgoing partner should also be prevented from disclosing information that is confidential to the partnership, and many agreements require such partners to return to the continuing partners all documents, records and other papers in their possession which relate to the partnership business. An outgoing partner may only be entitled to inform other continuing partners and not employees of his impending departure.

Dissolution and winding up [clause 25 of the model]

2.38   As noted above, the expulsion, retirement, death and bankruptcy of a partner will lead to the automatic dissolution of the partnership unless the agreement provides otherwise.

Dissolution may also be caused by expiration of the term of a fixed term partnership or, in the case of an indefinite term partnership, by any partner giving notice to the other partners of his intention to dissolve the partnership. If an individual partner has power to dissolve the firm unilaterally, and thus perhaps to force a sale of the firm's assets, including goodwill, he will have a very powerful weapon in the event of a dispute. To avoid this, the partnership agreement should normally provide that the partnership may only be dissolved if dissolution is approved by all or a significant majority of the partners.

Section 35 of the *Partnership Act 1890* provides that any partner may apply to the court for a decree of dissolution of a partnership in one of a number of situations, including where:

(*a*) a partner becomes permanently incapable of performing his part of the partnership agreement;

(*b*) the conduct of a partner is felt to be prejudicially affecting the conduct of the business, or a partner conducts himself in such a way that it is not reasonably practicable for the other partners to carry on business with him;

(*c*) the partner is persistently in breach of his obligations under the partnership agreement or the business of the partnership can only be carried on at a loss; or

(*d*) it is just and equitable that the partnership be dissolved.

The partner seeking dissolution cannot be the partner creating the reasons for dissolving the partnership. Dissolution may also be brought about by rescission for fraud or misrepresentation or by repudiation of the partnership agreement.

The agreement should set out the procedures to be followed on dissolution and should state how specific partnership assets (e.g. goodwill, the name and the firm's intellectual property rights) are to be dealt with on winding up. It will often be appropriate for the partnership agreement to provide for goodwill etc. to be sold to the highest bidding group of former partners, in the event of a dissolution.

Mediation and arbitration [clause 26 of the model]

2.39 To prevent a public airing of partnership disputes in the court and to encourage the preservation of relations between partners wherever possible, it is usual to include in a modern partnership agreement a private dispute resolution process.

An arbitration clause will provide for any dispute to be heard in private by an arbitrator or panel of arbitrators. In the case of a professional partnership, provision is often made for the arbitrator to be appointed by the President of the relevant professional body, or of the Chartered Institute of Arbitrators. The parties may provide that the arbitration rules of an arbitration institution will regulate the procedures to be adopted for the arbitration. The rules relating to arbitration proceedings are contained in the *Arbitration Act 1996* and in a substantial body of court decisions.

In the hope of restoring the trust and confidence that underlies the successful partnership relationship and to keep dispute resolution as inexpensive, quick and informal as possible, mediation may be used. Mediation involves a neutral third party who clarifies the objectives of the parties, seeks to find common ground between them, does not impose a solution on them and encourages them to resolve their points of difference by agreement in a way which avoids more formal means of dispute resolution, such as arbitration or court proceedings. It is possible to include a requirement that any dispute must first be referred to mediation. Mediators can be appointed with the assistance of, among other bodies, the Centre for Dispute Resolution. In case a mediation proves unsuccessful, the partnership agreement will also need to provide for a form of binding dispute resolution by arbitration or the courts.

Furthermore, the partnership agreement can require that technical matters, valuation issues and other matters relating to the exercise of professional judgement or expertise should be referred for expert determination. This method of dispute resolution is particularly helpful for dealing with disputes about matters relating to accounting standards and practice. The agreement should specify how the expert is to be chosen and what issue is required to be determined and should confirm that the expert does not act as arbitrator. It should also specify that the expert's decision is final and binding.

Alterations to the partnership agreement [clause 27 of the model]

2.40   In the absence of any contrary agreement, the partnership agreement can only be changed by unanimous agreement. This may cause considerable practical problems if a dissident minority stand in the way of a change which is viewed as important by the vast majority of the partners. It is therefore common to provide for the agreement to be capable of being altered by a particular majority, say 75% or 90% of the partners.

Other clauses

2.41   The partnership agreement may deal with many other issues in particular cases, including the following.

(*a*)   Holidays and other leave such as sick leave, sabbaticals and maternity leave.

(*b*)   Partners' pensions, life assurance and health insurance. For a fuller discussion of these issues see Chapters 15 and 26.

(*c*)   Cars provided to partners.

(*d*)   The right of partners to the provision of free services for themselves and their families perhaps subject to an overall limit.

(*e*)   Costs of drawing up the partnership agreement.

(*f*)   Whole agreement clause providing that the terms of the partnership agreement govern the firm to the exclusion of all earlier agreements except where otherwise stated.

PARTNERSHIP AGREEMENT CHECKLIST

2.42 It may be helpful to refer to the following checklist when reviewing a partnership agreement or preparing a new one.

1. The partners
(1) Are there more than 20 partners? If so, is the partnership exempt from restrictions on numbers? (2) Do all the partners have the necessary professional qualifications and, where appropriate, the qualifications required to carry on investment business under the *Financial Services and Markets Act 2000*?
2. The business of the firm
(1) What will the firm's business be? (2) What sort of majority will be required if the firm is to change the nature of its business?
3. The name of the firm
(1) Under what name will the firm carry on business? (2) Does the name comply with the *Business Names Act 1985*? (3) Does all the firm's stationery comply with the *Business Names Act 1985*? (4) Has the name been protected by registration as a service mark wherever necessary? (5) Does the name comply with any contractual obligations owed to associated firms and others?
4. Duration of the partnership
(1) Does the agreement make clear when it is to take effect? (2) Should the partnership be expressed to exist for a fixed term? (3) Has it been made clear, where appropriate, that death, retirement, expulsion and bankruptcy will not lead to dissolution of the firm? (4) Has it been made clear, where appropriate, that the firm cannot be dissolved except by specified majority decision?
5. Place of business
(1) Where will the firm carry on business? (2) If new partnership premises are to be established, what kind of majority will be required for the decision to be effective?

6.	Partnership property and goodwill
	(1) Is it clear what assets are partnership assets?
	(2) Do the partnership premises belong to the firm or to individual partners?
	(3) If the partnership premises belong to an individual partner, should the firm enter into a lease or licence enabling it to occupy the property? Will it pay rent? What other terms should apply to the firm's right to occupy the premises?
	(4) How is any interest in land held? If held in the name of a trustee or nominee for the partnership, what happens if the trustee or nominee dies or retires?
	(5) Does the goodwill associated with the partnership business belong to the firm as a whole?
	(6) Should any other important partnership assets (e.g. wholly-owned companies) be mentioned?
7.	Partnership capital
	(1) How much capital will the firm require?
	(2) How is partnership capital to be contributed?
	(3) In what shares should partnership capital be owned?
	(4) Should partners receive any interest on capital, whether correctly provided or over-provided?
	(5) Should partners be obliged to pay interest on capital under-provided?
	(6) What happens to the capital of a partner on his death, retirement or expulsion?
	(7) When will the firm's capital increase, and how will this be decided?
	(8) Will changes in profit-sharing ratios affect capital-sharing ratios, and what contributions and withdrawals should be made when profit shares change?
	(9) Should the firm's assets be re-valued from time to time, and should the amount of any increase or decrease be credited or debited to capital accounts?
8.	Profits and losses
	(1) How are profits and losses to be computed in the firm's accounts (e.g. on an earnings, cash receipts or bills delivered basis)?
	(2) How are profits to be shared?
	(3) How are losses to be shared?
	(4) Are any partners to be entitled to a first guaranteed slice of profits, and if so what happens if there is a shortfall?
	(5) Is there to be any additional reward for good performance, and if so how is this to be achieved?
	(6) Should partners account to the partnership for, or retain personally, any remuneration earned through directorships and other external offices and employments?

9.	**Drawings**

(1) How much can partners draw on account of their profit shares each month?
(2) What happens if a partner has drawn too much?
(3) What happens if, when the accounts are prepared, it emerges that a partner has drawn too little?
(4) Should there be a compulsory retention for the tax liabilities of individual partners and if so how should it be calculated?

10.	**Books and accounts**

(1) Where will the books be kept?
(2) Who will have access to the books and when?
(3) What will be the accounting reference date?
(4) Who will be the firm's accountants?
(5) Should the accounts take into account goodwill?
(6) How will the accounts be agreed?
(7) Will the accounts and partnership returns be available by the statutory self-assessment deadlines?
(8) Will the records meet the statutory requirements (e.g. production of a partnership return and a partnership statement setting out the income and expenses of the partnership)?

11.	**Partnership bankers**

(1) Who will be the firm's bankers?
(2) Who has authority to sign cheques, and for how much?
(3) How many partners have to sign each cheque, and should this vary according to the amounts involved?
(4) Will client accounts be needed?

12.	**Insurance**

(1) Has provision been made for professional indemnity insurance?
(2) Has provision been made for public liability insurance?
(3) Has provision been made for employer's liability insurance?
(4) Has provision been made for insurance of valuable partnership assets?
(5) Should any other form of insurance be provided for, e.g.
- key-man insurance
- permanent health insurance

13. Duties
(1) Is it clear that a partner must act with the utmost good faith? (2) Is it clear that partners must devote their full time and attention to the business? (3) Has flexibility been included where necessary to enable partners to pursue agreed outside interests? (4) Has provision been made, where appropriate, to prevent partners entering into other hazardous business ventures, such as underwriting at Lloyd's? (5) Has provision been made to prevent partners assigning or charging their share of the partnership? (6) Has provision been made for partners to comply with professional and regulatory rules? (7) Has provision been made for partners to keep partnership information confidential?
14. Management and decision-making
(1) What decisions require the approval of a simple majority of the partners? (2) What decisions require the approval of a special majority of the partners? (3) Should a partner be unable to vote on certain resolutions, e.g. a resolution to expel him? (4) What are the rules for the conduct of partnership meetings? (5) Should any management decisions be delegated to the senior or managing partner or a committee or committees? (6) Has a Precedent Partner been appointed for tax return purposes?
15. New partners/salaried partners
(1) What sort of majority is required for the appointment of new partners? (2) What capital will have to be contributed by a new partner? (3) What will the new partner's share of profits be? (4) What documentation should be signed by a new partner? (5) How will salaried partners be appointed?

16. Outgoing partners

(1) When can partners be expelled, and what majority decision is required?

(2) Should provision be made for partners to be suspended in appropriate circumstances, and what majority decision is needed?

(3) At what age should partners have to retire?

(4) Should a majority of partners be entitled to require a partner to retire early, and if so in what circumstances and what period of notice is required?

(5) Will retired partners have a right to participate in any consultancy arrangements?

(6) How can partners retire early?

(7) Should the partnership have the ability to exclude a partner from the firm's offices, from its clients and from its employees, where that partner has given notice to leave to join a competitor?

17. Entitlement of outgoing partners

(1) Will a retiring partner's share accrue automatically to the shares of the continuing partners, or will the continuing partners have an option to acquire it?

(2) How will the firm finance the payment of an outgoing partner's share of the firm?

(3) Should the payment of an outgoing partner's capital be made in instalments?

(4) How and when will an outgoing partner be paid his entitlement to profits?

(5) Will any revaluations be required when computing the value of a retiring partner's share in the firm?

(6) Should an outgoing partner or his dependants be entitled to an annuity from the firm?

(7) Should an outgoing partner have a consultancy arrangement with the firm after his retirement?

(8) What will happen to any property belonging to the firm but held in the outgoing partner's name following his retirement?

(9) What will happen to books and papers belonging to the firm and in the custody of the outgoing partner after his retirement?

(10) Should the outgoing partner be indemnified in respect of all debts of the firm, whether past or future? What if a particular liability arises through his own fault?

18. Restrictive covenants

(1) Will an outgoing partner be prevented from competing with the firm?

(2) Will an outgoing partner be prevented from soliciting clients and employees of the firm?

(3) Will an outgoing partner be prevented from representing himself as a partner in the future?

(4) How long should the restrictive covenants bind the partner?

19. **Dissolution**
(1) Should the agreement prevent dissolution on the expulsion, retirement, death or bankruptcy of a partner?   (2) Will the firm dissolve on the termination of a fixed term?   (3) Should the agreement prevent an individual partner dissolving the firm?   (4) How should partnership assets be treated on a dissolution?
20. **Arbitration**
(1) Has provision been made for disputes to be resolved by arbitration (and possibly mediation)?   (2) Who is to appoint the arbitrator or mediator?   (3) What rules will govern the arbitration or mediation proceedings?   (4) Can the arbitrator or mediator dissolve the firm?
21. **Alterations to the partnership agreement**
(1) What partner majority will be required to amend the agreement?
22. **Other clauses**
Has provision been made for the following matters?   • Holiday entitlements.   • Sick leave and the consequences of long-term absence.   • Sabbatical leave.   • Maternity leave.   • Life insurance and health insurance of partners.   • Savings by partners for their retirement.

Chapter 3

Liabilities of Partners and Partnerships

General liabilities of partnerships

3.1   Traditionally, young professional people have sought the status and rewards that are associated with becoming a partner in their firm. More recently, the risks associated with partnerships have been the cause of great concern. Some firms have faced claims that substantially exceed their insurance cover. There have been some high profile partnership failures, in some cases leading to personal bankruptcies. This chapter outlines the way in which the law deals with the liabilities of partnerships and refers to some of the problems that might be encountered in practice.

Power of partners to bind the firm

3.2   The general principle of agency in the context of partnerships is set out in *section 5* of the *Partnership Act 1890*. It is worth repeating that section in full.

'Every partner is an agent of the firm and his other partners for the purpose of the business of the partnership; and the acts of every partner who does any act for carrying on in the usual way business of the kind carried on by the firm of which he is a member, bind the firm and his partners, unless the partner so acting has in fact no authority to act for the firm in the particular matter, and the person with whom he is dealing either knows that he has no authority, or does not know or believe him to be a partner.'

This provision contains the following elements:

(*a*)   *Actual authority.* Something done by a partner on behalf of his firm which is within the scope of his actual authority always binds the firm. This is so even if the action concerned falls outside the usual course of business of the firm. For example, if a firm of chartered accountants decides to hold a dinner dance for its staff, it might decide to authorise one of the partners to organise the evening. Even though the organisation of dinner dances might not be in the usual course of the firm's business, the firm would be bound by the acts of the organising partner since they would fall within his actual authority. Furthermore, the organising partner will be entitled to require the other partners to contribute their fair share of the costs.

(*b*) *Implied authority.* An act done in order to carry on business of the kind carried on by the partnership in the usual way binds the partnership even if the partner concerned had no actual authority to bind the firm, unless the third party knows that the partner does not have the requisite degree of authority, or does not know that he is a partner. However, in these circumstances, the partner may have to indemnify the firm against any loss incurred by his actions. Whilst a partner in a firm of chartered surveyors specialising in land agency might not have actual authority to turn his hand to valuation work, if he does advise on valuation work his firm will be bound, unless he is in fact 'moonlighting' in his own capacity and makes that clear to the client.

It follows that if a partner does something without authority and outside the ordinary course of the firm's business, the firm will not be bound, except perhaps on the grounds of 'holding out' (see 3.3 below).

Furthermore, *sections 7* and *8* of the *Partnership Act 1890* expressly protect the firm where a partner purports to bind the firm in circumstances where it ought to be obvious that the transaction is unconnected with the partnership business, or where the third party knows that the act contravenes an agreed restriction on the partner's purported authority. For example, if an architect agrees to make a loan to a builder without the authority of his partners, the firm is unlikely to be bound. Similarly, in *Hirst v Etherington anr. [1999] 3 All ER 797, CA*, the Court of Appeal held that it was not possible to rely on an undertaking where, having regard to the nature of the underlying transaction, it is clear that a solicitor should not have given such an undertaking. The decision in *Hirst* on this point was cited with approval in *Antonelli v Allen [2000] All ER (D) 2040*.

Holding out

3.3   Even where a person is not a partner at all, he may incur liability if he is held out as such. The general principle of holding out in the context of partnerships is set out in *section 14* of the *Partnership Act 1890* which commences as follows.

> 'Every one who by words spoken or written or by conduct represents himself, or who knowingly suffers himself to be represented, as a partner in a particular firm, is liable as a partner to anyone who has on the faith of any such representation given credit to the firm.'

Liability under this section will arise where the following elements are present.

(*a*) There must be a holding out. The person concerned must either hold himself out as a partner or allow himself to be held out as such by a partner. Holding out does not have to take any particular form, and can be done in writing, orally or even by conduct.

(*b*)   There must be a reliance on the holding out. The third party must actually know that the person is held out as a partner, and rely upon it.

(*c*)   There must be credit given to the firm. This expression should be given a wide meaning, and extends to any transaction giving rise to an obligation on the firm's part.

Liability through holding out could occur even where no partnership exists at all, but a third party is led to believe that one exists, and even where the person who is 'held out' as a partner exceeds the authority actually conferred upon him.

The decision in *Nationwide Building Society v Lewis [1998] 2 WLR 915* confirmed that liability for professional negligence could be attributed to a salaried partner who is held out as a partner of the firm. In that case, the salaried partner was not liable in negligence because the plaintiff could not show any reliance on the salaried partner being held out as a full partner. The Court of Appeal found that a plaintiff would have to establish reliance on that holding out in order to be able to recover from the salaried partner.

A salaried partner is defined in this book as a salaried employee who may be held out as a partner. Sometimes the term is used for an equity partner whose profits consist principally of a fixed or prior share. Salaried partners may incur liabilities to the outside world under the holding out principle, which is why the full partners normally agree to indemnify them against any such liability arising which is not their own fault.

Contracts

3.4   A partner can generally bind his firm by contract under the principles discussed above. Even where there is no actual authority, there will generally be implied authority to issue invoices, to open bank accounts in the firm's name, write cheques and to borrow money for the purposes of the business. There will also be implied power to hire and fire employees and to effect insurance. However, implied powers are always subject to the requirement that the action taken should not be unusual in the context of the firm's business. Furthermore, there is no general implied power to commit the firm to guarantees, or to a mortgage of the firm's property. Perhaps the most common forms of contract binding the firm, where problems can arise, are leases and bank accounts.

Section 9 of the *Partnership Act 1890* provides that all partners are jointly liable for the debts of the partnership (but jointly and severally in Scotland). Joint liability means that an individual partner can be sued and found liable for the whole debt, but that partner would have a right to recover from the other partners the contribution which they are obliged to make to ensure that profits and losses are shared in accordance with the partnership agreement (see 3.12 below).

Leases

3.5   Most professional partnerships occupy leasehold premises. Where there are more than four partners, *section 34(2)* of the *Law of Property Act 1925* provides that the leasehold property cannot be vested in more than four partners, and very often four partners are therefore identified to act as nominees. Under normal principles of privity of contract, the nominee partners are liable on the tenant's covenants in the lease throughout the term of the lease, notwithstanding the dissolution of the partnership or the assignment of the lease to a third party.

The liability of the other partners to the lessor depends on the form of the lease. If it is a deed, and only the four nominee partners are parties, the lessor may have no contract with the unnamed partners. This is because there is generally no implied authority to bind a firm by deed. Furthermore, under common law as preserved by *section 6* of the *Partnership Act 1890*, even if the nominee partners had express authority from the firm and even if the deed makes it clear that the nominees are acting on behalf of the firm, the firm may not be bound unless the covenant is expressed to be made by the firm, and not merely on its behalf. If it is not a deed, the firm (i.e. the partners at the time when the lease is entered into) will be bound if the nominee partners had express or implied authority to enter into the lease, and the existence of implied authority to do so may depend upon the nature of the firm's business, the length of the lease and other factors.

Even if the firm is not bound as far as the lessor is concerned, the partnership agreement will generally give the nominee partners a right of indemnity from the firm. Nevertheless, problems can arise for nominee partners, who may have no right of recourse against anyone who was a partner at the date of the lease but has since retired, and who may have difficulties enforcing the indemnity if the partnership has been dissolved.

In order to avoid these problems, from the point of view both of the landlord and of the nominee partners, modern leases generally provide for all the partners to guarantee the obligations of the nominee partners, or to be parties to the lease and bound by its covenants. Provision is also often made for new partners to enter into guarantees and for retiring partners to be released from their obligations, usually subject to the number of partners remaining in the partnership being greater than a stated minimum. Alternatively, a nominee company may be substituted for the nominee partners, with the individual partners entering into the lease as guarantors.

Bank loans

3.6   When money is borrowed by a partnership, everyone who is a partner at the date when the debt is incurred will normally be subject to the obligation to repay. Retiring partners will remain bound unless expressly released, although they will normally be entitled to an express or implied indemnity from the continuing partners. New partners will have no direct obligation to the lender, unless they expressly or impliedly agree with the lender to be bound, but they will generally agree to indemnify the other partners in respect of their respective shares of the firm's liabilities, including the loan. The repayment of a partnership debt by one partner extinguishes the liability of the firm as a whole if the object of the payment is to repay the debt, or if partnership funds are used.

It can be very difficult to decide who is responsible for the outstanding debit balance of an overdraft facility where partners come and go and the firm is then dissolved. It is then necessary to match drawings under the facility, with amounts paid in to reduce the borrowing, in order to determine who is responsible for the outstanding amount. Amounts paid into the account will generally be treated as discharging the earliest amounts borrowed under the facility.

In order to reduce some of these difficulties, many loan documents provide for outgoing partners to be released from all their obligations, and for all new partners to sign documents agreeing to be bound, subject perhaps to the total number of partners remaining above a particular level.

Duration of a partner's liability

3.7 A new partner is not liable to third parties for the debts of the firm incurred before he became a partner merely by reason of the fact that he becomes a partner. [*Partnership Act 1890, s 17(1)*]. This is so even where the incoming partner contracts with his co-partners to contribute to a share of pre-incurred liabilities. However, the partnership agreement will generally provide for him to contribute a share of those liabilities to the extent that they are to be taken into account in computing the profits and losses of future years. The agreement may also provide for incoming partners to undertake direct contractual obligations, for example to bankers and lessors.

When a person ceases to be a partner, the authority of the continuing partners to bind him and his authority to bind the firm will both come to an end. However, third parties dealing with the partnership may be entitled to assume that the outgoing partner remains a partner (i.e. there may be continuing ostensible authority) until actual notice is given of the change. [*Partnership Act 1890, s 36(1)*].

Notice is not required to prevent liability for future obligations [*s 36(3)*] being incurred:

(*a*)   on the death of a partner;

(*b*)   on the insolvency of a partner; or

(*c*)   on the retirement of a truly dormant partner, who was not known to the outside world to be a partner.

Furthermore, *section 36(2)* of the *Partnership Act 1890* provides for an advertisement in the London Gazette (or Edinburgh Gazette in Scotland) to be sufficient notice of partnership changes to anyone who had no dealings with the firm before the date of the change concerned. Even so, it is important, for the protection of the continuing partners and of the outgoing partner alike, that an advertisement should be placed in the London Gazette, and that the main suppliers and creditors of the firm should be notified of the change.

It is also important that the outgoing partner should not be held out as a continuing partner, e.g. by omitting to change the notepaper or the list of partners at the principal office.

A partner who ceases to be a partner does not automatically cease to be liable for partnership debts incurred before he ceased to be a partner (although he would normally have an express or implied right of indemnity against his former partners). That is why the personal representatives of deceased former partners are sometimes unable to distribute a deceased former partner's estate for many years. If the firm faces claims in respect of a period before the deceased former partner left the firm, which exceed the available insurance cover, and the continuing partners of the firm are unable to meet the claim in full, the estate of the deceased former partner could be exposed to liability. If the personal representatives have made distributions, they may face personal liability. Of course, the creditor, the continuing partners and the outgoing partner can agree that the outgoing partner will be released, and provisions to this effect are frequently included in leases and loan facility letters. Indeed, *section 17(3)* of the *Partnership Act 1890* expressly recognises that this may be achieved by express agreement, or inferred from the course of dealing between a creditor and the firm as newly constituted.

Unless expressly released, a former partner cannot regard himself as free from claims relating to his period as a partner until those claims have been satisfied, become statute barred, or have otherwise lapsed.

Limited partnerships

3.8   An important exception to the rule that all partners are jointly liable for obligations incurred by the firm is a limited partner in a 'limited partnership' formed under the *Limited Partnerships Act 1907* [the *1907 Act*] (see Chapter 22, Taxation of Corporate Aspects). A limited partnership is no more than an ordinary partnership which satisfies certain characteristics required by the *1907 Act*. The Law Commission also published a consultative document ('Limited Partnerships Act 1907', A Joint Consultation Paper, the Law Commission (Consultation Paper No 161) and the Scottish Law Commission (Discussion Paper No 118)) on 28 September 2001, and the report which is expected in early 2003 will also cover limited partnerships.

A limited partnership must consist of one or more general partners and one or more limited partners. A general partner is liable for the obligations of the firm in the same way as a partner of any other partnership. A limited partner is only liable for the debts of the firm to the extent that he has agreed to contribute to its capital or withdrawn capital from it and under *section 4(2)* of the *1907 Act* a limited partner must contribute at least a nominal amount of capital to the partnership. A limited partnership must be registered with the Registrar of Companies, and only benefits from limited status at a time when all the requirements of registration have been met. The information on the register consists of:

(*a*)   the firm name;

(*b*)   the general nature of its business;

(*c*)   the principal place of business;

(*d*)   the full name of each partner;

(*e*)   the term, if any, of the partnership and the date of its commencement;

(*f*)   a statement that the partnership is limited and a description of every limited partner as such; and

(*g*)   details of the sum contributed by each limited partner and whether paid in cash or otherwise.

It is arguable that limited liability of limited partners is lost if the information held by the Registrar becomes out of date and/or inaccurate, by virtue of *section 5* of the *1907 Act*.

Generally speaking there is no obligation to file accounts (unless the general partner is itself a limited company in which case the general partner will be required by the *Partnerships and Unlimited Companies (Accounts) Regulations 1993* to produce and file a full set of accounts for the partnership). General partners can become limited partners and vice versa provided that the required details are registered, although a general partner who becomes a limited partner should take the same precautions as a general partner who retires (see 3.7 above). A company can be a general or a limited partner.

Section 6 of the *1907 Act* provides that a limited partner has no implied power to bind the firm, and cannot take part in the management of the partnership business. The partnership agreement can give express authority to the limited partner to act on behalf of the firm, in which case the firm will be bound by his actions in the same way as it would be bound by the acts of any employee or other agent. The danger from his point of view is that his actions will amount to management of the partnership business, thus forfeiting the benefit of his limited liability status. The *1907 Act* contains no definition of what is meant by 'taking part in the management of the partnership business', but it is generally thought that being involved in anything which amounts to an 'ordinary matter connected with the partnership business' will be likely to amount to taking part in management.

If it were not for *section 6* of the *1907 Act* limited partnerships might be a very helpful way of limiting partners' liabilities. For example, it might be possible to form a limited partnership with a corporate general partner which also enjoyed limited liability (although such a structure would now be subject to the provisions of the *Partnerships and Unlimited Companies (Accounts) Regulations 1993.*

The fact that the limited partners are unable to participate in management has effectively restricted limited partner status to passive investors, rather than active professional partners. (See 3.20 below on Jersey Limited Liability Partnerships and Chapter 4 on GB Limited Liability Partnerships.)

Concerns may also arise in relation to the classification of the limited partnership as a collective investment scheme for the purposes of *section 235* of the *Financial Services and Markets Act 2000,* and compliance with the consequent regulatory requirements. The characteristics of a collective investment scheme are: (i) that the contributions of the participants and the profits or income out of which payments are made to them are pooled; and (ii) that the property in question is to be managed as a whole by or on behalf of the operator of the scheme.

Since limited partners are excluded from participating in the management of the affairs of the partnership, and the general partner is regarded as the operator of the scheme, a limited partnership will be a collective investment scheme unless exempted for constituting a particular type of arrangement. Such arrangements are listed in the Schedule to the *Financial Services and Markets Act 2000 (Collective Investment Schemes) Order 2001.* Paragraph 9 of that Schedule applies if each of the participants carries on a business other than certain types of regulated activity and enters into the arrangements for commercial purposes related to that business, so that the limited partnership is ancillary to their separate non-regulated business. Other relevant arrangements that do not constitute collective investment schemes include where each of the participants (including the general partner) is a company in the same group.

If the partnership constitutes a collective investment scheme, the general partner must, unless it already has appropriate authorisation, seek authorisation under the *Financial Services and Markets Act 2000* to operate collective investment schemes. Alternatively, the practice of many general partners is to delegate the functions which constitute regulated activity to an appropriately authorised firm. Authorisation is generally sought from the Financial Services Authority, and this is a procedure which can take six months or more. Otherwise, the operation of the partnership will be illegal and the partnership agreement may be unenforceable.

In addition, the marketing of unregulated collective investment schemes (which would include limited partnerships) is very difficult within the UK regulatory framework unless marketing is limited to institutional investors only.

Wrongful acts and omissions

3.9   The principles that govern the treatment of wrongful acts and omissions, like torts and frauds, are set out in *section 10* of the *Partnership Act 1890* which reads as follows:

'Where, by any wrongful act or omission of any partner acting in the ordinary course of business of the firm, or with the authority of his co-partners, loss or injury is caused to any person not being a partner in the firm, or any penalty is incurred, the firm is liable, therefore, to the same extent as the partner so acting or omitting to act.'

As in the case of *section 5* of the *Partnership Act 1890* and contracts (see 3.4 above), a partner must be acting with the authority of the firm or in the usual course of business, if the firm is to incur liability.

There are many examples of cases in which a firm has been held liable for torts committed by partners acting in the usual course of the business. Perhaps the most relevant one in the context of a professional partnership is that of a tortious claim in respect of negligent advice. For example, if a solicitor fails to act on instructions to draw up a will and the testator dies, the disappointed beneficiaries may be able to recover from the solicitor and his firm.

The scope of *section 10* was considered by the Court of Appeal in *Dubai Aluminium Co Ltd v Salaam and Livingston [2000] 3 WLR 910, CA*. It was held that the meaning of 'wrongful acts or omissions' should be widely construed and its applicability should not be confined to torts properly so called and frauds. Consequently, provided that the partner so acting was acting in the ordinary course of the partnership's business, the co-partners of a person who incurred liability as a constructive trustee could, if circumstances indicated, also be liable under *section 10*. At the date of writing, the appeal to the House of Lords has been heard (June 2002) but the judgment is not yet available. *Section 10* and the judgment of the Court of Appeal in the *Dubai* case were considered further in *Walker v Stone [2001] 2 WLR 623*. *Walker* raised the question of whether a breach of trust by a partner in a firm of solicitors acting as trustee for a family trust fell within the ordinary course of business of the solicitors' firm. It was held that it fell outside the ordinary course of the business of the firm and, therefore, the firm could not be held vicariously liable for the wrongdoing of the partner by virtue of *section 10*.

Misapplication of money and property

3.10   *Section 11* of the *Partnership Act 1890* provides that where one partner acting in the scope of his apparent authority receives the money or property of a third person and misapplies it, or a firm in the course of its business receives money or property of a third person and misapplies it while in the firm's custody, then the firm is liable to make good the loss.

Once again the underlying principles that lie behind *sections 5* and *10* of the *Partnership Act 1890* apply, in that the firm is only liable where the money is received within the scope of the partner's express or implied authority and it also has to be in the context of the carrying on of the partnership's usual business. Thus, if a client pays money to an architect to enable the firm to discharge a quantity surveyor's bill on his behalf, and the architect uses the money for his own purposes, the architect's firm will be liable for the loss. However, if the money was received to enable the architect to place a bet on a horse on the client's behalf, the firm would not be liable.

Breaches of trust

3.11   *Section 13* of the *Partnership Act 1890* provides that:

'If a partner, being a trustee, improperly employs trust property in the business or on the account of the partnership, no other partner is liable for the trust property to the persons beneficially entitled therein.'

However, there are a number of provisos. *Section 13* does not prevent the trust money being followed and recovered from the firm if it is still in its possession and under its control. In addition, it does not affect any liability incurred by any partner by reason of his having notice of the breach of trust.

Most professions have their own rules which tend to be more stringent than the general provisions in *section 13*. Therefore, any potential transgression is likely to involve relevant rules of professional conduct as well as liabilities for breach of trust.

Sharing of liabilities

3.12   As far as third parties are concerned, any partner is liable, without limit, for the firm's debts incurred when he was a partner. However, it is open to the partners to agree between themselves how liabilities are to be borne. This is generally achieved through the sharing of profits and losses. The partnership's liabilities will be reflected in its profit and loss account and will therefore lead to an increased loss or decreased profit to be shared between the partners as noted in Chapter 6, Profit Shares. The sharing of profits and losses is deemed by *section 24(1)* of the *Partnership Act 1890*, to be equal unless the partnership agreement provides differently. In many cases, the most important aspect of a partnership agreement is the removal of this presumption of equality. It is also thought that a consistent contrary course of conduct, such as sharing profits and losses exactly in proportion to unequal capital contributions, will operate to disapply *section 24(1)*.

However, where a partner incurs a liability for the firm which falls outside the scope of his actual authority, the other partners will generally be entitled to seek an indemnity from him in respect of that liability, assuming that he has sufficient assets to meet his obligations. Similarly, the partners will often agree to indemnify non-partners who might be held out as partners, e.g. salaried and retired partners. The partners will also generally agree to provide for certain liabilities (e.g. claims for professional negligence) through insurance. Further discussion of professional indemnity insurance is set out in Chapter 15, Insurance.

National and international organisations of partnerships

3.13   The demand for nationwide and international professional services has led to the development of national and international organisations of professional firms. Sometimes, these organisations are no more than alliances between different firms, who agree to refer work to one another, to share training and technical facilities and to adhere to common standards of service. In some cases the member firms practise under the same name, often in many different countries, and in others member firms practise under their separate names in conjunction with a shared name or acronym common to all. Membership of some organisations implies agreeing to a measure of contribution to national, or international, profits and losses. Even where there is no such provision it can be important to determine whether one member firm can be liable for the obligations incurred by another.

This will generally depend upon two issues.

(*a*)   Is the organisation itself a partnership? If there is a partnership between two member firms, or between the individual partners of each of the member firms, then the partners of one firm may be liable in respect of the obligations of the other, under ordinary principles of partnership law.

(*b*)   Is the organisation held out as a partnership? If a client is able to establish that he instructed one member firm in reliance on a holding out of all member firms as partners in one large member firm, all the member firms may be jointly liable.

The difficulty in practice tends to be reconciling two conflicting objectives. On the one hand, member firms will wish to present themselves as part of a wider organisation which can meet all the clients' needs, and which has a homogeneous corporate image in the market place. This will obviously increase the 'holding out' risk. On the other hand, each member firm will wish to isolate itself from the financial problems of the others by emphasising its separateness. (See also Chapter 5, International Aspects.)

Limiting liability by contract

3.14   An obvious way for a firm to control exposure to claims by third parties is to include a term in its conditions of business or letter of engagement limiting liability to a particular sum.

The extent to which this can be a solution to the problem of unlimited liability depends to a large extent on whether clients are prepared to agree to such limitations. However, it is now becoming much more common for professional firms to limit their exposure to claims by contract. For example, the maximum liability is often limited to a multiple of the fee, to an insurable amount, or to loss of a particular description. Clauses of this nature may be subject to statutory control under the *Unfair Contract Terms Act 1977*. For example, any exclusion clause contained in a firm's written standard terms of business must be reasonable having regard to all the circumstances, such as the availability of insurance. [*Unfair Contract Terms Act 1977, ss 3* and *11*]. It is therefore essential to seek legal advice before relying on such clauses.

Section 60(5) of the *Solicitors Act 1974* provides that any provision limiting the liability of solicitors in contentious business is void. *Section 310* of the *Companies Act 1985* prevents accountants from limiting their liability as auditors.

Other methods of protection of partners

Insurance

3.15   Professional indemnity insurance remains a very important means of protection and for further discussion of this, see Chapter 15. Some professional firms may be unable to obtain adequate cover for certain high-risk areas of practice, such as auditing. Insurance cover is provided on a 'claims made' basis – i.e. a given policy covers claims made in that policy year, not negligent advice given in that policy year. Even if negligent advice is given in a year when the partnership has adequate cover, that cover may no longer be available by the time the claim is made. As a result of the problems with professional indemnity insurance in the market some partnerships have set up their own captive insurance companies, or mutual insurance companies shared with others, to provide for future uninsured claims. (See 15.12 below.)

Professional indemnity policies only cover professional indemnity claims and cannot protect against the claims of banks, landlords and other general trade creditors. Care must also be taken when taking on lateral hire partners from firms against which claims are existing or likely. In some circumstances, for example, where the number of partners taken on exceeds a threshold or the merged firm will use the other firm's name or former premises, it may be that such potential liabilities will need to be insured by the acquiring firm by virtue of the applicable professional indemnity insurance regulations. See, for example, clauses 1.4 and 8.18 of the minimum terms and conditions of professional indemnity insurance in Appendix 1, Solicitors' Indemnity Insurance Rules 2001.

Debts

3.16   Although all partners are jointly liable for the partnership's debts, partners can agree to share responsibility for debts in any way they like. Careful drafting of the partnership agreement can provide protection for particular partners through indemnities and profit and loss sharing arrangements. Of course, an individual partner will still be fully responsible for the partnership debts as far as third parties are concerned, and the value of his rights against fellow partners will depend on whether they have sufficient personal assets to meet claims brought by him under the partnership agreement.

Asset protection

3.17   Asset protection involves the transfer of assets to a spouse, or into a trust for the benefit of the partner and his family. The intention is to protect those assets from creditors and ensure that they are available for the partner's family should the worst happen. These arrangements involve substantial commercial and even potential criminal risks.

Incorporation under the Companies Acts

3.18   Accountants and solicitors can now incorporate their practices as Companies Acts companies like most other professionals. The benefit of incorporation is that third parties can only recover from the assets of a limited liability company and not from the personal assets of the members of the company (i.e. the former partners).

Even after incorporation, directors or employees whose personal negligence leads to loss may be personally liable either to the company under their employment contracts or to the aggrieved third party in tort. However, at least incorporation protects those director shareholders who were not themselves involved in giving negligent advice.

Incorporation as a company can only provide protection in respect of liabilities arising after incorporation and the former partners will remain responsible for liabilities arising before incorporation, including obligations under leases and bank loans entered into before that date unless the landlord or bank can be persuaded to enter into fresh arrangements with the new company. In that situation, banks may request personal guarantees from directors and shareholders.

Another possible approach is for a partnership to incorporate the part of its business which is most prone to professional indemnity claims (e.g. the audit practice of an accountancy firm). However, partial incorporation needs to be structured very carefully to ensure that a third party cannot argue, for example, that he thought he was dealing with the partnership or that the company itself has a claim against the partnership. Otherwise, the third party may be able to pierce the ring-fence provided by the company. The company must ensure that it clearly operates discrete services on its own behalf and that it employs all persons providing advice on that area of the business itself, in order to minimise the risk of claimants piercing the ring-fence that protects individual partners from claims after partial incorporation.

Incorporation has very important tax consequences and these are considered in Chapter 21.

GB limited liability partnerships (LLPs)

3.19 GB LLPs are considered in Chapters 4, 13 and 23 and a model LLP agreement is provided in Appendix 5.

Jersey and other foreign law limited liability partnerships

3.20 In the State of Jersey it is also possible to establish a limited liability entity which has legal personality separate from its members. The partners are not liable for the debts of the partnership in excess of their capital contributions, except in respect of their personal defaults or loss caused by them. This is an important exception to the limitation of liability; the law only protects innocent partners. The law does not protect the partnership's assets from creditors. However, limited partners will be able to participate in the management of the firm unlike in the case of a limited partnership where they must take no part in the management of the partnership's activities.

In addition, a partnership registering in Jersey as an LLP will be required to make a £5 million provision (a bond, or guarantee or other financial instrument) which would be available to meet the claims of any creditors to the extent that those claims are uninsured or cannot be met by the partnership assets. The Finance and Economics Committee of the States of Jersey may change this figure as it thinks appropriate. The purpose of this bond is twofold: firstly, it is supposed to offer partnership creditors a greater measure of protection in the event that they make a successful negligence claim against the partnership, and secondly, it is designed to deter small and medium-sized professional practices from seeking registration. The Jersey authorities have indicated informally that they are only seeking applications from partnerships of significant size and good repute.

Two other features of the Jersey law, which both flow from the distinct legal personality conferred on the LLP, are firstly, that the admission and retirement of partners will not affect the existence or status of the partnership, and secondly, that contracts made with the LLP will be made with it as an entity, and not with the partners themselves.

It is thought that the English Courts are likely to respect the limited liability of Jersey limited partners of a partnership in this form. For example the case of *JH Rayner (Mincing Lane) v Department of Trade and Industry [1990]*

2 AC 418 involved the International Tin Council, a body with separate legal personality under an English Statute but established by international treaty. It was not a company. The House of Lords held that its members were not liable in respect of contracts entered into by the International Tin Council itself.

In addition, in *Johnson Matthey and Wallace Ltd v Ahmad Alloush and others (1984) 135 NLJ 1012*, the Court of Appeal held that, if the members of a foreign entity with separate legal personality are given limited liability under the law of its establishment, that limited liability will have extra-territorial effect and will therefore be respected by the English courts.

Therefore, since the Jersey law provides for the key characteristics of separate legal personality and limited liability, it seems that Jersey limited liability partnership status should provide real protection before the English courts.

The question then arises whether the Jersey limited liability partnerships will be treated as partnerships or companies for the purposes of UK tax law. The Inland Revenue indicated in December 1996 that it would treat Jersey LLPs as companies rather than as partnerships for tax purposes. However, the Court of Appeal declined to decide the point as the Inland Revenue had only stated an intention, rather than ruling an actual tax liability. The risk of unfavourable tax treatment has so far deterred UK firms from becoming Jersey LLPs.

It is, however, also possible to form an LLP under the law of many states in the United States of America, including New York and Delaware, and one major UK law firm is understood to have registered as an LLP under the law of one of these states. Presumably, the Inland Revenue and the Law Society of England and Wales will have both accepted that the LLP is to be subject to taxation as a partnership.

However, the *Uniform Partnership Law*, on which the state laws are based, expressly provides that a partner remains liable for his own negligence and for the negligence of those under his supervision. Furthermore, it is understood that a partnership constituted under the US system is not a body corporate (unlike a GB LLP) and in some states (e.g. New York) a partnership can convert into an LLP simply by changing the proper law of its agreement to the law of the relevant state and registering as an LLP in that state. There are doubts about whether the partnership will be 'substantively separate' for its limited liability to stand up in the courts of England and Wales. Professional advice should be obtained before adopting this kind of structure.

Insolvency of partners and partnerships

Reasons for insolvency

3.21 A number of partnerships have suffered financial difficulties in recent years. Many firms have undertaken fixed overheads in better times, which are now difficult or impossible to reduce, despite falling turnover and pressure on profit margins. For example, many firms have entered into leases in respect of their premises which can run for up to 25 years and contain upwards-only rent review clauses. The market demands that many professional support staff are entitled to relatively high salary levels with little or no discretionary or bonus element. Many firms have committed themselves to making inflation adjusted annual payments to their former partners and their spouses. Some firms have very substantial borrowings, in addition to individual partners' borrowings taken up in order to finance the acquisition of their homes and their shares of equity in the partnership. In these circumstances, a downturn in business can be catastrophic. Once a firm's profits are under pressure, those partners who are practising in an area which remains profitable are often not prepared to continue to work hard for little reward. Such partners may be tempted by an offer from a competitor firm which remains more profitable, with the consequence that a dwindling group of partners remains responsible for the same fixed overheads. Once the spiral of decline has started it can be very difficult indeed to pull out of it.

Action required

3.22 A well-managed firm ensures that it has accurate and detailed management information available at all times, which will enable it to detect a downturn in profits very early on. It can then respond, e.g. by investing in new business areas, by carefully controlling costs, by supporting and encouraging partners to enable them to achieve maximum profitability, and perhaps by encouraging underperforming partners to leave. In some cases, it may be appropriate at an early stage to try to prevent the spiral accelerating by all the partners mutually agreeing that there are to be no resignations, or reduced drawings, for a period which is thought to be sufficient to enable the business as a whole to weather the crisis. It is essential that the financial position of the firm should be monitored closely during a difficult period, and that appropriate insolvency advice should be obtained. Individual partners will be subject to the provisions of the *Insolvency Act 1986* relating to bankruptcy offences, including the offences relating to obtaining credit and failure to keep proper accounting records. It should also be borne in mind that, in the event of an insolvency, the court now has power to make a disqualification order against a partner whose conduct as an officer of the partnership makes him unfit to be concerned in the management of a company, although it is understood that such a disqualification order will only have the effect of preventing the partner from acting as a director of a limited company and not from acting as a partner during the period of disqualification. It is also possible that the wrongful and fraudulent trading provisions of the *Insolvency Act 1986* could apply to a partner if the partnership goes into liquidation, although this is by no means clear.

Voluntary arrangements

3.23   It will rarely be in the interests of creditors to force a professional firm and its members into insolvency, which may prevent the partners from practising under their professional rules and therefore destroy their earning power on which creditors depend. Recognising that fact, *Article 4* of the *Insolvent Partnerships Order 1994* provides that the provisions of the *Insolvency Act 1986* dealing with company voluntary arrangements will now apply to insolvent partnerships (subject to some modifications). Essentially, voluntary arrangements involve debtors agreeing new terms for the repayment of debts with their creditors under the supervision of a qualified insolvency practitioner, and the 1994 Order facilitates voluntary arrangements with a firm as a whole, which may be easier to achieve than a series of interlocking voluntary arrangements with each member of the partnership. The procedure is that, if the proposed arrangement is approved by a majority of over 75% in value of those creditors attending and voting at a special creditors' meeting (whether in person or by proxy), then all creditors of a partnership who were given notice of the meeting and were entitled to vote will be bound by the arrangements. In this way, the partnership may avoid being wound up, and be able to trade out of its difficulties.

The *Insolvency Act 2000* contains provisions which, when they are brought into force, will introduce a new moratorium on creditor action for certain eligible companies whilst proposals are put together for a voluntary arrangement. By virtue of the *Insolvent Partnerships (Amendment) (No 2) Order 2002*, the moratorium will also be available to eligible partnerships whilst they are putting together a proposal for a partnership voluntary arrangement. The *Insolvency Act 2000* also contains provisions which would make the voluntary arrangement binding on all creditors, not just those with notice of the meeting, if the requisite majority votes in favour of the proposals.

Administration procedure

3.24   The *Insolvent Partnerships Order 1994* also provides that the administration procedure available to companies under the *Insolvency Act 1986* will now also be available to partnerships. An administration order may be made by the court if it considers that it is likely to achieve one or more of the three statutory purposes set out in the *Insolvency Act 1986*, namely the survival of the whole or any part of the partnership business as a going concern, the approval of a voluntary arrangement or the disposal of the partnership's property in a more advantageous way than would be the case on a winding up.

An administrator, who must be an independent insolvency practitioner, will have control of the partnership during the course of the administration and while the administration order is in force no order can be made for the winding up of the partnership. Furthermore, no steps may be taken to enforce any security over the partnership property, and no other proceedings can be commenced or continued against the partnership, without the leave of the administrator or the consent of the court. This provides a useful breathing space during which the administrator can attempt to achieve the purpose for which the administration order was made.

It should be noted that far-reaching reforms to the *Insolvency Act 1986* have been made in the *Enterprise Act 2002*, expected to come into force in 2003. These reforms will streamline the administrative process by introducing a new out-of-court route into administration in addition to the existing court route into administration. The purposes for which an administration order can be obtained will also be replaced with a single, three-part purpose with the primary emphasis on rescue. Although the *Enterprise Act* refers to corporate insolvency (rather than partnership insolvency), it is to take effect by amending the provisions of the *Insolvency Act 1986* and so, by virtue of the *Insolvent Partnerships Order 1994*, the new streamlined administration procedure will also be available to partnerships.

Winding up

3.25   If all else fails, the creditors or the partners themselves may be forced to petition for a winding up. There are various different ways in which a partnership can be wound up. Following the *Insolvency Act 1986* and the *Insolvent Partnerships Order 1994* all partnerships of whatever size are now subject to the regime affecting unregistered companies. This regime is concurrent with the provisions relating to the insolvency of individual partners, and it is possible to present an application to wind up a partnership as an unregistered company concurrently with insolvency petitions being presented against two or more of the partners. It should be noted, however, that it is possible for a partnership to be unable to pay its debts for the purposes of the *Insolvency Act 1986* notwithstanding that the value of the assets of one partner are greater than the partnership's liabilities. It makes no difference that the creditors of the partnership have full recourse against that partner. A detailed review of the law of insolvency in relation to partnerships is outside the scope of this book. However, broadly speaking, the partnership's assets are used first to meet the debts of the partnership, and only then to meet the separate debts of individual partners. The separate estates of the individual partners are used first to meet individual debts and only then to meet debts of the partnership.

Insolvency falls outside the terms of reference of the Law Commission's recent consultation documents (as mentioned above in paragraphs 1.1 and 3.8) but during the consultation phases it was recognised by many that the insolvency regime applicable to partnerships is unsatisfactory in a number of respects. A separate consultation was therefore undertaken under the aegis of the Insolvency Court Users' Association and it is hoped that proposals for the reform of the law of insolvency as it relates to partnerships will be brought forward at the same time as the Law Commission's other proposals.

Professional implications of insolvency

3.26   Insolvency may have serious implications under the professional rules applicable. For example, under *section 15(1)* of the *Solicitors Act 1974*, a solicitor's practising certificate is automatically suspended if he is adjudicated bankrupt, and remains suspended until the bankruptcy is annulled.

The suspension is advertised in the London Gazette and it is an offence for a solicitor to practise during this period. The Adjudication and Appeals Committee of the Law Society's Regulation Unit has power to hear applications to have a practising certificate reinstated notwithstanding bankruptcy, and quite frequently allows practising certificates to be reinstated, subject to conditions, in advance of the bankruptcy so that the practice is not interrupted.

Similarly, under Bye-law 7(a) of the ICAEW Principal Bye-laws, a chartered accountant automatically ceases to be a member of the institute on his bankruptcy. The council has power to readmit former members on the terms they think fit.

In either case, the bankruptcy may trigger the automatic dissolution of the firm under *section 33* of the *Partnership Act 1890*, subject to contrary agreement.

If a partner enters into a voluntary arrangement he is likely to avoid these professional problems, although the professional body is still likely to take note of the partner's conduct. For example, a solicitor's practising certificate will not be suspended but the Solicitors Disciplinary Tribunal has power to impose conditions on the solicitor concerned. Furthermore, the Law Society has power to intervene in the solicitor's practice, and will do so if it considers that there is evidence that clients' money may be at risk.

Chapter 4

Limited Liability Partnerships

4.1   Limited liability partnerships ('LLPs') were introduced into English law by the *Limited Liability Partnerships Act 2000* (the *'LLP Act'*), which received Royal Assent on 20 July 2000 and was brought into effect by ministerial order on 6 April 2001.

The explanatory notes which accompany the *LLP Act* (paragraphs 11 and 12) note that the idea emerged out of the 1996 Department of Trade & Industry ('DTI') feasibility investigation of joint and several liability, carried out by the Common Law Team of the Law Commission, and a DTI consultation document in 1997. The opportunity was taken to consult on the possibility of introducing LLPs to the law of Great Britain, against a background in which Jersey was working on implementing its own LLP legislation in order to meet the perceived needs of the accountancy profession.

The *LLP Act* applies to England, Wales and Scotland but not Northern Ireland (except that the tax provisions will apply in Northern Ireland to LLPs formed elsewhere in the UK) and is accompanied by the *Limited Liability Partnerships Regulations 2001* (the *'LLP Regulations'*) and the *Limited Liability Partnerships (No 2) Regulations 2002* which came into force on 6 April 2001 and 2 April 2002, respectively. These provide for the regulation of limited liability partnerships by applying to them, with modifications, the appropriate provisions of the existing law which relates to companies and partnerships largely contained in the *Companies Act 1985*, the *Insolvency Act 1986*, the *Income and Corporation Taxes Act 1988* and the *Taxation of Chargeable Gains Act 1992*.

The Limited Liability Partnership (Northern Ireland) Bill is currently before the Northern Ireland Assembly. That Bill is expected to receive Royal Assent at the end of 2002 and the Act should be operational in early 2003.

The basic structure

4.2   The name 'limited liability partnership' reflects the historical context, but in fact an LLP is much more like a company rather than a partnership. It is a separate legal entity and a body corporate able to enter into contracts and hold property in its own right. It continues in existence despite any change in membership and third parties contract with the LLP rather than with the individual members. Members of an LLP, like shareholders of a company, generally (subject to the rules on insolvency and especially to a special 'clawback' regime which applies to LLPs only) have limited liability in the event of insolvency of the LLP. LLPs, like companies, have the ability to do anything which a partnership could have done. Partnership law generally has no application to LLPs, unless otherwise specified in the *LLP Act*, but large sections of the *Companies Act 1985* and the *Insolvency Act 1986*, as they apply to companies, are adapted for the purposes of LLPs. For example, an LLP will be required to file audited accounts and an annual return (subject to special rules for small LLPs) at Companies House.

Nevertheless, there are important differences between LLPs and companies. There is no share capital and no requirement for capital maintenance. An LLP must carry on a business, unlike a company which may be passive, and limited liability will not be maintained if there is only one member. There is no requirement to file the agreement between the members at the Companies Registry, unlike the Memorandum and Articles of Association of a company. One of the most significant differences between an LLP and a company is that members of an LLP will generally be taxed as if they were partners in a partnership and it is anticipated that in these circumstances the courts will be able to draw on the law relating to partnerships, as well as to companies, in the absence of any case law relating to LLPs. LLPs are also subject to a unique new 'clawback' rule in the event of insolvency. Further details are provided in the following paragraphs.

What is a Limited Liability Partnership?

4.3   An LLP is a body corporate with legal personality separate from that of its members and which is formed by being incorporated under the *LLP Act*. [*Section 1(1)* and *(2)*]. It has unlimited capacity [*section 1(3)*] and is therefore able to undertake the full range of business activities which a partnership can undertake. The members have 'such liability to contribute to its assets in the event of [the LLP] being wound up as is provided for by virtue of this Act'. [*Section 1(4)*]. There is no express statement that members will have limited liability, but since the Act provides for members to be agents for the LLP and not one another (see the *LLP Act s 6* and see 4.10 below), and the Regulations introduced in relation to the *LLP Act s 14* apply the insolvency regime applicable to companies with some important modifications, the effect is to give members limited liability in a similar way to shareholders in a company – hence the name 'limited liability partnership'.

Furthermore, in order to eliminate the risk that members might otherwise incur joint and several liability through the common law rules on mutual agency, it is expressly stated that partnership law does not apply to LLPs except as expressly provided by the *LLP Act* or any other enactment. [*Section 1(5)*]. The only provisions based on partnership law are the 'default provisions' applicable to the extent that there is no members' agreement, as discussed at 4.19 below.

When is LLP status available?

4.4   For an LLP to be incorporated 'two or more persons associated for carrying on a lawful business with a view to profit must have subscribed their names to an incorporation document'. [*LLP Act s 2(1)(a)*]. It will be noted that the wording is similar to *section 1* of the *Partnership Act 1890* and that partnership case law would probably be used as a guide to interpretation accordingly. It is intended that LLPs should only be available in circumstances where there might have been a partnership, so paragraphs 1.2 to 1.4 inclusive of Chapter 1 will be equally applicable to LLPs. As a result of the 'business' requirement, therefore, LLPs will not be suitable for non-profit making organisations like clubs and charities or arrangements where there is no 'business', such as mere asset holding structures, or where there is no profit motive, as in mutual trading arrangements. However, the LLP structure is available to any business conducted by two or more persons all of whom have a view to profit and is not, as was at one stage suggested, restricted to the regulated professions.

Solicitors

4.5   The Law Society replaced the Solicitors' Incorporated Practice Rules 1988 and enabled solicitors to practice as LLPs. Solicitors who wish to incorporate themselves as LLPs will need to obtain recognition from the Law Society as a recognised body as well as satisfying the usual incorporation requirements (see 4.6 below). A solicitors' LLP should first be incorporated by registering itself with the Registrar of Companies and then the incorporated LLP should apply to the Council of the Law Society for recognition in accordance with *Rule 2(1)* of the *Solicitors' Incorporated Practice Rules 2001* before it starts to practice. Application is made to Companies House by way of Form LLP1 which must be signed by one of the LLP's members on behalf of the LLP.

Where a solicitors' LLP does not obtain recognition as a recognised body it will be in breach of the Solicitors' Practice Rules and will commit an offence under sections 20–24 *of the Solicitors Act 1974.*

The *Solicitors' Incorporated Practice Rules 2001*, which were made on 19 March 2001 by the Council of the Law Society, regulate the incorporated practices of solicitors in England and Wales. As well as specifying that before a body corporate commences business as a solicitor it must obtain recognition as a recognised body, they also set out requirements which are specific to recognised bodies. The result of this is that a solicitors' LLP will be subject to a greater number of rules than other LLPs.*

---

*For more information on solicitors' LLPs see the Information Pack on Incorporated Practices [Limited Liability Partnerships], revised February 2002 and published by Professional Ethics.

Incorporation of an LLP

4.6 An 'incorporation document' (Form LLP2) signed by the persons associated to carry on the lawful business with a view to profit, or an authenticated copy, must be delivered to the Registrar. *[LLP Act s 2(1)(a)* and *(b)]*. In addition, a subscriber to the incorporation document, or a solicitor engaged to form the LLP, must file a statement that the requirements of the *LLP Act s 2(1)(a)* are satisfied. *[LLP Act s 2(1)(c)]*.

The incorporation document must be in a form approved by the Registrar, and state

(*a*)   the name of the LLP;

(*b*)   whether the LLP will have a registered office situated in England and Wales, in Wales or in Scotland;

(*c*)   the address of the registered office;

(*d*)   the name and address of each of the members on incorporation; and

(*e*)   the names of the designated members or that all the members are to be 'designated members' (*LLP Act s 2(2)* and see 4.12 for a discussion of designated members).

Making a false statement will be an offence punishable by imprisonment or a fine. *[LLP Act s 2(3)* and *(4)]*. Thus, care needs to be taken to ensure that the incorporation document is correct and that the requirements of *section 2(1)(a)* really are satisfied.

Assuming the Registrar is satisfied that the requirements of the *LLP Act s 2* are met, he then registers the incorporation document, and issues a certificate of registration which is conclusive evidence that the LLP has been incorporated by the name specified in the incorporation document. *[LLP Act s 3]*.

Name and registered office

4.7 The *LLP Act s 1(6)* introduces the Schedule to the Act, which contains provisions relating to the name and registered office of an LLP. The name of the LLP must include the expression 'Limited Liability Partnership', 'LLP' (in upper or lower case) or Welsh equivalents. There are rules allowing intervention by the Secretary of State where names are confusing, too similar to the names of other existing LLPs or companies registered at Companies House, or offensive. LLPs must have a registered office at all times in Great Britain and the incorporation document has to state whether it is in England and Wales, in Wales, or in Scotland. Notice has to be given of changes of registered office. It is notable that it is not necessary for an LLP to have an actual place of business in the UK.

Membership of an LLP

4.8   Initially, the members are those who subscribe their names to the incorporation document, assuming they are still living or in existence [*LLP Act s 4(1)*], but any other individual or company can become a member of the LLP if so agreed with the existing members. The agreement to introduce the new member, rather than registration of a new member with the Registrar of Companies, creates the new membership but the appointment of a new member must be notified to the Registrar within 14 days. [*LLP Act s 9(1)(a)*]. Any change in the name or address of a member must also be notified, but within 28 days. [*LLP Act s 9(1)(b)*]. Notification has to be made in a form approved by the Registrar [*LLP Act s 9(3)(a)*] and must be signed by a designated member or authenticated in the manner approved by the Registrar. [*LLP Act s 9(3)(b)*]. Failure to comply with these rules is an offence. [*LLP Act s 9(4)*]. A member ceases to be a member on death or dissolution of that member or in accordance with agreement with the other members, and in the absence of agreement to the contrary, a member can cease to be a member on giving 'reasonable notice' to the other members. [*LLP Act s 4(3)*]. Fears were expressed during the consultation process that, in view of the existence of the LLP as a separate legal entity, the LLP and each member might have the relationship of the employer and employee, thus fundamentally altering the relationship between the member and his firm. Accordingly, an express provision has been included to the effect that a member of an LLP is not regarded for any purpose as employed by the LLP, unless he would have been regarded as employed by the LLP if he and the other members were in fact partners in a partnership. [*LLP Act s 4(4)*]. This provision is, therefore, slightly unsatisfactory given that partner and employee status are, generally, mutually exclusive. The effect appears to be that the member will not be an employee by reason only that he is a member of the LLP, but he may be an employee as well as a member if he has a contractual relationship with the LLP which amounts to a contract of employment. The statutory employment rights will be of equal application to employed members. Care must be taken in drafting the members' agreement to avoid an employment relationship unless employed status is intended. It is notable, however, that the Inland Revenue appears to accept that the partnership tax treatment for such members will be preserved, even if they are also deemed to be employees, as in their view the relevant taxation sections take precedence over *LLP Act s 4(4)*.

Relations between members, and between the LLP and the members

4.9   Except as otherwise expressly provided in the Act, relations between members and between the LLP and its members, are to be governed by agreement between the members, or between the LLP and the members, or in the absence of agreement, by the *LLP Regulations 7* and *8* which contain the default regime (similar to the default regime applicable to partnerships) and which provide that:

'7. The mutual rights and duties of the members and the mutual rights and duties of the LLP and the members shall be determined, subject to the provisions of the general law and to the terms of any LLP agreement, by the following rules:

(1) All the members of a limited liability partnership are entitled to share equally in the capital and profits of the limited liability partnership.

(2) The LLP must indemnify every member in respect of payments made and personal liabilities incurred by him:

   (*a*) in the ordinary and proper conduct of the business of the LLP; or

   (*b*) in or about anything necessarily done for the preservation of the business or property of the LLP.

(3) Every member may take part in the management of the LLP.

(4) No member shall be entitled to remuneration for acting in the business or management of the LLP.

(5) No person may be introduced as a member or voluntarily assign an interest in an LLP without the consent of all existing members.

(6) Any difference arising as to ordinary matters connected with the business of the LLP may be decided by a majority of the members, but no change may be made in the nature of the business of the LLP without the consent of all members.

(7) The books and records of the LLP are to be made available for inspection at the registered office of the LLP or at such other place as the members think fit and every member of the LLP may when he thinks fit have access to and inspect and copy any of them.

(8) Each member shall render true accounts and full information of all things affecting the LLP to any member or his legal representative.

(9) If a member, without the consent of the LLP, carries on any business of the same nature as and competing with the LLP, he must account for and pay over to the LLP all profits made by him in that business.

(10) Every member must account to the LLP for any benefit derived by him without the consent of the LLP from any transaction concerning the LLP, or from any use by him of the property of the LLP, name or business connection.

8. No majority of the members can expel any member unless a power to do so has been conferred by express agreement between the members.'

It will be noted that these provisions are broadly based on the provisions of *sections 24* and *25* of the *Partnership Act 1890*.

The Regulations also include minority protection in a similar form to *section 459* of the *Companies Act 1985*, which allows a member to apply for a court order where the LLP's affairs are conducted in a manner which is unfairly prejudicial to the interests of the members generally or some part of them. This provision may, however, be excluded by the unanimous decision of the members and it is usual to include a provision to that effect in the members' agreement. As can be seen, the *LLP Regulations* only set out the most basic rules regulating relations between members, which will rarely be sufficient or, in most cases, appropriate and will at best constitute only a basic code for the simplest situation. Furthermore, the general guidance of the rules of equity and law governing partnerships is expressly excluded by the *LLP Act s 1(5)* and there will be no general duty of good faith between members and only the most basic minority protections. In these circumstances, a detailed and comprehensive members' agreement will, in practice, be essential in order to avoid uncertainty and the risk of litigation (see 4.19 below and Appendix 5).

Relationship with third parties – limited liability

4.10   As the name 'limited liability partnership' implies, the key objective of the legislation is to create limited liability for members of the LLP, and as noted at paragraph 4.3 above this is achieved by a combination of the *LLP Act s 1*, which provides for the LLP to be a separate legal person and for partnership law (and therefore rules about mutual agency between partners and joint and several liability) to be excluded and the *LLP Act s 6* which provides (at *sub-section (1)*) for members to be agents of the LLP. Nowhere is it provided that there is any implied agency between the members themselves. Therefore, when a member enters into a contract with a third party on behalf of the LLP, the member generally binds the LLP and not the members personally. Thus the LLP, and not the members will be bound. Furthermore, as noted in paragraph 4.18 below, there are limited obligations on the members to contribute to the assets of an LLP on its insolvency. The effect is to create a limited liability regime which is very similar to that applicable to companies under the *Companies Act 1985* (but note the unique 'clawback' rule discussed in paragraph 4.18 below).

While third parties will generally only have contractual claims against the LLP, and not its members, a member who is personally negligent or who otherwise causes loss to clients of the LLP or third parties may still be personally liable in tort (as is noted in paragraphs 15 and 16 of the explanatory notes to the *LLP Act*). In the House of Lords case of *Williams v Natural Life Health Foods Ltd [1998] 1 WLR 830*, it was held that in deciding whether a person is personally liable to a client, the courts will have regard to various factors including whether that person has assumed a personal responsibility for the advice given so as to create a special relationship, whether the client has in fact relied on the advice and whether that reliance was reasonable (paragraph 16 of the explanatory notes to the Act). The factors outlined in *Williams v Natural Life Health Foods Ltd* were recently applied by the High Court in the case of *Partco Group Ltd and Another v Wragg* and *Scott [2002] 1 Lloyd's Rep 320.*

Following on from *Williams v Natural Life Health Foods Ltd*, in *Merrett v Babb [2001] 3 WLR 1* the Court of Appeal widened the concept of the assumption of personal responsibility with regard to professional individuals. The Court of Appeal considered that the defendant would not necessarily have actively to assume responsibility for the advice, but that such assumption of personal responsibility may be recognised or imposed by law by reference to the nature of the relationship. The question was stated as being whether the professional is to be taken to have assumed responsibility to the client to guard against the loss for which damages are claimed. In *Merrett v Babb* the claim arose from a negligent property valuation that was prepared for the lender, but also supplied directly to the buyers by the individual property surveyor in his own name. Even though there was no direct instruction from the borrower to the surveyor (having been instructed by the lender), as a matter of fact the borrower had relied upon the professional skill and care expected of a surveyor and of that individual as a member of that profession and that it was reasonable for them to have done so in the circumstances.

The implication of *Merrett v Babb*, therefore, is that it will be easier to establish personal responsibility in the case of members of a professional LLP because of the fiduciary duties between client and member which could easily constitute a special relationship with direct and personal exchanges between them.

It should be noted that the LLP will not be bound where a member deals with a third party if the member in fact had no authority to act on behalf of the LLP in that way and the third party either knows that the member has no authority, or does not know or believe him to be a member of the LLP. [*LLP Act s 6(2)*]. However, if a member commits a wrongful act or omission in the course of the LLP's business or with its authority, the LLP will be liable in any event. [*LLP Act s 6(4)*]. Because of the implied agency of members, it will be very important to ensure that the authority of members is clearly defined in the members' agreement.

Third parties are entitled to assume that a member is still a member, even if they have in fact ceased to be a member, unless they have actual notice that the member has ceased to be a member or the Registrar of Companies has been notified that the former member has ceased to be a member. [*LLP Act s 6(3)*].

It may be possible in practice to counteract the assumption of a personal duty of care by providing in all contracts with clients that no individual member assumes a personal duty of care to that client (thus excluding an action for negligence against the member personally), or excluding liability for any breach of the duty by the LLP or by individual members, although the *Unfair Contract Terms Act 1977* will apply in both instances and such provision may be ineffective unless they can be shown to be reasonable.

Ex-members

4.11   The *LLP Act s 7* applies where a member ceases to be a member in accordance with the agreement with the other members, or on death or dissolution [i.e. under *LLP Act s 4(3)*] or where his interest vests by operation of law in a third party on death, or insolvency, or where he has assigned the whole or any part of his share in the LLP to a third party. [*LLP Act s 7(1)*]. Thus, ceasing to be a member depends on these events rather than any entry on the register. The former member or his successor is prevented from interfering in the management or administration of the business or affairs of the LLP [*LLP Act s 7(2)*], but this does not affect any right to receive a payment from the LLP. [*LLP Act s 7(3)*]. Thus former members and their successors in title continue to have the economic rights associated with membership, but will not hold any other rights, and the successor will not automatically become a member itself. Of course, the other members may agree to admit the successor in title as a member of the LLP [*LLP Act s 4(2)*] whereupon the successor in title will have all the rights of membership. It is important that the members' agreement should set out the rights and obligations of the parties where a member ceases to be a member, dies, becomes bankrupt or assigns his membership rights.

In contrast, a shareholder of a company continues to have full economic and voting rights until he ceases to be registered as a shareholder upon his successor or assignee successfully applying to be registered in his place. The right of a successor or assignee to be registered as a shareholder will depend upon the terms of the company's articles of association. These are implied by regulations contained in *Table A* of the *Companies Act 1985*, if not otherwise expressly provided in the company's articles of association.

Designated members

4.12   The *LLP Act* introduces the concept of 'designated members' and the explanatory notes to the *LLP Act* explain that in general the role of designated members is to perform the administrative and filing duties of the LLP. However, the provisions of the *Companies Act 1985* and *Insolvency Act 1986*, as applied to LLPs by the *LLP Regulations* under the *LLP Act*, impose additional tasks on the designated members in respect of which they represent all members of the LLP including the signing of the LLP's filed accounts. The following is a list of the obligations of the designated members, the relevant Schedule to the *LLP Regulations* and the section of the *Companies Act 1985* or the *Insolvency Act 1986* which (as amended) create these obligations:

Examples of duties and liabilities of a designated member include obligations:

(1)   to register and certify the transfer of debentures correctly regardless of the terms of the LLP agreement. Failure to do so results in the designated members being liable to a fine [*s 183 Companies Act 1985* to *s 185 Companies Act 1985*];

(2) to keep accounts in accordance with *s 221 Companies Act 1985*. Failure to do so results in the designated members being guilty of an offence and liable to a fine or imprisonment [*s 221 Companies Act 1985*];

(3) to keep accounting records in accordance with requirements under *s 222 Companies Act 1985*. Failure to do so results in the designated members being guilty of an offence and liable to a fine or imprisonment [*s 222 Companies Act 1985*];

(4) to comply with the requirements of *s 231(6)(b)* of the *Companies Act 1985*. Failure to do so results in the designated members being liable to a fine for the period of default [*s 231 Companies Act 1985*];

(5) to approve and sign annual accounts. Approving accounts which do not comply with the necessary requirements results in the designated members being guilty of an offence and liable to a fine [*s 233 Companies Act 1985*];

(6) to ensure that the auditor's report is in the correct form and to ensure that the auditor signs the report. Failure to do so results in the designated members being guilty of an offence and liable to a fine [*s 236 Companies Act 1985*];

(7) to ensure that all members of the LLP receive a copy of the accounts and the auditor's report. Failure to do so results in the designated members being guilty of an offence and liable to a fine [*s 238 Companies Act 1985*];

(8) to comply with a request from a person entitled to receive a copy of the accounts and the auditor's report. Failure to do so results in the designated members being guilty of an offence and liable to a fine for the period of default [*s 239 Companies Act 1985*];

(9) to ensure statutory accounts or non-statutory accounts (as the case may be) are in the correct form. Failure to do so results in the designated members being guilty of an offence and liable to a fine [*s 240 Companies Act 1985*];

(10) to ensure annual accounts and auditor's report are delivered to the Registrar. Failure to do so results in the designated members being guilty of an offence and liable to fine for the period of default [*s 242 Companies Act 1985*];

(11) to ensure that the accounts are correct. If the accounts are found to be defective following an application to court by the Secretary of State for a declaration that the submitted annual accounts are defective, the designated members have the liability to pay the costs for the preparation of new accounts and to pay the costs of the court application if submitted annual accounts are found to be defective [*s 245B Companies Act 1985*];

(12) to deliver annual returns to the Registrar and in the form required. Failure to do so results in the designated members being guilty of an offence and liable to a fine for the period of the default [*s 363 Companies Act 1985*];

(13) to appoint auditors [*s 385 Companies Act 1985*];

(14) to notify the Secretary of State that his power to appoint auditors under *s 387 Companies Act 1985* has become exercisable. Failure to do so results in the designated members being guilty of an offence and liable to a fine for the period of the default [*s 387 Companies Act 1985*];

(15) where the LLP is a subsidiary undertaking of a parent, to supply information to the parent's auditors and failure to do so results in an offence and liability to a fine or imprisonment [*s 389A Companies Act 1985*];

(16) to give notice to the auditor of its removal [*s 391A Companies Act 1985*];

(17) to deliver a notice of an auditor's resignation to the Registrar. Failure to do so results in the designated members being guilty of an offence and liable to a fine for the period of default [*s 392 Companies Act 1985*];

(18) to convene a meeting of the members if requested by resigning auditor. Failure to do so results in the designated members being guilty of an offence and liable to a fine [*s 392A Companies Act 1985*];

(19) to submit a proposal for voluntary arrangement to nominee [*s 2 Insolvency Act 1986*];

(20) to sign statutory declaration of solvency. Failure to do so results in the designated members being guilty of an offence and liable to a fine for the period of the default [*s 89 Insolvency Act 1986*];

(21) to lay statement of affairs before the creditors. Failure to do so results in the designated members being guilty of an offence and liable to a fine [*s 99 Insolvency Act 1986*].

Designated members may, in relation to some of these duties, have a defence to liability if it is shown that he is not 'in default'; that is, he had not knowingly and wilfully authorised or permitted default or contravention of the relevant statutory provision.

In addition, the designated members powers include:

(1) Power to fill casual vacancies in the office of auditor [*s 388 Companies Act 1985*];

(2) to fix remuneration of the auditors [Schedule 2, *regulation 4* and *s 390A Companies Act 1985*];

(3) to give notice to the Registrar of removal of auditor. Failure results in the designated members being guilty of an offence and liable to a fine for the period of the offence [*s 391 Companies Act 1985*].

Initially, the designated members are those identified as such in the incorporation document, but members become and cease to be designated members in accordance with the members' agreement. [*LLP Act s 8(1)*]. Unless there are at least two designated members, or if the incorporation document states that every member of the LLP is to be a designated member, then all the members from time to time are designated members. [*LLP Act s 8(2) and (3)*]. It is therefore important that the members' agreement should deal with the identity of the designated members.

The LLP can notify the designated members from time to time to the Registrar. [*LLP Act s 8(4)*]. Anyone who ceases to be a member automatically ceases to be a designated member [*LLP Act s 8(6)*] and this takes effect as if included in the incorporation document. Where anyone becomes or ceases to be a designated member, the Registrar must be notified within 14 days [*LLP Act s 9(1)(a)*] but where all the members from time to time are designated members, there is no need to give separate notice of changes of designated members just because members change. [*LLP Act s 9(2)*]. Again, failure to comply is an offence. [*LLP Act s 9(4) and (6)*].

Membership changes

4.13 As noted at paragraph 4.12 above, changes of members and designated members, and in the name or address of the member, must be notified to the Registrar within the specified time period set out in *section 9*.

Taxation of LLPs

4.14 See Chapter 23.

Application of Company Law

4.15 As mentioned above, the *LLP Regulations* apply large parts of the *Companies Act 1985* and the *Insolvency Act 1986* to LLPs with appropriate modifications. *LLP Regulation 3* covers the application to LLPs of the rules on accounts and auditing. *LLP Regulation 4* covers the application to LLPs of other provisions of the *Companies Act 1985*. *LLP Regulation 5* covers the application to LLPs of certain provisions of the *Insolvency Act 1986*. *LLP Regulations 6* and *7* deal with 'default' rules to apply to relations between members except as otherwise expressly agreed, and is broadly based on certain provisions of the *Partnership Act 1890*.

Further amendments have been made in the *Limited Liability Partnerships (No 2) Regulations 2002.*

Accounts and audit

4.16   See Chapter 12.

Application of the Companies Act 1985 (other than accounts and audit requirements)

4.17   As mentioned above, *LLP Regulation 4* applies certain specified provisions of the *Companies Act 1985* to LLPs. It also sets out how those provisions are to be interpreted in relation to LLPs within the scope of the Act. The relevant provisions of the *Companies Act 1985* are listed together with modifications in *Schedule 2* to the *LLP Regulations.*

Any person involved with the establishment or operation of an LLP will need to familiarise themselves with all the relevant provisions of the *Companies Act 1985.* The following is a summary of some of the most significant provisions of this legislation which apply to LLPs.

Section 24: An LLP will require a minimum of two members in order to carry on business lawfully.

Sections 36–42: The rules regarding formalities for execution of documents, presumptions of due execution and use of seals apply to LLPs. A contract entered into on behalf of an LLP before its incorporation has the effect of giving personal liability to the person purporting to contract on behalf of the LLP [*section 36C*].

Sections 183–185 and 190–197: Provisions relating to the transfer, certification and regulation of debentures will apply to any such instruments issued by an LLP.

Sections 348–350: The name of an LLP must be clearly displayed outside any premises. Its name, registered address and number and place of registration must be clearly printed on all formal correspondence and documentation issued by the LLP.

Sections 363–364: Provisions establishing the requirements for annual delivery of relevant information relating to the LLP to the Registrar of Companies.

Sections 384–385, 387–392A and 394–394A: In general, LLPs will be required to appoint auditors. The designated members have primary responsibility for this. Related provisions regarding auditors' access to information, attendance at meetings, remuneration and resignation also apply, with modifications. Small and dormant LLPs are exempt from the requirement to appoint auditors (see Chapter 12 for relevance of this).

Sections 395–408 and 410–423: Any charge (for example by way of security) made over assets of an LLP must be registered with the Registrar of Companies. This is often done by the beneficiary of the charge but the LLP itself has the legal obligation to ensure registration. A charge not registered within the relevant time limits may be void.

Sections 425–427: These provisions are available to regulate compromise arrangements between an LLP and with its creditors and/or the members and provide a framework for other arrangements and reconstructions of the LLP.

Sections 431–441 and 447–452: Provisions enabling the LLP or its members to apply to the Secretary of State to appoint an inspector to investigate the affairs of the LLP. In order for LLP members to do this, the application will have to be made by at least one-fifth of the registered members.

Sections 459–461: These are minority shareholder protection provisions which enable a member to apply to the court for an order on the grounds of unfair prejudice to the interests of some or all of the members in the conduct of the LLP's affairs. The application of these provisions to the LLP can be excluded by unanimous agreement of the members.

Sections 651–658: The Registrar of Companies has the power to strike off the register any LLP which he has reasonable cause to believe is not carrying on a business or operating.

Sections 704–715: Administrative provisions relating to the Registrar of Companies and the filing of documents.

Sections 736–736B: The definitions of 'subsidiary', 'holding company' and 'wholly-owned subsidiary' will be relevant to the relationship between an LLP, its subsidiary and parent companies and LLPs. The provisions of the *Companies Act 1985* have been modified to take account of the differences in membership structure between a company and an LLP.

More recently, *Companies Act 1985 ss 723B–723F* have also been applied to LLPs by the *Limited Liability Partnerships (No 2) Regulations 2002*. These sections enable members to apply for confidentiality orders where appropriate.

Other definitions applicable to the sections of the *Companies Act 1985* which will apply to LLPs are also relevant.

Insolvency of LLPs

4.18   The *LLP Act* provides for the introduction of regulations relating to the insolvency and winding up of LLPs. [*LLP Act s 14*]. It also provides for regulations to be introduced in relation to the insolvency and winding up of 'oversea limited liability partnerships' – i.e. limited liability partnerships incorporated or otherwise established outside Great Britain but having a connection with Great Britain. *LLP Regulation 5* applies large sections of the *Insolvency Act 1986* to LLPs, subject to the various amendments set out in *LLP Regulation 5(2)* and *Schedule 3* to the *LLP Regulations*.

A detailed view of the insolvency regime which applies to limited partnerships is outside the scope of this chapter. The following is only a summary.

(1) *Insolvency procedures*

LLPs are broadly subject to the same insolvency procedures as companies including:

(*a*) voluntary arrangements;

(*b*) administrations;

(*c*) receiverships; and

(*d*) liquidation (although members are free to determine how and when an LLP is voluntarily wound up without any necessary formality).

(2) *Adjustment of prior transactions*

The insolvency regime for LLPs also contains provision for the adjustment of prior transactions taking place in the period leading up to insolvency. As in the case of companies there are four principal categories into which transactions which may be set aside by a liquidator fall:

(i) transactions at an under value, i.e. gifts or transactions for insufficient consideration;

(ii) preferences, i.e. anything done or allowed to be done which has the intended effect of putting a particular creditor or guarantor in a better position than he would have been in on an insolvent liquidation;

(iii) floating charges created within 12 months of the onset of insolvency except to the extent that the charge secures new indebtedness;

(iv) transactions entered into for the purpose of putting assets beyond the reach of a person who also is making, or may make, a claim or of otherwise prejudicing the interests of such a person in relation to a claim.

There are detailed time limits within which claims to set aside such transactions must be brought except in the case of category (iv), which is available without time limit.

(3)   *The position of the members*

As in the case for directors of companies, members or shadow members of LLPs may be ordered to contribute to the assets of an insolvent LLP in the following cases:

(*a*) misfeasance;

(*b*) wrongful trading;

(*c*) fraudulent trading.

However, the *LLP Regulations* introduce a new *section 214A* to the *Insolvency Act 1986*, relating to the 'adjustment of withdrawals' or 'clawback'. This is unique to LLPs and applies to a member or shadow member where, in the course of winding up it appears that during the period of two years ending with the commencement of the winding up he withdrew for his own benefit property of the LLP.

If the liquidator proves to the satisfaction of the court that at the time of the withdrawal the member or shadow member knew or had reasonable grounds for believing that the LLP was at the time of its withdrawal unable to pay its debts, within the meaning of *section 123* of the *Insolvency Act 1986*, or became so unable to pay its debts after the assets of the LLP had been depleted by the withdrawal and any other withdrawals made by members contemporaneously with that withdrawal or in contemplation when that withdrawal was made, the court can order the member to make such contributions to the LLP's assets as it thinks proper. For these purposes, a withdrawal occurs if property of the LLP is withdrawn in the form of share of profits, the payment of interest on a loan to the LLP or any other withdrawal of property. Aggregate contributions cannot exceed withdrawals made during the two-year period prior to a winding up. In making such an order, the court must decide whether the particular member knew or ought to have concluded that there was no reasonable prospect of avoiding insolvency. A member will be expected to reach the conclusions that a reasonably diligent person would reach with the same level of experience as that member and, if higher, the actual level of knowledge and skill of that member.

In addition, it should be noted that a member may be liable under the common law for negligence if he fails to show the degree of care and skill reasonably expected from a person of his knowledge and experience.

The *Company Directors Disqualification Act 1986* is also applied to LLPs and will enable the court (on the application of the DTI) to impose a disqualification order on any member (not just the designated members) of an LLP from being concerned in any way in, or taking part in the promotion, formation or management of any LLP or company if the member is found culpable of improper conduct leading up to the insolvency of the LLP.

All these rules will apply equally to members and shadow members. A shadow member is defined as 'a person in accordance with whose directions or instructions the members of the LLP are accustomed to act' (but so that a person is not a shadow member by reason only that the LLP members act on his professional advice).

(4)   *Conduct when an LLP is in difficulty*

The overall effect of the proposed insolvency regime for LLPs is that all members of an LLP in financial difficulty will be in a very similar position to directors, although they will also face the additional risk of clawback of their drawings for a potentially lengthy period. Considerable care must therefore be taken in such circumstances, and it will generally be essential for members to seek appropriate professional advice.

The Members' Agreement

4.19   There is no statutory requirement of an agreement between members although, as noted at paragraph 4.9 above, *LLP s 5* provides for mutual rights and duties of an LLP and its members to be governed by agreement between the members or, in the absence of agreement, by the regulations discussed in that paragraph. *Paragraph 17* of the explanatory notes to the *LLP Act* notes the 'clear advantages in having a formal written agreement between members to regulate the affairs of the undertaking and to avoid disputes between them', and that 'the formal procedures needed to establish an LLP, including the need for an application to the Registrar of Companies, are likely to encourage the members to set up a formal arrangement before the LLP commences business'.

The very elementary nature of the default provisions contained in the Regulations and the specific exclusions of the partnership law in all other respects means that a members' agreement will, in practice, be very important indeed (see paragraph 4.9). The members' agreement should be drawn up and signed before registration of the LLP in order to ensure that the rights and obligations of the members are clear before any statutory duties are assumed.

In the case of the partnership which is to convert into an LLP, the starting point is likely to be the firm's existing partnership agreement, but every provision of the partnership agreement will need to be reviewed for a number of reasons.

(*a*)   Unlike a partnership, but like a company, the LLP itself will be a legal person. The relationship between the members and the LLP will have to be spelt out, as well as the relationship between the members themselves. Every provision of the partnership agreement will have to be looked at again to see whether the members, the LLP or both should be able to enforce it. The Act expressly provides that an agreement made between members before incorporation of an LLP can bind the LLP itself. [*LLP Act s 5(2)*].

(*b*)   It will also be very important to ensure that limited liability protection is preserved. Partnership agreements generally provide for partners to contribute to losses, and to indemnify retiring partners against future losses. If the LLP has power to require members to contribute to losses, the limited liability of the members will be destroyed.

(*c*)   It will also be necessary to think carefully about the position of salaried and fixed share partners. The equivalent for LLPs will be members who are registered as members of the LLP, but who do not contribute capital and are entitled only to a salary from the LLP, or a salary plus a small share of profits.

(*d*)   The absence of a fallback on partnership law means that it will be important to consider whether there are any potential areas for dispute which are not covered by the partnership agreement and where the uncertainty could lead to the risk of litigation.

(*e*)   Finally, LLPs are obliged to file information with the Registrar of Companies, to appoint designated members and so on and the members' agreement should cover who are to be the designated members, who is to be responsible for filing this information and who is generally responsible for ensuring compliance.

The LLP Agreement

4.20   As referred to in 4.9 above, a detailed and comprehensive members' agreement will be the best way of regulating relations between the members of an LLP. A model LLP agreement can be found at Appendix 4 of this book. In most cases where a partnership is to convert into an LLP, the existing partnership agreement will be the starting point especially as it reflects the arrangements with which partners are familiar and in which the firm's culture is based. However, to reflect the fact that the LLP is a body corporate there will have to be some important modifications:

(*a*)   Perhaps the most obvious change is the terminology – 'partners' will be 'members' and the 'partnership' or 'firm' will be the 'LLP'. Some converted partnerships also feel it appropriate to use 'corporate' terminology, so that, for example, 'senior partner' could become 'chairman' or 'chief executive'.

(*b*)   Significantly, the parties to the agreement should include the LLP itself as well as the members. This is because the LLP, having separate legal personality, will be undertaking and owed duties as an independent entity as well as the members. For example, the LLP may be providing an indemnity to the members and the members may be obliged to contribute to the LLP's capital.

(c)   The Agreement will need to provide for the appointment, removal and additional duties of statutory designated members. The LLP should also indemnify these members in respect of their personal liability inherent in that position provided they act reasonably.

(d)   Provision should be made for the manner in which a new member is to be admitted, and membership is to cease. [See *LLP Act s 4(2)*].

(e)   The agreement should make it clear that the statutory requirements for record keeping etc. are to be adhered to.

(f)   The auditing/accounting provisions will need to reflect the relevant *Companies Act 1985* requirements which apply to LLPs.

(g)   The extent of each member's authority to the LLP should be specified.

(h)   The concept of 'dissolution', as it applies to partnerships, does not apply to LLPs, so provisions in the Agreement should deal with the winding up of the LLP and will need to reflect the relevant *Insolvency Act 1986* requirements. The winding up clause will probably be very different from that in the existing agreement. In particular, provision should be made for the mechanics by which the LLP and its members will determine that a voluntary winding up should occur and whether and to what extent members are to contribute to a winding up. Provision will normally be made for contribution of a normal sum to ensure that members are contributories for the purposes of *Insolvency Act 1986 s 79*, and individual members can therefore petition the court for a winding up.

(j)   The Agreement should also make it clear whether balances on a partner's account with the firm constitute equity (on the one hand) or debts owed to the member (on the other). The significance of this is that the member will be able to prove the amounts owed to them as debts in competition with other unsecured creditors of the LLP.

(k)   The Agreement should also contain a simple procedure for its alteration, perhaps giving the members of the board the power to authorise 'non-substantive' changes and a particular majority to effect more important changes. This will make it easier to adapt the agreement as the law and practice in relation to the LLPs develops and snags emerge; and

(l)   Members will often wish to deal with minority protection expressly in the members' agreement, and to exclude *Companies Act 1985 s 459*.

Why would an existing professional partnership wish to convert into an LLP?

4.21   LLP status has a number of advantages, including the following:

(a)   Limited liability – only a member who is personally negligent will be potentially exposed to claims in tort, and even this may perhaps be eliminated through carefully worded engagement letters (see paragraph 4.10 above).

(*b*) An LLP will be able to contract in its own name so that there will be no need to deal with novation of contracts every time partners retire or are appointed. Neither will there be a complex web of indemnities between generations of partners (see Chapter 3).

(*c*) The LLP will have unlimited capacity, including the ability to grant floating charges (see paragraph 4.3 above).

(*d*) There will be no limit on partner numbers, even for firms which are not already exempted, although as noted at paragraph 1.11 above that may be a temporary benefit.

However, there may be a number of reasons why a firm will decide not to convert, and these are discussed in the following section.

What might prevent a partnership converting?

4.22 Potential barriers to conversion include the following:

(*a*) **Current partners** – most partnership agreements will require a very substantial majority before the partnership can dispose the whole of its business and be dissolved. Some even require unanimity, and unanimity will be required if there is no partnership agreement. Is there a danger that a disaffected minority may use the exercise of an effective veto as a weapon in a dispute on something completely unconnected? It is important to think through the decision that will be required and how to achieve it.

(*b*) **Retired partners** – in many cases retired partners are entitled to an annuity from the current partners. Sometimes they are even given the right to a lump sum if the firm is ever dissolved or its business transferred, and this may give retired partners an effective veto. In these circumstances their agreement should be obtained, and ideally they should be asked to release the partners from their personal obligations in return for a covenant from the LLP. However, the obligation to pay the annuities will then have to appear on the LLP's balance sheet (see (*e*) below) and in many cases it may be appropriate for the LLP members to retain the liability to pay the annuities personally out of their profit shares, with the LLP having no liability at all. Arrangements will have to be made to release retiring members and bind incoming members.

(*c*) **Banks** – banks are likely to have two levels of exposure, loans to partners individually to finance their capital contributions and facilities provided to the partnership itself. In an ideal world, the bank will be asked to provide facilities to the LLP, rather than to each individual member of the LLP who would then have a personal liability, and to release the partners personally from any continuing liability. However, banks are likely to view lending to LLPs in much the same way as they regard lending to companies and may insist on security and on continuing personal guarantees from the partners. Their attitude will depend very much on their perception of the firm and its management. Some of the larger and better quality firms may be able to take facilities without any requirement for personal guarantees.

(*d*) **Landlords** – landlords generally have direct personal covenants from at least some of the partners, who, in turn, have rights of contribution from the other partners. In many cases landlords will be reluctant to give up these rights and may insist on being given equivalent protection in the form of personal guarantees. Some far-sighted firms may have negotiated leases in a form which allows them to substitute the LLP as tenant unilaterally. Either way, the position of landlords needs to be considered.

(*e*) **Accounts** – the requirement of filing accounts may be a major issue for many firms. Furthermore, the requirement that the accounts show a 'true and fair view' may be a barrier to conversion. If provision has to be made on a capitalised basis for retired partners' annuities, or vacant property, will this make the LLP's balance sheet look so bleak as to preclude incorporation at all? Can the offending liabilities be kept off the balance sheet of the partnership and retained by the partners, or can other steps be taken to address the problem? These issues need to be reviewed with the firm's accountants.

(*f*) **Clients** – experience suggests that limited liability in itself is unlikely to lead to the loss of clients, provided that it is handled carefully. Clients tend to choose their professional advisers on the strength of the relationship and their track record, rather than because each partner will be jointly and severally liable if something goes wrong. But, especially if the firm is heavily dependent on a small number of major clients, it will be as well to sound major clients out before incurring substantial expense.

(*g*) **Tax and regulations** – more complex overseas structures may be required if LLP status is adopted. For example, a firm with overseas offices which incorporates as an LLP may find that it is treated as a company for tax purposes in some countries, and may be prohibited from practising at all in others by local regulations.

Incorporating an existing partnership business as an LLP

4.23   This will involve four key steps:

(1)   Drawing up the members' agreement;

(2)   Registration of the LLP;

(3)   Transfer of the business of the partnership to the LLP; and

(4)   Winding up the old partnership.

The steps to be taken to register the LLP are discussed in paragraph 4.6 above. Issues arising on drawing up a members' agreement are discussed at paragraph 4.9 above. A model LLP Agreement is attached as Appendix 5 and a commentary of that document is contained in paragraph 4.20.

Turning to the business transfer, it was decided very early on to make incorporation as an LLP equivalent to incorporating as a company. Accordingly, the business of a partnership will actually have to be transferred to the LLP. This is thought to make it much less likely that foreign courts will refuse to recognise the limited liability of an LLP, any more than they would in the case of a company, and contrasts with the situation in most states of the USA where application is simply made to register an existing partnership as an LLP.

The following issues arise as a result:

(*a*)   The assets which are to be transferred to the LLP must be identified and, if third party consents are required, the consents obtained. Some assets may deliberately be left behind in the partnership – for example it may be appropriate to leave some debtors in the partnership so that the cash eventually realised could be used to pay creditors (to the extent that the LLP does not undertake to pay creditors pursuant to the transfer agreement).

(*b*)   It will be necessary to identify liabilities and obligations of the partnership which are to be assumed by the LLP, and any which are to be retained by the partnership. If a particular liability is to be transferred, in some cases it may be sufficient for the LLP simply to covenant to indemnify the partners in the partnership in respect of those liabilities. In other cases it may be desirable to ask the third party creditors concerned to release the partners in the partnership from liability, in return for a substitute covenant from the LLP. Unless creditors (like banks or landlords) release the partners from the partnership they will remain at risk from personal claims even after incorporation as an LLP. This means that there may have to be detailed negotiations with major creditors who may, in some cases, insist on continuing liability from the partners.

(*c*)   Clients will have to authorise the assumption of responsibility for client assignments by the LLP and to release the partnership. In the case of audit assignments shareholder consent will be required. Where no authorisation is forthcoming, the partnership will have to complete that assignment (either directly or through the agency of the LLP).

(*d*)   Employees of the partnership who are to transfer to the LLP will need to be identified. It is likely that all or most of the business of the partnership will be transferred to the LLP. In this case it should be expected that all the employees of the business will transfer automatically to the LLP by operation of law pursuant to the *Transfer of Undertakings (Protection of Employment) Regulations 1981*. Under these regulations the LLP will have responsibility generally for employees from the date of the transfer. It may be appropriate for the LLP to assume in addition all past liabilities of the partnership to employees. The detail of this and any divisions of liabilities and indemnities between the partnership and the LLP should be set out in the transfer agreement.

(e) Other contracts. Contracts entered into on behalf of the partnership in relation to the operating requirements of the business may or may not require the consent of the third party to assignment. This will need to be checked and consideration given to whether consent should be sought in advance of assignment to the LLP. For general contracts it may be appropriate to assign without prior consent and for the LLP to indemnify the partnership in relation to ongoing obligations and (possibly) past obligations (although it should be noted that the former partners will then remain liable under the contracts). The partnership should hold the relevant contracts on trust for the LLP. If contracts are still to be performed at the point where the original partnership is to be dissolved, then the assignment may need to be perfected at that time.

(f) Consideration. If all the partners in the partnership become members of the LLP with interests in the same proportions, the 'consideration' for the transfer to the partnership will, for each partner, be his membership of the LLP. The situation will be more complex if the proportionate shares are altered or some partners do not go forward as members of the LLP.

(g) Stamp duty and VAT. See Chapter 23.

(h) Regulatory issues may also be important. For example, if the partnership is authorised under the *Financial Services and Markets Act 2000*, the *Consumer Credit Act 1974* or similar legislation, the same authorisation will have to be obtained for the LLP before it starts business. If the firm has overseas offices it will need to think about local rules.

The final act is to wind up the old partnership. In some cases, even after the business has been transferred to the LLP, the partnership may be left with assignments to run off, debts to collect, creditors to pay and potential exposure to past claims where the transfer of these assets and liabilities to the LLP is impossible or undesirable. Some issues may take years to work themselves out. Sometimes the old partnership may deliberately be left in place for years, so that it can deal with liabilities which are to be kept off the LLP's balance sheet, such as retired partners' annuities.

It will be important to agree before incorporating an LLP how the business of the partnership is to be wound up, and the insurance arrangements to be put in place to cover any residual liability in respect of professional indemnity claims against the partners. In practice, running off of the old partnership business is likely to be undertaken by the LLP as agent for the partners at the date of incorporation and it is important to ensure that the LLP has the necessary authorisations and access to sufficient finance to enable it to conduct this process efficiently and smoothly.

Chapter 5

International Aspects

Introduction

5.1   Successful UK professional partnerships often seek to expand overseas, for two principal reasons.

(*a*)   *Servicing UK clients' international needs.* UK clients of the partnership may have international needs which cannot be serviced effectively from the UK. The partnership may therefore need to develop a capability in the relevant locations.

(*b*)   *Exploiting international marketing opportunities.* An overseas presence may be essential in order to capitalise on opportunities to sell the firm's skills to new clients overseas.

Different approaches to developing an international capability

Worldwide partnerships

5.2   One way to develop an international capability is for the parent UK partnership to set up local branch offices overseas while remaining a single worldwide partnership. Most of the large City of London law firms have expanded internationally in this way. The overseas branch offices can be staffed either by posting from head office or by local recruitment or a combination of both. In some territories, because of local practising or tax problems a branch may not be utilised: a locally incorporated company might be formed. This company would normally be owned by the partnership itself or by a UK company owned by the partnership.

Multinational organisations of independent firms

5.3   An alternative approach is to meet the need for overseas expansion by forming alliances with local firms overseas, and developing a multi-national organisation of independent firms. Often such organisations agree to use a common 'brand' name. There may or may not be some sort of worldwide 'umbrella' entity. There will (or should) certainly be a series of inter-firm agreements governing the relationship (including the secondment of partners and staff) between the separate parts of the multinational organisation. Most of the larger international firms of chartered accountants have developed in this way.

European Economic Interest Groupings (EEIGs)

5.4   The formation of an EEIG can be an attractive means for a UK partnership to establish links in other European Union member states without losing individual identity and independence although an EEIG cannot be established for the purpose of profit-making activities.

Developing a worldwide partnership

Need for local law advice

5.5   Before establishing any permanent presence in an overseas jurisdiction, the local conditions will have to be studied and local advice obtained. Some of the key factors to be considered are set out below.

(*a*)   *Licences to practise.* Local law may impose restrictions on the practice of certain professions by foreign nationals and licences may be needed. In some jurisdictions (e.g. in Japan) it may not be possible to open a branch office of the worldwide partnership and the local law may force the use of a separate entity under local control.

(*b*)   *Partnership law.* Local rules on the rights and obligations of partners, both between themselves and in relation to clients and other third parties should be considered. It will be important to put in place appropriate professional indemnity arrangements having regard to local conditions.

(*c*)   *Immigration and employment law.* Local law may impose restrictions on partners and staff from the UK going to the new country to live and work. If staff are to be recruited locally, local advice on the applicable employment regulations will be needed.

(*d*)   *Property law.* The branch office will need premises from which to operate. Local advice will be needed on the full range of property issues, e.g. applicable landlord and tenant rules, occupier's liability and health and safety regulations.

(*e*)   *Tax.* Local advice will be needed on the foreign tax treatment of the profits and losses of the branch office, and the foreign personal tax position of the partners and staff posted there. UK tax factors will also have to be considered.

Profit sharing and status

5.6   When expanding overseas the question of the status of the personnel in the overseas office and the profit and loss sharing rules applicable to them will be of key importance. Assuming there remains a single worldwide partnership a number of options are available.

(*a*) *Worldwide equity partners.* Full equity partners of the worldwide partnership could be posted to or recruited to run the overseas office, sharing worldwide profits and losses together with all other partners. Special additional remuneration arrangements may be needed (e.g. 'expatriate package' for those posted overseas or modified profit shares taking into account local profitability) depending on local conditions. The worldwide equity approach may be the least divisive initially but can lead to problems if the contribution made by an overseas office is very different from the contribution made by other offices.

(*b*) *Local equity partners.* Partners in the overseas office could be restricted to sharing in the profits and losses of that office (an 'eat what you kill' approach). Alternatively, part of the profits or losses of the overseas office could be allocated for sharing only between the partners in that office, the balance forming part of a worldwide pool. The approach adopted will be a matter for agreement.

(*c*) *Salaried partners and employees.* The partners staffing the overseas office could be salaried partners, who are held out to the outside world as partners, but paid a salary rather than having a profit share. This approach may not, however, satisfy the requirements of the partners concerned and some equity participation or salary reflecting profitability may become essential to retain them. The overseas office will need staff. These may be employed directly by the partnership or by a service company established in the jurisdiction and owned by the partnership.

UK tax consequences of a single worldwide partnership

5.7   The main advantage of a single worldwide partnership is that the results of the operation in overseas branches will normally be treated as an extension of the UK partnership's trade and not a new trade. Accordingly, the loss (or profit) of the overseas branch (before deducting local partners' share of profits and allowances treated as profit share) is part of the taxable profit in the UK. When an overseas branch starts up it is likely there will be a UK tax advantage as initially the branch is likely to operate at a loss. However, a non-resident individual partner in the worldwide partnership would be liable to UK income tax on his or her profit share in the partnership, in the same manner as a UK partner. This may be advantageous or disadvantageous, depending on where the overseas partners are based. For example, in the Netherlands the locally based equity partners may be exempt from Netherlands tax on their UK source income, with the result that they may suffer a lower effective rate of tax. In Hong Kong, exposure to UK taxation may lead to a higher effective rate of tax.

Partners assigned to an overseas branch are often made salaried partners to avoid exposure to UK tax. So long as the individual becomes non-resident by spending at least one complete tax year outside the UK and the duties are wholly rendered outside the UK, his or her salary (and bonus) would be liable to local taxation only. For capital gains tax purposes partners resident and ordinarily resident outside the UK are still liable to the tax on disposal of partnership assets because of the situs of the partnership in the UK. For other assets the liability to capital gains tax continues; the charge arises on the partner's return to the UK if that occurs within five complete tax years of the partner's date of departure from the UK.

For legal purposes, it is normal in the UK for the members of the UK partnership to be restricted to individuals. However for some professions a non-resident partner's interest might be held through a non-resident corporation or even a non-resident trust. In such cases, the corporation and the trust are liable to income tax at the basic rate (and not at the higher rate) on their share of partnership profits arising. This is on the basis that the corporation and/or the trust are managed and controlled outside the UK and, in the case of a foreign corporation, has no branch, agency or place of business in the UK. If the foreign corporation has such a branch, then its profit share becomes liable to corporation tax.

Local tax advice has to be taken in the particular territory in which the branch is set up. In some circumstances, the office can be characterised as a representative office and hence under the appropriate double tax agreement (if one exists) would be exempt from foreign tax. The double tax agreement would also give the UK partnership the opportunity to credit against UK income tax, the foreign taxes chargeable on the same income. The credit is restricted to income tax on the foreign source of income and to the top rate of income tax. If the foreign tax is at a higher rate than UK income tax no credit is obtained for the excess.

In some territories local tax advice and other factors, such as practising rights, would mean that for that territory's tax position a local company might be used. Dividends from such a company paid to a UK resident partnership of individuals do not carry with them the right to any underlying tax credit for the tax suffered in the foreign country: tax credit is restricted to withholding tax on the dividend. Accordingly, such a company would be held by a UK incorporated and resident company so that that company would obtain underlying tax credit as well as tax credit for withholding tax as dividends paid. In addition, the partnership would endeavour (within arm's-length pricing criteria) to charge costs incurred in the UK to the foreign firm.

Sharing liabilities

Holding out

5.8   The general principles of holding out have been considered in 3.3 above. Where personnel in an overseas office are referred to as 'partners' in the partnership, even though they may not have full or any equity (profit sharing) participation, they will be potentially liable as partners and will have implied authority to bind the partnership as partners. Appropriate indemnity provisions will be needed in the partnership agreement.

Partnership agreement

5.9   The arrangements for sharing liabilities and losses must be spelled out in the partnership agreement with as much clarity as the provisions on profit sharing. If partners in the overseas office have limited or no profit sharing rights, they should likewise have limited or no liability for losses as between the partners, and should have appropriate indemnities from the other partners. If profits are shared internationally, losses should usually be shared in the same way. If loss sharing is to be local, special provisions will be needed in the partnership agreement to achieve that result.

Central controls

Decision making and local autonomy

5.10   The partnership agreement will have to spell out how the decision-making apparatus applies to the overseas office. While the worldwide partnership as a whole will wish to retain control over many of the most important matters, e.g. the appointment of new partners in the overseas office, other decisions regarding local management may well be delegated to the local office. It may be appropriate to impose some reporting requirements on the local partners.

Indemnity insurance

5.11   It will probably be essential (and, in the case of many professional partnerships, required under the applicable professional rules) for the overseas offices to be covered by appropriate professional indemnity insurance. Local law and market conditions will need to be checked in this respect.

Name and goodwill

5.12   The use of the firm name and ownership of goodwill will be of critical importance. Assuming that local law allows the local office to practice under the name of the international firm, the partners in the worldwide partnership will want to ensure that the name and goodwill remains owned by them and cannot be exploited by the partners in the local office if they break away. Therefore, the partnership agreement should make clear that the name and goodwill are owned by the partners of the international firm, even if no value is attributed to them in the partnership accounts.

It would be prudent to register the name locally as a trade or service mark if the local conditions allow.

The local partners should be subject to central 'quality control' to avoid any damage to the firm's reputation as a result of disparities in standards of services available from different offices. Furthermore, it is an essential principle of trade mark law that the owners of the mark retain the right to monitor and control the quality of the goods or services for which the mark in question is being used. Failure to do so may undermine the enforceability of the registration and associated legal rights. It may be appropriate for service standards to be set out in a form of memorandum or charter for adoption by each office.

Preventing breakaways

5.13   The worldwide partnership will, after investing in overseas offices, want to ensure that those offices (if successful) do not break away from the firm as a whole, or at least that the potential damage if they do break away is minimised.

(*a*)   *Motivation and reward.* The most effective way to prevent individual partners in overseas offices, or even entire overseas offices, from breaking away from the parent firm will be to motivate and reward the local partners sufficiently. Shared goals and genuine mutuality of interest will be the best cement. For further information see Chapter 11, Human Resource Management.

(*b*)   *Restrictive covenants.* Restrictive covenants can be an effective way of preventing former partners and employees from soliciting clients of the firm and exploiting the goodwill of the firm for their own benefit or the benefit of a competitor. It will be necessary to consider the local rules on restrictive trade practices.

Multinational organisations of independent firms

Ownership of name and international branding

5.14   It is often important that a multinational organisation of independent firms (whether formed by merger or by the establishment of a network of related but independent local offices) develops a strong international image, which will help member firms attract and retain clients. The ownership and protection of the name and goodwill will be key issues.

Different organisations adopt different approaches to the problem. One approach is for all the member firms in the organisation to transfer their rights in a particular name or acronym to a central entity established in a country with favourable tax laws (which could be a company, foundation or trust). That entity then licenses the use of the name back to the various firms which participate in the multinational organisation for a fee, which is used to meet central costs. The name should be protected by registering all appropriate trade or service marks. The central entity must impose strict quality control procedures to ensure that the reputation of the organisation is maintained and that its ownership of the name (and associated trade or service mark registrations) and goodwill is retained and remains enforceable. Agreement will be needed on the ownership of the entity and for whose benefit the name and goodwill are held if the multinational organisation structure breaks up.

An alternative approach is for one of the firms in the multinational organisation (the dominant or founder firm) to retain ownership of the name but to licence it to the other participants, perhaps directly or perhaps through a central entity, which rests above it and the other member firms as an international co-ordinator. Again, the use of the name and the licensing arrangements will have to be carefully spelled out and policed to ensure continued protection of goodwill and its ownership, and the appropriate trade and service marks should be registered. It will be essential in either case for appropriate 'recapture' provisions to be included in the arrangements, so that the name and goodwill remain in the multinational organisation when member firms break away.

Profit and cost sharing

5.15 The agreements between the firms constituting the multinational organisation will need to spell out the profit and cost sharing arrangements. It may well be agreed that some costs, e.g. relating to training and know-how development should be shared on a central basis with all member firms contributing to a central fund. This could be consideration in return for the use of the name or could form an independent obligation.

In some cases, member firms may pay a small commission on fees referred from other member firms to the organisation; they may even agree to share profits and losses on a worldwide basis to a greater or lesser extent. Care would be needed to ensure there was no worldwide partnership which could lead to one member firm incurring liability for the defaults of another (see Chapter 3, Liabilities of Partners and Partnerships). In addition, care should be taken that each member firm is taxed in its territory on its profit and obtains a deduction for contributions and losses. Furthermore the firms should not expose themselves to overseas tax by the existence of the multinational organisations.

Sharing of liabilities: holding out and ring fencing

5.16 Assuming that the multinational contractual association between independent firms does not amount to a full partnership, it is possible that the use of a common name and the projection of a common identity will lead to a claim that the multinational organisation is held out as being an international partnership. The consequences of this are discussed in Chapter 3. The member firms should take steps to minimise the holding out risks, for example, by making clear in their contracts with clients, customers and suppliers that it is the relevant local firm which is contracting, not any multinational firm. The agreements between the member firms should also make clear that liabilities incurred are to be borne only by the firm which incurred them.

Escape routes

5.17 It may become necessary or desirable to expel a member firm, or a member firm may want to withdraw from the multinational organisation.

(*a*) *Expulsion*. The terms on which a member may be expelled should be spelled out in the agreements between the firms. Provisions will be needed regarding the recapture of the shared name and goodwill for the benefit of the continuing members (or for distribution if the entire organisation breaks up). Restrictive covenants should be imposed and consideration given to the enforceability of these provisions in all the relevant jurisdictions.

(*b*) *Voluntary withdrawal*. Provision may be included for voluntary withdrawal of member firms. Again, provisions for recapture of the name, goodwill and restrictive covenants will be needed. Similarly, if an individual partner in a member firm is also a partner in another connected firm, or has economic interests in another entity within the multinational organisation, it may be desirable to deem withdrawal from one firm to be withdrawal from the entire structure.

(*c*) *Cost of finding successor and financial penalties*. On expulsion or withdrawal of a member firm, it may be necessary to find a new firm to join the organisation in order to ensure continuity of cover for clients in the relevant jurisdiction. Therefore, it may be appropriate to impose the cost of finding a successor, and any other consequential loss, on the former member firm. Some organisations incorporate provisions for a departing firm to be liable to pay a sum calculated according to a formula, perhaps a multiple of fees for business referred to that member firm in the past year or two. A provision providing for payment of a liquidated sum on a breach of the international agreement may well be unenforceable under English law as a penalty, unless it represents a genuine attempt to pre-estimate loss suffered as a result of the breach. On the other hand, a provision for the payment of a particular sum, where a firm withdraws contractually from the organisation is likely to be enforceable.

(*d*) *Restrictive covenants*. Restrictive covenants should be imposed on the activities of an expelled or withdrawn member firm to prevent continued use of the international name, and poaching of clients referred by other member firms. The same considerations as discussed in Chapter 23, Partnership Changes, will apply to the enforceability of such covenants, which will depend on the law chosen by the member firms to govern the relationship between themselves and the enforceability of judgments under that law in the jurisdictions where the breaches occur.

European Economic Interest Groupings (EEIGs)

Formation

5.18   EEIGs are unincorporated associations formed by co-operation between two or more commercial organisations based in the EU and are designed as convenient structures to carry on co-operative activities of existing enterprises. Professional firms in member states thinking of forming an EEIG should check their own professional rules to see if they allow formation.

An EEIG must comprise at least two members based in a different EU member state. Each member must be registered and formed according to the laws of one of the member states and must have its central administration, i.e. place of central management and control, within the EU. Any legal body (including a company or partnership) which carries on any industrial, commercial, craft or agricultural activity or provides professional or other services in the EU can therefore form an EEIG with at least one other similar body. The activities of an EEIG must relate to and be ancillary to the economic activities of its members but it should not be established for profit making activites. An EEIG cannot therefore be established to carry on a business wholly unrelated to that of its members.

EU member states can grant EEIGs the status of legal personalities and in the UK a registered EEIG is accorded a legal personality and the status of a 'body corporate'. There is nothing that prevents an EEIG from being subsequently incorporated and becoming an autonomous economic entity.

EEIGs cannot employ more than 500 persons, exercise any form of control over the management of their members, have any ownership interest in their members, be a member of another EEIG, and may not invite invitations from the public to invest in them. Neither may an EEIG be used to make loans to directors or transfer property from a company to a director that would otherwise be prohibited.

Formalities

5.19   The members of an EEIG are bound together by a 'contract of formation'. The contract of formation must include the name of the EEIG, the official address of the grouping, the names and details of the group members and the objects of the EEIG. Typically the contract of formation will also include terms governing the sharing of profits and losses of the EEIG and the allocation of the EEIG's assets on termination, and rules on meetings and voting powers. It may provide that one or more particular members can exercise more than one vote, although no one member may exercise a majority of the votes.

The words 'European Economic Interest Grouping' or 'EEIG' must be included in the name. The name cannot include 'limited', 'unlimited', or 'public limited company' or their abbreviations.

The members of the EEIG must appoint managers to operate the EEIG on a day-to-day basis.

The contract of formation must be registered in the state in which the EEIG has its official address. This is either where the EEIG has its central administration or where one of its members has its central administration, as long as the EEIG carries on an activity there. Registration in England and Wales is at Companies House, Cardiff and registration in Scotland is at Companies House, Edinburgh. A fee of £20 is payable on registration. If the EEIG opens an 'establishment' in a member state other than the state in which it is registered then that establishment must be registered in that other state.

The creation and termination of an EEIG must be publicly announced in official publications. The relevant publication in England and Wales is the London Gazette. Various changes and other events must also be announced in these publications.

Further formalities in the running of an EEIG include registering details of the appointment or removal of managers; amendments to the formation contract; details of any judicial decision nullifying the EEIG; and notification of a member's assignment of all or part of its participation in the EEIG. The obligations are no more onerous than those imposed on a limited company registered in the UK.

Liabilities

5.20   An EEIG can sue and be sued and make contracts. The members of an EEIG have joint and several liability for its debts and other liabilities. Such liability will remain with any outgoing member who incurred liability before cessation of membership. Furthermore, unless exempted in the formation contract an incoming member will be liable for debts previously incurred. Such liability can be avoided or at least apportioned by drafting the EEIG contract in such a way as to ensure that each member of the EEIG will share only a pro rata liability.

Accounts and taxation

5.21   An EEIG is not subject to any accounting or auditing requirements such as the submission of an annual return. However, an EEIG registered in the UK is required to make a return to the Inland Revenue. Profits and losses resulting from the activities of an EEIG are taxable in the hands of its members as if the profits and gains had accrued to them directly.

Multinational partnerships

Regulatory environment

5.22   Professional restrictions often prohibit or impose conditions on the entry into partnership by UK professionals with foreign-qualified professionals in the same or other fields. Foreign-qualified professionals may be required to register with the relevant UK professional body.

The *Courts and Legal Services Act 1990, s 66*, removed the statutory restrictions on UK-qualified solicitors, barristers and notaries entering into partnership with non-qualified persons, whilst giving power to the relevant professional bodies to prohibit or regulate the creation of any such partnerships. However, care should be taken to ensure that the foreign-qualified person is not, by virtue of entering into partnership with UK-qualified professionals, regarded as holding himself out as having a UK qualification. In order to avoid this, foreign-qualified persons may be required to register with the relevant professional body. Partnerships between solicitors and registered foreign lawyers and/or registered European Lawyers are permitted and such a partnership is known as a multinational partnership. The registered foreign lawyer should be registered with The Law Society and will be regulated under the same rules and principles as solicitors in England and Wales. They must pay contributions to the Solicitors Compensation Fund.

Financial and investment-related professionals may be required to be qualified or registered under particular statutory provisions, which may prohibit partnership between a qualified and a non-qualified person. Medical professionals cannot generally enter into partnership with non-qualified persons.

Chapter 6

Profit Shares

Agreeing sharing ratios

6.1   As indicated in 2.9 and 2.10 above, *section 24* of the *Partnership Act 1890* states:

'...subject to any agreement expressed or implied between the partners ... all the partners are entitled to share equally in the capital and profits of the business, and must contribute equally towards the losses whether of capital or otherwise sustained by the firm.'

In practice there are very few partnerships where profits are shared equally, and this is because there has been an alternative agreement, either in permanent form or in the provision of a mechanism for regularly reviewing and agreeing profit shares. One such mechanism, a compensation committee that makes recommendations to the partnership, is suggested in 7.7 below.

Part of the difficulty in agreeing profit shares is that it is impossible, in most cases, for any partner to be objective as to what he considers his share should be, for example whether he measures his entitlement by his assessment of his past and present contribution, his perceived value in the market place or what he requires to meet his living expenses. Indeed in a typical partnership, the sum of the profit sharing percentages that would be proposed by each partner in respect of their own share would be considerably in excess of 100% and may even approach 200%.

However, it is likely that the firms that will continue to prosper in the competitive environment which currently exists, are those that are able to develop compensation systems for partners that are seen to be as fair as possible and properly reward partners for activities that increase the firm's profits generally.

Criteria for fair profit shares

6.2   These will vary very much from firm to firm. However, it is perhaps reasonable to break down criteria for rewarding partners into a number of different elements. Twelve such elements for a particular firm may be:

(*a*)   Past performance that has generated goodwill for the firm and thus, to some extent, the ability to earn current profits.

(*b*)   The provision of capital to the firm.

(*c*)   The skill of individual partners in attracting new business for themselves and other partners.

(*d*)   The amount of fee income brought into the firm bearing in mind the profitability of that work.

(*e*)   The number of hours of work successfully billed to and collected from clients and the recovery rate of such time.

(*f*)   The satisfaction of a partner's clients in relation to work done.

(*g*)   Contribution to the management of the firm or its individual departments.

(*h*)   Housekeeping skills in billing and collecting fees to minimise use of working capital.

(*j*)   Success in developing the skills of other partners and staff.

(*k*)   Contribution to the firm's external reputation through participation in high profile activities.

(*l*)   Intellectual and technical contributions.

(*m*)   Other intangible qualities that increase the partnership's strength.

Measurement of criteria

6.3   Some of these elements may be fairly judged using objective criteria but many can only be viewed subjectively. Even with objective criteria information is often unreliable or inadequate. Often several different partners rightly claim some responsibility for the generation of new work. In other cases where responsibility is claimed, it may in fact be the firm's reputation that was the key determinant in new work coming in and the recipient partner may simply be the lucky first port of call.

Judgement of criteria

6.4   It is important not to place too much reliance on any one factor as this may lead to undesirable behaviour by partners which would be detrimental to the firm. For example, if a partner felt he was judged simply on fee income, then the temptation could be to hog work for himself. In addition, too much reliance on chargeable hours may leave little time for other activities which in the long run may be more valuable to the firm. Alternatively, simply keeping an existing continuing client satisfied may be just as important as gaining a new client of equal value to the firm. Therefore, appropriate weight needs to be given to each factor considered relevant.

Further factors should be considered when deciding fair methods of profit sharing. For example, it may benefit a firm of solicitors to provide some less profitable services, e.g. residential conveyancing, and it would be unfair to penalise an individual partner for his responsibility for providing those services.

Finally some regard needs to be paid to profit shares in earlier years and likely shares in future ones to avoid wild fluctuations. Whilst it may be motivating to appear more highly valued, it is likely to be demotivating to appear less highly regarded.

Partner mobility

6.5   A fair approach to profit sharing is particularly important in an age of increased partner mobility. The system should prevent partners leaving partnerships simply because they feel they could get a 'fairer' reward elsewhere, and it should attract new partners who will need a certain remuneration level to be persuaded to join the firm. However, it is also important that the new partner's package should not upset the existing remuneration structure unduly as this may cause unnecessary friction.

Commonwealth approach

6.6   Some firms find a semi-scientific assessment of fair profit shares all too difficult and have fixed percentages or formulae based on seniority. Such bases have the possible advantage of reducing time spent arguing, as debates may take place only every few years, and the partnership spirit and co-operation between partners and departments may be engendered. There may also be peer pressure to ensure underperforming partners contribute in proportion to their share. However, often an underperforming partner does not recognise failings that may be seen all too clearly by his peers. Therefore, fixed percentages and seniority schemes tend to work best in very profitable firms where all partners can be satisfied with their lot.

Equal shares

6.7   In the life of a partnership, an equal sharing system is usually found at the beginning of a firm's life. Two or more individuals come together, recognise that their compatible qualities will lead to a successful business, and often, in the absence of knowledge or detailed consideration, or without the ability to devise an alternative basis, opt for equal sharing of profits. For example, two partners will take 50% of the profits each, or four partners 25% each etc. Such founder partners of a successful firm are likely to be highly influential in the development of the firm for many years and, as a firm grows, successfully retain significant rights for themselves. This may be no more than their proper reward for the entrepreneurial flair that created the firm in the first place.

Unequal shares

6.8   As a firm develops unequal shares may be the next step. This could be because of a mutual recognition, after a period, that the contribution of each partner to the generation of profits is not equal and equal sharing is unfair. This change may come about easily by agreement or when it becomes clear to the partners that the business will not thrive and prosper with unfair profit sharing and the only way to hold the business together is by adjusting profit shares. More often, particularly if the founder partners are few in number, the development to an unequal sharing system comes when the first new partner is admitted to the partnership, generally as a 'junior partner'.

A simple profit sharing example

6.9   To illustrate we will consider a new partnership with a simple profit sharing basis over a number of years.

Stage 1

A partnership with two partners, A and B, introduce C as a new junior partner. A and B who had 50% each of the equity each, after four years' successful practice, each offer 10% of the profits to C with the resulting profit shares.

Partner	Year 1	Year 4
A	50%	40%
B	50%	40%
C	—	20%
TOTAL	100%	100%

Part of the justification may be that C is unable to contribute capital, or not on the scale provided by A and B. However, as the matter is to be settled by agreement, A and B may make any offer they like to C. If C is an existing employee and the terms offered appear better than remuneration as a salaried employee, he is likely to accept.

Stage 2

As the partnership develops and prospers, new partners may be admitted with profit shares coming mainly or exclusively from A and B. For example, a new partner D may be offered an 8% share and E a 6% share in year 7 giving profit shares as follows:

Partner	Year 1	Year 4	Year 7
A	50%	40%	33%
B	50%	40%	33%
C	—	20%	20%
D	—	—	8%
E	—	—	6%
TOTAL	100%	100%	100%

Stage 3

Subsequently F, G and H are admitted in year 10 with 4% shares each coming from A, B and C unequally by agreement. This gives rise to respective shares of:

Partner	Year 1	Year 4	Year 7	Year 10
A	50%	40%	33%	28%
B	50%	40%	33%	28%
C	—	20%	20%	18%
D	—	—	8%	8%
E	—	—	6%	6%
F	—	—	—	4%
G	—	—	—	4%
H	—	—	—	4%
TOTAL	100%	100%	100%	100%

We have thus seen how a successful two-partner firm became an eight-partner firm over a ten-year period. How the firm develops from here may depend very much on the ages, personalities and ability of the partners together with the success of the business. For example, H may feel well rewarded with a profit share of 40,000 per annum but resent the fact that the two most senior partners take profits of 280,000. Equally A and B may be concerned about the future succession to the practice, and the ability of the remaining partners eventually to repay them their capital, let alone any value for the goodwill they have built up either in capital profits or through annuities if their partnership agreement so allows. The pressure is thus on for a new basis for sharing of profits and a negotiation amongst the partners.

Points scheme

6.10 It may be here that a points scheme comes into its own. Such schemes are particularly common amongst firms of solicitors and may be called lock-step arrangements. They often work as follows.

Partners are awarded a particular number of points. Each partner's profit share is then calculated according to their number of points, expressed as a percentage of the total number of points held by all the partners.

Therefore, our points scheme example partnership may negotiate initial points and these percentages as follows.

Stage 1

Partner	Year 11
A	20%
B	20%
C	17%
D	12%
E	10%
F	7%
G	7%
H	7%
TOTAL	100%

Stage 2

The scheme involves each partner gaining two points a year up to a maximum of 20. New partners will be introduced with seven points. A number of new partners join, I in year 13, J and K in year 14, L in year 15 and M and N in year 16. Two partners also retire, A in year 15 and B in year 16. This leads to a change in profit shares as on the following page:

Partner	Year 12		Year 13		Year 14		Year 15		Year 16	
	Points	%	Points	%	Points	%	Points	%	Points	%
A	20	20	20	16.8	20	13.7				
B	20	20	20	16.8	20	13.7	20	13.4		
C	17	17	19	16.0	20	13.7	20	13.4	20	12.4
D	12	12	14	11.9	16	11.0	18	12.1	20	12.4
E	10	10	12	10.1	14	9.6	16	10.7	18	11.2
F	7	7	9	7.5	11	7.5	13	8.7	15	9.3
G	7	7	9	7.5	11	7.5	13	8.7	15	9.3
H	7	7	9	7.5	11	7.5	13	8.7	15	9.3
I			7	5.9	9	6.2	11	7.4	13	8.1
J					7	4.8	9	6.1	11	6.8
K					7	4.8	9	6.1	11	6.8
L							7	4.7	9	5.6
M									7	4.4
N									7	4.4
TOTAL	100	100	119	100	146	100	149	100	161	100

Thus by year 16 succession is achieved, A and B have retired, C has become the most long-serving and probably senior partner, the partnership grows and the differential in profit shares is reduced and is related to seniority within the partnership.

Interesting features

6.11   This scheme has a number of other interesting features.

(*a*)   As a partnership grows, even though an individual increases his number of points, his profit share may fall, e.g. D in years 13 and 14.

(*b*)   The more junior members of the partnership's profit sharing percentage rises more rapidly than those nearing the plateau of 20 points.

(*c*)   Partners feel secure as their points rise each year, or at least the plateau does not fall.

(*d*)   The growth in the number of partners in the partnership will probably be possible as a result of rising profits. Otherwise the firm may well feel there is not 'room' for new partners. Thus even if a partners' profit sharing percentage is falling, commonly his share of profits may rise in monetary terms.

Escalators and ladders

6.12   Escalators and ladders are both points schemes. The scheme described in 6.9 was an escalator scheme, as the increase in points was an automatic process (two points per year leading in the seventh year to full equality with the most senior partners). This is a typical scheme, although the initial share in this case was only seven points, giving a differential of profit shares of almost three to one between the most junior and senior partners. The level of such differentials may depend on the profitability of the firm. More commonly, in a firm of solicitors, the starting point would be, say, 13 points (giving a differential of about 1.5 to 1 between lowest and highest sharing partners). The partners in this escalator scheme would move one point a year, to reach full equality with the senior partners in seven years.

The essential difference between a ladder scheme and an escalator scheme is that the more junior partner must exert some effort to climb the ladder, as opposed to rising automatically to the desired destination. This means that additional points are only awarded on the basis of perceived merit or, for example, by meeting defined targets. This will be assessed by the managing partner, the compensation committee or the firm generally. Arguably a ladder scheme carries with it the means to financial motivation and therefore may be better for the partnership. However, if an individual partner fails to climb a ladder that his peers are climbing, he may be demoralised to the detriment of the firm.

Discretionary elements

6.13   As we have seen, a ladder scheme has a discretionary element to it, as there is a decision needed as to whether a particular partner is judged to merit the additional point and thus move up the ladder. However, the amount of profit share subject to discretion is limited.

A firm may feel a greater element of profit sharing needs to be discretionary. For example, if a firm takes the view that unequal shares is the appropriate profit sharing method and regular renegotiations are too divisive or damaging to the firm, it may consider that creating annual discretionary bonuses would be motivating and an appropriate means for rewarding partners' activities that significantly benefit the firm. Such a bonus scheme typically involves 5–10% of profits being set aside and distributed to a small number of partners judged to have materially increased profits for the firm, where partners feel that the basic profit sharing arrangements are not fair.

Fixed shares and prior shares

6.14   A fixed or prior share of profits is a first charge on the firm's profits. Often a firm will consider equal prior shares as minimum 'salaries' to reflect time spent and work done, as opposed to the profitability of the firm. Such a scheme is a useful mechanism for ensuring junior partners still receive suitable remuneration in years when the firm's profits are low. An alternative is a safety net with a minimum level of profit for each partner (subject to the overall level of profits being adequate for each partner to receive a minimum share). Fixed shares can also be used to reflect particular onerous responsibilities, e.g. as senior partner or managing partner, where an additional 'salary' may be considered appropriate. Finally fixed shares may be the principal element of the profit sharing of mezzanine partners. If a profit sharing agreement provides for fixed or prior shares, consideration needs to be given to how it should operate in the case of losses or inadequate total profits.

Interest on capital

6.15   If all capital is provided equally, in accordance with profit sharing ratios, there is no need to pay interest on capital. However, capital is often provided in a different ratio to profits. This may be because more junior partners do not have access to sufficient capital or borrowing powers. In the interest of equity, it is necessary to consider paying interest on capital. Such 'interest' is treated as a prior share of profits for both accounting and tax purposes.

Consideration needs to be given to the rate of interest payable on such capital. Arguably it should be at least equal to the individual partner's borrowing costs to provide such capital. Growing partnerships, and all partnerships in an era of inflation, tend to have a growing requirement for capital to finance the business's working capital requirements. In the absence of an interest provision, particularly if capital is not to be provided completely in accordance with profit shares, it may be hard to persuade partners to raise the additional capital the firm needs. Different partners may have different, borrowing costs depending on their personal circumstances and, if interest is to be paid, it may need to be at a standard rate, e.g. bank base rate plus 2%. There is an argument that such capital should merit a much higher rate of return representing, as it does, risk equity.

There is also a good argument for paying interest on undrawn profits to encourage partners to keep funds in the business, as opposed to withdrawing them the moment they are released. If interest on such balances is paid at, say, bank base rate, both the firm and the individual may benefit. The firm benefits (and the partners generally benefit) because the firm may be financed with a permanent overdraft at an interest cost above base rate, and the partner benefits if he otherwise would have simply placed the funds on deposit in his own name at a rate of interest typically less than base rate. However, if partners choose to leave undrawn profits in the business, it may be a less secure loan than to a bank or building society.

Finally the interest on capital concept can be used to deal with other partnership issues involving equity between partners – e.g. motor cars, which are an emotive subject in many partnerships. Different amounts spent on individual cars can be treated as 'negative capital' giving an interest charge against individual profit shares.

Workers and owners

6.16   As indicated earlier, partners in a professional firm have the characteristics of both owners and workers. The analogy in a corporate environment is shareholders and employees. It is possible, and reasonable, to divide profit sharing into these two elements. In particular, it is generally hard to justify very large discrepancies in the profit share element between junior and senior partners which relate to how hard each works. The justification must relate more to both the value of that work with clients and contacts built up over many years, and the fact that more senior partners own a greater proportion of the business. If this is accepted, and it is not necessary for the junior partners, at least initially, to own the business and provide capital in the same proportions in which income is shared, schemes can then be devised that will enable junior partners to build up their capital over a period through retention of their profits or otherwise.

Salaried partners

6.17   The term 'salaried partners' is used in this book to describe senior employees held out by the practice as partners by 'being on the notepaper'. Such individuals do not strictly share in the profits at all. However, the term may also be used to define those partners whose profits consist principally of a fixed or prior share, with only a very small proportion of profits after fixed shares. Such partners have 'security' of profit share, as their 'take' in financial terms is not very dependent on the overall level of profits.

Losses

6.18 It is necessary to agree on the basis on which losses are to be shared. If this is not done the provisions of *section 24* of the *Partnership Act 1890* come into play. These provide that losses are to be shared equally. Whilst professional partnerships may not normally contemplate making losses, they can arise – possibly as a result of a professional negligence claim greater than the level of insured cover. Normally losses are shared on the same basis as profits (after any fixed or prior shares).

Capital profits and losses

6.19 The partnership agreement may provide that capital profits and losses are shared differently from revenue profits and losses. Capital profits and losses arise on disposals of capital assets, e.g. investments, properties or goodwill. Capital profits and losses would normally be shared on the basis on which capital is held which, as indicated in 6.16 above, may be different from revenue profit sharing.

Summary

6.20 As a collection of individuals, every partnership is different and it is not possible to be prescriptive about how profits should be shared. There are many different bases in common use. Nevertheless firms should be aware that the basis can have a significant effect on the partnership's success because of the motivating or demotivating effect of the basis on individual partners.

Chapter 7

Management

Decision taking

7.1   As we have seen in 2.23 above, *section 24(5)* of the *Partnership Act 1890* provides that, '... subject to any alternative agreement between the partners, every partner may take part in the management of the business'.

This is normally impractical for medium-sized or large partnerships. In smaller firms of perhaps up to eight or ten partners, it sometimes remains possible for all the partners to be involved in the management of the business. In such firms it can be practical for decisions to be taken on management issues at daily, weekly or monthly meetings of all general or equity partners.

Senior partner

7.2   However, even in small partnerships, the position of a senior partner is generally recognised as one that carries particular responsibilities for the firm as a whole. Such responsibilities generally extend to chairing partners' meetings, resolving partnership conflicts and disputes, where possible, and acting as the principal ambassador for the firm with the outside world, including the firm's professional body.

Committees

7.3   As a partnership grows, it becomes normal for decision-making functions to be devolved from the whole partnership to a number of committees. These would typically include a finance committee and a committee overseeing administration. There may also be committees responsible for the running of individual departments or functions, as well as a policy committee to which the more important decisions are devolved. An alternative structure involves an executive committee or board to whom important powers are delegated.

All powers of such committees would normally be devolved from the partners by one or more resolutions or in a general meeting. The partnership may reserve certain powers or require certain decisions, for example, on capital expenditure or the admission or expulsion of partners, to be referred to themselves for final decisions.

Whilst such committees have the advantage of being able to involve partners in decisions, all too easily, such committees can behave in the ineffective way, so graphically described in *The Law* by Professor C Northcote Parkinson (Penguin Books). This can lead to a paralysis of decision-making.

Managing partner

7.4 As a partnership grows further, the number of committees may increase until the firm reaches a critical size, typically perhaps 15 to 20 partners, when it becomes practical to appoint a managing partner (who may, or more usually may not, be the senior partner) for whom managing the firm can become a fairly full-time occupation. In addition to a managing partner, the governance or constitutional set-up can have a significant impact on the performance of firms. Even with a full-time managing partner, it is normal to involve a number of partners to some extent in the running of the practice.

The length of appointment as managing partner, and the powers attached to the post, vary from firm to firm. Typically, the position may be held for between two and five years, with perhaps the need for re-election, although there seems to be a trend towards longer terms for managing partners or even a career role.

Partnerships need to consider carefully who to choose as managing partner. Personal qualities rather than technical abilities are the key determinant. A managing partner generally takes a considerable risk in giving up his client base and he will deserve and welcome the commitment of the partnership to making his role a success.

Outsiders

7.5 An alternative route for a firm is to have a professional manager. However, as the post-holder will usually not be qualified in the professional discipline of the firm, his status will be an issue. It is often very hard for such an individual coming in from outside to obtain the full confidence of the partners.

Another way in which an outsider may be involved in a senior capacity is as chairman of the firm, a role in lieu of the position of senior partner. Such an individual must be highly respected to enable the role to work. The responsibilities would typically be similar to those of a senior partner, although it is likely that a firm choosing this route would be looking for such an individual to have additional skills.

Partnership governance

7.6 It is often helpful to divorce the positions of managing partner and senior partner. This enables the managing partner to have a separate sounding board. The senior partner will also generally be a conduit for channelling other partners' views. This more formal structure with a managing partner/ senior partner relationship mirrors a corporate structure with a chief executive or managing director/chairman relationship. The managing partner/director's powers are generally attenuated and made accountable through the senior partner/chairman role.

As a professional firm grows larger, it tends to resemble a corporate entity, except that in a professional firm all partners are effectively both senior executives and shareholders. However, the unlimited liability consequences of the partnership vehicle will typically mean that, even in their shareholder role, partners are more active and interested than shareholders in companies.

To complement the roles of managing and senior partners in a larger firm, it is normal to have a board of partners or an executive committee that may be elected. Such a board may consider having non-executive members in order to make good use of outside experience. Even with this structure there are likely also to be other committees involving partners in decisions related to functions or departments. In any event, it is usual to have at least an annual meeting of all partners, akin to a company AGM. This meeting will be responsible for approving accounts and may be involved for example in electing board and committee members and approving remuneration arrangements.

The particular structure chosen by any partnership will depend on history, the personalities of the partners and the stage of development of the partnership. In the author's view, partnerships that thrive and prosper will be those with good management. This generally means the partnerships that are able to create structures that enable good and timely decisions to be taken.

Compensation committee

7.7 As discussions involving remuneration or profit sharing can be highly divisive matters, one way of reducing the risk of damaging disputes is to devolve responsibilities for relevant recommendations to a compensation committee. Typically, such a committee will include both partners chosen because they are highly respected, and partners representing different groups or interests in the partnership.

Administration

7.8 Below partnership level, there will be senior staff involved in administrative and support functions. Typically, they will not have the qualifications to be partners and careful consideration needs to be given to their status to ensure that they can work effectively. The most senior and effective members may best be motivated with some form of stake or profit share in the firm, such as a profit-related bonus. Such staff will report to the managing partner, other partners or committees, depending on the partnership structure.

Partnership secretary

7.9 A common and well-recognised role is that of the partnership secretary. In some firms, this will be the most senior administrator, with responsibilities akin to those of a company secretary. This role generally involves attending meetings of partners, including in some cases committees of partners, recording decisions and ensuring that they are implemented. This role may be combined with others, for example responsibility for personnel, premises or insurances, depending on the size and structure of the partnership. It is, however, increasingly common to divorce this role from that of heading up the finance function.

Head of finance

7.10 This role can have a variety of alternative titles, director of finance, partnership accountant or financial controller, depending on the size and structure of the partnership and the degree of delegation from the partners. It is a critical role for any professional firm.

The head of finance will generally control day-to-day liaison with the partnership's bankers and be responsible for the proper financial record-keeping of the business and the annual accounts. He will also have the job of providing the firm's decision-makers with accurate and timely financial and other management information. External accountants may support and supplement this role. In a smaller firm, the individual may be responsible for computer support as well.

If the partnership chooses to delegate a considerable degree of responsibility for finance, then the individual's calibre must be very high. A good finance director will have to think strategically and the partners will increasingly rely on him for advice.

Other positions

7.11 These will vary from firm to firm and depend on the extent to which individual partners fill management functions. Other common senior roles in the larger firms will include head of personnel, head of marketing and head of information technology, exact titles may also vary.

Departments

7.12 It is common for a professional firm of any size to divide itself internally into a number of departments. Typically, this will depend on the type of work. For example, a law firm may be divided into litigation, commercial, property and private client departments, with partners and staff allocated to departments according to their specialities. Similarly, a chartered surveyors' firm may be divided into residential property and commercial property, each subdivided according to property management, development or broking activities. Normally, one partner (typically called the head of the department) will take overall responsibility for the performance and management of each department. The firm's information systems will need to be designed to produce financial and other information on a departmental basis.

A departmental culture may be good for accountability and team building, as each department becomes a profit centre. Nevertheless, overemphasis on departmental culture may breed infighting, particularly if some departments, whilst essential for the firm, are known to be less profitable or loss leaders.

Equally, overemphasis of the autonomy of departments and their role as separate profit centres will be damaging when clients need to be serviced by more than one department in the firm. Similarly, if departments are allowed complete autonomy in their marketing activity, confusing messages may be given to clients and the outside world.

To counter some of the effects of departmental marketing, specialist cross-departmental groups of partners and staff, perhaps organised on an industry or other grouping from which clients come, may be needed to spread knowledge and ensure that a firm's resources are efficiently deployed.

The administrative and support functions may also be subdivided into departments, for example finance, marketing, information technology and personnel.

Partners' meetings

7.13   The structure of the firm may mean that not all partners are fully involved in management. Nevertheless they invariably have certain powers of at least a reserve nature that will need exercising occasionally. Whilst sometimes this can be achieved through using written resolutions, normally there would be a partners' meeting which provides a forum for discussion as well as sometimes acting as a 'safety valve' mechanism.

The particular powers reserved to the partners as a whole will be determined in the constitution of the partnership. This is likely to include admission and expulsion of partners, election of the board, choice of managing and senior partners, mergers, opening and closing branches or departments, approval of expenditure above a certain level and possibly choice of the firm's professional advisers. Particular majorities may be needed, especially on such sensitive items as elections or the expulsion of a partner. It may be wise to provide a mechanism for secret voting.

Conduct of partnership and committee meetings

7.14   As noted in 2.25 above there is little statutory guidance on how such meetings are to be conducted. Much will depend upon the detailed guidelines that may be set out in the partnership agreement or be a matter of custom and practice. Effective meetings will depend primarily on the skill of the meeting chairman to set the agenda and guide debate. Whilst it is important to allow all present to have a full say, most attendees will be very busy and the chairman must be able to keep a balance between very full debate and ensuring that the meeting is not unnecessarily prolonged.

To ensure that action follows decisions taken by committees, accurate minuting of such meetings by the partnership or committee secretary and follow up by the meeting chairman and other partners or staff involved will be needed.

Functions of management

7.15   Management's functions may be defined as setting objectives, organising the business to meet such objectives, communicating those objectives to personnel and motivating them, measuring performance of parts of the business and taking necessary corrective action. To be able to do this, management must exercise control over the firm's affairs.

Within a professional firm, these functions are modified by the nature of the firm, its profession and the people in the firm. For example, the management of partners is always a delicate matter. The qualities that attract able individuals to practice in a profession may be such that subtle techniques need to be used by management to modify behaviour. Professional firms often attract successful partners who are 'prima donnas' who are difficult to manage. Such partners may see management's role as simply ensuring necessary support. Nevertheless management has a valuable role to play in assisting every partner to develop personally for the benefit of the firm.

Co-ordinating the activities of different departments to avoid duplication or conflicts will be a management responsibility. Further management responsibilities in professional firms are quality control and risk management.

Planning and implementation

7.16   Strategic planning is important for the success of most organisations including professional firms. The end product of the process may be longer-term objectives. For example, these could include merger proposals, specific diversification of the firm's business through acquisitions of partners or practices, opening new branches in the UK or overseas, making strategic alliances or developing new specialities. (See Chapter 8.)

In the shorter term, all well-run organisations need annual budgets and targets with regular monitoring of performance against such budgets and targets. (See Chapter 14.)

Financial control

7.17   A prime function of management of a partnership, particularly as any partner may commit the partnership to liabilities, is to exercise proper control over the finances of the firm. Adequate procedures need to be in place to control expenditure and commitments, including offers of employment. Management will take responsibility for record-keeping and should have delegated responsibility for the partnership, with limits of responsibility and requirements to report to the partners generally. (This is discussed in greater detail in Chapter 14.)

Marketing

7.18   New profitable business is the life blood of a firm that relies on a number of discrete assignments. For those firms with continuing work for clients, new business is the prerequisite to a growing firm and is necessary to replace lost business. In practice most firms generally have a mixture of discrete assignments and continuing work for clients, but all firms need to consider how to attract new clients.

Marketing has become increasingly important for the success of professional firms as constraints placed by professional bodies have been steadily reducing. Whilst specific marketing may be the responsibility of individual fee earning departments, central management's role, apart from providing support, is that of co-ordination and general promotion of the firm. (This is discussed in greater detail in Chapter 9.)

Information systems

7.19   For professional firms, information systems may represent a major investment of capital and commitment to revenue expenditure. Management must take overall responsibility for this and ensure that the investment provides an appropriate return. (See Chapter 10.)

Personnel

7.20   Professional firms are people businesses and both partners and staff are demonstrably the major asset of a firm. To ensure the best return on the investment in this asset, careful attention needs to be paid by management to motivation, remuneration, timing and development of partners and staff. (See Chapter 11 for further detail.)

Quality control

7.21 Management must take overall responsibility for the quality of advice or other services provided by a professional firm to its clients. Typically, detailed responsibility is delegated to fee earning departments. This is partly to ensure the firm has happy clients, willing to pay professional fees. In the light of the growth of claims for professional negligence, it is also particularly important as part of the risk management role that the firm's management must adopt. Management will have responsibility for liaising with the firm's insurers. This is addressed in Chapter 15. Some firms may wish to introduce formal quality systems such as ISO 9000 both to reassure management as to the quality of work undertaken, and as part of a marketing drive to win new clients.

Premises

7.22 Management will need to ensure that there is an adequate amount of appropriate space for the firm in suitable offices in the right location. Premises are often a difficult issue for a partnership because they involve uncertain long-term commitments and liabilities that may outlive the working lives of individual partners. Provision of suitable space for partnerships whose business is expanding (or contracting) can also be difficult and expensive. The opposite position is that premises may provide financial benefits for partners and partnerships at the times in the property cycle when significant inducements are offered to incoming tenants. The value of these inducements needs to be carefully balanced against the long-term liabilities.

Compliance with professional requirements and other legislation

7.23 Management will have overall responsibility for ensuring that the firm, its partners and staff comply with the responsibilities placed on them by the professional bodies of which they are members. This may extend to reports to such professional bodies, subscriptions, licences, registrations, and meeting obligations such as Continuing Professional Education etc. A stream of new regulatory and criminal statutes place onerous obligations on professional firms, and management will need to ensure the firm complies with these as well as other legislation, for instance, employment law and health and safety legislation.

Chapter 8

Strategic Planning

Introduction

8.1 This chapter is intended as a general introduction to the concept and process of strategic planning in a partnership. An in-depth analysis of the theory, methodologies and jargon of strategic planning is available in countless management books. This chapter has been written for the reader who probably has no previous direct experience of strategic planning but who wants a broad and practical understanding of it. Those intending to lead the development of a partnership's strategic plan, or likely to be heavily involved in the planning team, should follow this chapter with further reading, training and advice from appropriately experienced consultants.

There is a fair amount of scepticism about the use of strategic planning. Partnerships have generally been less inclined to develop strategic plans than other types of business. This scepticism is often because of a number of factors which might include the following:

(*a*) fears that the results of the work will be worthless;

(*b*) the fact that a previous strategic planning exercise has produced a voluminous tome which now gathers dust on the shelf; or

(*c*) concern that discussion about the firm's direction and priorities will lead to unseemly squabbles.

In short, partners often feel strategic planning will be a worthless exercise involving uncomfortable navel gazing. These fears are fair ones. However, we believe that, if it is approached in the right way, strategic planning can have significant tangible benefits both immediately and in the long term.

What is strategic planning?

8.2 At its simplest, strategic planning is thinking about how the partnership is to move from where it is today to where it wants to be at some future point. However, strategic plans have characteristics which differentiate them from other tactical plans.

(*a*) They tend to be about longer-term direction. For most partnerships, the most appropriate planning horizon is no more than five years. The majority of strategic plans probably look forward three years.

(*b*) Strategic plans always involve change. Any partnership which aspires to both survive and thrive will need to plan to change to meet the needs and pressures of a dynamic business environment. This is one of the many challenges of strategic planning. Handled inadequately, the planning process can cause a sense of unease and uncertainty in the partnership. This potentially negative aspect of strategic planning can stop businesses initiating or fulfilling a vital process – planning their long-term future.

(*c*) The final strategies and plans are heavily influenced by the values and aspirations of partners, staff and others involved in the process. Therefore, despite objective analysis of the firm's internal and external situation, there remains considerable subjectivity in the selection of the preferred strategy.

(*d*) The resultant actions are often complex because of the range of integrated issues which usually need to be addressed. These generally include marketing, human resources, business processes, finances, property and information systems.

(*e*) Strategic plans may create a high degree of uncertainty because they attempt to match the firm's activities and capabilities to a fast-changing environment. The shorter the plan's time span the more certainty there can be about the outcome.

Why develop a strategic plan?

8.3 Strategic planning can be beneficial to partnerships of all sizes and in any sector, in good times and in bad. Some of the potential benefits include the following.

(*a*) Ideas and initiatives are generated during the analysis, debate and discussion processes. Action, with immediate benefits, is often stimulated even before the strategy is completed.

(*b*) Partners and staff are given confidence in the future of the firm. This can inspire greater levels of motivation, commitment and teamwork.

(*c*) It helps to anticipate external changes which may be either opportunities or threats. This might, for example, allow the partnership to target new market opportunities before competitors or avoid exposing the firm to unnecessary risks.

(*d*) Resources can be planned more effectively. A clear view of the future for the firm might assist improved decision-making in terms of, for example, information systems, skills, numbers of staff, marketing, financing and property.

(*e*) It helps to resolve some of the debates and arguments which might have constrained the firm from making important decisions or even very basic ones.

(*f*)   The plan acts as a management tool – driving action and providing a basis for measuring the performance of the firm.

An effective strategic planning process can produce a coherent strategy for the firm, which gives it a competitive advantage in the market place. This is likely to provide immediate and practical benefits and increase the likelihood of achieving partners' common ambitions. There is no doubt that a partnership can go a long way without going through a strategic planning process. But perhaps it would go further and faster in the right direction with one?

Who should be involved?

8.4   Everybody should be involved, although each person will be involved in different ways. Levels of involvement can be broadly segmented into three – planning, consulting and communication.

Planning

8.5   Here, we are referring to the team of people who will be directly involved in designing and leading the strategic planning process. It is vital that this team is carefully selected to ensure that it has an appropriate mix of personalities, business and creative/analytical skills, and 'political' representation from across the firm. Teams comprising solely of equity partners rarely have the mix needed. It is usually advantageous to have a team of 4–8 people. This might include some salaried partners and senior managers.

The planning team should ideally be led by the senior partner (chairman) or managing partner (chief executive). A valuable external and objective perspective can be added by co-opting people from outside the firm, e.g. either a consultant or the equivalent of a non-executive director, if the firm has one.

Consulting

8.6   The planning team will wish to consult colleagues across the firm. In an ideal world, it is best to give everybody an opportunity to contribute to the strategy development at some stage in its formulation. This encourages greater 'ownership' and commitment to the strategy. Such consultation might take place through a variety of processes such as group discussions, personal interviews/meetings and formal staff surveys. However, consultation with every member of staff is often not feasible. The planning team will need to ensure that the consultation net is thrown wide enough and that all key players are given an opportunity to contribute.

Communication

8.7   It is vital to communicate and 'sell' the strategy across the firm. The senior partners, management and planning team must demonstrate their commitment to the plan. Communication, through presentations and discussion, should ensure that there is understanding of the firm's direction and of each person's and department's role in it. It is surprising how many firms claim to have a strategy but their staff have no knowledge of its existence, let alone what it is. The need to communicate does not imply, of course, that certain plans and issues should not remain confidential to a smaller group of people.

The strategic planning process

8.8   The strategic planning process is never exactly the same from firm to firm. There is no single correct process. The process must be designed to take the following factors (among others) into account:

(*a*)   the size of the firm;

(*b*)   the complexity and sensitivity of the issues which need to be addressed;

(*c*)   the availability of internal and external data;

(*d*)   the firm's experience of planning;

(*e*)   existing planning and budgeting processes;

(*f*)   the firm's culture;

(*g*)   competitive pressures; and

(*h*)   changes, and the speed of change, in the firm's operating environment.

It is vital to map the strategic development process at the outset. It is easy to lose your way unless there is a clear understanding of the steps and timetable. It is also important not to forget that as you move through the strategic planning process, you will often want to reconsider assumptions, options and conclusions, or address new issues which arise.

Another danger with the process is that, understandably, the people involved are distracted by day-to-day issues which need to be addressed. This often causes significant delay. In addition, planners may not have time to think and develop the creative ideas which are so often essential to producing a strategy which is appropriate to a dynamic and highly competitive environment. One potential solution is to appoint an external person to facilitate the process and to keep the team on track.

Whatever the nature of the strategic planning process undertaken to suit the firm, the following are some of the factors that are usually considered:

(i) *Aspirations/objectives.* In any partnership (and most businesses) key drivers to a strategy are the aspirations and personal objectives of the key internal stakeholders (e.g. partners, managers, staff). Any strategy which does not take these into account is likely to be doomed. Therefore it is vital that aspirations and objectives are understood.

(ii) *Mission and values of the firm.* There is normally considerable scepticism about the purpose and value of a 'mission statement' and it may be best to avoid that term. Nonetheless, some firms benefit from developing some form of written statement which summarises their firm's broad aims and philosophies in terms of, for example, markets, geography, services and values. Such a statement will provide the context for the development of the detailed strategy and plan.

(iii) *Internal analysis.* This should identify the firm's internal resource strengths and weaknesses in relation to the competition and the likelihood of future change in the external environment. It will involve the gathering and interpretation of information relating to, for example, people (attitudes, numbers, skills, training etc.), property, management information and quality of services and client care, information systems and finances.

(iv) *External analysis.* A practical strategy must be based on an objective understanding of the business environment at three levels: the macro-environment, competitors and clients. Analysis of the macro-environment will involve examining the social, political, technological, economic and legal factors that may make an impact on the market place. Also important is an analysis of both existing competitors and potential competitors to examine such issues as:

(*a*) their relative strengths and weaknesses;

(*b*) what they are doing new or differently; and

(*c*) their potential plans for the future.

Clients are, of course, fundamental to the future success of the firm. Client analysis would aim to answer questions such as:

(I) how they perceive the firm and its strengths and weaknesses;

(II) how their needs might change in the future;

(III) how they would like to see the firm develop in the future in terms of, for example, the range of services and method of service delivery; and

(IV) how perceptions, needs and other factors vary across different types of client and market segments.

This external analysis will enable the firm to get the future changes to and needs of the business in perspective and take a view on the opportunities and threats that may arise in the future.

(v) *Strategy development.* This stage will involve consideration of all the data gathered to date. The aim of this stage is to reach broad agreement on issues such as:

(A)   the firm's goals/objectives;

(B)   the current situation, perhaps defined in terms of a SWOT analysis (strengths, weaknesses, opportunities and threats);

(C)   critical success factors or issues which need to be addressed if the firm is to move successfully from its current position towards its objectives; and

(D)   review of options for business development, possibly evaluated against various scenarios such as for example changes in the law, government, technology and the economy.

(vi)   *Action planning.* Having agreed the broad strategy, it is important to develop a detailed action plan, incorporating clear responsibilities, timings and costs.

(vii)   *Monitoring and review.* Strategic planning should not be a one-off exercise which is undertaken every few years. There should be regular monitoring of a partnership's performance against the agreed performance targets and milestones. The strategy will probably require regular modification and refinement as performance targets are exceeded or missed and as the market and environment change

The agreed strategy should not be set out in a lengthy and verbose document. A summary for internal consumption is often appropriate. This should include key elements of the strategy (goals, objectives, SWOT, strategic paths). It is very important that it also includes the action plan and performance targets which the firm is aiming to achieve as the partnership moves towards its longer term goals.

Typical components of a strategic plan

8.9   These components consist of:

(a)   *Performance review.* A review of recent performance (overall, and in key areas of activity, e.g. products, customers, finances, people etc.).

(b)   *Environment analysis.* Review of trends in the operating environment, e.g. social, legal, economic, political, technological. Review of competitors. Review of the markets, customer segments and relevant trends etc. Identification of key opportunities and threats.

(c)   *Internal analysis.* Review of the firm's resources (e.g. people property, finances, products, services, information systems etc.) to identify principal strengths and weaknesses relative to the market place.

(d)   *SWOT analysis.* Summary of principal strengths, weaknesses, opportunities and threats.

(e)   *Vision/Mission/Aims.* A statement of the firm's longer term aspirations/aims values etc.

(f)   *Strategy.* A series of strategic (or policy) statements regarding key issues such as markets/customers; products/services; quality; people; information systems; finances; method of development; property; and geography (location, target areas). Options which might have been considered could be covered in this section.

(g)   *Objectives/performance indicators.* A series of measurable objectives (or performance indicators) against which progress can be monitored.

(h)   *Implementation plan.* Key actions with details of people responsible, timings and resource implications.

(i)   *Appendices.* Appendices might be required, e.g. financial forecasts/ scenario analyses; market data; sales data etc.

Common pitfalls

8.10   Some common pitfalls that firms experience during the strategic planning process are given below.

(*a*)   Inadequate internal consultation and consensus.

(*b*)   Preparation is delegated with insufficient top management involvement and commitment.

(*c*)   Too much time and effort spent on producing a voluminous report.

(*d*)   The time frame of the plan is too short term (e.g. 1–2 years rather than 3–5).

(*e*)   The plan is reliant on anecdotal and qualitative data which have not been substantiated with quantitative/objective data.

(*f*)   Lack of market and environment analysis.

(*g*)   The planning process goes on for too long (e.g. 12 months rather than 3 months). People become bored with it and the plan is out-of-date before it is finished.

(*h*)   Failure to monitor progress against measurable milestones.

(*i*)   Failure to review the strategy each year.

(*j*)   Failure to communicate the strategy internally.

(*k*)   Failure to incorporate a costed action plan with clear responsibilities.

(*l*)   Failure to recognise the full range of key issues because the planning team was too narrow in its background and outlook.

(*m*)   Failure to consider the aspirations and objectives of all stakeholders.

(*n*)   Potential future scenarios were not considered.

(*o*)   Inadequate challenge of the strategy in terms of feasibility and practicality.

(*p*)   Failure to develop and/or review the firm's strategy until the firm is in difficulty.

Chapter 9

Marketing

Introduction

9.1   In recent years, marketing has become an important practice management issue. This is due to several factors including:

(*a*)   an increase in competition;

(*b*)   an increasingly sophisticated client base who select providers of professional services on criteria other than just habit or price; and

(*c*)   a reduction in the regulations governing the ways in which professional practices promote their services.

In response, a number of partners have started to read up on this subject. However, many of the books dealing with marketing are founded on the theory and practices of large corporations. As a result such publications are not always very helpful to professional partnerships. This chapter cannot cover marketing in the same depth as general marketing texts but it highlights some of the key issues for busy partners.

What is marketing?

9.2   Within many professional partnerships, there is often still a considerable level of resistance to marketing. Many firms associate it purely with the production of glossy brochures, professional pitch presentations and mailshots. Although such activities may be the more visible aspects of marketing, they do not represent the full range of activities which the subject embraces. It is this common misconception that leads to confusion and can create scepticism about marketing and the view that it is 'not for this firm' or that the firm 'cannot afford to do it'.

There have been many definitions of marketing by various academics and consultants. Marketing can be summarised as something which:

(*a*)   places clients at the heart of the organisation and highlights the importance of understanding their needs;

(*b*)   is about allocating the firm's resources to continue satisfying clients' identified needs;

(c)   is about communicating the benefits of using one firm rather than another in a competitive market place;

(d)   is concerned with meeting the organisation's goals which, in the case of professional firms, centre on the long-term stability of the business and the generation of profit.

However, perhaps the best and most succinct definition comes from the Chartered Institute of Marketing which states: 'Marketing is the management process responsible for identifying, anticipating and satisfying customer requirements profitably.'

Key goals

9.3   The key goals of a marketing-orientated practice can be broadly summarised as follows:

(a)   to retain the firm's profitable clients;

(b)   to generate more profitable business from existing clients; and

(c)   to attract new clients to use the firm's services.

In order to achieve these goals, firms need to:

(i)   review the market place and identify those market segments which demonstrate similar characteristics (e.g. location, size, activities of clients);

(ii)   understand the needs of clients in each segment;

(iii)   target those market segments whose characteristics best match the firm's skills, resources and services;

(iv)   continue developing products and services to meet the needs of clients in the target segments;

(v)   communicate with potential clients in the target segments, highlighting the benefits of using the firm;

(vi)   understand and manage clients' expectations about the service they require and then ensure that clients are delighted because the firm's service exceeds these expectations; and

(vii)   monitor regularly service performance against client needs and expectations.

Therefore, marketing is much more than advertising, press releases and high-pressure selling. It is central to all business activity, and is already being undertaken by nearly all professional firms. It is not something that can be allocated to one partner or a department but must be embraced by everyone, from the senior partner to the most junior employee. It is only once this has been accepted that the marketing potential – and indeed the full potential of the firm – can be realised.

Understanding the external environment

9.4   If a firm is to achieve long-term success it is critical that it has a clear understanding of the external environment (see also Chapter 8, Strategic Planning, 8.8(iv)). Key questions for the firm might include, for example:

(a)   *The market.* How big is it? What are the key segments? Which segments are growing or declining? How will the market and the business environment change?

(b)   *Client organisations.* Who are they? How many are there? What are their needs and how well do we satisfy them?

(c)   *Competitors.* Who are they? How big are they? What services do they provide and to whom? How do they charge for their services? What are their relative strengths and weaknesses?

(d)   *Legislation.* What are the likely legal and/or political changes that will affect the market? Will that effect be positive or negative?

Sources of information

9.5   There are a variety of sources of information a firm might use to gain a better understanding of the external environment. These include the following.

(a)   *Monitoring the trade press.* Most business sectors have a range of publications which provide informed comment on key developments within the market.

(b)   *Desk research.* A wide variety of published research papers are available at business libraries, as well as direct from research agencies and trade associations.

(c)   *Competitors.* Information on competitors can be derived from their brochures, annual reports, advertisements, newsletters etc. as well as through direct contact as a 'mystery shopper'.

(d)   *Clients.* Information can be gained from clients on a structured basis, through targeted surveys, or through informal discussion as part of day-to-day business dealings.

(e)   *The Internet.* There is a vast amount of information on the Internet. Nowadays this will probably be the most efficient and effective first place to look for information about almost anything!

(f)   *Internal sources.* All members of the firm, particularly those with direct contact with clients, are likely to gain useful external information on what is happening in their professional world. By creating effective internal channels of communication, such data can be used to contribute to a firm's understanding of the market.

Having gathered the data, it is important to analyse the information carefully to see how the firm can enhance its services and market position, and counter potential threats from its competitors and others.

Marketing planning

9.6 Once the firm has a clear understanding of its market place, it can start compiling a marketing plan. This section will specify some of the key elements of the marketing plan but, first, it is worth considering the benefits of what some partners may regard as a time-consuming and unnecessary distraction from revenue earning work. These are as follows.

(*a*) A marketing plan will help the firm to decide where it is going and to set specific and measurable objectives.

(*b*) Documenting the plan will help to build consensus among the partners.

(*c*) The plan will identify what individual members of the firm have to do so the firm can achieve its goals.

Producing a plan

9.7 In the partnerships that prepare a marketing plan, it is often left to one individual to undertake the analysis and prepare the document. Although there are significant benefits in a single partner co-ordinating the production of the overall plan, it is strongly recommended that all service providers are involved in the development of marketing plans for their respective areas. This will encourage greater realism and make people more committed to the final marketing strategy and its objectives.

Contents of a plan

9.8 Each partnership will develop a plan format to suit its own requirements but, in the case of a professional service, this will usually include the following:

(*a*) SWOT analysis (summary of the current position);

(*b*) service/product range;

(*c*) target clients;

(*d*) the basis of charging for products/services;

(*e*) promotion and communication;

(*f*) key objectives; and

(*g*) action plan.

SWOT analysis

9.9 The partnership will need to complete an audit of its marketing-related activities before it starts to compile a marketing plan. Many firms find the SWOT analysis a useful shorthand for summarising their current position and a constructive starting point for developing the future marketing direction of the practice. SWOT analysis identifies the relative internal strengths and weaknesses of the partnership, as well as the key external (i.e. market/ environment related) opportunities for, and threats to, the business.

The value of the SWOT analysis is that it provides an agreed position from which the marketing plan and its key objectives can be developed. The hypothetical example below demonstrates some of the points that may be included in a summary SWOT analysis.

An example SWOT analysis, ABC partnership.

Strengths	Weaknesses
• Wide service range • Quality of service • Local market profile/reputation • Consistent income growth • Structured promotional programme • Blue chip client base • High level of retained clients	• Lack of service specialism • High concentration of client income • Low conversion rate of new sales leads • Poor cross-selling of services to existing clients • Poor understanding of clients' future needs • Uncompetitive pricing
Opportunities	**Threats**
• Market growth for XYZ services • Expand into: – other UK regions – Europe • Develop a service specialisation	• Increasing level of competition • Loss of key staff to competitors • Reduced demand for certain services as a result of new technologies

Service/product range

9.10   One of the most difficult aspects of marketing in a professional practice is that the service or product range is often relatively intangible. For example, it is probably harder to specify and define the service range of a management consultancy or solicitors' practice than it is to identify the product range of a manufacturer, where you can see and touch the goods that are produced.

Therefore, from the outset, a professional practice needs to identify and clearly define the full range of services that it offers. Surprisingly, this often has the benefit of gaining internal consensus among the partners on the firm's activities as well as assisting the communication of the service/product range to existing and potential clients. In defining the range, consideration should be given to:

(*a*)   the scope of activities;

(*b*)   the client benefits derived from using the service/product; and

(*c*)   how the service/product differs from, and (one hopes) is superior to, competing services/products.

Assuming the firm delivers more than one product or service, it may then be appropriate to prioritise the range. This will help management allocate resources appropriately (e.g. investment in staff, equipment, etc.) and also assist in focusing the external communication of the firm by defining what the firm 'stands for'. For example, a solicitors' practice may be able to provide a wide range of services, but it may wish to be known primarily for its expertise in commercial work, especially litigation, mergers and acquisitions.

How partners go about prioritising their services will vary, but it may involve judging how their practice services or departments compare with each other in terms of:

(i)   the profitability of the service;

(ii)   the level of technical skill within the firm;

(iii) the growth potential within the market place;

(iv)   market share; and

(v)   the level of competition.

Clients

9.11   Marketing plans should confirm precisely the firm's target audience for each product/service. Having reviewed the market place, the partners will have identified various market segments. Given that firms have limited resources, each of these sectors must then be prioritised so that the firm focuses on the most appropriate opportunities.

The criteria by which the partners undertake such prioritisation will vary. The client sectors may be chosen according to, for example:

(*a*)   the relative number of potential clients in each sector;

(*b*)   the firm's existing experience in serving each particular sector;

(*c*)   the perceived competition in each sector;

(*d*)   the relative costs associated with targeting and serving the selected market segments; and

(*e*)   the geographic concentration of clients.

An example of targeting

9.12   It is often useful to build a client profile so as to ensure the accuracy of targeting and to build internal consensus regarding the 'ideal' client. For example, an insurance broker wishing to sell life assurance cover might target:

(*a*)   private individuals;

(*b*)   men and women between 25 and 35 years old;

(*c*)   individuals located within a 30-mile radius of the office; and

(*d*)   those earning over £35,000 per annum.

Alternatively, a firm of engineers might target:

(i)   manufacturing businesses;

(ii)   organisations with a turnover of over £5 million;

(iii)   businesses located in the West Midlands; and

(iv)   firms with limited internal technical skills and resources.

The development of detailed target client profiles will enable all members of the firm to define their audience and will improve the accuracy of the organisation's targeting.

Pricing

9.13   Although many partners will consider that how the firm prices its services and products is an integral part of the financial business plan, pricing too plays a key part in the organisation's marketing. From a marketing perspective, the partners need to look at pricing from the clients' point of view. How does the firm compare with the prices set by our competitors? Given the quality of our service, do clients think that we give value for money? Does the firm charge by the hour, or is there a fixed price for a standard service? Can discounts be offered for volume purchases or early settlement? Agreement on pricing policy will also help to determine the image of the firm in the market place. For example, a firm that charges high prices will be perceived differently from a firm with a low pricing policy.

The partners need to answer these sorts of questions in the marketing plan in order to clarify how the income of the practice will be derived.

As an aside, it is worth noting that many firms do not review their prices often enough. An annual review of charge-out rates is a minimum requirement.

Promotional activity

9.14 All marketing plans include a promotional or communications programme designed to attract profitable new clients and retain existing ones. Before undertaking specific communication activity, partners must agree the key messages the firm must communicate to its clients and potential clients. To be effective, such messages need to concentrate on the major criteria by which clients choose professional practices. They should also be areas where the firm believes it is better than its rivals.

For example, key messages might include:

(*a*)   the widest range of services;

(*b*)   the quickest service;

(*c*)   the cheapest price; and/or

(*d*)   the most local/convenient service.

Once the key messages have been agreed, they should be clearly and consistently communicated across all media. There is a wide and varied choice of media available to professional practices. Selecting the right medium for a particular firm will depend on the resources available, the clients being targeted and the promotional objectives and messages that the firm wants to get across. Some of the more common promotional tools are noted below, together with some of the typical advantages and disadvantages experienced by partnerships who have used them, although these will obviously vary from practice to practice and partner to partner.

Analysis of common promotional tools

Promotional tool	Advantages	Disadvantages
Advertising	• Communicates message to a wide audience • Can build awareness and profile quickly	• Relatively high cost • Requires specialist implementation skills • Services may be too technically complex to communicate in an advert
Brochures	• Can give the firm 'stature' and credibility • Opportunity to convey potentially complex messages • Flexibility of use (e.g. in meetings, at presentations, in mailings)	• Relatively high cost • Difficult to keep up to date (e.g. new services, personnel, clients etc.)

Promotional tool	Advantages	Disadvantages
Direct mail	• Relatively low cost • Messages can be personalised • Easy to monitor activity's effectiveness	• Traditionally, response rates are low (c.2%) • May require follow up to be effective (e.g. by telephone)
Entertainment	• Opportunity to build client/contact relations • Variety of options (e.g. lunch, golf days) to suit all clients and budgets	• Can require a significant time investment • Some clients/contacts are becoming resistant to entertainment
Exhibitions	• Ability to target specific sectors • Brings the service provider into direct contact with potential purchasers	• Support material can be expensive • Requires significant time investment
Newsletters	• Flexible format for regular contact • Updates clients/contacts on issues and news • Builds credibility • Relatively low cost	• Time investment required to write articles • Regular production required
Personal selling	• Can be low cost • Ability to tailor the message to suit each contact	• Individuals may require training • Potential personal resistance to a 'sales' role
Press relations	• Can demonstrate technical expertise • Builds profile and credibility • Low costs	• Time investment required to target editors and write articles • May need to support editorial copy with paid advertising
Seminars	• Opportunity to demonstrate technical skills • Builds personal profile and credibility • Brings service provider into direct contact with potential purchasers	• Requires significant management time • Speakers may require training in presentation skills

Promotional tool	Advantages	Disadvantages
Website	• Makes information about the firm widely available • Can allow feedback from, and interaction with, visitors • Can be tailored to suit the profile and needs of many different types of audience	• Needs resources to keep it fresh and updated

Website

9.15   Many professional firms now have sites on the World Wide Web. A website can be a very effective tool for providing information about the firm to clients, potential clients, suppliers, potential recruits, journalists and others. Typical information might include: details about services and specialist expertise, a profile of the firm and its people, articles, press releases and commentary on topical issues. Websites can also provide effective means for delivering services and for engaging clients and others in an ongoing relationship with the firm.

Producing a website is now fairly easy. But many are often quite poor as all they do is replicate existing brochures or newsletters. Before producing a site, ensure that you 'surf' the Web to get a feel for what good and bad sites are like, and seek professional advice to ensure that you make the most of the new technology. Some characteristics of the best websites are that they:

(*a*)   are easy to navigate and use;

(*b*)   have up-to-date information;

(*c*)   are quick to download;

(*d*)   have sufficient quantity of relevant information;

(*e*)   have some degree of interactivity.

Assessment of promotional tools

9.16   Whatever combination of promotional tools is used by the firm, it is important that the source of new business is tracked to establish the effectiveness of each communication channel, so that the overall promotional programme can be reviewed and developed.

It is strongly suggested, particularly for smaller, low profile firms, that a structured programme of promotional activity is agreed for a year. This will encourage the partners to undertake business development activity continuously and not solely when the level of chargeable time starts to dip. Although this may mean spending time writing mailshot letters or entertaining potential clients when the partner is already busy and probably wishes to concentrate on delivering the service, it should help to ensure that periods of 'feast and famine', so often experienced by smaller firms, are reduced.

Client care

9.17   Although proactive promotional activity is important, it must be recognised that the best source of business is from existing clients. Satisfied clients stay with your firm and can give it additional work. Delighted clients will also talk positively about your firm and recommend it to potential new clients. Thus, whatever your firm might invest in promotional activities, it must keep focused on delivering exceptional client care and service in order to delight its existing clients.

The firm should ensure that it knows what aspects of service are important to clients generally and also to specific clients. Perceptions of service quality should be monitored. Your quality of service goals will need to be supported by appropriate attitudes, behaviours and skills; investment will be needed to develop and maintain the appropriate culture, resources and skills to deliver exceptional service.

Branding

9.18   The issue of branding is becoming increasingly important to professional firms. Brand is not just about logos and visual image. Brand is about the awareness and perceptions of the firm in the minds of clients, potential clients, staff and others with an interest in the firm (e.g. intermediaries, regulators, financial institutions, and potential employees).

A strong brand can give benefits to clients and other stakeholders as well as to the firm. For clients, a strong brand can, for example, provide them with reassurance about quality, it can facilitate decisions when selecting a supplier and it can give psychological satisfaction by association. For the firm, a strong brand can, for example:

(*a*)   attract profitable clients;

(*b*)   enhance client loyalty;

(*c*)   help to achieve higher fees;

(*d*)   increase the value of the firm;

(*e*)   assist with recruitment, motivation and retention of staff.

Some key issues to consider for effective brand development include:

(i) ensuring that top management are directly involved with, and are seen to lead, the brand development and management process;

(ii) understanding, measuring and monitoring the brand in terms of awareness of the firm and how the firm is perceived amongst key groups (this will normally involve qualitative and/or quantitative research);

(iii) developing a brand strategy in terms of how the firm wishes to be perceived, and how it wants to differentiate itself, in the minds of key audiences;

(iv) ensuring that the firm's values, culture and strategy are consistent with the brand strategy, and vice versa;

(v) ensuring that all communications and other direct contact (e.g. telephone handling style, offices, client care) with clients and others are consistent with the brand strategy and with each other;

(vi) communicating with and training staff about the brand strategy and their role in implementing it.

Setting objectives

9.19 A notable omission from many marketing plans is a section on objectives – the goals the marketing plan has been designed to achieve. Objectives, like the marketing plan itself, can cover a variety of time periods. Typically, however, objectives are normally set for the forthcoming twelve months and probably for the medium term, say three years. The objectives set will vary, depending on the partnership, but they will probably include the following indicators or dimensions:

(*a*) income and profitability;

(*b*) clients (e.g. total number, number of new clients, new geographic regions);

(*c*) products/services (e.g. income/profit from each service/product, launch of new products/services);

(*d*) communications activity (e.g. campaign activities, goals, expenditure and messages);

(*e*) pricing/charging (e.g. achievement of rate increases etc.).

SMART objectives

9.20 Objectives can be set for almost any area of marketing activity but in order for them to be effective, they should be SMART, i.e.

(*a*) Specific – the objectives should be clearly defined.

(*b*) Measurable – each objective should be measurable (e.g. number of cases, value of income etc.).

(*c*) Achievable – the objectives must be achievable, given the skills and resources of the firm.

(*d*) Relevant – the marketing objectives should be relevant to the long-term strategy of the partnership.

(*e*) Timely – the timeframe for achieving each objective should be clearly defined.

Action plan

9.21   The difference between a marketing plan which is an academic document and one which is a valuable management tool is often the inclusion of a practical action plan. The action plan should be driven by the marketing plan's objectives. In order to ensure the action plan is focused and easy to manage, it is suggested that it is constructed under the following headings:

(*a*) specific activity to be undertaken;

(*b*) marketing objective to which the activity relates;

(*c*) who is responsible for undertaking the activity;

(*d*) the time by which the activity should be completed; and

(*e*) an estimate of the resource implications/budget for undertaking the specific activity.

Organisation

9.22   For marketing to be effectively planned and implemented it is very important to clarify the marketing organisation, particularly the responsibilities each person across the firm has for marketing. A common problem occurs when a firm appoints a Marketing Partner and/or a Marketing Director (or Manager/Executive) and then many partners and staff think that they no longer have to do it!

More and more firms are taking on marketing professionals in-house to help plan and implement marketing. This is an important investment for any firm. The longevity of a marketing professional in a firm is often not very great (frequently less than a year). To help to avoid this problem, ensure that before recruiting someone there is an agreed job description, performance objectives and candidate profile, and that the partners and senior managers understand and are committed to the post.

Review and monitoring

9.23   The marketing plan of any professional partnership can never be set in stone. The market will change, clients will require new products/services, the firm's objectives will evolve. It is therefore important that the marketing plan is regularly reviewed. This will ensure that:

(*a*)   marketing activity continues to capitalise upon business opportunities;

(*b*)   the marketing plan supports the partnership's business strategy; and

(*c*)   specific action which has been designed to achieve defined objectives is actually being undertaken within the timescales and resource constraints agreed.

The review period will largely depend on the dynamics of the market place and the firm's strategy. However, it is suggested that the plan is reviewed annually, with individual supporting activity reviewed on a monthly basis.

Internal marketing

9.24   Internal marketing is also an important concept for professional firms. The concept includes, for example:

(*a*)   ensuring that everybody in the firm has a clear understanding about the firm's positioning in the market and its proposition (e.g. key values, competitive advantages/strengths and principal messages);

(*b*)   ensuring that people internally have an appropriate understanding of the full range of services provided by the firm and of recent successes/ achievements;

(*c*)   providing means for all partners and staff to provide their ideas about how the firm can improve its service and about new market opportunities;

(*d*)   developing client care and other relevant marketing skills. Firms often set internal marketing objectives with an associated action plan covering, for example, internal communication and training.

Summary

9.25   Marketing is a broad and potentially complex subject and this chapter has only begun to scratch its surface. However, we hope it has pointed to some of the priority issues which should be considered by partnerships which wish to achieve long term success in the market place. There are a number of key points to remember.

(*a*)   Understand your clients and potential clients, particularly with regard to:
  (i)   their current and future needs;
  (ii) the key criteria by which they select a supplier of professional services;
  (iii) what they think of your firm's services and quality of client care.

(*b*) Continually monitor trends in the market place to identify new opportunities and potential threats to the business.

(*c*) Define and prioritise the firm's service range.

(*d*) Agree the firm's key promotional messages and ensure they are consistently communicated in all media and by all members of the firm.

(*e*) Develop an agreed marketing plan which includes objectives and a detailed action plan.

(*f*) Ensure that everybody in the firm understands their role and responsibilities with regard to marketing.

(*g*) Regularly monitor the effectiveness of the marketing plan in achieving the stated objectives and refine it, as appropriate.

(*h*) Focus the firm's business development activity on the following groups, in order of priority:

    (i) existing clients, to ensure that they are provided with excellent service in order to retain their custom and to ensure that their needs are understood so that other services which the firm can provide are introduced to them, as appropriate;

    (ii) intermediaries who may recommend your firm and influence purchasing decisions (e.g. accountants, lawyers, agents etc.);

    (iii) potential clients.

(*j*) Involve everyone in the marketing of the business.

Chapter 10

Information Systems

Introduction

10.1   Good financial and management information, produced on a timely basis, is vital for modern partnerships. Proper information will help partners plan and monitor their business, and assist the decision-making process. The right computer systems can assist with the preparation of this information.

In many professions, computers are not just a means for recording information about the activity undertaken, but are vital tools of the trade. Nearly all businesses now use word processing software and more specialised document management systems are common in legal practices. Computer aided design (CAD) software is extensively used in architectural practices, and spreadsheet software is used throughout accountancy firms. In addition, many partners and professional staff now have desktop access to external e-mail and fax systems, and they are increasingly able to access office based systems direct from remote sites using a telephone land-line or a mobile phone.

Many firms not only have an Internet website for external visitors, but also an internal intranet or even an extranet for access by clients. Some firms are now evaluating the risks and rewards of e-commerce transactions on the Internet.

Scope of computer systems in professional practices

Time recording

10.2   In professional firms, time is the most valuable resource of partners and professional staff. To maximise fees for any given activity, even if fees are not charged exclusively on a time basis, it is a prerequisite that a full record is kept of the time each fee earner spends on both client and non-chargeable activities, and that this information is produced promptly. For partnerships of any size, it would be too time consuming to collate this information manually and errors may occur. Therefore, the use of a computer system becomes a necessity.

The speed and ease with which time information can be input are important considerations. Systems developed for some professions enable the fee earner to record time using hand-held systems or to use a scanning device that records bar codes attached to covers of files. The information can then be directly downloaded to the main computer system. It is increasingly common for staff to input the data from remote sites, including for instance their home. However, most professional firms still rely on traditional timesheets. There are a number of issues to consider when selecting a time recording system including the suitability of the base unit for charging time (e.g. minutes, six minutes, quarter hour) and the ability of the system to record different charge-out rates for different staff on similar activities. For instance, in a solicitors' practice, the legal aid charge-out rates will usually differ from those applied to non-legal aid work.

Work in progress

10.3   If the time records are computerised, then it is a logical extension for the amount of fees rendered to be offset against the time input, to provide an indication of time still to be billed. Disbursements chargeable to clients should also be recorded. Reports that combine information about unbilled time and disbursements can then be used in most professional practices as billing guides for raising fee notes. When selecting software to perform this function, it is important to ensure that reports produce sufficient detail about billed and unbilled staff time, and that the software processes under/over recoveries on interim and final fee notes in the way the partnership requires.

Features checklist—Time recording and work in progress software

General	Essential	Desirable	Not required
Integration with payroll and ledgers Timesheet frequency Base unit of time Expenses/disbursements Non-chargeable time			
Data entry Timesheet media Speed of data entry Narrative Charge-rates specified by: —staff member —staff grade —client —job type Charge-rate changes			

	Essential	Desirable	Not required
Processing			
Write-off procedures			
On account/final fee notes			
Valuation of partner time			
WIP valuation at cost			
Reporting			
Summaries			
Full detail			
Department totals			
Client totals			
Job analysis			
Billed and unbilled time			
Prior year or period information			
Billing guides			
Under/over-recoveries			
Recoverable disbursements			
Budgets, actual, variances			
Exception reports			

Financial accounting and reporting

10.4   If fee note details have been recorded for work-in-progress purposes, then duplication can be avoided if the fee ledger itself is computerised. For partnerships with a reasonable volume of transactions, it is sensible to computerise all the day books and the ledgers. Other accounting areas may warrant computerisation, including the payroll (if there are sufficient employees to merit this) and the fixed asset register.

It is sometimes suggested that accounts ledger software is all very similar and there are few real differences. However, features such as departmental reporting and multi-currency accounting are found in some ledger accounting packages but not in others. Therefore, some care must be taken in assessing the suitability of software for performing even relatively straightforward tasks.

The speed with which data can be input onto a computer may not appear to be any faster than writing out the details of transactions in traditional ledgers and day books. However, the major benefit from using a computer arises when reports are required. Many packages have a limited range of standard reports already prepared. However, in many partnerships, the requests for information are likely to be diverse. They can range from detailed queries from fee earners about individual client accounts to aggregated summaries for the management about the performance of the partnership as a whole.

Features checklist—Financial accounting software

General	Essential	Desirable	Not required
Accounting periods Password protection Integration with other modules Ledger codes: —Client and office accounts —Structures Multiple currency Internet enabled			
Data entry Batch posting Posting to future or past periods Sales or purchase invoices Single entry WIP update for expenses Cash book postings Cash allocation Journal postings: —multi-line —recurring —reversing Narrative			
Processing VAT cash accounting Brought forward or open item accounts Interest calculations Profit-share calculations			
Reporting Fee note production Cheque printing Aged debt listing Cash flow analysis Bank reconciliation Account history Audit trail Repeat period ends Consolidation By office, division Content and layout Budget, actual, variances Period, year to date, last year to date Report generator Data export to word processor or spreadsheet software Spooling to disc			

It is therefore likely that the content or layout of the standard reports are not what is needed, or that the reports do not incorporate the full range of analyses and ad hoc queries that may be requested from time to time. To mitigate these difficulties, packages often contain a report generator facility or a third party add-on product that enables users to design their own reports. The report generator may only permit reports to be designed using data from one part of the software, or alternatively it may allow data to be extracted from across the full range of the software.

Executive information systems

10.5   In the past, access to financial data tended to be restricted purely to the finance department or to partners. This was partly due to the traditional perceived need for privacy. But it was also due to the inability of software to present financial information in a manner comprehensible to non-financial persons.

Business executives then started using software that gave easy access to previously closed databases of financial information. This enabled both financial and non-financial data to be interrogated and presented in a visual way, comprehensible to people without a financial background. Other features that became more common included the ability to 'drill-down' to discover the detail behind any aggregated data. This type of software became known as an 'executive information system' or 'EIS', but could be more accurately described as an enterprise information system.

Contact databases

10.6   Existing clients and contacts are the principal sources of new work for a partnership. It is therefore important that information on them is kept up-to-date and accurate, and is disseminated to all who would benefit from it. Many partnerships consider that the need to share information about clients and contacts justifies having a computerised database that centralises all knowledge about a particular client or contact and his business. It can also be used for marketing purposes to ensure that the contact is managed properly, with invitations to selected events, and is sent appropriate publications produced by the firm, or given a periodic telephone call. Such software is often described as customer relationship management software, although in its broadest sense this describes software that records data about any contact or transaction with a new or potential customer. As with any database, keeping it up-to-date takes administrative effort. It also requires the active co-operation of partners and other staff who should supply and update the required information.

Word processing

10.7   In some firms, there was a reluctance to replace the typewriter but, as costs fell and technology improved, most soon acquired a word processing capability. Earlier word processors were dedicated machines designed purely for that purpose which tended to run in a proprietary environment. Nowadays most word processing is performed using standard packages operating on personal computers. Many firms think it is a good idea to use one of the standard packages as this increases the chances that new staff or temporary assistants will already have the necessary skills. The use of a standard package also reduces the risk of compatibility and formatting problems when transmitting a document by e-mail. For these reasons the legal profession is now tending to standardise on 'Microsoft Word'.

The functionality of word processing packages has improved to such an extent that many are now quasi-desktop publishing packages. However, this increased functionality has led to a need for hardware with an ever higher specification. Often, professional firms wishing to upgrade their word processing software or other office software are inhibited by having to replace the hardware on which it runs.

Spreadsheets

10.8   The basic design of spreadsheets has changed little since they were first launched in the late 1970s. However, spreadsheet packages now typically have additional features including graph facilities and a multi-sheet capability, as well as tools such as a spellchecker. Many spreadsheet packages also claim to have database features, although in reality these are quite primitive compared with designed database software.

Spreadsheet software is designed for the preparation of tabular analyses of financial data, and is ideal for budgets, forecasting, and sensitivity analyses. In partnerships, profit share allocations are often calculated on a spreadsheet. Spreadsheets are also often used to remedy the shortfalls in the content or presentation of reports produced by accounting software, and are extensively used by accountants.

Increasingly important is the ability to transfer data involving tables of information to and from other packages such as accounting software or word processing documents. Dynamic links permit data to be transferred and then to change automatically if the data in the linked software also changes. Other links are less sophisticated, and might just comprise a file transfer routine or an import/export process without any subsequent update.

Desktop publishing

10.9   Many firms use desktop publishing (DTP) software to produce good quality proposals, newsletters, and printer-ready copy. However, for other firms, word processing software is sufficient. DTP packages tend to divide into two types. The first includes large numbers of graphic images and fonts suitable for the creative design of single sheet documents. The second type has features that can be applied to multi-sheet documents, e.g. for producing booklets. DTP software is particularly memory and processor intensive, and a high-specification machine is sometimes necessary. Even with the right tools, it is very easy to produce desktop published documents that have an adverse visual effect. To use DTP software effectively, you need to have a member of staff with a good design sense who does not get carried away by the wide range of graphic images available.

Presentations

10.10   The need for slides or slide handouts at initial proposal meetings, or when presenting results to clients, is now well recognised.

Presentation software is available which makes the preparation of quite sophisticated outputs a relatively straightforward task. A number of different templates are usually provided, with varying backgrounds, bullet-point styles and slide transition characteristics.

Simple uncluttered slides can often be a more powerful tool than slides that appear very 'busy'. This is another situation where good design sense is required.

Electronic mail and voice communications

10.11   Electronic mail enables messages to be sent to other users. These systems either permit messages within the office environment across an existing network, or across the public telephone network using one of several e-mail carrying services.

Electronic mail can be advantageous in offices where many messages are generally sent or received and there is no need to send a hard copy of the message. However, e-mail systems presume that most people sending or receiving messages have ready access to a computer although this is becoming less of an issue as time passes. Mobile phones are now getting the capability to receive e-mails, although improvements in transmission times and quality are still required. The cost of installing an e-mail system can be quite high if it becomes necessary to purchase a number of additional computers purely to accommodate its usage. The introduction of an e-mail system also requires disciplined administration to ensure that messages received from outside mailboxes are not left unread.

Voice and data communications were previously viewed as completely discrete services but are now starting to share common equipment and lines. Firms are starting to review their telecommunications and information strategies in tandem, and to address such issues as how partners and staff can most efficiently be contacted when away from the office or in meetings. Message systems such as voice-mail are becoming increasingly common, typically including a switchboard operator diverting the caller to an answer-machine facility specific to the member of staff. These messages can then be heard when the staff member returns to his desk, or alternatively be accessed remotely by dialing in to the office.

Document management

10.12 As the volume of document files increases on networks and other multi-user systems, it becomes harder to manage, control and retrieve files. A well-developed file-naming convention will help. However, document management software exists which allows the user to develop a profile for each document. It uses information such as subjects and keywords, and then allows the document to be retrieved using these search criteria. Such software can often also be used for version control to monitor the history of document amendments, as well as identifying documents due for archiving.

Workgroup software or 'groupware' enables users to share and comment on each other's documents without necessarily updating the document itself. At a later stage the document author can review the comments and decide what further changes are required.

External databases

10.13 Professional firms are increasingly being offered access to databases of information maintained by third parties such as newspaper and book publishers, or more specialised sources. The number of these third party database information providers is growing. The advantage of these databases is that they enable firms to access and extract more information than could be maintained internally, and will usually be more up-to-date. Well-established services for particular professions include LexisNexis Butterworths Tolley, which offers a legal information service for lawyers covering UK and European Union case law and a range of other statutory and non-statutory document sources. Company financial information is provided by services such as Extel or Reuters, often with the choice of direct access via a modem, a CD ROM that is updated regularly or e-mail newsfeeds. CD ROM discs are now being used in professional firms as a more portable substitute for traditional reference books and manuals, enabling fast searches for material which contains specified key-words. In addition, increasing amounts of information are being made available on the Internet.

Internet, intranet and extranet

10.14 At its most basic level, the Internet is a large international network connected together using existing communication links around the world. The most widespread use of the Internet has until recently been electronic mail. However, in the last few years the World Wide Web ('the Web') has been the main reason for the Internet's rapid growth.

The Web comprises large numbers of computers worldwide which work together to provide a common graphical interface to an enormous database of text, pictures, sound and video. The user can access pages of a website computer anywhere in the world. Businesses can implement their own website so that information about the business can be accessed by other Internet users. Apart from marketing and promotion activities, the Internet can be used to access newsgroups and on-line databases.

Most Internet users are connected to the Internet by modem from their own computer to an Internet gateway computer run by an Internet Service Provider ('ISP'). Larger businesses may have direct access to the Internet, but will need to provide sufficient capacity for a number of remote Internet users to access the system (for instance, to visit the business website).

An 'intranet' is in effect a business-wide implementation of the Internet from which the public is excluded. Uses include sharing manuals and documents that are updated centrally (for instance telephone lists, staff handbooks), helpdesk questions and answers, and as a method for distributing software updates.

The term 'extranet' merely recognises that many businesses are opening up their intranets to suppliers, customers and other contacts. Uses can include providing customer support, or giving clients direct access to project documents. Confidentiality is an important issue to be considered when implementing an extranet.

E-commerce

10.15   E-commerce is a term used to describe the use of the Internet to sell products or services. In theory, e-commerce should provide a global presence at a reasonably low cost. However the difficulty for professional firms is identifying services that can sensibly be sold over the Internet.

The e-commerce market is generally split into two categories: the retail end where goods and services are being sold to consumers ('B2C'), and transactions between businesses ('B2B'). The future expected growth of e-commerce is enormous even allowing for slower than expected take-off in certain sectors.

Perceived difficulties include poor security and lack of privacy, as well as slow response times. Major increases in available bandwidth are now occurring, which will help resolve the speed problems, and also act as the spur to provide other new services. Security fears may hold back growth, although the increasing sophistication of firewall software and encryption tools will help mitigate some of these concerns.

Some firms are now starting to offer services such as on-line wills and contracts, and even divorces. It is too early to ascertain the long-term viability of these services.

There has been a great deal of publicity about 'm-commerce' (the use of mobile phones to transmit transactions) and WAP ('wireless application protocol') mobile phones. Generally the small screens, slow response times and the inability to handle graphics have resulted in relatively disappointing levels of activity. However it is expected that later generations of mobile phones will remedy many of these shortfalls, particularly when 3G technology becomes widespread.

Types of software

Packaged software

10.16 Most purchased software is based on an existing package written by a software house that is sold to any number of potential customers. There are several advantages with packaged software. It is normally cheaper than bespoke software (because of the economies of scale) and takes less time to get up to speed. Usually, many of the programme 'bugs' will already have been identified and corrected. There should also be the opportunity to contact and/or visit existing users of the software to discover how well it works in other businesses. However, the principal disadvantage of packaged software is that the customer is using a product that has not been specifically written for his particular business. So he will have to accept that it will probably not meet all his firm's individual requirements.

Bespoke software

10.17 Software written specifically for a particular customer is known as bespoke software. Its advantage is that, if it performs as expected, it will fit the requirements of a particular business much more closely than packaged software. However, the risks of developing bespoke software are much greater than when buying package software. There is a danger that the costs will overrun, that the software will not be delivered on time or that it will fail to satisfy the specified requirements.

The development of bespoke programmes will probably involve a much higher degree of managerial involvement and require close supervision. Legally watertight contracts on a fixed-cost basis are advisable, with penalties for failure to deliver software that satisfies the specified requirements within an agreed timescale.

Any significant bespoke programme is usually developed in two stages. The first stage involves the preparation of a functional specification detailing the features of the proposed new software, including screen and report content and layouts. An alternative approach involves the supplier developing a prototype of the software. The second stage involves the programming itself.

Bespoke programmes are sometimes combined with a package solution if software is already available that satisfies part of the overall requirement.

Alternatively, if a package already exists that satisfies most but not all of the requirements, the packaged software may be modified. When bespoke or modified software is acquired, it is particularly important to review the adequacy of future support arrangements. This is because a buyer of customised software will be heavily dependent on the software provider and it will be much harder to rearrange support with another supplier later on.

General purpose software

10.18 Software that is designed for use in a wide range of different business environments is often described as general purpose software. However, this terminology can be misleading since no software package is suitable for all businesses.

Accounting software

10.19 Some professional firms use the same general purpose accounting software as commonly sold to the corporate sector. In relation to the ledgers, the only differences between the requirements of the partnership and a company might be the need to replace the share capital account with a number of partner capital and drawings accounts, and to perform separate calculations of the journals necessary to record profit sharing arrangements.

However, many firms find general purpose accounting software does not have suitable time recording or billing features for a professional firm. Often the time recording function only appears as a relatively insignificant part of a wider-ranging job cost module typically designed for manufacturing organisations, and the timesheet entry screens are not designed to allow large amounts of data to be input with the minimum keystrokes. In addition, time summary reports sometimes provide an overall total for net unbilled work in progress, but do not show sufficient information for billing purposes about which staff time has been billed and which has not.

Professional firms are often more discerning about the presentation of fee notes to clients than a company raising invoices in a typical manufacturing or distribution environment. Therefore, the content and layout of invoices produced from standard company orientated packages may not be considered appropriate. The recording and recharge of disbursements by professional firms is another area which may not be adequately satisfied by standard general purpose software.

Vertical market software

10.20 Software written for a specific profession or business is usually described as 'vertical market' software. The advantage of such software is that it should be more suitable for the businesses at which it is targeted. For instance, software written for the legal profession will probably include client account features not found in other software. On the other hand, software developed for surveyors and estate agents will typically include a property management capability. In addition, software for architects normally contains project information analysed into RIBA work-stages.

As vertical market software is targeted at a smaller overall market, it tends to be more expensive than the equivalent general purpose package. In addition, suppliers are also likely to be more specialised and could be financially less stable.

Integrated software

10.21 A problem faced by many partnerships is that a great deal of financial and other data is kept in different places, by different partners and members of staff. It is not unusual for the partnership to have separate systems for ledger accounting, work in progress, publication mailing, marketing and archiving. Each partner and fee earner may also have a separate card index for their own client bases.

Maintaining the same data on separate systems is inefficient. Perhaps the most common example of duplicated data in a professional practice will be client details. It is likely that a client's name, address, telephone number and so on, is held in several separate databases. When these details change, it is not unusual to discover, for example, that some correspondence continues to be sent to an old address because not all the separate databases have been updated. This can give an adverse impression of the firm's efficiency. Separate work in progress and ledger software is also common, and leads to duplication.

Integrated software is designed to reduce these problems by ensuring that data is only entered onto a system once, with the entry of an amendment in one part of the software automatically updating the other functions. Recent software has often been developed so that all information is stored in one central database. Specific applications then extract and analyse data as required and present it either on the screen or in a report. After the core database has been acquired, it is usual for any additional applications to be purchased as individual modules which, when installed, integrate with the system as a whole.

Voice recognition software

10.22 Many people are still not confident about using computer keyboards. In the past there has been little alternative except to dictate tapes or handwrite text for subsequent word processing input by a secretary. Devices have been available for some time which attempt to recognise the human voice, and to directly convert speech into computer text. However, these devices were not initially very successful, since they required the operator to talk very slowly in 'dalek-like' speech, and the word conversion success rate was low. The technology is now much improved, and the use of voice recognition software is becoming more commonplace in the professions. Relatively high-specification machines are required, but the time taken for a computer to recognise a particular human voice is reducing, although still not insignificant. For many people this is starting to become a viable method for communicating with their computer.

Networks, minicomputers and Windows™

Networks

10.23   A network is usually made up of a fileserver connected to a number of microcomputer workstations and other peripheral devices, such as printers. If the fileserver is 'dedicated', it acts as a repository for the data which is to be shared by the workstation users, and controls access and requests for files. A 'non-dedicated' fileserver will also act as a workstation. However such fileservers are only advisable on small, low usage networks.

Networks are often introduced to enable several personal computers to share relatively expensive resources such as laser printers or access to communications facilities, such as a fax modem. They typically exist in the office environment where the software being used comprises mainly desktop tools such as word processing and spreadsheets. In such cases, the processing of data will occur on the workstation, with the data file only being transferred across the network from/to the file server when it is being retrieved or saved.

Minicomputer and open systems

10.24   The minicomputer has traditionally been considered the alternative multi-screen configuration to the network. It comprises a relatively large computer connected to dumb terminals, with all the processing and data handling functions being performed centrally.

In the past, there was a cost advantage when large numbers of users were connected, as dumb terminals were cheaper than PC workstations. However the difference is no longer so great. The use of dumb terminals can also lead to considerable strain on the central computer when processor-intensive applications such as spreadsheets and word processors are being used. However, the minicomputer configuration may still be appropriate, for instance, where access is required to a large central database with many accounting applications.

In practice, the differences between configurations of networked and minicomputer systems are no longer so clear-cut, since the dumb terminals connected to the minicomputer have often been replaced by personal computers. The end result is that users can often now get the best of both worlds.

Reference is often made to the term 'open systems'. In its broadest sense, this refers to an environment where software is portable between a range of different hardware platforms and where there are standards for transferring information between databases. Previously, every hardware manufacturer appeared to develop their own proprietary operating system and software was rarely transferable.

However, open systems has become a phrase commonly associated with a minicomputer operating system known as Unix. Ironically, there are now several different variants of the Unix operating system, and it cannot be assumed that application software which runs on one version of Unix will automatically run on another.

Microsoft Windows™

10.25   From the time that the IBM PC was first launched until the late 1980s, the character-based MS-DOS operating system was the de facto standard for microcomputer operating systems. A PC operating environment called Microsoft Windows was subsequently launched. The use of a mouse, icons and a graphical user interface was revolutionary for the PC environment, although the Apple Macintosh had already been making use of these tools for some years.

Over the last few years, Windows has become the new standard PC operating environment, and most application software is being rewritten to take advantage of features such as the Windows' graphical interface, drop-down menus and improved data transfer. The launch of Windows 95 towards the end of 1995 complemented the existing version of Windows, and this has itself now been superseded by Windows 98, Windows 2000 and then Windows XP. These later versions provide some additional functionality, and increasing platform stability, but were often not immediately suitable for many businesses with a large installed base of existing microcomputers due to higher minimum recommended hardware specifications.

The need to upgrade an operating system is now often dictated by software providers who typically withdraw support for their packages running on older versions of an operating system.

The selection process

Strategy

10.26   Developing a computer strategy is an essential first step when deciding on the future direction for information systems in a partnership. Whilst the business managers may be aware of the more obvious shortcomings of an existing system, they often fail to appreciate the wider perspective when considering what information is required to plan and control the business.

A computer strategy should not be developed in isolation from the aims and objectives of the partnership's overall business plan. The computer strategy needs to react to and anticipate future changes in the direction of the business and its structure. Traditionally once the business objectives had been agreed, then decisions were made about the information that is required to enable the managers to achieve these objectives. However, for some businesses IT is now itself the driver for business change, and not just a provider of information. In these circumstances the computer strategy and the business plan may effectively be the same document.

The firm then has to assess the adequacy of its existing computer systems, and decide how it gets to where it wants to be in the future. This may involve deciding between having a new system or upgrading an old one. It may also be a good idea to consider the firm's telecommunication requirements at the same time, particularly if the partnership has more than one office. In smaller partnerships, the use of manual systems for certain functions may remain an option, particularly if the volume of transactions is relatively low.

An objective cost benefit analysis of the different alternatives may be difficult to achieve. Costs are relatively easy to quantify, but the benefits are often harder to measure. Outside professional advice may be needed.

Specification

10.27   Once a firm has decided to acquire a new system and knows what it wants that system to do, then the next step is usually to prepare a specification. This will define in detail what is required from the new system.

The specification often comprises a formal document called a 'Statement of Requirements'. This describes what is wanted in commercial terms and may contain very little technical computer terminology. The contents normally comprise the following.

(*a*)   *Introduction.* This section puts the proposed new system in context, and will comprise a summary of the business background, organisational structure, the scope of the system, areas of special importance and a brief outline of the existing systems.

(*b*)   *Commercial constraints.* This section emphasises the business environment in which the new system will operate. Any relevant hardware requirements are analysed, including reference to the number of screens at each location and the need for peripheral resources such as printers. Details of existing hardware should be provided if it is anticipated this will be incorporated into the new system. Any specific security and performance parameters should be highlighted, and it is helpful if the skills of the project management team and the eventual end users are summarised.

(c)   *System requirements.* This is the most important part of the Statement of Requirements. It should detail all the data that the new system ought to contain, as well as all relevant processing routines. The scope and content of required reports should also be analysed.

The primary aim of a Statement of Requirements is to communicate the firm's IT needs to potential suppliers in a clear, precise way. This approach should minimise misunderstandings and will be the yardstick against which potential solutions will be evaluated at a later stage. Ultimately, the Statement of Requirements will form an important part of the contract with the selected supplier.

Preparing the Statement of Requirements will involve meetings and discussions with all key departmental managers. As a result this process often provides a useful focus for the partnership when discussing and agreeing the requirements for the new system.

Supplier selection

10.28   Shortlisting suitable suppliers for tender is a vital part of the overall process. Knowledge of the business and the computer market must be applied and the shortlist should be software, not hardware driven.

Initially, the computer market place should be reviewed to assess the availability of suitable software packages, or those which provide the closest fit and which, if necessary, can be modified. After identifying likely software solutions, potential software suppliers can be shortlisted. A supplier who will try to understand your requirements, and not simply sell you a system irrespective of its suitability will be needed. Suppliers should also demonstrate in-depth experience of the proposed product. Such an initial shortlisting exercise should ensure that time is not subsequently wasted at a later stage.

The Statement of Requirements now becomes part of an Invitation to Tender, which will also detail the proposed selection and implementation timetable, as well as the key contract terms and the tender response. The Invitation to Tender will usually be sent to at least three shortlisted suppliers, and often more, depending on the overall value of the system. However, it is not helpful to adopt a scatter-gun approach since suppliers may decide that the cost/ success ratio is too high and therefore may not be prepared to devote the required resources to preparing a detailed response.

The tenders returned by the suppliers must be thoroughly reviewed. The evaluation should check the supplier's response to each stated requirement, taking care to look for any omissions.

Supplier tender checklist

Understanding of the business requirements
Overall solution fit
Quality of solution
Initial costs
Recurring costs
Financial stability of supplier
Quality of supplier staff and technical competence
Quality of implementation and training services
Quality of on-going support
Quality of documentation
Proposed timetable
Expansion potential and costs
Risk areas

Ideally, the tender evaluation process will identify two or possibly three suppliers who merit further examination. Demonstrations of any packaged software should now be organised, and contact made with existing users to ascertain their opinions about the supplier. As soon as a decision is made in principle, then all outstanding matters should be confirmed in writing and contracts reviewed in detail.

Contracts

10.29 Suppliers invariably offer their standard terms and conditions in the first instance. Not surprisingly, these are usually biased in their favour and often omit elementary protection for the purchaser. It is therefore wise to review contract terms from both a legal and a commercial viewpoint, particularly if a relatively high value is involved or if there is a significant degree of risk, such as with bespoke programmes.

Most supplier contracts are negotiable. For instance, the standard contract often specifies that final payment is due on delivery. This could cause problems as the purchaser will not, at that stage, have had the opportunity to test whether the system meets his stated requirements. It is quite normal for a retention to be negotiated, and for the final payment to be made when acceptance testing has confirmed that the system is working properly.

The contract should normally include a fixed cost for the supply of the deliverables, including services such as implementation, training and support. Suitable warranties, performance guarantees and a delivery timetable should be specified. The purchase contract should also specify the nature and cost of ongoing computer support, including any likely future price increases. It may also be appropriate to include an escrow agreement within the contract to ensure the source code of any software is available in the event that the supplier ceases trading, particularly if bespoke software is being bought.

If a completely new system (including both hardware and software) is being acquired, then there are often significant advantages in obtaining all parts of the system from one source under a 'turnkey' contract. This ensures that one supplier has sole responsibility for ensuring that all elements of the system work properly. It also means that a failure to supply one part of the overall system in accordance with the terms of the contract can result in the supplier having to pay the purchaser compensation based on the whole value of the system. This makes it much harder for a supplier to agree to pay compensation for one unsatisfactory element of the system (e.g. any software that fails to perform in accordance with the contract) while insisting that the customer hangs on to other parts of the system (e.g. the hardware) which do meet the contractual terms.

It may be appropriate for a lawyer to review the contract(s) if there is any chance that the matter may end up in the courts. To minimise legal costs, always ensure that the lawyer has previous experience with reviewing computer contracts.

Selecting smaller systems

10.30   Performing all the recommended selection procedures can be a time-consuming process. If the value of the system is relatively low, and only standard package software is being supplied, then it may not be appropriate to perform all these procedures in detail.

However, it will probably still be necessary to consider the principles underlying each procedure and how best to mitigate the risk of the wrong system being selected. For instance, whilst it may be inappropriate to prepare a complete Statement of Requirements detailing every part of the new system, the key areas and issues can be addressed in an extended letter to potential suppliers.

An alternative 'Request for Information' approach has been sponsored by The Business and Accounting Software Developers Association ('BASDA'). This essentially involves a streamlined selection process which is less time-consuming but arguably also provides less assurance for the purchaser as compared with the traditional ITT approach. More information can be obtained on the BASDA Help Line (tel 020 7734 7810; www.basda.org).

Sources of information

10.31   Whilst business managers may understand the principles of how to select a new system, they may nevertheless be unsure of the best way of obtaining information about the systems that are available.

(*a*)   *Directories.* There are several comprehensive computer and software listings available either electronically, on the Internet or in hard copy which detail the majority of the leading systems available in the United

Kingdom. These are usually indexed by business sector, and are often a useful way of ascertaining quickly the names of relevant packages and suppliers for a particular profession. Due to space constraints, these directories inevitably only contain very cursory information but this should be sufficient to enable a firm to draw up a list of suppliers who merit a visit to their website or a telephone call to ascertain further details.

(*b*) *Professional bodies.* Various professional bodies and trade associations have staff who deal with queries from their members about systems for their business sector, and these can be a useful point of initial contact. Many of the institutes, including the Institute of Chartered Accountants in England and Wales, give their members access to comprehensive software databases and reports about software written for a particular profession. Informal contact through regional or district societies can also be a useful way of ascertaining from like-minded professionals the names of suppliers worth considering and those best avoided.

(*c*) *Consultants.* Many business managers have neither the time, inclination nor confidence to select a suitable system. In these circumstances, they may look for third party assistance from a consultancy. However, although good consultancy advice can reduce the risk of a mistaken decision, it cannot guarantee that the right decision will be made. There are large numbers of consultants prepared to offer advice, but the quality varies and they are rarely cheap. Preliminary vetting will be required to ensure that the chosen consultants have experience in the relevant business sector and have a track record of satisfying their clients. Some assurance can be obtained if the consultants are themselves members of a professional body such as the Institute of Management Consultancy (tel 020 7566 5220; www.imc.co.uk). Always consider taking references from former clients and ensure that the scope and cost of the consultancy assistance are detailed in a letter of engagement.

Implementation

10.32 Selecting the right system is important. However, much can still go wrong if the implementation of the new system is not properly planned and controlled. There are a wide number of issues to consider, often within a very short timescale.

(*a*) *Personnel.* The selection and introduction of a new system will often impact on departments and their staff, right across the partnership. An overall project manager should be appointed who is prepared to encourage constructive comments and to listen to a wide range of opinions, but who is also prepared to take responsibility and make decisions. Within a partnership, this position would normally be held by a partner. Each individual's responsibilities during the implementation phase should be clearly defined. Proper training is essential for the success of a new system and a suitable training programme will be required for each affected member of staff. Any changes in job specification will require agreement with the staff concerned. Specific responsibilities will require allocation. For instance, a new network may require a network supervisor, whilst the task of controlling and monitoring a database may be devolved to a database administrator. A help desk may be required to deal with the inevitable volume of queries that will arise during the implementation of a new system.

(*b*) *Site.* Most computer systems now operate in a normal office environment, so there is less need these days for a separate computer room purely to ensure that proper temperature and air conditions are maintained. However, security issues may dictate that the computer is sited in a separate unit away from the main office. A clean power supply may be required. The introduction of a new system often involves comprehensive recabling of an office. It is usually preferable for cabling to be the responsibility of the new supplier, but sometimes a third party contractor is involved. This requires planning to ensure that there is the minimum disturbance and that the cabling is installed and fully tested prior to the computer system being delivered.

(*c*) *Media.* The new system may require the redesign of pre-printed computer stationery such as fee notes, and liaison may be needed with a printer to ensure that the stationery is available when required. Other computer stationery such as tapes, disks, toner and ribbons may be required.

Security

10.33 Computer data is often one of the most valuable assets in a partnership, and therefore proper procedures and controls are required to ensure its security. The importance of proper security over personal data was given statutory backing with the introduction of the *Data Protection Act 1984*, now superseded by the *Data Protection Act 1998*. The need to raise internal awareness about good security has led many partnerships to distribute a document detailing procedures to be followed by partners and staff. This typically deals with the following issues.

(*a*) *Physical security.* The best form of security involves controlling access to buildings where computers are used. This may be through the use of staff monitoring every entry point to the building or by some form of electronic access control system. Access to a computer room containing important minicomputer or mainframe installations may also be controlled by physical security. The firm may insist that its staff lock away any portable computers that are not in use.

(*b*) *Passwords.* Good security measures often include the use of passwords to control access to programmes or individual data files. Passwords are particularly important where access can be obtained to a computer system from remote sites via a modem. Staff must be encouraged to keep passwords confidential, but at the same time the password must be obtainable if for some reason the individual is uncontactable.

(c)   *Viruses*. These are software programmes designed to corrupt or destroy programmes and data. Sometimes the effects of a virus are immediately noticeable, or they may involve a more gradual and insidious process. They are usually transmitted on a floppy disk or via a modem. All computers are vulnerable to viruses, and special care must be taken when programmes or data is received from outside computer systems. Games software is a notoriously high risk area for viruses. It is strongly recommended that every organisation with valuable data acquires software which can both detect and destroy at least the most common viruses. Connection to the Internet is another way that viruses can be transferred, for instance through the use of e-mail attachments, and can also enable unauthorised hackers to access a partnership's computer systems. Firewall software is available which when properly configured helps minimise these risks.

(d)   *Backup*. All media (whether documents, tapes or disks) which contain sensitive information must be controlled and physically protected. Computer magnetic media is particularly vulnerable to unintentional corruption. Users maintaining data on a hard disk or on just one floppy disk must be encouraged to take a security copy on a regular basis, and to systematically rotate the backup disks or tapes.

(e)   *Disaster recovery*. Events in New York and the City of London over the last decade have emphasised the importance of fall-back systems if access to an office is denied for whatever reason. Many firms now understand the importance of documenting procedures to minimise the effects of such a situation arising. Copies of vital disks and tapes should be taken to a separate site on a regular basis, and key personnel should know their tasks and responsibilities in the event that the fall-back systems have to be used.

The Data Protection Act

10.34   The *Data Protection Act 1984* introduced the requirement for most information about living individuals held on computer to be registered with the Information Commissioner (formerly the Data Protection Registrar), even if it only comprised a name and address. Registration also became necessary if data about individuals is processed by a third party, such as a computer bureau. Failure to register, or to re-register every three years, could lead to a prosecution by the Information Commissioner against a partnership, followed by imposition of a severe fine.

There was previously no requirement to register manual records, e.g. a card index. However, the provisions of the EU Data Protection Directive have now been enacted in the United Kingdom, and the *Data Protection Act 1998* extended the scope of legislation to include certain manual records. Whilst there are some exemptions, as well as a three-year transitional period which ended in October 2001, many businesses considered it safer to prepare a catch-all registration rather than risk penalties for non-compliance.

The *Data Protection Act 1998* also specifies eight required principles of good practice. These refer to the need to collect and process data fairly and lawfully, and to ensure the data is accurate, relevant, protected by proper security and only disclosed to people described in the register entry.

The Act also gives rights to individuals about whom the information is recorded. They are entitled to see the information, challenge it and have it corrected or erased if appropriate.

It is common for the partner responsible for financial matters to also take overall responsibility for such tasks as ensuring that the *Data Protection Act 1998* registration is kept up to date. The Office of the Information Commissioner can be contacted at Wycliffe House, Water Lane, Wilmslow, Cheshire, SK9 5AF (enquiry helpline 01625 545745; website: www.dataprotection.gov.uk).

European Monetary Union

10.35 At the time of writing it is still not clear when, or if, the United Kingdom will participate in European Monetary Union ('EMU'). Businesses operating in countries such as the United Kingdom have to decide whether to adapt their accounting software to deal with the implications of EMU whilst the United Kingdom remains 'pre-in', or whether to wait for a firm decision about the United Kingdom joining EMU at a later date.

Overall business strategy regarding the Euro will be a major factor in determining the need for changes to existing software. Organisations that need to consider at an early stage how their systems will cope include businesses that transact with customers or suppliers using Euros, or who have group companies based in the Euro-zone, or financial institutions dealing in Euro-zone securities. Many partnerships will consider that there is little need to make system changes until the United Kingdom decides to join EMU, although it may be advisable to check suppliers' future plans for the Euro if the partnership is making a major investment in new software.

Chapter 11

Human Resource Management

Introduction

11.1 Human resource management concerns the management of people. Its principal purpose is to ensure that the employment, utilisation, motivation and management of people is undertaken in a manner which fully supports the achievement of business objectives in the short and longer term. Managing, improving and sustaining the performance of professional staff is a key issue for professional partnerships. Quality professional people are expensive and scarce. When highly motivated and effectively managed, they are the most important resource a firm has at its disposal and are the key to its success. This success is most likely to be achieved if a firm's human resource policies and procedures are based upon and make a significant contribution to the achievement of its corporate objectives and strategic plans.

Human resource planning

11.2 The aim of human resource planning within a professional practice is to:

(*a*) define manpower requirements (how many people are required to manage and staff the practice); and

(*b*) identify the various types of people the practice needs (the technical and managerial competencies that staff must possess now and in the future).

Human resource systems

11.3 In common with other types of organisation, professional practices need programmes to recruit, reward, develop and manage performance. These programmes are often referred to as human resource systems.

The two key programmes for a professional partnership are as follows.

Reward management

11.4   Remuneration systems must be designed to motivate and reward partners and staff appropriately for their contribution to achieving the firm's goals.

Performance management

11.5   The aim of a performance management system is not simply to maintain levels of performance but to support their continuing improvement. Performance management is concerned with:

(*a*)   setting of performance objectives;

(*b*)   measuring their achievement; and

(*c*)   rewarding the achievement of objectives.

Criteria for setting objectives

11.6   The criteria for setting objectives for partners usually include some or all of the following:

(*a*)   billable hours worked;

(*b*)   hours billed;

(*c*)   effective hourly rate for business generation;

(*d*)   client responsibility;

(*e*)   non-billable hours, such as:

(i) firm management;

(ii) client development;

(iii) professional activities.

(*f*)   delegation and effective utilisation of other staff;

(*g*)   billing efficiency and debtor collection;

(*h*)   length of time spent with the firm;

(*j*)   reputation; and

(*k*)   quality of work.

The criteria may also include a number of fairly broad categories, e.g.

(A)   co-operation with other partners;

(B)   leadership ability;

(C)   dedication and efficiency;

(D)   training;

(E)   client management;

(F)   business development; and

(G)   historical contribution.

Reward management

11.7   Reward management focuses on the design, implementation and management of remuneration systems that support the achievement of the firm's business objectives. In order to do this, the systems must ensure that pay levels for partners and staff are competitive and fair. They must also ensure that reward is linked to contribution, and performance.

Overall aim of reward management

11.8   The principal aim of reward management is to attract, retain and motivate staff of the quality needed by the practice, in order to achieve its stated business objectives. A reward system must have three qualities.

(*a*)   *It must be competitive.* High calibre people are scarce. They are also fully aware of their value to the practice and expect to be rewarded accordingly. To attract and retain them, it is necessary to match market rates. Information on market rates can be gathered from a variety of sources including: job advertisements; remuneration consultants; published surveys; 'salary club' surveys; and bespoke surveys. It will usually be necessary to use a combination of these sources to discover the range of salaries/remuneration packages for a particular job. This kind of research will not, however, tell firms the exact market rate for the job – there is no such thing – but, having discovered the right salary range, a firm can then decide how much it wants to pay within those limits.

(*b*)   *It must be fair, and regarded by partners and staff as fair.* If it is perceived to be unfair it will demotivate staff and could lead to expensive discrimination claims.

(*c*)   *It must be able to provide rewards which are directly linked to levels of performance.*

Reward structures

Partner remuneration

11.9   This is the subject of considerable debate. It can sometimes cause animosity and upheaval in a professional partnership. However, these feelings are seldom due solely to the fact that some partners believe they are being inadequately rewarded compared with others in the firm. Partners who are unhappy about remuneration levels may also feel that there are problems in the systems used to determine their profit reward, or that the firm as a whole is not generating a satisfactory level of income.

Systems used to reward partners often seem to bear little relationship to the stage of the firm's development, except in a very broad sense. Younger and smaller firms tend towards the more straightforward systems, although there are also a number of larger partnerships which take this approach. The key lesson is that a firm must design and implement the reward system which is most beneficial to its own particular circumstances.

However, remuneration systems must be considered from a positive and constructive standpoint. The firm should look beyond the difficulties that may be encountered when changing existing arrangements. The new system may bring benefits to the firm which may outweigh the practical difficulties of implementing change.

Detailed consideration is given to profit sharing in Chapter 6, Profit Shares.

Professional fee earning staff

11.10   The criteria for setting objectives outlined in 11.6 above can also be used as the basis for setting and evaluating, through the normal appraisal process, the performance of other professional fee earning staff. These can then be used as the basis for determining the level of a performance related bonus element included within the normal remuneration package. When determining the performance related element in professional staff remuneration packages it is essential the performance related bonus is based upon a number of guiding principles. An effective performance related reward scheme for professional staff should:

(*a*)   be part of total remuneration and be used to motivate and reward excellent performance;

(*b*)   be based on performance targets that reflect the firm's business objectives;

(*c*)   be based on both quantitative and qualitative performance measures that are non-discriminatory;

(*d*)   produce rewards at a sufficient level to motivate over the defined period;

(*e*)   be affordable and beneficial to the practice as a whole; and

(*f*)   be simple to communicate, administer and manage.

Scheme design

11.11   The feasibility of including a performance related element in professional staff's remuneration package will depend on whether satisfactory responses can be obtained to the following questions.

(*a*)   Who is to be included in the scheme?

(*b*)   What are the most appropriate performance measures?

(*c*)   What standards of achievement are required for each measure?

(*d*)   To what extent will the measures be particular to each member of the scheme?

(*e*)   What is the scale of reward for achievement?

(*f*)   What types of reward will be used?

(*g*)   How will the scheme be communicated?

(*h*)   How will the scheme be managed, maintained and reviewed?

Profit related pay

11.12   At one stage profit related pay (PRP) became a common feature of many remuneration packages and professional partnerships of all sizes were quick to take advantage of the tax benefits available under these schemes. Whilst, the tax effective nature of these schemes has now been removed, some employers have continued with the schemes as they enable reward to be linked to the firm's financial performance. This allows staff at all levels to share in the profitability of the firm they work for.

Flexible benefits

11.13   With the phasing out of tax free PRP and the general tightening of the labour market, a number of firms have turned towards flexible benefit schemes as a way of attracting and retaining staff.

Flexible benefit schemes allow employees to choose the benefits they want from a range of choices so that the benefits they receive more closely match their individual needs. Schemes are tailored to each individual company and, as the purchasing power of organisations can often exceed that of the individual, firms can offer access to benefits such as healthcare, dental cover and critical illness cover at lower rates than the individual could achieve by going to the providers direct.

Other popular options are allowing staff to 'buy' extra holiday or 'sell' holiday in excess of the statutory minimum which they do not wish to utilise.

Legislation

11.14   There has been an increasing amount of legislation introduced in recent years that affects employees and firms need to consider the impact of these developments and how they will be implemented. Some of the key pieces of recent legislation are as follows:

(*a*)   Disability Discrimination Act 1995.

(*b*)   Employment Rights Act 1996.

(*c*)   Data Protection Act 1998.

(*d*)   Public Interest Disclosure Act 1998.

(*e*)   Working Time Regulations 1998.

(*f*)   Employment Relations Act 1999 (incorporating parental leave requirements).

(*g*)   Human Rights Act 1998.

(*h*)   Regulation of Investigatory Powers Act 2000.

(*j*)   The Part-time (Prevention of Less Favourable Treatment) Regulations 2000.

In addition, firms need to consider the impact of many significant decisions made recently by the courts and employment tribunals. This area of law is evolving rapidly and firms are strongly advised to seek specialist advice with regard to employment-related issues. Finally, firms will need to ensure that they comply with legislation in respect of Stakeholder Pensions, a subject dealt with in detail in Chapter 26.

Recruitment

Determining manpower needs

11.15   Professional firms need to formulate as part of their business plans not only what is to be achieved but who is to be responsible for achieving it. This process has two stages.

(*a*)   Determining the manpower requirements necessary and the competencies which staff must have if a firm's business objectives are to be achieved.

(*b*)   Analysis of the competencies which already exist within the firm and how they might be utilised most effectively.

This process will provide the necessary information to identify present and future manpower requirements and the possible need to recruit staff to satisfy any current shortfalls either in numbers of staff or in particular skills areas.

Recruitment steps

11.16   Recruitment needs to be conducted in a systematic, logical and objective fashion. In order to recruit successfully it is necessary to:

(*a*)   analyse the job the firm is seeking to fill;

(*b*)   prepare a detailed job description; and

(*c*)   prepare a person specification.

Job analysis

11.17   This establishes precisely the job's tasks and activities. It is necessary to establish the following:

(*a*)   Job title.

(*b*)   An organisation chart showing principal and secondary reporting lines.

(*c*)   A definition of the overall purpose of the job.

(*d*)   A definition of the job holder's responsibilities and accountabilities.

(*e*)   Performance criteria – fee income, chargeable hours, business development activities etc.

(*f*)   Particular requirements, e.g. the ability to manage people.

(*g*)   Special circumstances, e.g. travel away from home.

Job description

11.18   A job description should detail the following:

(*a*)   The job title.

(*b*)   Basic organisation and reporting lines.

(*c*)   Statement of the overall purpose of the job.

(*d*)   List of key responsibilities and tasks.

(*e*)   Decision-making authorities.

(*f*)   Job dimensions: numerical measures reflecting the size of the job (e.g. budgets, turnover, profits, number of staff, geography).

Person specification

11.19   The person specification is used in conjunction with the job description for the following purposes:

(*a*)   drafting job descriptions;

(*b*)   briefing recruitment consultants, if appropriate;

(*c*)   providing selection criteria;

(*d*)   detailing information which needs to be given to the candidate.

The information contained in a person specification would typically include:

(i) skills/expertise;

(ii) qualifications;

(iii) previous training;

(iv) experience;

(v) personal attributes;

(vi) promotion/career development opportunities;

(vii) terms and conditions.

Finding suitable candidates

11.20 When seeking to fill a particular vacancy, a number of potential sources exist. The most widely used methods include:

(*a*) internal candidates;

(*b*) advertising;

(*c*) recruitment consultants;

(*d*) executive search consultants;

(*e*) internet advertising.

Internal candidates

11.21 It may be considered that the ideal candidate for a vacancy already works for the firm. However, it is prudent to check this is indeed the case. Internal candidates' qualifications should be compared with the job specification. This will either confirm their suitability or demonstrate that they are perhaps not ideal candidates.

Advertising

11.22 Although there are specialised recruitment advertising agencies, a firm may decide to do this themselves. If so, a number of points should be considered when drafting the advertisement. A poorly drafted advertisement can lead to too many unsuitable applicants or too few suitable ones.

(*a*) A job advertisement must be designed in such a way as to gain:

  (i) attention;

  (ii) interest;

  (iii) action.

(*b*) The advertisement will usually include:

  (i) a summary of what the job entails;

  (ii) the qualifications/experience required;

  (iii) location;

  (iv) remuneration package.

(c) The advertisement should also detail how potential candidates should respond, e.g.:

    (i) full CV;

    (ii) request for an application form;

    (iii) letter of application;

    (iv) e-mail application attaching a CV.

(d) Discrimination in recruitment advertising. It must be remembered that it is unlawful to discriminate in recruitment advertisements:

    (i) advertisements must not seek to discriminate against candidates on the basis of their sex, marital status, race, religion or disability;

    (ii) candidates who feel that they have been discriminated against may complain to the Equal Opportunities Commission (EOC) or the Commission for Racial Equality (CRE).

Some publications will no longer accept advertisements which specify an age requirement.

EOC and CRE codes of practice

11.23 Codes of practice have been published by the EOC and CRE. These codes suggest that:

(a) advertisements should not be confined to areas or publications which would exclude or reduce the number of applicants from a particular racial group;

(b) employers should avoid stating requirements such as:

    (i) length of residence;

    (ii) experience in UK.

(c) qualifications obtained overseas that are fully comparable to those required are fully acceptable;

(d) advertisements also state that both men and women may apply.

Recruitment consultants

11.24 A number of points should be considered when deciding upon and using a selection consultancy.

(a) Use consultants that you have used in the past, and who have given good service and know your sector.

(b) Obtain recommendations from other professional firms.

(*c*) Identify those selection consultancies which have particular experience in your sector.

(*d*) Ensure that you meet the consultant who is actually going to perform the assignment.

(*e*) Once a recruitment consultant has been selected, confirm the terms of the appointment. This includes preparation of the person specification, advertising and the basis on which the candidate shortlist will be compiled.

(*f*) Establish the basis on which fees and expenses will be charged.

(*g*) Use the consultant's experience and expertise in drawing up the job description, person specification and level and content of the remuneration package.

(*h*) Obtain written confirmation of the terms of reference for the assignment.

Executive search consultants

11.25 Commonly known as head hunters, this type of consultant approaches candidates directly. They are of most value when there are only a limited number of potential candidates. However, head hunters should be used with care as their fees are high and results cannot be guaranteed. The basis on which head hunters should be selected is the same as for recruitment consultants (see 11.24 above).

Recruitment/selection procedures

11.26 It is essential that those responsible for performing selection interviews do so in an objective and consistent manner and in such a way that information is collected and recorded about each candidate. The following points are key areas to consider.

(*a*) *Attainments.* Educational, technical and professional.

(*b*) *Special aptitudes.* Particular skills/competencies required for the job.

(*c*) *Interests.* Particular interests outside the work field which may be of value.

(*d*) *Interpersonal skills.*

(*e*) *Circumstances.* What in terms of personal circumstances the job will demand.

The formulation of a detailed job description and person specification, and the collection of data during the actual interview, will make it easier to reach an objective decision about which candidate will best satisfy the firm's requirements.

Training and development

11.27 As with other human resource systems the provision of cost effective training and development activities is dependent upon a structured approach. To be effective, training needs to be designed specifically to support the achievement of the firm's business goals.

A structured approach

11.28 This involves:

(*a*) identifying training needs;

(*b*) planning the appropriate training activities;

(*c*) implementing the training; and

(*d*) evaluating the results.

Identifying training needs

11.29 A number of approaches exist for identifying training needs. However, all these approaches begin with a study of the job description. This focuses training provision on the key tasks, responsibilities and objectives which the job holder must satisfactorily achieve.

Analysis of job/role requirements

11.30 This involves identifying:

(*a*) the job's component parts;

(*b*) the tasks the job holder has to perform;

(*c*) the key responsibilities at each stage.

An analysis of job/role requirements ensures that training directly supports the achievement of the firm's business objectives. It also avoids providing training that might be generally useful but which has little or, at best, minimal impact on the job holder's performance.

Training activities

11.31 It is vital that training activities achieve measurable results in a cost effective manner. It is also essential that training disrupts the job as little as possible and that it equips those being trained with practical and versatile tools which will enhance job performance as much as possible.

The success of development and training activities is determined by the presence of certain key characteristics. These include the following:

(*a*)   Training activities must fully support the firm's business, e.g.:

    (i)   goals;

    (ii)   objectives;

    (iii)   opportunities.

(*b*)   Training and development processes are integrated with:

    (i)   formal training;

    (ii)   on-the-job training;

    (iii)   career planning; and

    (iv)   succession planning.

(*c*)   Training and development activities are:

    (i)   appropriate to staff needs;

    (ii)   based on managerial reality.

(*d*)   Outputs are measured by:

    (i)   evaluation of training/development activities; and

    (ii)   annual appraisal.

Training and development activities

11.32   While most people still associate training with the provision of formal courses, a wide number of other options exist. Choosing the right approach obviously depends on the type of training to be provided, as well as the intended audience.

Off-the-job programmes

11.33   Group activities such as courses, workshops, group exercises and business simulations that take place away from the working environment.

Presentations

11.34   Information-delivering activities that can take place internally or externally. They include events such as seminars, lectures, conferences and meetings.

Career planning

11.35   Planned career development activities including job rotation and secondment.

Personal initiative

11.36 Activities that individuals can initiate for themselves, such as distance learning, open learning and interactive video programmes.

Coaching and mentoring

11.37 Coaching and/or general guidance from a senior individual from within the organisation and who is not normally the person's direct line manager.

Secondments

11.38 Periods of time spent in other areas of the organisation or with other organisations (e.g. suppliers, partners, clients).

Evaluation

11.39 It is essential to evaluate the effectiveness of training and development activities. This will involve more than simply getting participants to complete the usual end-of-course assessment form. Although these forms will tell you about a participant's reactions to the actual training event, they cannot tell you whether the training will have a significant impact on his job performance.

To know that, you have to look at how well he/she does their work after he/she has been on the course. This is most easily done through the annual appraisal process, although it is advisable to review the performance of staff who have recently received training within two to six months of their having completed the course. This should ensure that training is producing demonstrable results and making a real impact on staff performance.

Investors In People

11.40 The Investors In People initiative was originally introduced in 1990 and the latest version of the Standard (IIP80D) was launched in April 2000.

An increasing number of professional service firms have either been recognised or are currently seeking accreditation as Investors In People.

The Standard is about investing in people to achieve success and being able to see what has been achieved. It is built on four principles:

(1) *Commitment.* Commitment to developing people in order to achieve the organisation's aims and objectives;

(2) *Planning.* Clarity about the organisation's aims and objectives and what its people need to do to achieve them;

(3)   *Action*. People are developed effectively in order to improve the organisation's performance;

(4)   *Evaluation*. The organisation understands the impact of its investment in people on its performance.

Potential Investors in People are assessed against twelve indications of good practice which underpin the four principles.

More information can be obtained from Investors in People UK, 7–10 Chandos Street, London W1M 9DE, tel 020 7467 1000, www.investorsinpeople.co.uk

Chapter 12

Accounting

Introduction

12.1   This chapter examines the accounting requirements of a partnership and the basis of preparation of financial accounts. It includes a review of the main items in a firm's balance sheet. In addition, it will deal with the use of service companies and internal audit.

The advent of the *Limited Liability Partnerships Act 2000* brought into being the existence of Limited Liability Partnerships ('LLPs'). Chapter 4 of this book sets out the nature of an LLP, the fact that it is more like a company than a partnership in a number of respects and the legal framework under which LLPs will operate. The accounting implications of operating as an LLP are set out in chapter 13.

Under *section 28* of the *Partnership Act 1890*, 'Partners are bound to render true accounts and full information of all things affecting the partnership to any partner or his legal representatives'.

In addition to the legal requirements to maintain accounts, case law has developed further obligations on partners to maintain accounts. It is the duty of continuing or surviving partners to maintain accounts of the partnership so that it is possible to show the financial position at each date and the ownership of the partnership. Recognising in practice that some firms are less organised than is desirable, for example where accounting records have not been maintained, or are so poorly maintained as to be unintelligible or have been destroyed or wrongfully withheld, subject to the direction of the court, those partners responsible for such a situation will be considered at fault. Where all the partners are at fault, this rule cannot be applied (*Walmsley v Walmsley (1846) 3 Jo & Lat 556*).

With regard to the right of inspection, *section 24(9)* of the *Partnership Act 1890* states that 'partnership books are to be kept at the place of business of the partnership (or the principal place if there is more than one), and every partner may, when he thinks fit, have access to and inspect and copy any of them'.

Whilst a partner cannot restrict access by his colleagues to the accounting records by keeping matters of a private nature within them, it is open to a partner himself to agree not to inspect the partnership's accounting records and to accept accounts prepared on his behalf (*Freeman v Fairlee (1812) 3 Mer 29*).

It is acceptable for a partner to engage an agent on his behalf to inspect the books and records of the firm, provided the agent is a person to whom no reasonable objection can be taken by the other partners (*Bevan v Webb [1901] 2 Ch 59*). As would be considered fair and just, access may be denied if the use of an agent is not reasonably required or the inspection is sought for an improper purpose. Naturally, the improper use of information so obtained is unlawful.

As mentioned in 2.12, the partnership agreement should include a clause on annual accounts. This clause should include reference to the date to which the annual accounts will be prepared, the scope of any third party examination and the scope of the information which should be included in the accounts. It should also make clear that before the accounts are binding on the partners as between themselves, they have to be signed by all of the partners, unless there are provisions in the partnership agreement for approval by the majority and signing by a specific number of partner(s) on behalf of all.

The annual accounts will show how the partners stand as regards outsiders and as regards each other, and will also be required for tax purposes whilst the underlying accounting records should be maintained to such a standard that they disclose with reasonable accuracy at any time the financial position of the partnership.

Partnership property

12.2 It is open to the partners to agree between themselves what assets are to be treated as partnership property. *Sections 20* and *21* of the *Partnership Act 1890* (see Appendix 1) provide a statutory framework which is helpful in considering what is and what is not partnership property when the appropriate treatment is ambiguous. However, where specific agreement exists, whether express or implied, that agreement will prevail over statute.

In the absence of an express agreement, the sections of the *Partnership Act* referred to above highlight the important factors to consider. These are:

(*a*)   the circumstances of the acquisition, in particular the source from which it was financed;

(*b*)   the intention of the acquisition; and

(*c*)   the manner in which the property has subsequently been dealt with.

By agreement between the partners, they may change the ownership of property, from partnership property to the separate property of a specified partner or partners or vice versa.

Information in the partnership accounts

12.3   General partnerships are not subject to the same rigorous rules relating to the standardised presentation of balance sheets, or the same standard accounting policies, as are companies. The format of balance sheets is thus very much a function of precedent, the particular requirements of the firm or the advice of their accountants. Particular accounting policies, partly driven by their tax consequences, may make a partnership's accounts appear very different from that of a corporate entity or indeed those of another partnership.

However, it is becoming more commonplace to provide greater disclosure within accounts to enable partners to have a good understanding of the financial performance of the firm and its standing at the year end date. There is also an increasing tendency to adopt the use of accounting policies which are generally accepted accounting practice ('UK GAAP').

The annual accounts of a partnership will typically include the following:

(*a*)   statement of approval of the accounts by the partners;

(*b*)   report of the accountants or auditors;

(*c*)   balance sheet;

(*d*)   profit and loss account; and

(*e*)   notes to the accounts, including accounting policies.

Included as Appendix 6 is an example set of partnership accounts.

Accounting policies

12.4   The accounting policies are the specific accounting bases judged to be appropriate to the circumstances of the partnership and which are adopted by the partnership for the purpose of preparing its accounts.

Accounting bases are diverse and numerous and because they have evolved in response to many types of businesses and transactions, there may justifiably exist more than one recognised basis for dealing with particular items.

If the partnership wishes its accounts to show a true and fair view it will need to prepare them in accordance with UK GAAP which would mean adopting the provisions of the *Companies Act 1985* together with the pronouncements issued by the Accounting Standards Board ('ASB'), including Statements of Standard Accounting Practice ('SSAPs'), Financial Reporting Standards

('FRSs') and other components of generally accepted accounting principles. This would however reduce the scope of the partnership to decide upon alternative accounting policies.

Accounting policies are discussed in detail under each separate balance sheet and profit and loss account heading in the paragraphs that follow.

Accounting concepts

12.5 Two accounting concepts play a pervasive role in the preparation of the accounts of any entity including partnerships. These are going concern and accruals.

The going concern concept assumes that the partnership will continue in operational existence for the foreseeable future and that there is no intention to curtail materially the scale of the partnership's activities.

The accruals concept recognises that the profit or loss for a period is the difference between income and expenditure – not the difference between cash receipts and payments. The accruals concept involves matching income with the costs incurred in producing that income.

In addition in selecting accounting policies a partnership needs to judge their appropriateness against the following objectives:

(i)   Relevance.
(ii) Reliability.
(iii) Comparability.
(iv) Understandability.

Financial information is relevant if it has the ability to influence the economic decisions of users and is provided in time to influence those decisions.

Reliable financial information should be neutral, free from material error, complete and where any uncertainty exists they should be prepared on a prudent basis.

Comparability of financial information can usually be achieved through the consistent application of accounting policies year on year and disclosure.

The information which is contained in the accounts of a partnership should be capable of being understood by those with a reasonable knowledge of business and accounting. The special interest of partners in the financial performance of the partnership means that those responsible for the preparation of the accounts need to be prepared to explain the content in non-technical terms.

Role of accountants and auditors

12.6   The role of the accountants when undertaking work for general partnerships is governed not by statute but by the instructions of each particular firm defining the scope of the work to be done and by the nature and extent of the records to be made available.

The Institute of Chartered Accountants in England and Wales (ICAEW) has considered it appropriate to issue a practice statement 'Reports on accounts computed by Accountants' (AUDIT 1/95) covering such situations. The Institute of Chartered Accountants in Scotland has also issued similar guidance. The statements emphasise the need for a clear understanding of the scope of the work to be undertaken and that an engagement letter should be put in place to formalise the arrangements agreed with the client.

Any report issued by a firm of accountants will make clear the extent of the responsibilities which they accept for the accounts prepared by them and will provide an opinion only on accounts which they have audited or where additional relevant responsibilities have been agreed.

An audit is an independent examination and expression of opinion on the accounts of an enterprise. Companies and LLPs are required to have their accounts audited by a firm of registered auditors, except where the company or LLP is dormant or where it meets certain criteria relating to the value of total assets and turnover, whilst general partnerships are not subject to a statutory audit requirement. However, some general partnerships may be required either by the regulatory authority or by a term in their partnership agreement, to have an audit. In addition, provision of audited accounts by a specific date after the year end may be a condition of the granting of a loan by a bank or other lending institution.

Accounts prepared but not audited

12.7   Where accountants have been instructed to prepare accounts but not to audit them, their report will be headed 'Accountants' report' and may be in the following form:

Example 1

Accountants' report to the partners of ABC

'As described in the partners' confirmation on page [ ], you have approved the accounts for the year ended [ ] on pages [ ] to [ ] for which you have sole responsibility.

At the request of the partners we have carried out the following limited procedures, sufficient to report our opinion. Our procedures consisted only of comparing the accounts with the accounting records kept by the partnership, and making such limited enquiries of the partners as we consider necessary for the purpose of our report. These procedures did not constitute an audit of the accounts and provide only the limited assurance expressed in our opinion. In particular, our report does not provide any assurance that the accounting records and the accounts are free from material misstatement.

In our opinion the accounts are in accordance with the accounting records maintained by the partnership.'

Accounts audited

12.8   Alternatively, if the partnership accountants are obliged by the partners to undertake an audit, if the deed expressly requires an audit, or if it is required by the regulatory authority, the form of report may be similar to a report to a company, but suitably amended. Such a report may be:

Example 2

Independent auditors' report to the partners of ABC

'We have audited the accounts of ABC for the year ended [ ] on pages [ ] to [ ]. These accounts have been prepared under the historical cost convention and the accounting policies set out therein.

Respective responsibilities of partners and auditors

As described in the partners' confirmation, the partners are responsible for the preparation of the accounts in accordance with United Kingdom Accounting Standards.

Our responsibility is to audit the accounts in accordance with relevant legal and regulatory requirements and United Kingdom Auditing Standards.

We report to you our opinion as to whether the accounts give a true and fair view.

Basis of audit opinion

We conducted our audit in accordance with United Kingdom Auditing Standards issued by the Auditing Practices Board. An audit includes examination, on a test basis, of evidence relevant to the amounts and disclosures in the accounts. It also includes an assessment of the significant estimates and judgements made by the partners in the preparation of the accounts, and of whether the accounting policies are appropriate to the partnership's circumstances, consistently applied and adequately disclosed.

We planned and performed our audit so as to obtain all the information and explanations which we considered necessary in order to provide us with sufficient evidence to give reasonable assurance that the accounts are free from material misstatement, whether caused by fraud or other irregularity or error. In forming our opinion we also evaluated the overall adequacy of the presentation of information in the accounts.

Opinion

In our opinion the accounts give a true and fair view of the state of the partnership's affairs as at [ ] and of its profit [loss] for the year then ended and have been properly prepared.'

Report by accountants with a hybrid role

12.9   As the firm is able to decide the scope of the work the partnership accountant may have a hybrid role. For example, they may conduct procedures on the consolidation process, on the allocation of profit and the compilation of partners' accounts but only undertake accounting work on a sample of branch accounting records and returns. Where such a situation exists, the accountants would usually issue a report in the form of a letter to the partners in the following format.

Example 3

Terms of reference

'This report has been prepared in accordance with our terms of reference dated [ ].

The procedures performed as detailed below are those agreed with the partners.

The procedures have been carried out for the information of the partners.

Procedures performed

We have re-performed the consolidation workings prepared by the partnership by comparing the amounts for the individual partnerships and subsidiaries included therein to their underlying financial statements and re-performing calculations for mathematical accuracy.

[etc]

Findings

List of factual findings including details of errors and exceptions found.

Our procedures did not constitute an audit or review and should not be relied upon to provide the same level of assurance. Had we performed additional procedures, other matters might have come to light that would have been reported.

Our report is prepared solely for the confidential use of the partners. It may not be relied upon by the partners for any other purpose whatsoever. Our report must not be recited or referred to in whole or in part in any other document. Our report must not be made available, copied or recited to any other party without our express written permission. [Accountants] neither owe nor accepts any duty to any other party and shall not be liable for any loss, damage or expense of whatsoever nature which is caused by their reliance on this report.'

Consolidated accounts

12.10   The partnership may own a business undertaking, either in the form of another partnership or a company, over which it has a degree of influence or control.

As general partnerships are not bound by the regulations that apply to companies, they do not normally prepare group accounts where their investment in a company is considered to warrant the definition of subsidiary or associated company. However, consideration should be given to the way in which accounts are prepared to ensure that partners are provided with sufficient financial information to enable them to assess the firm's and the subsidiary's financial performance. Where there are close trading relationships, it may be appropriate to prepare accounts which aggregate the results and assets and liabilities of the separate entities.

The Financial Reporting Standard (FRS) 9 Associates and Joint Ventures applies to companies incorporated under the *Companies Act 1985*. The principles laid down in it are, nevertheless, applicable to financial statements of any entity, which invests in another entity or entities.

In some cases, partnerships or other non-corporate joint ventures can have features which justify accounting for a proportionate share of individual assets and liabilities as well as profits or losses.

Conversely, a partnership may be owned by a company. The Financial Reporting Standard (FRS) 2, paragraph 16 defines undertakings as 'a body corporate, a partnership or an unincorporated association carrying on a trade or business with or without a view to profit'. It follows that the parent or investing company is required to adhere to the requirements of FRS 2 and FRS 9 when drawing up its own accounts and will consolidate the accounts of the partnership in accordance with the relevant accounting rules.

Management accounts

12.11 The scope and nature of the information which will be included in the management accounts will depend upon factors such as the size of the partnership, the frequency of preparation of the accounts, the users of the accounts and the timetable for their preparation. It is common practice to prepare accounts on a monthly basis.

It is important to recognise that the usefulness of the accounts as a management tool is affected by the timeliness of their preparation. Production within a few working days of the previous month end will involve estimating certain figures which, in time, may be assessed more accurately. However, it is possible to interpret the firm's financial performance very shortly after the period end, particularly if the partnership's income is based on time costs recharged to clients. For those firms whose income is based on long-term contract fee income, the production of management information should be geared towards accurate reviews of the progress on contracts which may take place throughout the month following the accounting period end.

The accounts should be drawn up using the same accounting policies and bases as the firm adopts for its annual accounts. However, a thorough review of such items as professional indemnity claims and bad debt provisions may be undertaken on a quarterly or six monthly basis rather than throughout the year.

The management accounts will present work in progress in a different manner to the annual accounts. The valuation of work in progress is discussed in 12.19 below, but suffice to state at this point that for management accounts purposes, it is appropriate in those businesses whose income is based on time costs recharged to clients, to monitor the sales value of the work undertaken rather than the direct cost of such work.

The information provided should enable active management of working capital and comparison of actual performance against budget, in terms of income, expenditure and working capital. With those objectives in mind, a monthly management accounts pack could contain the following information:

(*a*)   written report from the finance committee or finance partner/director;

(*b*)   profit and loss account, both for the period and cumulative, compared to budget and the prior year, analysed by department/activity, as appropriate;

(*c*)   analysis of chargeable time for staff, both for the period and cumulative to date compared to budget;

(*d*)   summary of aged work in progress analysed appropriately, or summary of contracts in progress, comparing actual and budget figures for both income and costs;

(*e*)   summary of aged debtors and disbursements;

(*f*)   summary of major debtor balances and commentary on long outstanding amounts;

(*g*)   summary balance sheet; and

(*h*)   cash flow statement, both for the period and cumulatively, compared to budget.

The commentary should highlight key information, report trends and focus on areas which are not performing to expectation. Care should be taken to focus on the key performance indicators of the firm and not to overload the recipient with unnecessary information. The use of graphical analysis and exception reporting can assist this process.

The balance sheet

12.12   Each firm will prepare an annual balance sheet that portrays, at a moment in time, a statement of the firm's capital, its assets and liabilities. It may be helpful to look at a fairly comprehensive partnership balance sheet showing a variety of features, some of which may be present in the balance sheet of an individual firm. An example is shown under Appendix 6, together with the related notes.

Because there are no statutory requirements covering the preparation of the accounts of a general partnership, the example showing a fairly full form of professional firm's accounts may not be typical.

However, the content and form of the accounts of an LLP have to conform to the Regulations. As already mentioned, these adopt the objective requirements of the *Companies Act 1985*, SSAPs, FRSs and other pronouncements, including the proposed LLP SORP.

The accounting items relating to a number of balance sheet headings are considered in the following sections of this chapter.

Goodwill

12.13   Goodwill is the difference between the value of a business as a whole and the value of its separable net assets. Goodwill may therefore be positive or negative.

Goodwill cannot be separately realised from the business as a whole. It is this characteristic which distinguishes it from all other items which may be included in the accounts of a partnership. In addition, there is generally no reliable or predictable relationship between the value of goodwill and any cost which may have been incurred. Intangible factors which cannot be valued are likely to contribute and the value of goodwill may fluctuate widely over time. In short, the assessment of the value of goodwill is highly subjective.

(*a*)   *Purchased goodwill.* Purchased goodwill is established when a firm purchases goodwill from partners or former partners who own such goodwill personally or when a business combination is accounted for as an acquisition. If a partnership purchases another business, and when acquisition accounting is used, goodwill represents the difference between the fair value of the purchase consideration and the fair value of the net assets acquired. One of the main practical problems that partnerships may encounter will be the valuation of the purchase consideration. Where businesses have been 'acquired' and the consideration is the granting of a profit share in the enlarged business, it may be appropriate to determine how much, if any, of that profit share represents payment for the business acquired and how much is compensation for services in the future.

If profit shares of the enlarged business granted to partners of the acquired partnership represent, exclusively, compensation for services after the acquisition date, the fair value of the assets acquired would be treated as capital contributed, and if there are no costs of acquisition, there would be no goodwill arising.

(*b*)   *The accounting treatment of goodwill.* If goodwill appears on a partnership balance sheet at all, it is likely to relate to historic cost rather than an assessment of its current value. In some cases goodwill is not shown either because the firm deliberately chooses not to recognise it, or because it is an asset which is expressed to be owned individually by the partners, rather than by the partnership.

FRS 10 sets out the accounting treatment for goodwill and the commentary which follows sets out the broad principles which general partnerships should treat as best practice.

It is accepted practice that purchased goodwill is not normally carried in the balance sheet as a permanent item unless it can be justified that no diminution in the value of the goodwill has occurred. Where goodwill is to be eliminated from the balance sheet it is normally done either by an immediate write-off against the partners' capital or current accounts or by amortisation through the profit and loss account over its estimated useful economic life. Negative goodwill, which arises where the aggregate of the fair values of the separable net assets acquired is greater than the value of the consideration given, should be credited directly to the partners' capital or current accounts or a separate reserve.

If the decision is made to amortise purchased goodwill, the useful economic life should be estimated at the time of acquisition. If it is considered at any time that there has been an impairment in the value of purchased goodwill, it should be written down to its estimated recoverable value. It is open to the partnership to adopt the immediate write-off treatment for one acquisition and the amortisation treatment for another acquisition.

However, some firms may be able to justify retaining purchased goodwill as a permanent item in the balance sheet. In particular, its value may go some way towards creating a more realistic cost of capital to incoming partners, as this sum is often only fixed to ensure the firm is adequately financed rather than to reflect a true value of the business. In addition, an immediate write-off of goodwill will have an impact upon all partners where a change in profit sharing ratios occurs. If the write off of goodwill does not reflect the economic reality of the situation, then certain partners will suffer unduly, whilst others will benefit correspondingly.

Whilst many firms request partners to contribute a capital sum on entry which may be subsequently increased or decreased depending upon their profit sharing ratio, certain firms have adopted a more scientific approach by which partners have to contribute capital. Such goodwill may be based on a multiple of a number of years' profits with the effect that a new partner would contribute capital in relation to the profit goodwill calculation at the time and a retiring partner would be paid out on a similar basis. The effect is to create goodwill in the balance sheet following the revaluations on partnership changes; each partner's capital will represent his share of the goodwill of the firm at a point in time, and will consist of paid up capital and capital derived from revaluations.

(c) *Ownership of goodwill.* Goodwill, where it is considered to be an asset of the partnership and shown on the balance sheet, is normally owned by the partners in their capital or profit sharing ratios. However, it may be held in a ratio different from both capital or profit sharing arrangements. On retirement a partner would be entitled to be paid for his share of goodwill, subject to the existence of any contrary agreement. Similarly, a partner joining a firm will acquire a share in the goodwill and can be required to pay for it. Where goodwill is held by the partners off the balance sheet a separate record needs to be maintained of the transactions between partners.

Tangible fixed assets

12.14 Tangible fixed assets includes such items as property, motor vehicles and the equipment, computers, fittings and furnishings used in the business. Fixed assets are those which are intended for use on a continuing basis in the enterprise's activities.

(a) *Depreciation.* The standard accounting procedure is to include such items at cost less an amount provided for depreciation. Depreciation should be allocated so as to charge a fair proportion of the cost of the asset to each accounting period expected to benefit from its use.

In general, this has lead to a standard approach such that depreciation is often charged on a straight line basis and at rates that are broadly consistent for each of the different types of assets. For example, motor vehicles are written off over four years, furniture, fixtures and fittings over five to ten years and computers over three years, although there is justification for smaller portable computers to be written off over a two-year period.

In the case of leasehold property, it is appropriate to write off the cost of the asset over the period of the lease, where this is a short leasehold of less than 50 years remaining. Depreciation on freehold property and long leasehold property is usually provided at the rate of 2% per annum.

(b) *Revaluing fixed assets*. It has also become more commonplace for businesses to revalue their fixed assets, in particular freehold and leasehold property, and to incorporate these revalued amounts in their financial statements. This gives useful and relevant information to users of accounts provided the revaluations are kept up to date.

Should a policy of revaluing assets take place, perhaps in order to create equity between partners arising from the increase in the value of the underlying property, it will have implications on partners' capital accounts and may create the need for property reserve or asset revaluation accounts. In addition, it may involve an increase in the capital contribution required from new partners and increased payments being made by the firm to departing partners.

An example of the accounting treatment accorded to a fixed asset revaluation is shown below.

Example 1

A freehold property with a cost of £2,500,000 has been depreciated at 2% per annum over nine years, and has a book value of £2,050,000. The partnership has decided to show the property at its current market value at 30 April 2003 of £3,550,000 to ensure the accounts more closely reflect the value of the partnership assets for the purposes of incoming and outgoing partners. The revaluation reserve of £1,500,000 represents partners' capital.

See next page for details.

	As at 30 April 2003 (pre-revaluation)	Revaluation adjustments	As at 30 April 2003 (post-revaluation)
	£'000	£'000	£'000
Fixed assets			
Freehold property – at cost/valuation	2,500	1,050	3,550
– less depreciation to date	(450)	450	–
– net book value	2,050	1,500	3,550
Net current assets	1,650	–	1,650
	3,700	1,500	5,200
	£'000	£'000	£'000
Partners accounts			
Freehold property – capital	2,000	–	2,000
– property revaluation reserve	–	1,500	1,500
– current	1,700	–	1,700
	3,700	1,500	5,200

Property ownership

12.15   In certain partnerships, the property occupied by the firm may be owned, not by the partnership as a whole, but by some of the individual partners only. Careful consideration must be given to the disclosure an accounting treatment of the property in these circumstances and on the impact on the partnership's business. For instance, it may be appropriate to adopt a formal lease between the firm and the property owning partners. In addition, the net investment in the properties held by certain partners may be shown separately in the accounts under a property reserve account. There have been a number of instances where property ownership has resulted in complex and difficult relationships developing and it may be necessary to adopt strict commercial arrangements to ensure the firm's business is not jeopardised by such ownership.

Leased assets

12.16 It is good accounting practice to capitalise assets used by the firm which are funded through finance leases based on the requirement set out in UK GAAP . The corresponding lease obligations are included as a creditor in the balance sheet, net of finance charges. Amounts paid are apportioned between the finance element which is charged as interest to the profit and loss account and the capital element which reduces the lease obligations.

It is considered technically more accurate to charge a greater cost of interest at the start of the lease, perhaps using a 'sum of the digits' calculation, rather than spreading the finance cost evenly. The cost of operating leases is charged to the profit and loss account evenly over the lease term.

Investments

12.17 Investments in quoted or unquoted companies are often stated in the firm's balance sheet at cost. Under UK GAAP, it is necessary to write down cost if it is considered there is an impairment in the value of the investment below cost. Where the underlying balance sheet value is different from market value, revaluations may be considered necessary in order to maintain equity between incoming and outgoing partners. With quoted investments, this is a straightforward task. With unquoted investments this may be a more complicated exercise, although in certain circumstances a value equivalent to the net assets of the company may be relevant, such as for holdings in service companies. Alternatively, the value of an investment in an unquoted company could be based on a multiple of the company's earnings, subject to certain adjustments, or on the company's dividend flow.

The valuation of unquoted investments is a subject in itself and the reader is advised to undertake further research before coming to a conclusion as to which basis to adopt for the purposes of the partnership accounts.

A revaluation would be shared between all of the existing equity partners in their capital or profit sharing ratios. The accounting treatment would be to increase the value of the investment held in the balance sheet and create a revaluation reserve as part of the partners' capital in the firm, similar to a property revaluation reserve.

On a change of profit sharing ratios and on the entry of new partners or exit of departing partners, an existing revaluation reserve will need to be reallocated, much along the same lines as is necessary for the reallocation of goodwill in the same circumstances. This will involve a transfer between partners, which can be dealt with between existing partners either by cash or through current account transfers, but in respect of incoming and outgoing partners it would represent a cash transaction. A significant revaluation will require considerably larger transfers and cash injections and payments. This may cause difficulties for a new partner attempting to finance his capital calls but where the investment pays dividends it may be reconciled as representing the purchase of his share of the dividend stream.

Normally each change in profit sharing ratio is considered by the Inland Revenue to be a commercial transaction between partners and therefore is not subject to capital gains tax except on leaving the partnership (Statement of Practice D12).

However, where there has been a revaluation of assets, Statement of Practice D12 cannot apply and each change in a partner's share of that asset will represent a transaction for capital gains tax purposes and the tax implications of this are considered in Chapter 19.

In considering whether or not to revalue an investment, a partnership should consider its intention with regard to the investments. If the investment is part of its core business of providing services to clients, then the justification for revaluation would be reduced if the dividend flow compensates the partners for much of their investment. However, if it is likely that a sale of the business is anticipated in perhaps five to ten years time, it may help to adopt a revaluation basis in order to maintain equity between partners.

Work in progress

12.18 Work in progress is time which has been spent by the partnership's staff on client affairs, which has not yet been invoiced to the client. Work in progress, unbilled disbursements and unpaid invoices often represent the majority of the working capital of a professional firm. The existence of working capital is due to the time-lag between performing a piece of work and being paid for it. The largest item of expenditure in the profit and loss account of a professional partnership will be staff salaries. The majority of employees of a professional partnership will be paid monthly in arrears. Therefore, if the partnership is paid by its clients more than 30 days after the work is performed, it will need to find cash, usually from reserves or borrowings, to pay its staff until the clients' money is received.

Valuation of work in progress

12.19 The method of valuing work in progress in the annual accounts, and the method used for tax purposes, may differ from the method which is used to value work in progress in the management accounts. Often, the valuation of work in progress in the annual accounts is based on an historic calculation, sometimes in accordance with SSAP 9, where work in progress is recorded at the lower of cost and net realisable value. In certain partnerships, no value has been ascribed to work in progress in the balance sheet, although the introduction of the 'catching-up-charge' for tax purposes, described in 17.14, has led some firms to adopt new accounting policies.

For those firms which wish to recognise in their annual accounts the value of work undertaken but not yet billed to clients, it is necessary to adopt an approach to the valuation of this work. There are two distinct approaches which are dependant upon the type of business undertaken by the firm. In both cases, equity partners' time would be recognised in the management accounts, but in the annual accounts it would be usual to only recognise it when it is invoiced to clients. Unlike employees and salaried partners who are paid a salary, there is no direct cost associated with equity partners.

(*a*)   *Time costs recharged to clients.* For partnerships whose income is based on time costs recharged to clients, work in progress for management accounts purposes normally comprises hours spent multiplied by the relevant charge-out rates, less provisions where it is not expected that the full value can be recovered. The valuation of work in progress may, therefore, be as follows.

	£
Time costs incurred by individuals at charge rates	420,000
Provision to reduce work in progress where time costs exceed realisable value	(20,000)
Value of work in progress (for management accounts)	400,000
less equity partners'/members' time	(100,000)
	300,000
less profit element of time costs, say 30% of charge rates	(90,000)
Value of work in progress (for year end accounts)	210,000

(*b*)   *Income is fee or value based.* For those professional partnerships whose income is fee or value based, e.g. architects or consulting engineers, such work in progress will be derived by including hours spent on a job at cost (normally the direct cost of salaries together with direct overheads) and profits will be taken on a prudent basis through the period of the contract. The normal route is to take little or no profit in the early stages of the contract and build up the level of profit considered to have been earned as the job nears completion. It is appropriate to provide losses once these are foreseeable.

If a general partnership wished to follow UK generally accepted accounting practice as adopted by UK companies and LLPs, it would follow the basis, rather simply outlined above, which is set out more fully in SSAP 9, 'Stocks and long-term contracts'.

As part of the changes in the provisions for calculating work in progress for tax purposes, the Inland Revenue sought to apply SSAP 9 to partnerships and it was concluded that for tax purposes, the time of partners and overheads applied to partners' time should not be included in the work in progress balance. Since partners' remuneration is a share of the profit of the partnership, partners do not have a direct cost which is capitalisable for the purposes of work in progress.

Furthermore, SSAP 9 states that where the business carries out long-term contracts and it is considered that their outcome can be assessed with reasonable certainty before their conclusion, the attributable profit should be calculated on a prudent basis and included in the accounts for the period under review. The profit taken needs to reflect the proportion of the work carried out at the accounting date and to take account of any known inequalities of profitability in the various stages of a contract. The procedure to recognise profit is to include an appropriate proportion of total contract value as turnover in the profit and loss account as the contract activity progresses. The costs incurred in reaching that stage of completion are matched with this turnover, resulting in the reporting of results that can be attributed to the proportion of work completed.

In calculating the carrying value of work in progress under SSAP 9, consideration must be given to the extent of conditional and contingent fees. Conditional fees may be defined as fees which can be billed once certain conditions are met. In general, the uncertainty surrounding conditional fees is only the timing or quantum of billing rather than the ultimate realisation of income. It is generally clear that a bill will at some stage be raised and therefore a writing-down to below cost of the work in progress on conditional fees is likely to be inappropriate.

By contrast, contingent fees depend on the satisfactory occurrence of defined but uncertain events. It may be a 'no win, no fee' arrangement. Alternatively an aggregate potential fee may comprise an agreed base to which a success fee may be added. The difference between the two would constitute a contingent success fee, and would usually be written down to nil value, as a prudent assessment would conclude that the potential net realisable value was nil.

The value of work-in-progress at any accounting date – and therefore the period in which profit is recognised – may be affected by the time elapsed before the accounts are finalised since a view has to be taken at that time on the status of conditional and contingent transactions. This is because SSAP 17 'Accounting for Post Balance Sheet Events' requires events arising after the balance sheet date to be taken into account when they provide evidence of conditions existing at that date.

Debtors and disbursements

12.20   Debtors represent the value of trade debtors, prepayments and other amounts recoverable by the firm, such as disbursements. They include the value of payments made by the firm on account of costs which will benefit a future accounting period, including normal overhead expenditure together with such items as rent deposits.

On a regular basis, provision should be made for irrecoverable debtors and disbursements. For the purposes of the firm's annual accounts, it is more tax efficient to specify particular debts to provide against, but for management accounts purposes it may be considered sensible to build up a general provision month by month.

Liabilities

12.21   Whilst recognising that the definition of the accruals concept established under UK GAAP need not be applied strictly to general partnerships, it is worthwhile considering the point at which liabilities and costs should be recognised in the firm's accounts (see 12.5 above).

FRS 12 'Provisions, Contingent Liabilities and Contingent Assets' sets out criteria used to decide whether a provision for a liability should be made in the accounts. While the application of FRS 12 is unlikely to present any unusual conceptual problems other than in the case of annuities, applying it fully to LLPs or general partnerships may require a significant change from current practice.

Historically, partnership accounting has focused heavily on the concept of equity between partners and different year groups of partners since there are often different partners and/or differing profit shares in successive years. Consideration of equity has often overridden the concept of prudence resulting in major liabilities being spread over several periods, often to match the cash flow, rather than being fully provided when known.

The sharing of profits will usually be governed by the partnership agreement. As a result the accounting for profit and its cash distribution can be based on different accounting policies. In effect, if there is a view that the accounting treatment is inconsistent with equity between partners, the profit distribution can be amended to reflect that. Under the concept of prudence, it is recognised that provision should be made for all known liabilities (both expenses and losses), whether their amount is known with certainty or is a best estimate based on the information available.

(*a*)   *Contingencies*. It is appropriate to take into consideration contingencies existing at the balance sheet date when preparing financial statements. The term 'contingency', when used in the preparation of accounts, is normally applied to a condition which exists at the balance sheet date, where the outcome will be confirmed only on the occurrence or non-occurrence of one or more uncertain future events. Estimates of the outcome and of the financial effect of contingencies should be made by the partnership. These estimates will be based on consideration of information available up to the date on which the financial statements are approved and will include a review of events occurring after the balance sheet date. For example, if there is a substantial legal claim against a firm, the factors to be considered would include the progress of the claim at the date on which the financial statements are approved, the opinion of legal experts or other advisers and the experience of the firm in similar cases.

The appropriate treatment of a contingency existing at the balance sheet date would be considered in the light of its expected outcome. In addition to accruals, under the fundamental concept of prudence contingent losses would be accrued where it is probable that a future event will confirm a loss which can be estimated with reasonable accuracy at the date on which the financial statements are approved.

A contingency may be reduced or avoided because it is matched by a related counter claim or claim by or against a third party. In such cases any accrual would be reduced by taking into account the probable outcome of the claim.

(*b*) *Liabilities of incoming and outgoing partners.* A person who is admitted as a partner into an existing firm does not thereby become liable to the creditors of the firm for anything done before he became a partner. However, by novation, he may take over the liabilities of the existing firm and make himself liable to the creditors. Novation implies an agreement with the creditors, either expressed or inferred from conduct. Similarly, a partner who retires from a firm does not therefore cease to be liable for partnership debts or obligations incurred before his retirement. However, he may be discharged from any existing liabilities by an agreement to that effect between himself, the members of the firm as newly constituted and the creditors. (See 2.23 above.)

(*c*) *Bank overdrafts.* Bank overdrafts are technically repayable on demand and are therefore shown under current liabilities, although it is recognised that in practice banks relatively rarely demand immediate repayment.

(*d*) *Longer term loans.* Many firms will be partially financed by longer term finance. This may be loans of perhaps five years or ten years duration. The rate of interest payable on the loans may be fixed. Such a form of finance can give great stability to the finances of the partnership. Such loans would be disclosed separately in the firm's accounts as long-term liabilities.

(*e*) *Professional indemnity insurance and claims.* The professional indemnity (PI) insurance arrangements of a partnership should ensure that claims made against it are minimised and it is able to meet claims as they fall due. This subject is addressed further in Chapter 14.

A partnership should regularly review its level of PI cover and assess whether it is sufficient to meet potential claims, taking into account expert advice from the firm's broker on aspects of the amount of cover available and its cost. The partners need to assess the adequacy of the firm's own resources to meet known claims. The firm should have procedures which require all partners to report immediately any matter which may lead to a claim being made and should have a standard approach to dealing with requests for information and in the handling of such claims. Any views expressed by the partners to third parties should be considered carefully in the light of the firm's professional indemnity position, as unguarded comments may give rise to liability.

Provisions should be made in the accounts of the firm for potential claims, and it is sensible to be cautious in the level of provisions made always bearing in mind the need to maintain equity between partners. As a minimum, it would be best practice to provide on matters for which the insurance company itself has made provision and such consistency of treatment is a useful argument when negotiating the tax treatment of the provision with the Inland Revenue. In normal circumstances, it is appropriate to provide the value of the firm's excess. The firm should review its recent claims history and each individual claim currently in progress and consider, on a claim by claim basis, the appropriate quantum of any provision that should be set aside.

(*f*) *Pension liabilities.* The partnership may have set up a staff pension scheme. It is normal practice for the annual costs of any defined contribution schemes to be charged to the profit and loss account as they arise. Whilst these types of schemes are becoming more prevalent, there continue to exist many defined benefit schemes. Accounting for the pension costs of these schemes can be more complex but in principle the costs of pensions would be charged to the profit and loss account in accordance with the recommendation of qualified actuaries and any funding surpluses or deficits that may arise would be amortised over the average service life of the members of the scheme. In those circumstances where partnerships are required to prepare accounts which give a true and fair view, they will additionally need to comply with, as a minimum, the disclosure requirements of FRS 17 'Retirement benefits'.

(*g*) *Annuities.* The principles of FRS 12 will apply to firms' post-retirement arrangements for partners where a true and fair view is to be expressed on the accounts. They apply except where valuable services proportionate to the consideration paid continue to be provided by the former member, such as under consultancy terms. Individual consideration will have to be given to the precise terms of annuity arrangements.

In the case of general partnerships the obligation to pay annuities to former partners may rest with the partners individually rather than the partnership itself which merely discharges the partners' personal obligations as agent. The personal rather than collective nature of the annuity obligation in such instances is borne out by the tax treatment of annuities (as an individual charge on personal income rather than as an expense of the whole partnership) and by case law.

Consistent with the concept that liability for annuities may rest with individuals and not with the business entity, it is possible that some firms do not have an actual or constructive liability for annuities payable by predecessor partners and/or general partnerships, even though they may, as agent for the members, disburse the related cash to the annuitant.

Although the details of annuity arrangements are numerous, they are often classified generally into two categories: 'fixed' and 'profit-based' annuities.

Fixed annuities are amounts payable to former partners that are fixed at the time of retirement. The amounts may be fixed by reference to historical earnings (for example, a percentage of the final year's profit share) or fixed at an amount, which may or may not be index-linked or linked to a measure independent of the firm's future profit. The period for which they are payable may or may not be fixed.

Profit-based annuities are those where former partners may receive, in effect, a share of the firm's ongoing profits, by way of a preferential first share, profit-points, profit-related bonus or some other mechanism. Such profit-based annuities may be contingent upon the future profits of the firm (for example, a percentage of profit, if any) or upon the firm generating sufficient profits to cover the annuity (for example, an amount payable subject to the firm earning a certain amount of profit). Such annuities may also be capped as a proportion of future profits in future years. In these cases the amount subject to abatement may or may not be carried forward for possible future payment. It will usually be the case that should no profits or minimal profits be generated, there will be no liability to the annuitant in respect of that accounting period. The calculation of profit for this purpose may be based on the profit shown by the firm's financial statements for period(s) post retirement, or on another agreed basis of determining profit for the purpose.

The accounting for annuities and similar amounts will vary according to the terms of the arrangements. It is possible that it may be appropriate solely to provide in the accounts for fixed share annuities and not for profit-based annuities, although for LLPs the accounting requirements are clearly defined and are discussed in more detail in 13.9.

(*h*)   *Other provisions.* As the preparation of general partnership accounts are not constrained by legal or accounting directives, it is open to firms to make provisions for foreseeable expenditure or costs on a particularly prudent basis. Such provisions are sometimes used as a means of restricting partners' profit distributions and controlling cash flow. Particular examples include future significant spending on information technology or property.

(*j*)   *Financing.* It is common practice within partnerships for partners to borrow to fund their capital and similar interests in a firm. Such arrangements may involve a firm entering into guarantees, indemnities or undertakings toward the lender concerned.

If the firm has entered into any guarantee or indemnity with respect to the borrowings of a partner or partners personally, the existence of such guarantee or indemnity where material could be disclosed either as a note to the accounts (where it is unlikely that the guarantee or indemnity would be called) or within provisions where there is an actual or constructive liability as defined under FRS 12 or it is probable that the guarantee or indemnity will be called.

Partners' accounts

12.22 Partners' accounts represent how the net assets of the business are financed by the partners. The partners' accounts (as shown in Appendix 6) are on the balance sheet as capital accounts, current accounts and, in some cases, taxation and other reserves. Former partners' accounts may be included or, alternatively, shown under current or long-term liabilities.

It has been noted in the paragraphs above that certain assets may be understated in the accounts of the firm. The other side of the equation, if all assets were fully and fairly stated, would be increases in the value of partners' equity through increases in the value of capital and current accounts or other reserves.

Understating assets, and hence the value of the individual partner's share of the business, may not be significant to many partners as it simply represents deferral of profits which they will receive in later years. However, it may be more significant to partners approaching retirement who may not be partners of the firm in later years when the profits are eventually recognised in the accounts. The view is often taken, on grounds of consistency, that partners may benefit when they join the partnership from such deferral, and must pay the price in loss of uplift in value when they leave.

Alternatively, the lost value is recognised in other ways, for example in annuities to former partners, payments for goodwill or simply higher profit shares in the last few years as a partner.

Capital and current accounts

12.23 In some firms, partners' capital is merged with the current accounts. Where it is separated, such capital accounts are intended to segregate an amount that is chosen to represent the 'permanent' capital of the business. In practice, even where such segregation has taken place, a significant proportion of current accounts often represent fairly permanent capital in that they may not be drawable by the individual at the moment the amounts are credited to their current accounts.

An element of a partner's profit share is usually credited monthly to enable drawings to be made on account during the year. The balance of the partner's share of profits would be credited annually after the final accounts are agreed; in practice this means that profits not drawn during the year become a source of capital for the firm.

Capital accounts may consist of both paid up capital, represented by cash paid in, and unpaid capital. This situation may exist where changes in the partnership profit sharing arrangements give rise to revaluations of goodwill. Where such changes are dealt with through a goodwill account the transactions between partners will not be represented by cash, except in the case of incoming and outgoing partners.

In some firms, current accounts may be used to settle partners' benefits, such as health care, motor vehicle expenses and home telephone bills (to the extent that such items are not allowable against tax) and life assurance together with interest on borrowings incurred to fund a partner's capital contributions.

Current accounts for junior partners are sometimes allowed to run temporarily in debit whilst they contribute their capital at the same time as enabling them to maintain an acceptable level of drawings.

Interest may be paid on the balances on both capital and current accounts. Where the ratio of such balances is not consistent with profit sharing ratios, it enables equity to be maintained between partners. It also has the added benefit that it acts as an encouragement to leave funds in the business; the firm could justify paying a rate above that which could be earned by each partner on his own account but less than the partnership's cost of borrowing.

Taxation reserves

12.24   Historically, unpaid income tax and provisions for taxation have been significant sources of finance for a professional partnership. Most partnerships will have a tax reserving policy. In as much as tax provisions are debited to current accounts that partners may otherwise be allowed to draw upon, a prudent basis of providing for taxation liabilities that may be uncertain and dependent on future events is not only a sound policy for the security of the partnership, but also tends to make policies to retain cash resources within a partnership easier to 'sell' to the partners.

Under the current self-assessment tax regime described in 17.2 onwards, income tax liabilities are individual liabilities, rather than joint and several partnership liabilities as they were under the old regime. Some firms allow partners to draw their share of profits to meet individual liabilities, in which case care needs to be taken to consider the impact this will have on the financing of the business.

It is best practice to provide on a prudent basis and to disclose in the balance sheet under current liabilities that element of the taxation provisions which is due and payable within the next twelve months. The excess element of reserves would normally be considered to be the 'prudent' element and it is considered reasonable to disclose the amount under partners' reserves, although variations on where these amounts are disclosed on the balance sheet are common.

Amounts owing to former partners

12.25 Some firms allow for the prompt repayment of capital and undrawn profits held within a partnership to outgoing partners. More often, in order to protect the capital base of the firm, there will be a delay between the time a partner leaves and the time he receives the full amount owing to him. In some cases this can be several years, with or without interest paid on outstanding amounts. Whilst for most firms this is not a significant source of finance, it can be important in smaller firms where a number of senior partners have retired or otherwise left the firm.

The profit and loss account

12.26 There is no standard form of profit and loss account for partnerships but it is sensible to identify expenditure into groups of overhead costs for the purposes of the financial accounts, as shown in the model example of accounts included as Appendix 6.

Other accounting policies and disclosures

Post balance sheet events

12.27 It is appropriate that events arising after the accounts date be reflected in financial statements if they provide additional evidence of conditions that existed at the balance sheet date and materially affect the amounts to be included in the accounts. A post balance sheet event is an event which occurs between the balance sheet date and the date on which the financial statements are approved by the partnership.

Events which would normally give rise to an adjustment in the accounts include the following:

(a)   the purchase price or sale proceeds of assets purchased or sold before the year end is finally determined;

(b)   a property valuation or the receipt of the financial statements for an investment provides evidence of an impairment in value;

(c)   the receipt of evidence that the previous estimate of accrued profit on a long-term contract was materially inaccurate or where the realisable value on debtors becomes known with greater accuracy;

(*d*) an amount received or receivable became known in respect of insurance claims which were in the course of negotiation at the balance sheet date; and

(*e*) the discovery of errors or frauds which show that the financial statements were incorrect.

However, it would not normally be considered appropriate to adjust for such items as mergers or acquisitions, losses of fixed assets or stocks as a result of a catastrophe such as a fire or flood and changes in foreign exchange rates.

Related parties

12.28 The provisions of FRS 8 'Related Party Disclosures' will apply to partnership accounts prepared under UK GAAP. A firm which is under the common control of another firm, company or other entity will be a related party to that other entity. The fact that some partners are partners of another partnership does not in itself make the businesses related parties; the extent of common control determines this.

The controlling party and ultimate controlling party of a firm, if one exists, would be disclosed in accordance with FRS 8. This would include an individual or entity which had the ability to control the firm, though that party may not be entitled to the majority of profits or have invested the majority of capital.

Foreign currency translation

12.29 During an accounting period, a firm may enter into transactions which are denominated in a foreign currency. The result of each transaction would normally be translated into the firm's local currency using the exchange rate in operation on the date on which the transaction occurred. However, if the rates do not fluctuate significantly, an average rate for a period may be used as an approximation. Where the transaction is to be settled at a contracted rate, that rate would be used.

An exchange gain or loss will result if the transaction is settled at an exchange rate which differs from that used when the transaction was initially recorded, or, where appropriate, that used at the last balance sheet date. An exchange gain or loss will also arise on unsettled transactions if the rate of exchange used at the balance sheet date differs from that used previously. Such gains and losses are recognised as part of the profit or loss for the year.

The investment by a head office branch in the affairs of an overseas branch is in the net worth of its branch rather than a direct investment in the individual assets and liabilities of that branch. The foreign branch will normally have net current assets and fixed assets which may be financed partly by local currency borrowings and in its day-to-day operations the foreign branch is unlikely to be dependent on the reporting currency of the leading office.

In these circumstances, the amounts in the balance sheet of a foreign branch should be translated into the reporting currency of the leading office using the rate of exchange ruling at the balance sheet date. Exchange differences will arise if this rate differs from that ruling at the previous balance sheet date or at the date of any subsequent capital injection or reduction. Amounts in the profit and loss account of a foreign branch should be translated at the closing rate or at an average rate for the accounting period.

Use of service companies

12.30   If a partnership is able to divert profits into a service company and use these for financing the business, it is far more efficient than for partners to do so out of taxed profits.

Service companies have become significantly less valuable for this purpose since income tax has been charged at a top marginal rate of 40% and corporation tax at a lower marginal rate of 20% (the lowest marginal corporation tax rate is 0%, but rises to 20% where profits chargeable to corporation tax exceed £50,000). Nevertheless, a retained 80% (or up to 100%) of profits for working capital requirements in a company is better than the 60% rate for profits retained within a successful firm. There are, however, a number of tax traps to be avoided.

The arrangements generally involve wholly owned service companies employing the firm's staff and possibly providing other services to the partnership with a profit margin over direct cost. The accumulated profits can be used either to purchase assets used in the firm's business (which can be made available to the partnership for a further fee) or to provide working capital to the firm.

To preserve equity between partners, if a firm's profits are to be diverted to a service company, it may be necessary to revalue the shares in the firm's accounts to their underlying asset value.

Internal audit

12.31   Internal audit provides a supporting service to those managing a partnership. It is independent of operational responsibilities and is used to provide objective analyses and recommendations in respect of activities appraised, which can lead to improved efficiency and effectiveness. Internal audit should be seen as a service to management and will be set up to assist in the process of monitoring performance to help achieve the operational targets and plans. In addition, in today's highly regulated climate, it is used as a means of monitoring adherence to the stated policies of the firm and in risk management.

The need for internal audit

12.32 The need for an internal audit function within a partnership will depend upon the size and complexity of the organisation. The role of internal audit is both a protective role, providing positive reassurance to management at differing levels, and a proactive role, contributing to improvements in operational performance. The scope of the internal audit function will be determined by those managing the partnership. The management team may decide that they require ad hoc reviews from time to time of particular aspects of the partnership's operation. In this case, the reviews would probably be performed most cost-effectively by external auditors. Alternatively, if an on-going review of the partnership's operations is required, an internal audit function within the partnership would probably be more appropriate.

The scope of an internal audit may include all or some of the following:

(*a*)   accuracy of records;

(*b*)   security of assets;

(*c*)   prevention of waste, errors or fraud;

(*d*)   compliance with established control procedures;

(*e*)   adherence to policy objectives;

(*f*)   reliability of management reporting;

(*g*)   adequacy and effectiveness of control systems; and

(*h*)   economy, efficiency and effectiveness of operations, including examination of value for money.

Internal audit can be used as the management function which monitors the continuing validity of management control systems and effective compliance. In undertaking these tasks, the internal auditor has the ability to spot opportunities for strengthening systems, streamlining procedures, for reducing duplication and waste, and to suggest ways in which the business can become more efficient and cost effective.

When management accept internal audit assurances and recommendations they are placing considerable confidence in the auditor's judgement. There has to be a sound basis for that confidence. In order to be constructive, recommendations and judgements arising out of the internal audit function must be unbiased and therefore can only be made by taking an objective view. Internal auditors must be independent of the operations being audited and must be seen to be independent. Any suggestion of conflicting interests undermines their credibility.

In order to demonstrate both independence and competence, it is usual to appoint an internal audit committee which would report regularly to the partnership as a whole or to the management committee. The auditors would be expected to have competence in the audit skills of observation, analysis and judgement but they must demonstrate understanding of the business environment and management philosophy. In addition, diplomatic and presentational skills are necessary to persuade others of the need to adopt recommendations which may result in significant change and, potentially, a reorientation of people's attitudes.

The ability to influence management to overcome inertia and maintain motivation in a new direction requires independence of thought and some degree of seniority.

Internal audit is essentially a critique which involves three fundamental procedures:

(i) obtaining evidence;

(ii) forming judgements and opinions based on the evidence; and

(iii) reporting those opinions.

The results of every internal audit assignment must be reported. If an audit examination uncovers significant weaknesses, management should be alerted as early as possible. However, in all cases, there should be a final report which is formal, written and signed and appropriate follow-up procedures should exist to implement agreed recommendations.

Chapter 13

Accounting for Limited Liability Partnerships

General accounting requirements

13.1   The accounting requirements for LLPs are set out in *LLPR 2001, Regulation 3* and *Schedule 1*. These regulations take *Part VII* of *CA 85* (accounts and audit) which deals with the requirements to prepare accounts, together with the relevant *Schedules [4, 4A, 5, 7, 8, 8A* and *10A]* which detail the content of those accounts and makes such modifications as are necessary to deal with the particular circumstances of LLPs.

For the first period after incorporation the accounting reference date of an LLP (i.e. the date to which the accounts are prepared) is the last day of the month in which the anniversary of its incorporation falls. In the absence of any application to shorten or lengthen the accounting period (see below), the first accounting period will start on the date of incorporation and end on that accounting reference date. The first accounting period cannot be shorter than six months nor longer than 18 months. Subsequent accounting periods will then cover a year from the date of the end of the previous accounting period unless an application is made to amend the accounting reference date.

The members are responsible for preparing at the end of each financial year a profit and loss account and balance sheet which give a true and fair view of the state of affairs of the LLP at the end of the financial period and of the profit or loss for the financial period. A report to the members (Members' Report) is also required. The form and content of the balance sheet, profit and loss account and notes to the accounts is set out in legislation. The fact that the accounts are required to give a true and fair view means that they also have to comply with all extant SSAPs, FRSs and UITF Abstracts. Therefore, where required, they will also need to include a Cash Flow Statement and Statement of Total Recognised Gains and Losses.

Where, at the end of the financial period, an LLP is a parent undertaking, both individual and group (consolidated) accounts are required.

The accounts are required to be approved by the members and signed on their behalf by a designated member. A copy of the accounts together with the audit report is required to be sent to every member within one month of approval. The designated members are responsible for delivering the accounts to the Registrar of Companies – in practice this will most probably be delegated to one person. Delivery to the Registrar must take place within ten months of the period end.

Where an LLP is within certain size criteria measured by reference to turnover, total assets and number of employees it may be eligible to file abbreviated accounts with the Registrar of Companies, although it will have to produce full accounts for the members.

Statement of recommended practice – accounting by limited liability partnerships ('the SORP')

13.2 The SORP does not provide details of all of the reporting requirements which are applicable to LLPs, but it does provide interpretation of those accounting standards where there are specific issues regarding their application to the circumstances of an LLP. There is a requirement within the SORP that the note to the financial statements which deals with accounting policies should refer to the LLP's compliance with the SORP, together with any non-compliance and the reasons.

Areas dealt with within the SORP are as follows:

- The contents of the annual report and financial statements. This section is fairly general and the SORP does not include an example set of accounts.

- Membership remuneration and interests.

- Retirement benefits.

- Taxation.

- Stocks and long-term contracts.

- Business combinations and group accounts.

- Provisions and other implications of FRS 12.

- Related parties.

These are discussed in further detail in the following sections.

An example set of accounts is set out as Appendix 6.

The requirement to appoint auditors

13.3 Unless entitled to the exemptions included in the legislation, all LLPs are required to appoint auditors and have their accounts audited. Exemption from audit is available for LLPs with turnover of £1 million or less and a balance sheet total (total assets before taking account of liabilities) that does not exceed £1.4 million. The exemption, however, is not available where the LLP is:

(*a*)   involved in banking or insurance;

(*b*)   enrolled under the list maintained by the Insurance Brokers Registration Council under *section 4* of the *Insurance Brokers (Registration) Act 1977*;

(*c*)   authorised under the *Financial Services and Markets Act 2000*;

(*d*)   a parent or a subsidiary unless:

  (i) throughout the financial period in which it was a subsidiary it was dormant; or

  (ii) it is a parent or subsidiary in what is defined as a small group.

An LLP which is exempt from audit is still required to file accounts with the Registrar of Companies and must also circulate a full set of the accounts to each member.

Accounting for members' interests

13.4   Within the balance sheet, amounts relating to the interaction of the LLP with the members are recorded in one of two places.

(*a*)   *Loans and other debts due to members* – amounts which are debts owed by the LLP to the member, for example profit allocations not covered by drawings.

(*b*)   *Members' other interests* – includes capital introduced by members, unallocated profits, any revaluation reserves and other reserves which have been set aside from profits (for example to cover the cost of retirement benefits).

The way in which the elements of members' interests are required to be presented within the balance sheet differs from that adopted by partnerships. Loans and debts due to members, which are broadly analogous to current accounts, are required to be presented as liabilities as they represent obligations the LLP owes to the members. In a partnership they are presented as part of the interests of the partners alongside capital accounts. The effect of this on the balance sheet is illustrated in the table below.

Partnership		LLP	
	£		£
Net assets	600	Net assets	600
		Loans and other debts due to	
		members	(350)
Total	600		250
Capital accounts	100	Capital accounts	100
Current accounts	350		
Other	150	Other	150
	600		250

The SORP also requires that total members' interests be presented in the accounts by showing the sum of amounts due to members and members other interests as a memorandum item on the balance sheet.

The SORP requires the accounts of the LLP to include a comprehensive statement of the components of members' interests and movements during the year. The format for that reconciliation is proscribed by the SORP and an example is contained in the accounts in Appendix 6.

Profit allocations

13.5   The basis on which profits will be allocated to individual members will be governed by the members' agreement. The amount of that profit for any particular year will however be known only when the accounts have been finalised. There is, therefore, an issue as to when the profits made by the LLP become a liability due to the members.

Legal advice taken during the development of the SORP concluded that 'the profits of an LLP are only converted into a debt due to its members when the members have agreed to divide the profits among themselves'. Therefore, this would imply that unless this had happened at the year end through some form of automatic agreement to divide profits within the members' agreement, the profits due to members should not be regarded as a liability. The question then arises as to where unallocated profits should be included within the accounts. Considering the analogous position with a company, undistributed profits would be included within the profit and loss reserve.

The Regulations do not permit an LLP to have in its balance sheet a separate heading 'Profit and loss account', therefore unallocated profits would be included within 'Other reserves'.

Following this interpretation would result in the accounts of a large number of LLPs showing, at the end of the financial year, a figure for amounts due to members which does not reflect the profits to be distributed for the year and an amount of members' other interests which is inflated by those profits. This would result in the accounts giving a misleading view of the real financial position of the LLP which could well be in conflict with their requirement to give a true and fair view.

The very nature of an LLP means that it intends to distribute its profits for any particular year to the members and as such this constitutes a constructive obligation to those members. Accordingly, the profits of any one year whether allocated to the members of the LLP or not, subject to any amounts retained, should be regarded as a liability to the members in that year and be included in the balance sheet within debt due to members.

Borrowings of members

13.6   Within partnerships it is common practice for the partners to borrow in order to fund their interests in that partnership. These arrangements frequently involve the partnership entering into a guarantee, indemnity or similar arrangement with the provider of the funding. Similar arrangements arise in LLPs.

The fact that the members' interests have been funded by way of borrowings is not of itself something which requires disclosure in the accounts. Instead it is necessary to look at the extent of the LLP's obligation to the provider of finance and how this should be treated. In the rare circumstances where the LLP has an obligation to repay the loan, then a provision should be recognised in the LLP's accounts. More commonly, the LLP will have guaranteed the borrowings but will only be liable if the member defaults on the loan. In these circumstances the resultant 'contingent liability' should be disclosed in the accounts.

Loans and other debts due to members

13.7   The SORP requires that the notes to the accounts disclose where amounts due to members would rank on a winding up in relation to other unsecured creditors. In the absence of any agreement to the contrary, amounts due to members will rank equally with other creditors.

Members' remuneration

13.8   The way in which members are remunerated will vary between LLPs but will reflect the fact that the members are in the position of both owning the LLP and, usually, working within it. The distinction between the rewards received as a result of ownership interests and those received from employment could well be ambiguous.

Whilst the intention will be for the members to share in the profits of the LLP, varying proportions of this may be 'guaranteed' in the form of fixed payments. A further complication is that it is possible for a member to also be an employee of the LLP and in these circumstances there will be a contract of employment between the LLP and the member.

The ways in which members may obtain reward for their involvement with the LLP are as follows.

(a)   *Allocation of profits* – Members are awarded a share of the profit made by the LLP. The basis of allocation will vary but will typically be based on a formula linked to the capital introduced by the member. Other factors such as seniority may also be included within the calculation.

(b)   *Fixed amount* – Members may be 'guaranteed' a certain amount of remuneration each year either within the membership agreement or through individual arrangements between the LLP and the member. This amount will be paid to them irrespective of the level of profits made by the LLP.

(c)   *Combination of fixed amount and allocated profit* – In addition to receiving a fixed amount, members may also receive an allocation of the profit remaining after paying such amounts.

(d)   *Drawings* – During the year members may be entitled to receive cash from the LLP in lieu of remuneration they either expect to receive or which relates to an earlier year. Such amounts are referred to as drawings. Receipt of drawings will be particularly common where remuneration is either all, or predominantly all, in the form of profit share.

The way in which members' remuneration is accounted for depends on whether it is 'salaried remuneration' or profit share. The Regulations require that the profit and loss account disclose a total for 'Profit or loss for the financial year before members' remuneration and profit share'. Salaried remuneration of members should be shown immediately after this, with the remainder being profit or loss available for division among members.

Salaried remuneration is defined in paragraph 17 of the SORP and in essence comprises any amount of remuneration a member is entitled to which is fixed and paid irrespective of the amounts of profit earned by the LLP.

The following table reproduced from the SORP summarises the treatment of members' remuneration:

Nature of element of a member's remuneration:	Treat as:
Remuneration that is paid under an employment contract Other payments, representing a debt of the LLP not arising from a division of profits	Expense, described as 'Salaried remuneration of members', and deducted after arriving at 'Profit for the financial year before members' remuneration and profit shares'
Fixed (or first) share of profits, representing a debt arising from a division of profits Profit-share, representing a debt arising from a division of profits	Allocation of profit

The notes to the accounts should analyse salaried remuneration of members between that which is paid under an employment contract and other. The average number of members during the year should be disclosed in a note to the accounts. Whilst not required by either the Regulations or the SORP, the members may wish to include details of average members' remuneration. Where this option is taken, the SORP states that it should be calculated by reference to the disclosed average number of members and the amount of 'profit before members' remuneration and profit shares' shown in the profit and loss account.

Where the profit of the LLP before members' remuneration and profit share is greater than £200,000, the notes to the accounts are required to disclose the remuneration of the member with the highest entitlement to profit. As well as profit share and salaried remuneration from the LLP this will also include any amounts paid to the member by a subsidiary undertaking or other third party. The member does not have to be named.

Retirement benefits

13.9   The accounting treatment of retirement benefits within LLPs is probably one of the most complex areas. The accounting requirements with respect to retiring members, in particular, was the subject of much debate during the development of the SORP and the solution is not entirely in accordance with general accounting requirements applied to other types of entity.

Retirement benefits payable to former members will be of one of the following two types:

(*a*)   *Pre-determined* – An amount which is fixed at the time of retirement (annuity). This may, for example, be by reference to the profits earned in the last year of membership. Alternatively it could be a fixed sum, which may be index-linked or linked to some other measure which is independent of the profits of the LLP.

(b) *Profit-dependent* – An amount which effectively results in the member continuing to receive a share in the profits of the LLP post retirement. This amount may be subject to some level of cap. There are a wide range of methods used to provide profit-dependent benefits and these may include arrangements whereby the LLP has to achieve a certain level of profits before any payment is made.

Irrespective of whether a retirement benefit is pre-determined or profit-dependent, provision should be made in the accounts for the present value of the best estimate of the future payments to, or in respect of, former members. Where the effect of the time value of money is considered to be material the provision should be discounted. A consequence of the requirement to make provision for retirement benefits is that LLPs with profit-dependent retirement benefit schemes will need to make an assessment of their future profits in order to determine the level of provision. Whilst there will have to be a certain amount of subjectivity attached to these estimates it should be possible for the LLP to determine the range of potential outcomes from which a provision could be calculated.

The SORP does not require a provision to be made to reflect an estimate of the liability with respect to the retirement benefits promised to existing members. In not requiring any provision in these circumstances, the SORP is at odds with generally accepted accounting treatment.

The retirement benefits provided to a former member on retirement are not related to the current year's performance, but represent a reorganisation of members' interests and the reflection of the continuing relationship the retired member has with the LLP. Accordingly, in the period that the member retires a transfer should be made from members' interests (either from other reserves or a reserve set aside for the purpose by the members). This transfer should be recorded as a loss in the Statement of Total Recognised Gains and Losses. Subsequent amendments to the liability should be charged to the profit and loss account as part of operating profit.

The position within the balance sheet of the liability to pay retirement benefits will depend on the extent to which it is a fixed amount. Where it represents a fixed amount it should be included either within 'creditors falling due within one year' or 'creditors falling due in more than one year', dependent on when the amounts are due for payment. Where the amount is not fixed, but represents the best estimate of the future liability, it should be disclosed as a separate category within 'provisions for liabilities and charges'.

Work in progress

13.10 Accounting standards require that work in progress be included in the balance sheet at the lower of cost and net realisable value. SSAP 9

'Stocks and work in progress' defines cost to include not only materials (unlikely to be relevant to the majority of LLPs) but also direct labour and overheads.

Direct labour should include the cost of those employees who have been directly involved in the provision of the related service. The employees' cost should include not only their wages or salaries, but also other employment costs such as National Insurance and pensions. Where members' time is included within work in progress it should only be valued to the extent that the members receive salaried remuneration. Amounts received by members by way of profit allocation should be excluded from the valuation of work in progress.

SSAP 9 also requires that all 'direct' overheads should be included within the valuation of work in progress. Irrespective of whether the time input by a member is included within work in progress, the general accounting requirement to match costs and revenues means that any overhead related to the member's time should be included in the valuation.

Provisions

13.11   In accountancy the term 'provision' can be used in two separate sets of circumstances. Firstly there are adjustments which are made to the amounts at which certain assets are included within the accounts. For example, 'provision for bad or doubtful debts' or 'provision for obsolete stock'. These are accounting adjustments and are not strictly provisions at all – this term is reserved for those items which can be included on the balance sheet within the heading 'provisions for liabilities and charges'. The accounting rules with respect to the recognition of such provisions are extremely strict and are set out in FRS 12 'Provisions, contingent assets and contingent liabilities'.

Before an LLP can recognise a provision within its accounts it must be able to satisfy each of the three criteria set out in FRS 12:

(i)   there must be a legal or constructive obligation at the balance sheet date as a result of an event occurring before that date;

(ii)   it must be probable that there will be a 'transfer of economic benefits' (e.g. paying cash) to settle the obligation; and

(iii)   a reliable estimate can be made of the amount involved.

A constructive obligation arises where, through custom and practice, the LLP has created a valid expectation on the part of the third party that their claim will be met.

Where the obligation to pay only becomes apparent after the balance sheet date, but it clearly arises as the result of an event before that date, a provision should be recognised. For example, an unexpected legal claim might be received after the balance sheet date in respect of damage alleged to have occurred before that date. In these circumstances a provision would be recognised, but it would not be acceptable to create a general provision for possible legal claims arising from work performed.

Related parties

13.12 LLPs are required to comply with FRS 8 'Related party disclosures'. The objective of FRS 8 is 'to ensure that financial statements contain the disclosures necessary to draw attention to the possibility that the reported financial position and results may have been affected by the existence of related parties and by material transactions with them'. The FRS requires disclosure of a material transaction undertaken by the LLP with a related party, irrespective of whether a price is charged.

Where the LLP is controlled by another party, disclosure is required of that controlling party, irrespective of whether a transaction has taken place with it.

FRS 8 defines two or more parties as being related when at any time during the financial period:

(i)　one party had either direct or indirect control of the other party; or

(ii)　the parties were subject to common control from the same source; or

(iii)　one party had influence over the financial and operating policies of the other party to an extent that that other party might be inhibited from pursuing at all times its own separate interests; or

(iv)　the parties, in entering into a transaction, are subject to influence from the same source to such an extent that one of the parties to the transaction has subordinated its own separate interests.

Certain parties are deemed to be related:

(*a*)　The LLP's ultimate and intermediate parent undertakings, subsidiary undertakings and fellow subsidiary undertakings.

(*b*)　The LLP's associates and joint ventures.

(*c*)　The investor or venturer in respect of which the LLP is an associate or a joint venture.

(*d*)　The directors of ultimate and intermediate parent companies.

(*e*)　Pension funds for the benefit of employees of the LLP or of any entity that is a related party of it.

(*f*)　Predecessor partnerships of the LLP.

Certain further parties are presumed to be related, unless it can be proven that neither party had influenced the financial outcome of a transaction.

(A)　The key management of the LLP and the key management of its parent undertaking or undertakings (key management are those persons in senior positions having authority or responsibility for directing or controlling major activities and resources). An entity managing or managed by the LLP under a management contract.

(B) Members of the close family of any individual above.

(C) Partnerships, companies, trusts and other entities in which any individual or member of the close family of the above has a controlling interest.

FRS 8 also includes the presumption that the directors of a company are related parties. This presumption should not be interpreted to mean that all members of an LLP should be automatically regarded as related parties. Whether the members are related will depend upon the degree of control they have over the day-to-day activities of the LLP. In a small LLP it may be the case that all the members are directly involved in its management and as such should be regarded as related. However in a large LLP management may be devolved to a small number of members who should be presumed to be related, whereas the remainder will probably fall outside the definition. The reference to key management in FRS 8 means that designated members will usually be related parties.

For each related party transaction the following should be disclosed:

   (i) The name of the related party.

  (ii) A description of the relationship between the LLP and the other party.

 (iii) A description of the transaction.

 (iv) The amounts involved.

  (v) Any other elements of the transaction necessary for an understanding of the financial statements.

 (vi) The amounts due to or from related parties at the balance sheet date and provision for doubtful debts due from such parties at that date.

(vii) Amounts written off in the period in respect of debts due to or from related parties.

Transition from partnership to LLP

13.13   The transition from partnership to LLP should be accounted for using the merger basis so long as it meets the criteria to be treated as a group reconstruction set out in FRS 6 'Acquisitions and mergers'. FRS 6 is worded in the context of corporate entities and states that in order to qualify as a group reconstruction 'the ultimate shareholders must remain the same, and the rights of each such shareholder, relative to the others, should be unchanged' immediately before and after the transaction.

Putting this definition into the context of a partnership, in order for the transfer to an LLP to qualify as a group reconstruction and hence for merger accounting, the interests of members in the LLP should be in the same proportions as their 'share' in the partnership immediately prior to transfer. Both the amount of capital introduced and profit sharing arrangements will need to be taken into account when determining if the criteria have been met.

The application of this requirement means that transition to an LLP should not be combined with the retirement or appointment of partners or members, nor should the relative benefits of partners/members be altered at this stage. Such changes may also have consequences in respect of the exemption from stamp duty on incorporation. However, the Inland Revenue have stated that they will accept that there can be a change of partners taking place the instant before or after incorporation. The Stamp Office are likely to ask to see all associated documents affecting the change in membership prior to and/or after incorporation

Where the requirements of FRS 6 are not met, the transfer should be accounted for as an acquisition and the assets and liabilities transferred would need to be restated to their fair values and the 'consideration' for the acquisition determined by reference to the value of the business of the partnership transferred. Goodwill will arise as a consequence of the difference between the two values and this will have to be recognised on the balance sheet and amortised through the profit and loss account of the LLP. For professional practices, the value of the business taken as a whole compared to the value of its underlying assets and liabilities could well be significantly different. The amount of goodwill, and the impact on the profit and loss account, could be substantial.

On transferring assets and liabilities to the LLP, the amounts at which they are initially recorded in the accounts should be calculated by reference to the accounting policies to be adopted by the LLP. Dependent on the policies adopted, these could vary significantly from those shown in the accounts of the predecessor partnership. This will be particularly relevant where the partnership had prepared accounts for its own purposes other than on the 'true and fair' basis, making adjustments to that basis only for the purposes of its tax return. Areas where differences are most likely to arise are as follows:

(*a*) Provisions for retirement benefits to former partners to the extent that the liability to meet the cost is transferred to the LLP.

(*b*) Valuation of work in progress.

(*c*) De-recognition of provisions which do not meet the definition within FRS 12 (for example provisions for possible future PI claims).

The SORP requires that single-entity LLPs formed from the transfer or incorporation of an existing entity, should present comparative pro-forma information for the previous period. The SORP does however permit an exemption to this where the time and cost involved in collating the necessary information is considered to be excessive. The corresponding amounts should be stated using the same accounting policies as those adopted by the LLP. For the reasons discussed above the amounts shown by the comparative figures may differ from those in the equivalent partnership accounts resulting in a consequent difference between partners' interests and members' interests. This difference should not be reflected in the accounts of the LLP which should be prepared on the basis that the LLP has always existed and always prepared accounts in accordance with its selected accounting policies.

Where a group transfers to LLP status, FRS 6 requires that comparative figures be presented for the previous year. These will not be pro forma and will, therefore, fall within the scope of the audit report.

Chapter 14

Financial Management

Introduction

14.1   This chapter examines the budgeting process appropriate for a professional practice, the funding of partnerships and deals with banking issues, including financial products and treasury management.

Budgets

14.2   Chapter 8 looked at the need for a business to produce an overall strategic plan, recognising the need to consider the resources necessary in order to achieve the objectives. The plan should ideally cover a three to five year period and include broad reference to the financial needs of the business.

The strategic plan should be supplemented by a three to five year financial forecast based on a reasonably small number of broad assumptions. Its purpose is to demonstrate the financial implications of the partnership achieving its objectives over the given period.

Objectives and definitions

14.3   The firm should produce an annual budget which is much more detailed than a long-term financial forecast. The objective of the budget is twofold. First, it is the means by which the objectives in the long-term plan can be converted to a detailed financial action plan. Secondly, it is a way of monitoring the partnership's financial performance on a regular basis.

Generally, a forecast estimates the future state of the market and the economy and is used for long or medium range planning. However, a budget is a far more detailed document that includes a monthly analysis of fees, salaries, overhead costs, cash flows, capital expenditure and working capital requirements.

Budgets provide a clear picture of the partnership's likely financial performance. They enable a view to be taken of income and overhead levels, likely profitability, capital expenditure and cash flow requirements. Preparing a budget provides a planning discipline that is useful in short-term decision-making and in controlling the allocation of resources. It also quantifies the likely effect of action plans. In addition, particularly for those whose performance might be assessed by reference to budget, it provides stimulation and motivation for the achievement of a good performance in the year. It is also a useful communication tool within the firm and is a key means of maintaining a focus on achieving the firm's aspirations throughout the financial year.

Perhaps more than any other financial tool used by a professional firm, the budget is able to affect the attitudes and behaviour of partners and senior members of staff. The purpose of the budget should also be to motivate and research has shown that budgets tend to improve performance. In order to extract the maximum benefit, it is essential that each of the departments within the firm takes ownership of their particular part of the budget.

Budgets must be set at a level that is realistically achievable but nevertheless demanding, rather than be a statement of the ideal which all involved know to be unachievable. Demanding, but achievable budgets tend to motivate, whilst less demanding or unrealistic targets have an adverse effect on performance. Care should be taken when setting and comparing budgets for different departments which may have differing levels of profitability but all contribute to the firm, in some cases in a way that cannot be shown in the budgets, such as giving the firm a high profile. Care must also be taken when a budget is not met. A critical approach may demotivate, and other factors, such as performance against the previous year, or factors outside the control of the firm, should also be taken into account when reviewing results. Ultimately, it is important that the budget is considered to be binding and attracts personal commitment from partners and senior staff.

Budget preparation

14.4   There are a number of critical steps to ensure that the budget process provides the greatest possible benefit to the firm. A formal budget committee will often need to be established to coordinate the budget process, although this role may be taken by the firm's finance committee. Members of this committee will vary according to the size of the partnership, the nature of its business and its management structure. However, in general, it is likely to include representatives of the executive management, department heads and accounting staff.

Key steps will include:

(*a*)   The committee, with guidance from the partnership board or management committee, should establish initial guidelines which can be used by departmental heads to prepare individual departmental budgets. The main parameters will include overall salary increases, charging structures and particular target growth rates for certain departments.

(*b*) A timetable should be issued for the preparation of relevant information, reviewing first draft budgets and discussing with each department head the basis upon which their budget has been prepared.

(*c*) The accountant or finance partner should co-ordinate the timetable and produce the first draft firm-wide budget.

(*d*) The finance committee or management board should consider the first version of the firm-wide budget to ensure inconsistencies and anomalies are removed and the budget is consistent with the firm's long range plans. Discussions with department heads are likely to take place as the overall aspirations of the firm are matched to each fee earning department's ability to deliver.

Content

14.5 The main elements of a budget include a detailed profit and loss account for the period and a cash flow statement. In a professional practice, the key areas of focus will include: the profit and loss account, the amount of value locked up in work in progress and debtors, the capital expenditure budget and the financing facilities available to the firm.

The cash flow budget should be compared with the bank and other facilities available to the firm. The variation between these two numbers should be taken into account when finalising the budget for the year and determining the firm's banking arrangements.

Budgeting income

14.6 Within a professional practice, the income element of the budget is a key issue. This figure can be uncertain, due to external factors such as decisions taken by competitors, the general state of the economy, the effectiveness of advertising and marketing activities and the stability of clients. Estimating professional practice income will often involve forecasting the value of time input and projecting the anticipated level of recovery of this time. However, in transactional based practices, such as agency work for chartered surveyors and corporate finance work for lawyers, it is difficult to estimate with any degree of certainty the projected fee income over the forthcoming year. History and past experience may show that fee income will continue to come from a number of sources and, with a proper understanding of the market place within which the firm operates, this should be a good base from which to develop the budget.

When preparing a budget, partnerships should first consider the key drivers of their income generation. For some this may be based on success fees or commission. However, for most firms the number of billable hours that individual employees can work during the year will be the key driver of income. One of the key factors in a profitable partnership is the extent to which professional staff are utilised in chargeable time working on behalf of clients. Clearly, the higher the utilisation of the individual the more profitable and productive he will be.

Utilisation rates will depend on the seniority of the person involved; partners will spend more time on business development and management issues than junior staff. Partnerships should generally aim to achieve the highest level of utilisation possible without the firm becoming an unpleasant place to work. Therefore, when preparing an income budget it is appropriate to consider potential chargeable hours by individual multiplied by the charge-out rate.

Charge-out rates are normally expressed as a rate per hour or day. Firms will set rates to reflect their own cost structure and what the market will accept. One method is cost plus pricing. In simple terms, this means calculating the cost of servicing a client and then adding a fixed percentage to cover overheads and a further percentage to provide a profit. Provided that the percentage uplift to cover overheads and profit reflect fairly on the working practices of the firm, the relevant fee will represent the firm's expected profits on each transaction. However, partnerships which only utilise this approach risk being out of touch with the market place. They may miss the opportunity for extra profits by undercharging for the real value of their work or, alternatively, find that where there is a lack of work they miss the opportunity of making a contribution to fixed overheads because they do not accept work for which they cannot achieve full recovery of their normal charge-out rates.

The market place for professional partnerships is changing dramatically and firms' pricing policies must move to meet market needs. However, it is essential that firms set charge-out rates for each of their professional employees and monitor and record the time charged by them to particular contracts or transactions. By setting charge-out rates that reflect a fair proportion of overheads and profit and taking into account each person's salary costs, the firm will determine the cost of undertaking work for clients. In current market conditions, when bidding for proposals or undertaking work for clients, charge-out rates will provide an indication of the cost of the work and the effect of the pricing policy on the profits of the firm.

Budgeting costs

14.7   The main cost elements will be staff costs, followed by premises. It should be reasonably straightforward to budget for these costs over the next twelve months as, in the short term, they are essentially fixed. Where this is not the case, the financial effect of decisions that have been taken in respect of levels of human resources, premises and other overheads should be factored into the budget.

Management accounts

14.8   Once partners and staff are aware that budgets have been set and that their performance will be gauged against them, they will generally work to increase the probability of making budget and avoid alternatives which reduce it. The successful use of budgets as a control mechanism to improve the financial performance of the business depends on whether each department takes ownership of the costs under its control. However, mitigating factors should also be considered, such as costs outside the control of the department and other priorities and responsibilities which may direct partners' attention away from client activity. In addition, the quality of the work being undertaken should not be ignored. Finally, it is often the case that the costs of support departments within the firm, such as marketing and personnel, attract particular attention and the effectiveness of their activities should be evaluated.

The budget should be reviewed on a monthly basis to compare actual results against expectations. An efficient way of doing this is to prepare management accounts which compare the budget and actual results for the period and for the year to date and include, where appropriate, the results of the prior year. A commentary highlighting the key areas where results do not meet expectations should be attached.

The monthly review of results should not only encompass the income and costs but also, particularly in professional practices, certain balance sheet items. The commentary should address capital expenditure and the level of lockup included in work in progress and debtors. The main determinant of liquidity within a partnership is the extent to which time has been incurred on client affairs but has yet to be billed and collected and the management of the firm's investment in this working capital is crucial to the control of cash and borrowing requirements.

At the conclusion of this chapter are some example schedules for a set of management accounts. These show the way a profit and loss account may be presented, together with the additional balance sheet information which is needed.

Management of work in progress

14.9   The management of work in progress in a professional firm has as much to do with managing the client relationship as it has to do with a well-run accounts department. Before accepting and starting work for a client, the fee earner should, if possible, provide the client with a quote for the work and agree a billing and payment schedule. If at any stage it appears possible that actual costs will exceed the budget, the client should be advised and a revised billing and payment schedule agreed. It is vital that professional staff manage effectively client's expectations, not only on delivery and quality of professional work, but also in terms of fee arrangements.

Disbursements incurred by a partnership on a client matter should be invoiced on a regular basis to ensure the firm does not fund excessive amounts of expenditure on behalf of a client.

The use of bar graphs of the monthly value of work in progress, perhaps analysed by department, can assist control. Alternatively, contracts can be monitored by line graphs that compare cumulative actual costs with budgeted costs month by month.

Management of debtors

14.10   Fees and disbursements should be billed to clients on a regular basis in order to ensure cash is collected in a timely manner. It is appropriate to have a standard procedure for chasing up unpaid bills, through the issue of monthly statements, reminders and solicitors letters. Again, the monitoring of debtor days, perhaps by individual fee earners, will enable the firm to maintain better control on its working capital.

Cash flow forecast

14.11   In order to manage the cash requirements it is usual to review the cash position on a regular basis, perhaps weekly but certainly no less than monthly. The forecast cash flow statement will be based upon information extracted from the income and expenditure budget over assumptions on debt collection and payments to suppliers, the capital expenditure budget and partners' drawings and tax payments.

The more sophisticated the cash flow document is, the more effective it will be as a management tool. Whilst it can be difficult to forecast the cash flows arising out of income, taking into account seasonal variations and detailed assumptions, monitoring the results against these expectations on a regular basis enables the firm's financing requirements to be managed effectively. It also provides credibility when exhorting fellow partners to increase their billing and debt-collection levels.

Variances which will occur between budget and actual must be considered carefully and action taken when appropriate. Some differences may merely be caused by timing whilst others will arise from a difference in volume, perhaps caused by excess business or lack of it, both at income and cost level. As the projection of income will influence the level of associated costs, if the income forecast is grossly inaccurate, the operating and cash budgets will fail to produce a realistic plan for the period. Therefore, it is essential to undertake regular reviews of the budget, which may involve rolling forward the actual cash balance every month. This has the advantage that cash forecasts will never get hopelessly out of line, as can happen if they are prepared only once a year.

Funding of partnerships and banking matters

Choosing a banker

14.12 As partnerships are very different in structure, law and operation to limited companies, the firm would benefit from dealing with a banker who understands the peculiarities and nuances of professional partnerships.

It is important that the banker understands how a partnership operates and, in particular, understands:

• the *Partnership Act 1890*;

• the *Limited Partnerships Act 1907*;

• the *Limited Liability Partnerships Act 2000*;

• the proposals and implications for the limiting of liability;

• how a firm finances its fixed assets and working capital;

• accounting and taxation principles and ongoing developments thereof; and

• how the economic cycle affects each profession.

Factors for success

14.13 The relationship between the firm and its banker, and the support that the firm receives, can be crucial to its success. The partners should be aware of the importance of this relationship and ensure that communication of key results and decisions is maintained.

In particular, the firm should look to demonstrate the following:

Management

(*a*) an understanding of the performance on both a client by client basis and a departmental basis;

(*b*) remuneration and training packages that ensure low staff turnover and the retention of key personnel, particularly major fee earners;

(*c*) an appropriate, responsible and managed approach to Professional Indemnity issues with adequate cover;

(*d*) efficient cost control systems to monitor overheads relative to fees;

(*e*) regular production of management accounts for partners and the bank on a timely basis including accurate and sufficiently detailed data;

(*f*) good credit and accounting control, particular in terms of:

(i) cash and cash flow management;

(ii) prudent and regular provisioning bases;

(iii)   efficient billing and cash collection procedures.

Structure

(*a*)   a workable partnership agreement;

(*b*)   taxation and drawings policies which are equitable between partners and prudent in terms of future liabilities and working capital requirements;

(*c*)   realistic policies for repayment of capital and current accounts as partners retire;

(*d*)   appropriate finance for known increases in capital expenditure;

(*e*)   efficient use and cost effective nature of property commitments;

(*f*)   procedures to avoid partners over-extending their personal financial position.

Market

(*a*)   market awareness;

(*b*)   good reputation within the market place;

(*c*)   expertise within the firm's chosen field(s);

(*d*)   the ability to retain and build on client relationships.

While a firm may strive to achieve these goals, its ability to deal with a changing working environment will impact on the banker's assessment of creditworthiness. How the firm deals with the following issues will therefore be of interest to bankers:

- Peer group competition and the impact on fee incomes;

- General decline in client loyalty makes markets more competitive and restricts profit growth;

- The cyclical nature of the market place and the type of work undertaken, such as consulting work;

- Potential downsizing to improve lacklustre performance.

The manner in which each firm deals with these issues will be influenced by its size and its extent of sophistication. However, the basic principles still remain.

Partners' financing

14.14   This chapter has so far considered the relationship between the firm and the banker, which will influence the level of finance available. An additional influence is the level of resources made available by the stakeholders to finance the business, represented by the partners' accounts shown on the balance sheet.

Partners' capital

14.15   There is no statutory or other requirement to use capital accounts to finance a firm. If, however, the firm chooses to use such a method, the partnership agreement will often contain a clause setting out details of the capital contributions to be made by the partners. If not, the partners are expected to contribute equally. The partners' capital represents the long-term capital base of the business; it also represents the cost of an individual's entry into the partnership which is returned upon retirement, subject to increases or decreases during the lifetime of the partner.

The capital to be put up by each partner may be based upon historic precedents within the firm. However, a number of partnerships also determine capital based on the level of profitability so that it reflects more closely the partner's share of the goodwill and value of the firm. Under this arrangement, capital may be calculated as a multiple of a number of years' profits. This approach takes into account that a new partner is buying into an existing business with a value attached.

Therefore if, on his retirement, the business has expanded and become more profitable, he will be due his share of that enhanced value by way of the revised calculation of his capital. In this situation, whilst the balance sheet of the firm shows the considerably higher partners' capital base, it will also show a value under goodwill to reflect the non-cash element.

Where capital is held in profit sharing ratios, it is often unnecessary to provide for interest to be paid. However, as capital and remuneration arrangements become more complex, it may be appropriate to allocate a prior share of profits as interest.

A new partner may find it prohibitively expensive to provide his share of capital immediately on joining, and the firm may consider that an incoming partner should be allowed to subscribe his share over a period of years by, for instance, not withdrawing part of his profit allocation. Alternatively he may use his own personal wealth, savings, mortgage or other assets, or he may take out a personal bank loan (see 14.34 below).

Depending on the availability of tangible assets as security, the bank may prefer to assist a partnership via personal loans to individual partners in addition to lending on the partnership account. If lending unsecured to a partner, the facility made available may only cover part of the overall requirement.

Partners' undrawn profits

14.16   In addition to the fixed capital provided by partners to fund the business, it is also common for partners to support the business through profits earned and left undrawn on current accounts. Every firm needs a policy on the level of partners' drawings. It is usual to provide that each partner may draw a sum on account of profits each month which represents a conservative estimate of his likely profit share for the year, subject to deduction of other expenses incurred on his behalf, e.g. health insurance, and after deduction of pension contributions and taxation.

There are many different practices as to when partners receive their profits over and above their monthly cash drawings. It is usual for firms to wait until the annual accounts have been produced when final profit shares have been agreed and taxation provided in accordance with the firm's policy. Partners may then be entitled to draw the balance due to them in their current account. However, some firms will be able to make payments of the partner's profits on account, perhaps after the six-monthly management accounts have been prepared, and again in stages during the preparation of the final annual accounts. The timing and extent of profit distributions will reflect historical practice, the level of partners' capital, third party finance and the cash flow forecasts.

As the current accounts also provide a form of financing the firm, most partnerships would expect partners' current accounts to remain in credit.

Where overdrawn current accounts occur, these should be dealt with carefully as they may give rise to tax difficulties. There may be particular cirumstances which have led to a partner's account being overdrawn and partnerships can, of course, agree specific procedures to deal with such a situation. Overdrawn balances may often arise on the more junior partners' accounts, where capital contributions are being transferred from the current account.

Retentions

14.17   A firm may also wish to restrict profit distributions by way of retentions, for example where cash resources need to be built up for the purposes of funding capital payments to departing partners.

Partners' taxation reserves

14.18   The accounting policy for providing for tax can vary from firm to firm. Best practice is to disclose on the balance sheet the tax payable within twelve months as a current liability, and to disclose the excess tax provisions in the partners' accounts. Firms which have a prudent policy for providing for tax, reduce the amount of cash available to partners on account of taxation payments which will be made perhaps one or even two years after the relevant profits have been earned. To the extent that such amounts are set up well in advance of the payments to the Inland Revenue, it would be considered reasonable to refer to these balances as part of the partners' financing of the firm, i.e. capital, rather than as creditors.

Financing by creditors

14.19   Creditors can provide a source of funding through the negotiation of terms of credit and the use of the related credit periods. The major creditors of partnerships are usually staff and taxes which, apart from partners' taxation, do not provide much scope for credit beyond the usual monthly cycle, although there may be opportunities to utilise payments to suppliers of other services.

Products and services available from financial institutions

Introduction

14.20   Whilst there are a number of partnerships which have, for historical reasons, always retained surplus cash balances within the firm, it is now much more common for banks and other providers of finance to be used in addition to funds provided by the partners themselves.

The following highlights specific issues the firm should be aware of when considering a type of finance.

Working capital/short term finance

14.21   Bank overdrafts are the most widely used form of external finance used by professional firms with nearly all using or having access to such facilities. Whilst they are technically repayable on demand and negotiated with the bank on what is normally an annual basis, they are often used to provide the whole of a firm's external funding requirements. Firms which operate using external finance on a permanent basis may find that overdraft funding provides an essential element of their financing facilities. However, short- and medium-term loan facilities may also be needed to meet non-working capital requirements and it should be borne in mind that overdrafts should never be regarded as a substitute for adequate medium-term finance.

The principal costs of an overdraft will be the variable interest rate, generally calculated on a day-to day basis with reference to the bank's base rate, together with an additional facility fee, usually a fixed percentage of the maximum facility. The overall interest rate charged by the bank will vary, depending on a number of criteria, including the historic and perceived profitability of the firm, its gearing levels, its length of relationship with the bank, its prospects, the quality of financial information it produces, and finally on the level of security provided to the bank.

Term finance

14.22   In general, loans are often used to finance specific capital expenditure, such as the cost of fitting out premises or enhancements to the firm's computer systems. A loan can be tailored to meet customers' capital expenditure needs and loan facilities should be allied to the life expectancy of the asset or work being undertaken. In practice, medium-term finance loans are usually put in place for a period of up to seven years and repayments are made on a regular basis to include both interest and capital. The interest cost can be either fixed at the beginning of the period of the loan or can be linked to the bank's own base rate in much the same way as an overdraft. The cost of a loan is likely to be greater than for an overdraft as the bank is making a longer term commitment. The extra cost borne by the firm should be taken into account when considering the value of the benefit of the bank's commitment and the reliability of this source of finance. When considering this, the firm should carefully review the terms of the loan. Term documentation is more complex than for overdrafts and other demand facilities, as numerous terms and conditions are included defining how both sides will act during the term of the loan, and setting out what will happen if the loan falls into default.

The Government Loan Guarantee Scheme, which is available for small firms only, is appropriate in situations where serviceability is proven but conventional security has been exhausted. The Small Firms Training Loan can be used by firms with less than 50 employees to meet the cost of training. This product offers preferential pricing and a capital and interest payment holiday.

Hire purchase and leasing

14.23 Hire purchase and leasing facilities are available with the former having the benefit of attractive capital allowances to reduce the tax liability.

Hire purchase and leasing arrangements can be set up quickly and generally offer fairly flexible repayment terms. The security for the advance is provided by the asset being purchased. Leasing, while more commonly used as medium-term finance, can also provide shorter-term funds.

The cost of such finance is often more competitive than overdrafts, but is only available for the funding of specific capital items rather than general working capital needs. As a result, firms have used hire purchase and leasing finance principally for motor vehicles, computer equipment and major office refurbishment.

Guarantees

14.24 In general, where firms have overseas offices it may be necessary for banks to provide cross-border bonding or guarantees. In particular, requests may be received to provide guarantees in favour of overseas banks, to cover advances and general banking facilities provided by those banks. Guarantees may also be required to cover lease obligations on commercial premises. Where firms are involved in competitive tendering for overseas contracts there may be a need for UK and overseas contract bonding facilities to be confirmed as part of the tendering process.

Contract hire and vehicle management services

14.25 Contract hire financial arrangements include a fixed monthly charge to reflect the capital costs of the vehicle, maintenance and depreciation. The contract would normally include a pre-determined mileage limit for each vehicle for the contract period.

On termination of the hire period, the contractor checks the condition of the vehicle and may look for a contribution in respect of damage beyond normal wear and tear, but otherwise would not look for further payments. Where the firm breaks the hire contract part way through the period, a payment would be due based on a number of months' hire charge.

The major benefits are that the firm knows the costs at the start of the contract period and so will not suffer from excess depreciation or maintenance expenditure, and the maintenance arrangements themselves are taken entirely out of the firm's hands, with commensurate savings and reduction in administration.

Firms which run fleets of ten or more vehicles can also be considered for specialist vehicle funding and management services such as accident management and vehicle rescue and recovery at competitive short-term rental rates.

Invoice discounting and debt factoring

14.26 Funds can be advanced against invoices (often up to 80% of invoice value) immediately upon agreement of the facility and, in the case of factoring, the factor (usually a bank group company) takes on the responsibility of the sales ledger management, credit control and debt collection. Facilities can be varied to cover all invoices for all buyers, all invoices for agreed buyers or selected invoices for agreed buyers. Both UK and overseas invoices can be covered by such facilities. Such financing arrangements would be most beneficial for firms that are expanding rapidly and require facilities to finance the increasing levels of their work in progress and debtors arising from this expansion. Factoring is becoming increasingly competitive and fees of about 2–3% of invoice value are the norm, together with a charge for cash advances. However, factoring has disadvantages such as the loss of immediate contact with the client, who may (unfairly) see factoring as a sign of financial weakness. Credit insurance is also available, either to cover this type of finance or as a stand alone product. For a fixed premium dependent on turnover, debtors are insured up to agreed limits per buyer and debt recovery is handled by the insurer.

Payment and cash management services

14.27 A full range of inward and outward payment facilities is available for sterling, euro and foreign currencies both within the UK and abroad. Electronic payment methods are increasingly being used with direct links between the firm and its bank, providing the facility to make payments directly into the banking system, to retrieve information on bank accounts, to reconcile accounts and download information directly into certain accounting software packages. For larger firms there is a range of options for cash pooling and netting.

Treasury management

14.28 Summarised below are a number of the options available to professional firms considering an appropriate place to deposit funds.

14.29 Cash flow budgets should reveal, among other things, the value of funds available for short-term investment. A professional partnership should take opportunities to manage money effectively over short periods of time. This may mean investing overnight, or for longer periods where appropriate, into the money markets to obtain the best rate for the funds. Funds should be placed with creditworthy institutions. The overall aim should be to secure the maximum interest possible, consistent with a satisfactory level of risk and the required degree of liquidity.

When considering the appropriate investment method, the certainty and accuracy of the cash budget will determine the amount and the length of time for which funds are available for investment. In addition, where there is any possibility that cash may be required prematurely to make unexpected payments, consideration must be given to the costs in the event of an early termination of the investment arrangement. Differences between investment opportunities arise principally over rates of interest, periods to maturity and the risk element. In broad terms, the shorter the life of the investment, the lower the interest earned and the riskier the investment, the higher the interest earned.

Banks can arrange for cleared funds in excess of a predetermined amount to be transferred automatically on a daily basis from the partnership's current account to an interest earning account. In addition, where the firm holds money on behalf of clients in general client accounts, they should discuss with the bank ways in which these funds can be used to offset, for interest purposes only, the cost of any borrowings the firm may have.

The professional partnership, like any business, should be actively managing its cash balances on a regular basis to ensure that it is obtaining the best use of its funds out of the money market and banking system and minimising the interest costs incurred on borrowings.

Managing surplus funds

Bank deposits

14.30   A range of commercial bank deposit products are available:

- variable rate deposit accounts including instant access, for relatively small balances;

- money market term deposits can be arranged at a fixed interest rate for a fixed period of between one day and five years. Withdrawals are not normally possible until the end of the term. The interest rate will depend on the length of the term and the size of the investment;

- certificates of deposit are issued by clearing banks. These carry a fixed rate of interest and are for a fixed term, normally between three months and five years, but can be sold by the investor during the term through the London discount market.

The minimum investment for money market deposits is £25,000 (one month), whereas certificates of deposit require a minimum investment of £100,000.

Special arrangements are also available for a firm's clients' money whereby interest can be earned on cheque accounts. On groups of clients' accounts higher interest rates can be obtained than would be available on each individual account.

Building society deposits

14.31   Competition for investors' deposits amongst building societies and between building societies and banks is keen, and as a result there are many different schemes.

Some societies (and banks) now offer accounts linked to a bank account with automatic transfers between the accounts as required. This is a useful way for firms to ensure that excess funds in a bank account can immediately be transferred to the building society.

Money market accounts

14.32   Several financial institutions, among them unit trust groups, merchant banks, finance houses and several commercial clearing banks, offer schemes which provide access to money market rates of interest for deposits which are not fixed. Withdrawals are allowed. The rates of interest available fluctuate with the London money market rates and the terms and conditions can vary substantially from scheme to scheme, so careful review of the terms and conditions is required.

Treasury bills

14.33   Treasury bills are issued by the Bank of England and are Government guaranteed. They are issued at a discount and redeemed at par after 91 days. The bills can be bought or sold on the discount market at any time until redemption.

Personal financing to partners

14.34   Banks often provide facilities to partners personally in addition to, or instead of, providing facilities to the firm directly and there are a number of related issues which arise. If structured correctly the funds lent to partners and used in the business will qualify for tax relief in respect on the interest charges arising on personal borrowing.

It is important that the firm makes the bank aware of the total facilities available to the firm and to the partners as a whole, when banks are considering the partner's own personal position. It is vital for a banker to establish the proportion of partnership capital which has been funded by personal loans to the partners, before a decision on financing can be made.

While joint and several liability in professional partnerships is attractive to a bank, partners may have committed personally or have ring-fenced their private assets without a banker's knowledge. It is therefore the overall position which will be considered when assessing where to position facilities.

The partner may find that the bank would prefer to arrange any new partnership debt with the partners personally if there is personal tangible security available, rather than lend directly to the firm.

If the firm were considering refinancing which involves new facilities with the bank, then it may also be a good opportunity to consider recycling partners' capital as this may enable the individual partners to structure their borrowings more tax efficiently. Care must however be taken to ensure that any such recycling is undertaken correctly as this is an area that the Revenue often review and will seek to deny tax relief for interest if it is undertaken incorrectly.

Security

14.35   When lending unsecured to the partners personally to fund partnership capital, the bank may prefer to lend only part of the overall requirement and therefore it may be necessary for the partner to provide part of the requirement from his own personal assets. Life cover should also be available to the bank to ensure that the partner's personal debts to the bank are cleared by the life assurance on death to avoid recourse to the firm or to the estate.

A banker may require a formal assignment of partnership capital to ensure that he has priority over other creditors in the event of death or bankruptcy.

The partner can choose between several different types of facility when arranging finance and should be aware of the different characteristics of each. In particular:

- term borrowing (over 364 days) tends to be more expensive than short-term borrowing;

- margins on loans linked to LIBOR can be lower than margins on base-rate linked loans;

- uncollateralised borrowing is more expensive than secured debt;

- financial strength of the partner will impact upon the rate of interest charged by the bank;

- the lower the perceived risk to the bank the lower the cost will be;

- facility arrangement fees are usually a feature of lending products and are most often calculated as a percentage of the maximum facility amount.

Practical considerations by banks

14.36 When the firm or partners individually consider appointing a new bank, there are a number of issues that the bank itself will want to consider. In particular:

(*a*) the type of profession and the economic conditions that affect it;

(*b*) the recent performance of the firm as evidenced by the financial accounts;

(*c*) the accounting policies used in arriving at these accounts, particularly the more subjective areas such as work in progress and provisioning;

(*d*) the partners' stake in relation to external finance and the overall level of gearing;

(*e*) professional indemnity history and outstanding or threatened claims;

(*f*) the taxation position of the firm and the manner in which it is accounted for in the firm's accounts;

(*g*) personal banking facilities;

(*h*) any recent press coverage or industry knowledge of the firm.

Partnership structures and legal matters in relation to banks

14.37 *Section 5* of the *Partnership Act 1890* sets out that the general principle of agency applies in the context of partnerships. This means that the bank could simply assume that, provided a partner acts within his actual authority or acts in the ordinary course of the partnership's business (implied authority), the partner's actions will bind the other partners jointly.

Even where there is no actual authority, in practice it is generally assumed that there is implied authority invested in the partner to open bank accounts in the firm's name, write cheques and borrow money for the purposes of the business.

In practice, reliance on implied powers is not generally satisfactory to a bank. A bank can ensure that the liability of all the partners is incurred by carrying out transactions only upon the express authority of all the partners, or pursuant to a mandate signed by all the partners.

Where persons hold themselves out as partners, they may incur the liability of the partnership. Common examples of these are 'salaried partners' who do not share in the partnership profits. However, commonly, the equity partners agree to indemnify such partners against liabilities arising against the partnership.

Extent and duration of an individual partner's liability

14.38   The laws dealing with a partner's liability are as follows:

In law any partner in a partnership is liable without limit for the partnership debts, except if he/she;

* is a minor;

* has limited liability under the *Limited Liability Partnerships Act 2000*;

* has limited liability under the *Limited Partnership Act 1907* (but in this case he/she will not be allowed to take part in the management of the partnership);

* has obtained the agreement of the individual clients of the partnership to a limited liability contract. This will apply only to those clients individually and not to all debts generally. Also, partnerships must not contravene the *Unfair Contract Terms Act 1977*, nor the *Solicitors Act 1974* which voids limited liability of solicitors.

In law, when a partnership borrows money, everyone who is a partner at the date when the debt is incurred will normally be subject to the obligation to repay. Retiring partners will remain bound but new partners will have no direct obligation to the lender.

Partners continue to be liable for the partnership's debts incurred before their death (or dissolution in the case of a partner which is a company), insolvency or until actual notice is given on their retirement or replacement.

The bank may control the duration and extent of any partner's liability through lending documentation signed by all the partners. For new partners, the bank could arrange for them to sign documentation agreeing to be bound to previously incurred partnership debt, and likewise arrange for retiring partners to be released from their liability.

Partnership property

14.39   Partners may agree amongst themselves what assets are to be treated as partnership property and may change the ownership of that property from partnership property to that of a specified partner or partners, subject to laws governing this area such as the *Law of Property Act 1925*.

Many professional partnerships occupy leasehold premises. The *Law of Property Act 1925* states that a leasehold (or indeed a freehold) property cannot be vested in more than four people, hence usually four partners are identified to act as nominees or, alternatively, the lease is held in the name of a nominee company. Generally, modern leases provide for the other partners to guarantee the obligations of the nominee partners.

Bank collateral

14.40   The firm should be aware of the following issues relating to any collateral that a bank may require:

(*a*)   security or charges given by the partnership to the bank should be executed or signed by all the partners on behalf of the partnership, or pursuant to the authority of all the partners;

(*b*)   security given by partners is generally taken in the same way as that given by tenants in common;

(*c*)   land vested in some of the partners as trustees for themselves and the other partners can be charged using special trustees' charge forms;

(*d*)   guarantees may be taken from parties other than the partners to secure partnership debt;

(*e*)   in some cases, the bank may obtain a formal assignment of a partner's partnership capital to secure the liabilities of that individual partner, and to prevent monies being released to third parties in the event of death or bankruptcy of that partner.

The bank may also require the firm to produce regular management accounts for its review as well as the annual accounts. The nature of the accounting policies and the sophistication of the regular reporting will influence the bank's reliance upon the accounts and hence the level of collateral that may be required.

14.41   Firms considering conversion to an LLP should review the impact of this new legal entity on its creditors, most notably the bank and the landlord:

(*a*)   Members of an LLP are not liable for the firm's debts, consequently the firm's bankers may seek individual recourse of the members.

(*b*)   Contingent liabilities will have to be declared and in some cases put onto the balance sheet and provided for (e.g. annuities to former partners). Also, members' undrawn profits or current accounts will no longer be shown as partners' funds but rather as liabilities of the LLP. Such a firm's balance sheets will look quite different post conversion to LLP and that may affect the perception of risk by the creditors, impacting the firm's credit rating and pricing.

(*c*)   An LLP does not have a share capital and there is no legal restraint on capital, or for capital maintenance requirements at all.

(*d*)   Creditors will be able to register a charge over the LLP assets, including a fixed and floating charge, although this is likely to have limited value given the nature of the assets and the circumstances at the time the charge may need to be relied upon.

There may be additional hidden costs of transition to an LLP due to the novation of many contracts, renegotiating leases and bank facilities, client appointments, public relations, stationery, new signage etc.

ABC Partnership – 'A' department

Management Accounts 2000/2001

	July 2000			July 1999	YTD July 2000		YTD July 1999
	Actual	*Budget*	*Variance*	*Actual*	*Budget*	*Variance*	*Actual*
Income							
Chargeable Time	**	**	**	**	**	**	**
Over/(Under) Recovery	**	**	**	**	**	**	**
Sundry	**	**	**	**	**	**	**
Costs							
Personnel	**	**	**	**	**	**	**
Establishment	**	**	**	**	**	**	**
Computer	**	**	**	**	**	**	**
Office	**	**	**	**	**	**	**
Finance	**	**	**	**	**	**	**
Other	**	**	**	**	**	**	**
Net Profit	**	**	**	**	**	**	**
Billing by Partners	**	**	**	**	**	**	**

	July 2000	June 2000		July 1999			
Working Capital							
Debtors	**	**		**			**
Provisions	**	**		**			**
Net Debtors	**	**		**			**
No of months fees	**	**		**			**
Work in progress	**	**		**			
Provisions	**	**		**			
Net work in progress	**	**		**			
No of months fees	**	**		**			
Total lockup	**	**		**			
No of months fees	**	**		**			

Capital Expenditure
Actual to date
Budget to date

Budget for year

Note: Costs would be analysed in detail on a supplementary schedule.

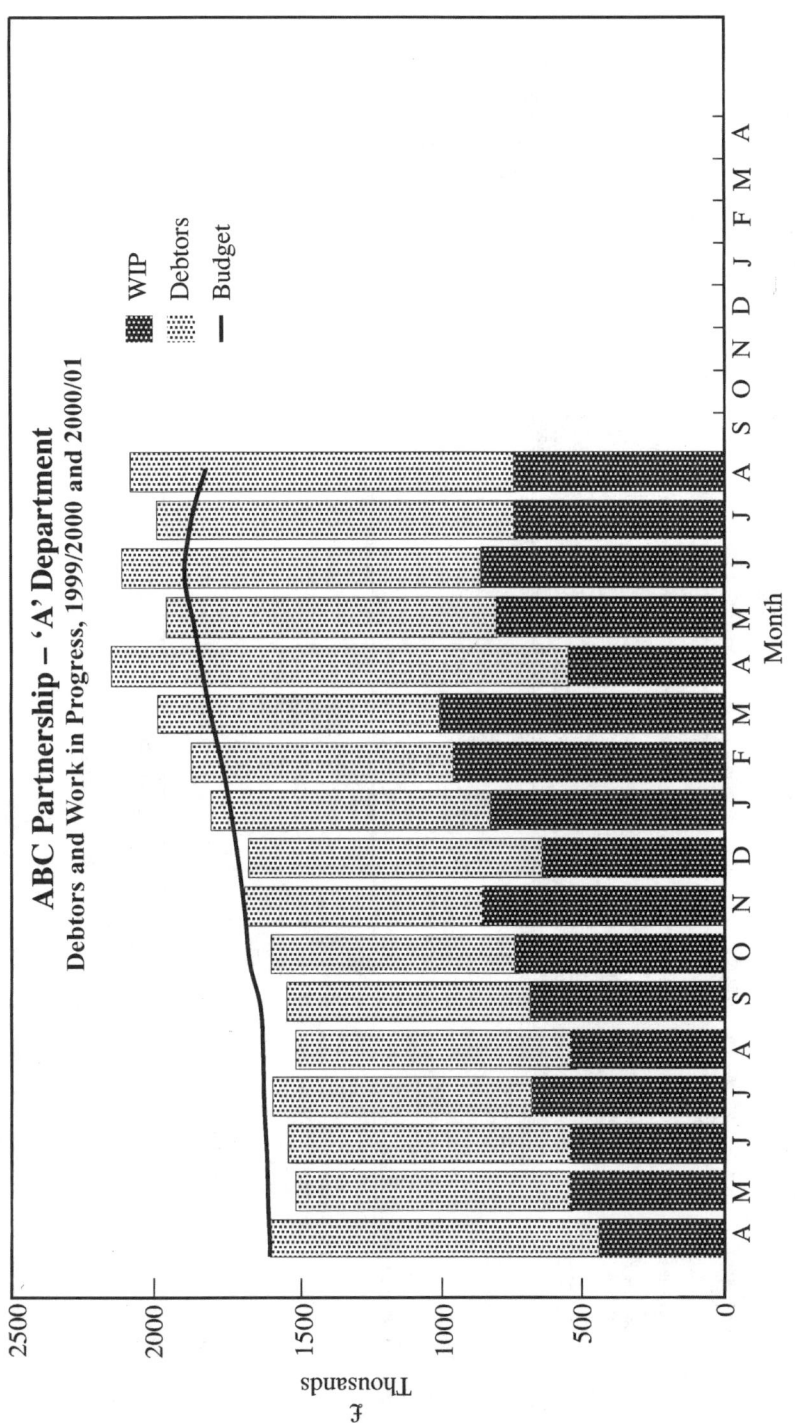

ABC Partnership – 'A' Department

Debtors and Work in Progress, 1999/2000 and 2000/01

ABC Partnership
A Department
Chargeable Time Summary

	May	Jun	Jul	Aug	Sep	Oct	Nov	Dec	Jan	Feb	Mar	Apr	YTD	Total Year
2000/01														
Compliance	280,000	403,000	407,000	⋮	⋮	⋮	⋮	⋮	⋮	⋮	⋮	⋮	1,090,000	
Ad Hoc	135,000	106,000	155,000	⋮	⋮	⋮	⋮	⋮	⋮	⋮	⋮	⋮	396,000	
	415,000	509,000	562,000	⋮	⋮	⋮	⋮	⋮	⋮	⋮	⋮	⋮	1,486,000	
Total Budget	415,000	466,000	457,000	308,000	395,000	345,000	333,000	243,000	356,000	368,000	383,000	333,000	1,338,000	4,402,000
Compliance %	67%	79%	72%	⋮									73%	
Ad Hoc %	33%	21%	28%	⋮									27%	
1999/2000 Actual														
Compliance	240,000	300,000	310,000	193,000	266,000	197,000	207,000	151,000	195,000	223,000	230,000	211,000	310,000	2,730,000
Ad Hoc	90,000	80,000	94,000	82,000	98,000	121,000	74,000	107,000	95,000	90,000	140,000	109,000	94,000	1,182,000
	330,000	380,000	404,000	275,000	364,000	318,000	281,000	258,000	290,000	313,000	370,000	320,000	404,000	3,912,000
Compliance %	73%	79%	77%										77%	
Ad Hoc %	27%	21%	23%										23%	

Chargeable Time - Variances

Bar chart — y-axis: 180,000 / 160,000 / 140,000 / 120,000 / 100,000 / 80,000 / 60,000 / 40,000 / 20,000 / —; x-axis: May, Jun, Jul, Aug, Sep, Oct, Nov, Dec, Jan, Feb, Mar, Apr. Legend: On Last Year, On Budget.

Chapter 15

Insurance

Introduction

15.1   The insurance requirements of professional partnerships are varied and a wide range of insurance covers are available. These are designed to protect the partnership itself, individual partners and employees. Each partnership must focus on the specific requirements of its business.

This chapter discusses the main insurance covers available.

(*a*)   Professional indemnity (PI) insurance.

    (i)   Purchasing PI insurance.

    (ii)   Description of a PI policy.

    (iii)   Key elements of a PI policy.

    (iv)   Selection of the sum insured and self-insured excess.

    (v)   Claims procedure.

(*b*)   Other insurances for professional partnerships.

    (i)   Office building.

    (ii)   Office contents.

    (iii)   Employer's liability.

    (iv)   Public liability.

    (v)   Money.

    (vi)   Motor.

    (vii)   Permanent health insurance.

    (viii)   Medical insurance.

    (ix)   Protection for dependants.

        (A)   Partners.

        (B)   Employees.

This list is not exhaustive. Firms may have specific insurance cover that is not mentioned. We make no excuse for concentrating on professional indemnity cover, which is essential to most professional partnerships.

Professional indemnity insurance

15.2 Professional indemnity insurance has been described as an insurance which indemnifies the professional against pecuniary loss resulting from their negligent act, error or omission which causes their client or a third party to suffer loss. The standard of care required of the professional is that of a person who is reasonably competent or skilled in that particular profession. Excellence is not required but merely the ability to exercise knowledge and skill by using a reasonable standard of care. It has been suggested that the professional should give the standard of professional service to their clients which they, when in the client's position, would be content to receive. Under English Law such a standard should avoid, or at least minimise, the risk of negligence. However, a professional could still be liable under the law of other countries as required standards may differ.

The need for PI insurance

15.3 Professional indemnity insurance is available to those individuals who provide a service, e.g. solicitors, doctors, accountants, architects and consulting engineers, to name but a few, and is intended to protect them against claims from aggrieved clients or third parties, primarily, but not now solely, based on allegations of negligence in the performance of their particular duties.

The last few years or so have seen an alarming increase in claims against professional people. In many cases, the insurance market has provided the means of absorbing these claims and continues to do so. Therefore, the decision to have a PI policy should form a crucial part of a firm's commercial thinking bearing in mind the increasing frequency of litigation.

Litigation is no longer the last resort for disgruntled clients who perceive they have received a substandard service or faulty advice, especially where these services have been provided for a fee.

The rules of certain professional institutes, including the Law Society and the RICS make PI insurance a requirement for some professions. While it is not a requirement for all professionals it is strongly advised for all firms which provide fee-based advice.

Even where the professional's innocence is upheld by a court, the costs of defending litigation can be very high and frequently could cost hundreds of thousands of pounds.

Purchasing PI insurance

15.4   Having decided to purchase a PI insurance policy, the first aspect to consider is the completion of the proposal form which must be submitted to the underwriters. The proposal forms are designed to give the underwriters an understanding of the firm so they can assess the degree of exposure which might be presented. Questions are asked about the particular business activities, the size and scale of operations and the firm's history.

The information given is extremely important because it is used by underwriters to rate the risk, and therefore determine the premium, as well as the terms and conditions of the policy. Therefore, proposal forms must be completed with great care.

Non-disclosure

15.5   Insurance contracts are treated by the courts as a contract of the utmost good faith. This means that it is incumbent upon the firm to provide all relevant material information to the underwriter on the risk which he is asked to accept. Therefore, any material non-disclosure or misrepresentation will entitle the underwriter to avoid meeting the particular claim he may be asked to consider, and he may be entitled to avoid the policy in its entirety.

Non-disclosure or misrepresentation does not have to be deliberate to enable the insurer to avoid the policy. A positive duty to disclose material facts is imposed, not just to answer the questions asked.

All those within the firm who could be aware of material facts must have the opportunity to disclose any matters which need to be disclosed to underwriters. Therefore, it is vital to circularise all appropriate partners, managers and employees before finally completing the proposal form. At renewal there is effectively a double duty to notify all claims or incidents which may give rise to claims during the policy period as well as disclose these incidents to the new insurer.

The duty of disclosure to the underwriters does not end with the completion of the proposal form but continues right up to the date when the policy commences, which could be a number of weeks later. Therefore, full disclosure and prompt reporting of all circumstances which constitute a claim or which might give rise to a claim are absolutely essential.

Differentiating risk

15.6   Completing a proposal form also gives the firm the opportunity to differentiate its risk from that of others in the same profession. Therefore, as much additional information as is appropriate must be provided. Some points of differentiation for underwriters are shown as follows:

(*a*)   Provide underwriters with a copy of the firm's operation and procedures manual.

(*b*)   Provide underwriters with details of the firm's approach to risk management.

(*c*)   Provide underwriters with a copy of your corporate brochure.

(*d*)   Try to meet with the underwriters to establish a face-to-face relationship.

(*e*)   Provide underwriters with copies of contract conditions used.

Access to underwriters

15.7   Considerably fewer underwriters write PI insurance than write some other general classes of insurance. A specialist market exists and incorporates many of the traditional large UK insurers supplemented by major Lloyd's participation and the involvement of the UK offices of large international insurance groups. Internationally, many countries have their own domestic PI market but only London and, to a lesser extent, USA markets operate globally and insure worldwide risks.

Description of a PI policy

15.8   Professional indemnity policies operate on a 'claims made' basis, i.e. any claim will fall to be dealt with under the policy in force when such claim is 'first made' by a third party and notified to the underwriters during the policy period. Claims made after the period will not be covered even if the work giving rise to the claim was performed in the period.

The assured should notify the underwriters as soon as any claim is made against them, and in some policies this is a condition precedent to the insurance coverage.

The aim of PI policies is to provide the assured with an indemnity in respect of the assured's legal liability to third parties for any third party claim which satisfies the following necessary requirements.

(*a*)   The third party claim must be for compensatory damages and such indemnity will include the claimant's costs, as well as the assured's costs and expenses of defending the proceedings. The question of costs is particularly important as claims against professionals generate substantial legal fees and expenses.

(*b*)   The claim must be made against the assured during the policy period.

(*c*)   The policy will provide an indemnity in respect of financial loss arising from any claim in respect of any legal liability arising out of the professional's activities and duties.

(*d*)   That the claim arises out of the provision of the services described in the proposal form. This is a particularly important point and the firm should ensure that the business description provided is wide enough to encompass all of its activities. This is something that should be reviewed annually when the policy is renewed. For example if a firm of solicitors takes the decision to offer personal financial planning services this should be notified to the insurer.

(*e*)   That the claim relates to a negligent act, error or omission which is alleged to have occurred after the retroactive date specified in the schedule of the policy.

The retroactive date limits the time from when the policy becomes effective, so the further the date goes back, the better. If possible, a policy providing full retroactive cover, without limitation, is of course preferable.

Important elements of a PI policy

15.9   These elements are comprised of the following.

(*a*)   Traditionally, policies are renewed annually. In certain cases the period can be extended but this is very rare.

(*b*)   The policy will generally only respond to claims brought anywhere in the world other than the United States of America and/or Canada. Cover can be extended where necessary.

(*c*)   The sum insured being provided can either be on an 'aggregate' or 'any one claim' basis. Having an aggregate sum insured costs less, but it also limits the sum insured available to pay claims in any one year to the limit chosen. For example, if a sum insured of £1,000,000 in the aggregate was chosen, this would be the maximum amount the underwriters would pay in any one year towards one claim or all claims notified to them during the policy period. Selecting the sum insured on an any one claim basis is the more expensive option, but allows the sum insured to apply to each claim that is notified during the policy period.

(*d*)   The policy will also cover all costs and expenses incurred by underwriters in the investigation, defence or settlement of any claim made against the firm. These costs and expenses can either be included within the sum insured or be in addition to that sum. The difference can be significant.

The more restrictive option is to have the costs and expenses included within the sum insured. This means that the sum insured the firm chooses can not only be eroded by damages awarded against them but also by costs and expenses incurred in defending the claim. The best cover option is to have the costs and expenses in addition to the sum insured.

(*e*)   It is generally a requirement for the assured to carry a self-insured excess or a deductible. By carrying a self-insured excess an assured has a vested interest in his own claims experience because each time a claim is made, he has to contribute towards it. It also cuts out nuisance claims being notified under the policy which, if frequent and involving underwriters in incurring costs to defend them, could influence the premium that they may charge when the policy renews.

(*f*) While some underwriters can be approached directly, the majority of policies are purchased via brokers who have access to all of the insurance underwriters both in the UK and overseas.

An assured who instructs a broker does not need to maintain a first class, professional broker capability and level of expertise within their organisation.

Why employ a broker?

15.10 Together with their broker a professional partnership should consider the following questions.

(*a*) What cover do we need?

(*b*) Which underwriter can offer the cover?

(*c*) Which underwriter can offer the broadest cover?

(*d*) Which underwriter is most competitive?

(*e*) Which underwriters have a reputation for not willingly paying claims?

(*f*) Where does one find the resources to arrange the cover and to negotiate claims settlements?

(*g*) How does one keep up with changes in the insurance market and the law?

(*h*) Have we examined all our options?

Selection of the sum insured and self-insured excess

15.11 Some professional bodies give guidance to their members on this subject, and this often takes the form of a multiple of the largest individual fee or annual fees. However, this is a very rough guide. Often this is a commercial decision weighing up price against exposure but, when doing so, the firm must bear in mind that the sum insured must be adequate for a settlement that may well be made years after the initial notification was made under the policy.

The decision should also be influenced by other exposure factors, such as the nature of the firm's work, where it is being done (e.g. the USA), the nature of the firm's clients, protection (if any) given by contractual terms, and current legal precedents.

When considering the appropriate level of self-insured excess, again it is important to weigh up the premium savings against the extra exposure that will have to be faced, usually on a per claim basis. The self-insured excess required by the underwriters depends upon various factors. These sums can range from a couple of hundred pounds to millions of pounds, depending on the size of the firm. If the self-insured excess requirement is potentially onerous, an alternative may be to establish a captive insurance company.

A captive insurance company

15.12 The objective of a captive insurance company is to create a formalised financing vehicle to support the firm's risk retention. The advantages and capabilities of such a vehicle over less formalised alternatives are as follows.

(*a*) It provides a central focus for implementing a firm's risk management strategy and complements the risk prevention efforts of management by providing a means of measuring the results of actions taken.

(*b*) It allows the firm to participate in a variety of ways in its own insurance programme and, to varying degrees, as an insurer that issues a policy for 100% of the risk, as a co-insurer alongside the conventional market or as a reinsurer.

(*c*) The firm can secure easier access to the reinsurance market which may be cheaper, more flexible and traditionally takes premiums in arrears, resulting in a cash flow advantage.

(*d*) By acting alongside and/or in substitution for conventional under-writers, it may be possible to exert a competitive influence when premium rates are competitive and a stabilising and smoothing influence when premium rates are increasing.

(*e*) It could, over a period of time, reduce the level of premium paid to the commercial insurance market, thereby reducing the costs to the firm.

If a firm decides that the captive insurance company option is viable for them then the specialist services of risk management advisers will be needed.

Claims procedure

15.13 It is now quite common for substantial claims to be made against professionals for a variety of complaints. Having a PI policy allows a firm to pass the claim to the underwriter who will manage the problem and, where appropriate, contest the third party claim. Cover is usually inclusive of legal costs which have been authorised by the insurer. It is the firm's responsibility to notify its underwriters as soon as a claim is made or as soon as it considers that there are circumstances which could give rise to a claim ultimately being made. Brokers can help with any notification given to underwriters, in its subsequent dialogue with them about the claim, and ultimately any settlement.

Once the claim is made or the circumstances which might give rise to a claim are notified to the underwriters, the underwriters have the right to appoint their own solicitors and/or specialist representatives to act on their behalf. In these circumstances, the firm must actively cooperate with the underwriters' appointed representatives to enable the claim to be efficiently and effectively defended. It is important that the firm does not make any admission of liability or offer of settlement without the concurrence of its underwriters. This would be contrary to the terms of the insurance policy and may in certain circumstances result in the rejection of the claim by the underwriters.

General insurance for professionals

Other insurances for professional partnerships

15.14   Partnerships can usually obtain most of the cover they need from a combined 'package' policy, available from many insurers. One document will provide most of the cover needed, e.g. office buildings, office contents, loss of income, employer's liability, public liability and money.

To ensure that the cover is purchased on the correct basis, points to consider include the following.

(*a*)   *Utmost good faith.* As is the case for PI insurance, general insurance contracts are determined by the doctrine of utmost good faith. The parties must disclose all material facts or the policy may be declared invalid. Particular care is needed to ensure that full and accurate details of the risk are provided, including previous claims. Where there is a question as to whether or not an aspect is material, it is best to disclose it.

(*b*)   *Underinsurance.* Office combined policies will usually provide for the replacement of property on a 'new for old' basis. Allowance should be made for telephone equipment and other property such as photocopying machines and computers leased or rented unless the rental agreement states otherwise. Therefore, the sum insured must reflect the new replacement cost of all the contents. If not the firm may be penalised should the firm need to make a claim.

(*c*)   *Definition of business.* The definition that appears on the policy must embrace all the firm's activities. If a loss occurs that is outside the definition the insurers may repudiate liability – a frequent omission is that of 'property owner', which is essential when buildings are owned.

(*d*)   *Claims reporting.* Whilst it has always been necessary to report claims promptly to comply with the policy conditions, this duty has increased following the Woolf Report. The most crucial area is that involving injury to employees or third parties where immediate notification to an insurance broker is essential.

(*e*)   *Terrorism.* The standard cover provided by an insurer is currently limited to £100,000 per policy or section of cover. For many firms this will be insufficient and it will be necessary to effect additional cover to ensure full protection. This can be either by a 'top up' of the existing cover or by a separate policy.

An hour or two should be devoted to fully reviewing the partnership's cover at least once a year to ensure that the cover is updated to reflect changes in the business.

Office buildings

15.15   Most policies will provide cover on an 'all risks' basis, rather than the contingency (e.g. fire, storm etc.) being specified. The cover operates in respect of all loss or damage, other than losses which are excluded. Therefore, the 'all risks' format is recommended and normally the difference in premium is small.

Buildings are usually defined to include outbuildings, walls, gates, fences and the owner's fixtures and fittings. Therefore, it is essential the sum insured is calculated accordingly with due allowance for professional fees and compliance with any local authority rebuilding requirements.

Exclusions

- Excess, usually £250.

- Damage caused by thieves (usually covered by the contents section).

- Storm damage to fences and gates.

- Breakage of glass (usually covered by the contents section, or this can be included separately).

- Maintenance costs (the loss must be fortuitous).

- Subsidence (can be added).

Extensions

- Subsidence.

- An index-linking of the sum insured.

Points to watch

- Some structures, particularly listed buildings, require special consideration to ensure the policy contains a local authority clause that allows for extra costs in rebuilding in accordance with revised planning requirements. Appropriate provision should be made within the sum insured.

Office contents

15.16   As with office buildings, the choice of cover is between 'all risks' and 'fire and perils'. The former is generally preferred. The office contents can normally be extended to include cover for reinstatement of documents including client files and title deeds, plans and the like in the firm's trust.

Exclusions

•   Excess, often £250.

•   Many policies will exclude theft losses which do not involve an actual break-in, i.e. a 'walk-in' theft is not covered.

•   Losses from unattended cars.

•   Electrical or mechanical breakdown, erasure of information, etc.

•   Theft of gold, silver, jewellery, etc. whilst unattended or outside a safe when the premises are closed.

Extensions

•   Some policies will provide for equipment such as laptop computers used away from the oce on either a temporary or permanent basis, but this should be checked. The firm may also need to include items that are used at an employee's private dwelling.

•   Damage to the building caused by thieves.

•   Cost of replacing locks following theft of keys.

•   Damage to glass.

•   Some policies give wider cover for computers, e.g. for reinstatement of data following erasure by any cause and increased cost of working cover following loss, damage or breakdown of the computer equipment. (A separate specialist policy may be the best option where high values are involved.)

Points to watch

•   Most policies provide cover for the contents whilst at the firm's specified premises with an extension for a lesser amount whilst at other locations in the UK. A few provide the extension for cover in Western Europe. Cover for contents temporarily in use anywhere in the world can normally be purchased if required for portable computers, etc.

•   Some policies require that computer equipment is specified within a separate sum insured.

•   Some insurers impose a minimum standard of security expected at the premises within the text of the policy. Frequently this is not well highlighted and could enable the insurer to repudiate a claim if the requirements are not being followed.

Loss of income

15.17 This provides an indemnity in respect of loss of income and the additional expenditure incurred in maintaining the business following a material damage loss. The cover operates for an agreed period following the loss, commonly 12–36 months.

Exclusions

- Losses which do not follow a claim under the material damage section.

- Losses which result from incidents at customers'/suppliers' premises (cover might be available if requested).

Extensions

- The accidental failure of electricity supply due to a fortuitous event at the power station.

- Accountants' costs in preparing a claim.

Points to watch

- Some policies provide automatic cover with a pre-set limit of indemnity. However, the 'average' condition normally still operates and therefore it is essential that the standard cover is in fact appropriate. Of course, if a 36-month indemnity period is given the sum insured must be at least three times the annual figure.

Employer's liability

15.18 This provides an indemnity in respect of the partnership's legal liability to employees in respect of death or bodily injury arising in the course of their work. The usual limit of indemnity is £10,000,000 for each occurrence.

Exclusions

- Injury sustained by manual workers (if you have any 'non-clerical' workers these must be disclosed to the insurer).

- Injury which occurs from activities outside the geographical limits of the policy. Usually insurers provide 'anywhere in the world cover' for business trips, so long as no manual work is involved.

- Injury to employees as passengers of motor vehicles (this will be covered under the motor policy). However, your legal liability to an employee who is driving a motor vehicle in the course of your business is covered under the employer's liability policy.

Extensions

- Most policies give a wide definition of 'employee' which includes work experience and voluntary workers.

- The legal costs in representation in respect of a prosecution under the Health and Safety legislation.

Points to watch

- Whilst the standard cover of £10,000,000 seems substantial, the limit may prove insucient if an incident occurs involving several employees, particularly if there is a delay in the case being decided by the court. Of course, it is the limit of indemnity in force at the time of the loss that is operative. 'Top-up' cover is available.

Public liability

15.19 The purpose of this section is to provide an indemnity to the firm in respect of its legal liability to third parties for bodily injury and loss/damage to their property. The limit of cover is normally £2,000,000 for each claim. (This limit should be treated as a minimum.)

Exclusions

- The excess, normally £250 in respect of third party property.

- Liability for loss/damage to goods in your custody and control. (Usually the exclusion does not apply to the personal effects of employees or visitors to the premises.)

- An incident that does not involve third party injury or damage.

- Liability in respect of any incident where the *Road Traffic Act* applies.

- The professional indemnity risk.

- Libel and slander.

- Breach of copyright.

Extensions

- Legal liability for injury or damage following the sale/supply of a product.

- Liability in respect of damage to rented premises (naturally the cover provided is that which is outside the requirements of any lease), i.e. if a lease makes you responsible to insure the building this extension will be insufficient.

- A cross-liability clause is needed where several companies are covered under the same policy. (This allows each company to claim indemnity against actions brought by others who are joint insured's under the policy – as if they had separate policies.)

Points to watch

- Many policies specifically exclude liability arising from manual work away from the premises.

Money

15.20   This section will provide cover for 'money' as per the policy definition. The usual definition is: 'Current coin, bank notes, currency notes, cheques, giro cheques, travellers cheques, bankers drafts, giro drafts, bills of exchange, money orders, postal orders, current postage stamps, unused units on franking machines, revenue stamps, National Insurance stamps, National Savings certificates, premium bonds, luncheon vouchers, trading stamps, consumer redemption vouchers, gift tokens, credit card sales vouchers, VAT purchase invoices, airline tickets, machine tokens and telephone cards.'

Exclusions

- Losses which exceed the limits of cover. Typically the following limits will apply as standard:

– Non-negotiables	£500,000
– Money in transit	£1,500
– Money on premises whilst open	£1,500
– Money in safe	£1,000
– Other money on premises when closed	£250
– Money at a private residence	£500

- Theft involving employees, unless not noticed within the 'discovery period' of the policy – this is usually seven days in most policies.

- An overnight theft loss from a safe when the keys are left on the premises.

Extensions

- Personal accident assault benefit, which provides a lump sum benefit for serious injury and a weekly disablement benefit following an assault on an employee whilst carrying the firm's money. It should be noted that frequently the standard benefit is for minimal sums but these can be increased at nominal cost.

Points to watch

- People travelling abroad on the firm's business will need additional cover as cover normally operates only in the UK (a Business Travel policy is usually best).

Motor

15.21   Motor insurance cover is available at four levels – comprehensive, third party fire and theft, third party only and fire and theft only (for vehicles which are 'laid up' and not in use).

Liability to third parties is included under all covers (except fire and theft only) in respect of all sums for which the firm may be legally liable. The limit of indemnity is normally £5,000,000 in respect of commercial vehicles and unlimited in financial amount for private cars and motor cycles.

Exclusions

* Excess, can be own damage only or all claims, and may apply to windscreens.

* Loss of use, depreciation, wear and tear, mechanical or electrical breakdown.

* Loss of value following repair.

* Loss or damage arising from theft or any attempted theft whilst the ignition keys have been left in or on your vehicle.

Extensions

* Rugs, clothing and personal eects.

* Territorial limits can be extended for foreign travel. EEC countries are included within a European certificate in respect of private car types whereas commercial vehicles are usually limited to cover in the UK, with prior notification required to extend.

* Unauthorised movement of third party vehicles.

* Contingent liability which provides an indemnity to the partnership in respect of a third party claim following an accident when an employee was using their own vehicle on the firm's business without proper motor insurance cover.

* Loss or theft of keys.

* Hire car provision either free of charge or at discounted rates.

* Breakdown assistance.

* Legal services and advice.

Points to watch

- Motor fleet insurance is generally only available where at least five vehicles are operated.

Permanent health insurance (PHI)

15.22 PHI is protection against loss of earnings in the event of sickness, injury or disability. It can be effected by individuals, partners or by companies or partnerships on behalf of their employees.

PHI for partners

15.23 The maximum amount of cover available to partners depends on their level of earnings. As earnings are assessed under schedule D, cover will normally be based on the certified profit and loss accounts together with the related Inland Revenue tax assessment by reference to gross profits less all expenses. The maximum level of cover is generally 50% of earnings. This limit is set by the various insurance companies which offer PHI for partners and it is possible, in certain circumstances, to negotiate a slightly higher maximum level of cover (say 65% of earnings).

Should the PHI benefit become payable it is paid directly to the partner and is free of any income tax liability.

For high earners benefits may be restricted by a maximum cover ceiling which varies between insurance companies. Benefits from all PHI policies are normally taken into account in calculating maximum benefits. The limits are set so as not to discourage an individual's financial incentive to return to work.

At the outset of the policy it is necessary to select a 'waiting period'. This is the period during which an individual is unable to work before payments commence. The longer the waiting period, the cheaper the premium. Waiting periods are commonly four weeks, 12 weeks, 26 weeks or 52 weeks.

Another aspect which affects the level of premiums charged is the occupation of the individual. Insurers categorise occupations into classes on a scale of one to four, one being the lowest risk, e.g. administrative duties, and four being the highest risk. Age at commencement and sex also affects the rate of premium as does an individual's state of health, as the policy has to be underwritten.

In the event of a claim, benefits are normally paid weekly or monthly. Benefits cease when the individual is able to return to work, dies or on the selected termination date, whichever is the earlier. The maximum age to which a policy can be written is State Pension Age.

It is possible to select a policy which automatically increases claims in payment by a fixed percentage such as 3%, 5% or 7% or in line with the Retail Prices Index (RPI). It is also possible to choose a policy under which cover increases by a fixed percentage or in line with RPI. Normally the premiums for these policies will rise in line with both the increase in cover and age.

Some policies will pay claims if the individual is unable to follow his/her own occupation prior to the sickness, injury or disability whilst for other policies claims will only be paid if the individual is unable to follow any occupation for which they are qualified.

If the individual is able to return to work but only on a part time basis or has to take a less well paid job, a proportion of the benefit will normally be paid.

Taxation

15.24   There is no tax relief on personal contributions. Following the *Finance Act 1995* benefits paid from April 1996 will not be taxed.

Group permanent health insurance

15.25   A group PHI policy is an arrangement set up by an employer for its employees to replace salary in the event of sickness, injury or disablement resulting in the individual being unfit for work. Economies of scale mean that premium rates for group PHI cover are cheaper per individual than the cost of individual policies. Many partnerships establish such schemes for their employees. The same pricing principles applies to group PHI schemes as for individual policies in that the average age and sex of the employees will be considered as will the occupations of the employees and the length of the 'waiting period'.

In addition to insuring a percentage of each employee's salary (sometimes called salary continuance benefit), it is possible to insure the employer pension contributions, either based on salary prior to disability or on notional pay in line with what the employee would have earned had he/she been fit to work. If the pension scheme is contributory, the employee pension contributions will normally be deducted from the salary continuance benefit. It is also possible to insure the employer's national insurance contributions but the employee's national insurance contributions would be recovered from the salary continuance benefit.

The maximum level of cover is normally 75% of salary less the State Long Term Incapacity Benefit (SLTIB). The example below shows how this works.

Example

	£
Salary £30,000 pa × 75% =	22,500
Less SLTIB (2000/01)	3,510
PHI benefit payable	18,990

Group PHI will normally be designed so that the 'waiting period' (the period during which an individual is unable to work before payments commence) coincides with the period during which the firm continues to pay an employee who is unfit for work.

There are three main types of group PHI scheme.

(*a*) *Flat pay*. This scheme provides a fixed percentage of pre-disability pay, usually 50%.

(*b*) *Integrated pay*. This type of scheme provides a fixed percentage of pre-disability pay less state benefit (normally the full single person's state incapacity benefit).

(*c*) *Net pay*. A net pay arrangement provides benefit based on a percentage of net pay (i.e. after tax) less the state benefit the individual actually receives.

It is possible to select cover which increases in payment either by a fixed percentage or in line with the Retail Price Index (RPI).

For schemes with a small number of employees, (normally fewer than two) the premium is costed each year based on the cover and age of employee, waiting period and termination date. The termination date will normally be state pension age but it is possible to effect limited payment which will limit a benefit paying period to two or five years.

For larger groups of employees, normally two or more, the premium is costed on what is known as a flat rate basis. This means that the premium is calculated as a percentage of the total sum assured and is normally guaranteed for a two-year period provided that there is not a material change in membership.

Free cover limit

15.26 Group schemes provide a free cover limit which is the level of cover that the insurer is prepared to offer without requiring evidence of health. Cover in excess of the free cover limit is underwritten, which means that the individual is required to provide details of his state of health and may also be required to undergo a medical examination and other tests.

Taxation

15.27 Premiums paid by the employer are allowable as a business expense and are not taxed as a benefit-in-kind on the employee. Generally any benefit payments are taxed under PAYE when passed to the employee.

Finance Act 1995

15.28 Since April 1995 changes have been made to the state provision of incapacity benefit (previously invalidity benefit). The method of testing whether an individual is entitled to state benefit has changed and it is now far more difficult to qualify. In addition, state incapacity benefit has ceased to be tax free and is now taxed as income. As a result insurance companies are redefining the integrated pay formula, although the way in which they will do this has yet to be decided.

Reducing partners' PHI costs

15.29 Many insurers of group schemes will allow a separate class of benefit to be created for partners which sits on top of the employee group PHI arrangement. In this way partners can benefit from group premium rates and free cover levels. However, the cost of the cover is the partner's personal responsibility and in all other aspects the benefits are treated as though they are arising from an individual policy.

Private medical insurance

15.30 Private medical insurance provides for the cost of medical treatment and hospitalisation. Typically, the providers of such cover are provident associations such as BUPA. Various levels of cover are available so that a choice can be made as to the hospital to be used and, to some extent, the type of treatment covered by the insurance. For example, some providers permit dental and oral maxillofacial treatment and procedures to be included in the cover as a matter of course, whereas others insist that cover for such treatment and procedures can only be provided as a 'bolt on' feature.

The provider will specify the maximum cost which can be covered and this might be, say, £250 for a minor operation up to, say, £3,000 for a complex operation. The costs specified will usually include the fees of the surgeon, anaesthetist and aftercare.

It is possible to arrange for immediate members of the family (spouse and children) to be included in the arrangement and some providers will allow non-married partners to be included.

Clearly the cost of the insurance varies with the level of cover chosen. The cost of medical insurance for partners is not allowed against tax as a business expense and the individual partner is responsible for his share of the premium cost, which would normally be deducted from his profit share.

Many partnerships put in place group arrangements for their employees. The cost of the arrangement is allowed as a business expense and any employee earning in excess of £8,500 per annum would be liable to pay income tax on the cost of providing the insurance as it is treated as a P11D benefit. The cost to the employer is allowable as a business expense.

Partners can normally effect cover for themselves through the employee arrangements but their tax position would be exactly the same as for an individual policy. The major benefit to the partner is that this results in a substantial reduction in the premium payable.

Protection for dependants

Partners

15.31   Any life assurance taken out by a partner to cover dependants is normally effected via individual life assurance policies (see also Chapter 26) with the partner being responsible for maintaining premium payments.

Before considering the most appropriate policy it is important to consider objectives. For example, if the requirement is to ensure that dependants are left with sufficient income to maintain their standard of living, it is important to assess the level of the income requirement and then capitalise this on the basis of annuity factors at the time.

The next question is to consider the term of the cover. If it is to provide for dependants whilst children are in full time education the policy term could be linked to when the youngest child might leave university. As a rule of thumb most families' insurance requirements are at their height between the ages of 30 and 50, reduce between 50 and 60 and increase after 60 when issues such as inheritance tax planning raise their head.

The simplest form of life cover which provides a lump sum on death is term assurance. This is one of the cheapest forms of cover as benefits are paid on the death of the life assured within a specified period and at the end of the period the cover simply expires with no investment value. There is no tax relief on premiums paid to the policy unless it is taken out under personal pension plan provisions (see 25.2 and 25.3). However, the proceeds will be free of all tax if the policy is properly established in trust.

Placing a policy in trust for beneficiaries ensures that benefits will not form a part of the deceased's estate. Failure to place benefits under trust could result in inheritance tax being paid if the deceased's estate exceeds the inheritance tax threshold. The trust can be discretionary, which is favourable for term assurance policies as they have no investment value, or a flexible interest in possession trust, a *Married Women's Property Act* trust or other absolute trust. Writing the policy in trust ensures that the proceeds are paid in accordance with the policyholder's wishes.

There are several types of term assurance: the most common is level term assurance, where the level of cover is set at the commencement of the policy and it remains unchanged until the term of the policy, which is selected at the outset, expires.

To protect the cover from inflation, there is the option of taking out an increasing term assurance. As the name implies, the original sum assured may be increased at a fixed rate or in line with the RPI each year during the term of the policy.

An option to renew the policy at the end of the term may be attached to term assurances. Another option available is to convert the policy to either endowment or whole of life policies. These options have to be selected at the commencement of the policy. At the end of the term the option to renew or convert will be available without any further medical underwriting but the premium will be based on premium rates and the age of the life assured at that time. These options can be useful where cover may be required for longer than the original selected term, but premium rates are more expensive than for level term assurance.

Family Income benefit may be taken out to provide an income instead of a lump sum on death. Again, at commencement the benefit and term must be selected. The benefit on death will be paid in the form of annual or monthly income from the date of death to the end of the term of the policy. It is, in effect, the same as lump sum assurance cover, but paid out in the form of a regular tax free income.

It is also possible to provide for partners' death-in-service under an unapproved group life scheme. This offers the normal benefits of a unit-costed group arrangement, such as levels of free cover (which can be extremely valuable) and simplified administration plus an averaged cost for the partnership grouping which may undercut the individual policy pricing. However, there are severe tax penalties on second and subsequent deaths in any grouping. This necessitates specialised advice to devise an effective strategy for the arrangement.

Employees

15.32   A partnership is allowed to provide death in service benefits for its employees. Benefits can be in the form of a lump sum, spouse's pension and/ or dependant's pension. The maximum lump sum that can be paid is four times final remuneration. Any spouse's/dependant's pension cannot be more than two thirds of the deceased employee's maximum prospective pension and the continued total of any spouse's/dependant's pensions must not exceed this maximum prospective pension.

The cost of providing the benefit is tax deductible as a business expense in the partnership accounts. Death in service schemes are established under trust and the partnership can appoint the trustees of the scheme. Employees should be encouraged to complete a 'nomination' form detailing to whom they would like the benefits to be paid in the event of death. The trustees would take these wishes into account when distributing the lump sum benefit in the event of a claim. The lump sum benefit is paid to beneficiaries free of inheritance tax.

The principal advantage of a group arrangement apart from the tax deductibility of premiums centres on the relatively cheap cost of cover (in comparison to individual policies) and the fact that these schemes provide a free cover level so that benefits below this level do not require underwriting regardless of the health of the individual.

Most partnerships will wish to provide cover for employees as it is the cheapest form of employee benefit, does not require a great deal of administration and helps ensure that their employees' dependants are adequately covered in the event of the employee's death in service.

Critical illness cover

15.33   Critical illness cover has been available in the UK for some ten years and until recently there has been little evidence that employers or individuals have been enthusiastic about effecting critical illness policies. However, market penetration is currently around 10% of the working population so it is clear that it is a growing market.

Generally it is not considered to be as vital as other forms of benefits such as pension, life assurance and permanent health cover. Many people confuse the benefits being provided by permanent health cover and critical illness. Permanent health cover as described above is designed to pay a regular income which can continue up until retirement for someone who is unable to carry on with their occupation. The illness concerned may not necessarily be life threatening.

Critical illness cover is designed to pay a lump sum, free of tax, in the event of one of a defined list of critical illnesses being diagnosed. Generally the medical conditions concerned are severe and potentially life threatening. The attraction of a tax free lump sum in the event of a critical illness is the fact that it could be used for purposes such as repayment of a mortgage or other debt or to help fund private medical care.

The IFA Association Critical Illness working party has agreed with a number of insurers in this market place seven core illness definitions in their policies which are listed below:

(i) Cancer.

(ii) Heart attack.

(iii) Kidney failure.

(iv) Major organ transplant.

(v) Coronary artery bypass surgery.

(vi) Multiple sclerosis.

(vii) Stroke.

In addition, many policies will provide cover in the event of total permanent disability (TPD).

More recently, model wordings for 13 non-core conditions have also been agreed with the insurers and these cover areas such as loss of limbs or deafness where specific levels of additional cover can be provided. In addition model wordings have been agreed in relation to the nine exclusions listed below explaining in what circumstances they will apply:

(1) Aviation.

(2) HIV/AIDS.

(3) Criminal acts.

(4) Living abroad.

(5) Drug abuse.

(6) Self-inflicted injury.

(7) Failure to follow medical advice.

(8) War and civil commotion.

(9) Hazardous sports and pastimes.

Many potential policyholders have felt that the lack of more precise wordings has impacted upon the growth in the market so these model wordings will in due course set minimum standards although providers will be free to offer additional cover if they wish.

For group schemes, premiums paid by the employer are tax deductible but taxed as a benefit in kind on the employee. Many group schemes nowadays are established as voluntary arrangements whereby the employee pays for the cover, normally as part of a flexible benefits package so that the premium is deducted from the payroll, and the employee then benefits from lower group rates.

In partnership situations professional partners will in most cases effect individual critical illness policies and set the level of cover to meet liabilities which might present a problem in the event of a critical illness diagnosis such as repayment of a loan or payment of school fees. The premiums paid to individual policies are not tax deductible but the benefit in the event of a claim is again tax free. Some insurers will offer group policies to partnerships which can be very cost efficient.

In many respects critical illness cover is likely to grow in popularity as most people will have friends or relations who have been affected by a critical illness so that the validity of the cover is apparent. To some extent the market place is still in its infancy and it is important therefore to effect policies with companies who have good claims payment records combined with competitive premium rates. Critical illness cover certainly complements a protection package which should also comprise life cover, private medical insurance and permanent health cover.

Chapter 16

Control of Clients' Money

Fundamental principles

16.1 Solicitors, chartered surveyors, chartered accountants and estate agents and those partnerships engaged in the provision of financial services are subject to client money rules issued by the relevant professional or regulatory bodies. Certain basic principles are common in all the various rules.

(*a*) Client money must be separated and distinguished from partnership money by the use of different bank and building society accounts.

(*b*) Proper books of account must be maintained.

(*c*) Client account balances belong to the individual clients. It is their money and can only be used as directed by them. Use of one client's money to settle the liability of another client is not permitted.

(*d*) When client money is held or received, an accountants' or auditors' report must be submitted stating whether client money rules have been complied with.

The main objective of the various rules is therefore to ensure fair treatment of clients' money and to maintain adequate book-keeping and recording systems in order to avoid any confusion of clients' money with the partnership's own money.

The Financial Services and Markets Act 2000

16.2 The *Financial Services and Markets Act 2000* (*FSMA 2000*) replaced the *Financial Services Act* (*FSA 1986*) during 2001. *FSMA 2000* has replaced all of the Self Regulating Organisations and the Securities and Investments Board with one statutory regulator, the Financial Services Authority (FSA).

Where firms do not carry out mainstream investment business (as defined by FSA), but whose only investment business arises in the context of the provision of professional services, these businesses will continue to be regulated by their Designated Professional Body (DPB) (formerly known as their Recognised Professional Body (RPB)), such as the ICAEW or the Law Society. Where firms carry out mainstream investment business, they will be regulated directly by the FSA. The ICAEW regulate their members' investment business through the Financial Services (Investment Business Clients' Money) (Chartered Accountants) Regulations 1988 and the Institute's Investment Business Regulations. Both these regulations interact with, and must be considered alongside, the Institute's Investment Business Clients' Money Regulations. For client monies that do not fall within the definition of investment business client monies, the Client Money Regulations apply and it is these which are summarised later in this chapter.

The Law Society currently regulates its members' investment business through the Solicitors Investment Business Rules (SIBR), which came into force in 1990 but for which an updated version, the SIBR 1995, came into force in June 1996.

If a partnership is already a member of a DPB, it should first consider seeking authorisation to carry on that type of investment business from its current regulator. In certain circumstances, where the new type of investment business is significantly different from its current business or is considered to be mainstream investment business, it may be necessary to seek membership of the FSA, in order that the new investment business can be properly regulated. Some professional bodies are not currently DPBs. Therefore, partnerships that are members of these bodies will need to apply to the FSA if they wish to carry out investment business.

This chapter does not seek to review in detail the DPB's regulations dealing with investment business but to concentrate on clients' monies generally and, in the following paragraphs, to comment on the regime operated under the umbrella of the *FSMA 2000*.

Separation of clients' money and assets

16.3   The regulatory body that the partnership applies to has a responsibility to protect investors or, in other words, the partnership's clients. Therefore, the regulatory bodies have developed detailed rules to cope with the situation where the partnership holds money or assets on behalf of its clients. The basic principle behind the client money and asset rules is to safeguard and protect any clients who have deposited funds or assets, such as securities, with the partnership. This is done by separating out clients' funds and assets into bank accounts that include the words 'client account' in the title of the accounts and are supported by trust letters to ensure that, if a partnership is wound up, the clients' funds and assets are segregated from the assets of the partnership, with only the latter being available to settle outstanding partnership liabilities.

A partnership may conduct investment business without the need to hold clients' funds and assets, although in certain circumstances the type of business operated will be made more efficient if they hold such funds or assets. The right to hold clients' money and assets can be requested in the initial application or in a separate extension of permitted business after the investment business has been set up.

Financial resources

16.4   As well as rules covering the holding of client money and assets, the FSA has developed financial resources rules with which the partnership must comply. The requirement of FSA members to maintain certain levels of financial resources is designed to ensure that any member participating in investment business has sufficient assets to support the business. This should protect the investors from poorly run or inadequately financed investment businesses and reduce the likelihood of such an operation being wound up at short notice.

When a partnership's application to FSA has been accepted, it will be given a permitted level of business that imposes constraints on the scope of the investment business that the partnership can operate. The level of financial resources required by the FSA is linked to this permitted business level, with more risky types of business requiring higher levels of financial resources.

Once a partnership has calculated its financial resources requirement, it must ensure that its actual financial resources remain in excess of this requirement. The method of calculating the actual financial resources is set out in the FSA's rulebook. Certain assets and liabilities of the partnership may be disallowed in these calculations and, as a general rule, the more risky the type of business, the more liquid the assets of the partnership must be.

The type of financing the partnership selects and the assets in which it invests is, therefore, crucial to the financial resources calculation. As a result, the partnership must consider the level of financial resources that the investment business will require before deciding whether to apply for authorisation to undertake the investment business.

The partnership must report its financial resources position to the regulator on a regular basis that can range from monthly to annually, depending on the regulator and the type of business operated. However it must also monitor the level of financial resources on a day-to-day basis and therefore have the necessary systems in place to do so. If at any point the partnership finds itself with a financial resources deficit, it has a duty to notify the regulator immediately.

Conduct of business

16.5   One of the key principles underlying the formation of the FSA was to protect investors. The FSA requires the maintenance of high levels of standards among their members as one of the key ways to ensure that this protection exists, with an emphasis on senior management being responsible for ensuring the high standards are maintained. Each member must comply with the rules set out in their rulebook that cover this area. Generally, these rules are known as the Conduct of Business rules and cover the level and type of professional standards with which the member must comply. Conduct of Business rules can be unspecific, but instead give a general indication of what the FSA expects. Despite this, they are still just as important an area of the FSA's rulebook as any other area, because the maintenance of high standards is seen by the regulator as an important method of preventing mistreatment of the client or investor.

Monitoring

16.6 As already stated, if a partnership is regulated by FSA, it must monitor its level of financial resources on a day-to-day basis. This is just one section of the rulebook with which the partnership must demonstrate compliance on a regular basis. Procedures adopted by the partnership as required by the rulebook must be documented in a formal manner in a compliance and procedural manual. This manual also sets out the ways in which the partnership intends to ensure that the procedures adopted comply with the rulebook. The manual will detail the regular checks that must be carried out by the partnership to monitor this compliance. While it is the partners who are directly responsible for compliance with the rulebook and ensuring that these checks are carried out, the partnership must appoint a compliance officer who oversees the whole compliance operation.

In addition to the internal monitoring that must take place, there are two external types of monitoring. The first is by the regulatory body itself. The FSA carries out regular visits to their own members to ensure that they are complying with their rules. The second is by auditors appointed by the partnership. The auditors have a duty to report to the regulatory body on certain aspects of financial resources, internal systems and client money.

Summary

16.7 Business that is regulated under *FSMA 2000* can be a profitable area for partnerships. However, this type of work is considered high risk and will lead to additional costs being incurred. These costs include the additional financial resources that must be put in place to meet the requirements and the increased administration costs, both internally, as more time must be devoted for compliance, and externally, in fees to both the regulator and professional advisers. It is, therefore, an area that must be thought through in great detail prior to any decision being made.

Professional requirements

16.8 Partnerships of solicitors, chartered surveyors and estate agents and chartered accountants may often receive and hold money belonging to their clients. The handling of this money is regulated by the professional bodies of which the partners are members.

Law Society

Introduction

16.9   Solicitors are responsible for large sums of their clients' money. The Law Society's rules aim to prevent the solicitor mixing his own money with that of the client. The Law Society monitors its members to ensure that the handling of money is being carried out in accordance with the rules. This is normally achieved by an annual report by an independent reporting accountant.

Even though authority may be delegated to one partner, responsibility for maintaining a proper book-keeping system is shared by all (including salaried partners). Any misappropriation or error by one partner is therefore the responsibility of all the partners. All partners are responsible for ensuring that any breaches of the rules are immediately remedied.

Current rules

16.10   Rules dealing with money belonging to solicitors' clients are made under the *Solicitors Act 1974* and are as follows.

(*a*)   Solicitors' Accounts Rules 1998 (SAR).

(*b*)   Rules 14 and 26 of the Solicitors' Investment Business Rules 1995.

(*c*)   Rules 9(3) and 12–16 of the Solicitors' Overseas Practice Rules 1990.

The Solicitors' Accounts Rules

16.11   The SAR includes the following definitions:

(*a*)   *Client* – 'any person on whose account a solicitor holds or receives a client's money'.

(*b*)   *Client account* – 'a current or deposit account at a bank or deposit account with a building society in the name of the solicitor or his or her firm in the title of which the word "client" appears'.

(*c*)   *Clients' money* – 'money held or received by a solicitor on account of a person for whom he or she is acting in relation to the holding or receipt of such money either as a solicitor, as agent, bailee, stakeholder or in any other capacity'. Excluded are:

(i)   'money held or received on account of the trustees of a trust of which the solicitor is a controlled trustee'; or

(ii) 'money to which the only person entitled is . . . one or more of the partners in the firm'.

Clients' money

16.12   Whilst clients' money is defined in 16.11 above, specific instructions from a client take precedence over the rules. These instructions may be in writing or acknowledged in writing.

In general a solicitor cannot treat himself or herself as a client or conduct personal or office transactions through a client account. There are however some exceptions, as follows.

(*a*)   If a firm is acting in a conveyancing transaction on behalf of both a principal and his or her spouse (not being a partner in the firm), the firm is acting for both jointly and the matter must be conducted through a client account.

(*b*)   If a conveyancing matter involves a building society or other lender for whom the firm is also acting, that part of the transaction involving the lender's money must be dealt with through a client account.

(*c*)   Where the firm conducts a conveyancing transaction on behalf of an assistant solicitor, he should be treated as a client and any money should be kept in a client account, even if it is the assistant solicitor who is handling the matter. Money held by a solicitor in respect of PAYE and VAT is not the client's money and should not be processed through a client account.

Stakeholder money is client money unless it is placed in an account operated jointly by two firms. The latter is not client money because it is not under the control of either firm. This applies equally to any money held jointly with a third party. It is best practice for jointly held money to be recorded separately in the accounting records.

Payments into a client account

16.13   The rules specify circumstances in which money must or may be paid into a client account. No other receipts are permitted to be paid in.

(*a*)   Client money received must be paid into a client account. This must be done without delay, which in normal circumstances means the day of receipt or the next working day.

(*b*)   Money that may be paid into a client account at the discretion of the solicitor is:

(i) trust money;

(ii) firm's own money for the purpose of opening or maintaining an account;

   (iii) money to replace any sum withdrawn in contravention of the rules;

   (iv) mixed receipts which contain a proportion of client money;

   (v) settlement of bill of costs, provided this money is withdrawn within seven days.

Withdrawals from a client account

16.14   The rules detail when money may be paid from a client account. Other withdrawals are not permitted without the express permission of the Law Society Council. The rules allow clients' money to be paid from a client account as follows:

(*a*)   to or on behalf of the client;

(*b*)   for the reimbursement of the solicitor provided the client's authority has been obtained;

(*c*)   for the solicitor's fees but only after a bill or written intimation of a bill has been delivered by him to the client;

(*d*)   into another client account.

Other payments allowed include:

   (i) payments of trust money;

   (ii) repayment of the firm's own money when no longer required;

   (iii) repayment of money paid in contravention of the rules.

As noted above it is at the discretion of the solicitor whether these are paid into a client account in the first instance.

Books of account

16.15   Solicitors are required to keep accounting records showing their dealings with all clients' money. The rules require that these records are properly written up at all times. The records should include for each client:

(*a*)   a client cash account or a column of a cash book;

(*b*)   a client's ledger or column of a ledger.

The records must be such that the account balance on each client's ledger can be extracted. Dealings with non-client money should be maintained separately but in the same manner.

In addition solicitors are also required to keep a record of all bills of costs which distinguish profit costs and disbursements and all written intimations delivered by the solicitor to his or her clients.

At least once in every five weeks the solicitor is required to:

(i) compare the total balances shown by the clients' ledger accounts (including trust money) with cash account balances;

(ii) prepare reconciliation statements explaining any differences;

(iii) reconcile the cash account balances to the balances shown on bank statements and building society pass books.

The reconciliation statements must be preserved. Other documents required to be preserved are as follows:

(A) accounting records for six years;

(B) bank statements for six years;

(C) all paid cheques for two years (these can be held by the bank);

(D) copies of bank withdrawal authorities for two years.

Interest

16.16   The rules detail the circumstances in which a client should receive interest on clients' money.

(*a*)   When the solicitor places the money on deposit in a separate designated account he must account to the client for the interest earned on it. In certain circumstances set out in the rules, he must also account for a sum equivalent to the interest which would have accrued if the money received had been kept on deposit, or its gross equivalent if the interest would have been net of tax.

(*b*)   Where sums are not held in a separate designated account, interest is based on the amount and the time held as set out in the rules.

Except as provided by these rules, a solicitor is entitled to retain personally interest on clients' money placed in a general client account. However, where there are variable balances, or the money is held intermittently with no individual sum within the table in the rules, interest should be accounted for when it is fair and reasonable. The fair and reasonable basis also applies to money transferred to or from a designated account while it is undesignated. Detailed rules concerning the relevant rate of interest are also set out in the rules.

The accountant's report

16.17   Within six months of the end of the financial year, every solicitor who handles clients' money or money subject to a controlled trust, is required to submit to the Law Society an accountant's report certifying that he or she has complied with parts A and B, rule 24(1) of part C, and part D of the SAR. The report must be delivered once in each period from 1 November to 31 October. The accounting period to which the report relates must normally cover not less than twelve months and should correspond to the period for which the accounts of the partnership are ordinarily made up. However, some flexibility may be allowed in the first period with the agreement of the Law Society.

Part F of the SAR sets out the nature and scope of the work to be carried out by the reporting accountant, including: who is qualified to give an accountant's report, the work that the accountant must perform on the client and office accounts for both client money and controlled trust money, when an accountant's report is required, and the format of the accountant's report. The rules do not require a *Companies Act* style audit of the solicitor's accounts nor do they require that accounts be prepared. The rules specify a test examination of the solicitor's accounts. Evidence of failure to comply with the SAR by such tests would lead to further testing to ascertain the extent and reasons for the failure.

The accountant is required to extract or check the extractions of balances on the client ledger on at least two dates selected by him or her during the accounting period. At these dates the accountant must compare the total liabilities to clients with the cash account balances of client accounts. He or she must also reconcile those cash account balances to those confirmed direct to him or her by the bank or building society.

A solicitor may decline to produce to the accountant any document which the accountant may consider it necessary to inspect, on the grounds of confidentiality between the solicitor and client. In these circumstances, the accountant must qualify the report to that effect, setting out the circumstances.

In many practices, clerical and book-keeping errors will arise. In the majority of cases these may be classified by the reporting accountant as trivial breaches. The reporting accountant is not required to report on trivial breaches due to clerical errors or mistakes in book-keeping, provided that they have been rectified on discovery and the accountant is satisfied that no client has suffered any loss as a result.

To report under the SAR, a reporting accountant must be a member of the ICAEW, ICAS, ICAI, the Association of Chartered Certified Accountants or the Association of Authorised Public Accountants. The reporting accountant must not have been disciplined by his professional body and must not be a partner or employee of the solicitor.

The accountant must also be either a registered auditor under *section 35* of the *Companies Act 1989*, an employee of the registered auditor, a partner or employee of a partnership which is a registered auditor, or a director or employee of a company which is a registered auditor.

The accountant is required to use an appropriate work programme and to complete and sign a checklist produced by the Law Society. This is kept by the solicitor for three years and has to be produced to the Law Society on request.

The checklist is effectively a summary of the work required under the SAR. There are two conclusions for each test:

(*a*)   whether the test is satisfactory; and

(*b*)   if not, whether the breaches should be notified in the accountant's report.

The checklist also requires cross-references to the accountant's own working papers.

The reporting accountant is required to report on material departures from the Law Society guidelines for procedures and systems for accounting for clients' money. The reporting accountant is not required to undertake a detailed check on compliance with these guidelines. Instead, the accountant only needs to report those matters which come to their attention during the course of the work required under the SAR.

The SAR require the rights and duties of the reporting accountant to be set out in a letter of engagement with standard terms, giving the accountant a right to report directly to the Law Society where there appears to be cause for concern, and a duty to report on termination of the appointment.

The terms of engagement also include:

(*a*)   the requirement for the accountant to produce the 'checklist' to the solicitor; and

(*b*)   the requirement to provide any further relevant information to the Law Society on request in response to a whistle-blowing report.

The letter of engagement has to be signed by the solicitor (or a partner or director of the firm) and by the accountant. Both parties must keep it for three years from the termination of the engagement and produce it to the Law Society on request.

The accountant has the right to report the following matters direct to the Law Society:

(*a*)   evidence of theft or fraud affecting clients' money or money subject to a controlled trust;

(*b*)   any other information likely to be of material significance in determining whether any solicitor is a fit and proper person to hold clients' money or money subject to a controlled trust.

The accountant also has a duty to report directly to the Law Society if his appointment is terminated following:

(*a*)   the issue of a qualified accountant's report;

(*b*)   the indication of an intention to issue such a report; or

(*c*)   the raising of concerns prior to the preparation of an accountant's report.

The reporting accountant is also given a measure of protection from breaching client confidentiality. The solicitor has to confirm in the letter of engagement that he waives his right of confidentiality in respect of any report made, document produced or information disclosed to the Law Society, provided that such reports, etc. are made in good faith. This applies even if the accountant is later shown to be mistaken in his belief that there was cause for concern.

Controlled trusts

Definitions

16.18   'Controlled trustee' is defined as meaning a solicitor who is a sole trustee or co-trustee only with one or more of his partners or employees. A 'controlled trust' is defined as a trust of which a solicitor is a 'controlled trustee'. 'Trustee' includes a personal representative.

'Trust money' is defined as money which is held or received by a solicitor which is not client's money and which is subject to a trust of which the solicitor is trustee, whether or not he or she is a controlled trustee.

Treatment of controlled trust money

16.19   Where a controlled trustee holds or receives trust money that money is to be paid in to a separate controlled trust account for that particular trust, unless it is paid into a client account.

Controlled trust money is required to be treated substantially in the same way as client money except for the payment of interest and reconciliations for passbook operated accounts. Rule 24, SAR regarding the payment of interest on client accounts does not apply to controlled trust accounts. Where monies are held in passbook operated accounts, the reconciliations referred to in 15.15 are required to be performed once every fourteen weeks rather than once in every five weeks.

When controlled trust money is paid into a client account, the record-keeping obligations are the same as those set out in 16.15 above.

The Royal Institution of Chartered Surveyors

Introduction

16.20 Chartered surveyors, as part of their work, often receive and hold money belonging to their clients. The handling of client money is regulated and independent reporting accountants are used to monitor compliance in much the same way as solicitors. The most established of the professional bodies is the RICS which has the most comprehensive rules. The rules of the Incorporated Society of Valuers and Auctioneers and National Association of Estate Agents are based on the RICS rules to a greater or lesser extent and therefore only the RICS rules are considered here.

Current rules

16.21 Rules dealing with clients' money are as follows.

(*a*) Members' Accounts Regulations (MAR).

(*b*) Accountants' Report Regulations (ARR).

It should be noted that unlike the SAR, the MAR have no statutory authority. However the rules were made by powers vested in the RICS royal charter, and therefore have the force of bye-laws.

Key definitions in the Members' Accounts Rules

16.22 The MAR provides a number of definitions. These include the following.

(*a*) *Client* – 'any person or body for whom a member or his practice is acting in any capacity; and any other person or body on whose behalf the member holds or receives clients' money'.

(*b*) *Client account* – 'a current or deposit account at a bank or building society into which clients' money is paid'.

(*c*) *Discrete client account* – 'a client account into which clients' money is paid which belongs exclusively to one client'.

(*d*) *Client's money* – 'any money received or held by a member or his practice over which he has exclusive control and which does not belong to him, or his practice or a connected person'.

(*e*) *Exclusive control* – 'means that control of clients' money is restricted to a member, connected persons and employees of his practice'.

Clients' money

16.23 The definition of clients' money is extremely wide (see notes to definitions MAR) but does not include money to which the only person

269

beneficially entitled is the member himself. This means that a member cannot treat himself or herself as a client and as a consequence cannot conduct personal or office transactions through a client account. In addition, where a practice acts as managing agent in respect of properties owned solely by one or several of the partners of the practice, any money received is not clients' money and should not be placed in a client account. Where, however, properties are owned jointly by a principal of a practice, with a person other than a principal, the principal is trustee with the co-owner. A trustee is not beneficially entitled to money held for another person. He is acting for the trust and such money must be paid into a client account.

The definition of clients' money excludes money over which members do not have exclusive control. This means that if a client can separately withdraw money from an account, it is not clients' money for the purposes of the Regulations. Members who operate such accounts must notify their clients in writing that they are not regulated by the MAR and therefore not covered by the Clients' Money Protection Scheme of the RICS. Members are required to retain a copy of the written notice with their own records for production to their reporting accountants and, if necessary, to the Institution's Investigating Accountant.

The word 'client' and the name of the member's practice must appear in the title of every client account. The title of a discrete client account must in addition also bear the full name of the client.

Payments into a client account

16.24   The rules specify circumstances in which money must be or may be paid into a client account. No other receipts are permitted to be paid in.

(*a*)   Client money received must be paid into a client account. This must be done without delay which in normal circumstances means the day of receipt or the next working day.

(*b*)   Money that may be paid into a client account at the discretion of the surveyor is:

(i)   the firm's own money for the purpose of opening or maintaining an account;

(ii)   money to replace any sum withdrawn in contravention of the rules;

(iii)   mixed receipts which contain a proportion of client money.

Withdrawals from a client account

16.25   The rules detail when money may be paid from a client account. Other withdrawals are not permitted without the express permission of the council. The rules allow:

(*a*)   Client's money to be paid from a client account as follows:

    (i)   to or on behalf of the client;

    (ii)   for the reimbursement of the surveyor's proper expenses;

    (iii)   for the surveyor's fees;

    (iv)   into another client account.

(*b*)   Other payments allowed include:

    (i)   repayment of the firm's own money when no longer required;

    (ii)   repayment of money paid in contravention of the rules;

    (iii)   repayment of the proportion of a mixed receipt which is not clients' money as soon as the member's entitlement can be quantified.

Books of account

16.26   Members are required to keep accounting records showing their dealings with all clients' money and any other money dealt with by members through a client account. The rules require that these records are properly written up at all times. The records should include for each client:

(*a*)   a client cash account or a column of a cash book;

(*b*)   a client's ledger or column of a ledger.

The records must be such that the account balance on each client's ledger can be extracted.

At least once in every 14 weeks the member is required to:

    (i)   compare the total balances shown by the clients' ledger accounts with cash account balances;

    (ii)   prepare reconciliation statements explaining any differences; and

    (iii)   reconcile the cash account balances to the balances shown on bank statements and building society pass books.

The reconciliation statements must be preserved. Members are encouraged as a matter of good practice to carry out monthly reconciliations.

Members are required to maintain a list of all persons for whom he or she has been holding clients' money and a list of all the bank and building society accounts in which client money is held. The list should include bank details and should be maintained for six years. Other documents required to be preserved for six years are:

(A)   accounting records; and

(B)   bank statements and building society passbooks.

Interest

16.27 Unlike the Law Society, the RICS does not provide detailed guidance on interest on clients' money. Chartered surveyors, like chartered accountants are bound by the decision in *Brown v CIR [1965]*, that a person acting in a fiduciary capacity cannot retain interest earned on another's money that he is holding. Thus, without the client's specific authority, all interest earned is clients' money and must be credited to the client concerned. There are exceptions relating to clients' money set out in the *Estate Agents Act 1979* (see 16.31 below), stakeholders' money and instances where specific authority is given by the client.

Overdrawn accounts

16.28 Members are not allowed to withdraw money for or on behalf of a client if that amount exceeds the total money held on behalf of that client. Overdrawing means that other clients who have deposited money with the member are subsidising that client, which is a misuse of client money.

However, the MAR allows a member to pay client money into a discrete client account (providing he has written instructions to do so) and then to pay money out of that account which causes the account to become overdrawn, providing certain further correspondence is in place. This correspondence comprises a letter from the member to the client and one from the client to the member. The first letter informs the client that he has requested the account become overdrawn, what the bank's charges will be, that the client will be bound to reimburse the member and that the account will not be covered by the RICS' client money protection scheme. The second letter authorises the withdrawal leading to the overdraft and undertakes to reimburse the member for the bank charges.

It should be noted that client accounts held in connection with instructions governed by the *Estates Agents Act 1979* must never be overdrawn.

The accountant's report

16.29 Within six months of the end of his financial year, every member who handles clients' money is required to submit to the RICS an accountant's report certifying that the member has complied with the MAR. The accounting period to which the report relates must normally cover not less than twelve months. It should correspond to the period for which the accounts of the partnership are ordinarily made up. The accountant's report should be completed on the standard form issued by the RICS.

The ARR for RICS members closely follows those for solicitors and reference should be made to 16.17 above. However there are some differences as follows.

(*a*)   The rules for solicitors require all balances to be extracted, whilst the rules for chartered surveyors allow a test extraction.

(*b*)   The rules for solicitors require a perusal of office records, whilst the rules for chartered surveyors require a test examination (a clearer but less onerous requirement).

(*c*)   The reporting accountant is permitted access to all relevant documents under the rules for chartered surveyors.

Auctioneer's dispensation

16.30   Members who are livestock and chattel auctioneers can apply for exemption from the MAR in respect of monies placed into accounts operated exclusively for the purposes of the sale room business. To obtain permission from the RICS to be exempt, members must subscribe to a scheme for the protection of client money which provides at least as much protection as the RICS' own scheme. Unless the auctioneer is a livestock auctioneer, all other money is subject to the MAR.

For livestock auctioneers only, client money not covered by any scheme of protection can be operated outside the MAR. The member is required first of all to notify the RICS of his intention to be exempt and, secondly, to notify clients in writing that the MAR do not apply to such an account and that the monies held in it are not covered by the RICS' client money protection scheme. To satisfy the requirement of notification in writing, the member is allowed to make a prominent public display of this notice in the sale room. It should be noted that the accountant is required to verify this display.

A member who is a livestock or chattel auctioneer is permitted to keep monies belonging to himself, his firm or his company in the same bank account as monies held on behalf of clients. Such mixed accounts must be appropriately identified and operated exclusively for purposes connected with the conduct of the member's livestock market (and other live or dead stock sales) or chattel sale room business. To take advantage of this dispensation members must receive prior authorisation from the RICS, for which the member will have to demonstrate that such monies are protected under a compensation scheme offering at least as much protection as the RICS' client money protection scheme. It should be noted that the MAR apply in all other respects to this money.

Estate agents

Introduction

16.31   The *Estate Agents Act 1979* (*EAA*) and the accompanying Estate Agents (Accounts) Regulations 1981 (EAAR) impose a statutory duty to pay into a separate client account without delay any pre-contract and contract deposits.

A pre-contract is a payment which a prospective buyer pays to an estate agent:

(*a*)   in whole, or in part, as an indication of his intention to acquire an interest in land;

(*b*)   in whole, or in part towards meeting any financial liability which would arise once unconditional contracts are exchanged; or

(*c*)   in relation to a connected contract.

A contract deposit is defined as being any sum paid by a prospective buyer which, in whole or in part is, or is intended to form part of the consideration of an interest in land, and is paid on or after the time unconditional contracts are exchanged.

Any contract or pre-contract deposits must be paid without delay into a separate client account with an institution authorised by the EAAR. The account must include the name of the person or firm engaged in 'estate agency work' and have the word 'client' in the title. The client account must never hold money which the estate agent has received for any other purposes. This money will however be subject to the client money rules of the NAEA, RICS and ISVA. The EAAR strictly regulate when payments may be put into or drawn out of a 'statutory' client account.

Payments into a client account

16.32   The following money may be paid into a client account:

(*a*)   all contract and pre-contract deposits;

(*b*)   the minimum necessary to open, or maintain, the account; and

(*c*)   any sum needed to rectify an error immediately upon discovery.

Withdrawals from a client account

16.33   Money may only be withdrawn from a client account in the following cases:

(*a*)   where it is properly required for payment to, or on behalf of the person entitled to ask for it;

(*b*)   for payment of any remuneration or reimbursement of expenses in relation to estate agency work provided the estate agent is entitled to the payment and it is made with the agreement of the client;

(*c*)   in the exercise of any lien to which the agent is entitled;

(*d*)   for transfer to another client account;

(*e*)   to remove the minimum sum which was non-client money used to open or maintain the account; or (*f*) to rectify a mistake when non-statutory client money has been paid into a client account in error.

Books of account

16.34 The regulations do not specify what books should be kept but specify what information the estate agent should record. At any time these must show that the estate agent has paid the money into a statutory client account and show and explain readily all subsequent dealings with that money. In particular these records must show:

(*a*) the full title of the client account;

(*b*) the authorised institution where it is held;

(*c*) the amount received;

(*d*) the name and address of the payer;

(*e*) whether the sum received is a contract or pre-contract deposit;

(*f*) in either case, whether it includes any sum in respect of a 'connected contract';

(*g*) if the sum includes any money which is not statutory clients' money, and if so, for what purpose and in what form that part is received;

(*h*) the interest in the land to which the sum relates;

(*j*) the identity of the person wishing to dispose of the relevant interest in the land;

(*k*) the capacity in which the sum is received;

(*l*) if the payee is himself an agent, the identity of the person for whom the sum is being received; and

(*m*) the date of receipt.

Interest

16.35 Under the EAAR anyone who holds clients' money in the course of estate agency work which exceeds £500 must account to the person for interest which has been or would have been earned, unless the amount involved is less than £10.

The accountant's report

16.36 'Statutory client accounts' must be audited within six months of the end of an accounting period, which must not exceed twelve months. The auditor must report to the estate agent whether, in his opinion, the requirements of the Act and of the EAAR have been observed or substantially observed. The auditor can report substantial compliance if, in his opinion, they have been so observed, or complied with except for trivial breaches – for example due to clerical errors or mistakes in book-keeping – all of which were rectified on discovery, and none of which resulted in any loss to the person entitled to the money.

The Act does not specify any particular form of Auditors' Report, but a model form has been produced by the accountancy bodies. As the Act is worded the auditor has considerable responsibility. If the estate agent's accounting system is non-existent, then it may be necessary to examine every file to check compliance.

It should be noted, however, that since the 1970s when the majority of estate agents made it standard practice to take deposits, this is an area where practice has changed significantly. There has been a greater resistance to taking pre-contract deposits as a result of intervention of solicitors and many firms have decided against taking them.

Institute of Chartered Accountants in England Wales

Introduction

16.37   The 'Clients' Money Regulations' introduced in April 1992 are applicable to all United Kingdom, Isle of Man and Channel Island offices of firms of chartered accountants, as defined below, and are set out in the Institute's 'Members Handbook'. However, the regulations do not apply to monies defined as 'investment business clients' monies' under the Investment Business Regulations. The main elements of the Client's Money Regulations are summarised below.

Key definitions

16.38   These definitions are as follows.

(*a*)   *Clients' money* – 'money which a firm holds or receives for or from a client and which is not immediately due and payable on demand to the firm for his own account and money held by a firm as stakeholder. Fees paid in advance for professional work agreed to be performed and clearly identifiable as such shall not be regarded as "Clients' Money" for the purposes of the "Chartered Accountants' Clients' Money Regulations"'.

(*b*)   *Clients' bank account* – 'an account in the name of the firm separate from other accounts of the firm which may be either a general account or an account designated by the name of a specific client and includes the word "client" in its title'.

(*c*)   *Firm* – 'a sole practitioner who is a Member, or a partnership or a body corporate comprised in whole or in part of Members, the main business of whom or of which is that of a public accountant'.

Payments into a client account

16.39   The regulations specify details of what must be and what shall not be paid into a client account as follows:

(*a*)   Clients' money received must be paid forthwith into a client account.

(*b*)   If money for any one client in excess of £10,000 is held or expected to be held then the money should be held in a designated client account.

Withdrawals from client account

16.40   The regulations set out the only permitted circumstances for withdrawing client money. These include:

(*a*)   monies paid into the client account in error;

(*b*)   non-client money paid in as part of a remittance consisting of client and non-client funds;

(*c*)   surplus funds remaining on the account after all amounts due to the client have been repaid to them;

(*d*)   money properly required to be paid to or on behalf of the client;

(*e*)   money required to pay the firm's fees, providing the firm has given the client a statement showing details of the work carried out, provided these have been agreed by the client, thirty days have lapsed since the statement has been delivered to the client, and the fees have been accurately calculated in accordance with a formula agreed in writing by the client; and

(*f*)   money properly transferred into another client account.

Records and reconciliations

16.41   Accountants are required to keep proper books of account showing their dealings with all client money. Cheques endorsed over to clients must be recorded, except for firms handling monies in an insolvency capacity provided other appropriate controls are implemented. Each client bank account is required to be reconciled against the clients' ledger at least every six months and records should be kept of such reconciliations.

Interest

16.42   The firm is required to pay interest over to the client, unless agreement not to do so has been effected in writing with the client. The client bank account must be an interest bearing account if 'material interest' would be likely to accrue. The regulations provide explanatory notes that set out as a guide minimum balances and lengths held for determining 'material interest'. The regulations are therefore reasonably concise and no reporting requirements exist. The regulations concerning client monies in relation to investment business are separately dealt with under the Financial Services (Investment Business Clients' Money) (Chartered Accountants) Regulations 1988 and the Institute's Investment Business Regulations.

Chapter 17

Taxable Income and Allowable Expenses

Types of income

17.1 The bulk of the income of a professional partnership is likely to consist of fees for services to clients and customers. However, many other kinds of receipt may in practice find their way into a firm, for example, interest on cash deposits, dividends from investments and rental income. Partners may also generate income from individual activities which they are obliged under the partnership agreement to put into the common pool.

The income tax system in the United Kingdom is a 'schedular' system which divides various types of income between Schedules set out in the relevant legislation. It is important to understand under which Schedule a particular item of income falls, because the rules which determine how much of it is taxable vary from one Schedule to another.

The main Schedules

17.2 The main Schedules relevant to partnership income are as follows.

(*a*) Schedule A, which covers rental income and most other kinds of property income.

(*b*) Schedule D, which covers income from the carrying on of a trade, profession or vocation, but also other kinds of income including interest.

(*c*) Schedule E, which covers income from offices and employments.

(*d*) Schedule F, which covers dividends from UK companies.

Schedule D

17.3 Schedule D, which is of most importance to partnerships, is divided into six sub-sections or 'Cases'.

(*a*) Case I, which covers profits from the carrying on of a trade at least partly in the UK.

(*b*)   Case II, which covers profits from UK 'professions or vocations'.

In general the distinction between trades on the one hand, and professions or vocations on the other, is of little practical importance nowadays and the tax treatment of both categories of activity is the same. However, the rules introduced in the *Finance Act 1998*, which brought to an end the so-called 'cash basis', require the distinction to be made, since only firms carrying on professions or vocations were allowed to defer the additional tax arising when a change was made from the cash basis. This is explained in more detail below (see 17.13).

(*c*)   Case III, which covers interest from UK sources, such as UK bank deposit accounts, UK gilts or loan stock issued by UK companies.

(*d*)   Case IV and V, which both relate to income from foreign investments, but Case V also covers the profits of a trade or profession carried on wholly outside the UK.

(*e*)   Case VI, which covers any other income.

Case II

17.4   Professional partnerships, inevitably, will have most of their income taxed under Case II. This will cover the profits of the practice from providing services to clients and customers. It may, however, also include various other items, such as, in some circumstances, money received as compensation for lost profits, or the proceeds of sale of a block of fees to another firm. There are rules governing what can be deducted in calculating the Case II profit and these are described in 17.8 below.

Case III

17.5   Many partnerships invest surplus funds on deposit and the interest earned will be Case III income for tax purposes. However, solicitors receiving interest on clients' money are subject to special rules.

Investment property rental income

17.6   A firm may have investment property producing rental income which will be taxed under Schedule A, although by Inland Revenue concession, rents from surplus office space may sometimes be included with the Case II profit.

Income received as individuals

17.7   Partners may also receive income from professional engagements which are undertaken by them as individuals. For example, a solicitor may write a legal textbook, or a doctor undertake medical examinations for a life assurance company.

Many partnership agreements provide that income of this type must be brought into the 'common pool' and it may then be reflected, if significant, in the size of the individual's profit share. It thus becomes part of the firm's Case II income. If retained personally, however, it will need to be entered on the individual's tax return.

Some such 'personal' activities may in law be offices or employments within Schedule E; e.g. a solicitor or doctor who acts as a coroner or an accountant who acts as a director of a company. Income tax normally has to be deducted under a PAYE code number from the fees received, although small directors' fees can often be paid gross of tax and NICs if the directorship is a normal incident of the profession and the firm, and the fees are pooled under the partnership agreement. (See Chapter 19 for the NIC treatment of such fees.)

The impact of the 'IR35' rules which came in from 6 April 2000 may have to be considered in relation to some income of this kind, a matter which is discussed in Chapter 18.

Computing profits for Schedule D

17.8   It has always been necessary to make adjustments, for income tax purposes, to the results shown by the accounts of a professional partnership in order to comply with tax law. These adjustments can be very substantial, because many items included, quite properly, by accepted accountancy practice may not necessarily be taxable receipts or allowable deductions under tax law. The main types of adjustment are mentioned in 17.9 and 17.17 below but this is only a very general description of this subject. What all partners must remember, however, when they see their firm's signed accounts, is that the profit share shown as allocated to them will almost always be less than the amount on which they will eventually be taxed for the year. If the accounts show significant depreciation charges or general provisions (neither of which is allowable for tax purposes) the difference could be substantial. Of particular relevance here is the effect of Financial Reporting Standard (FRS) 12 'Provisions, Contingent Liabilities and Contingent Assets'. This is considered in more detail at 17.21.

For periods of account starting after 6 April 1999, *section 42* of the *Finance Act 1998* has introduced an additional requirement. This is that the profits must be computed on an accounting basis which gives a true and fair view, subject to any adjustment required or authorised by law in computing profits for tax purposes. In the Inland Revenue's view this is no more than a statutory recognition of what the law, as interpreted by the courts, has always required, but its practical effect is to import into partnership taxation computations many of the accounting principles which are required for companies, although partnerships are still not required to draw up accounts under the rules of the *Companies Acts*. One very important consequence concerns the treatment of work-in-progress and debtors. This is discussed in more detail below (see 17.10).

Taxable and non-taxable receipts

17.9   There is a basic distinction between transactions of a revenue and a capital nature. Generally, the former are part of the taxable Case II income, whereas the latter are not, although they may well have other taxation consequences.

Therefore, fees for professional work will normally be taxable under Case II, but if a motor vehicle owned by the firm is sold at a profit this will arise on a capital asset of the business and although it is excluded from the Case II result, the transaction will usually affect the firm's capital allowances computation. A profit on the sale of a property would equally be excluded from the Case II result but would enter into the partner's capital gains tax computation.

Some kinds of compensation payment may be 'revenue' in nature, e.g. where compensation is received for loss of profits when builders damage the firm's offices and staff cannot work normally, the proceeds merely fill a hole in the firm's profits and are taxed just like the profits they replace. However, where almost all of a firm's profit arises from a single source, such as an agency contract, which is then cancelled, compensation for this is likely to be capital in nature and not part of the Case II result (though again it may be liable to capital gains tax).

Many types of grants or subsidies are taxable receipts under Case II, especially if they are intended to assist with 'revenue' type expenses (such as salaries), but if they are to assist with the cost of a capital asset they are not part of the Case II result but instead deducted in calculating the capital allowances on that asset.

Recognising taxable income

17.10   In practice, the correct time when income should be recognised for tax purposes is often a more difficult problem than whether a particular receipt is taxable. This is because of the treatment of work-in-progress.

The basic rule

17.11   The basic rule is that a professional receipt should be recognised for income tax purposes when the recipient has done everything which he is obliged to do to earn it. Normally a professional person acting for a client will issue a bill for his services at an agreed time, or at agreed intervals, as work is done. Everything necessary to earn that fee has therefore been done when the bill is issued. Therefore, the correct treatment is to bring into the accounts all bills issued in the year (the 'earnings' basis or 'bills issued' basis) – which automatically means that the taxable result includes outstanding debtors, possibly subject to any specific write-offs or reserves for bad or doubtful debts.

The cash basis – the old system

17.12   However, in periods of account ending on dates up to and including 6 April 1999, some firms, by long-standing practice, were allowed by the Inspector of Taxes to submit accounts on a 'cash' basis, i.e. including only bills paid by clients in the year. The Inspector would not, however, allow this practice in the first three years of a new business. If the firm was allowed to switch to the cash basis after this period it had to undertake to issue bills at regular and frequent intervals, usually at least quarterly. The Inspector was obviously concerned to make sure that the firm was not deliberately delaying the issue of bills to defer tax.

After the third year, when the cash basis was in force – assuming the Inspector agreed – tax might be paid twice on the same amount: if a bill was issued for £100, say, in year 3 and included under the 'bills issued' basis of accounting in that year for tax purposes, but was then paid in year 4 by the client, it was taxed again in that year.

The statutory ending of the cash basis

17.13   Important changes were introduced by the *Finance Act 1998*. With effect from the first accounting period starting after 6 April 1999, the cash basis was removed as an option for professional partnerships. In this and later accounting periods, therefore, all firms need to bring in the value of work done, whether or not cash has been received by the year end, and work-in-progress at the year end, valued at the lower of cost or market value. As a transitional measure there was a 'catching up' tax charge to bring into account the value of debtors and work-in-progress which previously fell out of account.

The 'catching up' charge was treated as income arising on the first day of the first accounting period in which the new basis applied; since the adjustment gives rise to income taxable under Case VI of Schedule D, however, and since Case VI income is computed on a current year basis, the catching up adjustment was normally taxable in the 1999/2000 tax year, whereas the first tax year affected by the compulsory ending of the cash basis was normally 2000/01.

More details about the implications of the catching up charge and the ending of the cash basis appear below (see 17.14).

Work-in-progress in a tax context

17.14 Conventional accountancy practice requires the matching of costs with revenues in a period. Therefore, although a firm has not yet billed a client for a particular job (let alone been paid) costs have been incurred on salaries and other overheads in doing that work. So an adjustment must be made to remove these costs from the accounts at the end of the year, known as work-in-progress (WIP). The opposite adjustment is made in the following year to bring the cost into the right place to match the expected income. However, since the time of equity partners does not represent a true cost to the firm for tax purposes, chargeable time recorded by them does not need to be included in the WIP adjustment.

Example 1

Calculating profit for tax purposes

ABC & Co bill clients for £100 of work in year 1 but also have £20 of chargeable time recorded, by fee earners other than partners, for further clients at the year end which will be billed in year 2. They normally apply a mark-up of 66% to costs to arrive at their charge-out rates so this £20 represents £12 of costs. The method of calculating the year 1 profit for tax purposes will therefore be as follows.

Year 1

	£
Bills issued	100
Costs incurred (say)	(30)
	70
Add Closing WIP as above	12
Taxable profit before other expenses	82

In year 2, the work is completed and billed at £20 in addition to other work billed at £90. The taxable profit before other expenses will be as follows.

Year 2

	£	£
Bills issued		110
Less costs		(30)
Opening WIP	(12)	
Closing WIP	15	
Taxable profit		3
before expenses		83

The impact of the 1998 changes

The 'catching up' adjustments required by the above changes affect firms which were previously on a 'pure' cash basis, i.e. which brought in only cash received in the year from clients and excluded both closing debtors and WIP. However, they can also affect firms which used various 'hybrid' bases falling short of a full 'earnings' basis. In some cases debtors were included in full, but no WIP (often called the 'bills delivered' basis); in others some recognition was given to WIP, but it fell short of including the cost (or market value, if less) of all time charged by fee-earners other than partners, perhaps bringing in merely an agreed percentage of fees earned.

In both cases, an adjustment needed to be made to bring into account for tax purposes the amounts which previously fell out of account. Normally this consisted of any debtors and/or WIP which were not recognised for tax purposes at the end of the last accounting period which ended after 6 April 1999. From this adjustment there may also have been a deduction for fees received in advance in the last 'pre-adjustment' accounting period; such fees would have been taxed under the cash basis but on a full earnings basis they would be attributed to the next year, and without this adjustment they would have been taxed twice.

In addition, the adjustment may have had to take expenses into account if these were also previously dealt with on a cash basis. For example, if rent is paid in advance, the last 'pre-adjustment' accounts may have included some rent which is attributable to the following year on an accruals or earnings basis of accounting. To prevent a double tax deduction, such amounts would have been added into the catching up adjustment. A converse (negative) adjustment might have been needed for expenses paid in arrears, since otherwise they might not achieve a tax deduction at all.

To give a simple example:

Example 2

XYZ and partners draw up accounts to 30 April each year, and were previously on a pure cash basis both for income and expenses, excluding WIP and debtors.

At 30 April 1999 the records show the following:

	£
Unpaid fees, i.e. debtors	10,000
WIP of fee-earners other than partners	5,000
Fees received in advance for uncompleted work	500
Rent paid in the year which relates to periods after 30 April 1999	1,000

The catching up adjustment would bring in the debtors and WIP, and the advance rent, as positive adjustments, and the advance fees as a negative adjustment, as follows:

	£
Debtors	10,000
WIP	5,000
Advance rent	1,000
Less advance fees	(500)
Total positive adjustment	15,500

So there will be additional taxable income of £15,500 for the partners. Example 3 below indicates how this is actually taxed.

In the next accounting period, ending on 30 April 2000, the full earnings basis would have applied. The firm would have brought into account the above debtors and WIP figures as opening (negative) adjustments, and at the end of the year they would have brought in the appropriate closing debtors and WIP figures. Thus increases in those figures over the year would have increased the taxable profit for the 2000/01 tax year, and reductions would have decreased it. The catching up adjustment thus achieved the transition to the full earnings basis of computation.

The catching up adjustment does not, however, create income which was all taxed in 1999/2000. A special relief recognises the fact that very large one-off amounts might otherwise have to be paid in tax by those who happen to be partners at the transition, whereas the benefit of untaxed debtors and WIP will have been enjoyed in previous years by their predecessors. This spreads the charge over ten tax years, from 1999/2000 to 2008/09. In each of those years except the last, the charge will be 10% of the adjustment or, if less, 10% of the firm's taxable profits before capital allowances. In the final (tenth) year any remaining untaxed balance is taxed.

The charge is allocated among whoever happen to be the partners in each of those years, regardless of changes of personnel, in their respective profit sharing ratios. The charge is treated as pensionable income but is not liable to Class 4 NICs (see 20.13 below). This treatment will be applied automatically unless the partners in any particular year elect to accelerate the liability; they can do this in whole or part, but all partners must elect for the treatment. A firm which encountered losses might decide to accelerate the catching up charge, since losses can be offset against it. If the business ceases before the end of the ten-year period, the remaining 'instalments' continue to be taxed on the partners who were in office at the date of cessation.

Continuing the above example to illustrate this:

Example 3

The partners in the firm, X, Y and Z, share profits equally. If the business continues and there is no change of partners, each partner will be taxed under Case VI of Schedule D, for each year from 1999/2000 to 2007/08 inclusive, on one-third of 10% of £15,500, i.e. £516. If the firm's profits declined drastically so that in any year a partner's share of profits before capital allowances was less than £5,166, the charge would be on 10% of that profit share. In 2008/09 each partner would be taxed on any remaining untaxed balance of the initial allocation of £5,166 (one-third of £15,500).

Suppose, however, that X retires on 30 April 2002 and is replaced by A, who also takes a one-third share of profits. X will be taxed (assuming that the '10% of profits' override does not apply) on £516 each year for 1999/2000 to 2002/03 inclusive; then A will take over the liability and be taxed on the same amount from 2003/04 to 2008/09 inclusive.

Each annual instalment is taxable income of the year in question, so that the amount of tax paid will depend on tax rates, allowances, etc. at the time, and the relevant amount will have to be included on the partner's tax return each year. However, the spreading relief is in no sense 'a loan' by the Revenue, and provided that the tax is paid on time each year there will be no interest cost. In the absence of large losses or a large increase in personal tax rates, therefore, there would seem to be little reason for partners to elect to accelerate the catching up charge. Nevertheless, there may be equitable issues as to the position of incoming and outgoing partners during the ten-year period which could affect the decision.

Firms have had to decide how to provide for these additional tax bills, since they are not matched by any real profits coming in. This raises issues concerning taxation reserves.

Valuation of debtors and work-in-progress

17.15   The *Finance Act 1998* changes make the valuation of debtors and WIP very important for partnerships, both as regards the amount of the catching up charge and, going forward, the taxable profits in future years. It is now vital for firms, especially those previously on the cash basis, to have good systems for recording both of these items, and for reviewing them regularly; inadequate valuations will mean that taxable profits are understated and open the partners to Revenue investigation and possible penalties, but over-valuation will cause needless acceleration of tax bills.

Debtors should be valued with due regard to those which are considered doubtful or bad, and appropriate specific, documented provisions or write-offs should be made which can be deducted for tax purposes.

WIP must also be monitored carefully, and systems put in place which allow the selling value to be written down to cost or, if there is doubt as to recoverability, a lower market value figure. The system also needs to be able to exclude partners' time (see 17.14 above), since this does not have to be included for tax purposes.

In some professions additional factors will come into play here. For example, work undertaken on a contingency fee basis by lawyers and others may not require recognition for tax purposes until it is clear that any amount will be receivable. Legally aided work by solicitors, or fees subject to 'taxation' by the courts, may also require special treatment. Chapter 12 has further details on work-in-progress.

Non-professional income

17.16 The Case II tax calculation will also need to eliminate any 'non-Case II' income shown in the accounts, such as rent or interest. These amounts will be divided between the partners in the appropriate proportions and taxed on them separately under the appropriate Schedule and Case, e.g. Schedule A for rent and Case III of Schedule D for interest (see 17.2–17.5 above).

The Schedule A calculation may need to include an adjustment for reverse premiums or similar cash inducements paid by landlords to persuade a firm to occupy a property which might otherwise be difficult to let. These are taxed as if they were rental income received, but the tax bill will be spread over the period over which the receipt in question is treated as income in the accounts. The normal accounting treatment would be to treat it as arising evenly over the period of the lease, or if sooner, to the date of the next rent review, and the taxation treatment will follow this. (See 17.18(c) for the treatment of rent-free periods.)

Deductible expenses

17.17 As with taxable income (see 17.8 above) there is a mass of case law on the expenses which can be deducted in calculating the Case II taxable profit. However, here there are also statutory rules, although their interpretation often causes problems.

This is especially true of the rule which says that expenses not incurred 'wholly and exclusively ... for the purposes of the trade, profession or vocation' cannot be deducted.

This area is not discussed in detail here but a summary is provided of the most common expenses likely to be incurred and their likely tax treatment.

Normally allowable

17.18   These include as follows.

(*a*)   *Personnel and administration*

    (i)   Staff salaries (although there can be problems with salaries to partners' spouses who do not perform very substantial duties).

    (ii)   Staff benefit costs.

    (iii)   Staff training costs.

    (iv)   Pension contributions for staff (but not partners). Note that a deduction is only allowable if it is paid over by the year end.

    (v)   One-off payments for services, e.g. temporary staff and consultants.

    (vi)   Magazines, newspapers, etc. related to the business and possibly books (but see 17.23 below).

    (vii)   Stationery, printing, photocopying, etc.

    (viii)   Legal fees relating to staff matters, e.g. disputes about unfair dismissal, but not disputes with partners.

    (ix)   Employment agency and 'head hunters' fees relating to staff.

    (x)   Staff entertaining, provided that clients, contacts and other outsiders are not present.

(*b*)   *Marketing*

    (i)   Costs of producing brochures, advertisements, etc. for the firm and its services.

    (ii)   Fees of PR consultants, etc.

    (iii)   Some kinds of sponsorship (excluding entertaining) where there is a clear advertising aspect.

(*c*)   *Property occupied for the business*

    (i)   Rent (but not a premium on a lease). The timing of the rent deduction may be affected by any rent-free periods which are agreed with the landlord; the normal accounting treatment of these will be to spread the rent actually payable over the lease, after allowing for such inducements, evenly over the term, and tax relief will be given in the same way.

    (ii)   Repairs and redecoration (which often raises problems of definition on which there is much case law).

    (iii)   Rates.

    (iv)   Water charges.

    (v)   Lighting and heating.

(vi)   Cleaning costs.

(vii) Property insurance.

(viii) Reserves for leasehold dilapidations, providing that the firm will have a legal obligation at the end of the lease term, and the reserve can be calculated with sufficient accuracy. This is an area where expert advice is essential but it should be possible to provide for the whole expected liability at the start of the lease, subject to an annual review. See also 17.21.

(ix)   Reserves for expected losses on rented accommodation previously used for the business, which cannot be sublet, or only at a loss (see also 17.21).

(*d*)   *Finance*

(i)   Interest on the firm's borrowings, whether for working capital or the purchase of capital assets used in the business.

(ii) Specific bad or doubtful debts written off or provided against, so long as there is evidence to support this.

(iii) Professional indemnity premiums.

Normally disallowed

17.19   These include the following.

(*a*)   *Personnel and administration*
(i)   Expenses which have dual business/private purposes (though sometimes apportionment may be allowed, e.g. home telephones which are sometimes used for business calls).

(ii) Expenses for the maintenance of the partners personally, e.g. their personal drawings.

(iii) Partners' personal pension contributions.

(*b*)   *Marketing*

Entertaining of clients, potential clients and contacts (this is very widely defined and the argument that, say, a party for potential clients is 'advertising' is not accepted by the Revenue).

(*c*)   *Property*

(i)   Improvements and new building costs.

(ii) Lease premiums and associated legal costs.

(iii) Leasehold redemption reserves (but see 17.18(*c*)(viii) regarding dilapidation reserves).

(*d*)   *Finance*

(i)   Depreciation of fixed assets.

(ii) Interest on partners' personal borrowings (though this may be allowed against the borrowing partner's personal income).

(iii) General bad debt reserves, i.e. not against specific bad or doubtful debts.

(iv) Other non-specific reserves, e.g. retentions against possible unspecified negligence claims (though a specific and properly quantified provision for such claims should be allowed – possibly after a struggle with the Revenue).

(v) Taxes on profit, e.g. income tax, but employment costs such as employer's NICs are allowable.

(vi) Interest on overdue tax.

It should be stressed that this is only a very broad list and there are many individual exceptions and special cases.

Only revenue expenses

17.20   It is, of course, fundamental that only revenue expenses are allowed. Therefore, for example, although fees paid to professional tutors for staff training courses will be allowable in calculating the Case II profit, the purchase of a television set and video recorder on which training videos can be watched represents the acquisition of new capital assets and is not so deductible (although capital allowances should be available, see 17.22–17.29 below). This capital/revenue distinction is also relevant in deciding, for example, whether a piece of building work represents a repair (allowable) or an improvement (not allowable). In this case there are no capital allowances on capital expenditure so the distinction is of considerable practical importance.

It is the presence of 'nothings' – items of expense for which neither a revenue deduction nor capital allowances is available, such as property improvements and many legal costs relating to property matters – which makes the gap between the accounts profit and the taxable profit so crucial for partners. The choice of knowledgeable and effective advisers who can negotiate the many grey areas with the Revenue is most important.

Timing of deductions

17.21   As with receipts (see 17.10 above) there are rules about when an expense can be recognised for tax purposes as a Case II deduction. Broadly, an allowable expense can be deducted when it would be charged in the accounts according to ordinary accepted accountancy principles, unless there is a statutory provision to the contrary. In one decided case (*Gallagher v Jones [1993] STC 199*) the Court of Appeal held that it was correct to spread the rental payments for an asset over the terms of the lease even though the actual payments were largely front-loaded.

Reserves and provisions for expected future expenses may be disputed by the Revenue unless they can be justified under normally accepted accounting practice. Financial Reporting Standard (FRS) 12 deals with these items and requires that a provision can only be made where a business has a present obligation, legal or constructive, as a result of a past obligating event, and it is probable that a payment will be required to settle that obligation. The amount of that payment must also be capable of being reliably estimated. For tax purposes, the Revenue will accept a properly estimated FRS 12 provision provided that it does not conflict with any rule in the Taxes Acts. It should, therefore, be possible to obtain tax relief for a properly calculated provision for leasehold dilapidations, or expected losses from being unable to sublet surplus space. In the past the Revenue tended to dispute these and allow relief only on a 'paid' basis when expenditure was incurred.

Example 4

A profit computation adjusted for income tax purposes

The following example – necessarily oversimplified – shows how a firm's profit and loss account is adjusted to take account of some of the more common adjustments mentioned above.

Messrs Sue, Grabbit and Runne's profit and loss account shows, in summary, the following results for the year.

	£	£
Work done (adjusted for WIP)		400,000
Less		
Salaries and other staff costs	100,000	
Partners' motoring expenses	10,000 (*a*)	
Entertaining of clients and contacts	5,000 (*b*)	
Office rent	25,000	
Office repairs	1,000 (*c*)	
Specific bad debt provided	3,000 (*d*)	
General bad debt reserve	2,000 (*e*)	
Interest on overdraft	10,000 (*f*)	
Interest on partners' loans	5,000 (*g*)	
Depreciation of fixed assets	12,000 (*h*)	
Other allowable expenses	27,000	
		200,000
Profit divisible among partners		200,000

Notes

(*a*)   It is agreed with the Inspector that 50% of these expenses are 'private' so profit for tax purposes is increased by £5,000.

(*b*)   The entertaining expenses are disallowed by statute (see 17.19 above), increasing taxable profits by £5,000.

(*c*) All are 'revenue' items except for £600 which is in fact the cost of a new desk for a partner and is disallowed for the purpose of the taxable profit, but will qualify for capital allowances.

(*d*) If this all relates to specific debtors, properly evaluated, it should be allowed.

(*e*) The general bad debt reserve of £2,000 is disallowed in full.

(*f*) Interest on the firm's overdraft will normally be allowed (so long as partners' current accounts are not overdrawn).

(*g*) Partners' personal borrowing costs of £5,000 are not allowable in computing the firm's profit, but may be allowed against their personal tax bills.

(*h*) Depreciation of fixed assets is disallowed here but may be reflected in the capital allowances. (See 17.22.)

The 'tax-adjusted' profit is therefore £229,600.

From this amount any capital allowances (see 17.22 below) are then deducted.

Capital allowances

Introduction

17.22   As has been seen in 17.21 above, there are several types of capital expenditure for which no deduction is due when calculating Case II taxable profits, but where some relief is available by capital allowances. These in their different ways all give some relief for the capital cost of an asset over a period of time, and so the practical difference between a Case II deduction and a capital allowance is measured in terms of cash flow.

The tax system gives capital allowances on plant and machinery, industrial buildings, agricultural buildings, ships, scientific research, certain hotels, patent rights and other more rarely encountered assets. However, professional partnerships will be concerned normally only with allowances for plant and machinery, so what follows will concentrate on these.

Meaning of 'plant and machinery'

17.23   This expression has misleading overtones of large industrial processes. In fact, it was defined by the courts many years ago as 'whatever apparatus is used by a businessman for carrying on his business – not his stock in trade, which he buys or makes for sale; but all goods and chattels, fixed or moveable, live or dead, which he keeps for permanent employment in his business' (*Yarmouth v France (1887) 19 QBD 647*). In that case the item held to be plant (which will be used here as a shorthand expression) was a horse. Its modern counterpart, the motor vehicle, is another obvious case of plant. In the present context, the expression also clearly includes the array of machinery such as computers, fax machines, photocopiers and telephone apparatus found in a modern office. Perhaps less obviously, the courts have held that a library of law books would be plant for a lawyer (though in practice the whole cost may be written off as a Case II deduction – see 17.18 above). There is now special legislation for intangible assets such as software.

Arguments about what is plant usually centre on items which are arguably parts of buildings or closely associated with buildings. The courts have drawn a distinction between the physical setting in which a business is carried on, which cannot be plant, and functioning apparatus with which it is carried on, which may be plant. Thus, for example, an immobilised barge, used as a restaurant, was held not to be plant, but a dry dock in a ship building business was. These case law principles have been supplemented by detailed statutory rules, introduced after the Revenue had become concerned about the increasingly liberal trend of recent court decisions. These are currently enshrined in the *Capital Allowances Act 2001.*

Very broadly, the Act declares that no expenditure on the provision of a building can be plant, and the same applies to assets incorporated or normally in buildings. Specific items are listed which are not to be plant, and there are lists of items which may be.

This development has not helped to clarify an already vague area of tax law. Firms which are contemplating a major building project or the purchase of office buildings must take good advice on how they can maximise the element of cost which qualifies as plant – remembering that the element which does not, attracts no relief at all (see 17.20). In general, plant allowances will not be available for the cost of walls, floors, ceilings, doors or stairs; for mains services delivering water, electricity and gas; waste disposal, drainage and sewerage systems and fire safety systems such as escapes and fire doors (though there are some special reliefs where the fire authorities insist on such work being done and fire alarm systems and sprinklers do qualify). However, many specific items are allowed, including space and water heating systems, air-conditioning systems, most kitchen equipment and sanitary fittings, lifts (but not their shafts), burglar alarms, safes, advertising displays, and partitions which are intended to be moved around to reconfigure working spaces. Most of these items reflect court decisions in the taxpayer's favour.

How plant allowances are calculated – first-year allowances, writing-down allowances and the 'pool'

17.24 Assuming the expenditure in question is 'plant', the law then requires that it must belong to the partnership which acquired it as a consequence of capital expenditure having been incurred on it (other types of financing are considered below). Firms which qualify as 'small or medium sized' businesses can qualify for a first-year allowance on certain items of plant. This has been possible for purchases since 1 July 1997. Very broadly, a firm will meet these size criteria if, in the accounting period in question or the previous one, it meets two of the following three conditions:

• Turnover not exceeding £11.2 million

• Gross assets not exceeding £5.6 million

• Not more than 250 employees, taking the average monthly figures in the period in question.

Firms which qualify obtained a first-year allowance of 50% of the expenditure in question incurred between 2 July 1997 and 1 July 1998, and then 40% of expenditure after 1 July 1998. *Section 70* of the *Finance Act 2000* has extended this indefinitely. (Firms in Northern Ireland may qualify for 100% allowance in respect of expenditure incurred between 12 May 1998 and 11 May 2002, subject to detailed rules.) The first-year allowances are not available on motor cars, expenditure in the period in which a business ceases, and certain other assets which have a predictable life exceeding 25 years.

Where an asset qualifies for the 40% allowance in its first year, the balance of expenditure (60%) attracts writing-down allowances (WDAs) at 25% on the reducing balance in later years, along with expenditure which did not attract the first-year allowance as described below.

Expenditure on information and communication technology incurred by a small enterprise is eligible for 100% first-year allowances where the expenditure is incurred in the three years to 31 March 2003 (*section 45* of the *Capital Allowances Act 2001*). A 'small' enterprise is one which meets at least two of the following criteria in the period in which the expenditure is incurred or in the previous accounting period:

• Turnover is not more than £2.8 million

• The balance sheet total is not more than £1.4 million

• The average number of employees calculated on a monthly basis does not exceed 50.

The types of expenditure covered by the information and communication technology relief would include computers and associated equipment, including cabling and dedicated electrical systems; certain types of telephone and transmission devices and software for qualifying equipment.

There is also an Enhanced Capital Allowances scheme which lists classes of energy-saving technologies that can qualify for 100% first-year allowances. The types of energy-saving plant which can qualify have to be designated as such by Treasury Order. With effect from 5 August 2002 five new categories of technology were added which include such items as heat pumps for space heating, solar thermal systems and refrigeration display cabinets and compressors. Full details of the qualifying technologies and products are available on the Internet at www.eca.gov.uk. Advice can be obtained from the Environment and Energy Helpline (tel 0800 585794). With effect from 17 April 2002, the first-year allowance available on qualifying technologies was also extended to plant used for leasing.

Most expenditure on plant which qualifies for WDAs, along with the balance of expenditure which qualified for first-year allowances, goes into a 'pool' and the allowance is calculated on the total value of the pool after deducting items sold, destroyed or no longer used in the business. The sale price of items sold, or the open market value or insurance proceeds in other cases, has to be deducted. However, this cannot exceed original cost, since the purpose of the WDA is to allow tax relief for no more than the cost, and any 'profit' made may be subject to CGT.

'Non-pooled' assets and private use

17.25   Certain assets are not 'pooled' in this way because the WDAs given on them are calculated differently. The principle instances are motor cars (but not vans) which cost more than £12,000, where the WDA is limited to £3,000 (or 25% of the reducing balance if less), and other assets which are used partly for private purposes, where the WDA is restricted to the business proportion. Where there is such a restriction the whole (unrestricted) WDA is deducted from the brought-forward value to give the value to carry forward to the next year, so the effect is that allowances are lost permanently to the extent that there is private use. Short-life assets (see 17.27 below) are also excluded from the 'pool'.

Balancing adjustments

17.26   Where there is a sale or other event which requires a value to be deducted from the 'pool' (see 17.24 above) this may exceed the total 'pool' value. In that event, the excess is treated as taxable income and known as a 'balancing charge'. It simply claws back the tax relief which was given on the original expenditure to the extent that it has been recovered by selling the asset. A similar calculation applies where a 'non-pooled' asset is sold. Balancing charges on such assets, especially cars, are more common than balancing charges on the 'pool'. If the business has ceased, the market value of the 'pool' has to be deducted from its brought-forward value. This may give rise to a balancing charge or, if the market value is less than the brought-forward value, a balancing allowance, which simply gives additional relief for the paper loss thrown up on cessation in respect of those depreciated assets.

A balancing allowance can also arise on 'non-pooled' assets which are sold, but it cannot arise in respect of the 'pool' except on cessation. This has led to the creation of a useful facility to extract certain 'short-life' assets from the 'pool' – see 17.27 below.

Short-life assets

17.27 The standard method of giving WDAs at 25% on the reducing balance each year may give a reasonable result for assets such as office furniture and fixtures, which often have a fairly long life. However, the reducing balance method may not reflect the economic reality for 'short life' assets, such as much modern computer equipment. Therefore, it is possible to elect for specified classes of assets of this type to be 'depooled'. This will ensure that a balancing allowance can be given immediately on sale (see 16.26 above) instead of having to wait until the business ceases. This treatment has to be claimed within two years of the tax year of acquisition. It is not suitable for assets expected to last for five years or more, since after five years any remaining cost is transferred back to the general 'pool', nor can this treatment be applied to motor vehicles.

Other forms of ownership

17.28 Plant may not necessarily, of course, be purchased outright: it may be taken on hire-purchase or various types of lease arrangement.

Assets purchased on a hire-purchase contract with an 'option to buy' attract WDAs on the capital element, which is treated as all incurred when the asset is first taken over. The 'hire' element is relieved as a revenue expense. Sometimes a firm which leases a building is required under the lease to fit out the building with fixtures of various kinds. Broadly these are treated as belonging to the tenant, even though in law they belong to the landlord, as long as they are used in the tenant firm's business and allowances can be claimed accordingly, but when business use ceases (e.g. if the lease is given up) the balance of unrelieved expenditure passes to the landlord who may be liable to any balancing charge.

Making claims and method of giving relief

17.29 Capital allowances are given as an expense item (or in the case of balancing charges, as business receipts) in arriving at the taxable Case II profit: if there is a Case II loss, they are simply components in arriving at that loss, like any other deductible expense.

Claims to capital allowances have to be specifically made in tax returns, which must be submitted by 31 January after the end of the tax year.

Example 5

Typical computation of capital allowances

A partnership has the following transactions in plant during the year ended 30 April 2003:

		£
July 2002	Purchase of car for partner	16,000
Nov 2002	Purchase of plant	20,000
Dec 2002	Disposal of plant	30,000
Jan 2003	Disposal of office computer	3,000
Feb 2003	Purchase of office computer	8,000

Both the computers are treated as 'short life' assets (see 17.27 above).

The car acquired for the partner is used privately for 30% of the time.

The written-down value of the general pool brought forward as at 1 May 2002 is £180,000 and of the 'old' computer (1) £5,000.

	General Pool £	Computer (1) £	Computer (2) £	Car £	Allowances Given £
Written down value b/fwd	180,000	5,000	–	–	
Additions at cost	20,000	–	8,000	16,000	
	200,000	5,000	8,000	16,000	
Sale proceeds (restricted to original cost, if lower)			–	–	
	(30,000)	(3,000)			
Balancing allowance/ (balancing charge)		(2,000)			2,000
	170,000	–	8,000	16,000	
WDA @ 25%	(42,500)		(2,000)	–	44,500
WDA restricted 30% private use	–		–	(3,000)*	3,000
					(900)
WDA c/fwd	127,500	–	6,000	13,000	
Total allowances to be given as an expense in arriving at 2003/04 taxable profits					48,600

*The WDA is limited to £3,000 since the car cost more than £12,000 – See 17.25 above.

Chapter 18

Income Tax

Introduction

18.1   Up to and including the tax year 1993/94 partnerships were taxed on the so-called Preceding Year (PY) basis. This meant that the profits taxed in any tax year were those of the accounting period ending in the previous tax year, subject to special rules for commencements and cessations. The commencement rules normally involved the profits of some period being taxed more than once. This was balanced to some extent by the fact that the cessation rules allowed some profit to remain untaxed in the last few years. When there was a change of partner but the business continued, the default rule was that the business was regarded as ceasing for tax purposes. However, the partners could make a 'continuation' election which had the effect of disregarding the change for tax purposes and treating the business as continuing. This avoided the need to adjust the taxable profits of the penultimate and anti-penultimate years of assessment and was therefore used where this adjustment would have increased the tax bill.

This system underwent a fundamental change in the mid-1990s to the present Current Year (CY) system under which the profits taxed in any tax year are those of the accounting period ending in that year, with special rules when businesses, and partners, commence and cease. This change was part of the larger reforms introduced by the Self Assessment system, and took effect in stages. Its impact depended on the date a partnership business commenced. Details of how the changes took effect appear in the first and second editions of this book, but very broadly:

(*a*)   A business which commenced before 6 April 1994 normally came within the present system from 6 April 1997. 1997/98 is the first year whose taxable profits are based on the CY system.

(*b*)   A business which commenced after 5 April 1994 was within the CY system from outset.

(*c*)   For a business which remained on the PY system until 1997/98 there were special transitional rules for 1996/97 which were explained in the first two editions of this book.

No attempt is made here to describe the PY system in detail and reference should be made to standard tax textbooks if further information is required.

The present system of income taxation for partnerships

Overview of the present system

18.2   The main features of the present system are:

(*a*)   a current year ('CY') basis of assessment (see 18.3 below);

(*b*)   special commencement and cessation rules (see 18.5 and 18.9 below);

(*c*)   the concept of 'overlap' reliefs for profits taxed more than once (see 18.6 below);

(*d*)   individual accountability for partners' tax and the concept of treating each partner as carrying on a notional separate business (see 18.21 below);

(*e*)   Self Assessment compliance rules (see 18.32 below).

The 'CY' basis

18.3   The present system replaces the old preceding year ('PY') basis of assessment (see 18.1 above) with a current year ('CY') basis. Instead of being taxed on the profits of the accounting period ending in the previous tax year, partners are now taxed on the profits of the accounting period ending in the current year.

Payment of tax and choice of accounting dates

18.4   Tax is due under the present regime via an instalment system which requires a final payment by 31 January following the end of the tax year (see 18.32 below). It can be seen, therefore, that although the time-lag between the end of the accounting period and the date of payment of tax has been reduced compared to the old system (see 18.28 below), the choice of an accounting date early in the tax year still can have advantages. With a 30 April date, the final tax payment for 2002/03 is due on 31 January 2004, 21 months after the year end.

Commencement rules

18.5   The present system deals with the opening years in the following way.

(*a*)   *First tax year of business.* Based on the actual profit of that year, apportioned to 5 April.

(*b*)   *Second tax year of business.*

(i) If there is an accounting date in that year which falls less than 12 months after the starting date, the taxable profit is based on the first 12 months.

(ii) If there is an accounting date in the second year which is more than 12 months after the starting date, the taxable profit is based on the accounting period ending in the year. In other words, such a business reaches the 'CY' basis in the second tax year.

(iii) If there is no accounting date in the year (for example, where a business starts on 1 March 2002 and draws up a long account to, say, 31 December 2003) the 'fiscal year' basis is used.

(c) *Third tax year of business.* By the third tax year the business should reach the 'CY' basis if it has not already done so in the second.

Example 1

Start business on 1 May 2002 with 30 September accounting date

Bob, Carole, Ted and Alice started their firm on 1 May 2002 and draw up their accounts to 30 September each year, from 30 September 2002.

Their accounts show tax adjusted profits as follows:

1 May 2002 to 30 September 2002	£60,000
Year ended 30 September 2003	£108,000
Year ended 30 September 2004	£120,000

Their tax bills will be based on the following.

2002/03: (based on 1 May 2002 to 5 April 2003)	
Profit of initial period	£60,000
plus (say) $\frac{6}{12} \times$ £108,000	£54,000
	£114,000
2003/04: (based on year to 30 September 2003)	£108,000
2004/05: (based on year to 30 September 2004)	£120,000

Note that in practice apportionment of 'overlap' profits (see 18.6 below) is calculated in precise numbers of days rather than round months.

Also note that the accounting date in the second complete tax year, 30 September 2004, falls more than 12 months after the starting date and thus the firm reaches the 'CY' basis by its second tax year.

The profits of this second accounting period are, clearly, taxed 1.5 times – partly in 2002/03 and wholly in 2003/04. The treatment of this 'overlap' profit is discussed below (see 18.6 below and the example at 18.10 below).

Example 2

Start business on 1 March 2003 with 30 September accounting date

Atherton, Helsby and Cable started their firm on 1 March 2003 and also draw up accounts to 30 September, with the following profits.

1 March 2003 to 30 September 2003	£91,000
Year ended 30 September 2004	£144,000
Year ended 30 September 2005	£156,000

Their tax bills will be based on the following:

2002/03: (based on 1 March 2003 to 5 April 2003) (say) $\frac{1}{7}$ × £91,000	£13,000
2003/04: (based on 1 March 2003 to 28 February 2004 – see below)	
Profits of initial period	£91,000
plus (say) $\frac{5}{12}$ × £144,000	£60,000
	£151,000
2004/05: (based on year to September 2004)	£144,000
2005/06: (based on year to 30 September 2005)	£156,000

Here, the accounting date in the second tax year, 30 September 2003, is less than 12 months after the starting date and thus the first 12 months' of profit is taken. The 'CY' basis is not reached until the third tax year.

As in the previous example, some profits 'overlap' – here the periods from 1 March to 5 April 2003 (falling in 2002/03 and 2003/04) and from 1 October 2003 to 28 February 2004 (falling into 2003/04 and 2004/05). This is discussed below (see 18.6 and the example at 18.10 below).

This multiple taxation of the same profits means that the legitimate minimisation of taxable profits in the opening periods remains very important. There are many ways in which this can be done, including the use as employees or consultants of those who may later become partners. This will reduce initial profits by their salaries or fees.

Overlapping profits

18.6   Both the examples in 18.5 above showed that the same profits can be taxed more than once. Whereas the old system compensated for this by not taxing a different slice of profit on cessation, however, the present system identifies the over-taxed profit – called an 'overlap' profit – and gives relief for those actual amounts later – either on cessation or if the accounting date is moved to later in the tax year. However, the rules do not give any relief for inflation, so the real value of this relief may be substantially eroded if it is not given until many years later.

Subsequent changes to a later accounting date

18.7 If no subsequent changes to a later accounting date in the tax year occur, the overlap relief will be given in full on cessation. If the accounting date is changed to a date nearer to the end of the tax year, a pro-rata fraction of the relief is given. A change to a 5 April date will result in the whole of the relief being given, but a change from, say, 30 September to 31 December, roughly 'half way' to 5 April, would release roughly half the accrued relief.

'Reward' for those with late accounting dates

18.8 The intention of this system is, quite clearly, to 'reward' firms who choose late accounting dates, with the consequent acceleration of the receipts to the Exchequer. When selecting accounting dates partners therefore need to bear in mind that the cash flow benefits of an early date may involve inability to recover 'overlap' relief until cessation. The minimisation of initial profits, and hence the amount of any overlap, is thus particularly important (see 18.5 above).

Cessations

18.9 In the tax year in which a partnership business ceases as a question of fact, the tax bills are based on the profits from the end of the last preceding basis period to the cessation date. The last preceding basis period may have ended in the previous tax year and the basis period could exceed 12 months, but the taxed profits may be reduced by 'overlap' relief from the opening years.

No revision of earlier years' assessments

18.10 There is no revision of any earlier years' assessments as there was under the old system. In addition, because no deemed cessation of the business occurs when there is a change of partners (see 18.25 below), the special cessation rules only become relevant when the business actually comes to an end.

Example 3

The overlap relief rules in relation to cessations

The following example illustrates how the overlap relief (see 18.6 above) feeds through into the treatment of cessations.

Bob, Carole, Ted and Alice (see Example 1), who started their business on 1 May 2002, decide to bring it to an end on 31 December 2005. Their profits from 1 October 2004 are as follows:

Year to 30 September 2005	£96,000
Period from 1 October to 31 December 2005	£24,000

The tax year of cessation is 2005/06, so the basis period for that year runs from 1 October 2004, immediately after the end of the basis period for 2003/04, to 31 December 2005, i.e. 15 months.

The profits taxed will be based on:

12 months to 30 September 2005	£96,000
3 months to 31 December 2005	£24,000
Total 15 months	£120,000

However, this is when the overlap relief from commencement is given. The period from 1 October 2002–5 April 2003, say six months, was taxed both in 2002/03 and 2003/04. So relief for this profit is now given as follows.

15 months profit to 31 December 2005 as above	£120,000
Less 6 months' profit from 'overlap' period	
as above, (say, $\frac{6}{12} \times$ £108,000)	£54,000
Total 9 months	£66,000

The tax bill for 2002/03 will thus be based on £66,000. Superficially it may seem that nine months of profit, corresponding to the (roughly) nine months from 6 April to 31 December, have been taxed, but the relief does not take the form of taxing only $\frac{9}{15}$ of the actual profits earned from 1 October 2004. It is based on the actual overlap profits from 2002/03. In the real world, Bob, Carole, Ted and Alice's firm might run for 40 years instead of less than four, and the real value of the 'overlap' profit of £54,000 in, say 2040 might have little impact on profit at that time. This is another argument for a late accounting date (see 18.8 above). It will also, of course, be important to record and carry forward any 'overlap' reliefs so that they are not overlooked.

When overlap relief exceeds the profits

18.11   The overlap relief is deducted from profits of the final tax year, as illustrated above, and if it exceeded those profits a 'loss' would be created, which could then be relieved against other income or in the various ways described below (see 18.17 below).

Changes of accounting date

18.12   Businesses are free to choose their own accounting date, despite the obvious inducement in the 'overlap rules' to choose a late date in the tax year, and in general this will be respected for tax purposes, but the Revenue have the power to disregard a change if certain conditions do not apply.

Conditions for change of accounting date

18.13   Except in the first three years of trading, in order to be a valid change of accounting date the following conditions apply:

(*a*)   the first period ending on the new date must be 18 months or less; and

(*b*)   notice of the change is given to the Inspector by 31 January following the 'year of change'; and

(*c*)   unless there has been no change under these rules in the previous five tax years (in which case no further steps are necessary), the Revenue is satisfied that there are bona fide commercial reasons (unconnected with tax) for the change.

If the above conditions are not satisfied, the results of the new accounting period must be apportioned across the old periods, so compliance with the above is highly advisable.

The 'year of change' is the first tax year in which accounts are drawn up to the new date, or, if there is a long gap so that there is a tax year with no accounting date, it means that 'blank' year. Therefore, if the change is from 31 December 2002 to 30 April 2003, 2003/04 is the 'year of change'. If the change is from 31 March 2002 to 30 April 2003, the 'year of change' is 2002/03.

The effect of changing the date

18.14   Assuming that these conditions are all met, the effect of changing the date will be that the tax bill for the 'year of change' will be based on the profits as follows:

(*a*)   if the period exceeds 12 months, from the end of the basis period for the immediately preceding tax year to the new accounting date in the year of change; and

(*b*)   in other cases, of the 12 months ended on the year of change.

To a later or earlier date

18.15   This is simpler than it sounds. If the change is to a later date in the tax year, the gap between the old and new dates will exceed 12 months. If it is to an earlier date, it will be less than 12 months. A change to a later date involves a basis period of more than 12 months and therefore 'overlap' relief can be deducted to reduce it to 12 months. A change to an earlier date leads to the extension of the 'gap' period to a full 12 months and therefore a further 'overlap' for relief later.

Example 4

Change of accounting date to later date

Atherton, Helsby and Cable (see Example 2 at 18.5 above) decide to change their accounting date from 30 September to 31 December. Their year to 30 September 2005 showed profits of £156,000 and their next accounts, for the 15 months to 31 December 2006, show profits of £240,000.

The 'year of change' is 2006/07, the first tax year in which the new date is used. So the bill for that year is based on 15 months from 1 October 2005 to 31 December 2006, less three months of 'overlap' relief from commencement. That 'overlap' profit was approximately:

1 March–5 April 2003 (say $\frac{1}{7} \times$ £91,000)	£13,000
1 October 2003–28 February 2004	
(say $\frac{5}{12} \times$ £144,000)	£60,000
Total	£73,000

So the 2006/07 tax bill will be based on:

15 months profit to 31 December 2006 as above	£240,000
less overlap relief £73,000 $\times \frac{3}{6}$	£36,500
	£203,500

The remainder of the 'overlap' relief (£36,500) is simply carried forward and can be given on another change to a later date (e.g. it would be fully available if that change was to 5 April, or in practice to 31 March), or on cessation.

Example 5

Change of accounting date to an earlier date

Suppose instead that Atherton, Helsby and Cable decided to change their accounting date to 30 June. Their next accounts after 30 September 2005 cover the nine months to 30 June 2006 and profits disclosed are £144,000.

2006/07 is still the 'year of change' but the 'gap' is less than 12 months from the old date. So 2006/07 is based on the 12 months to 30 June 2006, i.e.

$\frac{3}{12} \times$ £156,000	£39,000
plus 9 months as above	£144,000
	£183,000

There is now a new 'overlap', for the period from 1 July to 30 September 2005, producing £39,000 as above, which falls into 2005/06 and 2006/07. This is simply carried forward in addition to the relief accrued on commencement.

Revenue's view

18.16   These inducements to choose late accounting dates may well prompt a review of policy by firms which had high initial profits and thus high 'overlaps' on commencement. Fortunately, the Revenue is unlikely to regard a change to a later date as objectionable and for non-bona fide reasons. However, it should be relatively simple to make one change, since it is not necessary to show bona fide reasons unless there has been a change within the previous few years under the present system. Therefore, new businesses should be able to make a subsequent change to release large 'overlap' reliefs. Where profits fluctuate by high margins, good advisers would normally consider the impact of a change and make recommendations.

Losses

18.17   Business losses are relieved against other income for the tax year of loss or the previous year. Various permutations of claims are allowed.

Example 6

Options when making a loss

Dead, Beat & Co make a loss of £50,000 in their year to 30 September 2003. This is the basis period for 2003/04, so the tax bill for that year for the firm will be nil. Dead and Beat share losses equally. Dead has other (personal) income of £10,000 for 2003/04 and £15,000 for 2002/03 (this includes his share of the small profit the firm made in the year to 30 September 2002). He has the following options:

(*a*)   He can offset £10,000 of his share of the firm's loss (£25,000) against his 2003/04 income, reducing it to nil and reclaiming any tax already paid, and carry the balance (£15,000) forward to set against his share of future profits.

(*b*)   As (*a*) for 2003/04, but he can also carry back the balance of £15,000 to offset his other income of 2001/02. This will also be reduced to nil and tax paid be reclaimed. This uses up the whole of his losses, with nothing to carry forward.

(*c*)   He can set £15,000 of his losses against his 2002/03 income, claim relief as in (*b*) above, but then carry the remaining £10,000 forward. He might do this to avoid wasting other reliefs due in 2003/04 such as enterprise investment scheme investments or personal allowances.

Capital allowances

18.18   Capital allowances are given as a business expense, and balancing charges are treated as a business receipt. Thus the taxable profit figure will be net of allowances and include charges. If allowances are high enough they could, like any other expense, turn a profit into a loss.

Accounting period of more/less than 12 months

18.19   This does, however, mean that in accounting periods longer or shorter than 12 months, the allowances and charges have to be adjusted proportionately. In a six-month accounting period where expenditure of £10,000 is incurred on plant added to the 'pool', the writing down allowance (WDA) (see 17.24 above), normally 25% (i.e. £5,000), will become an expense of £2,500. In a 15-month period it would become ($\frac{15}{12} \times$ £5,000) £6,250. No accounting period can exceed 18 months for this purpose.

Expenditure allowed before it is incurred

18.20   The apportionment of accounting period profits into tax years can mean that expenditure in the first year of a firm's business can be allowed in a tax year before it was incurred.

Example 7

Relief in first tax year for item bought in second year

The firm of John Smith & Co began on 1 January 2002, and drew up its first accounts to 31 December 2002, spending £40,000 on plant and machinery on 1 December 2002. The accounts showed a profit of £110,000. After treating the capital allowances as an expense this becomes £100,000. Under the commencement rules (see 18.5 above) the first tax year, 2001/02, is based on the profits from 1 January to 5 April 2002, i.e. £25,000. This includes an element of relief for the plant and machinery even though it was not bought until 2002/03. This could allow a useful element of flexible planning in the first year, as the plant and machinery could be purchased when the partners' other income and circumstances for 2001/02 were already known.

How the income tax system treats partnerships

18.21   The changes described at the start of this chapter made a fundamental change in the tax treatment of partnerships. The old system taxed the profits of the firm as a unit and then allocated them between those who were partners in the tax year concerned, regardless of the identity of the partners in the basis period. There was joint and several liability in law for the resultant tax.

Key implications of the present system

18.22   Under the present system, however:

(*a*) Each partner is deemed to carry on a notional separate business, which begins when he joins the firm and ends when he leaves. The commencement, cessation and overlap rules will apply on an individual basis to these events.

(*b*) The profit is allocated among the partners according to their shares in the accounting period on which the tax year is based.

(*c*) Each partner is personally liable for tax on his share, but only for that tax.

Simpler allocation

18.23 In an ongoing firm with no partnership changes this system produces a simpler form of allocation.

Example 8

One partner reduces workload and profits

Peter, Paul and Mary have been in partnership for many years and until 30 April 2003 they share profits equally. On 1 May 2003, Peter decides to reduce his workload and profits are henceforth shared 10% to Peter and 45% each to Paul and Mary.

Profits are:

£180,000 to 30 April 2003
£200,000 to 30 April 2004.

The 2003/04 profits, based on the year to 30 April 2003, will be taxed as follows.

Peter	33.33%	£60,000
Paul	33.33%	£60,000
Mary	33.33%	£60,000
		£180,000

The 2004/05 profits, based on the following year, will be taxed as follows.

Peter	10%	£20,000
Paul	45%	£90,000
Mary	45%	£90,000
		£200,000

If Peter fails to pay the tax on his £20,000, Paul and Mary cannot be sued by the Revenue for this.

Adjustments

18.24 There may be adjustments for fixed shares such as salaries and partnership interest. These are made on the basis of the entitlement of the partners in the accounting period.

Leavers and joiners

18.25 This feature can become complex when partners join or leave a firm. The following example takes a firm from the commencement of the business through several partnership changes, to show how each partner is regarded as carrying on a notional separate business.

Example 9

Commencement of a partnership

Edwards, Bairstow and Harrison began practising as a professional partnership on 1 October 2000. Edwards contributed more capital than the others, so profits were initially split 50% to him and 25% each to Bairstow and Harrison.

Profits to 30 September each year are as follows.

2001	£270,000
2002	£300,000
2003	£320,000
2004	£360,000
2005	£375,000

(*a*) *Opening years*

The allocation of profits for tax purposes in the opening years follows the principles in 18.5 above.

Tax Year	Taxable Profits		Allocated		
			E	B	H
			£	£	£
2000/01	$\frac{6}{12} \times$ £270,000 = £135,000		67,500	33,750	33,750
2001/02	Year to 30 September 2001 = £270,000		135,000	67,500	67,500
Each partner also has a personal 'overlap' profit in respect of the period from 1 October 2000 to 5 April 2001 (see 17.9 above)			(67,500)	(33,750)	(33,750)

Each partner is treated as having begun his own notional profession on 1 October 2000.

(b)   *A new partner joins*

On 1 October 2002 the firm took in a new partner, Miss Rowlatt. Profits are now shared equally. Miss Rowlatt is regarded as beginning her own notional profession when she joins. However, she joins in 2002/03 so this is her first tax year, and the commencement rules apply to her share even though the others are taxed on the 'CY' basis. Miss Rowlatt's tax bill for 2002/03 is therefore based on the period from 1 October 2002 to 5 April 2003, during which she has a 25% share. So she will be taxed on 25% of $\frac{6}{12} \times$ £320,000, i.e. £40,000. This, of course, is based on the profits of the year to 30 September 2003.

The three original partners, however, are in the third tax year of their notional professions when Miss Rowlatt joins. For them, the basis period is the year to 30 September 2002 producing profits of £300,000. Their 2002/03 tax bills will be based on their profit shares in that year, i.e.:

Edwards	(50%)	£150,000
Bairstow	(25%)	£75,000
Harrison	(25%)	£75,000

Moving on to 2003/04, this is Miss Rowlatt's second tax year as a partner and her tax bill will be based on the year to 30 September 2003 (see 18.5 above). This gives her 25% of £320,000, i.e. £80,000. In addition, she also acquires a personal 'overlap' profit of £40,000 since the profits of her notional profession in the period from 1 October 2000 to 5 April 2001 have been taxed twice. The other partners will also have their tax bills based on the same year and will thus be taxed on £80,000 each.

To summarise the position for 2002/03 and 2003/04:

Tax Year	Taxable Profits		Allocated		
		E	B	H	R
		£	£	£	£
2002/03	Year to 30 September 2002 (£300,000)	150,000	150,000	150,000	–
	Period from 1 October 2002 to 5 April 2003 (25% × $\frac{6}{12}$ × £320,000)	–	–	–	40,000
2003/04	Year to 30 September 2003 (£320,000)	80,000	80,000	80,000	80,000
Personal 'overlap' to carry forward		(62,500)	(33,750)	(33,750)	(40,000)

(c)   *A partner retires*

On 30 September 2004, Edwards retires and the three remaining partners share profits equally thereafter.

Therefore, 2004/05 is Edwards' final tax year and his notional profession ceases. The cessation rules have to be applied to him only. His 2004/05 tax bill will therefore be based on the period from 1 October 2002–30 September 2004, i.e. 25% of £360,000 = £90,000. Now, however, he can deduct his 'overlap' profit from the first year of his notional profession, £67,500, to give him a net taxable profit of £22,500. The other partners are simply taxed on their shares of the profit of the same year.

Tax Year *Taxable Profit*		*Allocated*		
	E £	B £	H £	R £
2004/05 Year to 30 September 2004 (£360,000)	90,000	90,000	90,000	90,000
Less 'overlap' relief given on retirement	(67,500)			
	22,500	90,000	90,000	90,000
Personal 'overlap' relief carried forward	–	(33,750)	(33,750)	(40,000)

(d)   *Cessation of the whole business*

In the year to 30 September 2005 (profits £375,000) there are no changes in the firm, but there is a dispute shortly after this and the partners decide to go their separate ways on 30 April 2006. Profits from 1 October 2005 to that date are £90,000 (having been adversely affected by the internal bickering in the period).

The effect of this is that all the partners' notional professions are deemed to end on 30 April 2006 and 2006/07 is the final tax year for each. The cessation rules are applied and for each partner, the basis period for 2006/07 runs from 1 October 2005 to 30 April 2006. Each partner can deduct his or her accrued 'overlap' profits.

Tax Year	Taxable Profit	Allocated		
		B £	H £	R £
2005/06	Year ended 30 September 2005 (£375,000)	125,000	125,000	125,000
2006/07	1 October 2005–30 April 2006 (£90,000)	30,000	30,000	30,000
	Less personal 'overlap'	(33,750)	(33,750)	(40,000)
	Losses	(3,750)	(3,750)	(10,000)

It will be seen that the allowances for their 'overlaps' give each partner a loss in 2006/07 which can be used against any other income for the year or the previous year. If the losses were much larger they could claim 'terminal' loss relief against the previous three years' profits, i.e. 2005/04, 2004/05 and 2003/04.

Cessation in a successful partnership

18.26   In a more successful scenario, however, such a cessation could involve substantial tax bills. Suppose that this partnership had made profits of £480,000 in the period for 1 October 2005–30 April 2006. Each partner would have been taxed on £160,000 less 'overlap' relief. Each would have been a partner for only a month in 2006/07, yet would have been taxed on seven months' profit before 'overlap' relief, and that relief, on historical profits of an earlier period without indexation for inflation, would have been of much less value.

Retirement planning

18.27   This point needs to be borne in mind, since in the real world a partner might expect many more years of income from a firm and, in a successful career, would hope to retire with a much larger profit share, from a much larger pool of profits, than he started with. Provision will be needed for the substantial tax bills which will arise on retirement in such a case and the choice of retirement date will need careful planning.

Taxable and actual earnings compared

18.28   The present system produces a time-lag between when profits are earned and when they are taxed which still provides an incentive to select an accounting date early in the tax year.

Example 10

Time-lag between when profits are earned and taxed

The Taxwise Partnership (consisting of Mr Sharp and Mr Smart) has a 30 April accounting date. The partners' final tax bills will be payable on 31 January following the end of the tax year. The partners' 2003/04 tax bills will be based on the results to 30 April 2003 and the final payment date will be 31 January 2005 (see 18.32 below). However, 'interim' payments will be due on 31 January and 31 July 2004, based on the bills for 2002/03 (see 18.32 below). The choice of an early accounting date has therefore given the firm the use of the funds for 21 months, in so far as profits are rising so that they exceed what is needed for the interim payments. By contrast, a 31 March accounting date would have reduced this time-lag to just ten months.

The comparison

18.29   It is useful to compare actual and taxable income as follows:

Example 11

Actual and taxable income

Profits of the Taxwise Partnership are as follows:
Year ended
30 April   £

2003	350,000
2004	375,000
2005	400,000
2006	420,000

Assuming that the partners, Sharp and Smart, share profits equally, Mr Sharp's position is as follows.

Tax Year	*Income enjoyed* (A) £	*Income on which tax paid for year* (B) £	*'Tax deferred' income as % of* (A)
2003/04	187,500[1]	175,000[2]	6.6[3]
2004/05	200,000	187,500	6.25
2005/06	215,000	200,000	6.97

Notes
[1] Half of profit of the year to 30 April 2004.
[2] Half the profit of the year to 30 April 2003, taxed in 2003/04.
[3] £12,500 (£187,500 less £175,000), i.e. 6.6% of £187,500 is enjoyed in 2003/04 but not taxed until 2004/05.

Rising profits

18.30   Under the old 'PY' system the time-lag between the enjoyment of income and its taxation was often 12 months longer than it is now and the change to the CY system has reduced the opportunities for using tax-deferred income to fund working capital. This may increase the need for external financing. Fortunately, relief for interest on personal loans which are injected into the business is still available in full at marginal tax rates, on the basis of interest paid in the tax year.

Impact of substantial differences between taxable and actual profits

18.31   Another, less tangible but still important, feature of the CY system may be that the impact of substantial differences between the accounts profits and the taxable profits, due to tax adjustments, has become more noticeable (see 18.17 above). Under the old system, with early accounting dates, it could be almost two years before the effect of tax-related additions to the accounts profit 'came home' in tax bills. Under the CY system they now do so a year sooner and are much more likely to be fresh in partners' minds. The choice of advisers who can effectively negotiate the minimisation of these adjustments will therefore be even more important.

Tax payments – compliance and administration

18.32   Tax payments are due for a tax year by a final payment date of 31 January after the end of the year. However, two interim payments must also be made, on 31 January in the year and 31 July after its end. Each of these is based on half the partner's final tax bill for the previous year. Credit is given for these payments against the final bill on the following 31 January.

For the fiscal year 2002/03, tax will fall due for payment as follows:

1st payment on account	31 January 2003
2nd payment on account	31 July 2003
Balancing payment	31 January 2004*

*The 1st payment on account in respect of the 2003/04 year will also be due for payment on this date.

The interim payments on account also reflect any non-partnership income, such as bank interest, for the year, but not any capital gains. Tax on these is wholly collected in the final payment. If, because a partner's income has declined, the final bill is less than the interim payments, he will receive a refund (with tax-free interest). It is possible to reduce the interim payments if current income is thought to be reducing, but interest (and possibly penalties) can arise if this estimate proves incorrect.

Example 12

Timing of payments

Mr Sharp, of the Taxwise Partnership, has the following tax bills, on his income for 2003/04.

	£
On his share of the firm's profits (say)	70,000
On personal Schedule A income	5,000
	75,000

On his 2004/05 income and gains he has the following tax to pay.

	£
On share of profits	75,000
On Schedule A income	5,000
On capital gains (say)	10,000
	90,000

He will have to make the following payments for 2004/05.

	£
On 31 January 2005:	
Interim payment equal to half the previous year's tax (and see below)	37,500
On 31 July 2005:	
Second interim payment as above	37,500
	75,000

	£
On 31 January 2006:	
Final payment for 2004/05 on income and gains	90,000
Less interim payments as above	75,000
To pay	15,000

On 31 January 2005 Sharp will also have had to pay the final amount due for 2003/04 – the difference between £75,000 and the interim payments made in that year. On 31 January 2006 he will have to make the first interim payment for 2005/06.

Tax deducted at source

18.33   Credit is also given in the final bill for tax deducted at source, e.g. on UK bank interest or tax deducted under PAYE on director's fees, and for tax credits on UK dividends.

Late final payment

18.34 A late final payment, in addition to non-tax deductible interest at a rate which is usually in line with London Interbank Offered Rate (LIBOR), may incur a surcharge of 5%, which is doubled if payment is more than six months late.

Tax returns

18.35 The personal tax return is a 'self-assessment' return including income from all sources and capital gains, under which the partner must (unless he 'opts out' – see below) calculate the tax bill himself rather than having it calculated by the Revenue. This return is due by 31 January after the end of the tax year – the same date as the final tax payment date (see 18.32 above).

There is a penalty if the return is late, ranging from a flat £100 if it is even one day late, plus another £100 if it is six months late, to an amount of up to 100% of the tax due on the filing date if it is more than 12 months late. A taxpayer can 'opt out' of self-assessment and allow the Revenue to do the calculations, but he must then submit his return by 30 September after the end of the tax year, i.e. four months earlier than under self-assessment.

Partnership returns

18.36 A partnership must also submit a return, also due by 31 January after the end of the tax year. It includes a declaration of the names, residence and tax references of anyone who has been a partner in any part of the period to which the return relates, a statement of the tax-adjusted profit of the firm, the shares allocated to all partners, and other information, such as details of capital gains on business assets. It also includes basic information about turnover and profits, derived from the accounts: the accounts themselves are not required unless turnover exceeds £15 million. The person making the return also has to make a declaration that it is correct and complete to the best of his knowledge. The same penalty rules will apply (see 18.35 above) but if the return is late, the penalty is multiplied by the number of partners. Where the partner responsible for dealing with any matters relating to the partnership return ceases to be available to do so, the remaining partners must nominate a replacement as 'successor'.

Investigation into returns

18.37 A new code was introduced for Revenue investigations into tax returns and accounts at the same time as the self-assessment system. As a result the accurate and timely submission of computations has become very important. Even if the Revenue raises no queries on a firm's partnership return, the costs of an error could be considerable.

Example 13

Penalties for late submission of returns

Muddle, Shambles and Co is an old established firm with 25 partners. Its accountant, Ivor Crisis, prepares the firm's accounts and all the partners' individual tax returns. He is swamped with work in January 2003 and has not managed to collect all the information for the 2001/02 returns due on 31 January. Some partners are more dilatory than others and he decides to wait until he has each partner's figures – the last of which do not arrive until September. He then submits the partnership return and accounts plus 25 individual returns.

The delay means that the firm and the partners could incur the following fixed penalties (and possibly others, as the Inspector can ask the Appeal Commissioners for additional amounts in cases of long delay).

	£
Firm's return more than six months late (two penalties of £100 × 25 partners)	5,000
25 individual returns also more than six months late (£200 × 25)	5,000
	10,000

Therefore, firms must have an efficient system of compliance and competent professional help. The system also includes a tariff of penalties for inadequate business records, which must be retained for five years beyond the 31 January filing date each year, and since there are similar requirements for VAT (see Chapter 20), failure could be expensive.

Personal Service Companies ('IR35')

What IR35 means

18.38   Some complex rules were included in *Finance Act 2000* to counter perceived tax avoidance by 'Personal Service Companies', typically one-person organisations where the only shareholder also performs all the work which produces the profits. These could be used to control the amount and timing of the proprietor's remuneration for tax purposes, particularly by paying out profits in the form of dividends which do not incur National Insurance Contributions (NICs). The Revenue regarded many such proprietors as merely disguised employees of those for whom their company performed services, especially where the company had only one or a very few 'clients'.

From 6 April 2000 this perceived abuse has been countered by rules which have become known as 'IR35', after the number of the Budget Day Press Release in 1999 where they were first announced. Despite the references to companies, these rules can sometimes apply to partnerships.

The essence of IR35 is that it looks through the formal contractual relationship between the service company and its client, to the actual relationship between the person who performs the services ('the worker' – who may often be the proprietor of the service company) and the client. It then asks whether, in the absence of the service company, the worker would be, in law, an employee of the client. This question has to be answered using existing case law on the distinction between a contract of service (employment) and a contract for services (self-employment).

If the answer is that the worker would be an employee when the relationship is 'looked through', the service company is deemed to have made a payment of taxable Schedule E remuneration to the worker on the last day of the tax year in which the work is done. This requires the preparation of a 'deemed payment' calculation. This consists of the fees or other payments received from the client, less expenses which would be allowable if there really was an employment – such as travelling in the course of carrying out the work-pension contributions, any capital allowances which an employee could claim, NICs and a flat rate deduction of 5% (to cover all other expenses). The totals for all engagements which fall within IR35 have to be amalgamated and PAYE and employers' NICs calculated as if the amount was being paid out on 5 April as salary. Any PAYE and NICs which have actually been deducted in the year are credited. The net amount then has to be paid to the Revenue by 19 April after the year end. The liability for this payment falls on the service company, not on its clients.

How IR35 can affect professional partnerships

18.39   The Revenue was concerned that if the IR35 rules applied only to service companies they could easily be evaded by the use of service partnerships. Thus there are provisions which can catch partnerships, and they are so widely drawn that they can apply even where there is no intention to avoid or delay any tax payments.

Does IR35 apply to the work?

18.40   The first question to ask is whether the relationship between a partnership and any of its clients is such that the person or persons who do the work would be employees of the client, in the absence of the partnership (see above). Examples might include:

(i)   A firm of accountants is asked to lend a client the full-time services of a partner for 12 months to replace a Finance Director who has died suddenly.

(ii)   A firm of solicitors is asked to make a partner with a reputation for expertise in a particular specialism available to lecture several times a week and conduct tutorials at the local university in that subject, to cover for an academic who is taking sabbatical leave.

(iii) Another firm of accountants is asked to undertake high level financial modelling training for a group of senior executives in a client company, to replace the company's internal trainers who have been made redundant.

The fees received for work which is within the 'employment' category may fall within IR35, but this will depend on the status of the 'worker' and the nature of the firm, as explained below.

Does IR35 apply to the 'worker' and the firm?

18.41   IR35 can apply to the income from work within the 'employment' category if any of the following conditions apply:

(*a*)   The 'worker' is entitled to 60% or more of the profits of the partnership. For this purpose rights of relatives have to be counted as well – this includes a spouse, parent or remoter forebear, child or remoter issue, brother or sister. 'Spouse' also includes an unmarried partner with whom the 'worker' lives as man or wife.

(*b*)   Most of the profits of the firm are derived from engagements with a single client, or associates of that client, within the IR35 rules. 'Most' in this context is undefined and the Revenue have preferred to leave it open for negotiation.

(*c*)   The profit sharing arrangements are such that the income of any partner is based on the income generated by him in providing services through engagements within the IR35 rules.

'(*a*)' above will clearly apply to many family-based professional partnerships, as well as firms where one individual has a very large proportionate profit percentage.

'(*b*)' is aimed at specifically created devices to circumvent the rules, but could of course also apply if a separate firm was created, perhaps for regulatory reasons, to take on work which happened to fall within IR35. Where the client is a company, its associates include any person connected with the company as defined in *section 839* of *ICTA 1988*.

'(*c*)' is the least easy to understand. It appears to apply even if the income of a partner is 'based' to a small extent on IR35 income. However, it is thought that it is aimed at the direct passing through of IR35 income to the 'worker'. Unless either (*a*) or (*b*) is in point, it should not apply if the income of IR35 engagements is pooled in the normal way before profits are allocated.

Practical implications if IR35 applies

18.42   If IR35 does apply, separate records will be needed of the income and expenses involved and of who does the work. These will need to be kept on a tax year basis rather than an accounting year basis, as IR35 works on a cash basis rather than an accruals basis. This information will be needed to calculate the PAYE and NIC bill at 5 April each year. However, if the profits have been paid out as they come in with a PAYE and NIC deduction, no further payment will usually be needed.

The firm is entitled to deduct the deemed salary payment and the employer's NICs in calculating its taxable profits for accounting period in which the relevant 5 April falls. This means that a firm with a 31 March accounting date will always obtain relief for the payment one year late, and a change to 5 April might be considered if the amounts are material. If the deduction of this payment produces a loss, the partners cannot set this against their other income in the manner described above (see 18.17) – it can only be carried forward.

Partnership service companies and IR35

18.43   The above assumes that it is the partnership which provides services potentially within IR35. Many firms own companies which employ staff and provide common services, as well as perhaps holding properties from which the firm operates. These could, in theory, themselves be within IR35 if the work done through the company would represent an employment in the absence of the intervening company. However, the staff who actually provide the services in such companies will normally be paid through the PAYE and NIC system in the normal way for all the work they perform through the company, and no problems should therefore arise.

Where this is not the case, the IR35 rules can only apply to fees for work done through the company by individuals who hold, broadly, more than 5% of the ordinary share capital of the company, either alone or with associates. The latter expression includes not only relatives but also business partners. Thus, because one partner's ownership of service company shares will be attributed to all the other partners, it is likely that any fees for work done through a partnership-owned company by partners themselves will be within IR35 if the client relationship would be that of employer and employee in the absence of the company.

If this seems likely to be the case, it may be possible to avoid the rules by appropriate restructuring of the contracts. Failing this, the effects can be mitigated by making the maximum possible corporate pension contributions for those who undertake the work, since these are deductible in arriving at the amount which is subject to PAYE and NICs. Many of the running costs of the company – such as travelling and accommodation costs – can also be offset, and an additional 5% of the relevant fees can also be offset to cover other costs. IR35 is thus only likely to be a problem for partnership-owned companies where they receive substantial fees for work done by partners, or by staff with more than 5% of the shares who are not fully taxed under PAYE.

Revenue concessions

18.44   IR35 does not affect the Revenue practice of allowing small fees from directorships and other sources to be paid gross providing that they are pooled with profits before allocation (see 17.7 and 20.15).

Conclusions

18.45   Many firms will never encounter these complex provisions, but when they do apply their effects can be substantial. There are detailed rules affecting the calculation of the deemed payment required when IR35 'bites' and for partnerships in particular the treatment of expenses requires careful consideration. Instead of receiving fees which can be allocated, along with the rest of the general profit pool, among all partners, IR35 fees have to be taxed, in effect, as if they were paid as salary to a particular individual, and there will be interest and possibly penalty costs if the rules are not observed. Last but not least, an additional NIC cost on the relevant fees will be incurred which would not arise under normal rules. Family based firms, and smaller firms which could be caught by the 60% rule mentioned above, will therefore find it worthwhile to review current client engagements to see if any could fall within IR35, and if so, whether the contracts can be restructured. Larger firms may need to review profit sharing arrangements to ensure that even if they do have engagements within the rules, the income from them is genuinely pooled before profit shares are determined.

Chapter 19

Capital Gains Tax and Partnerships

This chapter outlines the main capital gains tax (CGT) issues which arise for partnerships and partners. This is a complicated subject, where there is not much statute law but a good deal of generally accepted Inland Revenue practice. Most of the practical problems arise when partners leave a firm or change their profit-sharing arrangements.

Partnership assets and the nature of a partner's interest

Basic points

19.1   CGT is a tax on gains on the disposal of assets, and according to the legislation 'all forms of property' are assets for CGT purposes unless specifically excluded. Clearly a firm's activities involve some assets which most people would describe as partnership assets, e.g. office premises and, perhaps, its goodwill. However, the partners also have rights under the partnership agreement (if one exists) which could be treated as assets. The combination of law and practice effectively:

(*a*)   disregards the firm as such, and deems all dealings in partnership assets as dealings by the partners;

(*b*)   treats each partner as owning a share of the firm's assets and therefore realising a share of any gains or losses when they are sold; and

(*c*)   makes the partners personally liable to CGT on their individual shares of any gains made on these assets (there has never been any joint liability here – contrast the position for income tax under the present regime).

How is a partner's share of gains calculated

19.2   A partner's share of any such gains will be his capital profit share as set out in the partnership agreement. If there is no agreement, or it does not specify any share, capital profits will be shared equally. Capital profit shares do not have to be identical to income profit shares. It is quite common to find that where for example, a partner puts a property into a firm, the agreement provides for capital profits or losses on its sale to be for the account of that partner alone.

Indexation and taper relief

19.3   Until 5 April 1998, indexation relief operated to remove the inflationary element of taxable gains. The acquisition expenditure (or 'base cost') of an asset was written up for tax purposes according to the increase in the Retail Prices Index between the date of acquisition and the date of disposal.

However, as a result of the *Finance Act 1998* indexation was 'switched off' at 5 April 1998 for individuals and partnerships. The relief which had accrued up to that date will still be available on a disposal after 5 April 1998, but it is not available on expenditure incurred after that date. Thereafter it is replaced by a new 'taper relief'. This operates by reducing the otherwise taxable gain – after any indexation up to 5 April 1998 for assets acquired before that date – by a percentage which increases the longer the asset is held. There are, in fact, two scales of tapering, one for business assets and one for other assets. The distinction between the two classes can be complex, but for the purposes of this chapter it will be assumed in the main that the asset being disposed of qualifies for the more generous business scale. That will be the case for a disposal of a partner's interest in a partnership, and of an asset which has been used, throughout its ownership (or throughout its ownership since 5 April 1998 if acquired earlier) wholly for the purpose of the firm's business. From 6 April 2000 it may also be the case with shares in trading companies owned by partnerships.

Even more generous taper rates have been made available for disposals after April 2002. These mean that for business assets held for just two whole years, an effective rate of CGT of only 10% will be available.

The taper scales which apply to disposals of business assets after 5 April 2002 are set out below. The amount of the relief depends on the length of the 'Qualifying Holding Period' (QHP); this is the number of complete years after 5 April 1998 for which the asset has been owned by the person disposing of it at the date of disposal. The table also shows the effective tax rate after taper relief, based on a 40% rate for a higher rate taxpayer:

Number of whole years in qualifying period	Percentage of gain taxed	Effective tax rate
Less than 1	100	40
1	50	20
2	25	10
3	25	10
4 or more	25	10

For non-business assets the scale is less generous:

Number of whole years in qualifying period	Percentage of gain taxed	Effective tax rate
Less than 3	100	40
3	95	38
4	90	36
5	85	34
6	80	32
7	75	30
8	70	28
9	65	26
10 or more	60	24

If a non-business asset was held at 16 March 1998 (the day before Budget Day) by the person disposing of it, an extra year's relief is given.

For disposals before 6 April 2000 the 'business' scale was also a ten-year one, with the effective minimum tax rate of 10% achieved only after ten years' ownership. No 'credit' is given for periods of ownership before 6 April 1998, since indexation operates for that period. Where an asset acquired before 5 April 1998 is sold after that date, indexation is calculated on the overall gain before taper relief, and taper relief is then applied to the indexed gain.

Finance Act 2000 also altered the definition of a business asset for taper relief purposes. Notably, in relation to partnerships, it provided that shares or securities in an unlisted trading company would become business assets in relation to periods after 5 April 2000, regardless of the percentage owned or whether the shareholder worked full time, or even at all, in the company's trade. Thus, shares in a partnership service company which carries on a trade, such as the provision of staff and services to the firm, should now qualify for the much more generous scale of business taper relief. However, the definition of a trading company for this purpose can be complex and expert advice is needed on what activities might prejudice the relief. Also, for periods of ownership before 6 April 2000 the shares might qualify only for the less generous non-business scale, unless the partner in question owned more than 25% of the voting shares, or, if less, was a full time employee of the company (not of the partnership). These conditions were rarely satisfied except in small firms, so the change is welcome.

An apportionment would be needed on the sale of service company shares held at 5 April 2000, which switched from non-business to business asset status as a result of these changes, between business and non-business periods; to achieve the minimum 10% tax rate, someone who owned shares which moved from the non-business to the business category would need to retain them until after 5 April 2010, after which the non-business period will drop out of the calculation. With good advice, however, it may be possible to accelerate the arrival of this minimum tax rate.

Disposals of partnership assets to the 'outside world'

19.4   There are normally few tax problems where a partnership asset is disposed of to a third party. The capital gain is calculated under the usual rules and then divided among the partners as indicated above (see 19.2 above).

Example 1

A disposal to a third party

Furniss, Dawson, Craven and White have been in partnership since 1984. They have always shared capital profits as to 40%, 30%, 15% and 15% respectively. In July 2003 they sell for £1,500,000 an office building acquired in July 1988 for £600,000 ('base cost'). The overall gain on the building is calculated under normal CGT principles but divided in appropriate shares, i.e.

	F 40% £	D 30% £	C 15% £	W 15% £	Totals £
Sale proceeds	600,000	450,000	225,000	225,000	1,500,000
Base cost	(240,000)	(180,000)	(90,000)	(90,000)	(600,000)
Indexation allowance to 5 April 1998 only, say 72% of cost	(172,800)	(129,600)	(64,800)	(64,800)	(432,000)
Indexed gains pre-taper relief	(187,200)	(140,400)	(70,200)	(70,200)	(468,000)
After taper relief*	46,800	35,100	17,550	17,550	117,000

*Each gain includes five years of taper relief at the 'business asset' rate, reducing the taxable gains to 25% of the indexed gains (see 19.3).

Each partner should include his share as above in his tax return, and tax will be payable by each accordingly.

Electing to 'rebase'

19.5   One important practical point needs mentioning here. If an asset was acquired before 31 March 1982 and is sold by the same owner after 5 April 1988, CGT law requires him to base his taxable gain on the value of the asset at 31 March 1982, if this produces a smaller gain or a smaller loss than taking historical cost. This process (called 'rebasing') cannot convert a gain into a loss or vice versa, merely reducing the gain to nil. A taxpayer can, however, elect to 'rebase' all his assets owned in a particular capacity to their 31 March

1982 value, to avoid this statutory comparison and the need to keep records of original cost. The election has to be made within two years of the end of the tax year in which the first disposal after 5 April 1988 (when the relevant law changed) of an asset held at 31 March 1982 occurred.

However, the Revenue regards assets owned by a person in his private capacity as separate from any in which he owns a share as a partner (and also separate from any he owns as a trustee). A partner might therefore find that he can still elect to 'rebase' his partnership assets to their 31 March 1982 values although he will now normally be too late to do so in relation to his other assets.

Reporting by the firm

19.6   Under the compliance regime for partnerships with effect from 6 April 1997, gains or losses on disposals of partnership assets must be reported by the firm on the new-style partnership return (see 18.35 above), quite separately from each partner's responsibility to report his personal gains or losses including shares of such disposals.

Transactions between partners

Change in capital income profit sharing ratios

19.7   When income profit-sharing ratios change, typically (but not only) when there is a change of partners, there may well also be a change of capital profit shares (see 19.2 above). This will affect the CGT base cost of each partner in respect of his share of any assets liable to CGT. Strictly, it amounts to a disposal by any partner whose share is reduced, and an acquisition by any whose share is increased.

Revenue practice

19.8   However, Revenue practice is not to make a CGT assessment on a partner who reduces his share in these circumstances, and to treat the transaction as giving rise neither to a gain nor a loss, subject to certain exceptions (see 19.11 and 19.12 below).

Instead, there is simply an adjustment to the base costs of all partners involved to reflect the altered entitlements to eventual capital profits. This takes account of the statutory indexation allowance.

Example 2

When a new partner is admitted

Instead of selling their building in July 2003, the partners in Furniss, Dawson, Craven and White (see the Example at 19.4 above) decide to admit a fifth partner, Templeman. Income and capital profits will henceforth be shared respectively 36%, 27%, 13.5%, 13.5% and 10%.

Assuming none of the exceptions in 19.11–19.12 below apply, no CGT assessments will be made and the following adjustments should be recorded to the partners' CGT base costs.

	F £	D £	C £	W £	T £	Totals £
Base cost b/f	240,000	180,000	90,000	90,000	–	600,000
'Disposal' to Templeman in July 2003	(24,000)	(18,000)	(9,000)	(9,000)	60,000	–
Revised base cost c/f	216,000	162,000	81,000	81,000	60,000	600,000

This calculation shows, as one would expect, that Furniss has 'disposed' of a 4% share (£24,000 being 4% of £600,000) since his profit share has declined from 40% to 36%. The other three original partners have respectively 'disposed' of 3%, 1.5% and 1.5%. Templeman has 'acquired' a 10% share of the original £600,000.

The effect of the indexation allowance and taper relief

19.9 However, this is not the whole story, because of the effect of the indexation allowance. Revenue practice here is to treat the inter-partner 'disposal' as taking place on a no gain/no loss basis after that allowance. If the property in the example above (at 19.4) is eventually sold, the partners will calculate their gains – assuming a sale in July 2004 for £2 million, with no further changes in the firm's constitution or sharing arrangements – as follows.

Example 3

	F (£000's)	D (£000's)	C (£000's)	W (£000's)	T (£000's)	Totals (£000's)
Base cost prior to July 2003	240	180	90	90	–	600
Indexation allowance to 5 April 1998 only, say 72% of cost	173	130	65	65	–	432
	413	310	155	155	0	1,032
Deemed disposals to Templeman July 2003	−41.28	−30.96	−15.48	−15.48	103.2	–
	371.52	278.64	139.32	139.32	103.2	1,032
Sale proceeds July 2004	720	540	270	270	200	2000
Indexed gains pre-taper relief	348.48	261.36	130.68	130.68	96.8	968
After taper relief*	87.12	65.34	32.67	32.67	84.7	302.5

*This example shows six years of taper relief for all the partners except Templeman, since all of them except him owned their interests at 5 April 1998 (see 19.3) and their gains are reduced to 25% of the indexed gains. Templeman, however, who only acquired his interest in July 2003, obtains only one year's relief.

In 2004/05 there will be CGT to pay by each partner as above, because this is a sale to the 'outside world' – unless the partners can claim any of the reliefs which are mentioned below (see 19.20 below).

Incidentally, although Templeman became a partner only in 2003, he effectively picks up a share of the indexation allowance which has accrued since 1988.

In practice, it is necessary to keep a record of the indexed base cost for each partner when there is a change in sharing ratios as this enables partners to see their true CGT base cost at any time. (There are some rather different rules, on which advice would be needed, where inter-partner transfers occurred between 6 April 1985, and 5 April 1988.) The same principle applies where there is a change in ratios within a partnership but no new partners join the firm.

Assets acquired before 1 April 1982

19.10 Further considerations can come into play where the asset in question was acquired before 1 April 1982. As noted above (see 19.5), 'rebasing' of CGT to this date will often mean that calculations are based on the value of the asset at 31 March 1982 rather than historic cost, with indexation also running from that date to 5 April 1998. As inter-partner transfers on a change of sharing ratios are treated as 'no gain/no loss' events (subject to the exceptions noted in 19.11–19.12 below), the base cost transferred between partners in such a case will be part of the value at 31 March 1982, plus indexation from that date, even where the transferee partner joined the firm long after that date.

If, in the above Example (see 19.9 above), the property had been acquired in, say, 1981, it is likely that Templeman, although he did not join until 2003, would inherit part of the 1982 value and indexation thereon up to 5 April 1998. This can still be an extremely valuable benefit when partners sell assets, though now limited by the 'freezing' of indexation at 5 April 1998.

Exceptions to the general rule

19.11   There are several exceptions to the general rule that inter-partner transactions in partnership assets take place on a 'no gain/no loss' basis. In these cases the transaction will normally be deemed to take place at the open market value of the asset concerned and tax may be payable by the disposing partner. These exceptions are:

(*a*)   where the parties are 'connected' with each other independently of the partnership, e.g. father and son; and

(*b*)   where a payment is made between the parties outside the accounts.

Detailed professional advice is needed in these situations.

Revaluations of assets

19.12   A further, and often more important, exception to the general rule is where partnership assets, for example property or goodwill, are revalued in the firm's accounts. This event does not have any CGT implications at the time, because nothing has been disposed of. However, when there is a later change in sharing ratios (whether between existing partners or on a partner joining or leaving), partners whose shares are reduced will be regarded as having realised a gain (if the revaluation was upwards) or a loss (if it was downwards). The logic behind this lies in the accounting entries made when a revaluation occurs. Where an asset is revalued upwards, anyone who was a partner at the time will be credited with the surplus according to his sharing ratio. If his share of capital profits is later reduced, without such treatment his potential CGT bill on a sale of the asset (or on leaving the firm – see 19.13 below) would also be reduced, yet his capital account would still show the revaluation surplus which could be enjoyed tax free.

Example 4

Revaluation of an asset

Sam and Janet have been in partnership for many years, sharing income and capital profits equally. They paid £20,000 for the goodwill of another practice which they took over in 1984. Until 1992 they showed this asset at cost in their accounts but then decided that since this side of the business had been very successful, they would revalue it to £100,000. £40,000 was credited to each partner's capital account. In December 2002 they admit a third partner, Arabella, and she takes a 20% share of profits with Sam and Janet reducing their shares to 40% each.

Sam and Janet are regarded, in 2002/03, as having each disposed of a 10% share of the goodwill to Arabella and as each making a capital gain as follows.

Deemed proceeds: 10% × £100,000	=	£10,000
Less 10% of original cost (£20,000)	=	(2,000)
and indexation thereon from 1984 to		
5 April 1998 (say 85%)		(1,700)
Capital gain		£6,300
Less four years' taper relief	=	£4,724
(see 19.3)		

This gain will be taxable in 2002/03 unless one of the relevant reliefs (see 19.20 below) applies.

Arabella is deemed to have a base cost of £20,000 (20% of £100,000).

It will be appreciated that this leaves the relevant partner with tax to pay, but no cash in his hand. Upwards revaluations should therefore be treated with great care since they may have unpleasant consequences in future. In this Example, Sam and Janet might have to withdraw funds from the firm, with consequent loss of working capital, to pay the tax. (See 19.16 below for the position when Sam retires.)

CGT implications of partnership retirements and goodwill

Typical arrangements

19.13 Firms make a wide variety of different provisions for a partner's retirement. The most common arrangements, however, are probably either:

(*a*)   the payment out of sums standing to the partner's credit (i.e. his capital and current account credit balances if any) but no payment for goodwill, together with an annuity; or (*b*)   a payment for goodwill, together with any credit balances as above, but no annuity – such a firm will have required partners to make their own pension arrangements out of their drawings.

No payment for goodwill

19.14   The first type of arrangement occurs either where no goodwill is thought to exist or where it is not recognised in the accounts as having any value, usually because it is declared in the partnership agreement as accruing to the firm as a whole. Where a partner leaves such a firm but the business continues, he will not have made any disposal of an asset recognised for CGT purposes. (The return of his capital and current account balances is simply, in effect, the withdrawal of his own money which has no CGT consequences – nor does it have any income tax consequences, because these funds include past profits on which he has already paid income tax.) However, advice will be needed, where a partner extracts assets (e.g. a property) in kind on retirement. See 19.18 below on the treatment of annuities.

The partner pays for goodwill

19.15   It might, of course, be the case that a partner in a firm of this type originally paid for a share of goodwill either when he joined the firm or perhaps when a new business was acquired (see the Example in 19.12), but this value has later been written down to zero because of a change of policy. In this event, a retiring partner might be able to claim a loss for CGT purposes, against any personal gains he makes in that or a later tax year, although the Revenue are likely to challenge this claim.

Payment for goodwill

19.16   In the second type of arrangement described above (see 19.13), the retiring partner will realise a taxable gain on his share of goodwill, calculated by taking the amount paid to him less his accumulated base cost on the principle already described for changes in profit shares (see 19.8–19.9 above). This is, after all, simply another such change, the retiring partner's share reducing to zero.

Example 5

Partner paid for share of goodwill on retirement

The partnership of Sam, Janet and Arabella which featured in the Example in 19.12 continues until July 2003 when Sam retires. He is paid £100,000 for his share of goodwill by Janet and Arabella, who henceforth divide profits equally. The CGT position is as follows:

	Sam £	Janet £	Arabella £
Share of goodwill before			
Arabella's admission (as 19.12)	10,000	10,000	–
Base cost used on disposal to			
Arabella	(2,000)	(2,000)	20,000
	8,000	8,000	20,000
Payment to Sam July 2003	(100,000)	50,000	50,000
Sam's gain	92,000		
Less indexation allowance			
(1984–5 April 1998) (say) 85%			
of £8,000	(6,800)		
Gain before taper relief	£85,200		
Remaining partner's base cost		58,000	70,000

Sam's taxable gain is reduced by five years of taper relief to £42,600.

Sam may well, however, be entitled to one of the reliefs mentioned below (see 19.20).

The payment of £100,000 to him would, of course, be justified only if Janet and Arabella considered that he might otherwise carry on working and entice clients away. By making such a payment they have in effect revalued goodwill again, and the consequences of this may have to be considered if the profit sharing ratios of Janet and Arabella are reduced later. (See 19.12 above.)

Other 'no gain/no loss' situations

19.17   It may be asked at this point what happens, on a partner's retirement, to his share of other assets of the firm, such as property. If that property remains in the firm, as it normally will, and no payment is made to the retiring partner, for CGT purposes, nothing happens. The transaction is simply regarded as a reduction in profit share to zero on the part of the retiring partner, giving rise to neither a gain nor a loss.

Example 6

Partner retires without property being sold

Returning to the firm of Furniss, Dawson, Craven, White and Templeman (see the Example at 19.9), suppose that the property is not sold in July 2004, but Furniss then retires. No payment is made to him in respect of his share of the property and the remaining four partners share profits thereafter as 36% to Dawson, 22.5% each to Craven and White and 19% to Templeman.

The position will be as follows.

	F (£000's)	D (£000's)	C (£000's)	W (£000's)	T (£000's)	Total (£000's)
Indexed base cost to 5 April 1998 (see 19.9)	371.52	278.64	139.32	139.32	103.2	1,032
'Disposal' by Furniss	(371.52)	92.88	92.88	92.88	92.88	–
Gain/loss to Furniss	NIL					
Base costs to c/f		371.52	232.2	232.21	96.08	1,032

The remaining partners have each increased their profit share by 9% of £1,032,000. Furniss has simply disposed of his share for its CGT base cost, in line with the treatment described earlier (see 19.9 above).

Annuities and CGT

19.18 Firms which do not make payments for goodwill to retiring partners tend instead to pay annuities in recognition of the retiring partner's contribution over the years. The Revenue will regard such payments wholly as income in the recipient's hands so long as they do not exceed a specified proportion of his recent shares of income profits. If more than these amounts is paid, the Revenue may treat the capitalised value of the annuity as consideration for a disposal of the partner's share of the firm's assets and CGT may be due accordingly.

Statement of Practice D12 revisited

19.19 In mid October 2002 the Inland Revenue released the long expected revised Statement of Practice D12 relating to the capital gains tax treatment of partnerships. The revised statement updates the original statement issued in January 1975 and reflects changes necessary in relation to the introduction of Limited Liability Partnerships (LLPs). The good new is that SP D12 will be extended to LLPs as long as they remain fiscally transparent. Fiscal transparency is only lost if the LLP ceases to carry on any trade or business with a view to profit and, even then, it can remain transparent whilst in the course of an orderly and bona fide winding up.

Of equal importance will be two new paragraphs inserted at the end of the statement dealing with partnership goodwill and taper relief. Where firms do not reflect the value of goodwill on their balance sheet or make payments between partners for goodwill then there will be no change in practice. However, where goodwill is included on a firm's balance sheet then this will be treated as a 'fungible' asset giving a more complex capital gains tax position than for those where goodwill is not so recognised. In essence, the new rules will mean that, where goodwill has been recognised on a firm's balance sheet, it will be treated as though goodwill was a holding of shares. This gives rise to different identification rules and potentially adverse taper relief implications, particularly where sales are made within a short period of the latest acquisition.

CGT reliefs for partners

19.20   Partners may be able to claim several valuable reliefs from CGT, some of which are deferrals of tax rather than exemptions. Basic points appear below, but the conditions are complex and expert advice should always be taken.

Rollover and holdover relief on replacement of business assets

19.21   Partners can 'roll over' the capital gains they make on their shares of the gain into the purchase of new qualifying assets.

Where a firm sells:

(*a*)   freehold land (or an interest in land such as a lease with more than 60 years to run), and/or buildings, which were occupied by the firm for its business; or

(*b*)   goodwill of the business (and several other kinds of asset which are unlikely to be found in a professional partnership, such as fixed plant and machinery, aircraft or satellites),

the partners can 'roll over' the capital gains they make on their shares of the gain on the purchase of new assets in the same categories. The new assets must be acquired during the period beginning one year before, and ending three years after the disposal of the old ones. Like-for-like replacement is not required (e.g. gains on a lease could be 'rolled' into an acquisition of goodwill, or vice versa). The effect is to reduce the base cost of the partners' shares of the new asset by their gains on the old assets. The relief is therefore a deferral of tax rather than an exemption, but if the new assets are later sold when retirement relief (see 19.24 below) is due, it may in effect turn into an absolute exemption. The scope for using this is however limited as retirement relief is being phased out by April 2003.

There are special rules which apply where:

(i)   the old asset has not been used wholly for the business;

(ii)   not all the sale proceeds are reinvested; or

(iii)   the new asset is a lease with less than 60 years to run – when tax on the gain may be deferred (holdover relief).

These can restrict or eliminate any deferral. The relief can also apply to an asset owned personally by a partner but used by the firm, e.g. office premises.

Where rollover relief is claimed on a new asset acquired after 5 April 1998, however, the base cost of the new asset for CGT purposes is reduced by the full untapered gain (after indexation up to 5 April 1998), and the taper relief for the new asset starts at the date of its acquisition. This means that all benefit of taper relief for the old asset is lost, and advice should be taken before deciding to claim rollover relief in these circumstances.

Gifts of business assets

19.22   Another type of deferral relief is available where an asset of a partnership business is given away. Here, the disposal is deemed to take place at market value but any gain can be deducted from the base cost of the donee. Normally, of course, professional partners will not be able to make such gifts under the partnership agreement. However, if a partnership decides to incorporate, this relief can be a useful way of passing assets to the successor company without immediate CGT bills arising. For more details see Chapter 21.

From 9 November 1999, this relief does not apply where the asset given away is shares or securities, and the donee is a company. This restriction was aimed at certain specialised methods of tax avoidance, but could also apply where a partnership holds shares, for example in a service company, and wishes to incorporate by means of a gift of assets to the new company. With careful planning it should be possible to resolve this problem.

Taper relief operates on gifts involving holdover relief after 5 April 1998 in a similar way to rollover relief (see 19.21 above), and this means that the benefit of taper relief which would otherwise have been available to the 'donor' is lost. Again, advice should now be taken when contemplating such transactions.

Reinvestment relief

19.23   A new type of CGT deferral relief was introduced in the *Finance Act 1998* which may be useful when partners leave a firm before they can claim retirement relief (see 19.24 below). This enables any capital gain, including one arising when a partner retires (see 19.13 above) or one of the exceptions to the 'no gain/no loss' rule for inter-partner transfers applies (see 19.11–19.12 above), to be deferred by the purchase of shares in an unquoted trading company. The time limits are the same as for the general rollover relief mentioned at 19.21 above.

This relief is now restricted to the subscription for new shares in companies which qualify under the Enterprise Investment Scheme, though it is not dependent on the availability of income tax relief on those shares.

Certain trades, notably those with a substantial property element such as property development and farming, do not qualify. The gain on the 'old' asset, such as a partnership interest, is not exempted from tax, but merely deferred until the new shares are sold, or certain other events occur, such as long-term emigration from the UK. Numerous other detailed rules apply, and advice should always be taken.

Retirement relief – types of relief available

19.24   Unlike the reliefs already mentioned, this is a permanent exemption from CGT. Its name is somewhat misleading since it is not always necessary for a partner to 'retire' in the everyday sense. The relief is available to a partner who, when aged at least 50, disposes of:

(a)   the whole or part of his interest in the firm (see 19.25 below); or

(b)   an asset which was in use for the purpose of the firm's business when that business ceased (see 19.26 below); or

(c)   an asset owned by him but used by the firm, either rent-free, or at less than a market rent (in the latter case relief may be reduced), as part of a withdrawal from the firm by the partner (see 19.27 below).

However, in the *Finance Act 1998* the Government decided to phase out this valuable relief between 1998 and 2003, as explained below (see 19.29).

Partner retiring and realising a gain

19.25   Category (a) above covers the normal case of a partner retiring and realising a gain, e.g. on his share of goodwill (see 19.16 above). It could also cover a partial realisation of goodwill while the partner continues to work as such, usually with a reduced profit share. However, it is important that the individual does not cease to be a partner before he makes his disposal, if he does, no relief is due (unless the whole business ceases – see 19.26 below).

The firm's business ceases

19.26   Category (b) covers the situation where a firm's business ceases, but disposals of partnership assets take place later. They must occur within twelve months of cessation, and the individual must have been a partner throughout the final twelve months of its life.

Partner personally owns the property

19.27   Category (c) assists where a partner owns, say, the business premises personally, allowing the firm to use it either rent-free or at less than market rent, and sells it (perhaps to the other partners) as part of his retirement plans. The precise scope of this rule is unclear and therefore the partner should make a disposal of all or part of his partnership interest within Category (*a*) at the same time as he sells the personally owned asset.

Retiring due to ill health

19.28 A special relief may be available if a partner under the age of 50 is forced to retire due to serious ill-health. This is the only situation where someone under 50 can claim the relief and he must completely retire from the firm, though it might be possible for him to continue to do some kinds of other work. Detailed medical evidence must be provided.

Amounts of relief available

19.29 The relief available depends on the size of the gains and the length of time the individual has been a partner. Someone who has been a partner for ten years or more could, up to 5 April 1999, claim relief on the whole of the gains up to £250,000 and on 50% of any gains between £250,001 and £1 million, which meant that up to £250,000 of CGT (at 40%) could be saved in this way. Someone who has been a partner for less than ten years will be entitled to proportionately reduced maximum amounts of relief, but no relief at all is due if he has been a partner for less than one year. In some cases, however, partnership service in a previous business can be added to increase the amount of relief due. This may assist where mergers occur.

Unfortunately, in his 1998 Budget the Chancellor announced that as a result of the new taper relief (see 19.3 above), retirement relief would be phased out over the period from 6 April 1999 to 5 April 2003. The maximum amounts mentioned above will be reduced as shown in the table below, according to the tax year in which the disposal occurs.

Tax year	£250,000	£1 million
1999/00	£200,000	£800,000
2000/01	£150,000	£600,000
2001/02	£100,000	£400,000
2002/03	£50,000	£200,000
2003/04 onwards	Nil	Nil

Where retirement relief does not fully cover a gain, taper relief will be given on the balance remaining.

It will be seen that the disposal needs to occur before 6 April 2003 to use the relief. This could well cause some partners over 50 to change their retirement plans, or to reduce their profit shares and realise goodwill early, even if they carry on working. For those who will still be under 50 at 5 April 2003, however, this previously very valuable relief ceases to be relevant. Where it is still available, good advice is needed, since the conditions can be much more complex than it is possible to describe in detail here.

Chapter 20

Other Taxes

This chapter briefly reviews taxes, other than income tax and capital gains tax, with which partnerships may be concerned. These are Inheritance Tax (20.1 below), Value Added Tax (20.7 below), PAYE and National Insurance Contributions (20.11 below) and Stamp Duty (20.16 below).

Inheritance tax (IHT)

IHT generally

20.1   IHT is payable, very broadly, on the value by which someone's 'estate' (i.e. the assets he possesses) is decreased either by gifts made in his lifetime or on death. Transfers during a person's lifetime to another individual, or to life interest or accumulation and maintenance trusts, are normally potentially exempt, which means that no tax is payable if the donor survives for seven years after the gift is made. However, lifetime transfers in relation to professional partnership assets will not normally be gifts, in this sense, because there will be no element of gratuitousness. Transfers between partners will normally be made in consideration of the respective services provided or capital contributions made, and absolute gifts will typically be prohibited by the partnership agreement. Therefore, attention here will be concentrated on transfers made when a partner dies.

Value of deceased partner's interest in the firm

20.2   When a person dies he is deemed to make a transfer, for IHT purposes, of all the assets he owned immediately before death. Therefore, if a partner dies, the value of his partnership interest, together with that of any asset which he owns but is used by the firm, will be liable to IHT, together with all his personal assets, less any debts owed. The net value of the estate is taxed, currently, at 40%, although this tax bill will often be reduced by the 'nil rate band' applicable to the first £250,000 (from 6 April 2002) of value. The exact liability will depend on any gifts made in the previous seven years and a number of statutory exemptions, the most important of which for present purposes is Business Property Relief (see 20.4 below).

Valuing a partner's interest

20.3 There can be complications in valuing a partner's interest in the firm for IHT purposes. The key feature is the procedure specified in the partnership agreement on a partner's death. It is rare nowadays for an agreement to specify that a firm is dissolved when a partner dies (though this is the legal position if there is no provision about death, see *section 33(1)* of the *Partnership Act 1890*) but if so, the deceased's share in all the partnership assets has to be valued together with any other amounts due, such as credit balances on capital and current accounts.

Usually, the agreement will provide that the firm will continue, but that an account is to be drawn up as at the date of death. This may require all the assets to be revalued, and for the deceased's estate to be paid out of that value. Alternatively it may provide for a payment to be made in respect of the deceased's share of the firm's assets or perhaps most typically nowadays it may state that goodwill accrues to the firm. In the latter case, the deceased's estate will only be entitled to the credit balances on his accounts (which may include items such as surplus tax and pension provisions). Provisions which compel the surviving partners to buy out the deceased's share cause problems with Business Property Relief – see 20.5 below. Normally, the Revenue will accept that the value of the deceased's partnership interest for IHT purposes is the amount which his estate receives for his share of the firm's assets and his capital and current account balances. There can, however, be complications where partners are 'connected' independently of the firm, e.g. in a family partnership. In any event, it is sensible to provide that any annuity payable on a partner's death is payable to the surviving spouse rather than the estate, because the value of the annuity rights will then normally be exempt from IHT.

Business property relief

20.4 Assuming that the relevant valuations have been established, the next step is to consider how much Business Property Relief (BPR) is due. BPR is given by a 100% reduction in the otherwise taxable value of the partner's 'interest in the business', and a 50% reduction for any land, buildings, machinery or plant owned personally by him, but used wholly or mainly for the firm's business immediately before his death. BPR is not due at all if the deceased had become a partner less than two years before his death. The 'interest in the business' is the value ascertained (see 20.3 above) and any personally owned assets attracting the 50% relief are valued at their open market value. 100% relief may also extend to minority shares in an unquoted partnership.

Assets, whether partnership assets or personally owned, which are neither used wholly or mainly for the business nor required for future use, are also excluded from BPR, which means it may be undesirable for a firm to hold long-term investment assets such as quoted shares or let property in its balance sheet. Substantial cash holdings which exceed any reasonably foreseeable business requirements should also be avoided.

Problems with the agreement

20.5   Problems can arise over BPR if the partnership agreement, or any side-agreement, provides that the continuing partners are required to buy out the deceased's share either at market value or according to a formula. The Revenue view is that this constitutes a binding contract for sale. Assets subject to such a contract are statutorily excluded from BPR, presumably because they are regarded as virtual cash-in-hand. Clauses which provide for the automatic accrual of the deceased's share to the surviving partners in return for a payment to the estate avoid this problem. An alternative, which achieves the same commercial effect, may be to provide for 'cross-options' under which the surviving partners may buy, and the estate may sell, within defined periods, though legal advice will be essential.

IHT planning

20.6   Currently BPR is extremely generous. In effect the value of a deceased partner's share in the business is exempt from IHT altogether. However, this relief can be put at risk in various ways, the most obvious being a change in the underlying assets of the partnership to non-qualifying assets. On the death of a retired partner IHT will be due since he will no longer have an interest in the business when he dies.

Value Added Tax

20.7   The general principles of VAT apply to partnerships in much the same way as to any other business. However, there are some issues specific to partnerships.

General background

20.8   For VAT purposes a partnership is a separate entity. Therefore, where a sole proprietor takes on a partner or where a partner retires leaving a sole trader, a business is deemed to be transferred for VAT purposes and a new registration is required. Changes in the composition of an existing partnership do not represent transfers of business. However, a retiring partner could cause two partnerships to become one for VAT purposes, e.g. where one firm consists of A, B and C, and the other of A and B, and C then retires.

Each partner is jointly and severally liable for any VAT liability and therefore a retiring partner remains liable until Customs & Excise are notified of his departure, even if this occurred at an earlier date.

It is possible to treat changes from sole trader to partnership status and vice versa as a 'transfer of a going concern' and therefore outside the scope of VAT. However application must be made to Customs & Excise for this treatment. Where a transfer of a going concern takes place, the purchaser should beware of the dangers of taking over a VAT registration number as this will make him liable for any VAT owed by the transferor. When a partner disposes of an interest in the assets of the partnership back to the remaining partners, this is treated as a withdrawal of capital rather than consideration for a supply, and is thus outside the scope of VAT.

Generally professional partnerships are involved in the supply of services rather than goods, and therefore it is important that the 'tax point' rules for the supply of services are understood to ensure the correct accounting for VAT. It is also important to remember that where a member of a partnership is also an officer of another organisation, e.g. a company director, fees paid will usually be treated as if paid for supplies by the partnership and therefore subject to VAT.

Partnership registrations

20.9   In some cases, a number of individuals operating together without a formal partnership deed are treated by Customs & Excise as deemed partnerships carrying on the business of a single taxable person. This is subject to a direction being made under the *Value Added Tax Act 1994 Schedule 1 para 2*. Directions are given in cases where business splitting or disaggregation has taken place, often in an attempt to keep below the VAT threshold. This is particularly common with husband and wife business activities, and in such cases it is important to look at the intentions of the individuals. For example.

(*a*)   Are profits shared gross or net of expenses?

(*b*)   Is there a written partnership agreement?

(*c*)   What do the annual accounts reflect?

(*d*)   How do business names appear on stationery?

(*e*)   In whose names are sales invoiced?

(*f*)   Who would be sued if an action was taken against the business?

(*g*)   Are separate bank accounts maintained?

(*h*)   Is there a common trading name?

(*j*)   How is the business taxed by the Inland Revenue?

If such a direction is made it cannot operate retrospectively.

In the case of limited partnerships, which involve at least one general partner and at least one limited partner, agreement should be reached with Customs & Excise on the basis of registration. Often two separate registrations will be needed.

Joint ventures tend to be treated by Customs & Excise as partnerships and registered as such. Administratively this is easier, but it does mean that Customs & Excise will treat all bodies as jointly and severally liable for debts. There are cases where a venture does not involve anything approaching a partnership. In such circumstances Customs & Excise may treat one party as receiving and supplying goods, and payments to and from other members as being consideration for services given and received. Care is needed, as, if the relationship is not clear, it may lead to situations where VAT is not charged where it should be or is recovered where it should not be. Co-owners of buildings and land are now registered by Customs & Excise as a single person and all interested parties will be treated as jointly and severally liable subject to a request by the beneficiaries to be registered, although there remains difficulty with bringing in the legislation on this issue.

Customs & Excise have provided their view on the VAT position of partnerships which become Limited Liability Partnerships (LLPs) (see Chapter 23) in Business Brief 3/2001. In these cases the change in structure should be treated as the transfer of the business as a going concern. Although the VAT number may be transferred to the LLP, the partnership cannot simply assume that the VAT registration is carried on uninterrupted. The old partnership must be deregistered for VAT and the limited partnership registered for VAT.

Other VAT points to consider

20.10   The rules on the recovery of input tax for partnerships are the same as those which apply to all businesses. However, it is worth noting that where exempt or partially exempt partnerships operate with service companies which recharge certain expenses, the non-recoverable VAT on the recharge will represent an expense to the partnership.

Partnerships should also note the need to account for output tax when assets are taken for personal use by a partner.

Another issue to consider is where partners hold various offices, including acting as clerk and/or treasurer of various local charities and societies, Customs & Excise may take the view that the partners have accepted the offices in the course or furtherance of their profession. This would result in the partnership being required to account for output tax on any payments which the partners received in relation to those offices. However, if it can be shown that the duties involved were a reflection of the personal standing of the partner involved and were of an administrative nature it may be possible to argue that the partnership should not be liable to account for output tax (see *Oglethorpe Sturton & Gillibrand* (*VAT tribunal decision 17491*)).

When a partnership comes to an end, the outgoing partner will remain liable for the VAT owed by a partnership until the date that Customs & Excise are notified of the partnership's dissolution. Until that date the partnership will be treated as continuing (see *Customs and Excise Comrs v Jamieson, Chancery Division [2001] SWTI 938*).

PAYE and National Insurance Contributions

PAYE and employer's NICs

20.11   Partnerships have the same obligations as other employers for the PAYE system and collection of employer's (Class 1, 1A and 1B) National Insurance Contributions (NICs). It should be noted that salaried partners are employees in law and their remuneration will therefore be subject to PAYE and Class 1 NICs.

Class 1 contributions apply to employee earnings and are divided into employee's (primary) and employer's (secondary) contributions. Class 1A contributions are payable by the employer only, on company cars, car fuel and other benefits in kind provided to employees. Class 1B contributions, again payable by the employer only, are part of a method of settling PAYE and NICs on certain employee benefits in the form of a PAYE Settlement Agreement (PSA).

Class 1 contributions may also be due on fees earned by partners if they arise from a client engagement which is caught by the IR35 rules which have applied since 6 April 2000 (see 18.38).

Class 2 and 3 NICs

20.12   As self-employed people, partners are subject to Class 2 NICS, which are paid at a flat rate (in 2002/03, £2 per week) unless profit shares are very small indeed (in 2002/03, £4,025 per annum) or they make a loss. These contributions secure entitlement only to state sickness and invalidity benefits, and the state retirement pension and widow's benefit. (They do not give a partner who is made redundant the right to claim unemployment related benefits, or a female partner the right to claim maternity benefit.) They are not deductible for income tax purposes and are now paid either quarterly or by direct debit. In some circumstances, e.g. where a partner has spent some years abroad and did not pay Class 2 contributions, it might be worth paying Class 3 contributions (£6.85 per week in 2002/03) to make up for 'lost' years – this can be done within six years of the year in question, subject to detailed rules.

Class 4 NICs

20.13 Class 4 NICs are simply income taxes by another name, as they secure no additional benefits. As self-employed people, partners are in principle subject to these, which are calculated as a percentage of a slice of their profit share for income tax purposes (in 2002/03, 7% of profits between £4,615 and £30,420, i.e. a maximum of £1,806.35). The profit share is adjusted for capital allowances, losses and interest on partnership capital loans. The contributions are paid along with income tax under Case II of Schedule D on the same payment dates.

Schedule E

20.14 Partners may also have income taxable under Schedule E (see 17.7 above), e.g. from directorships, which makes them liable to Class 1 employee's NICs. Class 1 NICs secure a much wider range of state benefits than Class 2 NICs or Class 4 NICs. Therefore it would be unfair for someone who has paid the maximum Class 1 NICs on Schedule E income, and Class 2 NICs as a self-employed person, to have to pay the full amount of Class 4 NICs as well. Therefore, Class 4 liability is limited by a complex formula, explained in *Tolley's Practical NIC Service*, section 20. Where this is likely to apply, the partner can apply for 'deferment' of Class 4 NICs. This in fact means exemption once it is established that the maximum Class 1 NICs have been paid for the tax year. Partners who are not resident in the UK, or who are aged over 65 (men) or over 60 (women) are not subject to Class 1, 2 or 4 NICs.

Remuneration from 'incidental' directorships

20.15 Some partners may acquire directorships as an incident of their professional work, e.g. with a client company. Where this is a 'normal incident' of the profession, as is generally the case, e.g. for accountants and solicitors, the amounts are an insubstantial part of the turnover of the firm, and the partner is required to account for the fees to the firm, fees for such directorships can be received without employer's or employee's Class 1 NICs being due. (A similar practice allows the fees to be paid without PAYE and instead included in the Case II results of the firm – see 17.7 above.) This concession continues despite the IR35 rules which have applied since April 2000 (see 18.38).

Stamp duty

Basic provisions

20.16 Stamp duty will be due in the normal way when a firm acquires assets by documents which require stamping. Duty will be payable (from 28 March 2000) at up to 4% of the consideration for freehold land and buildings and 0.5% for shares. Duty on the grant of a lease will also be payable, the rate depending on the term of the lease and the rent payable.

Where stamp duty is sometimes involved

20.17   Other transactions by the firm may sometimes involve stamp duty, e.g. work-in-progress by means of a document will involve duty at up to 4% of the consideration. It may be possible to mitigate this cost in some cases, on acquiring the business and assets of another practice, tangible assets such as furniture or cars can be transferred 'by delivery' (e.g. handing over the registration documents and keys for cars), and book debts can be collected by the vendor as agent for the buyer. Similar issues may arise on incorporation of a firm (see Chapter 21).

When a partnership is formed or new partners admitted

20.18   Duty should not arise when a partnership is formed, or when new partners are admitted, although this may involve legal documents of various kinds. However, it might be due if the transaction amounts to a sale, e.g. where an incoming partner who was previously a sole practitioner transfers work-in-progress or debtors to the firm in return for a credit to his capital account. It is common for a firm to hold any lease of its premises through a nominee company owned by the partners. This avoids the need for the lease to be assigned by a new document, carrying up to 4% duty, every time there is a change of partners.

Stamp duty into the future

20.19   Stamp duty is undergoing radical change. For example, the *Finance Act 2002* included eight sections concerned with stamp duty and stamp duty reserve tax. One notable change was that stamp duty ceased to apply to the acquisition of goodwill with effect from 23 April 2002. Other changes were anti-avoidance provisions.

Further changes are expected in the *Finance Act 2003* and as a result of the consultation arising from a Revenue paper entitled 'Modernising Stamp Duty on land and buildings in the UK', which was published in April 2002. If these proposals are taken forward, most classes of transfer will be removed from stamp duty leaving the charge as it currently exists as a form of property transfer tax. However, it remains to be seen exactly what changes will be implemented.

Chapter 21

Incorporation — Accounting and Tax Issues

Commercial reasons

21.1   An overview of the commercial reasons for considering incorporation of a professional partnership should include the following.

(*a*)   Limitation of liabilities.

(*b*)   Professional indemnity issues.

(*c*)   Property factors.

(*d*)   Ability to raise finance.

(*e*)   General management issues.

(*f*)   Stock exchange flotation.

Limited Liability Partnerships – LLPs

21.2   It has been possible to form or convert to a Limited Liability Partnership since 6 April 2001. This might be one alternative route for a partnership to incorporate in order to minimise the impact of professional indemnity and other liability problems. This is dealt with separately in Chapter 4.

Professional indemnity issues and limitation of liabilities

21.3   Professional indemnity issues have become more important as the commercial climate has become more litigious. The cost of professional indemnity insurance has become heavier. There have been claims many years after the event which incurred the loss, and this has increased the level of premiums. For example architects may have problems with defective buildings, sometimes designed many years in the past.

The incorporation of a professional partnership does not alleviate or alter the liability of pre-incorporation partners from their liability for such professional indemnity issues, but from the moment of incorporation there is a time cap on their liabilities. The limited liability of the incorporated professional firm provides the cap for post incorporation events. Professional indemnity insurance is still needed for the business, so that the cost may not change. One possibility is that some firms may choose to reduce the top level of professional indemnity cover relying on the limited liability cover of the incorporated business. However, those shareholders who are former partners can sleep more easily since they know they will not be asked for the possible excess over the limit of professional indemnity cover arising after incorporation.

Property

21.4 If a professional partnership is, for example, taking on a long lease, then each and every partner is jointly and severally liable for the rent, dilapidations payments and other onerous terms of the lease. For further discussion of the liabilities of partners and partnerships see Chapter 3.

Raising finance

21.5 A limited company is a more straightforward, easier legal entity for banks and lending institutions to deal with than a partnership. The ability, for example, to issue shares, loan notes and give charges over securities probably leads to the incorporated professional firm having the edge over a partnership. A commercial bank lending to a professional partnership will usually examine not only the partnership's balance sheet but also that of each individual partner. A company on the other hand would normally, depending on size and other factors, have its borrowings dealt with on a stand alone basis. The individual shareholder's position would be considered separately (and not collectively) and then, normally, only in the context of his or her application for finance for acquiring shares or making loans to the company.

Management

21.6 Whilst it is perfectly possible for a partnership to be run on corporate lines with a board elected from the partnership, it is much easier for the limited company to be so run in accordance with the normal Articles of Association derived from the *Companies Acts* which give a legal framework for management.

Stock exchange flotation

21.7 Some professions have allowed the share capital of their incorporated members to be quoted on the stock exchange. Therefore, stock exchange flotation and capital wealth creation for some of the members of the partnership who ultimately receive shares in the incorporated entity, must be considered as a major reason for incorporation.

Tax considerations on incorporation

Introduction

21.8 The major problems on incorporation arise because of the impact of UK taxation of income and gains arising up to and on the act of incorporation and the different treatment of the business after incorporation.

Cessation

21.9 Incorporation for income tax purposes by a professional partnership will be a cessation (see 18.9). The possibility arises for partners to utilise overlap relief against the final period's profits from the partnership. Care should be taken that there are sufficient profits to utilise such relief (see 18.9 and 18.11). If a partnership's taxation position is some years in arrear then estimation of the tax effect of incorporation may involve an extensive exercise to get the partnership's and partners' tax affairs up to date. This can give rise to a position where the tax position is imprecise and contains probability factors due to the presence of, for example, disputes regarding the treatment of expenditure or the analysis of items which are not clear.

Accounting basis

21.10 On incorporation, the accounts of the incorporated professional firm must be prepared under the constraints of the *Companies Act 1985*. Auditors may have to be appointed although the turnover limit for exemption from audit since 23 July 2000 is £1,000,000. Whilst the directors are responsible for the preparation of financial statements, the auditors have a responsibility to form an independent opinion on their statements. The opinion is that the accounts have been prepared in accordance with applicable accounting standards and the *Companies Act 1985* and that the auditors are able to report that they show a true and fair view of the state of the company's affairs at the accounting date.

This report should be contrasted with a professional partnership where as shown in Chapter 12, Accounting, the partnership does not need to have an audit, nor does an opinion have to be expressed (unless this is contained in the partnership deed) that the accounts of the partnership are prepared in accordance with applicable accounting principles or the *Companies Act 1985*. This particularly applies with regard to stocks and long-term contracts, SSAP 9, which is the Statement of Standard Accounting Practice on work in progress for an incorporated firm. Similarly, fee income has to be accounted for when it is delivered rather than on a 'cash' or any other basis. For a professional partnership which accounted for work in progress on a basis outside SSAP 9 and billings on an abnormal basis there would inevitably be an uplift of an amount which comes into charge to tax.

However, as outlined in Chapter 17, the *Finance Act 1998* introduced a new rule that the taxable profits of a professional firm must be computed 'on an accounting basis which gives a true and fair view, subject to any adjustment required or authorised by law in computing profits for those purposes'. This came into effect for the year (of assessment) ended 5 April 2000.

Accordingly, for incorporation now this aspect will not necessarily accelerate the charge to taxation although there may be an uplift resulting from, for example, the inclusion of partner time in work in progress. If there is an uplift in valuation of work in progress this can be taken either in the old partnership, i.e. pre-incorporation by a sale or transfer at a higher 'new' basis of valuation, or in the new corporation by a sale or transfer at the old basis of valuation followed by revaluation in the corporation. The uplift if taken in the partnership would be liable to income tax in the normal way as profits of the old partnership up to the date of cessation. If the uplift is accounted for in the professional corporation, then it would be liable to corporation tax with the trading results of the first accounting period in the normal way.

Treatment of work in progress and stock sales or transfers

21.11 Sections *100* and *101* of the *Income and Corporation Taxes Act 1988* provide a measure of symmetry in the treatment of work in progress and stock sales or transfers on incorporation: i.e. whatever figure is taken as the transfer value (unless it is unreasonable and excessive) is taken as the closing figure for income tax purposes in the partnership and the opening figure for the incorporated professional corporation for corporation tax purposes. This subject is dealt with in a Technical Circular TR 5/95 issued by the ICAEW in February 1995.

Alternative treatment for work in progess

21.12 Occasionally, on incorporating a professional partnership, the partners may not wish to dispose of the work in progress to the corporation. This may be because one near completed contract, for example, is particularly identified with one or two old or retiring partners in the context of a firm of architects. Instead the work in progress may be run off or collected subsequent to incorporation in which case the benefit of the sale accrues to the 'old' partners as a group. This transaction does not escape the tax net – such post-cessation receipts are dealt with as income under the regime for post-cessation receipts in *sections 103* to *109* of the *Income and Corporation Taxes Act 1988*.

Treatment of assets liable to capital allowances

21.13 The professional partnership which incorporates would normally have assets which would be liable to capital allowances. These may be transferred over from the partnership to the corporation without unfortunate tax consequences. Such assets probably have four different figures attached to them as follows.

(*a*)   The value shown in the books of the partnerships, i.e. usually cost less depreciation.

(*b*)   Their tax written-down value; this would normally be cost less annual allowances and be encapsulated in various 'pools' constituting the residue of expenditure.

(*c*)   Their market value; this would be determined by a sale to a third party (and would not be replacement cost or value).

(*d*)   Cost.

The *Taxes Act* allows assets which have been subject to capital allowances under the code for plant and machinery (i.e. computer equipment, cars and so on), to be transferred to the professional company at tax written-down value, if an election is made under *section 77* of the *Capital Allowances Act 1990*. The result of this is that there is no additional income or loss in this respect for the partnership as it incorporates, and the professional corporation takes over these assets for tax purposes at their tax written-down value. A similar election can be applied for industrial buildings and enterprise zone investments. Failing an election, the legislation would impute into the transaction the asset's market value. Given the nature of a professional partnership's assets this would be troublesome, e.g. on motor vehicles or computers, so that in almost all cases an election is made.

Goodwill and property

21.14   Other assets (which are not liable to capital allowances) and the goodwill of the firm have the capability of a market value significantly in excess of their cost. Furthermore goodwill may not be recorded in the partnership's accounts. The cost of land and buildings owned by a partnership may be shown in the books, and could even be depreciated, but the market value may be significantly above cost. If on incorporation the land, buildings and goodwill are transferred into the company which is going to carry on the professional business, a disposal has been made for capital gains tax purposes by the partnership. Capital gains tax will, therefore, be due on the increase in the value of the asset from its cost or 31 March 1982 value to its market value at the date of incorporation after indexation to 31 March 1998 and taper relief. In such a case, market value would have to be substituted because the partnership and the company which carried on the business will be connected persons and the transaction will therefore be deemed not to be at arm's length.

Applicable reliefs

21.15   Fortunately, there are several reliefs which apply or can be made to apply on incorporation of a professional practice. These usually avoid the problem of a capital gain and the resulting payment of tax. These are as follows.

(a) *Retirement relief – section 163* of the *Taxation of Chargeable Gains Act 1992*. This relief is being phased out and will cease to be available after 5 April 2003. This applies when an individual has attained the age of 50 or has retired on health grounds before 50. In the context of incorporation, it might be utilised by all the partners aged over 50, even though they might work full-time for the incorporated company after incorporation. This is because the relief exempts from capital gains tax for the year ending 5 April 2003, £50,000 of capital gains and then one half of the excess of the gains over £50,000 up to £200,000.

The phasing out of retirement relief is occasioned by the introduction of taper relief (see (d) below), but this new relief is given after retirement relief has been given. It may be possible to accelerate the use of retirement relief, but the provisions of this relief are complex and its utilisation involves satisfaction of detailed provisions contained in *Schedule 6* of the *Taxation of Capital Gains Act 1992*, which must be checked in every case.

(b) *Transfer for shares relief – section 162* of the *Taxation of Chargeable Gains Act 1992*. Under this section, a relief is given if a person (or persons) which is not a company, transfers to a company, a business as a going concern, together with the whole assets of the business for the issue of shares in that company. The relief is that the gain on the disposal into the company is calculated but is deducted from the cost for capital gains tax purposes of the shares issued. Effectively, the individual receives the shares at the same value for capital gains tax purposes as the old assets that were transferred into the company.

The relief can still be obtained if the cash element in the old partnership is not transferred into the company and under the Inland Revenue's Extra-Statutory Concession D32, the Revenue are prepared not to treat liabilities taken over by a company as consideration. Further, relief is not precluded if some or all liabilities of the business are not taken over by the company.

It should be noted that for taper relief purposes the taper clock does not continue through incorporation but a new qualifying period commences based on the issue of the shares in the company itself.

Before 5 April 2002, *section 162* relief had to apply to all partners on an incorporation. The *2002 Finance Act* provides an election for an individual partner to elect for the provisions of *section 162* not to apply. This may be beneficial where incorporation is followed by a sale of some or all of the shares received in order to maximise the relief from tax arising from the entitlement to business asset taper relief.

For the purposes of chargeable gains, the assets taken over by the company are acquired at their market value at the date of transfer and not their historic cost to the partnership. This can provide a useful tax-free uplift.

(c) *Relief for gifts of business assets – section 165* of the *Taxation of Chargeable Gains Act 1992.* This relief is claimable if a business asset is given to a trading company within the United Kingdom. The gain is held over and the trading company acquires the assets at the tax cost to the individual who disposed of the assets to the company for capital gains tax purposes.

Again, for taper relief purposes the taper clock does not continue through incorporation but a new qualifying period commences based on the acquisition of the shares in the company to which the assets have been gifted.

(d) *Taper relief – sections 121–126* of the *Finance Act 1998* and *sections 66* and *77* of the *Finance Act 2000.* As in (a) above, the *Finance Act 1998* phased out retirement relief and also stopped indexation relief at 5 April 1998. The Chancellor granted taper relief for disposals of assets. Professional partnership assets would generally qualify as business property and for such assets held on 6 April 2000 the relief could be 75% and hence only 25% of the gain would be chargeable if the disposal occurs after four years. From 6 April 2002 the qualifying period for business assets has been reduced to two years. Care should be exercised where the qualifying period straddles this change or where during the qualifying period the asset is deemed to be a non-business asset, since the maximum taper relief may not be obtained.

(e) *Enterprise investment scheme –* EIS relief. Individuals investing in an EIS qualifying company may defer gains to the extent of the investment. Hence the gain on incorporation might be deferred into the subscription for shares in the company formed. However, EIS companies do not include accountancy, legal or financial services companies so that in the context of a professional practice incorporating, only a few qualify.

For more details on taper relief and retirement relief see Chapter 19.

Annuities

21.16   It is difficult to predict what relief will best suit the incorporation of each and every professional firm. The problem is exacerbated if the partnership pays annuities, normally to former partners. The liability in the partnership deed to pay a future annuity to retiring partners can create significant tax problems. Although not recorded in the balance sheet of the partnership the current value of the future liability can be estimated and in the Inland Revenue's view this amount is consideration on incorporation. The assumption by the company of this liability is deemed to be consideration, as far as the old partners are concerned, on incorporation. It is not therefore met by the relief under *section 162*. Accordingly, the result would be a chargeable gain which should be liable to capital gains tax in those circumstances.

Comparison of tax costs of partnership versus company

Running tax cost

21.17 In deciding whether or not to incorporate, the tax cost on incorporation is a material factor. Another material factor is the running tax cost of the business as a company as opposed to a partnership. A partner's profit share is taxed at income tax rates up to the maximum of 40%. This is replaced with a salary, dividend and returns of interest which are all liable to income tax. The big difference that applies in a corporate setting is the fact that employers' National Insurance has to be paid on salaries distributed by a company to its employees. The additional tax of 12.8% (the employers' rate of National Insurance for 2003/2004) is a significant tax cost on incorporation. Turning to the impact of income tax versus corporation tax, the rates of corporation tax are as follows:

		Year to 31 March 2003
Standard rate of corporation tax	–	30%
Small companies rate	–	19%
Starting rate	–	0%
Starting rate profit limit	–	£10,000
Lower limit on small companies rate	–	£300,000
Upper limit on small companies rate	–	£1,500,000
Starting rate marginal rate	–	23.75%
Marginal rate of corporation tax	–	32.75%

Examples of the impact of the small company rate are as follows:

Year end		*31 March 2000*	*31 March 2001*
Chargeable profits	–	£500,000	£700,000
£300,000 @ small rate	–	£57,000	£57,000
Balance @ marginal rate	–	£65,500	£131,000
Total corporation tax	–	£122,500	£188,000
Effective rate of corporation tax	–	24.5%	26.86%

The limits, lower and upper, apply if there is only one company involved. If there is an associated company under common control, then the lower and upper profit limits are halved. If there are three associated companies, then the lower and upper limit for each company is divided by one quarter. It can be seen that if a professional practice incorporates and the profit (after distribution of salaries to the partners) is under £300,000, a lower rate of tax at 19% on retained earnings is a useful advantage of 21% over the top rate of income tax.

Dividends

21.18   A company has the option to pay dividends to its shareholders as an alternative to paying remuneration. A dividend, unlike remuneration, is not tax deductible from the company's profits. For the individual recipient there is a notional tax credit of $\frac{1}{9}$th of the actual dividend paid. The dividend plus tax credit will then be liable to tax at the top rate of 32.5%. For top rate taxpayers the calculation shows that as a percentage of the cash dividend the tax payable is at a maximum at 25% as follows:

Cash Dividends paid	£1,000
Income tax credit: $\frac{1}{9}$	111
Taxable Dividend plus tax credit	£1,111
Income Tax at 32.5%	£361
Tax payable after tax credit	£250
Tax payable as a percentage	25%

The pension contributor

21.19   The last factor in this context which may affect the decision to incorporate is the amount that can be contributed to a company pension scheme for an individual as opposed to the amounts that can be contributed by partners as individuals under personal pension policies (or the former retirement annuity policies). This is dealt with in Chapter 26, Retirement planning.

The overall position

21.20   It is difficult to generalise on the overall tax costs of operating a professional practice as a partnership as opposed to an incorporated entity; there is no simple rule and the financial dynamics of each business have to be considered. However the cost of National Insurance on salaries at 12.8% means that incorporation and then distributing all income as salaries/ emoluments increases the tax cost because of National Insurance which adds a surcharge of up to 12.8%. However if the incorporated business retains earnings then the tax charge can be reduced.

Interest relief

Purpose of borrowings

21.21   Inside a partnership, interest paid on its borrowings would be deductible if the borrowings were wholly and exclusively for the purpose of the professional activity carried on. If the borrowings are not exclusively utilised for business purposes, a certain amount of disallowance might occur in the partnership. For a corporation, interest relief on borrowings depends not on the fact that the interest is wholly and exclusively for the purposes of a trade, but that the interest is paid in respect of a loan relationship and/or a money debt. In a way, the criteria for deduction of interest are easier for a corporation than for an unincorporated partnership.

Funds borrowed by an individual

21.22 There is a difference between the criteria for interest relief on funds borrowed by an individual to lend to a partnership or a company or, alternatively, to invest in the capital of a partnership or shares in a company. The relief given in *section 362* is for interest on a loan to buy into or lend money to a partnership and is conditional on individuals concerned being partners and not withdrawing any capital from the partnership. The relief for interest on loans utilised to buy shares in a company or lend money to a company is more restrictive. The company concerned has to be close (or employee-controlled) and the definition of this is restrictive. Few incorporated professional firms meet this definition, see *section 361* of the *Income and Corporation Taxes Act 1988*. Furthermore, the individual either has to possess a 'material interest' (simply put, 5% of the capital) or he or she has to have worked for the greater part of his time in the actual management or conduct of the company or an associated company, see *sections 360(1), (2)* and *(3)* of the *Income and Corporation Taxes Act 1988*. This latter requirement can prove restrictive as the Inland Revenue have tried to interpret the requirement as relating to the management of the company as a 'whole' and a specialist technical director may not qualify.

Close company status

21.23 Close company status means that the incorporated professional firm has to be under the control of its directors who are participators, or of five or fewer participators taken together. For a partnership planning to incorporate, this is easy to achieve if there are ten or fewer partners but for larger partnerships, artificial means of making the corporation close may have to be used.

Partial incorporation

Disadvantages

21.24 Incorporating half or part of a professional practice would almost certainly be tax disadvantageous for two reasons. First, the capital gains exemption under *section 162* of the *Taxation of Chargeable Gains Act 1992* would not be available, as it refers to the whole assets of the partnership. Secondly, the division of a profession or business into two parts of which one is incorporated would almost certainly lead to the cessation of both parts of the business or profession for tax purposes (Statement of Practice 9/86).

Existing service companies

21.25   If a professional firm has a service company then this company may be used as the vehicle for incorporation using the provisions of *section 165* of the *Taxation of Chargeable Gains Act 1992*. This may have the benefit of being able to take advantage of the existing taper relief qualifying period for this company thereby resulting in a lower effective tax rate on a early sale of shares. The position of service companies and of associated trading companies is considered in more detail at 22.4–22.13. The service company or associated trading company may be used as the corporate vehicle for incorporation since usually the capital gains relief can be organised to apply to the share capital in the company. In addition, there would not normally be too many difficulties in arranging interest relief on the cost of former partners financing any share capital increase or loans to the company.

Chapter 22

Taxation of Corporate Aspects

Corporate partners

22.1   There is nothing in the *Partnership Act 1890* itself to prevent a company incorporated in the United Kingdom or elsewhere, being a partner in a partnership governed by that Act. However, for most professions the presence of a corporate partner is not allowed. Some professions do allow corporate partners, e.g. consulting engineers. The presence of a corporate partner can be useful to provide capital, but the liability of the corporation to the partnership debts is restricted to its own resources. The joint and several liability would normally stop at the resources of the corporate partner's capital and reserves.

Corporate partner's tax position

22.2   From a United Kingdom taxation viewpoint, a corporation incorporated in the United Kingdom is now always liable to corporation tax on global income. For a company which is a partner, following legislation which was introduced at the same time as the anti-avoidance legislation on limited partnerships, there is an overriding restriction on the quantum of loss relief given. This is contained in *section 118* of the *Income and Corporation Taxes Act 1988* and limits the loss again to the company's contribution to the partnership at the appropriate time of the claim.

Other rules for dealing with corporate partners

22.3   The other detailed rules for dealing with corporate partners are contained in *sections 114* and *115* of the *Income and Corporation Taxes Act 1988*. A partnership with a corporate partner has to adjust the partnership's total profits under corporation tax rules. Then the corporation is taxable on the share of the adjusted result of the partnership for each of its accounting periods. This would be a separate and distinct calculation to the adjustment of the total profit for income tax purposes which would be necessary for income tax purposes for the group of individual partners. In particular, in adjusting the profit for corporation tax purposes, all references to distributions, charges and capital allowances are initially disregarded. Then in the corporate partner's hands, an appropriate proportionate share of items such as charges and capital allowances are allowed as a deduction.

In general it is unusual for corporations to be members of a partnership. They would usually prefer to be engaged in joint ventures, because such entities do not have a 'joint and several' liability attached to them.

Service companies

22.4   Further details of service companies are found in 12.30 above. For a variety of reasons, including the perceived organisational cumbersomeness of large partnerships, there has been a trend over some years for so called 'service companies' to be utilised. They were commonly set up to enable the former tax benefits of profit related pay to be obtained. Service companies have traditionally been used for one or more of the following:

(*a*)   employ some or all the staff of a partnership;

(*b*)   own the partnership's plant, machinery, motor cars, etc.; and

(*c*)   own the property, take leases and generally deal with occupancy expenses.

Director status

22.5   The service company can also be used to provide director status for professionally unqualified employees so they can assume a role similar to that of a partner. The company clearly has to be funded to pay the payroll costs so, in general, a service company charges on a monthly basis the total costs of the payroll together with a profit margin.

Charges between practice and company

22.6   It is essential to ensure that charges made between the professional practice, the partnership and the corporation are on a consistent and reasonable basis. In the case of *Stephenson v Payne Stone, Fraser & Co* a firm of accountants incorporated a service company which provided the firm with premises and its services as secretaries, registrars and executors. In the first year, the service charge paid was 1.47 × the actual cost incurred for the provision of the services. In the second year the actual charge was less than the cost of the provision of the services, on the basis that the excess profit of the first year would be recouped. The High Court ruled that for tax purposes only the cost of the services plus a nominal profit could be charged across and could be properly attributed to the first year of operation. Therefore, care should be taken over the level of profitability in a service or an associated trading company, and that this is consistently applied.

Corporation tax

22.7   The profit retained inside the service company will be subject to corporation tax at the following rates:

		Year to *31 March 2003*
Standard rate of corporation tax	–	30%
Small companies rate	–	19%
Starting rate	–	0%
Starting rate profit limit	–	£10,000
Lower limit on small companies rate	–	£300,000
Upper limit on small companies rate	–	£1,500,000
Starting rate marginal rate	–	23.75%
Marginal rate of corporation tax	–	32.75%

For an example see 21.17. Depending upon the size of the profits of the partnership and the service company concerned, the lower rate on a profit of £300,000 can be a method for reducing the overall tax charge on the partnership.

The limits for application of the different rate of corporation tax are divided by two if the service company has an associated company and three if the service company has two associated companies and so on. 'Associated' is defined as being under common control and, for these purposes, the partners in a partnership are all associated. Any companies owned and controlled by the partners in a professional partnership will affect the availability of the small companies rate.

In particular, the recent case of *R v IRC, ex p Newfields Developments Ltd* highlights the scope of the potential attribution of associated companies within the partnership field. For example, some partners in a professional partnership may participate in another business partnership, such as one for the promotion of films, and it is unlikely that the partners concerned will know whether the other partners have a controlling interest in a company. Irrespective of this lack of knowledge the Revenue are likely to insist that the associated companies rules apply thus resulting in the higher rate of corporation tax applying.

Generally, corporation tax is payable nine months after the end of the accounting period of the company concerned. However, for companies whose profits exceed the upper limit the *Finance Act 1998* and regulations issued under its authority introduced a system of payments on account on a quarterly basis starting with the first payment on the fourteenth day of Month 7 of the accounting period. For associated companies the payment on account system applies to companies whose profits exceed the upper limit divided by the same number as above. In the context of a service company, care should be taken that its profitability and that of associated companies does not exceed the upper limit and hence accelerate the payment of tax by an average of ten months.

Profits for corporation tax purposes are computed on a form CT600 under CTSA, i.e. corporation tax self assessment, which form, together with the accounts (and usually a computer produced computation), are sent in to the Inspector of Taxes on an annual basis. The tax is now on a self-assessment system which, broadly speaking, follows the individual system. Payments of corporation tax are made to the Collector of Taxes.

Example 1

A tax reduction example

An example of the tax reduction arising from the use of a service company follows:

N & Co, consultants, have made a level profit of £2,000,000 per annum for some years. The firm incorporates a service company to employ all staff and the company makes a profit each year of:

(*a*)   £250,000;

(*b*)   £500,000; and

(*c*)   £750,000.

The profit margins are consistently applied and accepted by the Inland Revenue. Ignoring income tax reliefs, the lower rate bands and allowances that would accrue to the individual partners, the income tax position would be as follows:

	No service company £	*(a) Profit* £	*(b) Profit* £	*(c) Profit* £
Profit of service company	–	250,000	500,000	750,000
Profit in N & Co	2,000,000	1,750,000	1,500,000	1,250,000
Income tax at 40%	800,000	700,000	600,000	500,000
Corporation tax at 19% to limit of £300,000	–	47,500	57,000	57,000
32.75% on profit over £300,000	–	–	65,500	147,375
Total corporation tax liability	–	47,500	122,500	204,375
Total tax liability	800,000	747,500	722,500	704,375
Reduction achieved	–	52,500	77,500	95,625
Percentage reduction	–	6.56%	9.69%	11.95%

For reasons of simplicity this example ignores the impact of current year bases of assessment of the partnership's profits and the economic aspect of differing payment dates for income tax and corporation tax.

Financing problems

22.8   The use of a service company and the retention of lower taxed profits by the company can lead to financing problems. The surplus funds should not be lent to the partnership, since the Inland Revenue will charge 20% tax on the loan under *section 419* of the *Income and Corporation Taxes Act 1988* as a loan to participators and it is possible that deemed income arises to individual partners of a benefit charge on a proportionate part of the loan at the official rate of interest, currently 6.25%. If the loan is repaid and not outstanding nine months after the end of the company's accounting period, no tax is due; in addition, any tax already paid becomes repayable. There is an exemption under *section 420* of the *Income and Corporation Taxes Act 1988* for trading debt. This applies if the loan or debt arises from the supply by the services company of goods or services, in the ordinary course of its trade or business unless the credit given exceeds six months or is longer than that given to the company's customers. As most service companies would not have third party customers, invoices for supply of staff should be settled in less than six months. Surplus funds could then either be used to provide dividends to the shareholders, i.e. the partnership and hence the partners or be utilised to invest in partnership property.

Payment of dividends

22.9   The payment of a dividend will have to be reported on the form CT61.

On receipt of a dividend from its service company, the partnership is not itself liable to any further income tax. The income is excluded from the partnership's taxable profits and apportioned among the partners. If their incomes exceed the amount at which the 23% rate band becomes 40%, they will have a notional tax credit of $\frac{1}{9}$th of the actual dividend paid. The dividend plus tax credit will then be liable to tax at 32.5%, as shown below.

Example 2

	£
Dividend paid	
Apportioned dividend from service company	1,000
Add tax credit at $\frac{1}{9}$ of dividend	111
Income chargeable to tax	1,111
Income tax @ 32.5%	361
Less tax credit	111
Liability to tax	250

Utilising surplus funds

22.10   As an alternative to paying dividends a service company might utilise surplus funds to provide benefits for partners or could use them to incur entertainment or other disallowable expenditures. This is disallowable for both corporation tax and income tax purposes. The advantage here is that it may be possible that the disallowable expenditure incurred by the service company will be liable to the lower rates of corporation tax compared to the top rate of income tax. It is important to take good professional advice when considering such courses of action.

Provision of cars

22.11 Service companies have often been used to provide cars, not just for the employees of the firm, but also for the partners of the partnership, which would own the service company. The objective here is to put the possession of the car or the benefit of the car onto the basis for Schedule E, i.e. as for all employees rather than to have the complexity of being dealt with under the Schedule D Case 1 rules. Whether this is a positive income tax benefit to the individual partners is difficult to predict and will depend on the usage and expense of the car concerned for the individual. Each case has to be dealt with on its own merits, particularly following the new basis of charge on emission levels.

Plant and machinery

22.12 Where a service company owns plant and machinery and leases it across to the partnership, it would receive capital allowances in respect of that plant and machinery. In the case of items of expenditure which do not generate capital allowances, e.g. leasehold improvements, it may be advantageous if these are incurred in a service company, as optimally the lease charge would be both tax deductible in the partnership at a marginal rate of 40% and taxable at 19% (or 30%) in the company and be used to deplete the surplus of funds in the company. Again each case has to be judged on its merits.

Pensions

22.13 On the provision of pensions for employees, there is no real distinction between providing a scheme linked to a service company and one linked to the professional partnership. (See also Chapter 26, Retirement Planning, below.)

Associated trading companies

Expansion

22.14 When a professional partnership expands, opportunities may arise in associated areas of activity which may differ geographically or economically from the core professional activity. As an example, accountancy practices, solicitors and actuaries have tended to consider utilising separate companies for the provision of financial services. Having a separate company can also help in regulatory areas, as the company's activities could be 'ring-fenced' and better controlled than having the provision of financial services spread throughout the partnership. Another example could be when a civil engineering practice buys an incorporated civil engineer located in a different area of the United Kingdom. It would be difficult for corporation tax and capital gains tax reasons to disincorporate the entity, so trading through the associated trading company would continue.

Where care is needed

22.15   In service companies (see 22.8 above) care must be taken that cross-charging from either the partnership to the associated trading company or vice versa for the provision of services is consistently done on a fair basis. The associated trading company will either be indebted to the professional partnership or will be lending to it. Care should be taken that loans are not made by the company to the partnership to provide its long-term funding (i.e. the loan is outstanding for more than nine months after the end of the accounting period in which it is made) as the Inland Revenue would argue that these are caught by *section 419* of the *Income and Corporation Taxes Act 1988*. The result would be that tax at the rate of 20% would be deducted from the loan from the company to the partnership. It would be refunded when the loan was repaid, but would generally be a needless deposit with the Inland Revenue (see 22.8 above).

Funding for the acquisition of shares

22.16   Funding for the acquisition of shares in an associated trading company or lending to such a company, can be problematic. If this is done using partnership funds it could be deemed unnecessary for the partnership's business particularly if a minority interest in the associated trading company is involved. The result could lead to a restriction on eligibility for deduction for tax purposes of interest on the partnership overdraft or on partners' borrowings for the provision of partnership capital. Therefore it might be advantageous to have such an investment made by the partners directly, having withdrawn funds from the partnership.

Half-way to incorporation

22.17   Associated trading companies (and service companies) can be utilised as a half-way stage to incorporation of the professional practice, this is dealt with in Chapter 21.

Joint ventures

How they differ from partnerships

22.18   A joint venture should be distinguished from a partnership because although both are governed by contract and are between two or more parties, the parties agree typically to split expenses (and/or income) in a defined basis rather than profits (the result). The result in financial terms may be the same – if a joint venture between three parties has each entitled to 33% of the income and 33% of expenditure of the joint venture, then this is effectively identical to a partnership with a profit sharing/loss sharing ratio of one-third each. However, for tax and financial purposes the effect is different. For tax purposes the joint venture is not a separate and distinct taxable entity – if the participator in the joint venture is a professional partnership or a corporation it takes into its own accounts its share of the joint venture's income and expenditure. Commercially joint venturers are not jointly and severally liable beyond their share of the income and expenditure of the joint venture.

The construction industry

22.19   Joint ventures are common in the construction industry, and may be preferable to partnerships, since the start of a new joint venture is not necessarily thought to be that of a new trade. The result is that separate and new accounts for the new venture do not have to be prepared and none of the opening/closing years of assessment under the current year basis of assessment have to be invoked. A joint venture is usually looked at as being an extension of an existing trade. This has the additional advantage that there are no restrictions on the losses arising from a joint venture; it forms part of the general activities of the professional partnership.

Bank interest

22.20   Joint ventures usually have bank accounts which are joint accounts for the joint venturers. Care should be taken that the interest on cash deposits arising to the joint venture is included in the correct tax return periods of the joint venturers. This is a common cause of difficulties with such joint ventures.

Chapter 23

Taxation of Limited Liability Partnerships

Introduction

23.1   After substantial consultation between the Department of Trade and Industry, the Inland Revenue, Customs & Excise and interested professional bodies the *Limited Liability Partnerships Act* was published on 20 July 2000. The Act came into force from 6 April 2001 is supplemented by various regulations.

The LLP Act deals quite briefly with the taxation treatment of LLPs. This is because wherever possible, the intention is to align their taxation treatment with that of conventional unlimited partnerships, and thus to treat them as transparent for tax purposes.

Income tax

23.2   The LLP, like an unlimited partnership, will normally be subject to income tax on its profits rather than corporation tax.

The incorporation of an existing partnership business into a Limited Liability Partnership (LLP) will not be treated as a cessation for income tax purposes. Accordingly, the income tax treatment of partners in a partnership will be unaffected by the changed LLP status.

LLP tax return/partnership tax return

23.3   Providing there is no change of accounting reference date, it is likely to be acceptable to submit one return for the fiscal year affected by the transition of the partnership into an LLP part-way through the year. The annual return to the Inland Revenue will therefore set out the tax figures relevant to that fiscal year. The relevant level of disclosure on the return will be the same as that for the partnership tax return.

Assessable income

23.4   An LLP will be taxed on the profits arising during the accounting period ending during the relevant tax year. Accordingly, if an LLP has an accounting reference date of 30 April, the accounts for the year ended 30 April 2003 will produce the profits which will be assessable in the fiscal year 2003/04.

Commencement rules

23.5   When a new member commences his self-employment in an LLP, the income tax rules apply and therefore the new member will be assessed on his share of taxable profits arising in the business during the relevant tax year. For example if a new member was admitted to an LLP on say, 1 May 2003, his taxable profits for the fiscal year 2003/04 will amount to his share of the assessable profits of the LLP for the period 1 May 2003 to 5 April 2004. During the second year of the new member's self-employment of the LLP, he will be assessed on his share of the full year's profits of the LLP for the year ended 30 April 2004.

As a result of the opening year rules profits for the period 1 May 2003 to 5 April 2004, in the above example, will be assessed twice, in the first and second tax year. However, the underlying principle of self-assessment is that during an individual's self employment they will be taxed once and only once on the whole of their self employment income, not a penny more or a penny less.

Accordingly, the profits that are assessed twice in the opening years are termed 'overlap' profits. Relief for these overlap profits will crystallise in the final year of a member's participation in an LLP. This is described in more detail elsewhere in this book (see Chapter 18).

Overlap profits

23.6   The Inland Revenue has confirmed that the incorporation of the whole of the businesses of an unlimited partnership to an LLP will not trigger any recovery of overlap relief for members or partners.

Cessation

23.7   When a member leaves an LLP, he will be deemed to have ceased his self-employment in respect of the LLP business. As a result, the cessation rules will apply to the individual concerned with the release of his overlap relief being crystallised. In the year of cessation, the member is taxed on his share of the LLP's profits for the period since the end of the basis period for the previous tax year. In the case of a member who retires from an LLP on say, 30 September 2003, his previous tax basis period is the accounting period ended to 30 April 2002. Therefore, his basis period for the year of cessation (2003/04) is the 12 months to 30 April 2003 plus the five months to 30 September 2003. Against this profit is offset the overlap relief being crystallised.

There may be other problems, however, when an LLP ceases its business: see 23.18 below.

Annuities

23.8   The position regarding ongoing partnership annuities to former members of an unlimited partnership upon its incorporation into an LLP can be complex. It is, however, thought that income tax relief should still be given to the ongoing members of the new LLP as though these annuities were still being paid by the 'old' partnership.

It should also be possible to pay similar annuities to former members of an LLP and for the ongoing LLP members to obtain income tax relief.

Pensions

23.9   The same pension relief rules will apply to members of an LLP as to the partners in a partnership.

Members still claim income tax relief on RAPs/PPPs although PPPs are affected by the new pension rules which came into effect from 6 April 2001.

Loan interest relief

23.10   Although the original LLP draft bill excluded interest relief in respect of a loan taken out to fund a limited partnership, it was later amended to ensure that loan interest relief will continue to be available to LLP members, but see 23.12 below in relation to investment and property investment

Loss relief

23.11   Relief for losses should be available to members of LLPs which carry on a profession in the same way as it is available to members of an unlimited partnership. More complex rules apply if the LLP carries on a trade rather than a profession, which are beyond the scope of this book and on which professional advice should be taken.

Anti-avoidance provisions

23.12   The *Finance Act 2001* contained some measures designed to prevent tax loss through the use of LLPs. These anti-avoidance rules are aimed at investment and property investment LLPs. The anti-avoidance legislation ensures that:

(*a*) exempt bodies are taxed on any income from property they receive in their capacity as members of an LLP;

(*b*) the same consequences follow for shareholders in a company that disincorporates to form an LLP, as currently apply where a company disincorporates to form a partnership; and

(*c*) loans used to provide funds to purchase an interest in an investment LLP will not qualify for tax relief.

For these purposes an 'investment LLP' means an LLP whose business consists wholly or mainly in the making of investments and the principal part of whose income is derived therefrom. A 'property investment' LLP is an LLP whose business consists wholly or mainly in the making of investments in land and the principal part of whose income is derived therefrom.

Capital gains tax

23.13 Since the members of an LLP will be treated similarly to the members of unlimited partnerships, the existing rules in relation to partners' capital gains tax (CGT) will apply to the members of an LLP. Accordingly, the individual assets of an LLP are treated as though owned by the members in proportion rather than separately by the LLP itself. This can prevent many complexities particularly in areas where members join and leave an LLP or where there is a change in the profit and asset sharing ratios within the LLP.

The transfer of a business from a partnership to an LLP will have no effect for CGT purposes. The assets before transfer will be deemed to be owned by the partners individually and following incorporation, the assets will be owned by the members also individually, thus resulting in no disposal of assets for CGT purposes. Obviously, if there were to be a change in ownership ratios at the time of incorporation then chargeable gains might arise, subject to the application of the Statement of Practice D12, which has been revised to deal with LLPs (for the CGT rules applicable to partnerships and LLPs, see Chapter 19 of this book).

As a result of there not being a disposal by the partners on incorporation to an LLP, this transfer will not affect the availability of the indexation allowance for periods of ownership prior to 6 April 1998, or on the accrual period for taper relief purposes after that date. Equally, this will not be a disposal whereby former partners will be able to take advantage of the retirement relief provisions, which come to an end on 5 April 2003. However, where a member retires from an LLP before this date his qualifying period for retirement relief should run on across the date when the partnership converted to LLP status. With regard to the provisions on rollover relief, there are still some problems. It will apparently be possible to claim rollover relief to defer

CGT where a member of a LLP disposes of private assets and reinvests the proceeds in acquiring an interest in a LLP (see the explanation of this relief in Chapter 19).

Inheritance tax

23.14   Where an unlimited partnership becomes an LLP, a partner's period of ownership qualifying for business property relief (100%/50%) should not be interrupted and therefore his entitlement to such relief should not be affected by conversion.

All other applicable reliefs and exemptions for IHT purposes should remain available to members of an LLP.

Stamp duty

23.15   The *LLP Act 2000* includes an exemption specifically dealing with stamp duty on the incorporation of a partnership into a LLP. This exemption requires all the partners before the incorporation and all the members after the incorporation to be identical and to own identical proportions of the assets of the business both before and after the incorporation. In this event, there is no stamp duty on assets which are transferred from the 'old' partnership to the LLP for the purpose of its incorporation, provided that this transfer takes place within twelve months of incorporation.

National Insurance contributions

23.16   The *LLP Act 2000* includes a specific section, which states that members of an LLP will not be employed earners for the purpose of National Insurance contributions. This therefore means that members of an LLP will remain liable to Class 2 and Class 4 National Insurance contributions and not to the Class 1 (employee) contribution system. Equally, employer National Insurance contributions will not be payable in respect of a member's profit share.

Value added tax

23.17   An LLP will represent a separate legal entity, and therefore most or all of the assets and liabilities of an existing unlimited partnership will need to be transferred into the LLP. For VAT purposes, Customs & Excise have indicated that a transfer of a business or part of a business from a partnership to an LLP should amount to a transfer of a going concern and will therefore have no effect for VAT purposes. The VAT registration number may therefore remain unchanged for LLPs. Customs & Excise have indicated that LLPs should be registered as bodies corporate and provided they satisfy the control test in *section 736* of the *Companies Act*, then they may be entitled to join a VAT Group.

Cessation of the business of an LLP

23.18   An unfortunate aspect of the way in which the LLP Act was drafted can cause problems if a LLP ceases to carry on any trade, profession or other kind of business activity, but then there is a period during which it is wound up and dissolved. During this period, strictly, tax transparency is lost, and the LLP is taxed as a company, at corporate tax rates. More seriously, the rights of members would appear to be treated from that point as if they were shares, which could lead to double taxation when the LLP is finally dissolved and its assets distributed to members. It is understood, however, that the Inland Revenue will not apply the strict letter of the law regarding loss of transparency and the treatment of members' interests as shares where winding up takes place over a relatively short period, provided that it is done solely for commercial reasons and not for tax avoidance purposes. Also, any deferred CGT which members have claimed under the rollover relief rules would, strictly, appear to become taxable immediately on the cessation of any trade or business, even though no sale proceeds would be available.

Great care and professional advice should therefore be taken when contemplating the cessation of a LLP's activities.

Chapter 24

Partnership Changes

Planning for succession

24.1   In any partnership, planning for succession should be an issue for management and certainly in the forefront of the minds of the senior partners of the firm. Without younger partners willing and able to take on the more senior positions of responsibility in the firm, there can be no continuing business. Without a continuing business, it is unlikely that retiring partners will receive full or satisfactory return of capital contributions, annuities or payment for goodwill (depending on the nature of arrangements for retiring partners). Whilst there may still be satisfactory exit routes available with mergers or sale of the practice, such methods rarely produce full value in the case of a forced sale. Retired partners will also often have a vested interest in the firm continuing successfully so that it can maintain continuing professional indemnity cover.

A first step in planning for succession is an examination of the birth dates of all partners, together with planned retirement dates. This will show any bunching of retirements at particular times.

Plans for introducing new partners to the firm should bear in mind the likely retirement dates. Skeleton plans for transfers of responsibilities should be in place, not only to prepare for retirements or wind-downs in the run up to retirement, but also to cope with emergencies such as death, disablement or other early departures of partners.

Finally younger partners must eventually have the financial resources to take over the responsibilities for providing capital and enabling retiring partners to be bought out. This is a factor to be considered in profit sharing arrangements.

Admitting new partners

24.2   Each firm will have a procedure, formal or informal, for agreeing which individuals should be admitted as new partners to a firm. There may be separate procedures for admission as full partners and admission as salaried partners. This is likely to be a matter on which the whole partnership votes or otherwise has its say, although in large firms it is sometimes a matter reserved for management. The candidates will generally be senior employees but, increasingly, candidates are existing partners in other professional firms who, for whatever reason, wish to leave their existing practices and generally have been introduced to the firm by intermediaries. In most firms the issue of dissolution on admission of new partners will have been dealt with in the partnership agreement (see Chapter 2).

A new partner needs to absorb a significant amount of information prior to and at the time of admission. This will include details of the financial position of the firm, profit sharing arrangements, capital provisions by the new partner, his tax position and additional responsibilities. He or she would also be well advised to enquire generally into the nature of these arrangements, seeking information from existing partners in the firm and, possibly, seeking permission to obtain information from the firm's accountants.

Expulsion of partners

24.3   Power to expel a partner is a reserve power that most partnerships generally hope will never be needed. It is however a very powerful tool for management.

There will be no power to expel a partner without an express power in the partnership deed. It is sometimes said that professional partnerships find it very difficult to progress without the existence of this power. It is normally only exercisable with the consent of a significant proportion of the partnership's voting rights, generally at least 75%.

Providing the management has the full backing of most of the partnership, the very existence of this power will help give it the necessary clout to exercise delicate negotiations with any partner, both on the question of departure and, more generally, on profit-sharing arrangements or other major issues.

In practice it is rare for partners to be expelled and withdrawals or resignation are more normal.

Retirements

24.4   A wise partnership will write a retiring age into its partnership deed. Such ages are normally chosen at between 60 and 65. Modern professional partnerships have tended to do away with provisions for partners' annuities or consultancies on retirement. Instead they generally encourage or even require partners to make provision for their retirement during their time as a partner.

Many partnerships have restrictive covenants in their partnership agreements to discourage partners leaving to join other firms and minimise the damage when they do leave. Restrictive covenants are considered further at 2.36–2.37 above. The use of notice periods during which the retiring partner is excluded from the office, clients and employees, often called 'gardening leave clauses', has also proliferated as firms seek to prevent partners simply walking out to join their competitors. The combination of a notice period and restrictive covenants is a disincentive to poachers, as it can reduce the value of the incoming partner. Providing that the restrictive covenant and notice period are reasonable, they will generally be enforceable.

Demergers

24.5   A demerger is used to describe the situation when several partners in a firm, generally representing a branch or department, split away from the main firm to carry on their profession as a separate, smaller business. Such a circumstance may arise as a result of dissatisfaction over profit shares, how the firm is run or a desire for autonomy.

Mergers and team moves in partnerships

24.6   Mergers and team moves are becoming increasingly common in professional partnerships. Whilst within the corporate world many mergers would be classified as acquisitions, the partnership environment means that such transactions will nearly always be presented to clients (particularly of the smaller firm) as a merger.

A merger is the coming together of two or occasionally more professional practices. In many cases, mergers are more akin to takeovers. True mergers occur where the two firms are of similar sizes. Contested takeovers of the kind that occur with quoted companies are unheard of. This is partly because information about firms is closely held and partly because the merger is unlikely to be a success unless the majority of partners in both firms wish it to take place. However, in some mergers, it is a precondition of the deal that some partners are not included. Some partnership agreements now have provisions designed to prevent the movement of whole teams to rival firms, as this is perceived to be more damaging than the loss of a single partner.

A firm may decide to take a merger partner, or acquire a smaller practice, as a result of its strategic plan (see Chapter 8). Alternatively it may be approached and consider the merger a business opportunity. Whatever the reasons leading up to the merger proposal, a great deal of careful investigation and planning will be needed to ensure it is a success.

Why merge or acquire a team?

24.7   There are many reasons why a partnership may wish to seek a merger or team acquisition, which may include a wish to:

(*a*)   expand or diversify client base;

(*b*)   increase income or profit growth;

(*c*)   increase depth of skills;

(*d*)   increase range of services; or

(*e*)   expand/diversify geographically.

Care should be taken to consider other factors which may be seen by the merger partner as a weakness. Some mergers fail as they are undertaken in order to resolve problems through the merger which should be addressed internally. Typical issues which can have a negative impact on the merger process are:

(i) failure to keep up with growth of clients;

(ii) ageing senior partner or partners failing to grasp the succession problem;

(iii) failure to control the firm's finances;

(iv) unutilised office space, tied into a long leasehold;

(v) culture clash between the firms;

(vi) inadequate due diligence leading to unpleasant surprises about the other firm or its clients; and

(vii) establishing a commonality between the two sets of partners; will the merger be harmonious or will some partners continue to create difficulties for the new firm?

If problems such as the above exist it is better that they are considered and an action plan agreed before the merger process is entered into.

Merger issues

Third party advice

24.8   Lack of external advice is often cited as a reason for difficulties arising either during or after a merger. Firms should not be afraid of seeking advice from other members of their own profession more experienced in mergers subject to obtaining appropriate confidentiality agreements. External advice may be required on a number of separate and distinct areas and the use of an external independent adviser can, at times, assist in the negotiation process. He or she could be responsible for chairing meetings between the two parties and ensuring a proper exchange of information. It is important that information exchanged should be in a similar format ensuring accurate comparisons can be made. For example, there is no statutory format for a partnership's accounts and therefore each party may have accounting policies which may produce considerably different results from the same details. The independent adviser should also be required to consider areas of dispute with a view to providing a compromise solution acceptable to both parties.

Human resources

24.9   Interestingly the most common underlying reasons for post-merger failure revolve around people issues. Some of the areas which should be considered on or prior to the merger are as follows.

(*a*)   Remuneration and benefits. Should the best practices, and probably the most expensive, be adopted by the new firm?

(*b*)   Appraisal and grading systems.

(*c*)   Contracts of employment.

(*d*)   Manpower planning. Will some staff be surplus to requirements and how will this be dealt with?

(*e*)   Management structure and style.

(*f*)   New firm culture. Will this be dominated by one party and if so what will be the effect on the staff of the other party?

(*g*)   Managing internal communications and post transaction expectations.

Legal issues

24.10   As with all important transactions it is important to ensure that what has been agreed is properly documented. Whilst minor issues may be documented by way of agreed minutes, more major issues should be agreed by way of either amendments to or a new partnership agreement. Equally there are various other legal issues which will need to be fully considered, such as the Transfer of Undertakings regulations.

External and internal communications

24.11   The strategic reasons behind any merger will always include an aspect concerned with development of the external perception of the firm. It is therefore advisable to ensure that the merger is perceived in the market place as a significant move forward for the new firm.

Equally, communications with clients and staff should be considered carefully and worded to ensure a positive and constructive message is received.

Information technology

24.12   Most businesses are reliant upon information technology systems to run their finances, billing system, word processing and other key functions. It will therefore be necessary to consider the position of the new firm and, in particular, the following issues,

(*a*)   Are both parties using compatible equipment?

(*b*)   Should one of the existing systems be adopted? If so, when and how should this be implemented?

(*c*)   Is it appropriate to review the new firm's information technology structure with a view to adopting a more advanced and integrated system?

Property

24.13   Issues concerning property can often result in the failure of merger discussions. It is important that these are discussed at the start with consideration being given to areas where difficulties may arise. It may be worth seeking external advice to understand the size of any problem and what options may be available to resolve these issues. Possible options may include:

(*a*)   renegotiation of lease term;

(*b*)   renegotiation of rent payable; and

(*c*)   property swaps.

Tax problems with mergers

24.14   The merger of two firms (or more) is strictly an occasion where each firm ceases for the purposes of income tax assessments and a new business commences. The Inland Revenue have however issued a Statement of Practice (SP9/86) indicating that the continuation provisions might apply in certain circumstances.

However, tax problems can arise on a merger and some of these are as follows.

(*a*)   *The basis of assessment.* It is possible that both parties will be regarded as ceasing their respective businesses, or that one of them will cease but the other continues, or that both continue. The right answer will depend on the facts. In general when two firms in the same profession 'merge', even if they are of significantly different sizes, the Inland Revenue does not argue that either firm's business has come to an end as a question of fact. Instead it accepts that both businesses 'survive' inside the merged firm. Where it is clear that two firms with similar businesses have merged, the merged firm will now normally be taxed without any cessation adjustments. If the component firms have different accounting dates, there will be some complications in the year of merger, since at least one set of partners will have a change of accounting date. The rules outlined in 18.13–18.16 above may need to be applied and some 'overlap' relief may be generated or used.

(*b*)   *Catch-up-charge.* Some firms considering a merger may have a catch-up-charge which resulted from the requirement to produce true and fair accounts figures for taxation purposes. As a result there can be a spreading of this charge over a ten-year period up to the tenth anniversary of the charge, which will normally fall in the tax year 2008/09. The allocation of this catch-up-charge is, strictly, based upon the profit sharing arrangements between partners for the 12 months to each anniversary date. Thus in a merger position it can be seen that such catch-up-charges may be spread across a greater number of partners. Consideration will be needed in financial arrangements as to where the catch-up-charge falls after the merger.

(c) *Capital gains tax (CGT)*. On a merger the partners involved will make disposals for CGT purposes; their interests in their old firms, including partnership assets such as premises and goodwill, will be given up in consideration of obtaining interests in the post-merger firm. These are regarded as changes in profit-sharing ratios and will not usually give rise to any immediate tax bills because they will be treated as taking place at balance sheet values; see the outline of the CGT rules at 19.1. Sometimes, however, there may have been upwards revaluations of assets in the old firms which will mean that CGT may be due when partners reduce their respective shares as a result of the merger – for example where two firms both consisting of two equal partners merge, each partner's profit share will reduce from 50% to 25%. However, there are various CGT reliefs which may help here. Whatever the particular circumstances the parties need to be clear about the CGT effects of a merger before they commit themselves.

(d) *Other tax issues*. Other matters which will have to be addressed will include:

   (i) *VAT*. The taxable or exempt (or partially exempt) status of each firm, their respective VAT accounting periods and the question of cancellation of registrations will all have to be considered (see 20.7).

   (ii) *Tax provisions*. Pre-merger tax bills will eventually arrive for each constituent firm and the way in which the post-merger firm provides for these will have to be considered. Similar decisions will be needed about any ongoing commitments of the old firms, e.g. to retired partners or their surviving spouses.

This is only a general outline of the issues which arise and indicates that a careful eye has to be kept on tax issues throughout the merger process, with expert advice being essential.

The final phase

24.15 Assuming negotiations reach a successful conclusion and an agreement is signed, it is important to recognise that the process does not come to an end there. Both parties should continue to work together to establish proper integration and the new culture for the success of the new firm.

Chapter 25

Considerations on Becoming a Partner or Member

General and financial considerations

Introduction

25.1　Becoming a partner, or member, of a Partnership or Limited Liability Partnership is a career ambition for the majority of professionally qualified individuals who work within such businesses. Partnership signals to their contemporaries that they have made the grade. It indicates to their clients that they have the authority and experience to make major decisions on the client's behalf. It confirms that the individual's colleagues consider him or her sufficiently able and experienced to join them within the partnership. Partnership is a privilege that is not easily achieved and which cannot be taken lightly.

The various categories of partners are outlined in the glossary. This chapter is particularly concerned with those who are invited to become equity or full partners and is written from a prospective partner's perspective. However, a firm should address similar considerations when deciding who to admit to the partnership and what information it will need to make available.

Routes to equity partnership

25.2　There are generally two main routes to equity partnership.

(*a*)　Perhaps the most common is to progress from salaried partner to equity partner within the same firm. While salaried partners are able to make the same commitments on the firm's behalf as equity partners, they are either employees in the partnership or partners whose profits consist principally of a fixed or prior share and, therefore, generally make no contribution, or at least no substantial contribution, to the firm's capital. Nor do they have any significant share in the partnership's profits. After a period as a salaried partner, an individual may be invited to become an equity partner.

(*b*)　The second route is to be invited to join a partnership as an equity partner without going through the 'probation period' as a salaried partner. This may occur, for example, when a senior individual leaves one partnership and is invited to join another at a similar level. It may also occur when an individual joins a partnership from a senior non-partnership position, such as industry or local government.

What does equity partnership involve?

25.3   Becoming an equity partner requires a full understanding of the running of the partnership, its commitments and strategy. Although a new partner is often in a poor negotiating position and is not generally able to dictate terms, partnership is a serious commitment and a degree of due diligence is required. A responsible firm should respect the individual for asking reasonable questions. The following issues should be considered.

(*a*)   *The existing partners.* Who are they? Do you respect them? Are you happy to join them in a relationship which will involve you having joint and several liability for commitments they have entered into and will enter into? Most importantly, do you trust them? Becoming an equity partner involves a firm commitment from you, as well as from the present partners.

(*b*)   *The financial strength of the business.* Are you given access to financial information? How profitable is the partnership? Has it got a reasonable capital base? Has it got any unreasonable borrowings or long-term commitments? Are any bank overdrafts, loan facilities or other sources of finance in place for the foreseeable future? What are the terms on which partnership premises are occupied and when will they change? What is the position on retired partners' annuities? Are you confident that the partnership's finances are and will continue to be well managed?

(*c*)   *Professional indemnity insurance.* Is the present level of cover adequate? You should be able to review details of the cover and any outstanding claims. Is there a material level of uninsured potential liability?

(*d*)   *Capital requirements for individual equity partners.* How and when will you be required to contribute capital to the business? Many partnerships have arrangements in place that enable equity partners to borrow money and obtain tax relief on the interest or pay their capital in instalments out of profits.

(*e*)   *Profit sharing arrangements.* What arrangements are in place at present? Is there a lockstep system? How might this change in the future? Is it fair? Will it reward you adequately for your contribution? What is the policy on drawings on account of such profits? Will this meet your immediate requirements for income?

(*f*)   *Monthly income.* What effect will the change in status have on your monthly income? How are monthly drawings calculated? What events may reduce monthly drawings? When and what additional drawings will be allowed?

(*g*)   *Provision for taxation.* How is taxation provided for within the partnership? Who will be responsible for payment of tax liabilities on partnership income? If a full reserve is made for taxation on all profits earned, over what timescale will you be required to build up this reserve?

(*h*) *Associated companies.* Will the admission affect the taxation position of any company of which you are a shareholder, or control (see 22.7)?

(*j*) *Benefits and expenses.* How will pension contributions, private health insurance, permanent health insurance, critical illness insurance and life insurance be dealt with? Will you have a car paid for by the firm? A prospective partner is likely to require advice on his accrued rights under existing pension schemes as well as the position for the future.

(*k*) *The partnership agreement and other documentation.* Will you be able to review this fully before agreeing to become a partner? You should consider taking legal advice before signing the agreement.

(*l*) *Other partners' personal balance sheets.* Before joining the partnership, will you have access to any information on the financial position of existing partners? A new partner may wish to know whether the existing partners have been entering into asset protection arrangements that would reduce the partnership's ability to support future claims. This is a most delicate area and many firms do not provide the information to prospective partners.

(*m*) *Partnership decisions.* How are decisions made that affect the way the partnership is run? Is there a management committee or board? If so, who sits on it and for how long? Is there provision for rotation of positions on the committee? Who has the final say in setting the direction of the partnership? How would a new equity partner make his or her views clear? How confident are you in the effectiveness of the partnership management?

(*n*) *Strategy documents.* Does the partnership have a strategy document? Are you able to review this before signing the partnership agreement? It is important that a new partner understands what his colleagues are planning to do with the business and the way it will develop in the future.

(*o*) *Business winning and retaining.* What fee target will you be set? What will happen if the target is not met? If your initial role is to inherit and retain clients won by an existing partner who is approaching retirement, will you be penalised for not winning new business? If you are expected to develop clients in a new sector in which the firm has no existing reputation, has this been taken into account? How will you be supported in this activity?

(*p*) *Management.* What percentage of your time is likely to be spent on management? Are these and other non-chargeable activities recognised as valuable? Will you also be asked to take on specific non-chargeable responsibilities? If so, how are these activities recognised in the reward system?

(*q*)   *Retirement.* What are the terms on which you will be able to retire from the partnership in due course? What indemnities will be available for liabilities arising both before and after your retirement? Will there be continuing burdens such as restrictive covenants?

(*r*)   *Personal finances.* Should you consider rearranging your personal and family finances in the context of the proposed partnership?

(*s*)   *Advice.* Will you be able to have access to the firm's accountants or legal advisers to discuss any of the above? This is a route which professional firms are increasingly prepared to consider to ensure that a prospective partner fully understands the firm's finances and his rights and obligations. You may like to consider obtaining independent advice rather than dealing with the firm's professional advisers.

Limited Liability Partnerships

25.4   If being invited to become a member in a LLP then all the above considerations remain in point. However, in this instance the level of exposure will be capped, subject to any 'duty of care' liability, to your investment in the firm. You should consider how the LLP has been set up and its engagement terms with clients, suppliers and landlords to understand any potential liability that may go beyond the LLP. Equally you should be aware of any personal guarantees which partners have given in connection with the business. In view of the more restricted liability exposure it may be preferable to join a LLP rather than an unlimited liability partnership.

Conclusion

25.5   Becoming an equity partner or member is a serious business decision. You should satisfy yourself about as many of the above questions as possible before accepting partnership or membership. This is a decision for which only you can take final responsibility. It is also a decision in which you must allow trust and instinct to play a major part. In some firms it may be wiser to remain a salaried partner or even a well paid employee than to take on the responsibility of equity partnership if you are not comfortable with the replies to some of the above questions.

Chapter 26

Retirement Planning

Introduction to pension planning

26.1   This chapter covers the following areas.

(*a*)   Pension planning for partners and non-partners.

(*b*)   Implications of the *Pensions Act 1995* on pension schemes for employees.

(*c*)   The introduction of Stakeholder Pensions in April 2001.

Partners in professional firms cannot join corporate pension schemes because these are only open to people with earnings taxed under Schedule E. As a result, they have to make their own pension provision through personal pension arrangements.

Until the *Finance Act 1980*, there were severe restrictions on the maximum level of contributions that could be paid into personal policies. Under the retirement annuity provisions, there was a ceiling on maximum contributions of £3,000. However, the ceiling was abolished and professional partners were generally encouraged under the terms of their partnership deeds to make maximum pension provision each year.

The long-standing retirement annuity regulations were replaced in the *Finance (No 2) Act 1987* by the personal pension plan legislation which came into effect on 1 July 1988.

More recently, there has been a major change in the rules for carry back/carry forward for personal pension contributions as well as a variety of other amendments which are covered later in this chapter and which came into effect from 6 April 2001.

Retirement annuity policies

26.2   Following the personal pension plan legislation (see 26.1 above), no new contracts under the retirement annuity rules have been taken out since 1 July 1988. However, policyholders who hold such contracts may continue to invest in them.

Retirement annuity contracts are intended for the self-employed and those not in pensionable service. In corporate pension schemes, there are limitations on the level of income that can be drawn from the pension fund at retirement. In contrast the retirement annuity rules place limits on the contribution levels but not on the emerging pension. The maximum contributions are based upon a percentage of what are known as 'net relevant earnings' which are broadly defined as gross earnings less tax deductible allowances. The relevant contribution percentages are detailed below:

Age at start of tax year	*Maximum contribution percentage*
50 or less	17.5
51–55	20
56–60	22.5
61 or over	27.5

Full tax relief is given on contributions up to the allowable limits. The contributions are paid gross and tax is claimed back via the tax assessment (see 26.7).

Retirement under such contracts cannot be before the age of 60 or after 75. When the policyholder comes to draw benefits, it is possible to draw a tax-free cash sum which is calculated with reference to annuity rates at the time. The basic rule is that the tax-free cash sum must not exceed three times the annuity purchased by the balance of the fund. The type of annuity purchased is selected by the policyholder at retirement. It is possible to draw a pension even if the individual is continuing to work.

When death occurs before benefits are drawn from such policies, it is now usual for the whole of the accumulated fund to be paid as a lump sum. Many policies taken out in the 1970s and early 1980s, however, particularly those on a with-profits basis, do not pay out the full accumulated fund value in such circumstances, so policyholders with existing contracts are recommended to consider this particular aspect. The death benefit of these policies can be placed in trust for beneficiaries; and, if such action is taken, the proceeds on death do not form part of the deceased's estate for inheritance tax purposes.

As well as building up a pension fund through retirement annuity policies, the regulations also allow life assurance cover with tax-allowable premiums. Such premiums must not exceed 5% of net relevant earnings and are taken into account as part of the overall percentage contribution allowances detailed above.

In addition, where regular annual or monthly pension contributions are being paid, part of the contributions can be utilised to provide what is known as waiver of premium cover. This is in effect insurance against the possibility of disability which could result in earnings ceasing. In these circumstances the insurance cover provides for the policy to be automatically credited with the contractual premium during the period of loss of earnings or until the maturity of the policy, whichever is earlier. In this way pension rights can be maintained.

Some with profit policies contain guaranteed annuity terms which apply when the policy reaches maturity. At present, with low interest rates, we are in a scenario where these guarantees are often quite valuable. The terms of such guarantees should always be investigated at policy maturity dates.

Personal pension plans

26.3   As mentioned above (see 26.1), these were established on 1 July 1988 and the allowable contributions are again based on a percentage of net relevant earnings.

The meaning of 'net relevant earnings' here is slightly different from its definition in retirement annuity policies. However, the major differences are unlikely to apply in partnership situations as they relate to the non-allowance of share option gains in calculation of earnings. The relevant contribution percentages are listed below:

Age at start of tax year	Contribution percentage
35 or less	17.5
36–45	20
46–50	25
51–55	30
56–60	35
61 or over	40

For high earners, the personal pension plan legislation brought in the concept of an 'earnings cap'. This was set at an initial level of £60,000 for the 1989/90 tax year and it was intended to roughly rise in line with RPI each year, although in 1993/94 there was no increase. For the 2002/03 tax year, the earnings cap has been set at a level of £97,200.

Retirement benefits from personal pension plans can be drawn at any time between the ages of 50 and 75 and there is a strict limit of 25% of fund value on the amount of tax-free cash that can be drawn. The policyholder can select the type of pension annuity purchased with the balance of the fund.

In the same way as for retirement annuity contracts, policies can be placed in trust to avoid inheritance tax liabilities in the event of the policyholder's death before drawing benefits. Some personal pension providers have adopted standard rules produced by the Inland Revenue so that the policyholder simply completes a nomination form under a master trust. This nomination would normally be revocable by the policyholder in the event of a change of circumstances or requirements. Other personal pension providers operate in the same way as they do for retirement annuity policies, and issue individual trusts allowing the policyholder to select an appropriate beneficiary clause.

Until 5 April 2001, similar rules to the retirement annuity provisions operated for term assurance, where up to 5% of net relevant earnings could be used to provide life assurance cover with full tax relief on the premium. In addition, waiver of premium cover was available for regular annual or monthly payments.

However, with effect from 6 April 2001 for life cover under new personal pensions, the premium payable must not exceed 10% of contributions into personal pension plans. In addition, any waiver of premium effected must be by a stand alone policy and the premiums for this will not qualify for tax relief. Existing cover taken out prior to 6 April 2001 continues to qualify for tax relief and this also applies where options to effect life cover or waiver of premium under existing policies are exercised.

Drawing benefits from pension policies

26.4   There are a variety of options available when individuals decide to draw their pension from either retirement/annuity or personal pension policies, which are examined below.

(*a*)   *Annuity purchase.* When a policyholder comes to draw benefits from either a retirement annuity policy or a personal pension plan, most policies will permit what is known as an open market option to be exercised. This means that the policyholder can transfer the accumulated fund to another insurance company which may be offering more attractive annuity rates at the time, normally with no penalty being applied for the transfer. This flexibility can be extremely important as annuity rates can vary significantly from one company to the next. It is not unusual for those companies with good investment track records to have very poor annuity rates.

The policyholder can then choose the type of annuity purchased by his retirement fund. Typically, the questions which will need to be asked when the annuity is purchased are as follows.

(i)   Whether the annuity should include some provision for a spouse's pension.

(ii)   Whether any provision should be made for annual pension increases.

(iii)   Whether or not to include a minimum pension payment period, so that if the policyholder dies within this time the balance of the payments due within the period are paid to the estate either as a lump sum or as an ongoing pension for the remainder of the guarantee period.

Annuity rates for pensions are determined both by the policyholder's age at the time and also the level of market interest rates, in particular yields on long term gilts. Each additional option added to the annuity will have the effect of reducing the initial level of the annuity.

The important point here is that the policyholder needs to make no decision as regards the type of pension purchased until such time as benefits are to be drawn.

(*b*) *Segmentation.* Many pension policies contain the option for the policy to be issued as a number of identical segments. This means that if the total policy value is, say, £10,000 and there are ten segments to the policy, each segment is worth £1,000. The policyholder then has the option of cashing in, say, five segments to buy pension benefits and defer drawing from the remaining five segments until some time in the future. For those who do not require a high level of income from the outset, this flexibility could prove attractive.

(*c*) *Phased retirement.* Under this type of arrangement the policy would be divided into a greater number of segments, in many cases up to £1,000. Each year, a number of segments are encashed and the income that the policyholder requires is provided through a mixture of the tax-free cash sum available under those policies encashed and the annuity which is purchased.

This facility can be extremely useful for those seeking to provide a growing income as long as the underlying investment funds continue to grow and annuity rates generally do not fall. If interest rates remain static, one would expect annuity rates to improve each year due to age. The disadvantage of the staggered vesting option is that it is totally inappropriate for those who would like to generate a tax-free cash sum at the outset.

(*d*) *Income drawdown.* The *Finance Act 1995* introduced a new concept which is designed to provide policyholders with greater flexibility in the way in which an income can be drawn from a pension fund in an era of lower interest rates.

The intention is that the policyholder may defer the purchase of a conventional pension annuity until age 75. In the meantime, a variable level of income may be withdrawn from the accumulated pension fund, which will continue to remain invested on a tax exempt basis.

The principal attractions are:

(i) the timing of the purchase of an annuity will be left to the individual;

(ii) the level of income withdrawn each year may be varied at will between set parameters; and

(iii) the full tax free lump sum (up to 25% of fund value) may be taken at the outset.

(*d*)(i) *Timing of annuity purchase.* One of the disadvantages of conventional pension policies is that a pension annuity has to be purchased before the pension can commence, which is particularly unfortunate if interest rates happen to be low.

The drawdown facility will enable the individual to purchase the annuity at a time to suit himself (up to age 75), e.g. when annuity rates have improved due to higher interest rates or simply older age.

387

The conversion to a conventional annuity may be done on a piecemeal basis effectively creating a phased drawdown plan.

(*d*)(ii) *Income parameters.* The Government Actuaries Department has produced a table determining maximum income withdrawal rates for various ages and allowing for underlying interest rates. This will be applied to the value of the pension fund at the outset, i.e. when the tax-free cash sum or the first income instalment is paid. Thereafter the figure will be reviewed every three years. The income drawn each year can be between 35% and 100% of the maximum income figure.

The pension annuity factors are based on a single life pension with no provision for a spouse's pension.

(*d*)(iii) *Tax-free cash sum.* The disadvantage of the alternative option of 'phased retirement' is that the whole of the tax-free cash sum is not available at the outset. Thus, the availability of the full tax free cash sum under the income drawdown facility will be welcomed by those who may require funds to meet liabilities such as loan repayment when they retire.

(*d*)(iv) *Availability.* At present, this facility is only available under personal pension plans. Retirement annuity policyholders have to convert their plans to personal pension arrangements before they can take advantage of it. A drawdown facility now applies under occupational pension schemes, but it is far less flexible. As a result, where possible for those wishing to take advantage it is prudent to transfer the capital value of an occupational pension scheme into a personal pension plan prior to retirement. Once the facility has been selected and pension payments commenced it is now possible to transfer from one personal pension provider to another. However, this can only be organised after an initial twelve-month period.

(*d*)(v) *Position on death.* A conventional pension annuity must be purchased by the time the policyholder has attained age 75. In the event of death whilst income is still being drawn from the pension fund, a surviving spouse would have three options:

(1) to continue to receive a pension from the fund until such time as the surviving spouse or the deceased policyholder would have attained age 75, whichever comes earlier, by which time a conventional pension annuity must be purchased;

(2) to elect for the pension fund to be paid out as a lump sum, in which case it will be subject to a 35% tax charge. This benefit can be written under trust to include beneficiaries other than the surviving spouse. Whilst the payment still attracts tax at 35% the trust avoids an additional inheritance tax liability; and

(3) to purchase a conventional pension annuity. There is also scope for pensions to be paid from the fund to those who could be considered financially dependent on the policyholder.

Overall the income drawdown facility is a welcome addition to the range of options for drawing benefits from pension policies and it is likely to be particularly suitable for those retiring early when annuity rates are set at relatively low levels. In addition, the flexibility to vary income withdrawn each year could be a useful tax planning tool.

(*e*)   *Investment linked annuities.* Some insurance companies offer annuities which can be linked to the performance of selected investment funds. Those linked to with profit funds offer greater security and if investment targets are met there is the possibility of the pension increasing each year. By the same token, annuity levels can fall when targets are not met. With profit based annuities have a floor below which the annuity cannot fall. Unit linked annuities do not have any such floor and can therefore be more volatile as they are dependent upon underlying unit performance. When annuity rates are low, it is likely that investment linked annuities will be an attractive option to consider.

(*f*)   At present investors in either personal pensions or retirement annuities must buy an annuity by the time they attain age 75. There has been considerable speculation that this requirement may be abolished or the age limit may be extended. To date we have seen little evidence of any Government wish to make a change and the Treasury has been insistent that it is happy for insurance companies to produce creative annuity products which work within the existing legislative framework. There are some products of this nature now available but they are both untried and untested. In addition, because of their specialist, bespoke nature they are outside the scope of this chapter.

Tax treatment of pension contributions

Carry forward of pension allowances

26.5   The treatment of payments into personal pensions, but not retirement annuities, was changed with effect from 6 April 2001.

Under the retirement annuity regulations, it is possible to carry forward unused contribution allowances and pay them in a subsequent tax year. Unused relief may be carried forward for up to six years and relief given in the year in which the payment is made. In order to pick up unused relief, it is necessary first to clear the contribution allowance in the year of payment. Any contributions in excess of this figure are then utilised to clear unused relief starting six years previously and working forwards. The following example will help to illustrate how this operates in practice, and assumes there were no allowances available prior to 1996/97.

Example

	1997/98 £	1998/99 £	1999/2000 £	2000/01 £	2001/02 £	2002/03 £
Maximum contribution allowance	10,000	10,000	11,000	11,000	12,000	12,000
Contribution paid in year	5,000	5,000	5,000	5,000	10,000	22,000
Unused relief	5,000	5,000	6,000	6,000	2,000	(10,000)

As will be seen from the table, in 2002/03 an excess contribution of £10,000 has been paid which can be utilised to clear unused relief; firstly the unused relief allowance for 1997/98 and then the 1998/99 allowance. The unused relief for 1999/2000 to 2001/02 can be carried forward and can be cleared by the payment of any excess contributions in subsequent tax years.

For payments into personal pension plans after 6 April 2001 new provisions were introduced designed to integrate with the stakeholder pension proposals with the intention of simplifying the regime. Under stakeholder the traditional link between earnings and pensions was abolished for contribution levels up to £3,600 in any one tax year. As a result contributions can be made even where the individual has no earnings. All contributions to personal pensions regardless of whether they are in relation to self employed or employed earnings are paid net of basic rate tax with higher rate tax separately claimed.

If contribution allowances calculated by reference to age and earnings exceed the £3,600 figure the higher figure can be paid.

The main change impacting on calculation of available allowances was that rather than looking at relevant earnings in the year of payment the contribution can be based upon earnings in any one of the preceding five years if they were higher. The following example will help illustrate how this operates.

Tax year	Age at start of tax year	Maximum contribution % age	Net relevant earnings (£)
1997/98	41	20	55,000
1998/99	42	20	40,000
1999/00	43	20	50,000
2000/01	44	20	35,000
2001/02	45	20	40,000
2002/03	46	25	40,000

As we can see from the above table, earnings in the 1997/98 tax year are higher than in the 2002/03 tax year. Therefore, in 2002/03 a contribution of 25% of £55,000 can be paid, i.e. £18,750 without reference to any contributions which may have been paid against those earnings in 1997/98. In the 2003/04 tax year, if earnings were say £40,000, as the earnings in 1997/98 would have fallen out of account as they are now six years prior to the current year, contributions could be based on the earnings of £50,000 in 1999/2000.

Post retirement, if personal circumstances permit, personal pension contributions can continue to be paid for up to a further five years based on the final year of earnings or on earnings in the five tax years up to retirement. In any event contributions of up to £3,600 can be paid without reference to earnings as mentioned earlier.

Carry back of pension contributions

26.6 This provision gives the contributor the option of electing that any contribution paid in one tax year can be carried back to the previous tax year to be set against net relevant earnings for that year. It will be treated for tax purposes as though the payment was made in the previous tax year. Many contributors to pension contracts take advantage of this facility as they are unlikely to know by the end of the tax year the contribution allowance that they have available for that year. The self-assessment rules (which commenced from 1996/97) have altered the procedures, but the principle remains the same.

Self-assessment and carry back

26.7 As this is a complex topic, the following paragraphs pose various questions and then attempt to answer them.

Why the need for change?

The Revenue state that one of the central tenets of self-assessment is that any claim relevant to a period for which a return has been issued must be made in that return. Carry back claims are a clear exception to this rule which could, without any changes to the pre self-assessment rules, slow down the process of agreeing any particular year. It was therefore decided that whilst the relief will be quantified as though the pension premium had been paid in an earlier year, the actual granting of that relief will be given in the year of payment of the premium as a 'tax credit'.

How is the relief for premiums calculated?

The amount of any relief in respect of premiums carried back is still calculated as though the premium were paid in the previous tax year. Accordingly, the actual amount of tax relief due remains the same as in the pre self-assessment era. The issue that the Revenue seem to have overlooked is the cash flow effect, as it is necessary for individuals to pay the full tax liability for a tax year prior to obtaining relief for premiums paid and related back.

How is tax relief given under self-assessment?

The tax relief will be given in respect of a valid carry back claim either by a taxpayer including the claim in the return for the later year (i.e. the year of payment of the premium), or making a stand alone claim. There are three restrictions to this rule, which are:

(*a*) no repayment of tax will be made unless tax for the earlier year has been paid in full;

(*b*) if the liability for any year is outstanding, relief will be given by set-off;

(*c*) where there are no outstanding liabilities, relief will be given by repayment.

Will carry back elections affect payments on account?

No.

As the carry back relief is not given by adjustment to the self-assessment for either the year of claim or payment, it does not reduce the liability on which payments on account are based. Therefore, carry back elections will not affect payments on account.

Does this differ for premiums not carried back?

Yes.

Where relief is given for pension contributions made during the year of assessment, then such payments do have an effect on the tax due for the year of payment. As a result, pension premiums paid during the year of assessment, and not carried back, can reduce the payments on account for subsequent years and, possibly, for the year in question.

Does repayment supplement arise in respect of carry back claims?

As a carry back claim is a claim for the year of payment and the relief will not alter the amount of tax paid in respect of the self-assessment of the earlier year, no interest is payable until 31 January following the end of the year of payment of the relevant premium. For a stand alone claim, interest will run from the date on which the valid claim is made.

Retirement annuity premiums

I want to make an election – what action should I take?

Each payment of tax will be without the benefit of pension tax relief, so ensure a prudent tax provision is made throughout the year.

Premiums can be paid up to 5 April in a tax year and related back. If you want relief against the final tax payment on 31 January then the contribution should be paid before that date. Ensure the Self-Assessment Tax Return is submitted promptly. Stand alone elections may be more beneficial in some cases.

The election must be submitted by 31 January following the year of assessment in which the premium was paid.

Personal pensions including stakeholder

Do I still require the normal pension certificates?

The Revenue have stated that they will not require evidence of payments, e.g. PPCCs (Personal Pension Contributions Certificates) in support of carry back claims unless they wish to make an enquiry into the return. However, we recommend that certificates are obtained in order to comply with the record-keeping requirements under self-assessment.

An election to carry back personal pension or stakeholder contributions must be made on Form PP43 no later than the date the contribution is made. Higher rate tax can be claimed through completion of Form PP120 or the tax return.

Summary of planning points

- The use of carry back should be considered on a year by year basis.

- An election may be appropriate; a possible tax saving of up to 18% based on current tax rates if the marginal rate of taxation is lower than in the preceding year. This may be because of a change of legislation or merely a reduction of taxable income.

- Because of retirement, overseas secondment or some other reason an individual may have no relevant earnings in the year of payment; if so he or she will certainly benefit from a carry back.

- The date of payment and carry back election need to be selected carefully.

- Consider stand alone elections.

Retirement annuity policies versus personal pension plans

26.8   This section is relevant only to those who have existing retirement annuity policies as, otherwise, they will automatically fall under the personal pension plan regime.

The principal differences between the two types of contracts are as follows.

(*a*)   The different calculation of the tax-free cash sum, i.e. a strict 25% of fund value for personal pensions as opposed to the annuity based calculation for retirement annuity policies.

(*b*)   Personal pension plans permit retirement from 50 onwards, as opposed to 60 in the case of retirement annuity policies. (This can be circumvented simply by transferring from a retirement annuity policy to a personal pension plan policy, but this may involve a transfer penalty.)

(*c*)   The different contribution percentages (see 26.2 and 26.3 above).

(*d*)   The different tax rules both for actual payments and how they are calculated.

(*e*)   The imposition of the earnings cap for personal pension plan arrangements.

The difference in contribution percentages and the imposition of the earnings cap have meant that professional partners who are or potentially could be affected by the earnings cap need to consider carefully the planning of their pension contributions. This will be considered in the following sections.

Planning for retirement annuity or personal pension contributions

26.9   The carry forward rules now only apply to retirement annuity policies whereas carry back does apply to personal pensions as well and we now have the concept of basis years for personal pensions. These changes could have a major impact in assessing which option is best. However, for those who have existing retirement annuity policies, it is currently possible to designate individual tax years as either personal pension plan years or retirement annuity years. This would be important in years where earnings are well in excess of the earnings cap. For years which are designated as retirement annuity years, it is imperative that no contributions whatsoever are made to personal pension plans, including personal pension term assurance.

However, where one is taking advantage of personal pension plan allowances, it is possible to mix and match retirement annuity and personal pension plan contributions as long as the contributions paid to existing retirement annuity policies do not exceed the retirement annuity allowance for that year. In the following example, an individual has earnings of £50,000 and is aged 47. Under these circumstances, his contribution allowances would be calculated as follows:

PPP allowance (25% × £50,000) = £12,500

RAP allowance (17% × £50,000) = £8,750

On the basis of these figures, the individual could pay up to £8,750 to his existing retirement annuity policies. However to take advantage of the full PPP allowance, he must pay a PPP contribution of at least £3,750 (£12,500 less £8,750).

In comparing the benefits of retirement annuity and personal pension plan payments, great play is often made of the higher potential tax-free cash sum under a retirement annuity policy.

There are two important points to bear in mind here. Firstly, while this statement may have been true when interest rates were high, at the time of writing for anyone drawing benefits under the age of 68, the basic 25% tax-free cash sum rule for personal pensions is now higher as a result of falling long-term interest rates which have depressed annuity rates. Secondly, to take advantage of a higher tax-free cash sum under a retirement annuity, the pension annuity must be purchased with the insurance company through which the policy is held or it must be transferred to an existing retirement annuity policy with another company. The annuity would then be purchased through that company. This lack of annuity choice could mean that the annuity terms are far less favourable than those available on the open market. In conclusion, the tax-free cash sum argument for most policyholders is perceived rather than real.

Investment of pension contributions

26.10   Under the retirement annuity regulations, the bulk of pension contributions were invested via insurance company policies. But with the advent of the new personal pension plan legislation and regulations permitting banking institutions to provide pensions, a number of new providers have come into the market place. This has created new investment opportunities so that the investment options are now far wider than before. There are, in effect, three main categories of investment.

With-profits policies

26.11   The majority of insurance companies now offer unitised with-profit funds that operate differently from conventional with-profits funds. Conventional funds fall into three main categories:

(*a*)   *Conventional with-profits policies*

(i) Cash funding. These contracts provide a minimum guaranteed basic sum to which bonuses are added, and once bonuses have been added, they cannot be taken away. There is, therefore, a compounding effect in terms of investment return and many companies will pay terminal bonuses when the individual comes to draw benefits. Unlike annual bonuses, terminal bonuses are not guaranteed in any way.

(ii) Deferred annuities offering guaranteed cash conversion terms. Many old-style with-profits contracts were established on this basis and they offer a guaranteed pension at retirement age which increases each year as bonuses are added. At retirement, the policyholder is offered a guaranteed factor for converting the pension into a cash sum which can then be used to purchase pension benefits. At times of low interest rates at retirement, the guaranteed annuity may be an attractive option when compared with market annuity rates at the time.

(iii) Pure deferred annuities. This is exactly the same as above but with no guaranteed cash conversion factor.

(b) *Unitised with-profits policies.* The traditional with-profits arrangements are designed to smooth out the peaks and troughs of investment performance. In good investment years, part of the investment returns are held in reserve and these reserves are then used to maintain bonus levels in poor investment periods. The idea behind the terminal bonus is that it is a method of reflecting the true overall return on the contributions paid over the period of investment.

In essence unitised with-profits funds provide a minimum guaranteed rate of return which is topped up each year by additional bonus sums dependent upon investment performance. In theory, bonus additions could vary quite markedly from year to year. This is not the case with conventional with-profits funds, which is why so many companies have now abandoned the conventional with-profits fund as their actuaries prefer not to be tied to guaranteeing long-term bonus returns. Where there are existing policies linked to such funds, they can continue to remain invested in this way.

Overall, the attraction of with-profits arrangements is that they offer predictable returns and guarantees that investment values will not fall. So they are likely to appeal to the more security conscious investor or to the investor close to retirement.

Unit linked policies

26.12 Most insurance companies offer the option of investment in unitised funds that are very similar in terms of design to the structure of other collective investment vehicles such as unit trusts. In essence, there are a variety of investment options available, typically ranging from commercial property funds to specific sector funds investing in both UK and overseas equity markets. There is also the option of investing in a managed fund where the investment decisions and sector allocations are left to the insurance companies' own investment managers.

The policyholder can select the fund or funds into which his contributions are paid and units in the fund are then allocated to the policy. The charges inherent in the underlying funds are more transparent than in the case of with-profits arrangements and typically will involve the following.

(a) A bid/offer spread on the purchase of units, normally in the range of 5%.

(*b*)   An annual management charge for the pension fund itself, which will be in the region of 0.5% to 1.5%.

(*c*)   Monthly or annual policy fees.

In addition, there may be further charges, dependent upon whether contributions are paid on a regular or one-off basis.

Finally, there are factors applied to the contribution before units are purchased that can enhance or reduce the amount of each contribution utilised to purchase units. Generally speaking, the larger the contribution, the better the allocation terms.

Stakeholder pensions introduced a CAT mark standard for charging in that the overall product cost for stakeholder pension funds must not exceed 1% per annum of fund value. It is likely that charges in all personal pension plan investment will fall into line in due course.

The performance of the units is based purely on the performance of the underlying assets, with no guarantees of performance. Thus, there is more risk involved than in with-profits arrangements, although the potential is greater because there is no need to smooth out investment performance. All of the investment return, after the charges mentioned above, is translated into either an increase or decrease in unit price.

It is possible to switch between funds at any time at little or no cost. One can move from, say, a European equity fund into an American equity fund and typically pay a maximum cost of £25. This is excellent value, bearing in mind the costs of effecting such a switch in either shares, unit trusts or investment trusts.

At retirement, the value of the investment fund will, of course, depend upon the sectors which the policyholder has selected, the performance of the investment managers in those sectors and the timing of contributions paid. Many companies that offer unitised with-profits funds will allow switches between unit linked funds and unitised with-profits funds. This can be attractive to those approaching retirement. Companies with no with-profits funds will typically have a deposit or fixed interest fund which can enable policyholders to secure gains made in other sector funds as they approach retirement.

The longer the period of investment before retirement, the more attractive unit linked funds become. This is because they offer greater investment potential than with-profits funds, albeit at greater risk.

Self-invested personal pension plans

26.13   Some insurance companies have been offering self-invested facilities under pension arrangements (including retirement annuity policies) for many years. However, the ability to establish a pension fund which allows the policyholder either to manage the assets of the fund personally or to appoint his own fund manager has become a more established principle as a result of Joint Office Memorandum 101.

This relates to personal pension plan arrangements and permits policies to be established that allow the policyholder to purchase investments for his fund, in effect creating a personal pension portfolio of investments. The investment parameters allow investment in a wide range of sectors including stocks and shares, unit trusts and investment trusts, overseas stocks and shares, commercial property and derivatives.

There are certain specific exclusions such as the requirement that funds should not hold residential property nor should they trade with the policyholder or anyone connected with him in relation to any asset which he or any connected party has owned within the previous three years.

This type of fund is likely to appeal to professional investors or perhaps to professional partners who would like to club together to acquire a particular commercial property. It will also appeal to those who prefer the visibility of the charging structure and the control that such arrangements permit.

Payment of contributions

26.14   There are three basic options when it comes to paying pension contributions, namely, payment on a regular basis (either monthly or annually), recurring single premiums or one-off single premiums. The choice of contribution method can have a major impact upon both the flexibility and investment terms of the underlying policy.

(*a*)   *Annual or monthly premiums.* The facility to pay monthly or annual payments is useful for those who like the discipline of a regular commitment. However, there can be additional costs involved, as typically these policies pay higher levels of commission to intermediaries or direct salesmen and this cost is usually recouped through a capital levy. This affects the investment terms in relation to typically both the first and second years' premium payments. Such costs can be avoided by ensuring investment is made in pension plans which are based on stakeholder charges.

(*b*)   *Recurring single premiums.* This facility is becoming more common and can be applied either to annual or monthly premium policies. The idea here is that one avoids the capital levy charges, despite the fact that there is a regular premium commitment as each premium is treated as a one-off payment. In this way, penalties for early retirement can be avoided. Again stakeholder plans offer this contribution flexibility.

(*c*)   *Single premium contributions.* These are one-off payments which can be made at any time to the policy so there is no ongoing commitment. For those with variable relevant earnings, this flexibility can be crucial.

Generally, the investment terms are attractive for such payments as there are no capital levy charges, which can be a feature of regular payment policies.

Taking advice on investment of pension contributions

26.15 It is important that partners are encouraged to make adequate pension provision to ensure that, when they retire, their remaining partners do not feel that they have any moral obligation towards the retiring partner. Partnership annuities have largely been written out of partnership agreements and partners can only rely on the basic old age pension from the state. Most partnership agreements nowadays provide that partners should make minimum levels of pension contribution each year; and this should be monitored to ensure that partners are actually meeting this commitment.

The following table will help to illustrate the effect of delaying commencement of pension contributions. It is based upon a partner today earning £60,000 and shows the pension he may receive as a percentage of his final earnings, assuming that he pays the maximum pension contributions throughout.

Age at retirement	50	55	60
Partner aged 30	19.2%	45.6%	100%
Partner aged 35	8.6%	25.5%	66.5%
Partner aged 40	3.2%	13.2%	36.8%

So the 30-year-old partner who decides to defer paying any contributions until he is 35, and then pays the maximum contribution, would receive a pension when he is 60 reduced by one third because of the delay of five years. The table also illustrates that partners who wish to retire early must make an early start on pension payments.

In arriving at these figures, various assumptions have been made, principally in relation to investment returns, earnings inflation and the rate of increase in the RPI. The assumption is that earnings inflation will be broadly equivalent to investment returns and that the real return on investment is 2% per annum, which is well within the bounds of normal actuarial practice.

Pension planning for non-partners

26.16 Most partnerships will wish to provide pension benefits for non-partners and this can be looked at in a number of ways.

However, existing pension arrangements and any schemes which may be established in the future need to be assessed against the stakeholder pension provisions which came into effect from 6 April 2001. The provisions for stakeholder pensions were combined in the *Welfare Reform and Pensions Act 1999* and the *Stakeholder Pensions Schemes Regulations 2000*.

The main provisions are as follows:

(i) The employer must ensure that there is at least one registered stakeholder scheme available to all its relevant employees. Before designating the scheme the employer must consult with relevant employees and any organisations representing them.

(ii) The employer must provide its relevant employees with the name and address of its designated stakeholder scheme or schemes, and such other information as may be prescribed.

(iii) The employer must allow its designated stakeholder scheme or schemes reasonable access to relevant employees to provide information about the scheme.

(iv) The employer must offer payroll deduction on request.

(v) The employer must withdraw any scheme as its designated scheme if the scheme ceases to be registered with OPRA as a stakeholder scheme.

Rather surprisingly there is no requirement for the employer to contribute to a stakeholder scheme on behalf of any of its employees and there are exemptions from the stakeholder requirements in the following circumstances:

(i) Employers with fewer than five employees will be exempt from stakeholder requirements.

(ii) Employers do not have to provide access to stakeholder:

(A) for any employees whose earnings are below the lower earnings limit (LEL) in any week in the preceding three months (LEL is £89 per week for 2002/2003) or

(B) for any employee who has been employed for less than three months.

(iii) Employers who provide an occupational pension scheme or group personal pension scheme can also escape the obligation to offer access to a stakeholder scheme as long as certain criteria are met.

(*a*) *Occupational pension schemes*
To gain exemption from the stakeholder requirements, an employer's occupational pension scheme must meet the following criteria:

(i) Access to the scheme must be made available to all employees except those who are under age 18 or within five years of scheme retirement age.

(ii) Employees must not be made to wait for more than 12 months before they actually join the scheme (however, access need not be offered to an employee who has refused membership of the scheme in the past and is excluded from membership as a result).

(*b*)   *Group personal pension (GPP) schemes*
Employers running a Group Personal Pension Scheme can gain exemption from stakeholder requirements as long as the scheme meets the following criteria:

(i)   Access to the scheme must be made available to all employees aged 18 or over.

(ii) Employees must be offered access within three months of commencing employment.

(iii) The employer must make a contribution of at least 3% of their employees' basic salaries and reflect this in the employees' contracts of employment. There are further conditions covering issues such as when the employee becomes eligible to join the scheme and whether the employer requires a contribution from the employee.

(iv) The employer will operate payroll deductions to the GPP on request.

(v)   The scheme must impose no exit charges so that individuals can leave the scheme at no extra cost.

There are a wide range of additional requirements but probably the most interesting feature of stakeholder plans is that the maximum charge which can be levied is restricted to 1% per annum of fund value with no entry and no exit charges.

Other types of pension scheme

26.17   Pension provision for employees usually involves either the establishment of a group personal pension arrangement or a formal pension scheme. The impact of the stakeholder pensions requirements on these types of arrangement are discussed above. In both cases the contributions paid by the employer will be fully allowable as a business expense. Where formal pension schemes are established they will be subject to Inland Revenue regulations which restrict the maximum level of pension benefits which can be drawn at retirement, but funding possibilities for older employees are rather better than for personal pension arrangements.

Most schemes of this nature are now being established on what are known as 'money purchase principles' where there is no guarantee of ultimate benefit levels. Instead, the basic contribution level is set at a fixed percentage of annual salary, which is extremely helpful to the employer for budgeting purposes. Such schemes are subject to the full provisions of the *Pensions Act 1995* and are exempt from stakeholder if they offer membership to all employees except those who are under age 18 or within five years of scheme retirement age. The eligibility period for joining the scheme must not be more than 12 months.

A group personal pension plan on the other hand has no legal meaning, it is simply a vehicle for obtaining better terms for individual policies. In the light of stakeholder pension requirements the Group Personal Pension would meet requirements as long as the company's pension contribution for their employees is at least 3% of salary and employees can join within three months of joining the company.

In today's competitive environment for good quality staff, the employee benefits package is an increasingly relevant factor in overall remuneration so employers generally will wish to consider carefully the options available. The simple rule is that any schemes established for employees must be appropriate from the point of view of the cost, size and requirements of the company, as well as meeting the aspirations of employees in an era where future state pension benefits are likely to be scaled down.

Implications of the Pensions Act 1995 for occupational pension schemes

26.18   Employers who operate occupational schemes have to ensure compliance with the terms of the *Pensions Act 1995* which became fully effective on 6 April 1997. The Act codified much of the previous pensions legislation, including relevant sections of the *Income and Corporation Taxes Act 1988*. The Act introduced many new requirements for member protection whilst further increasing the responsibilities of trustees.

A powerful new 'watchdog', the Occupational Pensions Regulatory Authority (OPRA), was created to ensure compliance with the terms of the Act. Actuaries (for final salary schemes) and auditors, whom the Act requires to be appointed by trustees, are duty-bound to report non-compliance to OPRA, which could result in significant personal fines or even imprisonment for trustees.

The areas outlined below are those which impact upon most schemes. Advice should always be sought on application of the Act in respect of a particular scheme.

Member-nominated trustees (MNTs)

26.19   The Act introduced a requirement for MNTs for both final salary and money purchase schemes. Generally, MNTs must make up one-third of the total number of trustees, with a minimum of two, unless the scheme has less than 100 members, where the minimum is one. It is the duty of trustees to ensure that arrangements for member-nominated trustees are put in place, although the employer may make alternative arrangements so long as it undertakes a statutory consultation procedure with the members. Alternative arrangements may only be adopted where not more than 10% of the membership object.

MNT provisions were expected to change in 2002 or 2003, but amendments that were included (but not brought into force) in the *Welfare Reform and Pensions Act 1999* were put 'on hold' pending the outcome of the 'Pickering Review', a government-sponsored initiative to simplify UK pensions. The Review has now been undertaken although the Government has recognised that consideration of the proposals and subsequent inclusion of any elements into law will take some time.

As an interim measure, amending regulations were introduced, extending current arrangements to a maximum of ten years, rather than the six years that had been permitted by the *Pensions Act 1995*. However, any alternative arrangements that are adopted after 6 October 2002 may stand for a maximum of four years. It is anticipated that further legislation will be introduced from October 2006.

Professional advisers

26.20   The Act requires trustees to appoint a scheme actuary (final salary schemes) and an auditor. There is no restriction on the scheme's auditor being of the same firm as the sponsoring employer's accountant. Most trustees will also need to appoint a fund manager and legal adviser, although the latter need only be appointed by the trustees if legal services are required. Again, employer and trustees may have the same legal adviser, unless a conflict arises. The general guideline is that trustees must not take advice from anyone whom they have not themselves appointed. This would include their pension consultants.

Minimum funding requirement (MFR)

26.21   This applies to approved final salary schemes. The scheme's actuary is required to carry out a full MFR valuation every three years. If the MFR funding level falls below 90%, it must be restored to 90% within three years, with a funding plan put in place to achieve full funding within ten years. Achieving 90% funding may be through an injection of capital by the employer or through increases in the value of scheme assets. If the funding level is between 90% and 100%, action must be taken to restore the level to 100% within ten years. MFR is expected to be replaced by a new, scheme-specific, long-term funding standard, possibly as early as April 2004.

Contribution schedules

26.22   In the case of final salary schemes, the trustees and the principal employer will agree a schedule of contributions after each actuarial valuation, designed to meet ongoing funding requirements of the scheme. The schedule should reflect contributions payable over the next five years at a level which is also sufficient to meet MFR. The scheme actuary must 'sign off' the schedule, to the effect that he is satisfied that contributions will enable the scheme to at least meet the MFR. Annual re-certification of the contribution schedule is needed where a scheme is less than 100% funded on an MFR basis, for schedules which follow MFR valuations that are issued after 19 March 2002.

Payment schedules are required for money purchase schemes, showing contributions due and when payable, along with any other expenses if paid from the scheme. Contributions deducted for members must be paid into the scheme no later than 14 days after the end of the tax month in which the deduction is made (i.e. by the nineteenth of the following calendar month). The payment schedule will stipulate due dates for payment of members' and employers' contributions, which may be earlier than this date. Payment schedules must be reviewed annually.

Statement of investment principles (SIP)

26.23 Trustees of self-administered (non-insured) schemes are required to put in place a Statement of Investment Principles (SIP) which must be reviewed annually.

Essential content of the SIP is prescribed by the Act, with subsequent Regulations adding further items. In particular, the Statement must now include the trustees' policy on 'socially responsible investment' and their policy on voting shares. The recommendations of a recent 'Review of Institutional Investment in the UK' by Paul Myners, established principles (The Myners' Principles) which the British Government has urged UK pension scheme trustees to adopt. However, if the principles are not widely adopted as a matter of good practice, it is expected that the government will make adoption compulsory.

Myners' principles will impact significantly upon trustees' actions and will affect what additional information is disclosed in their SIP. Different principles and disclosures apply to final salary and money purchase schemes. Investment in an insurance company's managed funds does not necessarily constitute an 'insured' scheme, so care should be taken to ensure that an SIP is maintained, as appropriate.

Trustees' bank account

26.24 A bank account must be established by the trustees in all cases, excepting those rare situations where the insurer receives payments directly from the employer and all benefits are settled directly with members.

Report and accounts

26.25   Trustees must produce an annual report to members, together with full audited accounts or an auditor's statement in respect of the payment schedule (insured money purchase schemes).

The report and accounts (or auditor's statement) must be produced and 'signed off' within seven months of the end of each accounting period, which is normally the same as the scheme year.

Internal dispute resolution procedure

26.26   Trustees must establish a formal procedure that handles disputes between beneficiaries and the scheme trustees or managers, but not the employer. If a dispute cannot be settled through operation of the procedure, the member may still apply to the Occupational Pensions Advisory Service (OPAS) and, ultimately, the Pensions Ombudsman, who has wide powers to determine disputes. The Occupational Pensions Regulatory Authority may also be contacted by members, although it is likely that they will be redirected to OPAS and the Ombudsman, if the nature of the complaint falls within the Ombudsman's jurisdiction.

Contracting out

26.27   The state currently provides a basic flat rate pension, from state pension age, to all those who have paid sufficient National Insurance contributions (NICs) during their working life. An earnings-related component, the State Second Pension (S2P) is payable in addition. It is possible to contract out of S2P, in return for paying either reduced NICs or by redirecting part of the NICs already paid during the tax year, as described below.

Between 6 April 1978 and 5 April 1988, it was only possible to contract out through an occupational (final salary) pension scheme. Other forms of contracting out were available from 6 April 1988.

Until 5 April 1997, members of contracted out final salary schemes accrued Guaranteed Minimum Pensions (GMPs) within their occupational pension scheme. GMPs were intended to be roughly equivalent to the earnings-related pension given up through contracting out of the fore-runner to S2P, known as the State Earnings-Related Pension Scheme (SERPS).

The changes introduced from 6 April 1997 were as follows:

(*a*)   *Final salary schemes.* Contracted out final salary schemes stopped accruing GMPs. They must now comply with a prescribed quality test for contracted-out service after that date. The actuary will need to certify that the scheme provides benefits which are broadly equivalent to or better than a 'reference scheme'. GMPs already accrued will continue to be revalued in line with earnings until the member leaves contracted-out employment, at which point the scheme will normally revalue GMP at a fixed rate (4.5% in April 2002). Some schemes revalue GMPs in line with *section 148* of the *Social Security Administration Act 1992*, which approximates to full inflation-proofing. A further revaluation method, 'limited revaluation', is no longer available.

Contracted out National Insurance rebates will continue to be a flat rate for members of final salary schemes, although the employer's rebate has increased to 3.5% of middle band earnings (MBE). Employees continue to receive a rebate of 1.6%. The change to the employer's rebate coincides with the advent of the State Second Pension (S2P) as a replacement for the State Earnings-Related Pension Scheme (SERPS). MBE is earnings between the lower earnings limit and the upper earnings limit (£3,900 and £30,420 respectively at 6 April 2002).

(*b*) *Money purchase schemes.* Contracting-out through an occupational money purchase scheme is based on reinvestment of an age-related structure of rebates. Investment is made in two stages: 2.6% (1% employer, 1.6% employee) of MBE is paid at the time scheme contributions are made by the employer, with the balance (up to a total of 10.5%, depending on age) payable by the DSS after the end of the tax year. Subsequent to the *Pensions Act 1995* and changes made to the treatment of advance corporation tax, the Government Actuary's Department reviewed the structure of rebates, worsening the terms for contracted-out occupational money purchase schemes from 6 April 1999.

National insurance rebates are reviewed at least every five years, although a minimum of one year's notice is required before being implemented. The most recent change to rebates was in April 2002.

Equality

26.28   Schemes must treat men and women equally in relation to service after 17 May 1990. This means that they must have the same normal retirement age and be able to join the scheme on the same terms. Significantly, this legislation now overrides scheme rules.

Non-compliance

26.29   In some cases, non-compliance with the Act can result in the removal of a trustee and permanent disqualification from holding such a position in future. The Occupational Pensions Regulatory Authority can impose fines on employers and trustees. It may also report actuaries and auditors to their professional bodies. Trustees can be fined personally for breaches of the Act and may not be indemnified by the scheme against such fines, although many employers provide trustee indemnity either directly or through third party insurance. The most serious breaches can involve criminal charges and ultimately imprisonment, against which trustees may not legally be indemnified.

Chapter 27

Death of a Partner

Introduction

27.1 A partner's death can be extremely problematic for the partnership. Quite apart from the practical difficulty of providing a continuing high standard of service to the deceased partner's clients, the firm will have an urgent need to replace the capital contributed by the deceased partner. There may even be an automatic dissolution of the firm with the tax consequences that follow.

All partnerships, however large or small, should therefore consider the consequences of a partner dying in office and take steps to facilitate the continued smooth running of the business.

Automatic dissolution

27.2 Unless the partnership agreement provides otherwise, the death of a partner (including a general partner in a limited partnership) will cause an automatic dissolution of the partnership. [*Partnership Act 1890, s 33(1)*]. This is so even if the partnership agreement states that the partnership will exist for a fixed term and that term has not yet expired, but it does not extend to the death of a limited partner. [*Limited Partnership Act 1907, s 6(2)*]. A dissolution can cause serious difficulties between the continuing partners. For example, the agreement may contain an obligation to sell the goodwill at the highest available price, and a death may provide a recalcitrant partner with an opportunity to exploit this provision. In addition, a dissolution can have significant tax consequences. It is, therefore, important to include in the partnership agreement a provision that deals with the continuation of the partnership on the death of a partner. If, however, the death of a partner leaves only one surviving partner, there can of course be no continuing partnership and the provisions in the partnership agreement dealing with dissolution will then apply.

Since a limited partnership must have at least one general and one limited partner it follows that, where there were more than two partners, the death of a sole limited partner would have the effect of converting the limited partnership to a general partnership regardless of any provision in the partnership articles to the contrary, unless a new limited partner is immediately admitted to the firm to prevent this from happening. This may be of limited concern as the general partners carry the unlimited liability anyway. The same would happen on the death of a sole general partner, assuming that provision was made in the agreement that death of a general partner did not dissolve the partnership.

Partnership share of the deceased partner

27.3   The deceased partner's beneficial interest in the partnership vests in his personal representatives. However, if the partnership owns land and the partner who dies is one of those in whom the legal title to the land has been vested, then on his death legal title to the land will automatically devolve upon the other partners who share in the ownership of the legal title to the land on his death, the land remaining beneficially owned by the partnership.

The personal representatives have no power (unless expressly provided for by the deceased partner's will) to use assets of the estate in connection with a business venture, and will be personally liable for losses arising in respect of the deceased partner's partnership share after his death, if they use the assets in connection with the partnership without express authority in the will. The terms of the will may include a power for the personal representatives to carry on the business, or power for the deceased partner's capital contribution to remain in the business as a loan (bearing interest) to allow time for alternative arrangements to be made by the continuing partners. The provisions are unlikely to be mandatory, and personal representatives cannot therefore generally be obliged to continue in the partnership, although they may be liable in damages to the partnership if they fail to do so in contravention of an express term of the partnership agreement.

Subject to any contrary agreement with the continuing partners, personal representatives have no right to participate in the management of the partnership or to become partners. [*Partnership Act 1890, s 31*]. However, personal representatives can be admitted to the partnership as partners with the consent of the other partners. Where the personal representatives are admitted as partners they will, from the time of their appointment as partners, have personal liability for any liabilities incurred by the partnership. If they do became partners they do not automatically impose their personal liability onto the deceased partner's estate.

Return of capital and withdrawal of profits

27.4   It is important to ensure that the partnership agreement sets out clearly how the deceased partner's share of capital and past profits is to be realised by the personal representatives.

These provisions need to protect not only the estate of the deceased partner but also the ongoing partners. There should be provisions that deal with the amounts of capital and profits that can be withdrawn and the timing of any withdrawals, and particular care needs to be taken to reduce any cash flow problems that might arise as a result of the death.

The death of a partner before his retirement is a relatively unlikely occurrence, and it can therefore be reasonably inexpensive to fund the entitlement of his estate through life insurance. This is often achieved by each partner agreeing to effect insurance on his own life and to assign the policy to the firm. In the event of a partner's death, the firm can then apply the proceeds of the policy towards the entitlement of the estate in respect of capital and profits of the firm. In a company it is normal to insure the key players in order to protect the company's profitability in the event of their untimely death. However, in a partnership this type of cover is not available, as insurance companies do not view a partnership as a legal entity. Cover is, therefore, normally restricted to ensuring that funds are available to pay out the deceased partner's capital stake.

Sometimes more complex arrangements, involving the use of flexible trusts for the benefit of the firm and the deceased partner's estate, are used in order to make it easier to deal with changed circumstances, such as partners joining and leaving the firm. However care needs to be taken to ensure that the arrangements made do not amount to a gift with reservation of benefit, such that the proceeds of the policy and the partnership interest itself are both treated as forming part of the deceased partner's estate for inheritance tax purposes. Professional advice should, therefore, be obtained before entering into such arrangements.

How such cover is organised will depend upon the provisions in the partnership agreement covering withdrawal of capital (see 2.9). This may take the form of an automatic conversion of the deceased partner's share into an entitlement to the repayment of the sums standing to the credit of his capital and current accounts, coupled with the automatic vesting of his interest in the business in the continuing partners (an 'automatic accruer' arrangement). Alternatively, provision may be made for the estate to be obliged to sell the interest to the firm for cash (a 'buy and sell' arrangement). Sometimes provision is made for the firm to have an option, so that it can force the sale of the partnership interest to the firm for cash (an 'option' arrangement) perhaps coupled with the retired partner having a right to a dissolution if the option is not exercised so that he can realise the value of his interest either way. Ultimately, the choice of clause may be dictated more by inheritance tax than commercial considerations.

(*a*)   *Life assurance.* Where an automatic accruer provision exists each partner would take out life assurance cover on their lives to cover the value of their share in the partnership so that the proceeds of the policy would effectively pay out their interest in the firm. The deceased partner's interest in the firm would then be shared between the surviving partners on the basis of their interest in the partnership at the time. The cover could be written under trust for beneficiaries to avoid

409

inheritance tax and premiums would be a first charge on net distributable profits.

(*b*)   *Buy and sell agreement.* Because of inheritance tax complications it is unlikely that these agreements would be entered into. Where they do exist, normally in small partnerships, it is sensible to arrange policies in trust for surviving partners. To avoid any inheritance tax complications it is necessary to demonstrate that the arrangements are commercial (i.e. that all partners are unconnected and largely receiving similar benefits from the arrangement). Assuming that this is the case the premium payments for the policies will not be treated as gifts for inheritance tax purposes.

Inheritance tax – business property relief

27.5   In general business property relief at 100% is likely to be available on the net value of an interest in a partnership which forms part of the estate of the deceased partner, if and to the extent that he has owned it for at least two years prior to his death. If his share has increased as a proportion of the firm's capital during the two years prior to his death, relief will not be available to the extent of that increase.

However, it is important to note that where a partnership agreement contains a binding obligation on the continuing partners to buy, and on the deceased partner's personal representatives to sell, the deceased's interest, as in the case of a 'buy and sell' arrangement, the relief is not available. [*Inheritance Tax Act 1984, s 113*].

It is strongly arguable that an 'automatic accruer' arrangement is not the same as a binding obligation to sell the deceased partner's share, and that *section 113* should not apply in such cases. Indeed, the authors have received confirmation from the Capital Taxes Office that a particular automatic accruer arrangement will not prejudice full business property relief. While the answers given were (in accordance with the Revenue's usual practice) expressed to be limited to the circumstances of the particular case, it is thought to be likely that the Inland Revenue would normally adopt the same approach. Clauses 23(5)–(7) of the model partnership agreement set out in Appendix 4 operate as an automatic accruer arrangement if the words in square brackets are deleted.

The inheritance tax position can be put beyond doubt by the inclusion in the partnership agreement of an option arrangement. This would operate so that on the death of a partner his personal representatives would continue to hold the deceased's partnership interest, but the continuing partners would have an option to acquire his interest from the personal representatives. The personal representatives should also have the right to realise their interest in the firm, and this could be achieved either by giving the estate a cross-option entitlement or by providing for a dissolution, if the continuing partners do not exercise this option, but there would be no binding buy and sell arrangement as such. It is the Revenue's stated view that an option arrangement does not deny the availability of full business property relief. Clauses 23(5)–(7) of the model partnership agreement set out in Appendix 4 operate as an option arrangement if the words in square brackets are incorporated.

Loans

27.6 If individual partners borrow in order to introduce capital to the firm, and secure these loans on their other non-business assets, the loan should reduce the value of those assets for inheritance tax purposes and maximise the value of the business property relief applicable to their business assets. Ideally, the loan should actually be secured on non-business property, because otherwise the Inland Revenue may argue that the loan should be attributed rateably to the whole of the deceased partner's estate, including the business property.

Liability of personal representatives

Debts incurred prior to a partner's death

27.7 There may, of course, be internal partnership rules about the sharing of debts incurred prior to the death of a partner, but to the outside world the estate will remain jointly liable with the surviving partners in respect of liabilities of the partnership incurred before the date of death. This liability extends beyond simple debts to any torts, frauds or breaches of trust that are committed before the partner's death.

It follows that where the firm is known to face the risk of large uninsured claims at the date of death, the personal representatives must retain the whole of the deceased partner's estate in order to fund these potential liabilities. If the personal representatives make a distribution to the heirs, and the amount retained proves to be insufficient, the personal representatives will be personally liable for the shortfall up to the amount distributed.

Even in relatively straightforward situations, it may be prudent for the personal representatives to retain part of the estate to make provision for unknown partnership liabilities.

Debts incurred after a partner's death

27.8 *Section 36(3)* of the *Partnership Act 1890* expressly provides that the estate is not liable to third parties for partnership debts contracted after the date of death, except those properly and necessarily incurred in connection with the winding up of the partnership on the death of the partner. Furthermore, most partnership agreements provide that the deceased partner's estate owes no obligation to the other partners to contribute to liabilities incurred after death.

However, this is subject to any contrary agreement and the deceased partner's personal representatives may find that they became subject to liabilities incurred after death if, by their conduct, they effectively agree to become parties in that capacity. If the personal representatives are not expressly authorised to commit themselves in this way by the deceased's will, they may also incur personal liabilities for breach of trust and considerable caution is advisable.

The deceased partner's family

27.9   Busy partners are often far less effective in managing their own affairs than they are in looking after their clients. If a partner dies without making proper provision for his family, his partners may feel committed to ensuring that his family is looked after properly, and this can be expensive, both financially and in terms of management time.

Prevention is much better than cure, and many of the best run firms encourage their partners to provide for their families through appropriate pension and life insurance arrangements. For a fuller discussion of this, see Chapter 15. It is also important for family and firm alike that the partner's tax affairs can be wound up and his share of the firm's capital and profits distributed as soon as possible after his death. Many firms, therefore, also encourage partners to make well thought out wills, often appointing a continuing partner as one of the executors. It is important to be aware that conflicts can arise between the interests of the estate and the interests of the firm. Where an executor is a partner, therefore, the will should allow the executors to enter into contracts even where they have a personal interest, although the executors' overriding duty will be to act in the best interests of the beneficiaries, which may not necessarily be the best interests of the partnership.

Partnership Act 1890

1890 Chapter 39 – Royal Assent 14 August 1890

ARRANGEMENT OF SECTIONS

Nature of Partnership

1. Definition of partnership

(1) Partnership is the relation which subsists between persons carrying on a business in common with a view of profit.

(2) But the relation between members of any company or association which is—

(*a*) Registered as a company under the Companies Act 1862, or any other Act of Parliament for the time being in force and relating to the registration of joint stock companies; or

(*b*) Formed or incorporated by or in pursuance of any other Act of Parliament or letters patent, or Royal Charter; or

(*c*) A company engaged in working mines within and subject to the jurisdiction of the Stannaries:

is not a partnership within the meaning of this Act.

2. **Rules for determining existence of a partnership**

In determining whether a partnership does or does not exist, regard shall be had to the following rules:

(1) Joint tenancy, tenancy in common, joint property, common property, or part ownership does not of itself create a partnership as to anything so held or owned, whether the tenants or owners do or do not share any profits made by the use thereof.

(2) The sharing of gross returns does not of itself create a partnership, whether the persons sharing such returns have or have not a joint or common right or interest in any property from which or from the use of which the returns are derived.

(3) The receipt by a person of a share of the profits of a business is prima facie evidence that he is a partner in the business, but the receipt of such a share, or of a payment contingent on or varying with the profits of a business, does not of itself make him a partner in the business; and in particular–

    (*a*) The receipt by a person of a debt or other liquidated amount by instalments, or otherwise out of the accruing profits of a business does not of itself make him a partner in the business or liable as such.

    (*b*) A contract for the remuneration of a servant or agent of a person engaged in a business by a share of the profits of the business does not of itself make the servant or agent a partner in the business or liable as such.

    (*c*) A person being the widow or child of a deceased partner, and receiving by way of annuity a portion of the profits made in the business in which the deceased person was a partner, is not by reason only of such receipt a partner in the business or liable as such.

    (*d*) The advance of money by way of loan to a person engaged or about to engage in any business on a contract with that person that the lender shall receive a rate of interest varying with the profits, or shall receive a share of the profits arising from carrying on the business, does not of itself make the lender a partner with the person or persons carrying on the business or liable as such. Provided that the contract is in writing, and signed by or on behalf of all the parties thereto.

    (*e*) A person receiving by way of annuity or otherwise a portion of the profits of a business in consideration of the sale by him of the goodwill of the business is not by reason only of such receipt a partner in the business or liable as such.

3. **Postponement of rights of person lending or selling in consideration of share of profits in case of insolvency**

In the event of any person to whom money has been advanced by way of loan upon such a contract as is mentioned in the last foregoing section, or of any buyer of a goodwill in consideration of a share of the profits of the business, being adjudged a bankrupt, entering into an arrangement to pay his creditors less than twenty shillings in the pound, or dying in insolvent circumstances, the lender of the loan shall not be entitled to recover anything in respect of his loan, and the seller of the goodwill shall not be entitled to recover anything in respect of the share of profits contracted for, until the claims of the other creditors of the borrower or buyer for valuable consideration in money or money's worth have been satisfied.

4. Meaning of firm

(1) Persons who have entered into partnership with one another are for the purposes of this Act called collectively a firm, and the name under which their business is carried on is called the firm-name.

(2) In Scotland a firm is a legal person distinct from the partners of whom it is composed, but an individual partner may be charged on a decree or diligence directed against the firm, and on payment of the debts is entitled to relief pro rat from the firm and its other members.

Relations of Partners to persons dealing with them

5. Power of partner to bind the firm

Every partner is an agent of the firm and his other partners for the purpose of the business of the partnership; and the acts of every partner who does any act for carrying on in the usual way business of the kind carried on by the firm of which he is a member bind the firm and his partners, unless the partner so acting has in fact no authority to act for the firm in the particular matter, and the person with whom he is dealing either knows that he has no authority, or does not know or believe him to be a partner.

6. Partners bound by acts on behalf of the firm

An act or instrument relating to the business of the firm and done or executed in the firm-name, or in any other manner showing an intention to bind the firm, by any person thereto authorised, whether a partner or not, is binding on the firm and all the partners.

Provided that this section shall not affect any general rule of law relating to the execution of deeds or negotiable instruments.

7. Partner using credit of firm for private purposes

Where one partner pledges the credit of the firm for a purpose apparently not connected with the firm's ordinary course of business, the firm is not bound, unless he is in fact specially authorised by the other partners; but this section does not affect any personal liability incurred by an individual partner.

8. Effect of notice that firm will not be bound by acts of partner

If it has been agreed between the partners that any restriction shall be placed on the power of any one or more of them to bind the firm, no act done in contravention of the agreement is binding on the firm with respect to persons having notice of the agreement.

9. Liability of partners

Every partner in a firm is liable jointly with the other partners, and in Scotland severally also, for all debts and obligations of the firm incurred while he is a partner; and after his death his estate is also severally liable in a due course of administration for such debts and obligations, so far as they remain unsatisfied, but subject in England or Ireland to the prior payment of his separate debts.

10. Liability of the firm for wrongs

Where, by any wrongful act or omission of any partner acting in the ordinary course of the business of the firm, or with the authority of his co-partners, loss or injury is caused to any person not being a partner in the firm, or any penalty is incurred, the firm is liable therefor to the same extent as the partner so acting or omitting to act.

11. Misapplication of money or property received for or in custody of the firm

In the following cases; namely–

(*a*) Where one partner acting within the scope of his apparent authority receives the money or property of a third person and misapplies it; and

(*b*) Where a firm in the course of its business receives money or property of a third person, and the money or property so received is misapplied by one or more of the partners while it is in the custody of the firm;

the firm is liable to make good the loss.

12. Liability for wrongs joint and several

Every partner is liable jointly with his co-partners and also severally for everything for which the firm while he is a partner therein becomes liable under either of the two last preceding sections.

13. Improper employment of trust-property for partnership purposes

If a partner, being a trustee, improperly employs trust-property in the business or on the account of the partnership, no other partner is liable for the trust-property to the persons beneficially interested therein.

Provided as follows:

(1) This section shall not affect any liability incurred by any partner by reason of his having notice of a breach of trust; and

(2) Nothing in this section shall prevent trust money from being followed and recovered from the firm if still in its possession or under its control.

14. Persons liable by 'holding out'

(1) Every one who by words spoken or written or by conduct represents himself, or who knowingly suffers himself to be represented, as a partner in a particular firm, is liable as a partner to any one who has on the faith of any such representation given credit to the firm, whether the representation has or has not been made or communicated to the person so giving credit by or with the knowledge of the apparent partner making the representation or suffering it to be made.

(2) Provided that where after a partner's death the partnership business is continued in the old firm-name, the continued use of that name or of the deceased partner's name as part thereof shall not of itself make his executors' or administrators' estate or effects liable for any partnership debts contracted after his death.

15. Admissions and representations of partners

An admission or representation made by any partner concerning the partnership affairs, and in the ordinary course of its business, is evidence against the firm.

16. Notice to acting partner to be notice to the firm

Notice to any partner who habitually acts in the partnership business of any matter relating to partnership affairs operates as notice to the firm, except in the case of a fraud on the firm committed by or with the consent of that partner.

17. Liabilities of incoming and outgoing partners

(1) A person who is admitted as a partner into an existing firm does not thereby become liable to the creditors of the firm for anything done before he became a partner.

(2) A partner who retires from a firm does not thereby cease to be liable for partnership debts or obligations incurred before his retirement.

(3) A retiring partner may be discharged from any existing liabilities, by an agreement to that effect between himself and the members of the firm as newly constituted and the creditors, and this agreement may be either express or inferred as a fact from the course of dealing between the creditors and the firm as newly constituted.

18. Revocation of continuing guaranty by change in firm

A continuing guaranty or cautionary obligation given either to a firm or to a third person in respect of the transactions of a firm is, in the absence of agreement to the contrary, revoked as to future transactions by any change in the constitution of the firm to which, or of the firm in respect of the transactions of which, the guaranty or obligation was given.

Relations of Partners to one another

19. Variation by consent of terms of partnership

The mutual rights and duties of partners, whether ascertained by agreement or defined by this Act, may be varied by the consent of all the partners, and such consent may be either express or inferred from a course of dealing.

20. Partnership property

(1) All property and rights and interests in property originally brought into the partnership stock or acquired, whether by purchase or otherwise, on account of the firm or for the purposes and in the course of the partnership business, are called in this Act partnership property, and must be held and applied by the partners exclusively for the purposes of the partnership and in accordance with the partnership agreement.

(2) Provided that the legal estate or interest in any land, or in Scotland the title to and interest in any heritable estate, which belongs to the partnership shall devolve according to the nature and tenure thereof, and the general rules of law thereto applicable, but in trust, so far as necessary, for the persons beneficially interested in the land under this section.

(3) Where co-owners of an estate or interest in any land, or in Scotland of any heritable estate, not being itself partnership property, are partners as to profits made by the use of that land or estate, and purchase other land or estate out of the profits to be used in like manner, the land or estate so purchased belongs to them, in the absence of an agreement to the contrary, not as partners but as co-owners for the same respective estates and interests as are held by them in the land or estate first mentioned at the date of the purchase.

21. Property bought with partnership money

Unless the contrary intention appears, property bought with money belonging to the firm is deemed to have been bought on account of the firm.

22. Conversion into personal estate of land held as partnership property

Where land or any heritable interest therein has become partnership property, it shall, unless the contrary intention appears, be treated as between the partners (including the representatives of a deceased partner), and also as between the heirs of a deceased partner and his executors or administrators, as personal or moveable and not real or heritable estate.

23. Procedure against partnership property for a partners separate judgment debt

(1) After the commencement of this Act a writ of execution shall not issue against any partnership property except on a judgment against the firm.

(2) The High Court, or a judge thereof, or the Chancery Court of the county palatine of Lancaster, or a county court, may, on the application by summons of any judgment creditor of a partner, make an order charging that partner's interest in the partnership property and profits with payment of the amount of the judgment debt and interest thereon, and may by the same or a subsequent order appoint a receiver of that partner's share of profits (whether already declared or accruing), and of any other money which may be coming to him in respect of the partnership, and direct all accounts and inquiries, and give all other orders and directions which might have been directed or given if the charge had been made in favour of the judgment creditor by the partner, or which the circumstances of the case may require.

(3) The other partner or partners shall be at liberty at any time to redeem the interest charged, or in case of a sale being directed, to purchase the same.

(4) This section shall apply in the case of a cost-book company as if the company were a partnership within the meaning of this Act.

(5) This section shall not apply to Scotland.

24. Rules as to interests and duties of partners subject to special agreement

The interests of partners in the partnership property and their rights and duties in relation to the partnership shall be determined, subject to any agreement express or implied between the partners, by the following rules:

(1) All the partners are entitled to share equally in the capital and profits of the business, and must contribute equally towards the losses whether of capital or otherwise sustained by the firm.

(2) The firm must indemnify every partner in respect of payments made and personal liabilities incurred by him–

    (*a*) In the ordinary and proper conduct of the business of the firm; or

    (*b*) In or about anything necessarily done for the preservation of the business or property of the firm.

(3) A partner making, for the purpose of the partnership, any actual payment or advance beyond the amount of capital which he has agreed to subscribe, is entitled to interest at the rate of five per cent per annum from the date of the payment or advance.

(4) A partner is not entitled, before the ascertainment of profits, to interest on the capital subscribed by him.

(5) Every partner may take part in the management of the partnership business.

(6) No partner shall be entitled to remuneration for acting in the partnership business.

(7) No person may be introduced as a partner without the consent of all existing partners.

(8) Any difference arising as to ordinary matters connected with the partnership business may be decided by a majority of the partners, but no change may be made in the nature of the partnership business without the consent of all existing partners.

(9) The partnership books are to be kept at the place of business of the partnership (or the principal place, if there is more than one), and every partner may, when he thinks fit, have access to and inspect and copy any of them.

25.   Expulsion of partner

No majority of the partners can expel any partner unless a power to do so has been conferred by express agreement between the partners.

26.   Retirement from partnership at will

(1) Where no fixed term has been agreed upon for the duration of the partnership, any partner may determine the partnership at any time on giving notice of his intention so to do to all the other partners.

(2) Where the partnership has originally been constituted by deed, a notice in writing, signed by the partner giving it, shall be sufficient for this purpose.

27.   Where partnership for term is continued over, continuance on old terms presumed

(1) Where a partnership entered into for a fixed term is continued after the term has expired, and without any express new agreement, the rights and

duties of the partners remain the same as they were at the expiration of the term, so far as is consistent with the incidents of a partnership at will.

(2) A continuance of the business by the partners or such of them as habitually acted therein during the term, without any settlement or liquidation of the partnership affairs, is presumed to be a continuance of the partnership.

28. Duty of partners to render accounts, etc.

Partners are bound to render true accounts and full information of all things affecting the partnership to any partner or his legal representatives.

29. Accountability of partners for private profits

(1) Every partner must account to the firm for any benefit derived by him without the consent of the other partners from any transaction concerning the partnership, or from any use by him of the partnership property name or business connexion.

(2) This section applies also to transactions undertaken after a partnership has been dissolved by the death of a partner, and before the affairs thereof have been completely wound up, either by any surviving partner or by the representatives of the deceased partner.

30. Duty of partner not to compete with firm

If a partner, without the consent of the other partners, carries on any business of the same nature as and competing with that of the firm, he must account for and pay over to the firm all profits made by him in that business.

31. Rights of assignee of share in partnership

(1) An assignment by any partner of his share in the partnership, either absolute or by way of mortgage or redeemable charge, does not, as against the other partners, entitle the assignee, during the continuance of the partnership, to interfere in the management or administration of the partnership business or affairs, or to require any accounts of the partnership transactions, or to inspect the partnership books, but entitles the assignee only to receive the share of profits to which the assigning partner would otherwise be entitled, and the assignee must accept the account of profits agreed to by the partners.

(2) In case of a dissolution of the partnership, whether as respects all the partners or as respects the assigning partner, the assignee is entitled to receive the share of the partnership assets to which the assigning partner is entitled as between himself and the other partners, and, for the purpose of ascertaining that share, to an account as from the date of the dissolution.

Dissolution of Partnership, and its consequences

32. Dissolution by expiration or notice

Subject to an agreement between the partners a partnership is dissolved–

(*a*) If entered into for a fixed term, by the expiration of that term.

(*b*) If entered into for a single adventure or undertaking, by the termination of that adventure or undertaking.

(c) If entered into for an undefined time, by any partner giving notice to the other or others of his intention to dissolve the partnership.

In the last-mentioned case the partnership is dissolved as from the date mentioned in the notice as the date of dissolution, or, if no date is so mentioned, as from the date of the communication of the notice.

33. Dissolution by bankruptcy, death or charge

(1) Subject to any agreement between the partners, every partnership is dissolved as regards all the partners by the death or bankruptcy of any partner.

(2) A partnership may, at the option of the other partners, be dissolved if any partner suffers his share of the partnership property to be charged under this Act for his separate debt.

34. Dissolution by illegality of partnership

A partnership is in every case dissolved by the happening of any event which makes it unlawful for the business of the firm to be carried on or for the members of the firm to carry it on in partnership.

35. Dissolution by the Court

On application by a partner the Court may decree a dissolution of the partnership in any of the following cases:

(a) [. . .]

(b) When a partner, other than the partner suing, becomes in any other way permanently incapable of performing his part of the partnership contract:

(c) When a partner, other than the partner suing, has been guilty of such conduct as, in the opinion of the Court, regard being had to the nature of the business, is calculated to prejudicially affect the carrying on of the business:

(d) When a partner, other than the partner suing, wilfully or persistently commits a breach of the partnership agreement, or otherwise so conducts himself in matters relating to the partnership business that it is not reasonably practicable for the other partner or partners to carry on the business in partnership with him:

(e) When the business of the partnership can only be carried on at a loss:

(f) Whenever in any case circumstances have arisen which, in the opinion of the Court, render it just and equitable that the partnership be dissolved.

36. Rights of persons dealing with firm against apparent members of firm

(1) Where a person deals with a firm after a change in its constitution he is entitled to treat all apparent members of the old firm as still being members of the firm until he has notice of the change.

(2) An advertisement in the London Gazette as to a firm whose principal place of business is in England or Wales, in the Edinburgh Gazette as to a firm whose principal place of business is in Scotland, and in the Dublin Gazette

as to a firm whose principal place of business is in Ireland, shall be notice as to persons who had no dealings with the firm before the date of the dissolution or change so advertised.

(3) The estate of a partner who dies, or who becomes bankrupt, or of a partner who, not having been known to the person dealing with the firm to be a partner, retires from the firm, is not liable for partnership debts contracted after the date of the death, bankruptcy, or retirement respectively.

37. Rights of partners to notify dissolution

On the dissolution of a partnership or retirement of a partner any partner may publicly notify the same, and may require the other partner or partners to concur for that purpose in all necessary or proper acts, if any, which cannot be done without his or their concurrence.

38. Continuing authority of partners for purposes of winding up

After the dissolution of a partnership the authority of each partner to bind the firm, and the other rights and obligations of the partners, continue notwithstanding the dissolution so far as may be necessary to wind up the affairs of the partnership, and to complete transactions begun but unfinished at the time of the dissolution, but not otherwise.

Provided that the firm is in no case bound by the acts of a partner who has become bankrupt; but this proviso does not affect the liability of any person who has after the bankruptcy represented himself or knowingly suffered himself to be represented as a partner of the bankrupt.

39. Rights of partners as to application of partnership property

On the dissolution of a partnership every partner is entitled, as against the other partners in the firm, and all persons claiming through them in respect of their interests as partners, to have the property of the partnership applied in payment of the debts and liabilities of the firm, and to have the surplus assets after such payment applied in payment of what may be due to the partners respectively after deducting what may be due from them as partners to the firm; and for that purpose any partner or his representatives may on the termination of the partnership apply to the Court to wind up the business and affairs of the firm.

40. Apportionment of premium where partnership prematurely dissolved

Where one partner has paid a premium to another on entering into a partnership for a fixed term, and the partnership is dissolved before the expiration of that term otherwise than by the death of a partner, the Court may order the repayment of the premium, or of such part thereof as it thinks just, having regard to the terms of the partnership contract and to the length of time during which the partnership has continued; unless

(*a*) the dissolution is, in the judgment of the Court, wholly or chiefly due to the misconduct of the partner who paid the premium, or

(*b*) the partnership has been dissolved by an agreement containing no provision for a return of any part of the premium.

423

41. Rights where partnership dissolved for fraud or misrepresentation

Where a partnership contract is rescinded on the ground of the fraud or misrepresentation of one of the parties thereto, the party entitled to rescind is, without prejudice to any other right, entitled–

(*a*) to a lien on, or right of retention of, the surplus of the partnership assets, after satisfying the partnership liabilities, for any sum of money paid by him for the purchase of a share in the partnership and for any capital contributed by him, and is

(*b*) to stand in the place of the creditors of the firm for any payments made by him in respect of the partnership liabilities, and

(*c*) to be indemnified by the person guilty of the fraud or making the representation against all the debts and liabilities of the firm.

42. Right of outgoing partner in certain cases to share profits made after dissolution

(1) Where any member of a firm has died or otherwise ceased to be a partner, and the surviving or continuing partners carry on the business of the firm with its capital or assets without any final settlement of accounts as between the firm and the outgoing partner or his estate, then, in the absence of any agreement to the contrary, the outgoing partner or his estate is entitled at the option of himself or his representatives to such share of the profits made since the dissolution as the Court may find to be attributable to the use of his share of the partnership assets, or to interest at the rate of five per cent per annum on the amount of his share of the partnership assets.

(2) Provided that where by the partnership contract an option is given to surviving or continuing partners to purchase the interest of a deceased or outgoing partner, and that option is duly exercised, the estate of the deceased partner, or the outgoing partner or his estate, as the case may be, is not entitled to any further or other share of profits; but if any partner assuming to act in exercise of the option does not in all material respects comply with the terms thereof, he is liable to account under the foregoing provisions of this section.

43. Retiring or deceased partner's share to be a debt

Subject to any agreement between the partners, the amount due from surviving or continuing partners to an outgoing partner or the representatives of a deceased partner in respect of the outgoing or deceased partner's share is a debt accruing at the date of the dissolution or death.

44. Rule for distribution of assets on final settlement of accounts

In settling accounts between the partners after a dissolution of partnership, the following rules shall, subject to any agreement, be observed:

(*a*) Losses, including losses and deficiencies of capital, shall be paid first out of profits, next out of capital, and lastly, if necessary, by the partners individually in the proportion in which they were entitled to share profits:

424

(*b*) The assets of the firm including the sums, if any, contributed by the partners to make up losses or deficiencies of capital, shall be applied in the following manner and order:

1. In paying the debts and liabilities of the firm to persons who are not partners therein.

2. In paying to each partner rateably what is due from the firm to him for advances as distinguished from capital.

3. In paying to each partner rateably what is due from the firm to him in respect of capital.

4. The ultimate residue, if any, shall be divided among the partners in the proportion in which the profits are divisible.

Supplemental

45. Definitions of 'court' and 'business'

In this Act, unless the contrary intention appears–

The expression 'court' includes every court and judge having jurisdiction in the case:

The expression 'business' includes every trade, occupation, or profession.

46. Saving for rules of equity and common law

The rules of equity and of common law applicable to partnership shall continue in force except so far as they are inconsistent with the express provisions of this Act.

47. Provision as to bankruptcy in Scotland

(1) In the application of this Act to Scotland the bankruptcy of a firm or of an individual shall mean sequestration under the Bankruptcy (Scotland) Acts, and also in the case of an individual the issue against him of a decree of cessio bonorum.

(2) Nothing in this Act shall alter the rules of the law of Scotland relating to the bankruptcy of a firm or of the individual partners thereof.

48. Repeal

[. . .]

49. Commencement of Act

[. . .]

50. Short title

This Act may be cited as the Partnership Act, 1890.

Limited Partnership Act 1907

1907 Chapter 24 – Royal Assent 28 August 1907

ARRANGEMENT OF SECTIONS

1.   Short title

This Act may be cited for all purposes as the Limited Partnerships Act, 1907.

2.   Commencement of Act

This Act shall come into operation on the first day of January one thousand nine hundred and eight.

3.   Interpretation of terms

In the construction of this Act the following words and expressions shall have the meanings respectively assigned to them in this section, unless there be something in the subject or context repugnant to such construction:

'Firm', 'firm name', and 'business' have the same meanings as in the Partnership Act, 1890.

'General partner' shall mean any partner who is not a limited partner as defined by this Act.

4.   **Definition and constitution of limited partnership**

(1)   From and after the commencement of this Act limited partnerships may be formed in the manner and subject to the conditions by this Act provided.

(2)   A limited partnership shall not consist [. . .] of more than twenty persons, and must consist of one or more persons called general partners, who shall be liable for all debts and obligations of the firm, and one or more persons to be called limited partners, who shall at the time of entering into such partnership contribute thereto a sum or sums as capital or property valued at a stated amount, and who shall not be liable for the debts or obligations of the firm beyond the amount so contributed.

(3)   A limited partner shall not during the continuance of the partnership, either directly or indirectly, draw out or receive back any part of his contribution, and if he does so draw out or receive back any such part shall be liable for the debts and obligations of the firm up to the amount so drawn out or received back.

(4)   A body corporate may be a limited partner.

5.   **Registration of limited partnership required**

Every limited partnership must be registered as such in accordance with the provisions of this Act, or in default thereof it shall be deemed to be a general partnership, and every limited partner shall be deemed to be a general partner.

6.   **Modifications of general law in case of limited partnerships**

(1)   A limited partner shall not take part in the management of the partnership business, and shall not have power to bind the firm.
Provided that a limited partner may by himself or his agent at any time inspect the books of the firm and examine into the state and prospects of the partnership business, and may advise with the partners thereon.
If a limited partner takes part in the management of the partnership business he shall be liable for all debts and obligations of the firm incurred while he so takes part in the management as though he were a general partner.

(2)   A limited partnership shall not be dissolved by the death or bankruptcy of a limited partner, and the lunacy of a limited partner shall not be a ground for dissolution of the partnership by the court unless the lunatic's share cannot be otherwise ascertained and realised.

(3)   In the event of the dissolution of a limited partnership its affairs shall be wound up by the general partners unless the court otherwise orders.

(4)   [. . .]

(5)   Subject to any agreement expressed or implied between the partners–

(*a*)   Any difference arising as to ordinary matters connected with the partnership business may be decided by a majority of the general partners;

(*b*) A limited partner may, with the consent of the general partners, assign his share in the partnership, and upon such an assignment the assignee shall become a limited partner with all the rights of the assignor;

(*c*) The other partners shall not be entitled to dissolve the partnership by reason of any limited partner suffering his share to be charged for his separate debt;

(*d*) A person may be introduced as a partner without the consent of the existing limited partners;

(*e*) A limited partner shall not be entitled to dissolve the partnership by notice.

7. Law as to private partnerships to apply where not excluded by this Act

Subject to the provisions of this Act, the Partnership Act, 1890, and the rules of equity and of common law applicable to partnerships, except so far as they are inconsistent with the express provisions of the last-mentioned Act, shall apply to limited partnerships.

8. Manner and particulars of registration

The registration of a limited partnership shall be effected by sending by post or delivering to the registrar at the register office in that part of the United Kingdom in which the principal place of business of the limited partnership is situated or proposed to be situated a statement signed by the partners containing the following particulars:

(*a*) The firm name;

(*b*) The general nature of the business;

(*c*) The principal place of business;

(*d*) The full name of each of the partners;

(*e*) The term, if any, for which the partnership is entered into, and the date of its commencement;

(*f*) A statement that the partnership is limited, and the description of every limited partner as such;

(*g*) The sum contributed by each limited partner, and whether paid in cash or how otherwise.

9. Registration of changes in partnerships

(1) If during the continuance of a limited partnership any change is made or occurs in–

(*a*) the firm name,

(*b*) the general nature of the business,

(*c*) the principal place of business,

(*d*) the partners or the name of any partner,

(*e*) the term or character of the partnership,

428

(*f*) the sum contributed by any limited partner,

(*g*) the liability of any partner by reason of his becoming a limited instead of a general partner or a general instead of a limited partner, a statement, signed by the firm, specifying the nature of the change shall within seven days be sent by post or delivered to the registrar at the register office in that part of the United Kingdom in which the partnership is registered.

(2) If default is made in compliance with the requirements of this section each of the general partners shall on conviction under the Summary Jurisdiction Acts be liable to a fine not exceeding one pound for each day during which the default continues.

10. **Advertisement in Gazette of statement of general partner becoming a limited partner and of assignment of share of limited partner**

(1) Notice of any arrangement or transaction under which any person will cease to be a general partner in any firm, and will become a limited partner in that firm, or under which the share of a limited partner in a firm will be assigned to any person, shall be forthwith advertised in the Gazette, and until notice of the arrangement or transaction is so advertised, the arrangement or transaction shall, for the purposes of this Act, be deemed to be of no effect.

(2) For the purposes of this section, the expression the Gazette means–

In the case of a limited partnership registered in England, the London Gazette;

In the case of a limited partnership registered in Scotland, the Edinburgh Gazette;

In the case of a limited partnership registered in Ireland, the Dublin Gazette.

11. [...]

12. [...]

13. **Registrar to file statement and issue certificate of registration**

On receiving any statement made in pursuance of this Act the registrar shall cause the same to be filed, and he shall send by post to the firm from whom such statement shall have been received a certificate of the registration thereof.

14. **Register and index to be kept**

At each of the register offices herein-after referred to the registrar shall keep, in proper books to be provided for the purpose, a register and an index of all the limited partnerships registered as aforesaid, and of all the statements registered in relation to such partnerships.

15. **Registrar of joint stock companies to be registrar under Act**

The registrar of joint stock companies shall be the registrar of limited partnerships, and the several offices for the registration of joint stock companies in London, Edinburgh, and Dublin shall be the offices for the registration of limited partnerships carrying on business within those parts of the United Kingdom in which they are respectively situated.

16. Inspection of statements registered

(1) Any person may inspect the statements filed by the registrar in the register offices aforesaid, and there shall be paid for such inspection such fees as may be appointed by the Board of Trade, not exceeding one shilling for each inspection; and any person may require a certificate of the registration of any limited partnership, or a copy of or extract from any registered statement, to be certified by the registrar, and there shall be paid for such certificate of registration, certified copy, or extract such fees as the Board of Trade may appoint, not exceeding two shillings for the certificate of registration, and not exceeding sixpence for each folio of seventy-two words, or in Scotland for each sheet of two hundred words.

(2) A certificate of registration, or a copy of or extract from any statement registered under this Act, if duly certified to be a true copy under the hand of the registrar or one of the assistant registrars (whom it shall not be necessary to prove to be the registrar or assistant registrar) shall, in all legal proceedings, civil or criminal, and in all cases whatsoever be received in evidence.

17. Power of Board of Trade to make rules

The Board of Trade may make rules (but as to fees with the concurrence of the Treasury) concerning any of the following matters:–

(*a*) The fees to be paid to the registrar under this Act, so that they do not exceed in the case of the original registration of a limited partnership the sum of two pounds, and in any other case the sum of five shillings.

(*b*) The duties or additional duties to be performed by the registrar for the purposes of this Act;

(*c*) The performance by assistant registrars and other officers of acts by this Act required to be done by the registrar;

(*d*) The forms to be used for the purposes of this Act;

(*e*) Generally the conduct and regulation of registration under this Act and any matters incidental thereto.

Limited Liability Partnerships Act 2000

2000 Chapter 12 – Royal Assent 20 July 2000

ARRANGEMENT OF SECTIONS

431

Professional Partnership Handbook

Schedule

Names and registered offices

Part I — Names.

Part II — Registered offices.

Introductory

1. Limited liability partnerships

(1) There shall be a new form of legal entity to be known as a limited liability partnership.

(2) A limited liability partnership is a body corporate (with legal personality separate from that of its members) which is formed by being incorporated under this Act; and —

  (*a*) in the following provisions of this Act (except in the phrase 'oversea limited liability partnership'), and

  (*b*) in any other enactment (except where provision is made to the contrary or the context otherwise requires),
  references to a limited liability partnership are to such a body corporate.

(3) A limited liability partnership has unlimited capacity.

(4) The members of a limited liability partnership have such liability to contribute to its assets in the event of its being wound up as is provided for by virtue of this Act.

(5) Accordingly, except as far as otherwise provided by this Act or any other enactment, the law relating to partnerships does not apply to a limited liability partnership.

(6) The Schedule (which makes provision about the names and registered offices of limited liability partnerships) has effect.

Incorporation

2. Incorporation document etc.

(1) For a limited liability partnership to be incorporated —

  (*a*) two or more persons associated for carrying on a lawful business with a view to profit must have subscribed their names to an incorporated document,

  (*b*) there must have been delivered to the registrar either the incorporation document or a copy authenticated in a manner approved by him, and

  (*c*) there must have been so delivered a statement in a form approved by the registrar, made by either a solicitor engaged in the formation of the limited liability partnership or anyone who subscribed his name to the incorporation document, that the requirement imposed by paragraph (*a*) has been complied with.

(2) The incorporation document must —

(a) be in a form approved by the registrar (or as near to such a form as circumstances allow),

(b) state the name of the limited liability partnership,

(c) state whether the registered office of the limited liability partnership is to be situated in England and Wales, in Wales or in Scotland,

(d) state the address of that registered office,

(e) state the name and address of each of the persons who are to be members of the limited liability partnership on incorporation, and

(f) either specify which of those persons are to be designated members or state that every person who from time to time is a member of the limited liability partnership is a designated member.

(3) If a person makes a false statement under subsection (1)(c) which he —

(a) knows to be false, or

(b) does not believe to be true,
he commits an offence.

(4) A person guilty of an offence under subsection (3) is liable —

(a) on summary conviction, to imprisonment for a period not exceeding six months or a fine not exceeding the statutory maximum, or to both, or

(b) on conviction or indictment, to imprisonment for a period not exceeding two years or a fine, or to both.

3.   Incorporation by registration

(1) When the requirements imposed by paragraphs (b) and (c) of subsection (1) of section 2 have been complied with, the registrar shall retain the incorporation document or copy delivered to him and, unless the requirement imposed by paragraph (a) of that subsection has not been complied with, he shall —

(a) register the incorporation document or copy, and

(b) give a certificate that the limited liability partnership is incorporated by the name specified in the incorporation document.

(2) The registrar may accept the statement delivered under paragraph (c) of subsection (1) of section 2 as sufficient evidence that the requirement imposed by paragraph (a) of that subsection has been complied with.

(3) The certificate shall either be signed by the registrar or be authenticated by his official seal.

(4) The certificate is conclusive evidence that the requirements of section 2 are complied with and that the limited liability partnership is incorporated by the name specified in the incorporation document.

4. Members

(1) On the incorporation of a limited liability partnership its members are the persons who subscribed their names to the incorporation document (other than any who have died or been dissolved).

(2) Any other person may become a member of a limited liability partnership by and in accordance with an agreement with the existing members.

(3) A person may cease to be a member of a limited liability partnership (as well as by death or dissolution) in accordance with an agreement with the other members or, in the absence of agreement with the other members as to cessation of membership, by giving reasonable notice to the other members.

(4) A member of a limited liability partnership shall not be regarded for any purpose as employed by the limited liability partnership unless, if he and the other members were partners in a partnership, he would be regarded for that purpose as employed by the partnership.

5.   Relationship of members etc.

(1) Except as far as otherwise provided this Act or any other enactment, the mutual rights and duties of the members of a limited liability partnership, and the mutual rights and duties of a limited liability partnership and its members, shall be governed —

(*a*) by agreement between the members, or between the limited liability partnership, and its members, or

(*b*) in the absence of agreement as to any matter, by any provision made in relation to that matter by regulations under section 15(*c*).

(2) An agreement made before the incorporation of a limited liability partnership between the persons who subscribe their names to the incorporation document may impose obligations on the limited liability partnership (to take effect at any time after its incorporation).

6.   Members as agents

(1) Every member of a limited liability partnership is the agent of the limited liability partnership.

(2) But a limited liability partnership is not bound by anything done by a member in dealing with a person if —

(*a*) the member in fact has no authority to act for the limited liability partnership by doing that thing, and

(*b*) the person knows that he has no authority or does not know or believe him to be a member of the limited liability partnership.

(3) Where a person has ceased to be a member of a limited liability partnership, the former member is to be regarded (in relation to any person dealing with the limited liability partnership) as still being a member of the limited liability partnership unless —

(a) the person has notice that the former member has ceased to be a member of the limited liability partnership, or

(b) notice that the former member has ceased to be a member of the limited liability partnership has been delivered to the registrar.

(4) Where a member of a limited liability partnership is liable to any person (other than another member of the limited liability partnership) as a result of a wrongful act or omission of his in the course of the business of the limited liability partnership or with its authority, the limited liability partnership is liable to the same extent as the member.

7. Ex-members

(1) This section applies where a member of a limited liability partnership has either ceased to be a member or —

(a) has died,

(b) has become bankrupt or had his estate sequestrated or has been wound up,

(c) has granted a trust deed for the benefit of his creditors, or

(d) has assigned the whole or any part of his share in the limited liability partnership (absolutely or by way of charge or security).

(2) In such an event the former member or —

(a) his personal representative,

(b) his trustee in bankruptcy or permanent or interim trustee (within the meaning of the Bankruptcy (Scotland) Act 1985) or liquidator,

(c) his trustee under the trust deed for the benefit of his creditors, or

(d) his assignee,
may not interfere in the management or administration of any business or affairs of the limited liability partnership.

(3) But subsection (2) does not affect any right to receive an amount from the limited liability partnership in that event.

8. Designated members

(1) If the incorporation document specifies who are to be designated members —

(a) they are designated members on incorporation, and

(b) any member may become a designated member by and in accordance with an agreement with the other members,
and a member may cease to be a designated member in accordance with an agreement with the other members.

(2) But if there would otherwise be no designated members, or only one, every member is a designated member.

(3) If the incorporation document states that every person who from time to time is a member of the limited liability partnership is a designated member, every member is a designated member.

(4) A limited liability partnership may at any time deliver to the registrar —

    (*a*) notice that specified members are to be designated members, or

    (*b*) notice that every person who from time to time is a member of the limited liability partnership is a designated member,
and, once it is delivered, subsection (1) (apart from paragraph (*a*)) and subsection (2), or subsection (3), shall have effect as if that were stated in the incorporation document.

(5) A notice delivered under subsection (4) —

    (*a*) shall be in a form approved by the registrar, and

    (*b*) shall be signed by a designated member of the limited liability partnership or authenticated in a manner approved by the registrar.

(6) A person ceases to be a designated member if he ceases to be a member.

9.   **Registration of membership changes**

(1) A limited liability partnership must ensure that —

    (*a*) where a person becomes or ceases to be a member or designated member, notice is delivered to the registrar within fourteen days, and

    (*b*) where there is any change in the name or address of a member, notice is delivered to the registrar within 28 days.

(2) Where all the members from time to time of a limited liability partnership are designated members, subsection (1)(*a*) does not require notice that a person has become or ceased to be a designated member as well as a member.

(3) A notice delivered under subsection (1) —

    (*a*) shall be in a form approved by the registrar, and

    (*b*) shall be signed by a designated member of the limited liability partnership or authenticated in a manner approved by the registrar, and, if it relates to a person becoming a member or designated member, shall contain a statement that he consents to becoming a member or designated member signed by him or authenticated in a manner approved by the registrar.

(4) If a limited liability partnership fails to comply with subsection (1), the partnership and every designated member commits an offence.

(5) But it is a defence for a designated member charged with an offence under subsection (4) to prove that he took all reasonable steps for securing that subsection (1) was complied with.

(6) A person guilty of an offence under subsection (4) is liable on summary conviction to a fine not exceeding level 5 on the standard scale.

Taxation

10. Income tax and chargeable gains

(1) In the Income and Corporation Taxes Act 1988, after section 118 insert —

'Limited liability partnerships.

118ZA Treatment of limited liability partnerships.

For the purposes of the Tax Acts, a trade, profession or business carried on by a limited liability partnership with a view to profit shall be treated as carried on in partnership by its members (and not by the limited liability partnership as such); and, accordingly, the property of the limited liability partnership shall be treated for those purposes as partnership property.

118ZB Restriction on relief.

Sections 117 and 118 have effect in relation to a member of a limited liability partnership as in relation to a limited partner, but subject to sections 118ZC and 118ZD.

118ZC Member's contribution to trade.

(1) Subsection (3) of section 117 does not have effect in relation to a member of a limited liability partnership.

(2) But, for the purposes of that section and section 118, such a member's contribution to a trade at any time (the relevant time) is the greater of —

(*a*) the amount subscribed by him, and

(*b*) the amount of his liability on a winding up.

(3) The amount subscribed by a member of a limited liability partnership is the amount which he has contributed to the limited liability partnership as capital, less so much of that amount (if any) as —

(*a*) he has previously, directly or indirectly, drawn out or received back,

(*b*) he so draws out or receives back during the period of five years beginning with the relevant time,

(*c*) he is or may be entitled so to draw out or receive back at any time when he is a member of the limited liability partnership, or

(*d*) he is or may be entitled to require another person to reimburse to him.

(4) The amount of the liability of a member of a limited liability partnership on a winding up is the amount which —

(*a*) he is liable to contribute to the assets of the limited liability partnership in the event of its being wound up, and

(*b*) he remains liable so to contribute for the period of at least five years beginning with the relevant time (or until it is wound up, if that happens before the end of that period).

118ZD Carry forward of unrelieved losses.

(1) Where amounts relating to a trade carried on by a member of a limited liability partnership are, in any one or more chargeable periods, prevented from being given or allowed by section 117 or 118 as it applies otherwise than by virtue of this section (his "total unrelieved loss"), subsection (2) applies in each subsequent chargeable period in which —

(a) he carries on the trade as a member of the limited liability partnership, and

(b) any of his total unrelieved loss remains outstanding.

(2) Sections 380, 381, 393A(1) and 403 (and sections 117 and 118 as they apply in relation to those sections) shall have effect in the subsequent chargeable period as if —

(a) any loss sustained or incurred by the member in the trade in that chargeable period were increased by an amount equal to so much of his total unrelieved loss as remains outstanding in that period, or

(b) (if no loss is so sustained or incurred) a loss of that amount were so sustained or incurred.

(3) To ascertain whether any (and, if so, how much) of a member's total unrelieved loss remains outstanding in the subsequent chargeable period, deduct from the amount of his total unrelieved loss the aggregate of —

(a) any relief given under any provision of the Tax Acts (otherwise than as a result of subsection (2)) in respect of his total unrelieved loss in that or any previous chargeable period, and

(b) any amount given or allowed in respect of his total unrelieved loss as a result of subsection (2) in any previous chargeable period (or which would have been so given or allowed had a claim been made).'

(2) In section 362(2)(a) of that Act (loan to buy into partnership), after 'partner' insert 'in a limited partnership registered under the Limited Partnerships Act 1907'.

(3) In the Taxation of Chargeable Gains Act 1992, after section 59 insert —

'59A Limited liability partnerships.

(1) Where a limited liability partnership carries on a trade or business with a view to profit —

(a) assets held by the limited liability partnership shall be treated for the purposes of tax in respect of chargeable gains as held by its members as partners, and

(b) any dealings by the limited liability partnership shall be treated for those purposes as dealings by its members in partnership (and not by the limited liability partnership as such), and tax in respect of chargeable gains accruing to the members of the limited liability partnership on the disposal of any of its assets shall be assessed and charged on them separately.

(2) Where subsection (1) ceases to apply in relation to a limited liability partnership with the effect that tax is assessed and charged —

    (*a*) on the limited liability partnership (as a company) in respect of chargeable gains accruing on the disposal of any of its assets, and

    (*b*) on the members in respect of chargeable gains accruing on the disposal of any of their capital interests in the limited liability partnership,

it shall be assessed and charged on the limited liability partnership as if subsection (1) had never applied in relation to it.

(3) Neither the commencement of the application of subsection (1) nor the cessation of its application in relation to a limited liability partnership is to be taken as giving rise to the disposal of any assets by it or any of its members.'

(4) After section 156 of that Act insert —

'156A Cessation of trade by limited liability partnership.

(1) Where, immediately before the time of cessation of trade, a member of a limited liability partnership holds an asset, or an interest in an asset, acquired by him for a consideration treated as reduced under section 152 or 153, he shall be treated as if a chargeable gain equal to the amount of the reduction accrued to him immediately before that time.

(2) Where, as a result of section 154(2), a chargeable gain on the disposal of an asset, or an interest in an asset, by a member of a limited liability partnership has not accrued before the time of cessation of trade, the member shall be treated as if the chargeable gain accrued immediately before that time.

(3) In this section ''the time of cessation of trade'', in relation to a limited liability partnership, means the time when section 59A(1) ceases to apply in relation to the limited liability partnership.'

11. Inheritance tax

In the Inheritance Tax Act 1984, after section 267 insert —

'267A Limited liability partnerships.

For the purposes of this Act and any other enactments relating to inheritance tax —

    (*a*) property to which a limited liability partnership is entitled, or which it occupies or uses, shall be treated as property to which its members are entitled, or which they occupy or use, as partners,

    (*b*) any business carried on by a limited liability partnership shall be treated as carried on in partnership by its members,

439

(c) incorporation, change in membership or dissolution of a limited liability partnership shall be treated as formation, alteration or dissolution of a partnership, and

(d) any transfer of value made by or to a limited liability partnership shall be treated as made by or to its members in partnership (and not by or to the limited liability partnership as such).'

12. Stamp duty

(1) Stamp duty shall not be chargeable on an instrument by which property is conveyed or transferred by a person to a limited liability partnership in connection with its incorporation within the period of one year beginning with the date of incorporation if the following two conditions are satisfied.

(2) The first condition is that at the relevant time the person —

(a) is a partner in a partnership comprised of all the persons who are or are to be members of the limited liability partnership (and no-one else), or

(b) holds the property conveyed or transferred as nominee or bare trustee for one or more of the partners in such a partnership.

(3) The second condition is that —

(a) the proportions of the property conveyed or transferred to which the persons mentioned in subsection (2)(a) are entitled immediately after the conveyance or transfer are the same as those to which they were entitled at the relevant time, or

(b) none of the differences in those proportions has arisen as part of a scheme or arrangement of which the main purpose, or one of the main purposes, is avoidance of liability to any duty or tax.

(4) For the purposes of subsection (2) a person holds property as bare trustee for a partner if the partner has the exclusive right (subject only to satisfying any outstanding charge, lien or other right of the trustee to resort to the property for payment of duty, taxes, costs or other outgoings) to direct how the property shall be dealt with.

(5) In this section 'the relevant time' means —

(a) if the person who conveyed or transferred the property to the limited liability partnership acquired the property after its incorporation, immediately after he acquired the property, and

(b) in any other case, immediately before its incorporation.

(6) An instrument in respect of which stamp duty is not chargeable by virtue of subsection (1) shall not be taken to be duly stamped unless —

(a) it has, in accordance with section 12 of the Stamp Act 1891, been stamped with a particular stamp denoting that it is not chargeable with any duty or that it is duly stamped, or

(b) it is stamped with the duty to which it would be liable apart from that subsection.

13. **Class 4 national insurance contributions**

In section 15 of the Social Security Contributions and Benefits Act 1992 and section 15 of the Social Security Contributions and Benefits (Northern Ireland) Act 1992 (Class 4 contributions), after subsection (3) insert —

'(3A) Where income tax is (or would be) charged on a member of a limited liability partnership in respect of profits or gains arising from the carrying on of a trade or profession by the limited liability partnership, Class 4 contributions shall be payable by him if they would be payable were the trade or profession carried on in partnership by the members.'

Regulations

14. **Insolvency and winding up**

(1) Regulations shall make provision about the insolvency and winding up of limited liability partnerships by applying or incorporating, with such modifications as appear appropriate, Parts I to IV, VI and VII of the Insolvency Act 1986.

(2) Regulations may make other provision about the insolvency and winding up of limited liability partnerships, and provision about the insolvency and winding up of oversea limited liability partnerships, by —

    (*a*) applying or incorporating, with such modifications as appear appropriate, any law relating to the insolvency or winding up of companies or other corporations which would not otherwise have effect in relation to them, or

    (*b*) providing for any law relating to the insolvency or winding up of companies or other corporations which would otherwise have effect in relation to them not to apply to them or to apply to them with such modifications as appear appropriate.

(3) In this Act 'oversea limited liability partnership' means a body incorporated or otherwise established outside Great Britain and having such connection with Great Britain, and such other features, as regulations may prescribe.

15. **Application of company law etc.**

Regulations may make provision about limited liability partnerships and oversea limited liability partnerships (not being provision about insolvency or winding up) by —

    (*a*) applying or incorporating, with such modifications as appear appropriate, any law relating to companies or other corporations which would not otherwise have effect in relation to them,

    (*b*) providing for any law relating to companies or other corporations which would otherwise have effect in relation to them not to apply to them or to apply to them with such modifications as appear appropriate, or

    (*c*) applying or incorporating, with such modifications as appear appropriate, any law relating to partnerships.

16. Consequential amendments

(1) Regulations may make in any enactment such amendments or repeals as appear appropriate in consequence of this Act or regulations made under it.

(2) The regulations may, in particular, make amendments and repeals affecting companies or other corporations or partnerships.

17. General

(1) In this Act 'regulations' means regulations made by the Secretary of State by statutory instrument.

(2) Regulations under this Act may in particular —

(*a*) make provision for dealing with non-compliance with any of the regulations (including the creation of criminal offences),

(*b*) impose fees (which shall be paid into the Consolidated Fund), and

(*c*) provide for the exercise of functions by persons prescribed by the regulations.

(3) Regulations under this Act may —

(*a*) contain any appropriate consequential, incidental, supplementary or transitional provisions or savings, and

(*b*) make different provision for different purposes.

(4) No regulations to which this subsection applies shall be made unless a draft of the statutory instrument containing the regulations (whether or not together with other provisions) has been laid before, and approved by a resolution of, each House of Parliament.

(5) Subsection (4) applies to —

(*a*) regulations under section 14(2) not consisting entirely of the application or incorporation (with or without modifications) of provisions contained in or made under the Insolvency Act 1986,

(*b*) regulations under section 15 not consisting entirely of the application or incorporation (with or without modifications) of provisions contained in or made under Part I, Chapter VIII of Part V, Part VII, Parts XI to XIII, Parts XVI to XVIII, Part XX or Parts XXIV to XXVI of the Companies Act 1985,

(*c*) regulations under section 14 or 15 making provision about oversea limited liability partnerships, and

(*d*) regulations under section 16.

(6) A statutory instrument containing regulations under this Act shall (unless a draft of it has been approved by a resolution of each House of Parliament) be subject to annulment in pursuance of a resolution of either House of Parliament.

442

Supplementary

18. Interpretation

In this Act —

'address', in relation to a member of a limited liability partnership, means —

    (*a*) if an individual, his usual residential address, and

    (*b*) if a corporation or Scottish firm, its registered or principal office,

'business' includes every trade, profession and occupation,

'designated member' shall be construed in accordance with section 8,

'enactment' includes subordinate legislation (within the meaning of the Interpretation Act 1978),

'incorporation document' shall be construed in accordance with section 2,

'limited liability partnership' has the meaning given by section 1(2),

'member' shall be construed in accordance with section 4,

'modifications' includes additions and omissions,

'name', in relation to a member of a limited liability partnership, means —

    (*a*) if an individual, his forename and surname (or, in the case of a peer or other person usually known by a title, his title instead of or in addition to either or both his forename and surname), and

    (*b*) if a corporation or Scottish firm, its corporate or firm name,

'oversea limited liability partnership' has the meaning given by section 14(3),

'the registrar' means —

    (*a*) if the registered office of the limited liability partnership is, or is to be, situated in England and Wales or in Wales, the registrar or other officer performing under the Companies Act 1985 the duty of registration of companies in England and Wales, and

    (*b*) if its registered office is, or is to be, situated in Scotland, the registrar or other officer performing under that Act the duty of registration of companies in Scotland, and

'regulations' has the meaning given by section 17(1).

19. Commencement, extent and short title

    (1) The preceding provisions of this Act shall come into force on such day as the Secretary of State may by order made by statutory instrument appoint; and different days may be appointed for different purposes.

(2) The Secretary of State may by order made by statutory instrument make any transitional provisions and savings which appear appropriate in connection with the coming into force of any provision of this Act.

(3) For the purposes of the Scotland Act 1998 this Act shall be taken to be a pre-commencement enactment within the meaning of that Act.

(4) Apart from sections 10 to 13 (and this section), this Act does not extend to Northern Ireland.

(5) This Act may be cited as the Limited Liability Partnerships Act 2000.

SCHEDULE

Names and Registered Offices

PART I — NAMES

Index of names

1. — In section 714(1) of the Companies Act 1985 (index of names), after paragraph (d) insert —

'(da) limited liability partnerships incorporated under the Limited Liability Partnerships Act 2000,'.

Name to indicate status

2. — (1) The name of a limited liability partnership must end with —

(*a*) the expression 'limited liability partnership', or

(*b*) the abbreviation 'llp' or 'LLP'.

(2) But if the incorporation document for a limited liability partnership states that the registered office is to be situated in Wales, its name must end with —

(*a*) one of the expressions 'limited liability partnership' and 'partneriaeth atebolrwydd cyfyngedig', or

(*b*) one of the abbreviations 'llp', 'LLP', 'pac' and 'PAC'.

Registration of names

3. — (1) A limited liability partnership shall not be registered by a name —

(*a*) which includes, otherwise than at the end of the name, either of the expressions 'limited liability partnership' and 'partneriaeth atebolrwydd cyfyngedig' or any of the abbreviations 'llp', 'LLP', 'pac' and 'PAC',

(*b*) which is the same as a name appearing in the index kept under section 714(1) of the Companies Act 1985,

(*c*) the use of which by the limited liability partnership would in the opinion of the Secretary of State constitute a criminal offence, or

(*d*) which in the opinion of the Secretary of State is offensive.

(2) Except with the approval of the Secretary of State, a limited liability partnership shall not be registered by a name which —

(*a*) in the opinion of the Secretary of State would be likely to give the impression that it is connected in any way with Her Majesty's Government or with any local authority, or

(*b*) includes any word or expression for the time being specified in regulations under section 29 of the Companies Act 1985 (names needing approval), and in paragraph (*a*) 'local authority' means any local authority within the meaning of the Local Government Act 1972 or the Local Government etc. (Scotland) Act 1994, the Common Council of the City of London or the Council of the Isles of Scilly.

Change of name

4. — (1) A limited liability partnership may change its name at any time.

(2) Where a limited liability partnership has been registered by a name which —

    (*a*) is the same as or, in the opinion of the Secretary of State, too like a name appearing at the time of registration in the index kept under section 714(1) of the Companies Act 1985, or

    (*b*) is the same as or, in the opinion of the Secretary of State, too like a name which should have appeared in the index at that time,

    the Secretary of State may within twelve months of that time in writing direct the limited liability partnership to change its name within such period as he may specify.

(3) If it appears to the Secretary of State —

    (*a*) that misleading information has been given for the purpose of the registration of a limited liability partnership by a particular name, or

    (*b*) that undertakings or assurances have been given for that purpose and have not been fulfilled,

    he may, within five years of the date of its registration by that name, in writing direct the limited liability partnership to change its name within such period as he may specify.

(4) If in the Secretary of State's opinion the name by which a limited liability partnership is registered gives so misleading an indication of the nature of its activities as to be likely to cause harm to the public, he may in writing direct the limited liability partnership to change its name within such period as he may specify.

(5) But the limited liability partnership may, within three weeks from the date of the direction apply to the court to set it aside and the court may set the direction aside or confirm it and, if it confirms it, shall specify the period within which it must be complied with.

(6) In sub-paragraph (5) 'the court' means —

    (*a*) if the registered office of the limited liability partnership is situated in England and Wales or in Wales, the High Court, and

    (*b*) if it is situated in Scotland, the Court of Session.

(7) Where a direction has been given under sub-paragraph (2), (3) or (4) specifying a period within which a limited liability partnership is to change its name, the Secretary of State may at any time before that period ends extend it by a further direction in writing.

(8) If a limited liability partnership fails to comply with a direction under this paragraph —

    (*a*) the limited liability partnership, and

(*b*) any designated member in default, commits an offence.

(9) A person guilty of an offence under sub-paragraph (8) is liable on summary conviction to a fine not exceeding level 3 on the standard scale.

Notification of change of name

5. — (1) Where a limited liability partnership changes its name it shall deliver notice of the change to the registrar.

(2) A notice delivered under sub-paragraph (1) —

(*a*) shall be in a form approved by the registrar, and

(*b*) shall be signed by a designated member of the limited liability partnership or authenticated in a manner approved by the registrar.

(3) Where the registrar receives a notice under sub-paragraph (2) he shall (unless the new name is one by which a limited liability partnership may not be registered) —

(*a*) enter the new name in the index kept under section 714(1) of the Companies Act 1985, and

(*b*) issue a certificate of the change of name.

(4) The change of name has effect from the date on which the certificate is issued.

Effect of change of name

6. — A change of name by a limited liability partnership does not —

(*a*) affect any of its rights or duties,

(*b*) render defective any legal proceedings by or against it,

and any legal proceedings that might have been commenced or continued against it by its former name may be commenced or continued against it by its new name.

Improper use of 'limited liability partnership' etc

7. — (1) If any person carries on a business under a name or title which includes as the last words —

(*a*) the expression 'limited liability partnership' or 'partneriaeth atebolrwydd cyfyngedig', or

(*b*) any contraction or imitation of either of those expressions, that person, unless a limited liability partnership or oversea limited liability partnership, commits an offence.

(2) A person guilty of an offence under sub-paragraph (1) is liable on summary conviction to a fine not exceeding level 3 on the standard scale.

Similarity of names

8. — In determining for the purposes of this Part whether one name is the same as another there are to be disregarded —

(1) the definite article as the first word of the name,

(2) any of the following (or their Welsh equivalents or abbreviations of them or their Welsh equivalents) at the end of the name —

'limited liability partnership',
'company',
'and company',
'company limited',
'and company limited',
'limited',
'unlimited',
'public limited company', and
'investment company with variable capital', and

(3) type and case of letters, accents, spaces between letters and punctuation marks, and 'and' and '&' are to be taken as the same.

PART II — REGISTERED OFFICES

Situation of registered office

9. — (1) A limited liability partnership shall —

(*a*) at all times have a registered office situated in England and Wales or in Wales, or

(*b*) at all times have a registered office situated in Scotland, to which communications and notices may be addressed.

(2) On the incorporation of a limited liability partnership the situation of its registered office shall be that stated in the incorporation document.

(3) Where the registered office of a limited liability partnership is situated in Wales, but the incorporation document does not state that it is to be situated in Wales (as opposed to England and Wales), the limited liability partnership may deliver notice to the registrar stating that its registered office is to be situated in Wales.

(4) A notice delivered under sub-paragraph (3) —

(*a*) shall be in a form approved by the registrar, and

(*b*) shall be signed by a designated member of the limited liability partnership or authenticated in a manner approved by the registrar.

Change of registered office

10. — (1) A limited liability partnership may change its registered office by delivering notice of the change to the registrar.

(2) A notice delivered under sub-paragraph (1) —

(*a*) shall be in a form approved by the registrar, and

(*b*) shall be signed by a designated member of the limited liability partnership or authenticated in a manner approved by the registrar.

Model Partnership Agreement

[NOTE: This model agreement has been prepared by Allen & Overy and is for illustration only. Every firm's needs are unique and it is important to obtain legal and accounting advice when preparing a partnership deed.]

THIS DEED OF PARTNERSHIP is made on [   ], 20 [   ] BETWEEN the persons whose names and addresses are set out in Schedule 1:

WHEREAS:

(A) The parties carry on business together in partnership as [   ] and wish to enter into this deed for the purpose of setting out the terms and conditions under which they will carry on business together with effect from and including the Effective Date (as defined below).

(B) It is the intention of the parties that this document be executed as a deed.

NOW THIS DEED WITNESSES AND IT IS AGREED as follows:

1. Interpretation

(1) In this deed:

'**Accession Agreement**' means an agreement by which a New Partner accedes to the Partnership and to this deed and which states his initial Profit Share and capital contribution;

'**Accounts**' means the accounts of the Partnership prepared and approved in accordance with clause 8;

'**Accounts Date**' means [   ] in each year or such other date as may be decided by General Decision;

'**Accounting Period**' means the period of one calendar year ending on the Accounts Date, unless otherwise decided by General Decision;

'**Admission Date**' has the meaning given to it in sub-clause 17(1);

'**Appointment**' has the meaning given to it in sub-clause 13(1);

'**Approved Appointment**' has the meaning given to it in sub-clause 13(1);

'**Approved Liability**' has the meaning given to it in sub-clause 13(2);

'**Effective Date**' means [   ];

'**Former Partner**' means a person who ceases to be a Partner after the Effective Date for any reason (other than the dissolution of the Partnership) and includes the personal representatives of a Former Partner;

'**General Decision**' means a decision of the Partnership taken as a General Decision under clause 14;

'**Goodwill**' means the goodwill of the Partnership;

'**Losses**' means the revenue and capital losses of the Partnership as shown in the Accounts;

'**Management Committee**' means the members for the time being of the committee constituted under clause 16;

'**Managing Partner**' means the person who holds office as Managing Partner from time to time under clause 16;

'**New Partner**' means any person admitted as a Partner on or after the Effective Date under clause 17;

'**Non-Approved Appointment**' has the meaning given to it in sub-clause 13(1);

'**Partners**' means:

(*a*) those persons listed in Schedule 1; and

(*b*) every other person (excluding a Salaried Partner) who is admitted as a partner in the Partnership after the Effective Date

in each case only until he becomes a Former Partner and 'Partner' means any one of them;

'**Partnership**' means the partnership carried on by the Partners under this deed;

'**Partnership Accountants**' means [   ] or such other firm of chartered accountants as may be decided by General Decision;

'**Partnership Bank**' means [   ] Bank Plc or such other additional or substitute bank as may be appointed as banker to the Partnership by [General Decision/the Management Committee];

'**Partnership Business**' means the business and practice of [   ] and any other business or practice which the Partnership may resolve to carry on by [General/Special Decision];

'**Partnership Interest Rate**' means the base lending rate of the Partnership Bank plus [   ] per cent per annum or such other rate as may be determined by [the Management Committee/General Decision/Special Decision];

'**Partnership Name**' means the name of [   ] or such other name as may from time to time be adopted by [General/Special] Decision;

'**Partnership Premises**' means the offices of the Partnership specified in Schedule 2 and such other offices as the Partners from time to time by [Special/General] Decision decide will be used by the Partnership Business;

'**Profits**' means the revenue and capital profits of the Partnership Business as shown in the Accounts;

'**Profit Share**' in relation to a Partner means the percentage set out against his name in Schedule 1 or such other percentage as shall be determined from time to time under the provisions of this deed;

450

'**Retirement Date**' means the date when a Partner ceases to be a Partner and becomes a Former Partner by reason of death, expulsion, retirement or otherwise;

'**Salaried Partner**' means any person appointed as a salaried partner on or after the Effective Date by an employment contract made between him and the Partnership under clause 18;

'**Senior Partner**' means the person who holds offices as such from time to time under clause 16;

'**Special Decision**' means a decision of the Partnership taken as a Special Decision under clause 14; and

'**Unanimous Decision**' means a decision of the Partnership taken as a Unanimous Decision under clause 14.

(2) In interpreting this deed the following rules will be applied unless the context otherwise requires:

(*a*) words importing the singular include the plural and vice versa and words importing gender import all genders;

(*b*) references to any clause, sub-clause, schedule, paragraph or sub-paragraph are references to that clause in this deed, the sub-clause in the relevant clause in which it appears, a schedule to this deed or the paragraph or sub-paragraph in the relevant sub-clause, paragraph or schedule in which it appears and any schedules to this deed form part of this deed;

(*c*) references to statutory provisions, subordinate legislation or professional regulations will be construed as references to those provisions, legislation or regulations as they have been or may be amended or re-enacted or as their application is modified by other provisions from time to time;

(*d*) headings to clauses are for reference only and do not affect its interpretation;

(*e*) references to this deed or any other instrument include any variation, novation or replacement of any of them; and

(*f*) if a period of time is specified and is expressed to run from a given day or the day of an act or event, it is to be calculated exclusive of that day.

(3) In this deed, unless the context otherwise requires, any reference to:

an '**agreement**' also includes a contract, deed, licence, undertaking, or other document and includes that agreement as modified, novated or substituted from time to time;

a '**law**' includes common or customary law and any constitution, decree, judgement, legislation, order, ordinance, regulation, treaty or other legislative measure of England and Wales;

a '**person**' includes an individual and that person's executors and administrators;

'**professional regulations**' includes any directions, standards, rules or regulations of any professional bodies which govern the conduct of any Partner or Salaried Partner or of the Partnership;

'**rights**' includes authorities, discretions, remedies, powers and causes of action; and

'**tax**' includes any present or future tax, levy, duty, rate, charge, fee, deduction or withholding imposed, assessed or levied by any governmental agency in any part of the world (including national insurance contributions and any other social security or similar contributions wherever imposed) and any interest, penalties, fines, costs, charges and other liabilities arising from or payable in respect of that tax.

2. Commencement, Effect, Name and Duration

(1) With effect on and from the Effective Date, the Partners will carry on the Partnership Business in partnership under the Partnership Name in accordance with the provisions of this deed.

(2) The Partners agree that they will at all times comply with the provisions of the Business Names Act 1985 and of any regulation, instrument, rule or order from time to time and for the time being made under that Act.

(3) The Partnership Name and any abbreviation or combination of it or any registered trade or service marks including or associated with those names, abbreviations and combinations (in this sub-clause the '**Names**') and any logos or registered designs derived from or associated with the Names are assets of the Partnership and the use of the Names (or any interest in the Names) may only be licensed, sub-licensed, assigned, transferred or sold to third parties or otherwise disposed of as the Partnership may by [Special Decision] decide. No Partner may sell or dispose of the Names (or any interest in the Names) or use the Names save in connection with the Partnership Business.

(4) The Partnership will continue upon the terms of this deed for so long as there are at least two Partners or until dissolved under clause 25.

(5) No change in the constitution of the Partnership (whether by reason of death, retirement, expulsion or bankruptcy of any Partner, or appointment of a New Partner or otherwise) shall cause the dissolution of the Partnership.

3. Place of Business

The Partnership Business shall be carried on in the Partnership Premises.

4. Property and Liabilities

(1) All the assets of the Partnership, including (without limitation) the Goodwill, the Partnership Premises and all property for the time being used for the Partnership Business (other than property belonging personally to any Partner but kept by him upon the Partnership Premises), will be the property of the Partnership.

(2) Any asset of the Partnership not held in the names of all the Partners will be held upon trust for the Partnership by the person in whose name that

asset is held, and that person will be indemnified by the Partnership in respect of all liabilities arising in respect of that asset.

5. **Capital**

(1) The capital of the Partnership will be the sum of [   ].

(2) Each Partner will on the Effective Date be deemed to have contributed to the capital of the Partnership the amount set out opposite his name in Schedule 3.

(3) With effect on and from the Effective Date, the capital of the Partnership will be contributed by and belong to the Partners in proportion to their Profit Shares. Accordingly, on any change in the Partners' Profit Shares, any Partner whose Profit Share has increased will contribute in cash the corresponding amount as additional capital to the Partnership and any Partner whose Profit Share has decreased will be entitled to withdraw the corresponding amount from the capital of the Partnership and his capital account will be adjusted accordingly.

(4) The Partners may from time to time decide by [General/Special] Decision to increase or reduce the capital of the Partnership. Any additional capital which may be required will be contributed by the Partners, and any surplus capital no longer required will be repaid to the Partners, in proportion to their Profit Shares as at the date of that decision and each Partner's capital account will be adjusted accordingly.

(5) Where, within [   ] months of the time when the Accounts have been approved by the Partnership in respect of each Accounting Period under clause 8, a Partner is shown in the Accounts to have contributed an amount to the capital of the Partnership that is less than the amount which ought to have been contributed by him, the amount of such deficit will become a debt due by that Partner to the Partnership [and interest thereon will be payable to the Partnership at the Partnership Interest Rate].

(6) Subject to clause 23 (Former Partners and their entitlements) where, within [   ] months of the time when the Accounts have been approved by the Partnership in respect of each Accounting Period under clause 8, a Partner is shown in the Accounts to have contributed an amount to the capital of the Partnership that exceeds the amount which ought to have been contributed by him, the excess will be paid out to him as soon as is reasonably practicable with interest at the Partnership Interest Rate.

(7) Subject to clause 23 (Former Partners and their entitlements) and except as expressly provided in this deed or [with the agreement of the Management Committee/by Special Decision]:

(*a*) no Partner may draw out or receive back any part of his capital contribution to the Partnership during the continuance of the Partnership; and

(*b*) no Partner is entitled to any interest on the contribution made by him to the capital of the Partnership and no Partner is entitled to any interest on any amount lent by him to the Partnership.

453

6. Profit Shares and Losses

(1) The Profits and Losses of the Partnership are to be shared or borne by the Partners in proportion to their Profit Shares for the time being.

(2) On the Effective Date the Profit Shares allocated to each Partner are as specified in Schedule 1.

(3) The Profit Share allocated to any New Partner will be as specified in his Accession Agreement.

(4) The Partners may by [General/Special] Decision increase or reduce a Partner's Profit Share from time to time, such increase or reduction to take effect on and from a date specified in that decision.

(5) Each Partner will be reimbursed all reasonable and proper out of pocket expenses incurred by him in the performance of his duties under this deed or otherwise on behalf of the Partnership. Each Partner will provide to the Partnership appropriate records of his expenses within such period after the time when those expenses were incurred as the Management Committee may determine.

(6) Any liability occasioned by the fraud or dishonesty of a Partner must be made good by that Partner alone.

7. Drawings

(1) Subject to clause 9 (Provision for tax liabilities), the Partners may on account of their Profit Shares in the relevant Accounting Period make monthly drawings of such amounts as may from time to time be determined by [General Decision/the Management Committee].

(2) Within one month of the time when the Accounts have been approved by the Partnership in respect of each Accounting Period under clause 8, any Partner who is shown in the Accounts to have drawn any amount in excess of his share of Profits for that period, after provision for tax liabilities under clause 9, will refund that excess to the Partnership as soon as is reasonably practicable [together with interest on that amount at the Partnership Interest Rate for the period from the date when he is requested by the Management Committee to make the refund to the date of repayment].

(3) Unless otherwise determined by [Special Decision/the Management Committee], if a Partner is shown in the Accounts to have drawn an amount less than his Profit Share, after provision for tax liabilities under clause 9, that undrawn balance will be credited within one month of the time when the Accounts have been approved by the Partnership in respect of each Accounting Period under clause 8 to his current account with the Partnership [together with interest on that amount at the Partnership Interest Rate from such date as is determined by the Management Committee to the date of repayment]. When the Accounts for each Accounting Period have been approved under clause 8, each Partner may draw the amount of the credit balance on his current account as shown in those Accounts at the times and in the instalments determined by [General Decision/the Management Committee].

(4) Except as expressly provided in this deed, no Partner will be entitled to any interest on any undrawn balance of his share of the Profits.

(5) Losses will be debited to the current accounts of the Partners rateably in accordance with their Profit Shares. If the deduction of a loss from a Partner's current account results in a negative balance on that current account, that Partner will contribute to the Partnership on request by the [Management Committee] an amount equal to that negative balance.

8.   Accounts

(1) The Management Committee will ensure that proper books of accounts and records will be kept by the Partnership of all matters, transactions and things of any kind that are usually entered in such accounts by those engaged in a business similar to the Partnership Business (including details of acquisitions and disposals of Partnership assets).

(2) The Partnership will at all times comply with the requirements of [name of any professional or regulatory body regulating the Partnership] from time to time in force relating to the keeping of records and books of accounts.

(3) The Management Committee will ensure that the books and records kept under this clause, together with any supporting documentation relating to the Partnership Business (including all those records specified by law) will be kept for at least [six] years after the end of the relevant Accounting Period or for any longer period required by law. The books shall be kept at the Partnership Premises.

(4) Each Partner, his agents and the Partnership Accountants will have access to the books at all times, and may take copies or extracts as they think fit but will be required to treat all those copies and extracts as confidential to the Partners, their advisers and the Partnership Accountants.

(5) Subject to sub-clauses 23(1) and 23(2) at the end of each Accounting Period, Accounts will be produced for the Partnership, comprising a profit and loss account, balance sheet and any other information which the Partnership is required by law or professional regulation to produce from time to time. The Accounts will be prepared upon such basis and within such period, in accordance with generally accepted accounting principles and practices, as may be recommended by the Partnership Accountants or otherwise determined by General/Special Decision.

(6) No account will be taken in the Accounts of the value of Goodwill.

(7) As soon as the Accounts have been prepared, and not later than six months after the relevant Account Date, those Accounts will be submitted:

   (*a*) to each Partner; and

   (*b*) to any Former Partner in respect of whom a retention has been made under clause 9.

(8) The Accounts will be considered by the Partners at a general meeting and will only be binding on all the Partners once approved by [General/ Special] Decision. Once approved, the Partners hereby authorise any two members of the Management Committee to sign the Accounts on behalf of the Partnership.

(9) If the Accounts are not approved by [General/Special] Decision, any Partner may refer any point of dispute for resolution in accordance with clause 26.

(10) The books of accounts and records maintained for the purposes of complying with this clause will be subject to audit by the Partnership Accountants in respect of each Accounting Period.

9. Provision for Tax Liabilities

(1) Except as otherwise determined by the Management Committee the Partnership will retain[1] such proportion of each Partner's share of the Profits in any Accounting Period as the Management Committee recommend is appropriate to meet that Partner's individual tax liability (if any) in respect of those Profits.

(2) Sums retained in respect of a Partner under sub-clause (1) will (even if he has since become a Former Partner) be paid on his behalf to the relevant tax authority when and to the extent necessary to meet the liability for which retention has been made.

(3) Sums retained in respect of each Partner or Former Partner under sub-clause (1) will be paid or released to him only when and to the extent considered by the Management Committee to be in excess of the necessary retention. In the event of a dispute between a Partner or Former Partner and the Management Committee as to the amount of the retention that is necessary, the decision of the Partnership Accountants (acting as experts and not as arbitrators) will be final and binding in the absence of manifest error.

(4) The Management Committee will make its recommendations under sub-clauses (1) and (3):

(*a*) on a basis which is consistent between the Partners and Former Partners;

(*b*) assuming that all personal allowances and reliefs available to a Partner or Former Partner will be set against his income and gains from the Partnership before being set against other income and gains.

10. Bank Accounts

(1) The Management Committee will ensure that all bank accounts required for the purposes of or in connection with the Partnership Business will be maintained with the Partnership Bank and will include the Partnership Name. This requirement does not apply to an account in the name of a client of the Partnership.

(2) All Partnership receipts will promptly be paid into and deposited with the Partnership Bank to the credit of the Partnership.

(3) All cheques drawn on the bank accounts of the Partnership will be drawn in the name of the Partnership.

---

[1]Consider whether amounts retained should be retained as working capital of the partnership or kept in a separate fund.

(4) All cheques, bills of exchange and other bank transfers or other instruments pledging the credit or affecting the property of the Partnership will be signed on behalf of the Partnership by any [two] Partners unless otherwise decided by [General/Special] Decision.

(5) All monies and all securities received on behalf or for the account of a client or third party will (except as required for the matter in hand on behalf of that client or third party):

(*a*) promptly be paid or delivered to that client or third party; or

(*b*) be paid into or deposited with the Partnership Bank in a client account or statutory client account (as the case may be) which is separate and distinct from any account relating to the property of the Partnership; or

(*c*) otherwise be dealt with in a manner authorised by any law or professional regulations.

11. Insurance

(1) The Management Committee will ensure that the Partnership is insured against the following:

(*a*) employers' liability and any other liability against which it is required to be insured by any law or professional regulations;

(*b*) liability for professional negligence of the Partnership;

(*c*) liability of the Partnership to third parties for death, injury or illness, and for damage to third party property;

(*d*) loss or damage to Partnership assets, including Partnership Premises;

(*e*) liability of the Partnership as occupiers of the Partnership Premises; and

(*f*) such other risks as the Management Committee may determine.

(2) The Management Committee may arrange any insurance with any insurer, on the terms and subject to the conditions, exclusions, limits and deductibles (or any other self insurance or captive insurance arrangements), as it thinks fit.

(3) In respect of all insurances effected for the benefit of the Partnership the following will be treated as expenses of the Partnership:

(*a*) all premiums payable in respect of those insurances and all broker and adviser fees;

(*b*) all sums expended pursuant to any deductible or excess borne by the Partnership; and

(*c*) all sums expended for the account of the Partnership by reason only of the insufficiency of the limit of insurance or the failure (for any reason) of the insurers to meet any valid policy claim.

(4) The protection provided by any professional negligence or other liability insurance purchased for the benefit of the Partnership will extend to Former Partners to the extent of their individual liabilities as such. The benefit of that insurance and of any claim or recovery made under it, will

be held in trust for the Partners and Former Partners rateably with their respective shares of liability for the matter that was the subject of the insurance claim under this deed.

12. Duties

(1) Each Partner will at all times:

(*a*) act diligently in the conduct of the Partnership Business;

(*b*) act with the utmost good faith in all transactions relating to the other Partners and the Partnership;

(*c*) disclose to the Management Committee on request full details of all business transactions by him or at his direction for the account of the Partnership;

(*d*) provide the Management Committee with the information concerning the Partnership Business in his knowledge or possession that the Management Committee requests;

(*e*) comply with any law or professional regulations to which the Partnership or the Partner is or may become subject in that capacity and use reasonable endeavours to comply with any other law or contractual or other legal obligations of which he is aware;

(*f*) use the Partnership Name in all business transactions of the Partnership;

(*g*) except as otherwise determined by the Management Committee, account to the Partnership for any money or thing representing money including all gifts and legacies received from a third party in the course of the Partnership Business.

(2) Unless a [General Decision/the Management Committee] determines otherwise in any particular instance:

(*a*) subject to clauses 22 (Gardening Leave) and 28 (Holidays and Maternity Leave) each Partner will devote his whole time and attention to the Partnership Business during normal business hours and at any other time when it is necessary to do so to enable him to perform his duties to the Partnership or any of its clients;

(*b*) subject to clause 13 (Appointments and Approved Liabilities) a Partner will not become a sole trader or a partner in any business other than the Partnership Business or be a director of any company other than a company owned by the Partnership or be or become a member of Lloyd's or hold any shares in any company with unlimited liability;

(*c*) a Partner will not do or omit to do any act or thing the doing or omission of which will bring or tend to bring the Partnership into disrepute;

(*d*) a Partner will not, otherwise than as required by law, assign, declare any trust of, transfer or create a security interest over any legal or beneficial interest in his share in the Partnership or any part of the Profits of the Partnership;

(*e*) a Partner will not lend any money or other property of the Partnership or, in the context of the Partnership Business, give credit to or act for or have any dealing with any person, company or firm with whom the Management Committee has previously requested him not to deal; and

(*f*) except within his authority as Partner, insofar as his advisers and any court, expert or arbitrator need to be informed in order to resolve any dispute under this deed or as required by law, a Partner or Former Partner will not use to the detriment or prejudice of the Partnership (or divulge to any person other than another Partner in any way which could reasonably be foreseen to risk any detriment to the Partnership or any of its clients) any confidential information concerning the business, investment or affairs of the Partnership or any of its clients. In this paragraph '**confidential information**' includes (without limitation) any information relating to this deed, the Accounts, the books of the Partnership, the financial position of the Partnership, any decision of the Partnership (including a decision of the Management Committee) or any matter affecting the rights and obligations of the Partners or Former Partners or the management of the Partnership. However, a Former Partner may disclose the terms of the restrictions imposed on Former Partners under this clause and clause 24 (Covenants).

13. Appointments and Approved Liabilities

(1) (*a*) Partners must not accept or hold any charitable or non-charitable trusteeships, offices or appointments including (without limitation) appointment as a director of a company, an executor, an administrator or trustee of any will, estate or settlement ('**Appointments**') except in accordance with this clause.

(*b*) Unless otherwise agreed by the Management Committee, every Appointment will be deemed to be held for the account of the Partnership. Those Appointments that the Management Committee agree will not be held for the account of the Partnership are referred to in this clause as '**Non-Approved Appointments**'.

(*c*) A register (the '**Register**') of all Appointments will be maintained by the Management Committee specifying whether or not an Appointment is a Non-Approved Appointment or an Appointment held on behalf of the Partnership (an '**Approved Appointment**') and this Register will be open to inspection by all Partners.

(2) (*a*) If any Partner incurs a liability (otherwise than by reason of his own fraud or dishonesty) in connection with or as a result of an Approved Appointment (an '**Approved Liability**'):

(i) that Approved Liability and any costs or expenses incurred by that Partner in or about contesting, compromising, admitting or compounding it will be a liability of the Partnership;

(ii) that Partner will be entitled to the same rights of indemnity and contribution from the other Partners as if that Approved Liability had been incurred by him in the ordinary and proper course of the Partnership Business; and

(iii) that Partner must take such action at the expense of the Partnership as any insurer which is on risk in respect of the Approved Liability or the Management Committee may from time to time require to recoup all or any sums within the scope of this clause from any assets (other than his own) or from any person (other than himself) who may be liable in respect thereof and he must account to the Partnership for all sums so recouped.

(*b*) If any Partner incurs a liability in connection with an Appointment which is not an Approved Liability, the Partnership will have no responsibility for that liability and he will not be entitled to any rights of indemnity and contribution from the other Partners.

(3) All Approved Appointments other than those which are required to be held in the name of an individual must be held in the name of the Partnership and not in the name of any Partner.

(4) Unless otherwise agreed by the Management Committee, all fees, profits, remuneration, emoluments or other benefits received by a Partner (including, without limitation, all fees and payments received by a Partner arising from his acting as a company director or dividends or other payments received by virtue of a Partner holding shares in any company on trust for the Partnership) in respect of:

(*a*) any Approved Appointment, will be received by him for the account of the Partnership and must be paid by him to the Partnership within seven days of receipt;

(*b*) any Non-Approved Appointment, will not be received by him for the account of the Partnership but will be held for his own personal account.

14. Meetings and Procedures for Decision-Making

(1) A meeting of the Partners may be convened at any time by the Managing Partner, the Management Committee or on the written request of any Partner to the Management Committee.

(2) (*a*) Subject to paragraph (*b*), the Management Committee will in all cases determine the time, date and place of each meeting of the Partners and the nature of the business to be transacted.

(*b*) Any Partner may submit a matter for discussion at a meeting of the Partners to the Managing Partner before commencement of that meeting.

(*c*) Any meeting of the Partners shall be chaired by the Senior Partner.

(3) Subject to sub-clause (4), each Partner will have one vote at any meeting of the Partners.

(4) (*a*) The Senior Partner will have a casting vote where a deadlock exists and may cast his second vote as he thinks fit.

(*b*) No Partner who has been required to retire from the Partnership by a Special Decision under sub-clause 20(1), no Partner who has served a notice to retire as a Partner under clause 21 and no Partner who is absent from the Partnership under clause 22 (unless otherwise agreed by the Management Committee), will be eligible to vote for any purpose but no decision may adversely affect his interests without his written consent unless it applies fairly to all Partners.

(c) A Partner subject to a Special Decision under sub-clause 19(1) or sub-clause 22(2)(a) will not be entitled to vote on that matter.

(5) (a) Any Partner may be represented at any meeting by appointing another Partner as a proxy and that proxy will vote on the directions of the Partner in favour of or against any decision taken at the meeting. Written proof of appointment must be presented by that proxy to the chair of the meeting prior to commencement of the meeting.

(b) A vote cast by a proxy which complies with the terms of his appointment will count as the vote of the Partner making the appointment, and that Partner will be deemed for all the purposes of this deed to have been present at the meeting and to have voted on the matter.

(6) The quorum for any meeting of the Partners will be fifty per cent of all the Partners.

(7) A Unanimous Decision, a Special Decision and a General Decision will bind all Partners.

(8) (a) For a General Decision to be validly taken [seven] clear days' notice in writing must be given to all Partners. A lesser period of notice may be agreed in writing by [ninety per cent] in number of all Partners.

(b) General Decisions must be made at a meeting of the Partners on a show of hands by a simple majority of those Partners present and voting at the meeting (whether in person or by proxy).

(9) A Special Decision will be taken in the same way as a General Decision except that at least [seventy-five per cent] by number of all the Partners (whether present and voting or not) must be present at the meeting (whether in person or by proxy) and vote in favour of the resolution.

(10) A Unanimous Decision may be taken:

(a) at any meeting of the Partners on a show of hands provided all Partners vote in favour of the decision (whether in person or by proxy); or

(b) with the written approval of all the Partners in which case no meeting of the Partners is required for the making of that decision.

(11) The accidental omission to give notice of a meeting to, or the non-receipt of notice of a meeting by, any [two] or less Partners entitled to receive notice will not invalidate the proceedings of a meeting or a decision made by the Partnership.

15. Unanimous and Special Decisions

(1) In addition to any other matters referred to in this deed, the following matters will be determined by [Unanimous/Special] Decision:

(a) the transfer or vesting of any part of the Partnership Business to or into a body corporate, limited liability partnership or any analogous entity or the merger of the Partnership Business with that of any other person;

(*b*) any acquisition by the Partnership of any business or part of a business or company or part of a company for valuable consideration or any disposal by the Partnership of any business or part of a business or company or part of a company for valuable consideration;

(*c*) any acquisition or disposal of freehold or leasehold property.

(2) Except where otherwise specifically provided in this deed any matter connected with the conduct and management of the Partnership Business will be decided by the Management Committee which will exercise its powers and discretions in the best interests of the Partnership as a whole.

16. Managing Partner and Management Committee

(1) The Management Committee will be comprised of the Managing Partner and [   ] other Partners. With effect on and from the Effective Date the Management Committee will be comprised of the Partners specified in Part I of Schedule 5.

(2) Any decision of the Management Committee made in accordance with this deed binds the Partners and the Partnership.

(3) The quorum necessary at meetings for the transaction of business by the Management Committee is [   ] members present in person or by telephone.

(4) (*a*) A member of the Management Committee will cease to be a member on ceasing to be a Partner and on the [   ] anniversary of his most recent appointment but in the latter case shall be eligible for re-appointment. The Partners may from time to time by [Special/ General] Decision remove any member of the Management Committee and may appoint another Partner to replace that member so removed or to replace any member of the Management Committee who has ceased to be a member of the Management Committee for any other reason or appoint an additional member of the Management Committee. Nominations for all such appointments must be given to the continuing members of the Management Committee at least 14 days prior to a general meeting of the Partners.

(*b*) A member of the Management Committee may voluntarily stand down from the Management Committee on giving at least 2 months' notice to the continuing members and the Partners must replace that member in accordance with paragraph (*a*) above.

(5) Subject to sub-clause (6), the Management Committee will meet together for the despatch of business, adjourn and otherwise regulate its meetings as it thinks fit.

(6) Matters arising at any meeting of the Management Committee will be determined by a simple majority of votes of the members of the Management Committee who are present and voting thereon on the basis of one vote per member. For the avoidance of doubt, the Managing Partner will not have a casting vote for the purposes of this sub-clause.

(7) (*a*) With effect from and including the Effective Date, the offices of

Managing Partner and Senior Partner will be filled by the Partner specified in Parts II and III of Schedule 5 respectively. The provisions of sub-clause (4) will apply mutatis mutandis to the removal, retirement and appointment of the Managing Partner.

(b) The Managing Partner or the Senior Partner may delegate to any Partner anything required to be done by him and the actions of the delegate will bind the Partners and the Partnership as if they were carried out by the Managing Partner or the Senior Partner himself. In the absence of the Senior Partner, or if he is unavailable, and notwithstanding any delegation of his powers under this sub-clause, any notice required to be given to him must be given to any one or more of the other members of the Management Committee.

17. Admission of New Partners

(1) A New Partner may at any time be admitted by Special Decision which decision will specify his date of admittance to the Partnership (his **'Admission Date'**).

(2) The admission of a New Partner is conditional upon the execution by him of an Accession Agreement approved by the Partners (excluding the New Partner) by Special Decision, on or before his Admission Date or, if later, within [   ] months of the date of the decision referred to in sub-clause (1). This Agreement will then be construed as though he had been a Partner with effect from the Admission Date.

(3) The Accession Agreement will state the New Partner's initial capital contribution and his Profit Share. The Profit Shares of the existing Partners shall be reduced in proportion to their Profit Shares by the percentage necessary to accommodate the New Partner's Profit Shares.

18. Salaried Partners

(1) Any person may be employed as a Salaried Partner in the Partnership. The admission and the terms of admission of any Salaried Partner who is held out to be a Partner must be authorised by a [Special/General] Decision.

(2) The rights and obligations of any Salaried Partner will be governed by the agreement for employment made between him and the Partnership.

19. Expulsion

(1) A Partner will immediately cease to be a Partner upon being served with a notice in writing of a Special Decision expelling him following any of the events listed below:

(a) if he wilfully or persistently acts in a manner contrary to his material obligations under this deed or is guilty of any grave professional misconduct; or

(b) if he is convicted (unless quashed on appeal) of any criminal offence involving dishonesty; or

(c) if he commits any act of bankruptcy or is adjudicated bankrupt or enters into any composition, scheme or arrangement with his creditors or the equivalent in any relevant jurisdiction; or (*d*) if he creates or purports to create a security interest over any legal or beneficial interest in his share in the Partnership including (without limitation) his account with the Partnership or any part of the Profits of the Partnership for his separate debt; or

(*e*) if he has become incapacitated by mental or physical illness, ill-health, accident or otherwise from performing his duties, obligations or responsibilities hereunder for a continuous period of [   ] months.

(2) A Partner will immediately cease to be a Partner if the Partnership would otherwise be dissolved by operation of law because he has lost or fails to hold a relevant qualification or to satisfy a relevant professional regulation.

20. Compulsory Retirement and Retirement due to Age and Death

(1) A Partner will retire from the Partnership and cease to be a Partner and become a Former Partner on the earlier of his death and the expiration of six months from the date of a Special Decision requiring him to retire as a Partner.

(2) Unless otherwise determined by Special Decision a Partner will automatically retire from the Partnership, cease to be a Partner and become a Former Partner on the date on which he attains the age of sixty years.

21. Voluntary Retirement

Any Partner may retire from the Partnership by giving not less than [six] months' previous notice in writing to the Management Committee expiring on an Accounts Date (but any General Decision to amend the Accounts Date that follows such notice will not affect the date of expiry of the notice) except that the Management Committee may agree a shorter period of notice in any individual case whether or not expiring on an Accounts Date.

22. Gardening Leave and Suspension

(1) Where a Partner has been required to retire from the Partnership by a Special Decision under sub-clause 20(1) and where a Partner has served notice to retire as a Partner under clause 21, the Management Committee may direct by notice to him in writing that during the whole or any part of the period of his notice to retire the retiring Partner:

(*a*) will not enter any of the Partnership Premises;

(*b*) will not contact or have any communication (or may only communicate in specified ways) with any client or employee of the Partnership for any business purpose;

(*c*) will do, or omit from doing, all such things in connection with the Partnership Business as the Management Committee may reasonably require including, for example, carrying out administrative duties or working on non-client matters; and

(*d*) will be subject to the provisions of clause 24 (Covenants) (without prejudice to the application of that clause to him when he ceases to be a Partner).

(2) (*a*) Where there are reasonable grounds for believing that any of the events referred to in clause 19 may apply to a Partner, the Partners may by [Special/General] Decision decide that such Partner will forthwith take no further part in the Partnership Business for a specified period (not exceeding six months) or until further notice (not exceeding six months) on such terms as that decision shall determine.

(*b*) Without prejudice to the generality of paragraph (*a*), the decision may direct that the provisions of sub-clause (1) will apply to the suspended Partner.

(*c*) A Partner who is subject to this sub-clause will, at the expiration of six months from the date of the decision referred to in paragraph (*a*), be deemed to have retired from the Partnership unless that decision has ceased or been revoked at, or before, the expiration of that period.

(*d*) The revocation of a decision made under this sub-clause will be by [Special/General] Decision.

(3) During any period when sub-clauses (1) or (2) apply, the Partner concerned will continue to be entitled to his share of the Profits and liable for his share of Losses and to drawings on account of those Profits after providing for any amount owed by the Partner to the Partnership.

23. Former Partners and their Entitlements

(1) As quickly as is reasonably practicable following a Former Partner's Retirement Date of a Partner which falls other than on the Accounts Date, the Partnership Accountants will prepare Accounts in accordance with the provisions set down in clause 8 as at the Retirement Date for the period from the preceding Accounts Date to the Retirement Date.

(2) The interim accounts prepared under sub-clause (1) will be prepared on the same basis as the Accounts.

(3) Within two months of the Accounts being approved under clause 8 (or otherwise finally determined in accordance with the terms of this deed) (in the case of a Partner who ceases to be a partner on the Accounts Date) or the interim accounts being approved by [Special/General] Decision (in all other cases) and after providing for any amount owed by the Former Partner to the Partnership, the undrawn credit balance, if any, on the Former Partner's current account will be paid to the Former Partner.

(4) The Partners will [if they make the election specified in sub-clause (5)] pay to the Former Partner a sum equal to the balance, if any, standing to the credit of the Former Partner's capital account less the debit balance, if any, on his current account. Such payment will be made as follows:

(*a*) one half plus interest thereon at the Partnership Interest Rate will be paid [twelve] months after the Former Partner's Retirement Date;

(*b*) one half plus interest thereon at the Partnership Interest Rate will be paid [eighteen] months after the Former Partner's Retirement Date

provided always that in the event of the dissolution of the Partnership (otherwise than for the purposes of amalgamation or reconstruction) any outstanding balance due to a Former Partner will immediately become due and payable.

(5) The share of the Former Partner in the capital and assets of the Partnership will [if the Partners so elect by written notice to the Former Partner within six months of his Retirement Date and with effect from his Retirement Date] accrue to the Partners rateably in accordance with their Profit Shares.

[(6) If the Partners make no election under sub-clause (5) then the assets of the Partnership will be realised as soon as may be practicable and in any event within twelve months of the Retirement Date. Any surplus or loss on such realisation will be credited or debited to the capital accounts of the Partners and the Former Partner and the Former Partner will be entitled to be paid the balance standing to the credit of his capital account within eighteen months of his Retirement Date together with interest from the Retirement Date at the Partnership Interest Rate.][2]

(7) (*a*) Subject to paragraph (*b*) the Partners will indemnify each Former Partner against all liabilities of the Partnership including (without limitation) liabilities in respect of leases under which the Partnership Premises are held. If and to the extent that the Former Partner is entitled to any right of indemnity, reimbursement or contribution in respect of those liabilities from any person other than the Partnership or any Partner (whether under a policy of insurance or otherwise), he will disclose details of any such rights of reimbursement, indemnity or contribution, and any claim made under it, to the Partnership, which will be entitled to exercise those rights by way of subrogation.

(*b*) Notwithstanding paragraph (*a*) and unless otherwise agreed by [Special/General] Decision, each Former Partner will remain liable for that share of any liability arising by reason of his own professional negligence or breach of duty corresponding to the proportion which his Profit Share allocated to him at the time when the liability was incurred bears to the aggregate Profit Shares of all the Partners in the Partnership at that time.

(*c*) For the purposes of paragraph (*a*), any liability will be reduced to the extent that insurance cover would have been in effect in respect of it if a claim had been made in respect of it on the Former Partner's Retirement Date.

(8) The Profit Share to which a Former Partner was entitled immediately prior to his Retirement Date shall accrue rateably to the Profit Shares of the other Partners.

(9) A Former Partner will at all times comply with the obligations imposed on him as a Former Partner by this deed, including (without limitation) the obligations imposed by clauses 12 (Duties) and 24 (Covenants).

(10) A Former Partner is entitled to the payments described in this clause in full satisfaction of his interest in the profits of the Partnership, and in the Goodwill, the Partnership Name, Partnership Premises, the Partnership's furniture and equipment and other assets of the Partnership, and has no further rights in respect of those profits or assets.

---

[2]Words in square brackets to be deleted if automatic accruer is desired.

24. Covenants

(1) In this clause:

  (*a*) '**in any capacity**' means on that Partner's or Former Partner's own account, or jointly, in conjunction with, or on behalf of any other person, firm or company; and

  (*b*) '**Partnership Client**' means any individual, partnership, body corporate or unincorporated association who or which has been a client of the Partnership and for whom the relevant Partner had carried out work at any time in the period of [two] years before his Retirement Date except that each distinct business unit of a client will be treated for this purpose as a separate Partnership Client.

(2) A Partner or Former Partner will not, without the prior agreement of the Management Committee do any of the following:

  (*a*) for a period of [one] year from his Retirement Date act for, solicit or accept instructions from or provide legal services to, any Partnership Client in a way which is likely to compete with the business carried on by him as a Partner or by the Partnership immediately before his Retirement Date;

  (*b*) for a period of [one] year from the Retirement Date employ, solicit or endeavour to entice away, offer partnership or employment to or enter into partnership or any other commercial arrangement with any person who, at the Retirement Date was a Partner in, an employee of or consultant of the Partnership;

  (*c*) at any time after his Retirement Date and in any capacity:

    (i) represent himself as a Partner in, employee of or consultant to the Partnership or that he is in any way connected with, or has the authority to bind the Partnership or any Partner; or

    (ii) use the Partnership Name or any name which may in any way be confused with the Partnership Name.

(3) Each of sub-clauses (2)(*a*) to (*c*) inclusive constitutes a separate and independent restriction on each Former Partner so that, if one or more are held to be invalid or unenforceable for any reason whatsoever then the remaining covenants will be valid and enforceable to the extent that they are not held to be invalid or unenforceable.

(4) Upon any Partner becoming a Former Partner, all deeds, drafts, letters and other papers or records belonging to the Partnership or any Partnership Client or relating to any Partnership Client or prospective client of the Partnership will remain in the possession of, or be delivered by the Former Partner to the Partnership and, at the request of the Management Committee, the Former Partner will certify in writing to the committee whether or not he is in breach of this sub-clause.

(5) When a Partner becomes a Former Partner, due notice that he has ceased to be a Partner will be given in the London Gazette and (so far as is reasonably practicable) by a circular letter in such form and sent to such persons, companies and firms as the Management Committee will in their absolute discretion determine. If a Former Partner (who is still alive) shall refuse to sign the notice for insertion in the London Gazette the Managing

Partner may sign the name of the Former Partner on his behalf and each Partner irrevocably grants to the Managing Partner from time to time his power of attorney for the sole purpose of signing his name on such a notice and by way of security of his obligations under this sub-clause. Each Partner's power of attorney shall expire automatically 30 days after his Retirement Date.

25. Dissolution

(1) The Partnership may be dissolved at any time by a Special Decision or, if the Partnership then comprises only two Partners, by either Partner.

(2) Upon the dissolution of the Partnership for any reason all the assets of the Partnership (including the right to use the Partnership Name) will be realised and the proceeds remaining after the discharge of all liabilities to third parties (including any amounts outstanding to or in respect of any Former Partner) will be applied firstly in payment of the amount standing to the credit of the capital and current accounts of each of the Partners at the date of dissolution. Any balance will be distributed to the Partners in proportion to their respective Profit Shares at the date of dissolution.

(3) Sub-clause (2) will have no application if the Partnership is dissolved on or after the assignment of the whole or substantially the whole of the Partnership Business to a body corporate, a limited liability partnership or any analogous entity in consideration for the issue to the Partners, rateably in accordance with their Profit Shares, of shares, membership rights or analogous rights in that entity and the Partners will accept those shares, membership or other rights in full satisfaction of their interest in the Partnership and the Partnership's Business.

26. Arbitration and Dispute Resolution

(1) Where any question, claim, dispute or difference (dispute) arises between any of the Partners or Former Partners concerning or in any way arising out of this deed or the performance of the terms of this deed, those Partners or Former Partners will make a genuine effort to resolve the dispute without resorting to litigation, using the procedures set out in this clause.

(2) Any dispute in connection with this deed will be resolved as follows:

   (*a*) in accordance with sub-clause (3) below if the dispute relates to an accounting matter; or

   (*b*) in accordance with sub-clauses (4), (5) and (6) below, in the case of all other disputes.

(3) Disputes relating to an accounting matter will be referred, at the written request of any party to the dispute, for determination by an independent accountant (the '**Independent Accountant**') who is a member of the Institute of Chartered Accountants in England and Wales (the 'Institute') appointed by agreement between the parties to the dispute within seven days of delivery of the written request or (in default of agreement) appointed by the President for the time being of the Institute on the application of any party to the dispute. The Management Committee will determine whether a dispute concerns an accounting matter or not and its decision will be final in the absence of a manifest error. The determination

of the Independent Accountant is final and binding on all Partners and Former Partners. In determining the dispute, the Independent Accountant will act as an expert and not as an arbitrator. All costs incurred by the Independent Accountant will be borne by the parties to the dispute as determined by the Independent Accountant.

(4) Without prejudice to any right to seek interim relief all other disputes will be referred, at the written request of any party to the dispute, to mediation by a mediator appointed by agreement between the parties to the dispute within seven days of the written request or (in default of agreement) appointed by the Chief Executive for the time being of the Centre for Dispute Resolution ('**CEDR**'). The mediation will be conducted in London in accordance with the CEDR Model Mediation Procedure (together with any amendments and updates to that procedure that are adopted by the Management Committee before the appointment of a mediator in relation to a particular dispute), which is deemed to be incorporated in this deed. If an agreement is reached on the resolution of the dispute during the mediation, that agreement will be reduced to writing and, once signed by the parties to the dispute, will be binding on all the Partners. Unless concluded with a written legally binding agreement, the mediation will be conducted in confidence and without prejudice to the rights of any Partner or Former Partner in any further proceedings.

(5) Without prejudice to any right to seek interim relief in the event that the dispute has not been settled within sixty days after the appointment of the mediator, or if no request is made to refer that dispute to mediation, the dispute will be referred (by any Partner or Former Partner involved in the dispute) to arbitration in London to be conducted in the English language by a sole arbitrator appointed in accordance with the rules of the London Court of International Arbitration (the Rules) which Rules are deemed to be incorporated by reference into this clause.

(6) The Partners agree that any party to an arbitration under this deed may appeal against any award of an arbitrator on points of law.

27. Alterations

(1) Any of the provisions of this deed may be altered at any time by [Unanimous] Decision.

(2) Notwithstanding sub-clause (1), any of the provisions of this deed may be altered at any time by the Management Committee if the alteration is of a minor or technical nature which either is not materially prejudicial to the interests of any of the Partners or is to correct a manifest error. Any such alteration will be made on the terms and subject to the conditions that the Management Committee determines, will be notified to Partners as soon as possible and will be binding on the Partners when notified to them.

(3) No alteration of this deed will invalidate any prior act which would have been valid if that alteration had not been made.

28. Holidays and Maternity Leave

(1) In each calendar year, in addition to public and religious holidays, each Partner shall be entitled to take such annual holidays not exceeding [five] weeks in the aggregate [of which not more than [three] weeks may be

taken consecutively] or as shall be determined by [General/Special] Decision from time to time and may (subject to such determination) carry forward into the next calendar year any unused part of his entitlement.

(2) A female Partner may, in the event of her pregnancy and upon giving not less than [three months'] prior written notice of her intention to do so to the other Partners, take a period of maternity leave of not more than [four months'] duration and commencing not more than [four weeks] prior to the expected date of confinement.

29. General

(1) None of the rights or obligations under this deed may be assigned or transferred without a Unanimous Decision.

(2) Where an obligation is expressed to be undertaken by two or more parties they shall, unless otherwise expressly stated, be jointly and severally responsible in respect of it.

(3) This deed may be executed in any number of counterparts, all of which taken together shall constitute one and the same deed and any party may enter into this deed by executing a counterpart as a deed.

(4) This deed and its schedules and the documents referred to in it contain the whole agreement between the parties and supersede all previous agreements between the parties.

(5) Each of the parties acknowledges that in agreeing to enter into this deed he has not relied on any representation, warranty or other assurance except those set out in this deed.

(6) This deed is governed by and shall be construed in accordance with English law.

(7) Any notice required or permitted to be given under this deed shall be in writing and if posted by prepaid recorded delivery post to the last known address of the person to be served shall be deemed to have been duly served forty-eight hours after despatch.

(8) The parties agree that, subject to clause 26, the courts of England have exclusive jurisdiction in connection with this deed.

IN WITNESS of which each of the parties has executed this document as a deed the day and year first above written.

SCHEDULE 1

Partners

Name   **Address**   **Profit Shares**

SCHEDULE 2

Partnership Premises

Address

SCHEDULE 3

Name   **Initial Capital Contributions**

SCHEDULE 4

Part I

Initial Management Committee

Part II

Initial Managing Partner

Part III

Initial Senior Partner

SIGNED as a deed by   }

in the presence of:

Witness's
signature: . . . .

Name: . . . .

Address: . . . .

. . . .

. . . .

SIGNED as a deed by   }

in the presence of:

Witness's
signature: . . . .

Name: . . . .

Address: . . . .

. . . .

. . . .

SIGNED as a deed by   }

in the presence of:

Witness's
signature: . . . .

Name: . . . .

Address: . . . .

. . . .

. . . .

Appendix 5

Model Limited Liability Partnership Deed

[NOTE: This model deed has been prepared by Allen & Overy and is for illustration only. Every LLP's needs are unique and it is important to obtain legal and accounting advice when preparing an LLP deed.]

THIS DEED is made on [   ], 20 [   ] BETWEEN

(i) the persons whose names and addresses are set out in Schedule 1 (the **'Original Members'**); and

(ii) [   ] LLP, a limited liability partnership incorporated in England and Wales under the Limited Liability Partnerships Act 2000 with registered number [   ] and whose registered office is at [   ] (the **'LLP'**).

WHEREAS:

(A) The Original Members have incorporated the LLP and have agreed to carry on the business of [   ] through the LLP and wish to enter into this deed for the purpose of setting out the terms and conditions under which they will carry on business together with effect from and including the Effective Date (as defined below).

(B) It is the intention of the parties that this document be executed as a deed.

NOW THIS DEED WITNESSES AND IT IS AGREED as follows:

1. Interpretation

(1) In this deed:

'Accession Agreement' means a deed by which a New Member accedes to the LLP and to this deed and which states his initial Profit Share and capital contribution;

'Accounts' means the accounts of the LLP prepared and approved in accordance with clause 8;

'Accounts Date' means [   ] in each year or such other date as may be decided by General Decision;

478

'**Accounting Period**' means the period of one calendar year ending on the Accounts Date, unless otherwise decided by General Decision;

'**Admission Date**' has the meaning given to it in sub-clause 17(1);

'**Appointment**' has the meaning given to it in sub-clause 13(1);

'**Approved Appointment**' has the meaning given to it in sub-clause 13(1);

'**Approved Liability**' has the meaning given to it in sub-clause 13(2);

'**Auditors' Report**' means the report to the Members prepared by the LLP Auditors in accordance with clause 8;

'**Chairman**' means the person who holds office as such from time to time under clause 16;

'**Chief Executive**' means the member who holds office as Chief Executive from time to time under clause 16;

'**Companies Act**' means the Companies Act 1985 as it applies to limited liability partnerships, as replaced and amended from time to time and any regulations published pursuant thereto;

'**Designated Members**' means those Members appointed as such under clause 4 and registered from time to time at Companies House under sections 8 and 9 of the LLP Act;

'**Effective Date**' means [   ];

'**Former Member**' means a person who ceases to be a Member after the Effective Date for any reason (other than the winding up of the LLP) and includes the personal representatives of a Former Member;

'**General Decision**' means a decision of the Members taken as a General Decision under clause 14;

'**Goodwill**' means the goodwill of the LLP;

'**Insolvency Act**' means the Insolvency Act 1986 as it applies to limited liability partnerships as amended or replaced from time to time and any regulations published pursuant to that Act;

'**LLP Act**' means the Limited Liability Partnerships Act 2000 as replaced or amended from time to time and any regulations published pursuant to that Act;

'**LLP Auditors**' means [   ] or such other firm of chartered accountants as may be decided by General Decision;

'**LLP Bank**' means [   ] Bank Plc or such other additional or substitute bank as may be appointed as banker to the LLP by [General Decision/the Management Committee];

'**LLP Business**' means the business and practice of [   ] and any other business or practice which the LLP may resolve to carry on by [General/Special] Decision;

'**LLP Interest Rate**' means the base lending rate of the LLP Bank plus [   ] per cent per annum or such other rate as may be determined by [the Management Committee/General Decision/Special Decision];

'**LLP Name**' means the name of [   ] or such other name as may from time to time be adopted by [General/Special] Decision and notified to the Registrar of Companies under the LLP Act;

'**LLP Premises**' means the offices of the LLP specified in Schedule 2 and such other offices as the Members from time to time by [Special/General] Decision decide will be used by the LLP Business;

'**Losses**' means the revenue and capital losses of the LLP as shown in the Accounts;

'**Management Committee**' means the Members for the time being of the committee constituted under clause 16;

'**New Member**' means any person admitted as a Member on or after the Effective Date under clause 17;

'**Non-Approved Appointment**' has the meaning given to it in sub-clause 13(1);

'**Members**' means:

(*a*) the Original Members; and

(*b*) every other person (other than a Salaried Member) who is admitted as a member in the LLP after the Effective Date
in each case only until he becomes a Former Member and '**Member**' means any one of them;

'**Profits**' means the revenue and capital profits of the LLP as shown in the Accounts;

'**Profit Share**' in relation to a Member means the Percentage set out against his name in Part 1 of Schedule 1 or such other percentage as shall be determined from time to time under the provisions of this deed.

'**Retirement Date**' means the date when a Member ceases to be a Member and becomes a Former Member by reason of death, expulsion, retirement or otherwise;

'**Salaried Member**' means any person admitted on or after the Effective Date as a salaried member under an employment contract made between him and the LLP under clause 18;

'**Special Decision**' means a decision of the LLP taken as a Special Decision under clause 15; and

'**Unanimous Decision**' means a decision of the LLP taken as a Unanimous Decision under clause 15.

(2) In interpreting this deed the following rules will be applied unless the context otherwise requires:

(*a*) words importing the singular include the plural and vice versa and words importing gender import all genders;

(*b*) references to any clause, sub-clause, schedule, paragraph or sub-paragraph are references to that clause in this deed, the sub-clause in the relevant clause in which it appears, a schedule to this deed or the paragraph or sub-paragraph in the relevant sub-clause, paragraph or schedule in which it appears and any schedules to this deed form part of this deed;

(c) references to statutory provisions, subordinate legislation or professional regulations will be construed as references to those provisions, legislation or regulations as they have been or may be amended or re-enacted or as their application is modified by other provisions from time to time;

(d) headings to clauses are for reference only and do not affect its interpretation;

(e) references to this deed or any other instrument include any variation, novation or replacement of any of them; and

(f) if a period of time is specified and is expressed to run from a given day or the day of an act or event, it is to be calculated exclusive of that day.

(3) In this deed, unless the context otherwise requires, any reference to:

a '**deed**' also includes a contract, deed, licence, undertaking, or other document and includes that deed as modified, novated or substituted from time to time;

a '**law**' includes common or customary law and any constitution, decree, judgement, legislation, order, ordinance, regulation, treaty or other legislative measure of England and Wales;

a '**person**' includes an individual and that person's executors and administrators;

'**professional regulations**' includes any directions, standards, rules or regulations of any professional bodies which govern the conduct of any Member or Salaried Member or the LLP;

'**rights**' includes authorities, discretions, remedies, powers and causes of action; and

'**tax**' includes any present or future tax, levy, duty, rate, charge, fee, deduction or withholding imposed, assessed or levied by any governmental agency in any part of the world (including national insurance contributions and any other social security or similar contributions wherever imposed) and any interest, penalties, fines, costs, charges and other liabilities arising from or payable in respect of that tax.

2. Commencement, Effect, Name and Duration

(1) With effect on and from the Effective Date, the LLP will carry on the LLP Business under the LLP Name in accordance with the provisions of this deed.

(2) The LLP will at all times comply with the provisions of the Business Names Act 1985 and of any regulation, instrument, rule or order from time to time and for the time being made under that Act.

(3) The LLP Name and any abbreviation or combination of it or any registered trade or service marks including or associated with those names, abbreviations and combinations (in this sub-clause the '**Names**') and any logos or registered designs derived from or associated with the Names are assets of the LLP and the use of the Names (or any interest in the Names) may only be licensed, sub-licensed, assigned, transferred or sold

to third parties or otherwise disposed of as the LLP may by [General/ Special Decision] decide.

3. **Place of Business**

The LLP Business shall be carried on in the LLP Premises.

4. **Designated Members**

(1) The Designated Members on the Effective Date shall be the Members named in Schedule 3.

(2) A Designated Member will cease to be a Designated Member if he leaves to be a Member or if he gives at least [two] months written notice of his resignation to the LLP management. The Committee may by written notice remove a Designated Member and appoint another Member to replace any person who has ceased to be a Designated Member.

(3) The Management Committee shall ensure that at all times there are at least two Designated Members.

(4) The Management Committee and Designated Members shall ensure that notice of the appointment in sub-clause (1) and of any change in the Designated Members is delivered to the registrar of limited liability partnerships within fourteen days, as required by Section 9 LLP Act.

(5) The Designated Members shall have such duties as are specified in the LLP Act or otherwise at law and in this deed.

(6) The LLP shall indemnify each Designated Member and former Designated Member in respect of any personal liability arising as a result of his position as Designated Member, other than as a result of his fraud, wilful default or gross negligence.

(7) Unless otherwise stated in this deed or decided by the Members by [General/Special] Decision, the Designated Members are authorised to execute or authorise the execution of any documents or deeds on behalf of the LLP which has been approved by the Members or by the person or persons duly authorised to do so under this deed and shall ensure that all such documents (including promissory notes, cheques or similar bills) contain such details as required by Sections 349 and 351 of the Companies Act in legible form.

5. **Capital**

(1) The capital of the LLP will be the sum of [   ].

(2) Each Member will on the Effective Date contribute to the capital of the LLP the amount set out opposite his name in Schedule 4.

(3) With effect on and from the Effective Date, the capital of the LLP will be contributed by and belong to the Equity Members in proportion to their Profit Shares. Accordingly, on any charge in Members' Profit Shares, any Member whose Profit Share has increased will contribute in cash the corresponding amount as additional capital to the LLP and any Member whose Profit Share has decreased will be entitled to withdraw the

corresponding amount from the capital of the LLP and his capital account will be adjusted accordingly.

(4) The Members may from time to time decide by [General/Special] Decision to increase or reduce the capital of the LLP. Any additional capital which may be required will be contributed by the Members to the LLP and any surplus capital no longer required will be repaid to the Members by the LLP, in proportion to their Profit Shares as at the date of that of that decision, and each member's capital account will be adjusted accordingly.

(5) Where, within [   ] months of the time when the Accounts have been approved by the LLP in respect of each Accounting Period under clause 8, a Member is shown in the Accounts to have contributed an amount to the capital of the LLP that is less than the amount which ought to have been contributed by him, the amount of such deficit will become a debt due by that Member to the LLP [and interest thereon will be payable to the LLP at the LLP Interest Rate].

(6) Subject to clause 23 (Former Members and their entitlements) where, within [   ] months of the time when the Accounts have been approved by the LLP in respect of each Accounting Period under clause 8, a Member is shown in the Accounts to have contributed an amount to the capital of the LLP that exceeds the amount which ought to have been contributed by him, the excess will become a debt due to him from the LLP and will be paid out to him as soon as is reasonably practicable with interest at the LLP Interest Rate.

(7) Subject to clause 23 (Former Members and their entitlements) and except as expressly provided in this deed or [with the deed of the Management Committee/by Special Decision]:

(a) no Member may draw out or receive back any part of his capital contribution to the LLP; and

(b) no Member is entitled to any interest on the contribution made by him to the capital of the LLP and no Member is entitled to any interest on any amount lent by him to the LLP.

6. **Profit Shares and Losses**

(1) The Profits of the LLP are to be shared by the Members in proportion to their Profit Shares for the time being.

(2) On the Effective Date the Profit Shares allocated to each Original Member are as specified in Schedule 4.

(3) The Profit Share amount allocated to any New Member will be as specified in his Accession Agreement.

(4) The Members may by [General/Special] Decision increase or reduce a Member's Profit Share from time to time, such increase or reduction to take effect on and from a date specified in that decision.

(5) Each Member will be reimbursed all reasonable and proper out of pocket expenses incurred by him in the performance of his duties under this deed or otherwise on behalf of the LLP. Each Member will provide to the LLP appropriate records of his expenses within such period after the time when

those expenses were incurred as the Management Committee may determine.

(6) Subject to sub-clause (7), losses of the LLP shall be borne by the LLP but the Members may decide by [General/Special] Decision to increase their contributions to the capital of the LLP to meet that deficiency and any such decision shall bind all of the Members.

(7) Any liability occasioned by the fraud or dishonesty of a Member must be made good by that Member alone.

7. Drawings

(1) Subject to clause 9 (Provision for tax liabilities), the Members may on account of their Profit Shares in the relevant Accounting Period make monthly drawings of such amounts as may from time to time be determined by [General Decision/the Management Committee].

(2) Within one month of the time when the Accounts have been approved by the LLP in respect of each Accounting Period under clause 8, any Member who is shown in the Accounts to have drawn any amount in excess of his share of Profits for that period, after provision for tax liabilities under clause 9, will refund that excess to the LLP as soon as is reasonably practicable [together with interest on that amount at the LLP Interest Rate for the period from the date when he is requested by the Management Committee to make the refund to the date of repayment].

(3) Unless otherwise determined by [Special Decision/the Management Committee], if a Member is shown in the Accounts to have drawn an amount less than his Profit Share, after provision for tax liabilities under clause 9, that undrawn balance will be credited within one month of the time when the Accounts have been approved by the LLP in respect of each Accounting Period under clause 8 to his current account with the LLP [together with interest on that amount at the LLP Interest Rate from such date as is determined by the Management Committee to the date of repayment]. Amounts from time to time credited to a Member's current account with the LLP will be debts owed by the LLP to that Member. When the Accounts for each Accounting Period have been approved under clause 8, each Member shall be paid the amount of the credit balance on his current account as shown in those Accounts at the times and in the instalments determined by [General Decision/the Management Committee].

(4) Except as expressly provided in this deed, no Member will be entitled to any interest on any undrawn balance of his share of the Profits.

8. Statutory Accounts

(1) The Accounts of the LLP shall be made up to the Accounts Date in each year.

(2) A profit and loss account shall be taken in every year on the Accounts Date and a balance sheet as at the same date shall be prepared.

(3) The Designated Members shall, in compliance with the LLP Act and the Companies Act appoint the LLP Auditors as the auditors for each

Accounting Period of the LLP and shall have the power to fix their remuneration.

(4) The Designated Members shall ensure that the Accounts are drawn up in the format and giving the information required in the LLP Act and the Companies Act, and the Accounts shall be audited by the LLP Auditors. Except as otherwise required by law, the Goodwill shall not be attributed any value in the Accounts. The LLP Auditors shall report to the Members and will state, as set out in their letter of appointment, whether or not the Accounts give a true and fair view of the profit or loss of the LLP for the Accounting Period.

(5) The Designated Members shall ensure that all the necessary and proper financial records of accounts shall be kept to enable the Accounts to be made up as above and retained for at least six years after the end of the relevant Accounting Period or such periods of time as required by law at the registered office (or such other place as the Members may determine) of the LLP on behalf of the Members in compliance with the LLP Act and such records shall be available for inspection by each Member and by the LLP Auditors for the time being at all times. Each Member shall be responsible for ensuring that full and proper entries of all transactions entered into by him on account of the LLP are made.

(6) As soon as the Accounts have been finalised, and no later than three months after the Accounting Date, the Accounts and Auditors' Report will be distributed to each Member and will be presented at the next duly convened Members' meeting for approval. Once the Accounts have been approved by [General/Special] Decision they shall be binding on the Members, save in the event that an error be discovered, in which event such error shall be rectified in the manner required by the Companies Act.

(7) The Designated Members shall then sign the Accounts on the balance sheet as required by the Companies Act.

(8) The Designated Members shall in respect of each Accounting Period deliver to the registrar of limited liability partnerships a copy of the approved Accounts and Auditors' Report as required by the Companies Act.

(9) Where additional reporting or accounting information is required by the LLP Auditors to allow them to complete the Auditors' Report or comply with any statutory requirement to which the LLP is subject (including the provision of any information requested by the inspectors of the Department of Trade and Industry), that information will be provided by the relevant Member or Members at the expense of the LLP as soon as practicable.

9. Provision for Tax Liabilities

(1) Except as otherwise determined by the Management Committee the LLP will retain such proportion of each Member's Profit Share in any Accounting Period as the Management Committee recommend is appropriate to meet that Member's individual tax liability (if any) in respect of those Profit Shares.

(2) Sums retained in respect of a Member under sub-clause (1) will be debts owed by the LLP to the Member and will (even if he has since become a Former Member) be paid on his behalf to the relevant tax authority when and to the extent necessary to meet the liability for which retention has been made.

(3) Sums retained in respect of each Member or Former Member under sub-clause (1) will be paid or released to him only when and to the extent considered by the Management Committee to be in excess of the necessary retention. In the event of a dispute between a Member or Former Member and the Management Committee as to the amount of the retention that is necessary, the decision of the LLP Auditors (acting as experts and not as arbitrators) will be final and binding in the absence of manifest error.

(4) The Management Committee will make its recommendations under sub-clauses (1) and (3):

(*a*) on a basis which is consistent between the Members and Former Members;

(*b*) assuming that all personal allowances and reliefs available to a Member or Former Member will be set against his income and gains from the LLP before being set against other income and gains.

10. Bank Accounts

(1) The Management Committee will ensure that all bank accounts required for the purposes of or in connection with the LLP Business will be maintained with the LLP Bank and will include the LLP Name. This requirement does not apply to an account in the name of a client of the LLP.

(2) All LLP receipts will promptly be paid into and deposited with the LLP Bank to the credit of the LLP.

(3) All cheques drawn on the bank accounts of the LLP will be drawn in the name of the LLP.

(4) All cheques, bills of exchange and other bank transfers or other instruments pledging the credit or affecting the property of the LLP will be signed on behalf of the LLP by any [two] [Designated] Members unless otherwise decided by [General/Special] Decision. The Signatories shall ensure that such documents and instruments shall contain such details as are required by Sections 349 and 351 Companies Act in legible form.

(5) All monies and all securities received on behalf or for the account of a client or third party will (except as required for the matter in hand on behalf of that client or third party):

(*a*) promptly be paid or delivered to that client or third party; or

(*b*) be paid into or deposited with the LLP Bank in a client account or statutory client account (as the case may be) which is separate and distinct from any account relating to the property of the LLP; or

(*c*) otherwise be dealt with in a manner authorised by any law or professional regulations.

11. Insurance

(1) The Management Committee will ensure that the LLP and (in the case of paragraph (*b*)) its Members, [Salaried Members] and employees are insured against the following:

  (*a*) employers' liability and any other liability against which it is required to be insured by any law or professional regulations;

  (*b*) liability for professional negligence of the LLP or any of its Members, [Salaried Members] and employee fees;

  (*c*) liability of the LLP to third parties for death, injury or illness, and for damage to third party property;

  (*d*) loss or damage to LLP assets, including LLP Premises;

  (*e*) liability of the LLP as occupiers of the LLP Premises; and

  (*f*) such other risks as the Management Committee may determine.

(2) The Management Committee may arrange any insurance with any insurer, on terms and subject to conditions, exclusions, limits and deductibles (or any other self insurance or captive insurance arrangements), as it thinks fit.

(3) In respect of all insurances effected for the benefit of the LLP and its Members [Salaried Members] and Employees the following will be treated as expenses of the LLP:

  (*a*) all premiums payable in respect of those insurances and all broker and adviser fees;

  (*b*) all sums expended pursuant to any deductible or excess borne by the LLP; and

  (*c*) all sums expended for the account of the LLP by reason only of the insufficiency of the limit of insurance or the failure (for any reason) of the insurers to meet any valid policy claim.

(4) The protection provided by any professional negligence or other liability insurance purchased for the benefit of the LLP and its Members will extend to Former Members to the extent of their individual liabilities as such. The benefit of that insurance and of any claim or recovery made under it, will be held in trust for the Members and Former Members rateably with their respective shares of liability for the matter that was the subject of the insurance claim under this deed.

12. Duties

(1) Each Member will at all times:

  (*a*) act diligently in the conduct of the LLP Business;

  (*b*) act with the utmost good faith in all transactions relating to the other Members and the LLP;

  (*c*) disclose to the Management Committee on request full details of all business transactions by him or at his direction for the account of the LLP;

  (*d*) provide the Management Committee with the information concerning the LLP Business in his knowledge or possession that the Management Committee requests;

(*e*) comply with any law or professional regulations to which the LLP or the Member is or may become subject in that capacity and use reasonable endeavours to comply with any other law or contractual or other legal obligations of which he is aware;

(*f*) use the LLP Name in all business transactions of the LLP;

(*g*) not exceed the authority conferred on him by this deed when acting on behalf of the LLP;

(*h*) except as otherwise determined by the Management Committee, account to the LLP for any money or thing representing money including all gifts and legacies received from a third party in the course of the LLP Business; and

(*j*) not hold himself out as being in partnership with the LLP, or as being in partnership with or authorised to act as agent for any other Member or Former Member.

(2) The LLP shall:

(*a*) comply with the statutory duties imposed on it from time to time;

(*b*) indemnify the Members in respect of payments made and personal liabilities incurred by them:

(i) in the ordinary and proper conduct of the LLP Business; or

(ii) in or about anything necessarily done for the preservation of the LLP Business.

(3) Unless a [General Decision/the Management Committee] determines otherwise in any particular instance:

(*a*) subject to clauses 22 (Gardening Leave) and 28 (Holidays and Maternity Leave) each Member will devote his whole time and attention to the LLP Business during normal business hours and at any other time when it is necessary to do so to enable him to perform his duties to the LLP or any of its clients;

(*b*) subject to clause 13 (Appointments and Approved Liabilities) a Member will not become a sole trader or a member in any business other than the LLP Business or be a director of any company other than a company owned by the LLP or be or become a member of Lloyd's or hold any shares in any company with unlimited liability;

(*c*) a Member will not do or omit to do any act or thing the doing or omission of which will bring or tend to bring the LLP into disrepute;

(*d*) a Member will not, otherwise than as required by law, assign, declare any trust of, transfer or create a security interest over any legal or beneficial interest in his share in the LLP or any part of the Profits of the LLP;

(*e*) a Member will not lend any money or other property of the LLP or, in the context of the LLP Business, give credit to or act for or have any dealing with any person, company or firm with whom the Management Committee has previously requested him not to deal; and (*f*) except within his authority as Member, insofar as his advisers and any court, expert or arbitrator need to be informed in order to resolve any dispute under this deed or as required by law, a Member or Former Member will not use to the detriment or prejudice of the LLP (or divulge to any person other than another Member in any way which could reasonably be foreseen to risk any detriment to the LLP or any of its clients) any confidential information concerning the business, investment or affairs of the LLP or any of its clients. In this paragraph '**confidential information**' includes (without limitation) any information relating to this deed, the Accounts, the books of the LLP, the financial position of the LLP, any decision of the LLP (including a decision of the Management Committee) or any matter affecting the rights and obligations of the Members or Former Members or the management of the LLP. However, a Former Member may disclose the terms of the restrictions imposed on Former Members under this clause and clause 24 (Covenants).

13. Appointments and Approved Liabilities

(1) (*a*) Members must not accept or hold any charitable or non-charitable trusteeships, offices or appointments including (without limitation) appointment as a director of a company, an executor, an administrator or trustee of any will, estate or settlement ('**Appointments**') except in accordance with this clause.

(*b*) Unless otherwise agreed by the Management Committee, every Appointment will be deemed to be held for the account of the LLP. Those Appointments that the Management Committee agree will not be held for the account of the LLP are referred to in this clause as '**Non-Approved Appointments**'.

(*c*) A register (the '**Register**') of all Appointments will be maintained by the Management Committee specifying whether or not an Appointment is a Non-Approved Appointment or an Appointment held on behalf of the LLP (an '**Approved Appointment**') and this Register will be open to inspection by all Members.

(2) (*a*) If any Member incurs a liability (otherwise than by reason of his own fraud or dishonesty) in connection with or as a result of an Approved Appointment (an '**Approved Liability**'):

(i) that Approved Liability and any costs or expenses incurred by that Member in or about contesting, compromising, admitting or compounding it will be a liability of the LLP;

(ii) that Member will be entitled to the same rights of indemnity and contribution from the LLP as if that Approved Liability had been incurred by him in the ordinary and proper course of the LLP Business; and

(iii) that Member must take such action at the expense of the LLP as any insurer which is on risk in respect of the Approved Liability or the Management Committee may from time to time require to recoup all or any sums within the scope of this clause from any assets (other than his own) or from any person (other than himself) who may be liable in respect thereof and he must account to the LLP for all sums so recouped.

(*b*) If any Member incurs a liability in connection with an Appointment which is not an Approved Liability, the LLP will have no responsibility for that liability and he will not be entitled to any rights of indemnity and contribution from the LLP.

(3) All Approved Appointments other than those which are required to be held in the name of an individual must be held in the name of the LLP and not in the name of any Member.

(4) Unless otherwise agreed by the Management Committee, all fees, profits, remuneration, emoluments or other benefits received by a Member (including, without limitation, all fees and payments received by a Member arising from his acting as a company director or dividends or other payments received by virtue of a Member holding shares in any company on trust for the LLP) in respect of:

(*a*) any Approved Appointment, will be received by him for the account of the LLP and must be paid by him to the LLP within seven days of receipt;

(*b*) any Non-Approved Appointment, will not be received by him for the account of the LLP but will be held for his own personal account.

14. Meetings and Procedures for Decision-Making and the Chairman

(1) A meeting of the Members may be convened at any time by the Chief Executive, the Management Committee or on the written request of any Member to the Management Committee.

(2) (*a*) Subject to paragraph (*b*), the Management Committee will in all cases determine the time, date and place of each meeting of the Members and the nature of the business to be transacted.

(*b*) Any Member may submit a matter for discussion at a meeting of the Members to the Managing Director before commencement of that meeting.

(*c*) Any meeting of the Members shall be chaired by the Chairman.

(3) Subject to sub-clause (4), each Equity Member will have one vote at any meeting of the Members.

(4) (*a*) The Chairman will have a casting vote where a deadlock exists and may cast his second vote as he thinks fit.

(*b*) No Member who has been required to retire from the LLP by a Special Decision under sub-clause 20(1), no Member who has served a notice to retire as a Member under clause 21 and no Member who is absent from the LLP under clause 22 (unless otherwise agreed by the Management Committee), will be eligible to vote for any purpose but no decision may adversely affect his interests without his written consent unless it applies fairly to all Members.

(*c*) A Member subject to a Special Decision under sub-clause 19(1), or sub-clause 22(2)(*a*) will not be entitled to vote on that matter.

(5) (*a*) Any Member may be represented at any meeting by appointing

another Member as a proxy and that proxy will vote on the directions of the Member in favour of or against any decision taken at the meeting. Written proof of appointment must be presented by that proxy to the chair of the meeting prior to commencement of the meeting.

(b) A vote cast by a proxy which complies with the terms of his appointment ' will count as the vote of the Member making the appointment, and that Member will be deemed for all the purposes of this deed to have been present at the meeting and to have voted on the matter.

(6) The quorum for any meeting of the Members will be fifty per cent of all the Members.

(7) A Unanimous Decision, a Special Decision and a General Decision will bind all Members and the LLP.

(8) (a) For a General Decision to be validly taken [seven] clear days' notice in writing must be given to all Members. A lesser period of notice may be agreed in writing by [ninety per cent] in number of all Members.

(b) General Decisions must be made at a meeting of the Members on a show of hands by a simple majority of those Members present and voting at the meeting (whether in person or by proxy).

(9) A Special Decision will be taken in the same way as a General Decision except that at least [seventy-five per cent] by number of all the Members (whether present and voting or not) must be present at the meeting (whether in person or by proxy) and vote in favour of the resolution.

(10) A Unanimous Decision may be taken:

(a) at any meeting of the Members on a show of hands provided all Members vote in favour of the decision (whether in person or by proxy); or

(b) with the written approval of all the Members in which case no meeting of the Members is required for the making of that decision.

(11) The accidental omission to give notice of a meeting to, or the non-receipt of notice of a meeting by, any [two] or less Members entitled to receive notice will not invalidate the proceedings of a meeting or a decision made by the LLP.

15. Unanimous and Special Decisions

(1) In addition to any other matters referred to in this deed, the following matters will be determined by [Unanimous/Special] Decision:

(a) the transfer or vesting of any part of the LLP Business to or into a body corporate, limited liability partnership or any analogous entity or the merger of the LLP Business with that of any other person;

(b) any acquisition by the LLP of any business or part of a business or company or part of a company for valuable consideration or any disposal by the LLP of any business or part of a business or company or part of a company for valuable consideration;

(*c*) any acquisition or disposal of freehold or leasehold property.

(2) Except where otherwise specifically provided in this deed any matter connected with the conduct and management of the LLP Business will be decided by the Management Committee which will exercise its powers and discretions in the best interests of the LLP as a whole.

16. Management Committee, Chief Executive

(1) The Management Committee will be comprised of the Chief Executive and [   ] other Members with effect on and from the Effective Date the Management Committee will be comprised of the Members referred to in Part I of Schedule 5.

(2) Any decision of the Management Committee made in accordance with this deed binds the Members and the LLP.

(3) The quorum necessary at meetings for the transaction of business by the Management Committee is [   ] present in person or by telephone.

(4) (*a*) A member of the Management Committee will cease to be a member on ceasing to be a Member on the [   ] anniversary of his most recent appointment but in the latter case shall be eligible for re-election. The Members may from time to time by [Special/General] Decision remove any member of the Management Committee and may appoint another Member to replace that member so removed or to replace any member of the Management Committee who has ceased to be a member of the Management Committee for any other reason or appoint an additional member of the Management Committee. Nominations for all such appointments must be given to the continuing members of the Management Committee at least 14 days prior to a general meeting of the Members.

(*b*) A member of the Management Committee may voluntarily stand down from the Management Committee on giving at least two months' notice to the continuing members and the Members must replace that member in accordance with paragraph (*a*) above.

(5) Subject to sub-clause (6), the Management Committee will meet together for the despatch of business, adjourn and otherwise regulate its meetings as it thinks fit and may appoint one of their number as Chairman.

(6) Matters arising at any meeting of the Management Committee will be determined by a simple majority of votes of the members of the Management Committee who are present and voting thereon on the basis of one vote per member. For the avoidance of doubt, the [Chairman and] Chief Executive will not have a casting vote for the purposes of this sub-clause.

(7) (*a*) With effect from and including the Effective Date, the office of Chief Executive and Chairman will be filled by the Member specified in Part II and Part III of Schedule 5 respectively. The provisions of sub-clause (4) will apply mutatis mutandis to the removal, retirement and appointment of the Chief Executive and the Chairman.

(*b*) The Chief Executive or the Chairman may delegate to any Member anything required to be done by him and the actions of the delegate will bind the Members and the LLP as if they were carried out by the Chief Executive or the Chairman himself. In the absence of the Chief Executive or the Chairman, or if he is unavailable, and notwithstanding any delegation of his powers under this sub-clause, any notice required to be given to him must be given to any one or more of the other members of the Management Committee.

17. Admission of New Members

(1) A New Member may at any time be admitted by Special Decision which decision will specify his date of admittance to the LLP (his '**Admission Date**').

(2) The admission of a New Member is conditional upon the execution by him of an Accession Agreement approved by the Members (excluding the New Member) by Special Decision, on or before his Admission Date or, if later, within [   ] months of the date of the decision referred to in sub-clause (1). This deed will then be construed as though he had been a Member with effect from the Admission Date.

(3) The Accession Agreement will state the New Member's initial capital contribution (if any) and his Profit Share. The Profit Shares of the existing Members shall be reduced in proportion to their Profit Shares by the percentage necessary to accommodate the New Member's Profit Share.

18. Salaried Members

(1) Any Member may be employed as a Salaried Member by the LLP. The admission and terms of admission of any Salaried Member whose name is entered on the register at Companies House as a Member of the LLP must be authorised by a [Special/General] Decision.

(2) The rights and obligations of any Salaried Member will be governed by the agreement for employment made between them and the LLP.

19. Expulsion

(1) An Equity Member will immediately cease to be a Member upon being served with a notice in writing of a Special Decision expelling him following any of the events listed below:

(*a*) if he wilfully or persistently acts in a manner contrary to his material obligations under this deed or is guilty of any grave professional misconduct; or

(*b*) if he is convicted (unless quashed on appeal) of any criminal offence involving dishonesty; or

(*c*) if he commits any act of bankruptcy or is adjudicated bankrupt or enters into any composition, scheme or arrangement with his creditors or the equivalent in any relevant jurisdiction; or

(*d*) if he creates or purports to create a security interest over any legal or beneficial interest in his share in the LLP including (without limitation) his account with the LLP or any part of the Profits of the LLP for his separate debt; or (*e*) if he has become incapacitated by mental or physical illness, ill-health, accident or otherwise from performing his duties, obligations or responsibilities hereunder for a continuous period of [   ] months.

(2) A Member will immediately cease to be a Member if the LLP would otherwise be dissolved by operation of law because he has lost or fails to hold a relevant qualification or to satisfy a relevant professional regulation.

20.   Compulsory Retirement and Retirement due to Age and Death

(1) A Member will retire from the LLP and cease to be a Member and become a Former Member on the earlier of his death and the expiration of six months from the date of a Special Decision requiring him to retire as a Member.

(2) Unless otherwise determined by Special Decision an Equity Member will automatically retire from the LLP, cease to be a Member and become a Former Member on the date on which he attains the age of sixty years.

21.   Voluntary Retirement

Any Member may retire from the LLP by giving not less than [six] months' previous notice in writing to the Management Committee expiring on an Accounts Date (but any General Decision to amend the Accounts Date that follows such notice will not affect the date of expiry of the notice) except that the Management Committee may agree a shorter period of notice in any individual case whether or not expiring on an Accounts Date.

22.   Gardening Leave and Suspension

(1) Where a Member has been required to retire from the LLP by a Special Decision under sub-clause 20(1) and where a Member has served notice to retire as a Member under clause 21, the Management Committee may direct by notice to him in writing that during the whole or any part of the period of his notice to retire, the retiring Member:

(*a*) will not enter any of the LLP Premises;

(*b*) will not contact or have any communication (or may only communicate in specified ways) with any client or employee of the LLP for any business purpose;

(*c*) will do, or omit from doing, all such things in connection with the LLP Business as the Management Committee may reasonably require including, for example, carrying out administrative duties or working on non-client matters; and

(*d*) will be subject to the provisions of clause 24 (Covenants) (without prejudice to the application of that clause to him when he ceases to be a Member).

(2) (*a*) Where there are reasonable grounds for believing that any of the events referred to in clause 19 may apply to a Member, the Members may by [Special/General] Decision decide that such Member will

494

forthwith take no further part in the LLP Business for a specified period (not exceeding six months) or until further notice (not exceeding six months) on such terms as that decision shall determine.

(*b*) Without prejudice to the generality of paragraph (*a*), the decision referred to in paragraph (*a*) may direct that the provisions of sub-clause (1) will apply to the suspended Member.

(*c*) A Member who is subject to this sub-clause will, at the expiration of six months from the date of the decision referred to in paragraph (*a*), be deemed to have retired from the LLP unless that decision has ceased or been revoked at, or before, the expiration of that period.

(*d*) The revocation of a decision made under this sub-clause will be by [Special/General] Decision.

(3) During any period when sub-clauses (1) or (2) apply, the Member concerned will continue to be entitled to his share of the Profits and to drawings on account of those Profits after providing for any amount owed by the Member to the LLP.

23. Former Members and their Entitlements

(1) As quickly as is reasonably practicable following Retirement Date of a Member which falls otherwise than on the Accounts Date, the LLP Auditors will prepare interim accounts as at the Retirement Date for the period from the preceding Accounts Date to the Retirement Date.

(2) The interim accounts prepared in sub-clause (1) will be prepared on the same basis as the Accounts.

(3) Within two months of the approval of the Accounts (if the Member ceases to be a Member on the Accounts Date) or of the Interim Accounts being approved by [Special/General Decision] (in all other cases) and after providing for any amount owed by the Former Member to the LLP (if applicable), the undrawn credit balance, if any, on the Former Member's current account will be paid to the Former Member.

(4) The LLP will [if the LLP makes the election specified in sub-clause (5)] owe to the Former Member a sum equal to the balance, if any, standing to the credit of the Former Member's capital account less the debit balance, if any, on his current account. Payment of such amount owed will be made as follows:

(*a*) one half plus interest thereon at the LLP Interest Rate will be paid [twelve] months after the Former Member's Retirement Date;

(*b*) one half plus interest thereon at the LLP Interest Rate will be paid [eighteen] months after the Former Member's Retirement Date

provided always that in the event of the winding up of the LLP (otherwise than for the purposes of amalgamation or reconstruction) any outstanding balance due to a Former Member will immediately become due and payable.

(5) The share of the Former Member in the capital and assets of the LLP will [if the LLP so elects by written notice to the Former Member within six months of his Retirement Date] and with effect from his Retirement Date

accrue] to the Equity Members rateably in accordance with their Profit Shares.

[(6) If the LLP makes no election under sub-clause (5) then the assets of the LLP will be realised as soon as may be practicable and in any event within twelve months of the Retirement Date. Any surplus or loss on such realisation will be credited or debited to the capital accounts of the Members and the Former Member and the Former Member will be entitled to be paid the balance standing to the credit of his capital account within eighteen months of his Retirement Date together with interest from the Retirement Date at the LLP Interest Rate.][1]

(7) The LLP will indemnify each Former Member against all liabilities of the LLP. If and to the extent that the Former Member is entitled to any right of indemnity, reimbursement or contribution in respect of those liabilities from any person other than the LLP or any Member (whether under a policy of insurance or otherwise), he will disclose details of any such rights of reimbursement, indemnity or contribution, and any claim made under it, to the LLP, which will be entitled to exercise those rights by way of subrogation.

(8) The Profit Share to which a Former Member was entitled immediately prior to his Retirement Date shall accrue rateably to the Profit Shares of the other Members.

(9) A Former Member will at all times comply with the obligations imposed on him as a Former Member by this deed, including (without limitation) the obligations imposed by clauses 12 (Duties) and 24 (Covenants).

(10) A Former Member is entitled to the payments described in this clause in full satisfaction of his interest in the LLP, its profits, and in the Goodwill, the LLP Name, LLP Premises, the LLP's furniture and equipment and other assets of the LLP, and has no further rights in respect of those profits or assets.

24. Covenants

(1) In this clause:

(a) 'in any capacity' means on that Member's or Former Member's (who was an Equity Member) own account, or jointly, in conjunction with, or on behalf of any other person, firm or company; and

(b) 'LLP Client' means any individual, membership, body corporate or unincorporated association who or which has been a client of the LLP and for whom the relevant Member had carried out work at any time in the period of [two] years before his Retirement Date except that each distinct business unit of a client will be treated for this purpose as a separate LLP Client.

(2) A Member or a Former Member will not, without the prior deed of the Management Committee do any of the following:

---

[1] Words in square brackets to be deleted if automatic accruer is desired.

(a) for a period of [one] year from his Retirement Date act for, solicit or accept instructions from or provide legal services to, any LLP Client in a way which is likely to compete with the business carried on by him as an Equity Member or by the LLP immediately before his Retirement Date;

(b) for a period of [one] year from the Retirement Date employ, solicit or endeavour to entice away, offer membership or employment to or enter into membership or any other commercial arrangement with any person who, at the Retirement Date was a Member in, an employee of or consultant of the LLP;

(c) at any time after his Retirement Date and in any capacity:

    (i) represent himself as a Member in, employee of or consultant to the LLP or that he is in any way connected with, or has the authority to bind the LLP or any Member; or

    (ii) use the LLP Name or any name which may in any way be confused with the LLP Name.

(3) Each of sub-clauses (2)(a) to (c) inclusive constitutes a separate and independent restriction on each Former Member so that, if one or more are held to be invalid or unenforceable for any reason whatsoever then the remaining covenants will be valid and enforceable to the extent that they are not held to be invalid or unenforceable.

(4) Upon any Equity Member becoming a Former Member, all deeds, drafts, letters and other papers or records belonging to the LLP or any LLP Client or relating to any LLP Client or prospective client of the LLP will remain in the possession of, or be delivered by that Former Member to the LLP and, at the request of the Management Committee, the Former Member will certify in writing to the LLP whether or not he is in breach of this sub-clause.

(5) When a Member becomes a Former Member, due notice that he has ceased to be a Member will be given by the LLP to the Companies Registrar as required by the LLP Act.

25. Winding Up

(1) A [Special/General] Decision of the Members is required for a voluntary winding up under Section 84(1) Insolvency Act.

(2) The Designated Members shall file a copy of the determination made by Members for a voluntary winding up with the registrar of limited liability partnerships within 15 days from when it was made in accordance with Section 84(3) Insolvency Act and advertise the same in the London Gazette.

(3) The Designated Members shall (if they are satisfied that the LLP is able to pay its debts in full together with interest as described in Section 89(1) of the Insolvency Act) make a statutory declaration of solvency and file the same with the registrar of limited liability partnerships in accordance with Section 89 Insolvency Act.

(4) A liquidator may be appointed under Section 91 of the Insolvency Act by [Special/General] Decision of the Members.

(5) Upon winding up of the LLP:

(*a*) the Designated Members will procure the preparation of a set of accounts in accordance with generally accepted accounting practices in the UK. Those accounts will be available within 30 days of the date of winding up, and will subsequently be audited by the LLP Auditors; and

(*b*) all the assets of the LLP (including the right to use the LLP Name) will be realised and the proceeds remaining after the discharge of all liabilities to third parties (including any amounts outstanding to or in respect of any Former Member) will be applied firstly in payment of the amount standing to the credit of the capital and current accounts of each of the Members at the date of winding up. Any balance will be distributed to the Members in proportion to their respective Profit Shares.

(6) The LLP Business (or any of it) may be transferred to one or more limited liability partnerships, partnerships, bodies corporate or any analogous entity in consideration for the issue to Members of shares, membership rights or analogous rights in that entity which are broadly equivalent to their interests in the LLP upon such terms as shall be agreed by the Members.

(7) Each Member agrees to contribute £100 to the assets of the LLP on a winding up and shall be a contributory for the purposes of Section 79 of the Insolvency Act accordingly.

(8) The provisions of this deed shall remain binding notwithstanding that the LLP has been wound up or become insolvent in so far as the obligations and covenants set out in it remain or require to be performed.

26. Arbitration and Dispute Resolution

(1) Where any question, claim, dispute or difference ('**dispute**') arises between any of the Members, the Former Members and the LLP concerning or in any way arising out of this deed or the performance of the terms of this deed, those Members, Former Members and the LLP involved in that dispute will make a genuine effort to resolve the dispute without resorting to litigation, using the procedures set out in this clause.

(2) Any dispute in connection with this deed will be resolved as follows:

(*a*) in accordance with sub-clause (3) below if the dispute relates to an accounting matter; or

(*b*) in accordance with sub-clauses (4), (5) and (6) below, in the case of all other disputes.

(3) Disputes relating to an accounting matter will be referred, at the written request of any party to the dispute, for determination by an independent accountant (the '**Independent Accountant**') who is a member of the Institute of Chartered Accountants in England and Wales (the '**Institute**') appointed by deed between the parties to the dispute within seven days of delivery of the written request or (in default of deed) appointed by the

President for the time being of the Institute on the application of any party to the dispute. The Management Committee will determine whether a dispute concerns an accounting matter or not and its decision will be final in the absence of a manifest error. The determination of the Independent Accountant is final and binding on all Members and Former Members. In determining the dispute, the Independent Accountant will act as an expert and not as an arbitrator. All costs incurred by the Independent Accountant will be borne by the parties to the dispute as determined by the Independent Accountant.

(4) Without prejudice to any right to seek interim relief all other disputes will be referred, at the written request of any party to the dispute, to mediation by a mediator appointed by deed between the parties to the dispute within seven days of the written request or (in default of deed) appointed by the Chief Executive for the time being of the Centre for Dispute Resolution ('**CEDR**'). The mediation will be conducted in London in accordance with the CEDR Model Mediation Procedure (together with any amendments and updates to that procedure that are adopted by the Management Committee before the appointment of a mediator in relation to a particular dispute), which is deemed to be incorporated in this deed. If an agreement is reached on the resolution of the dispute during the mediation, that deed will be reduced to writing and, once signed by the parties to the dispute, will be binding on all the Members. Unless concluded with a written legally binding deed, the mediation will be conducted in confidence and without prejudice to the rights of any Member or Former Member in any further proceedings.

(5) Without prejudice to any right to seek interim relief in the event that the dispute has not been settled within sixty days after the appointment of the mediator, or if no request is made to refer that dispute to mediation, the dispute will be referred (by any Member or Former Member involved in the dispute) to arbitration in London to be conducted in the English language by a sole arbitrator appointed in accordance with the rules of the London Court of International Arbitration (the '**Rules**') which Rules are deemed to be incorporated by reference into this clause.

(6) The Members and the LLP agree that any party to an arbitration under this deed may appeal against any award of an arbitrator on points of law.

27. Alterations

(1) Any of the provisions of this deed may be altered at any time by [Unanimous] Decision.

(2) Notwithstanding sub-clause (1), any of the provisions of this deed may be altered at any time by the Management Committee if the alteration is of a minor or technical nature which either is not materially prejudicial to the interests of any of the Members or is to correct a manifest error. Any such alteration will be made on the terms and subject to the conditions that the Management Committee determines, and will be notified to Members as soon as possible and will be binding on the Members when notified to them.

(3) No alteration of this deed will invalidate any prior act which would have been valid if that alteration had not been made.

28. Holidays and Maternity Leave

(1) In each calendar year, in addition to public and religious holidays, each Member shall be entitled to take such annual holidays not exceeding [five] weeks in the aggregate [of which not more than [three] weeks may be taken consecutively] or as shall be determined by [General/Special] Decision from time to time and may (subject to such determination) carry forward into the next calendar year any unused part of his entitlement.

(2) A female Member may, in the event of her pregnancy and upon giving not less than [three months'] prior written notice of her intention to do so to the other Members, take a period of maternity leave of not more than [four months'] duration and commencing not more than [four weeks] prior to the expected date of confinement.

29. General

(1) None of the rights or obligations under this deed may be assigned or transferred without a [Unanimous/Special Decision].

(2) Where an obligation is expressed to be undertaken by two or more parties they shall, unless otherwise expressly stated, be jointly and severally responsible in respect of it.

(3) This deed may be executed in any number of counterparts, all of which taken together shall constitute one and the same deed and any party may enter into this deed by executing a counterpart as a deed.

(4) This deed and its schedules and the documents referred to in it contain the whole deed between the parties and supersede all previous deeds between the parties.

(5) Each of the parties acknowledges that in agreeing to enter into this deed he has not relied on any representation, warranty or other assurance except those set out in this deed.

(6) This deed is governed by and shall be construed in accordance with English law.

(7) Any notice required or permitted to be given under this deed shall be in writing and if posted by prepaid recorded delivery post to the last known address of the person to be served shall be deemed to have been duly served forty-eight hours after despatch.

(8) The parties agree that, subject to clause 26, the courts of England have exclusive jurisdiction in connection with this deed.

(9) Except as expressly stated in this deed, no third party shall have any rights in respect of this deed, whether pursuant to the Contracts (Rights of Third Parties) Act 1999 or otherwise.

(10) Section 459 of the Companies Act is excluded from operation by a minority of Members in respect of any resolution of the LLP or decision of the Management Committee pursuant to its powers under this deed or any other agent, delegate or sub-delegate of the Management Committee.

IN WITNESS of which each of the parties has executed this document as a deed the day and year first above written.

SCHEDULE 1

Original Members

Name   **Address**

SCHEDULE 2

LLP Premises

Address

SCHEDULE 3

Initial Designated Members

SCHEDULE 4

Name	Initial Capital Contributions	Initial Profit Share

SCHEDULE 5

Part 1

Initial Management Committee

Part II

Initial Chief Executive

Part III

Initial Chairman

SIGNED as a deed by   ⎱

in the presence of: ⎰

Witness's
signature: ....

Name: ....

Address: ....

....

....

SIGNED as a deed by   ⎱

in the presence of: ⎰

Witness's
signature: ....

Name: ....

Address: ....

....

....

SIGNED as a deed by   ⎱

in the presence of: ⎰

Witness's
signature: ....

Name: ....

Address: ....

....

....

SIGNED as a deed by   ⎱

[   ] LLP   ⎰   ....

acting by [   ]   ⎱

and [   ]   ⎰   ....

Appendix 6

ABC Partnership — financial statements for the year ended 30 April 2003

Professional Partnership Handbook

ABC Partnership

The accounts of ABC Partnership for the year ended 30 April 2003 as set out on pages 511 to 521 were approved by the Partners on 30 August 2003.

Partner A   . . . .

Partner B   . . . .

:
:
:
:
:
:
:

Partner Y   . . . .

Partner Z   . . . .

Report of the accountants to ABC Partnership

As described in the partners' confirmation on page 510, you have approved the accounts for the year ended 30 April 2003, comprising the profit and loss account, the balance sheet and the related notes 1 to 17.

In accordance with your instructions we have compared the accounts with the accounting records kept by the partnership and made such limited enquiries of the partners as are considered necessary for the purposes of this report. These procedures do not constitute an audit. Accordingly, we do not express an audit opinion on the accounts. Therefore, our report does not provide any assurance that the accounting records and the accounts are free from material misstatements.

In our opinion the accounts are in accordance with the accounting records maintained by the partnership.

Smith & Williamson   No 1 Riding House Street
Limited   London W1A 3AS

2 September 2003

ABC Partnership — profit and loss account for the year ended 30 April 2003

	Notes	2003 £	2002 £
INCOME			
Turnover	1	12,647,254	10,549,140
Closing work in progress		1,882,418	1,853,610
Opening work in progress		(1,853,610)	(1,777,515)
		12,676,062	10,625,235
Other income	2	145,781	131,247
		12,821,843	10,756,482
EXPENSES			
Staff expenses — fee earners	3	3,149,879	2,614,561
Staff expenses — non fee earners	4	1,030,337	876,652
Premises expenses	5	1,374,188	1,054,427
Professional indemnity insurance		509,746	421,274
General expenses	6	1,836,364	1,324,801
Financial expenses	7	398,137	367,574
Annuities to former partners		47,804	43,458
		8,346,455	6,702,747
PROFIT AVAILABLE TO PARTNERS	15	4,475,388	4,053,735

ABC Partnership — balance sheet as at 30 April 2003

	Notes	2003 £	2002 £
FIXED ASSETS			
Intangible	8	200,000	250,000
Tangible	9	2,100,772	1,929,759
Investments	10	30,695	30,695
		2,331,467	2,210,454
CURRENT ASSETS			
Work in progress		1,882,418	1,853,610
Debtors	11	3,804,664	3,102,428
Cash at bank		423,926	199,823
		6,111,008	5,155,861
CREDITORS: Amounts due within one year	12	(2,977,710)	(2,781,640)
NET CURRENT ASSETS		3,133,298	2,374,221
TOTAL ASSETS LESS CURRENT LIABILITIES		5,464,765	4,584,675
CREDITORS: Amounts due in more than one year	13	(1,200,000)	(1,100,000)
NET ASSETS		4,264,765	3,484,675
Financed by:			
PARTNERS' ACCOUNTS			
Capital accounts	14	2,500,000	2,220,000
Current accounts	15	1,764,765	1,264,675
		4,264,765	3,484,675
Client monies in hand		4,460,685	3,605,925

ABC Partnership — notes to the financial statements for the year ended 30 April 2003

1. **Accounting policies**

   The following accounting policies have been used in dealing with items which are considered material in relation to the partnership's accounts.

   (*a*) *Basis of accounting*

   The accounts are prepared using the historical cost basis of accounting except for certain fixed assets which are included at valuation.

   (*b*) *Turnover*

   Turnover comprises net invoiced values for services rendered in the ordinary course of business, excluding value added tax.

   (*c*) *Goodwill*

   Goodwill represents the excess over fair value of the cost of DEF Partnership. The cost is being amortised in equal amounts over a 10 year period.

   (*d*) *Tangible fixed assets*

   Depreciation is provided on all tangible fixed assets, except freehold property, at annual rates calculated to write off their cost, less estimated residual value, on a straight line basis, over their expected useful lives as follows:

Leasehold land and buildings	– Over the term of the lease
Fixtures, fittings and equipment	– 20% p.a.
Computers	– 25%–30% p.a.
Motor vehicles	– 25% p.a.

   (*e*) *Work in progress*

   Unbilled work has been included in these financial statements at the valuation made by the Partners, based on the lower of cost and net realisable value.

   (*f*) *Taxation*

   Full provision is made for income tax for the 2003/04 tax year, which is based on the profit for the year ended 30 April 2003.

   (*g*) *Leases*

   Rental costs under operating leases are charged to the profit and loss account in equal amounts over the periods of the leases.

   (*h*) *Pension costs*

   The partnership operates a pension scheme providing benefits based on final salary. The assets of the scheme are held separately from those of the partnership, being invested with an insurance company. Contributions to the scheme are charged to the profit and loss account so as to spread the cost of pensions over employees' working lives. The contributions are determined by a qualified actuary.

ABC Partnership — notes to the financial statements for the year ended 30 April 2003 (*cont*)

		2003	2002
2.	Other income	£	£
	Deposit interest	102,047	87,498
	Commissions	15,410	24,032
	Other income	21,867	16,405
	Directors fees	5,000	2,000
	Dividends on investments	1,457	1,312
		145,781	131,247
3.	Staff expenses — fee earners	£	£
	Salaries	2,677,398	2,222,377
	National insurance	283,490	235,310
	BUPA staff	12,500	11,000
	Temporary staff	32,795	22,205
	Recruitment costs	9,481	5,082
	Practising certificates	58,900	56,500
	Consultancy fees	50,500	41,328
	Costs, draughtsmans' fees	3,250	2,859
	Training	21,565	17,900
		3,149,879	2,614,561
4.	Staff expenses — non fee earners	£	£
	Staff salaries	896,393	762,687
	Temporary staff	41,214	35,067
	National insurance	92,730	78,898
		1,030,337	876,652
5.	Premises expenses	£	£
	Rent payable	618,385	527,215
	Repairs	219,324	158,164
	Rates and water	274,838	210,885
	Lighting and heating	48,098	42,178
	Insurance	34,900	33,200
	Professional fees	137,418	51,152
	Cleaning	41,225	31,633
		1,374,188	1,054,427

ABC Partnership — notes to the financial statements for the year ended 30 April 2003 (*cont*)

		2003	*2002*
6.	**General expenses**	£	£
	Accountancy and taxation fees	120,203	99,758
	Professional fees	69,195	36,510
	Hire of motor vehicles and equipment	126,730	80,736
	Office sundry expenses	202,768	152,149
	Photocopying	45,048	33,277
	Postage and courier charges	88,702	66,565
	Unrecovered expenses	101,367	76,038
	Computer expenses	202,770	123,178
	Other equipment	25,346	19,015
	Publications and subscriptions	76,037	57,057
	Stationery	214,311	171,167
	Telephone	189,251	142,600
	Travelling expenses	126,025	115,021
	Practising certificate—partners	40,810	36,625
	Entertainment	207,801	115,105
		1,836,364	1,324,801

		£	£
7.	**Financial expenses**	£	£
	Bank charges and interest	10,900	12,500
	Bad debts written off	32,597	27,500
	Provision for bad and doubtful debts	(15,950)	7,200
	Depreciation – furniture fixtures and equipment	129,781	95,868
	– computer	80,565	78,525
	– goodwill	50,000	50,000
	– motor vehicles	60,244	45,981
	– leasehold land and buildings	50,000	50,000
		398,137	367,574

ABC Partnership — notes to the financial statements for the year ended 30 April 2003 (*cont*)

8. Intangible fixed assets – goodwill

	£
Cost	
As at 1 May 2002 and 30 April 2003	500,000
Depreciation	
As at 1 May 2002	250,000
Charge for the year	50,000
As at 30 April 2003	300,000
Net book value	
As at 30 April 2003	200,000
As at 30 April 2002	250,000

9. Tangible fixed assets

	Leasehold land and buildings	Computers	Furniture fixtures and equipment	Motor vehicles	Total
COST	£	£	£	£	£
As at 1 May 2002	1,250,000	518,945	1,335,155	344,900	3,449,000
Additions	–	86,296	255,442	149,865	491,603
Disposals	–	(120,000)	(99,990)	(74,900)	(294,890)
As at 30 April 2003	1,250,000	485,241	1,490,607	419,865	3,645,713
DEPRECIATION					
As at 1 May 2002	300,000	209,561	837,755	171,925	1,519,241
Charge for the year	50,000	80,565	129,781	60,244	320,590
Disposals	–	(120,000)	(99,990)	(74,900)	(294,890
As at 30 April 2003	350,000	170,126	867,546	157,269	1,544,941
NET BOOK VALUE					
As at 30 April 2003	900,000	315,115	623,061	262,596	2,100,772
As at 30 April 2002	950,000	309,384	497,400	172,975	1,929,759

10. Fixed asset investments

	2003 £	2002 £
Investment at cost in ABC Services Limited (net asset value £110,000; 2002: £90,000)	30,695	30,695

ABC Partnership — notes to the financial statements for the year ended 30 April 2003 (*cont*)

11. Debtors	2003 £	2002 £
Trade debtors	3,043,732	2,342,870
Disbursements	342,420	381,291
Other debtors	152,186	147,097
Prepayments	266,326	231,170
	3,804,664	3,102,428

12. Creditors: Amounts falling due within one year

	£	£
Bank overdraft	109,554	155,632
Current portion of long term loans	407,914	334,184
Purchase ledger	119,110	111,265
Counsels' fees	372,215	347,705
Income tax (note 17)	1,118,847	963,435
Other taxation and social security	406,485	289,082
Other creditors and accruals	208,400	194,957
Fees received in advance	129,775	187,820
Former partners' loan accounts (current portion)	105,410	197,560
	2,977,710	2,781,640

13. Creditors: Amounts falling due after more than one year

	£	£
Long term loans	927,550	677,040
Former partners loan accounts	272,450	422,960
	1,200,000	1,100,000

The loans are secured on certain fixed assets and repayable in equal annual instalments up to 2009. Interest is charged at 2% over base rate.

ABC Partnership — notes to the financial statements for the year ended 30 April 2003 (*cont*)

14. **Partners' Capital Accounts**

	Balance as at 30 April 2002	Transfer from current account (note 15)	Repaid in year	Balance as at 30 April 2003
	£	£	£	£
Partner A	120,000	–	(120,000)	–
Partner B	120,000	–	–	120,000
:				
:				
:				
:				
:				
:				
Partner Y	–	60,000	–	60,000
Partner Z	–	60,000	–	60,000
	2,220,000	400,000	(120,000)	2,500,000

15. **Partners' Current Accounts**

	Balance as at 30 April 2002	Profit for the year	Transfer to capital account (note 14)	Drawings (note 16)	Provision for taxation (note 17)	Balance as at 30 April 2003
	£	£	£	£	£	£
Partner A	106,973	267,568	–	(226,292)	(67,951)	80,298
Partner B	87,916	232,345	–	(187,542)	(58,466)	74,253
:						
:						
:						
:						
:						
:						
Partner Y	–	109,723	(60,000)	(57,705)	(24,760)	(32,742)
Partner Z	–	109,723	(60,000)	(58,373)	(28,970)	(37,620)
	1,264,675	4,475,388	(400,000)	(2,545,377)	(1,029,921)	1,764,765

ABC Partnership — notes to the financial statements for the year ended 30 April 2003 (*cont*)

16. Partners' Drawings

	Cash drawings £	National insurance £	Pension and life policies £	Partners expanses £	Motor car cost (private element) £	Total £
Partner A	145,000	1,230	52,500	14,500	3,062	216,292
Partner B	140,000	1,230	25,500	6,500	4,312	177,542
:						
:						
:						
:						
:						
Partner Y	48,000	1,230	6,525	1,950	–	57,705
Partner Z	48,000	1,230	6,193	2,950	–	58,373
	2,100,000	32,000	277,928	99,995	35,454	2,545,377

ABC Partnership — notes to the financial statements for the year ended 30 April 2003 *(cont)*

17. Partners' income tax

Income tax balances at 30 April 2003

Balance sheet liabilities

	2001/02 £	2002/03 £	2003/04 £	Total Reserves 30/04/2003 £	Total Reserves 30/04/2002 £
Partner A	41,228	50,090	65,170	156,488	138,036
Partner B	35,291	49,815	57,050	142,156	125,133
. . . .					
Partner Y	–	1,740	22,100	23,840	43,125
Partner Z	–	2,100	29,505	31,605	4,059
	478,407	617,674	1,005,486	2,101,567	1,758,587
Tax paid	(646,643)	(336,077)	–	(982,720)	(795,152)
Tax payable/(repayable)	(168,236)	281,597	1,005,486	1,118,847	963,435

Income tax charge for the year ended 30 April 2003

	Current tax provision and prior year adjustments			
	2001/02 Case II £	2002/03 Case II £	2003/04 Case II £	Total £
Partner A	575	2,206	65,170	67,951
Partner B	195	1,221	57,050	58,466
Partner Y	–	1,740	22,100	23,840
Partner Z	–	2,100	29,505	31,605
	(4,455)	28,890	1,005,486	1,029,921
				(note 15)

Appendix 7

XYZ LLP—Report and Accounts For the year ended 31 March 200X

Contents
Designated members and advisers
Members' report
Statement of members' responsibilities in respect of the accounts
Auditors' report
Consolidated profit and loss account
Consolidated statement of total recognised gains and losses and
consolidated note of historical cost gains and losses
Consolidated balance sheet
Reconciliation of members' interests – group
Balance sheet
Reconciliation of members' interests – LLP
Consolidated cash flow statement
Notes to the consolidated cash flow statement
Notes to the accounts

Designated members and advisers

Designated members

A Designate
B Smith
C Jones

Registered office

1 The Long Street
Longtown
Longshire
LL1 1XY

Bankers

Big Bank plc
85 The Long Street
Longtown
Longshire
LL1 1YZ

Auditors

Stuart & Wilson LLP
5 The Short Street
Longtown
Longshire LL2 1AB

Solicitors

Wright & Prentice LLP
25 The Short Street
Longtown
Longshire
LL2 1BC

Registered number

OC3 54321

Professional Partnership Handbook

Members' report

The members present their report and the accounts for the year ended 31 March 200X.

Activities

The principal activity of the LLP continues to be accountants. The subsidiary, ABC Limited's, principal business is catering.

Review of business

In the opinion of the members the state of the company's affairs at 31 March 200X is satisfactory.

During the year the LLP acquired the entire share capital of ABC Limited. Further details can be found in note 2.

Results for the year and allocation to members

The profit for the year available for distribution to members was £708,000 (200Y: £557,000).

Of this £94,000 (200Y: £67,000) was transferred to the retirement benefit reserve to take account of future liabilities to retiring members.

[[   ] (200Y: [   ]) has been retained within the partnership to cover future development and growth requirements.][1]

Designated members

The following were designated members during the year:

A Designate
B Smith
C Jones

Policy with respect to members' drawings and subscription and repayment of members' capital

Members are permitted to make drawings in anticipation of profits which will be allocated to them. The amount of such drawings is set at the beginning of each financial year, taking into account the anticipated cash needs of the LLP.

New members are required to subscribe a minimum level of capital and in subsequent years members are invited to subscribe for further capital, the amounts of which is determined by the seniority and performance of those members.

On retirement, capital is repaid to members.

---

[1] Disclosure required where amounts are retained from profits.

Transfer of members' interests

During the year £15,000 was transferred from members' capital interests to debts due to members. Since the year end further amounts totalling £12,000 have been transferred.

Donations

During the year the group made donations for charitable purposes of £7,500.

Employee involvement[2]

There are quarterly briefing meetings for all employees at which a presentation is made covering the salient features of the management accounts, new work won and future plans. There is an opportunity at these meetings for employees to ask questions of the designated members.

All employees receive a monthly magazine which contains details of the performance of the group and items of general interest for employees.

Employment of disabled persons[2]

Full and fair consideration is given to the employment of disabled persons having regard to their particular aptitudes and abilities. Appropriate training is provided for disabled persons and this includes the re-training for alternative work of employees who become disabled.

Auditors

A resolution to reappoint Stuart & Wilson LLP as auditors will be proposed at the next members' meeting.

**Approved by the members
and signed on their behalf**

A Designate

Designated member

---

[2]Only required where there are more than 250 employees.

Statement of members' responsibilities in respect of the accounts[3]

Legislation applicable to limited liability partnerships requires the members to prepare accounts for each financial year which give a true and fair view of the state of affairs of the LLP and of the profit or loss of the LLP for that period. In preparing those accounts, the members are required to:

- Select suitable accounting policies and then apply them consistently;

- Make judgements and estimates that are reasonable and prudent;

- State whether applicable accounting standards have been followed, subject to any material departure disclosed and explained in the accounts[4];

- Prepare the accounts on the going concern basis unless it is inappropriate to presume that the LLP will continue in business.

The members are responsible for keeping proper accounting records which disclose with reasonable accuracy at any time the financial position of the LLP and to enable them to ensure that the accounts comply with the Limited Liability Partnerships Regulations. They are also responsible for safeguarding the assets of the LLP and thence for taking reasonable steps for the prevention and detection of fraud and other irregularities.

---

[3]This statement can alternatively be included within the members' report.
[4]Required only for large LLPs

Independent auditors report to the member of XYZ LLP

We have audited the accounts of XYZ LLP for the year ended 31 March 200X on pages [   ] to [   ]. These accounts have been prepared under the historical cost convention as modified by the revaluation of certain fixed assets and investments and the accounting policies set out therein.

Respective responsibilities of members and auditors

As described in the Statement of Members' Responsibilities the members of the LLP are responsible for the preparation of the accounts in accordance with applicable law and United Kingdom Accounting Standards.

Our responsibility is to audit the accounts in accordance with relevant legal and regulatory requirements and United Kingdom Auditing Standards.

We report to you our opinion as to whether the accounts give a true and fair view and are properly prepared in accordance with the Limited Liability Partnerships Regulations and also report to you if, in our opinion, the Members' Report is not consistent with the accounts, if the LLP has not kept proper accounting records, if we have not received all the information and explanations we require for our audit or if the information specified by law regarding members' remuneration is not disclosed.

We read the Members' Report and consider the implications for our report if we become aware of any apparent misstatements within it.

Basis of audit opinion

We conducted our audit in accordance with United Kingdom Auditing Standards issued by the Auditing Practices Board. An audit includes examination, on a test basis, of evidence relevant to the amounts and disclosures in the accounts. It also includes an assessment of the significant estimates and judgements made by the members in the preparation of the accounts, and of whether the accounting policies are appropriate to the LLP's circumstances, consistently applied and adequately disclosed.

We planned and performed our audit so as to obtain all the information and explanations which we considered necessary in order to provide us with sufficient evidence to give reasonable assurance that the accounts are free from material misstatement, whether caused by fraud or other irregularity or error. In forming our opinion we also evaluated the overall adequacy of the presentation of information in the accounts.

Opinion

In our opinion the accounts give a true and fair view of the state of the group and the LLP's affairs as at 31 March 200X and of the profit of the group for the year then ended and have been properly prepared in accordance with the Limited Liability Partnerships Regulations.

Stuart & Wilson LLP
Chartered Accountants   30 September 200X
Registered Auditors

Consolidated profit and loss account for the year ended 31 March 200X

	Notes	200X £'000	200X £'000	200Y £'000
Turnover	3	9,091		
– Acquisitions		153		
			9,244	8,490
Cost of sales			(5,879)	(5,565)
Gross profit			3,365	2,925
Administrative expenses			(2,497)	(2,164)
Other operating income			33	–
Operating profit		881		
– Acquisitions		20	901	761
Profit/(loss) on sale of fixed asset investments			38	–
Interest receivable and similar income			47	32
Interest payable and similar charges	6		(139)	(117)
Profit on ordinary activities before taxation	7		847	676
Tax on profit on ordinary activities	8		(3)	–
Profit for the financial year before members' remuneration and profit shares			844	676
Salaried remuneration of members	4		(136)	(119)
Profit for the financial year available for division among members			708	557

All of the LLP's operations are classed as continuing. [There were no gains or losses in either year other than those included in the above profit and loss account.][5]

---

[5]Disclosure required where there are no recognised gains and losses other than the profit or loss.

Consolidated statement of total recognised gains and losses for the year ended 31 March 200X

	200X £'000	200Y £'000
Profit for the financial year available for division among members	708	557
Unrealised surplus on revaluation of properties	237	–
Unrealised surplus on revaluation of investments	12	11
Transfer from members' interests on retirement of former member	(94)	(67)
Total recognised gains and losses for the year	863	501

Consolidated note of historical cost gains and losses

	200X	200Y
Profit for the financial year available for division among members	708	557
Difference between the historical cost depreciation charge and the actual depreciation charge for the year calculated on the revalued amount	15	–
Historical cost profit for the financial year	723	557

Consolidated balance sheet as at 31 March 200X

	Notes	200X £'000	200Y £'000
Fixed assets			
Intangible assets	10	109	23
Tangible assets	11	3,161	2,823
Investments	12	266	144
		3,536	2,990
Current assets			
Work in progress	13	514	348
Debtors	14	875	764
Cash at bank and in hand		211	299
		1,600	1,411
Creditors: amounts falling due within one year	15	(1,397)	(1,446)
Net current assets/(liabilities)		203	(35)
Total assets less current liabilities		3,739	2,955
Creditors: amounts falling due after more than one year	16	(509)	(645)
Provisions for liabilities and charges	18	(155)	(68)
Net assets before pension fund surplus/(deficit)[6]			
[Pension fund surplus/(deficit)][6]			
Loans and other debts due to members	19	(2,435)	(2,043)
Net assets		640	199
Members' other interests			
Members' capital		107	121
Revaluation reserve		260	11
Other reserves		273	67
		640	199
Total members' interests			
Loans and other debts due to members		2,435	2,043
Members' other interests		640	239
Amounts due from members		(14)	–
		3,061	2,282

The accounts were approved by the members on 30 September 200X and were signed on its behalf by:

A Designate
Designated member

---

[6]Position of net pension fund surplus/(deficit) where the LLP adopts the full requirements of FRS17.

Reconciliation of members' interests – group

	Members' capital £'000	Revaluation reserve £'000	Retirement benefits reserve £'000	Other reserves £'000	Total £'000	Loans and other debts due to members (note 19) £'000	Total £'000
Amounts due to members						–	
Amounts due from members						2,043	
Members' interests: balance at 1 April 200Y	121	11	67	–	199	2,043	2,242
Remuneration of salaried members, including employment and retirement benefit costs						136	136
Profit for the financial year available for division among members				708	708		708
Members' interests after profit for the year	121	11	67	708	907	2,179	3,086
Allocated profits				(502)	(502)	502	–
Surplus arising on revaluation of fixed assets		237			237		237
Surplus arising on revaluation of investments		12			12		12
Retirement benefits due to former members			94	(94)			
Introduced by members	73				73		73
Repayments of capital	(72)				(72)		(72)
Conversion of capital to debt	(15)				(15)	15	–
Drawings						(275)	(275)
Amounts due to members						(14)	
Amounts due from members						2,435	
Members' interests at 31 March 200X	107	260	161	112	640	2,421	3,061

Balance sheet as at 31 March 200X

	Notes	200X £'000	200Y £'000
Fixed assets			
Intangible assets	10	26	23
Tangible assets	11	3,018	2,823
Investments	12	556	144
		3,600	2,990
Current assets			
Work in progress	13	476	348
Debtors	14	754	764
Cash at bank and in hand		177	299
		1,407	1,411
Creditors: amounts falling due within one year	15	(1,287)	(1,446)
Net current assets/(liabilities)		120	(35)
Total assets less current liabilities		3,720	2,955
Creditors: amounts falling due after more than one year	16	(509)	(645)
Provisions for liabilities and charges	18	(153)	(68)
Net assets before pension fund surplus/(deficit)[6]			
Pension fund surplus/(deficit)[6]			
Loans and other debts due to members	19	(2,435)	(2,043)
Net assets		623	199
Members' other interests			
Members' capital		107	121
Revaluation reserve		260	11
Other reserves		256	67
		623	199
Total members' interests			
Loans and other debts due to members		2,435	2,043
Members' other interests		623	239
Amounts due from members		(14)	–
		3,044	2,282

The accounts were approved by the members on 30 September 200X and were signed on its behalf by:

A Designate
Designated member

---

[6]Position of net pension fund surplus/(deficit) where the LLP adopts the full requirements of FRS17.

Reconciliation of members' interests – LLP

	Members' capital £'000	Revaluation reserve £'000	Retirement benefits reserve £'000	Other reserves £'000	Total £'000	Loans and other debts due to members (note 19) £'000	Total £'000
Amounts due to members						–	
Amounts due from members						2,043	2,043
Members' interests: balance at 1 April 200Y	121	11	67	–	199	2,043	2,242
Remuneration of salaried members, including employment and retirement benefit costs						136	136
Profit for the financial year available for division among members				691	691		691
Members' interests after profit/(loss) for the year	121	11	67	691	890	2,179	3,069
Allocated profits				(502)	(502)	502	–
Surplus arising on revaluation of fixed assets		237			237		237
Surplus arising on revaluation of investments		12			12		12
Retirement benefits due to former members			94	(94)			
Introduced by members	73				73		73
Repayments of capital	(72)				(72)		(72)
Conversion of capital to debt	(15)				(15)	15	–
Drawings						(275)	(275)
Amounts due to members						(14)	
Amounts due from members						2,435	
Members' interests at 31 March 200X	107	260	161	95	623	2,421	3,044

533

Consolidated cash flow statement for the year ended 31 March 200X

	Notes	200X £'000	200Y £'000
Net cash inflow/(outflow) from operating activities	a	970	939
Returns on investments and servicing of finance			
Interest received		47	32
Interest paid		(127)	(107)
Interest element of finance lease rental payments		(10)	(10)
Net cash outflow from returns on investments and servicing of finance		(90)	(85)
Taxation			
Corporation tax paid		–	–
Capital expenditure and financial investment			
Payments to acquire tangible fixed assets		(324)	–
Receipts from sales of tangible fixed assets		96	–
Purchase of fixed asset investments		(110)	(75)
Purchase of trademarks		(14)	(10)
Net cash outflow for capital expenditure and financial investment		(352)	(85)
Acquisitions and disposals			
Purchase of subsidiary undertaking		(195)	–
Net overdraft acquired with subsidiary		(21)	–
Net cash outflow from acquisitions and disposals		(216)	–
Transactions with members and former members			
Payments to members		(347)	(264)
Contributions by members		73	59
Retirement benefits paid to former members		(10)	–
Net cash outflow from transactions with members and former members		(284)	(205)
Cash inflow before management of financing		28	564
Financing			
New long-term loans		50	100
Repayment of long-term loans		(29)	(35)
Repayment of capital element of finance lease rentals		(44)	–
Net cash (outflow)/inflow from financing		(23)	65
Increase in cash in the year		5	629

Notes to the cash flow statement

a	Reconciliation of operating profit to net cash inflow/(outflow) from operating activities	200X £'000	200Y £'000
	Operating profit	901	761
	Depreciation	343	321
	Amortisation of intangible asset	15	12
	Loss/(profit) on sale of tangible fixed assets	(38)	8
	Decrease/(increase) in work in progress	(124)	(115)
	Decrease/(increase) in debtors	68	72
	Increase/(decrease) in creditors	(195)	(120)
	Net cash inflow from operating activities	970	939

b	Reconciliation of net cash flow to movement in net debt		
	Increase in cash in the year	5	629
	Cash inflow/(outflow) from increase/(decrease) in debt	23	65
	Change in net debt resulting from cash flows	28	694
	Other non-cash items:		
	New finance leases	(28)	–
	Movement in net debt in the year	–	694
	Net debt at 1 April 200Y	(660)	(1,354)
	Net debt at 31 March 200X	(660)	(660)

c	Analysis of net debt	At 1 April 200Y	Cash flow	Other non cash changes	At 31 March 200X
		£'000	£'000	£'000	£'000
	Cash in hand, at bank	299	(88)		211
	Overdrafts	(242)	93		(149)
			5		
	Debt due after 1 year	(581)	29	100	(452)
	Debt due within 1 year	(40)	(50)	(100)	(190)
	Finance leases	(96)	44	(28)	(80)
	Total	(660)	28	(28)	(660)

Notes to the accounts for the year ended 31 March 200X

1   **Accounting policies**

The accounts have been prepared in accordance with applicable accounting standards and the requirements of the Statement of Recommended Practice 'Accounting by limited liability partnerships'. A summary of the more important accounting policies adopted are described below.

Basis of accounting

The accounts have been prepared under the historical cost convention, modified by the revaluation of certain tangible fixed assets and investments.

Basis of consolidation

The accounts consolidate the results and the assets and liabilities of the LLP and its subsidiary.

Acquisitions

On the acquisition of a business, fair values are attributed to the group's share of net separable assets. Where the cost of acquisition exceeds the fair values attributable to such net assets, the difference is treated as purchased goodwill and capitalised in the balance sheet in the year of acquisition. The results and cash flows relating to an acquired business are included in the consolidated cash flow statement from the date of acquisition.

Goodwill and other intangible assets

Goodwill arising on acquisition is the difference between the fair value of the consideration given and the fair value of the net assets acquired. It is included on the balance sheet and is being amortised over a period of 10 years. Trademarks are included at cost of acquisition and are depreciated over their estimated useful life of 3 years.

Fixed assets

Depreciation is provided on cost or revalued amounts in equal annual instalments over the estimated useful lives of the assets concerned. The following annual rates are used.

Fixtures and fittings	–	15% reducing balance
Office equipment	–	20% reducing balance
Motor vehicles	–	25% reducing balance

Investments

Investments in unit trusts are included at their mid-market value at the year end.

Investments in subsidiaries are included at cost less any provision for impairment.

Deferred taxation

Deferred tax is provided for on a full prevision basis on all timing differences which have arisen but not reversed at the balance sheet date. *[No timing*

536

differences are recognised in respect of (i) property revaluation surpluses where there is no commitment to sell the asset; (ii) gains on sale of assets where those assets have been rolled over into replacement assets; and (iii) additional tax which would arise if profits of overseas subsidiaries are distributed except where otherwise required by accounting standards.] A deferred tax asset is not recognised to the extent that the transfer of economic benefit in the future is uncertain. Any assets and liabilities recognised have not been discounted.

Members' remuneration

Remuneration is paid to certain members under a contract of employment and is included as an expense in the profit and loss account after arriving at 'profit for the financial year before members' remuneration and profit shares'.

In addition, the LLP agreement provides that fixed amounts, determined for each member each year, be paid to members, irrespective of the profits of the LLP. These amounts are also included within salaried remuneration of members.

A member's share in the profit or loss for the year is accounted for as an allocation of profits. Unallocated profits and losses are included within 'other reserves'.

Pension costs

Contributions to defined contribution schemes are charged to the profit and loss account as they become payable in accordance with the rules of the scheme.

Retirement benefits of former members

The retirement benefits of former members are determined annually based on a formula directly linked to the profits of the partnership. Provision is made at the date of retirement of the member for the estimated present value of the expected future payments to that member. On initial recognition the estimated current value of the future pension is transferred from members' interests to provisions for liabilities and charges. The unwinding of the discount of the provision to retirement benefits is charged to the profit and loss account and included in interest payable.

The liability is reassessed annually and any changes in the estimates are included within the profit and loss account.

Leases

Assets held under finance leases are included in fixed assets and the capital element of the related lease commitment is shown as obligations under finance leases. The lease rentals are treated as consisting of capital and interest elements. The capital element is applied to reduce the outstanding obligations and the interest element is charged against profit over the period of the lease.

Rental costs under operating leases are charged to the profit and loss account on a straight-line basis over the lease term.

Foreign currencies

Transactions denominated in a foreign currency are translated into sterling at the rate of exchange ruling at the date of the transaction. At the balance sheet date, monetary assets and liabilities denominated in foreign currency are translated at the rate ruling at that date. All exchange differences are dealt with in the profit and loss account.

Work in progress

Work in progress comprises direct staff costs and a share of overhead appropriate to the relevant state of completion of the related project. The relevant proportion of the salaried remuneration of members is included within work in progress. Members' profit allocations are excluded. The overhead attributable to all time incurred by members and included within work in progress is included within the valuation.

Turnover

Turnover, which excludes value add tax, represents the invoiced value of goods and services supplied.

2 Acquisitions

During the year the LLP acquired the entire share capital of ABC Limited for cash consideration of £195,000. In addition, the former shareholders of ABC Limited have been offered an enhanced allocation of profits in addition to that available to all members, which is calculated by reference to a formula linked to the financial performance of ABC Limited. An amount of £95,000, being the current best estimate of the amounts payable, is included in members' other interests. The acquisition has been accounted for using the acquisition method of accounting. The amount of goodwill arising as a result of the acquisition is £87,000. This is included on the group balance sheet.

The profits after taxation of ABC Limited were as follows:

	Profit after tax £'000
Results prior to acquisition	
1 April 200Y to date of acquisition	57
Preceding financial year ended 31 March 200Y	38

The following table summarises the adjustments made to the book value of the major categories of assets and liabilities acquired to arrive at the fair values included in the consolidated accounts at the date of acquisition.

	Book amount £'000	Revaluation £'000	Fair value £'000
Tangible fixed assets	115	35	150
Current assets	263	(42)	221
Creditors	(140)	(28)	(168)
	238	(35)	203
Consideration			
Cash (including acquisition costs of £35,000)		195	
Contingent consideration		95	
			290
Goodwill			87

The profit and loss account includes the following amounts attributable to the acquired business: turnover £153,000, cost of sales £58,000, gross profit £95,000, administrative expenses £75,000 and operating profit £20,000.

3	**Turnover**[7]	**200X** **£'000**	**200Y** **£'000**
	United Kingdom	7,296	7,660
	Other European countries	1,948	830
		9,244	8,490

4	**Information in relation to members**	**200X** **Number**	**200Y** **Number**
	The average number of members during the year was	8	7

	£'000	**£'000**
[*The average members remuneration during the year was*[8]		]

	£'000	**£'000**
Salaried remuneration of members		
Paid under employment contract	30	25
Paid under the terms of the LLP agreement	106	94
	136	119

The amount of profit attributable to the member with the largest entitlement was	125	108

5 **Employee information**

The average number of persons (including members with contracts of employment) employed by the LLP during the year was:

	200X **Number**	**200Y** **Number**
Selling and distribution	45	43
Administration	5	4
	50	47

	£'000	**£'000**
Staff costs for the above persons were:		
Wages and salaries	1,427	1,351
Social security costs	41	34
Pension costs	26	23
	1,494	1,408

---

[7]Analysis only required where there is more than one class of business, or geographical segment
[8]This disclosure is optional.

6	Interest payable and similar charges	200X	200Y
		£'000	£'000
	Bank loans and overdrafts	127	106
	On finance leases	10	10
	Unwinding of discount in relation to retirement benefits to former members	2	1
		139	117

7	Profit on ordinary activities before taxation is stated after charging/(crediting):		
	Depreciation		
	– owned assets	331	310
	– assets held under finance leases	12	15
	Goodwill amortisation	4	–
	Amortisation of intangible assets	11	12
	Auditors' remuneration		
	– audit	23	22
	– other services	21	12
	Hire of plant & machinery – operating leases	30	40

In addition, £10,000 paid to the LLP's auditors in connection with advice in respect of the acquisition of ABC Limited is included within acquisition costs (see note 2).

8	Tax on profit on ordinary activities	£200X	£200Y
		£'000	£'000
	UK corporation tax at 20%	3	–
	[Under/(over)provision in respect of prior years][9]		
	[Deferred tax]		
		3	–

The standard rate of tax for the year, based on the UK standard rate of corporation tax is 30%. The actual tax charge for the current and previous year is less than the standard rate for the reasons set out in the following reconciliation.

---

[9]Shows position of disclosure where required.

	200X £'000	200Y £'000
Profit on ordinary activities before tax	847	676
Tax on profit on ordinary activities at standard rate	254	203
Factors affecting charge for the period:		
Profits of LLP not chargeable to corporation tax	(252)	(203)
[Capital allowances for period in excess of depreciation][9]		
Expenses not allowable for tax purposes	1	
[Other timing differences][9]		
[Profit on sale of fixed asset covered by rollover relief][9]		
[Adjustments to tax charge in respect of prior periods][9]		
	3	

9   **Profit of the LLP**

As permitted by S230 Companies Act (as modified for application to LLPs), the LLP is exempt from presenting its own profit and loss account. The profit of the LLP for the financial year amounted to £691,000 (200Y: £557,000).

10   **Intangible fixed assets**

Group

	Goodwill £'000	Trademarks £'000	Total £'000
Cost			
At 1 April 200Y	–	33	33
Additions	87	14	101
At 31 March 200X	87	47	134
Amortisation			
At 1 April 200Y	–	10	10
Charge for year	4	11	15
At 31 March 200X	4	21	25
Net book value			
At 31 March 200X	83	26	109
At 31 March 200Y	–	23	23

---

[9]Shows position of disclosure where required.

LLP	Trademarks £'000
Cost	
At 1 April 200Y	33
Additions	14
At 31 March 200X	47
Amortisation	
At 1 April 200Y	10
Charge for the year	11
At 31 March 200X	21
Net book value	
At 31 March 200X	26
At 31 March 200Y	23

11	**Tangible fixed assets** **Group**	Freehold land and buildings £'000	Office fixtures & fittings £'000	Motor vehicles £'000	Total £'000
	Cost or valuation				
	At 1 April 200Y	2,542	1,189	443	4,174
	Additions	261	62	29	352
	Acquired with subsidiary	85	33	32	150
	Disposals	–	(77)	(50)	(127)
	Adjustment arising on revaluation	108	–	–	108
	At 31 March 200X	2,996	1,207	454	4,657
	Depreciation				
	At 1 April 200Y	519	598	234	1,351
	Charge for the year	60	206	77	343
	Disposals	–	(31)	(38)	(69)
	Adjustment arising on revaluation	(129)	–	–	(129)
	At 31 March 200X	450	773	273	1,496
	Net book value				
	At 31 March 200X	2,546	434	181	3,161
	At 31 March 200Y	2,023	591	209	2,823

Comparable amounts determined according to the historical cost convention.

	Freehold land and buildings £'000	Office fixtures & fittings £'000	Motor vehicles £'000	Total £'000
Cost	2,888	1,207	454	4,549
Accumulated depreciation	(554)	(773)	(273)	(1,600)
Net book value				
At 31 March 200X	2,334	434	181	2,949
At 31 March 200Y	2,023	591	209	2,823

The net book value of the group's office fixtures and fittings includes £35,000 (200Y: £42,000) in respect of assets held under finance leases.

LLP

Cost or valuation

At 1 April 200Y	2,542	1,189	443	4,174
Additions	261	62	29	352
Disposals	–	(77)	(50)	(127)
Adjustments arising on revaluation	108	–	–	108
At 31 March 200X	2,911	1,174	422	4,507

Depreciation

At 1 April 200Y	519	598	234	1,351
Charge for the year	58	203	75	336
Disposals	–	(31)	(38)	(69)
Adjustments arising on revaluation	(129)	–	–	(129)
At 31 March 200X	448	770	271	1,489

Net book value

At 31 March 200X	2,463	404	151	3,018
At 31 March 200Y	2,023	591	209	2,823

Comparable amounts determined according to the historical cost convention.

Cost	2,803	1,174	422	4,399
Accumulated depreciation	(534)	(770)	(271)	(1,575)
Net book value				
At 31 March 200X	2,269	404	151	2,824
At 31 March 200Y	2,023	591	209	2,823

Freehold land and buildings are held at a valuation. All such assets were given a full valuation at 31 March 200X, by Mssrs House & Co, Chartered Surveyors.

12 **Investments**
Group

	Unit trusts £'000
At 1 April 200Y	144
Additions	146
Disposals	(36)
Revaluation	12
At 31 March 200X	266

LLP

	Unit trusts £'000	Investment in subsidiary undertaking £'000	Total £'000
At 1 April 200Y	144	–	144
Additions	146	290	436
Disposals	(36)	–	(36)
Revaluation	12	–	12
At 31 March 200X	266	290	556

Investments in unit trusts are held to fund the LLP's liabilities to meet the future retirement benefits of members.

The LLP has the following investments in subsidiary undertakings:

	Country of registration	Activity	Portion of ordinary shares held
ABC Limited	England & Wales	Caterers	100%

13 **Work in progress**

	Group		LLP	
	200X £'000	200Y £'000	200X £'000	200Y £'000
Work in progress	514	348	476	348

544

14	Debtors	Group		LLP	
		200X £'000	200Y £'000	200X £'000	200Y £'000
	Trade debtors	545	509	441	509
	Amounts owed by subsidiary undertaking	–	–	86	–
	Amounts due from members	14	–	14	–
	Other debtors	220	167	138	167
	Prepayments and accrued income	96	88	75	88
		875	764	754	764

15 **Creditors: amounts falling due within one year**

	Group		LLP	
	200X £'000	200Y £'000	200X £'000	200Y £'000
Bank loans and overdrafts	339	282	284	282
Obligations under finance leases	23	32	23	32
Trade creditors	352	401	279	401
Amounts owed to subsidiary undertaking	–	–	104	–
Corporation tax	3	–	–	–
Other taxation and social security	318	345	274	345
[Retirement benefits due to former members][10]				
Other creditors	182	181	156	181
Accruals and deferred income	180	205	167	205
	1,397	1,446	1,287	1,446

16 **Creditors: amounts falling due after more than one year**

	Group		LLP	
	200X £'000	200Y £'000	200X £'000	200Y £'000
Bank loans and overdrafts	452	581	455	581
Obligations under finance leases	57	64	54	64
[Retirement benefits due to former members][10]				
	509	645	509	645

---

[10]Where the amount of retirement benefit is fixed it should be included within creditors rather than provisions (split between due within and due after one year).

17   **Borrowings**

	Group		LLP	
	200X **£'000**	**200Y** **£'000**	**200X** **£'000**	**200Y** **£'000**
Bank overdraft	149	242	138	242
Bank loan	642	621	601	621
(secured 0.5% above LIBOR)				
	791	863	739	863
Obligations under finance leases	80	96	77	96
	871	959	816	959
Due within one year	362	314	307	314
Due after one year	509	645	509	645
	871	959	816	959
Maturity analysis				
Within one year or on demand	362	314	307	314
More than one year but less than two years	294	325	294	325
More than two years but not less than five years	215	220	215	220
More than five years	–	100	–	100
	871	959	816	959

18   **Provisions for liabilities and charges**

Group

	Retirement benefits of former members **£'000**	Deferred taxation **£'000**	Total **£'000**
At 1 April 200Y	68		68
Subsidiary acquired	–	2	2
Profit and loss account charge	(2)	–	(2)
Transfer from members' interests	94	–	94
Applied	(7)	–	(7)
At 31 March 200X	153	2	155

Retirement benefits of former members.

The provision represents the present value of the expected liability for future payments to former members.

Deferred taxation

Provision for deferred taxation consists of the following amounts:

	200X £'000	200Y £'000
Capital allowances in excess of depreciation	2	–
Other timing differences	–	–
	2	–

LLP

	Retirement benefits of former members £'000
At 1 April 200Y	68
Profit and loss account charge	(2)
Transfer from members' interests	94
Applied	(7)
At 31 March 200X	153

19 **Loans and other debts due to members**

	Group & LLP	
	200X £'000	200Y £'000
Loans from members	1,176	819
Amounts owed to members in respect of profits *[Other[11]]*	1,259	1,224
	2,435	2,043
Falling due within one year	1,557	1,664
Falling due after more than one year	878	379
	2,435	2,043

Loans and other debts due to members rank equally with debts due to ordinary creditors in a winding up.

---

[11]Provide further information where amount is material

20 Pensions costs

The group operates a defined benefit scheme in the UK. A full actuarial valuation was carried out at 31 March 200Y and updated to 31 March 200X by a qualified independent actuary. The major assumptions used by the actuary were:

	At 31/03/0X	At 31/03/0Y
Rate of increase in salaries		
Rate of increased in pensions in payment		
Discount rate		
Inflation assumption		

The assets in the scheme and the expected rate of return were:

	Long term rate of return expected at 31/03/0X £'000	Value at 31/03/0X £'000	Long term rate of return expected at 31/03/0Y £'000	Value at 31/03/0Y £'000
Equities				
Bonds				
Property		————		————
Total market value of assets				
Present value of scheme liabilities		————		————
Surplus in scheme				
Related deferred tax asset		————		————
Net pension asset		════		════

Movement in surplus during the year

	200X £'000	200Y £'000
Surplus in scheme at beginning of the year		
Movement in year:		
Current service cost		
Contributions		
Past service costs		
Other finance income		
Actuarial gain	————	————
Surplus in scheme at end of year	════	════

The full actuarial valuation at 31 December 200Y showed an increase in the surplus from [   ] to [   ]. Improvements in benefits costing [   ] were made in 200X and contributions reduced to [   ] ([   ] of pensionable pay). It has been agreed with the trustees that contributions for the next three years will remain at that level.

21 **Operating lease commitments**

At 31 March 200X the LLP had annual commitments under operating leases as follows:

	200X Other £'000	200Y Other £'000
For leases expiring:		
Within one year	15	14
Between two and five years	25	36
	40	50

22 **Capital commitments**

	200X £'000	200Y £'000
Contracted but not provided for	40	150

23 **Contingent liabilities**

The LLP has guaranteed the borrowings of individual members taken out in order to fund their capital interests in the LLP. At 31 March 200X the total amount guaranteed was £175,000 (200Y: £165,000).

24 **Controlling party**

In the opinion of the members there is no controlling party as defined by Financial Reporting Standard No 8 'Related party disclosures'.

Glossary of key terms

Automatic accruer

Where a share of profits is allocated in accordance with the partnership deed. It is not dependent upon an individual's performance.

Buy and sell agreements

Where a partnership deed includes clauses whereby one partner is required to sell his interest in the partnership upon leaving and the other partners are required to purchase the interest from the departing partner.

Common property

This means there is a common ownership of property which does not necessarily itself constitute a partnership. Typically, in the case of partnerships, the business premises will constitute common property being owned jointly by the partners.

Corporate partner

A company, with either limited or unlimited liability, that can be a full partner or limited partner in the partnership.

Demerger

Occurs where there is a split in the partnership and partners leave taking with them segments of the business. Demerger normally means the cessation of one business and the commencement of two or more successor businesses.

Dissolution

Where a partnership is dissolved on the departure of one or more partners.

Drawings

Partners 'takings' from the business which are reflected in their current or other personal accounts and which are not therefore shown as an expense of the firm.

Equity partner

A partner who shares in the profits and losses of the business.

Escalators

Where a partner gains additional profit sharing points merely by remaining a partner for a set period of time. The increase in profit sharing points is not normally dependent upon performance.

550

European Economic Interest Grouping	A form of supra-national legal entity which is intended to facilitate the creation of the European single market. The EEIG is designed to enable businesses to co-operate at an international level.
Fixed share	Where a partner is entitled to a pre-determined amount of the firm's assessable profits.
Goodwill	The difference between the value of the business as a going concern and the value of its physical assets or, more specifically, the value of the name recognition, reputation and contacts of the firm. All businesses generate goodwill to some extent and in a professional partnership goodwill may be substantial although often not formally or fully recognised in the accounts of the partnership.
Holding out	A person holds himself out to be a partner if, by what he says, does or writes, he invites others to draw a conclusion that he is a partner. Typically this may be the value of his name being printed on the firm's notepaper with no indication that he is other than a partner. As a result he will therefore be jointly liable as a partner for his actions and those of his fellow partners.
Incidental directorships	Where a person is a director of a company which is incidental to their main business. These are often classed as non-executive directorships and would, for example, cover the position where a lawyer was a director of a client company.
Integrated software	Refers to software which has a number of different functions or purposes, but which only requires data to be entered once and which will automatically transfer relevant information between the different parts of the software.
Investors In People	Also known as IIP, this is the national standard for effective investment in people. It aims to encourage and recognise effective training and development.

Joint property	Where two or more individuals own property jointly they will not be partners for this reason alone, even if they share profits made by the use of the property.
Joint tenancy	A method in which assets are held jointly. Where an asset is held by joint tenants, the asset automatically passes to the other joint tenant(s) upon the death of one tenant. Husband and wife are presumed to own assets as joint tenants.
Joint venture	Where a joint business relationship is entered into but a partnership relationship is not intended and cannot be implied.
Ladders	Where a partner gains additional profit sharing points *provided* that certain criteria are met.
Limited Liability Partnership	A body corporate with legal personality separate from that of its members and which is formed by being incorporated under the *Limited Liability Partnerships Act 2000.*
Limited Partner	Means a partner whose liability is limited to his capital in the partnership under the *Limited Partnership Act 1907.*
Lockstep	A system of dividing the firm's profits between partners whereby each partner each year receives a pre-determined share based on the time each partner has served. This normally operates as an upward only ratchet for a number of years.
Managing partner	The partner who undertakes the day to day running of the business.
Merger	Where two or more businesses are brought together to form a single business. It is also something used to describe situations where a significant team joins an existing firm.
Minicomputer	A multi-user computer on which all processing is centralised. Traditionally the users accessed the minicomputer using dumb terminals, but now commonly done via a

PC. Not as large as a mainframe computer system.

Open systems

An environment where software is portable between a range of different hardware platforms, or where there are standards for transferring information between e.g. databases or user devices. Now often associated with the Unix operating environment.

Partners' accounts

Represent the amount due to partners (if for example they were to retire). Typically this amounts to both the equity partners' capital accounts and their current accounts. The capital accounts disclose the amount each partner has invested in the firm. Current accounts typically disclose share of profits, drawings, tax provisions and personal expenses.

Partnership

The relationship which exists between persons carrying on a business in common with a view to profit.

Partnership agreement

A written document setting out the rights and duties of all partners.

Partnership secretary

The partnership secretary is usually the chief administrative officer of the partnership.

Permanent Health Insurance

Insurance to protect an individual against loss of earnings as a result of ill health or incapacity.

Personal Pension Plans

Types of pension contracts where an individual pays a qualifying pension premium in a year of assessment under a contract made after 30 June 1988. The amount of a contribution paid in a year of assessment may, subject to certain limits, be tax deductible from the individual's taxable profits.

Points share

A method whereby the profits of the business or a part thereof, are shared between the partners according to points allocated to each partner out of a pool of points for the firm.

Prior share

The first slice of the assessable profit of the business before distributing the balance in the firm's profit sharing arrangements. Typically this will constitute a fixed sum required by each partner to provide an acceptable standard of living.

Professional indemnity insurance

Insurance obtained to protect the firm against a claim for professional negligence and public liability.

Profit

The net result of excess income over expenditure in any period.

Profit Related Pay

That part of the remuneration of an eligible employee paid under a Profit Related Pay ('PRP') scheme registered with the Inland Revenue.

Profit shares

The division of the business profits of the firm between the partners.

Restrictive covenants

Normally included in the partnership deed and reflect the agreement between partners not to undertake certain actions which may damage the ongoing business upon their departure.

Retention

When a sum of money is retained to cover any future liability which is not yet finalised.

Retirement annuities

Pension contracts of partners designed to provide for a pension on retirement. These must be made under contracts entered into before 1 July 1988.

Salaried partner

Is a person who is not recognised as a full partner but usually receives a salary and is thus generally treated by the Inland Revenue as an employee. Salaried partners often take on financial risks of the partnership without necessarily enjoying the compensatory privileges but usually receive indemnities from the equity partners.

Self-assessment	The new tax regime for individuals introduced from 1996/97.
Senior partner	The partner who is considered the most senior within a firm, either by age or importance.
Service companies	Companies which provide support services to the partnership for a management fee paid by the partnership to the service company.
Staggered vesting	Where the ownership of an asset passes over a period of time.
Stakeholder pension	A low-cost pension meant for people who currently do not have the right pension options available to save for their retirement. Unless exempt, all employers must offer their employees access to a stakeholder scheme.
Strategic plan	A plan setting out the strategy of the business.
Tenancy in common	A method in which assets are held jointly, such that a separate share can be disposed of in lifetime or on death as the person wishes. People other than husband and wife are presumed to own assets as tenants in common.
Time recording	An account maintained of people's time worked on a client's affairs. This can be used to identify the work-in-progress and total time spent on a job for billing purposes.
Utmost good faith	The law presumes that partners will exhibit the utmost good faith in their dealings with one another, i.e. each partner must act honestly and honourably towards the other partners in the firm and must not allow his own personal interest to conflict with those of other partners or the firm.
Vertical market software	Software written for a particular industry or profession, as compared with more general purpose software.

Winding up

The dissolution of the business whereby the partnership business ceases. Winding up the business involves realising all the assets, paying off the firm's debts and distributing any surplus to the former partners.

Worldwide partnership

A partnership which includes both UK and international branches/offices and therefore trades both in the UK and abroad.

Index